FULL DISCLOSURE

Editor of *The Sunday Times* for over a decade, Andrew Neil is the most successful and famous newspaper editor of his generation. In *Full Disclosure* he reveals the stories behind the headlines which dominated the eighties and early nineties – and gives a behind-closed-doors account of what it was like to be a key figure in Rupter Murdoch's huge global media empire.

Andrew Neil tells us of his battles with the Royal Family and the Thatcher and Major governments, and gives a unique, first-hand report of a decade of controversial scoops, campaigns and opinions which made him a household name in Britain, and *The Sunday Times* a paper admired and feared throughout the world.

For the paperback edition, Andrew Neil has written a new introduction to bring us up to date with the events of the past year, including the aftermath of his final split with Rupert Murdoch and his views on the relationship between Murdoch and Tony Blair.

ANDREW NEIL was born in 1949 and educated at Paisley Grammar School and then the University of Glasgow, from where he graduated in 1971 with an MA in politics and economics. He joined *The Economist* in 1973 and for ten years covered the main stories of the day from Belfast, London, New York and Washington. He became editor of *The Sunday Times* in 1983, expanding the paper in size and circulation so that a decade later it had seen off all its rivals and dominated the Sunday broadsheet market. In 1989 he launched Sky Television while still editing Britain's biggest-selling quality newspaper. At the end of 1994, at the peak of his success, he quit News International to embark on a new career as a writer, broadcaster and media consultant. He broadcasts regularly on both sides of the Atlantic and in 1996 became editor-in-chief of the *Scotsman*, *Scotland on Sunday* and the *European*. He now lives and works out of London, the south of France, Edinburgh and New York.

ANDREW NEIL

FULL DISCLOSURE

PAN BOOKS

First published 1996 by Macmillan

This edition published 1997 by Pan Books
an imprint of Macmillan Publishers Limited
25 Eccleston Place, London SW1W 9NF
and Basingstoke

Associated companies throughout the world

ISBN 0 330 34348 3

1 3 5 7 9 8 6 4 2

A CIP catalogue record for this book is available from
the British Library.

Phototypeset by Intype London Ltd
Printed and bound in Great Britain by
Mackays of Chatham plc, Chatham, Kent

‘Life on Andrew Neil’s paper was not dull. Nor is his book . . .’
Peter Cole, ‘Night and Day’, *Mail on Sunday*

‘A remarkable, honest account of his turbulent public and private life at the helm of what used to be the world’s greatest newspaper.’
Sunday Business

‘Neil has contributed an important chapter to our island’s chequered journalist history.’
Charles Wheeler, *TLS*

‘It is the most comprehensive, authoritative account of Rupert Murdoch’s personality and working methods so far written. Murdoch will not enjoy the portrait . . .’
Roy Greenslade, *Guardian*

Dedicated to my parents, Jim and Mary,

and to everybody who helped make

The Sunday Times THE Sunday papers

List of Illustrations

The author and publishers wish to record their thanks to the owners and copyright holders of the illustrations used in this book for permission to reproduce them.

Sources and photograph credits are set out in brackets after each illustration.

In the first plate section

Contents

Introduction to the Paperback Edition

'He was most upset by your book,' one of Rupert Murdoch's senior confidants reported privately in the aftermath of the autumn, 1996 hardback publication of *Full Disclosure*. 'So upset, in fact, that he couldn't think straight for almost three weeks. People found it impossible to deal with him, though few knew the reason.'

I expressed scepticism that my former proprietor could have been discombobulated by my literary efforts. The official word from London and New York was that Rupert had not even bothered to read the book.

Though I took that with several buckets of salt I agreed with Graydon Carter, the editor of *Vanity Fair*, who published a long extract from the book in his magazine: 'Journalists like us can't hurt people as rich and powerful as Murdoch,' said Graydon. 'Not unless you destroy their share price or kidnap their children.' Since I had done neither I assumed he would be privately intrigued by what I had written – and publicly indifferent.

'You don't understand,' my source at the Court of King Rupert continued. 'He's battling on too many fronts these days. Expanding his television interests in America and Asia. Trying to break into satellite TV in the US. Spending massively on expensive Hollywood movies. Fighting a costly newspaper price war in England. And *still* acquiring new assets.

'The markets are nervous about the insatiable demand for capital these projects will require of his company – and his never-ending expansionism is making him lots of enemies. Your book came at a highly sensitive time. It confirmed investors' fears about how News Corporation [the Australian-based holding company for Rupert's global empire] is a one-man band – and explained how that one man can't help acquiring and accumulating, whatever the cost. No wonder he was mad.'

There was some sense in this but I was still dubious that anything I had written could have put Rupert in the doldrums, even temporarily. His only certain reaction to the book (of which I am aware) was when the *Independent*, with its customary disregard for the facts on Murdoch/Neil matters, carried a story just before the book came out headlined: 'Murdoch: why I fired Neil'.

'I never fired Andrew,' he complained to an associate after seeing this report. 'He walked out on me.'

Rupert was right. I had left of my own volition and on my own terms. But that had not endeared me to him. Being fired by Rupert means there is always the chance you will be invited back into the News Corp fold, at his instigation and on his terms. Leave on your own terms and you risk his enmity. Why this should be I do not know: perhaps he hates the idea of people walking out on him before he has had a chance to fire them.

But deny Rupert the pleasure of sacking and you risk creating a simmering resentment at the top which permeates throughout the upper echelons of the company (as senior executives ape their master's voice) and makes you *persona non grata* throughout the Murdoch empire. The moment I parted company with Rupert in December, 1994 that was what happened to me.

*

THOUGH WE HAD separated on apparently amicable terms, both of us promising to keep in close touch and expressing the hope that we would soon have the opportunity to work together again, it quickly became clear that only one side meant it.

I began my new life of freedom at the start of 1995 excited by future prospects and keen to spread my journalistic activities into more entrepreneurial media ventures. I was approached in January by some Wall Street investors who wanted me to head up a bid for the historic news footage library owned by Twentieth Century Fox, News Corp's Hollywood studio. They reckoned that, with the millennium approaching, there was an international market for documentary material on the great events of the century.

It was an asset Fox was failing to exploit – indeed the original film was deteriorating in various Fox vaults. We proposed to digitize the whole library, thereby saving it for posterity, and to market it aggressively to television and film companies across the world. The investors had approached me because they thought (mistakenly as it turned out) I had a friendly entrée to the man at the top.

I made my initial pitch in a memo to Rupert, suggesting a decent price, a share of the profits and a generous buy-back arrangement should he want to own all of this asset again at some time in the future. It seemed a good deal for both of us. But there was no response.

Then word reached me of a revealing exchange at a *Times* board directors' lunch in Wapping. A mutual colleague who knew of my proposal remarked to Rupert across the table that it sounded like an interesting idea. 'Yeah,' drawled Rupert with a smug smile. 'But I'm not selling the library to Neil.' He then abruptly changed the subject.

I heard later that Rupert had instructed Fox to start exploiting the library itself. At least I had prompted the use (and the rescue) of an asset of historic importance. But the man who had shaken my hand only a month before and spoken such warm words about future co-operation never even bothered to reply to my memo.

If I had known his resentment towards me I would never have made the proposal in the first place. But within months of my departure I began to hear how he was becoming increasingly irrational towards me. It infuriated him, for example, that *The Sunday Times* still carried a weekly political column by me after I resigned as editor, even though it had been a key part of the severance package I had agreed with him.

My successor as editor, John Witherow, had to fend off regular complaints, not about its content (which Rupert had to admit he rather liked) but about its very existence in a newspaper he owned. When the editor and senior Wapping executives argued that a column by its ex-editor might possibly be an asset to the paper (never mind that he had personally agreed a two-year contractual arrangement to carry it), he would ask sullenly: 'OK. OK. But do we have to carry his picture so big?'

Since the photograph that accompanied my by-line was the size of a postage stamp, it was the sort of pathetic request that illustrates how petty big men can be when they do not get their way. But soon it was more than my picture which offended him.

Part of my new-found freedom I relished most was the ability to speak out on media matters without risking the wrath of a Murdoch transatlantic telephone call because I had offended his interests or opinions. In the summer of 1995 I was invited to give a lecture to the Royal Television Society. I chose to argue the case for diversity in the coming age of digital broadcasting. I argued that Rupert, through his 40 per cent stake in Sky Television, was set to dominate digital broadcasting and that British broadcasters, on existing plans, were destined to be also-rans.

I explained how Sky was already well advanced to launch over 200 digital satellite channels. It was better positioned than anybody else to provide the sort of premium programming – especially films, sports and special events – that viewers would pay most to see; and it commanded the technology to make it the digital gatekeeper for the new age of pay-TV. The danger was that Sky would control who could enter and that access would be on its terms.

A shortened version of my lecture was published in the *Independent* and there was some comment on it. But I attempted to do more than stimulate debate. Along with two other former senior executives of News International (the London arm of News Corp), I attempted to interest British broadcasters and publishers in the case for what we called a common digital platform: a set-top box which would decode signals from all potential sources of digital television – terrestrial, satellite or cable – and give homes efficient access to the Internet through their TVs. This would allow the various media players to compete with their programming on a level playing field, with no one group monopolizing the technology or the access to it.

It was a reasonable proposal, designed to ensure diversity and competition in the public interest. It was essentially the same sort of case that I had deployed against the established broadcasters when launching Sky against their opposition in 1989/90. But angry thunder could be heard emanating from New York.

Rupert was furious that three of his former executives had the temerity to challenge his planned digital dominance. I saw it as a legitimate business venture for me which had the additional advantage of guaranteeing diversity in a multi-channel world – a world in which Rupert would still be the biggest player, whatever the technology or regulations, because he had had the guts to risk all and be first. But he saw it as an act of treachery by former employees. The big guns were wheeled out to intimidate us.

A 'without prejudice' letter arrived from New York in August 1995 from Arthur Siskind, the executive vice president of News Corp and Rupert's most senior legal counsel. It 'advised' me to 'cease and desist' from further activity on digital television, threatening the 'seeking of damages and injunctive relief' if I refused. The letter argued that I was in breach of guarantees given at the time of my departure not to 'divulge any secret or confidential information' I had learned while in News Corp's employ.

Since I had ceased to be Sky's executive chairman early in 1991 and had never been a party to any information about digital broadcasting while working at either *The Sunday Times* or Sky (indeed the subject was never discussed) the premise of the letter was absurd. But Siskind, a somewhat brutal Murdoch courtier who likes to operate in the style of his master, nevertheless demanded that I give immediate 'written assurances' that I would not proceed with my digital venture. Similar letters went to my two associates.

It was an over-the-top response to an attempt to increase competition, something Rupert was supposed to support as much as me. But then he had also once said that 'monopolies are a terrible thing – unless you have one'. He clearly regarded our modest efforts as a threat to his satellite monopoly.

I resented the heavy-handed intrusion of his henchman and threw it into my bottom drawer, deciding not to dignify it with a reply. In the end my digital diversion came to nothing, not because of News Corp's antics but because British broadcasters did not have the guts to go head-to-head with Rupert in digital competition.

As time progressed I realized that the tentative connection

I still had with Rupert through my *Sunday Times* column would soon have to end. His displeasure with me had already seeped into the attitudes of his senior courtiers.

I was no longer someone to be seen with, much less thought a friend. Les Hinton, an old colleague from my days at Fox TV in New York and a supporter of my plans for a Fox news magazine show who was now running Wapping, apparently decided it was too dangerous to have lunch with me, despite several requests on my part. Sir Edward Pickering, another former colleague and Rupert's long-time Fleet Street confidant, later remarked to me wryly at a press lunch (where there was presumably safety in numbers): 'You were very kind to me in your book. It's done me no good at all!'

Unknown to me, I had also apparently been banned from appearing on Sky. When I was eventually interviewed on Sky News after a long absence I remarked to the correspondent that it was some time since I had been requested to comment on current events.

'We wanted to use you regularly,' said the Sky reporter, 'but every time you appeared a thunderbolt came from Sam Chisholm [the Rupert-appointed chief executive of Sky, who decided to depart Sky in the summer of 1997] warning that you should never darken our screens again. Even when you were the only commentator we could get to defend Sky from attack, we were bollocked for using you.'

At the Chelsea Flower Show in 1997 a Sky crew innocently asked for an interview. 'No point in talking to him,' shouted Adam Boulton (Sky's excellent political editor) cheerfully. 'Chisholm won't let him on.'

My broadcasting career somehow managed to survive the Sky ban. I suffered a far greater deprivation when they withdrew my complimentary Sky smart card, which unscrambled the various channel pictures on satellite TV. I had enjoyed a free subscription to Sky's multi-channel services since 1991, presumably in recognition of my efforts to get Sky off the ground when it looked like crashing on take-off. By a strange coincidence of timing it was withdrawn just as this book was being published.

More important matters had already come to a head in the run up to publication in the autumn of 1996. I offered *Full Disclosure* to *The Sunday Times* for serialization, regarding my old paper as the book's natural home since much of the content was to its greater glory. But the editor was in a difficult position and understandably declined: he knew that the last thing Rupert wanted to see was my book spread across his newspaper.[1]

---

[1] The book was instead serialized by the *Daily Mail*, an excellent fallback since it is a fine paper for which I then also wrote a weekly column and the editor seemed keen to have it. It published extensive extracts over five days, but in a curiously half-hearted fashion.

There was no pre-publication promotion to announce the impending serialization – not even in the *Mail*'s own pages – despite the large five-figure sum they had paid for it. Nobody could tell me when the serialization was going to run: even at 7 p.m. on the Sunday night before it had been tentatively scheduled for Monday publication, the duty editor could not say for sure if it would be published the next day. I had to catch a plane for Hong Kong that night not knowing if it would appear the next day.

It did – but without even a small billing on page one to indicate it was beginning inside. Nor was there any news story 'write-off' to draw readers' attention to it even though other papers had started to run numerous stories based on various parts of the book's contents. The extract on Murdoch had been strangely sanitized.

The rest of Fleet Street was mystified by this treatment, especially since controversy had already started to swirl publicly

I asked that, since my autobiography was not thought suitable for serialization, could he indicate if the contract for my column would be renewed (the existing two-year contract expired at end-1996). The editor demurred, saying it would be best to wait to see the reaction to the book's publication. I knew whose reaction he particularly had in mind. I decided to end my uncertainty and the editor's discomfort by taking the decision for him: I accepted an offer to become editor-in-chief of *The European* in London and *The Scotsman* and its sister titles in Edinburgh, resigning as a *Sunday Times* columnist in consequence.

But Murdoch's men had not quite finished with me. For no apparent reason, *The Times* ran a full-page interview with my former Indian friend, Pamella Bordes, accompanied by a massive picture of her (looking rather more matronly than I

---

about the book's publication. BBC Radio 4's *Today* programme even tracked me down in the Governor's office in Hong Kong for a ding-dong on the extracts with my old sparring partner, Peregrine Worsthorne. Other papers and broadcasters waded in. I watched with relish from the other side of the world as the controversies developed back home. Still the *Mail* continued its serialization *sotto voce.*

I suspected the proprietor's old-boy network at work. There is an unwritten understanding that proprietors do not make disclosures (especially not *Full Disclosures*) about other proprietors. Murdoch had recently forbidden the *Sun* to publish an extensive dossier in its hands about Lord Rothermere's late wife, a flamboyant society lady nicknamed Bubbles, involving her strange obsession with a so-called mystic who lived in a council house in Peckham. Perhaps the *Daily Mail* was paying off its proprietor's debt by making sure his paper did not dwell on what was most critical about Murdoch in my book. I doubt if his lordship was involved himself: more likely one of his courtiers concluded that downplaying my book would be judicious.

remembered her), just as *Full Disclosure* hit the bookshops. I have no doubt this was meant to embarrass me. But it failed: she had nothing new to say and my book contained a complete account of the Bordes affair anyway.

Then, just as I took up my new appointment The *Sunday Times Magazine* attempted to dig the dirt on my new proprietors, the Barclay brothers. That failed too: the profile rambled on page after page but contained no great revelations. When a mutual associate of the brothers and Rupert interceded on their behalf asking that the profile not be published, Rupert's reply was revealing: 'I never interfere in editorial matters [sic] – and anyway I don't like the fact they've hired Andrew Neil.'

No matter: the final connection with Rupert Murdoch had been severed, no doubt to his relief as much as mine.

*

BUT RUPERT MURDOCH never quite leaves you. Now that I have four editors reporting to me, I have copied his general approach in dealing with them (but without his notorious brand of telephone terrorism). I have agreed with them the broad outlines of what their papers should stand for and the strategic development of each title then left them to get on with it, becoming involved only when they need help or advice and when there are matters of importance to be decided – from launching a new section to which party each paper should support in a general election. That last decision is largely a matter for the individual editors but during the 1997 general election I made it clear that I expected to be consulted.

In Scotland all three editors opted to support Tony Blair. This caused me no problems. I had laid down that our titles must be broadly in favour of the market economy, defenders of the union between Scotland and England and prepared to tackle head on the many outdated Scottish shibboleths and collectivist attitudes which still dominate politics north of the border. None of this conflicted with backing Blair.

It is true that I remain unconvinced of the value of Scottish devolution, especially the particular scheme planned by Labour. But the case against home rule has been lost and the argument must now be about making it work. Its supporters say it will enhance Scotland's desire to stay part of the United Kingdom. Time will tell. The priority for the moment is to devise a devolution scheme designed to do precisely that.

As for Scotland's ruling collectivist consensus. Blair's own press officer described the largely old-fashioned, left-wing Scottish media to me as a 'bunch of unreconstructed wankers' and Blair himself told me he hoped I might be able to stir things up and help bring Scottish political opinion into the last decade of the twentieth century.

What I would not tolerate as an editor-in-chief is a newspaper under my ultimate control which advocated independence for Scotland. I find no conflict in being Scottish *and* British and neither do the majority of Scots. I believe in the United Kingdom. This was once the matter of an angry row with Rupert.

For purely opportunist reasons designed to increase the circulation of the Scottish edition of the *Sun*, Rupert had agreed to go along with the idea of turning it into a paper that supported the separatist Scottish Nationalists. I remember him outlining the plan to me with glee in the run-up to the 1992 general election, saying that there were no sales in Scotland for a paper that backed the Tories (which his English *Sun* continued to do) but that a Nationalist Sun would steal lots of readers from the pro-Labour *Daily Record*, Scotland's largest-selling downmarket tabloid.

I sat in sullen silence as he explained his thinking. I realized that, when his cheque book was talking, there was no point in arguing. But when the *Sun* went Nationalist, with pipers greeting Rupert in the Wapping boardroom and a special edition of the Scottish *Sun* jammed with 'here's tae us, wha's like us' tartan drivel, the Scottish edition of *The Sunday Times* also had its say.

'Enter the bar room cretin into Scotland's constitutional debate' was how the first line of *The Sunday Times* Scotland editorial greeted the *Sun*'s convenient conversion. Rupert was furious. He called in a temper to complain that, once again, I was 'beating up on the *Sun*'. I replied with equal fervour.

'You are advocating the breaking up of my country just so you can add to the *Sun*'s sales in Scotland,' I remonstrated. He started to justify his position, arguing that it would take votes away from Labour and might even help the Tories in Scotland. But I would have none of it.

'It is a disgraceful thing to do,' I continued, my anger rising as I spoke, 'and I will not be a party to such a policy. How would you feel if *The Sunday Times* started advocating the dismemberment of Australia?'

It was a low blow but Rupert realized my genuine outrage. He backed off, changed the subject and never raised the matter again. By the 1997 general election, with the Scottish Nationalists showing no signs of making a major breakthrough and Rupert increasingly taken with Tony Blair, the Scottish *Sun* was ordered to fall into line with its English sister paper and support Labour.

*

DESPITE OUR GENERAL falling out after my departure, Rupert and I made a remarkably similar transition from Thatcherite to Blairite after the 1992 election. We developed in our own separate ways a growing despair, culminating in disgust, at John Major's inability to provide a lead for either the country or his party (though unlike Rupert I had never supported him in the first place). Both of us came to see Tony Blair as a more credible heir to the Thatcher revolution than her Tory successor – though we also feared that the Labour party might inhibit Blair from fulfilling his potential.

The increasing anger, sometimes erupting in fury, which fuelled *The Sunday Times*' coverage of the Major government after its re-election in 1992 was an accurate reflection of the mood of Middle Britain, which refused to forgive Major or his party for causing so much unnecessary pain by making the recession far deeper than it need have been. Many natural Tory voters were also furious with a government which they had re-elected on the promise of tax cuts but which then proceeded to raise taxes again and again.

Though the recovery was well established by the time of the 1997 general election, even those who had voted Tory throughout the 1980s could not forget what Major had put them through in the recession. They wanted revenge – and took it with relish, wiping out the Tories as a credible party in the process.

With the hindsight of the 1997 Labour landslide, it is now clear that Major never recovered from the events described in the introduction to the hardback edition of this book. The ignominious ejection of sterling from the European exchange-rate mechanism (ERM) in the autumn of 1992 was John Major's defining moment, the beginning of the end for him. The public, of course, did not follow the intricacies of the exchange-rate mechanism. But Major had staked his reputation on the pound's membership of the ERM and come unstuck. Voters sensed that something had gone badly wrong, that the government had lost control of events. Major's reputation never recovered.

The Tory position was not helped by the government's refusal to take the blame for what had gone wrong, indicate any remorse, make even the vaguest of apologies. Instead, they blundered on, exuding a fatal mixture of arrogance and complacency which was to be their massive undoing. I argued many times with senior Tories that they were heading for a bad fall. Like a blind man staggering across the road in front of an oncoming double-decker bus, they could not see it coming. Even realists like Michael Heseltine insisted in private to me that, despite the polls, the Tories would still win the next election by 60 seats. They had been in power for so long they had become cocooned from the reality.

But voters live in the real world. If you won't take any blame for the recession which has hurt us so badly, concluded Middle Britain, then why should the Tories be given any credit for the recovery? Especially since, as *The Sunday Times* had pointed out in an editorial in 1993, the recovery was happening *despite* the government, not because of it. After all, with his trademark stubborn stupidity, Major had insisted again and again that if Britain left the ERM the country would go into deep decline. In fact, contrary to everything Major and his men told us, sterling's ejection was to mark the start of the recovery. No wonder voters were disinclined to give Major any credit.

Major's apologists argued that the Tory party had become impossible to run: it had divided into warring factions, especially over Europe, and Major did everything possible to keep the show on the road. This is nonsense. The Tories descended into civil war because there was a leadership vacuum at the top: their squabbling filled it.

The party had also been divided many times under Margaret Thatcher. But nobody was ever in doubt where the boss stood on any divisive issue. That helped to keep the dissidents in line. Because nobody was ever sure where Major stood on any issue, every Tory faction fought for his support, assumed it had his ear, speculated that they really represented his true position. Thus did Major's inadequacies as a leader fuel the fires of dissent.

In retrospect, it is clear Major made two fatal mistakes no previous Tory prime minister had ever managed: he alienated, to an unprecedented degree, a huge chunk of the Tories' natural constituency in Middle Britain with his economic policies; and he lost the Tory Press.

As his miserable administration dragged on, mired in sleaze, incompetence and division – and lacking any strategic direction or vision – it became depressingly clear that Major had been promoted above his abilities. The man should never have been prime minister in the first place. He had brought to its knees the most successful political party in the democratic world. It was time for a change, especially since Blair was saying many of the right neo-Thatcherite things on the economy, tax, the family and welfare.

*

WHEN THIS BOOK WAS WRITTEN Rupert Murdoch and Tony Blair were still wooing each other. I predicted that Rupert was moving towards endorsing Labour in the 1997 general election after almost two decades' solid support for the Tories but that he would probably hedge his bets by splitting his papers between the parties. In the event, the *Sun* and the *News of the World* (the two papers whose editorial lines are directly under his control) backed Labour. *The Sunday Times* stuck grudgingly with the Tories and *The Times* said vote for Eurosceptic candidates whatever their party (a feeble ploy which had zero impact).

A long courtship between Murdoch and Blair followed their first secret dinner date (revealed in this book) in the autumn of 1994. The extent of the ties that developed between New Labour and News Corp has never been fully revealed. In addition to regular meetings between the two top men, a network of contacts was established between senior company executives and Labour frontbenchers. Even the Murdoch family was brought into the act.

Lachlan, the son Murdoch has been grooming as his heir apparent, met Blair and got on as well with him as his father. Elisabeth, the daughter Murdoch thinks Lachlan should have to compete with for the succession, was also introduced to senior Labour figures, even though she has only a tentative grasp of British politics. She took to calling Peter Mandelson, Blair's senior spindoctor, 'my dear friend'. More serious contacts were established in regular meetings between Rupert's top managers and advisers, such as Irwin Stelzer, Sam Chisholm and Les Hinton, and Blair's men.

John Major watched the developing Murdoch–Blair love-in with a mixture of desperation and powerlessness. By now he realized that Rupert was so disgusted with his record as prime minister that no personal intervention on his part would make any difference. So he turned to Rupert's heroine, Margaret Thatcher, to keep the Murdoch papers Tory.

At Major's instigation Thatcher invited Rupert to a private dinner. Her task was to secure Rupert's assurances that he (and above all the *Sun*) would stick with the Tories. But she did not stick to her appointed mission. When Rupert voiced some reservations he still had about Blair it was Thatcher who came to his defence.

'Don't you worry about Tony Blair,' she said firmly to Rupert. 'He's a real patriot.'

It was not exactly what Major had intended Rupert to hear. Blair's pro-Europe policy, however, remained a major stumbling block for Rupert. 'It was *all* about Europe,' says one Murdoch man involved in many of the various meetings.

The Labour leader sought to reassure him that he would not be a soft touch for Brussels. He had already made it known privately to Rupert that he regarded it as unlikely, even undesirable, that Sterling would be among the first wave of currencies to join a single European currency. Behind closed doors he spoke to Murdoch's men about 'formidable obstacles', later going public with these very words. In a speech early in 1997, which was barely reported in the press but which did not go unnoticed in Wapping, Blair said that he did not regard the European social model as one that New Labour should follow.

Blair went the final mile for Rupert in an article for the *Sun* right at the start of the election campaign. He flew the Union flag and wrote in highly Eurosceptical tones. Rupert was delighted. He saw no reason to delay his endorsement for Labour any longer, especially since all the polls made Blair overwhelming favourite to be the next prime minister anyway. There were brownie points to win with New Labour, thought Rupert, by coming out for it now. Next day, 'The *Sun* backs Blair' was splashed across the tabloid's front page. The *News of the World* quickly followed suit.

The decision to place his two Tory tabloids – the biggest-selling in Britain – behind Blair and the Labour party was entirely Rupert's. Their editors played almost no part in the decision and many of the staff, especially on the *Sun*, were very unhappy about it. But they had no say in the matter and were never consulted.

The *Sun*'s respected political editor, Trevor Kavanagh, whom Murdoch holds in high regard, did mount a rearguard action to stop a Labour endorsement and his arguments had enough sway to force Rupert to hesitate. But when Blair presented himself as sufficiently Eurosceptic for the *Sun*, Kavanagh's objections were overruled. The unease among senior editors at the *Sun*, however, was reflected in the paper's lacklustre campaign coverage.

The *Sun*'s support was a real coup for Blair, who recognized its political importance in the 1980s as the paper that cemented its massive Middle England readership around Thatcher. He believed that it would be a matter of great symbolic significance – a sign that New Labour really was safe for the striving lower middle classes – if that same paper backed him in the 1997 election. It would confirm to many disillusioned Tories that he was indeed the true heir to Thatcher. He succeeded in his wish. But at what price?

I do not believe there was an explicit deal between Murdoch and Blair in which the *Sun* gave its support in return for promises that a Labour government would leave Rupert's British media empire alone. But there was an implicit understanding, never openly talked about between the two men but an understanding nevertheless.

Blair once said to me that 'how we treat Rupert Murdoch's media interests when in power will depend on how his newspapers treat the Labour party in the run up to the election.'

The remark illustrated his ability to play hardball when it matters that belies his 'Bambi' image. He was not insisting that Murdoch's papers had to endorse Labour to be left alone by a Blair government. But he was clear that if they beat up on Blair in the way they attacked Neil Kinnock in the 1992 election then who knew what a Labour government would have in store. 'We never really expected the *Sun*'s endorsement,' a senior Blair aide said to me. 'We would have been happy if it had treated us fairly.'

Rupert, for his part, had been ready to contemplate supporting Blair since he had first met him. His admiration for him grew almost as fast as his respect for Major plummeted. Except for Europe (and even that was finally resolved), few major issues separated them. Blair had no plans to legislate on the ownership of the press and with the regulation of satellite TV turned over to Oftel, the independent regulatory body, Murdoch seemed to have little to fear on the Sky Television front either.

Nor was Rupert out to secure any special favours from Blair. He realizes no government would allow him to own more national newspapers in Britain and he is no longer interested in acquiring terrestrial television stations (he makes more money than any of them from satellite). With his British newspapers prospering, Sky TV a goldmine and his likely domination of digital television, Murdoch now concentrates his time and treasure on developing his global, non-British interests. Murdoch's main aim was to ensure that the lucrative British arm of his media empire was safe from Labour assault. The status quo in media matters suits him: by aligning his two tabloids with Blair (which he was prepared to do on broad policy grounds anyway) he seems to have secured it.

As for Labour's plans to make union recognition easier – a policy that the Wapping management dreaded because they feared the unions would win any ballot of the print works – Rupert now believes that if the Wapping workers vote for union recognition it will be his management's fault for failing to create the sort of conditions in which a non-union environment can prosper.

Tony Blair should enjoy his honeymoon with Rupert Murdoch. It is unlikely to last long. The marriage might not have happened if Rupert had not been sure Blair was certain to win anyway – or been so thoroughly disgusted with the Tories. And Rupert is promiscuous when it comes to political support.

In Australia and America he has a track record of embracing politicians who can further his business interests – then dumping them when circumstances change or they've served his purpose. If Prime Minister Blair deviates from his pro-market promises or kowtows too much to Brussels then he will soon enough face the full wrath of the Murdoch press and rightly, for Blair will have reneged on what he promised publicly and privately in opposition. If the Tories become solidly Eurosceptic with a clear post-Thatcher agenda then Rupert will be tempted to return to the Tory fold.

If the Tories had chosen Ken Clarke to succeed John

Major, that would have given the Murdoch–Blair bandwagon fresh impetus: Rupert detests Clarke almost as much as Major. 'He's really a socialist,' he confided to me once – and, of course, he is seen as soft on Europe. Hence the Murdoch papers, without an agreed favourite of their own for Tory leader, rallied behind a 'Stop Clarke' campaign in the June, 1997 leadership contest.

William Hague, who emerged as the winner, does not excite Rupert. He knows nothing about him and his politics are too vague for his clear-cut right-wing leanings. Rupert came away from a dinner with Hague (organized by Brian Griffiths, who used to run Thatcher's Downing Street policy unit and sits on Times Newspapers board) during the Tory leadership contest saying he had been distinctly underwhelmed by him. In any case, Blair in power has so far exceeded Rupert's expectations, staying encouragingly Eurosceptic and making no concessions to the Labour Left. But, like everybody else who deals with Rupert, there comes a time when you are past your sell-by date.

'I've never seen anybody more astute at manipulating politicians to his advantage than Rupert Murdoch,' one of his most senior executives once told me. Blair should remember these words as he savours his days in the *Sun*.

*

RUPERT MURDOCH NEVER DID get round to launching the prime-time news magazine show he had sent me to New York to launch on his Fox Television Network in the summer of 1994. Those charitable souls in the British press who had mischievously written that it had been my inadequacies as a broadcaster which had killed the show (the London *Evening Standard* even concocted a story that I could not stop 'sweating' on air, a piece of journalistic fiction stolen from a scene in the film *Broadcast News*) have subsequently managed to ignore the fact that nobody was brought in to take over after my departure.[1]

Nor did Rupert's television executives in Los Angeles turn out to be right when three years ago, to bolster their successful attempts to kill the planned Fox news magazine, they predicted the demise of the news magazine as a programme format. In fact, news magazines have gone from strength to strength on the other American networks.

CBS's *60 Minutes* remains a huge ratings success, NBC's *Dateline* is expanding to four nights a week, a second night of ABC's *20/20* is being planned while *Primetime Live* (ABC) and *48 Hours* (CBS) all continue to rate well. Far from withering on the vine, there are now four news magazines among the twenty best-watched shows in America, which means they are doing better than most situation comedies and action-adventure shows. At the time of writing (June, 1997) an unprecedented ten hours of news magazine shows were being planned for American TV's prime-time autumn schedules.

The economics of news magazines are attractive: they cost about $400,000 an hour to produce, only around a third of the cost of a top-flight drama like *NYPD Blue*. They also help a network to define itself and give it character: nobody can quite remember which popular sitcom appears where but every American knows that *60 Minutes* belongs to CBS and *20/20* to ABC. And because they rate well, they are moneyspinners – so successful, in fact, that some networks

---

[1] The dismissive view of London's professional dividing classes was not shared by those who know a little more about American TV. After I had completed an interview for CBS's flagship *60 Minutes* in the autumn of 1996, the programme's veteran presenter, Mike Wallace, commented: 'Well, thank God Rupert did not put you up against us.'

are considering replacing their nightly newscasts with news magazines.

'There is no sign of slowing when it comes to prime-time news programmes,' wrote *Broadcasting & Cable* magazine in November, 1996. 'A news boom in prime time' was how the *Wall Street Journal* described it in the summer of 1997. Clearly Rupert should have proceeded with a Fox news magazine, with or without me. But Fox still has no news magazine of its own, nor any plans to produce one. Nor has Rupert succeeded in transferring the big audiences he won by buying the expensive rights to Sunday afternoon American football to his Sunday evening schedules.

Rupert's original plan had been to hold on to the afternoon football ratings with an early evening news magazine, just as CBS had built up its Sunday night for a generation by following the football with *60 Minutes*. But, after the cancellation of our news magazine, everything else Rupert tried bombed: costly game shows, sitcoms, action-adventure series – nothing seemed to work in that early Sunday night slot. For the last two years, commented the *Wall Street Journal* in the autumn of 1996, 'Fox has failed to find a successful 7 p.m. Sunday show to take advantage of its sports audience.'

At least the man who had done most to turn Rupert against our news magazine got his come-uppance. John Matoian, the hotshot TV executive Rupert had poached from CBS in the summer of 1994 to become president of Fox TV – the man who had opined so confidently on arrival that news magazines were dead – was 'let go' two years later (after the usual ritual denials that Rupert was finished with him), the fourth Fox president in seven years to bite the dust. One more Murdoch flavour of the month had passed his sell-by date.

It was another illustration of Rupert's uncertain touch when it comes to broadcasting. When I went to New York his strategy was to launch a weekly news magazine first, then a late-night daily news show and finally a 24-hour all-news channel. Within a year everything was back to front: the news magazine was abandoned, never to be revived, the daily news show (which he had wanted me to stay to do) was never even attempted – but he decided to leap straight into 24-hour news.

Fox News was launched late into an already crowded 24-hour news market (dominated by Ted Turner's CNN) in October 1996, to public and critical indifference. The channel's profile was not helped by the refusal of Manhattan's cable system, which was owned by Time Warner, who also happened to own CNN, to carry it. Cable distribution was difficult in other parts of America too but it was the lack of an outlet in Manhattan that hurt Rupert most: his news channel was invisible to the movers and shakers of the media capital of the world – especially the advertising agencies who control billions of advertising dollars.

There began an unseemly public slanging match between Murdoch and Turner, with much hurling of personal abuse and legal writs at each other. This provided some diverting entertainment for media folks though it did little to further Rupert's case. It confirmed his belief, however, that if he was to succeed in America's multi-channel environment he had to control his own means of distribution for his channels, just as he did in Britain. He resolved to create an American satellite TV system in the image of his British Sky.

*

THE BRITISH BROADCASTING establishment had laid down in front of Murdoch's Sky onslaught and let Rupert run over them. The great panjandrums of the BBC and ITV had originally sneered at Rupert's satellite schemes and sniggered as he looked like losing his shirt. But when Sky emerged as one of the most profitable TV ventures in the world, they were like rabbits mesmerized by his oncoming headlights, too terrified to move, much less compete with him.

When, with some former News International executives, I tried to launch a common digital platform that would allow British television to compete with Sky in the digital age, there was broad support for the concept. British TV executives knew that they had missed out on subscription and pay TV, the fastest growing streams of revenue, by leaving satellite to Sky. Digital TV was their second chance for a share of the pie.

They liked the idea of a common set-top box which would take all forms of digital TV and free them from reliance on Sky's scrambling and subscriber management systems. Seed capital was promised to proceed with its development in the summer of 1995. But when we pointed out that there was no point in developing the technology unless they started buying up the pay TV rights to the sort of programming – essentially films and sport – which would move the set-top boxes, they froze. It meant going head-to-head with Murdoch for programme rights.

The BBC was first to opt out: its dependence on limited public funds and inability to raise money on the capital markets will sadly condemn it to be an also-ran in the digital age. But even the more commercially-minded bosses of ITV balked at the prospect of competing with Murdoch. They were more at home making money out of their regional monopoly franchises.

Even the self-made, hard-headed giants of ITV, like Gerry Robinson (Granada/LWT/Yorkshire) and Michael Green (Carlton/Central), thought competing with Murdoch was beyond them. They settled for an alliance instead, joining with Sky to bid for terrestrial digital frequencies, with Sky clearly in the driving seat and set to make most of the money because it had the rights to the programmes for which people were prepared to pay. But American broadcasters are made of sterner stuff.

'In Britain he overwhelmed a complacent broadcasting establishment with his satellite service,' commented the *Wall Street Journal* in May, 1997, 'quickly signing up millions of subscribers by locking up exclusive movie and sports rights. But the US cable industry, with 65 million subscribers and $25 billion in annual revenues, is a far more aggressive rival in local markets – as well as Capitol Hill.'

Things went wrong for Rupert right from the start. Unlike in Britain, where he was the satellite-TV trailblazer, there were already three strong players in the market when he entered it. Rupert was scrambling to catch up. He was later privately to describe his delay in entering the US satellite market as 'one of my worst mistakes ever'. So he rushed into a billion dollar alliance with a tough, Tennessee-bred satellite-dish entrepreneur called Charlie Ergen, who began his business life hawking dishes in Denver.

The deal began unravelling almost before the ink was dry on their agreement.

Ergen's fledgling EchoStar satellite service was supposed to merge with News Corp's satellites and programming to form American Sky Broadcasting (ASkyB), which would provide 500 channels of crystal-clear CD-quality programmes all over America. But (surprise, surprise) Ergen and Murdoch quickly fell out. They had a fight over the encryption system: Rupert insisted on the one he was using in Europe and Asia. 'He can't fire me,' Ergen had said when the deal was signed 'and I can't fire him. It's like a marriage.' The poor chap thought that as chief executive of ASkyB he would be left to run the show: but Rupert, of course, had other ideas.

There were echoes in this of the abortive deal he did with Disney to launch Sky in Britain. For a white, Anglo-Saxon Protestant, Rupert has a curiously Mediterranean approach to deal making. For him, the real bargaining begins after the agreement is made. At Sky, he expected me to keep Disney as partners but ignore them in practice. That marriage ended in a $3 billion law suit. The Murdoch–Ergen 'marriage' ended without ever being consummated in a $5 billion law suit.

Rupert was also forced to face up to that fact that, for the first time, the markets were not prepared to go along with his expansionist plans. Investors regarded ASkyB as a huge black hole which would gobble up billions. He was embarking on his satellite strategy while still making other expensive acquisitions, from the Family Entertainment cable channel (cost: $1.7 billion) to the discount coupon business of the Heritage Media Corporation ($1.4 billion) to the Los Angeles Dodgers ($350 million) and various other sports acquisitions costing $800 million. The markets would not wear it: News Corporation's stock got hammered as investors decided to unload it. For the first time, Rupert was forced to worry about the reaction of his shareholders.

Rupert was also defeated on Capitol Hill. His plans to compete head-to-head with America's mighty cable companies required not just deep pockets but a favourable regulatory environment, as he had achieved in Britain. Rupert thought he had plenty of chips to cash in with a Republican Congress he had done much to cultivate. He did some of the lobbying himself. But he could not swing his plans politically. The cable companies, combined with the power of the local broadcasters, had too much clout on Capitol Hill.

'It was a confluence of events that Rupert had never faced before anywhere in the world,' said one of his close advisers later. 'His EchoStar deal was unravelling, nobody else wanted to be his partner, the markets gave him a huge thumbs down and he didn't have the politicians in his pocket the way he thought he did.'

It was a painful reality check for Rupert. Murdoch's men

had boasted that ASkyB would be a 'death star' for cable. Now he was capitulating to cable, forced to sue for peace on the best terms he could. Instead of providing an aggressive satellite competitor to America's cosy cable monopolies, which would have been greatly in the public interest, he reluctantly merged his satellite assets with PrimeStar, a satellite service owned by the cable companies – including arch-enemy Ted Turner – which concentrates on providing satellite channels to areas where cable is weak. It offers no threat to existing cable franchises and Congress could well veto the tie-up as anti-competitive. But, whatever the regulators decide, Rupert had been forced to cave in to a monopoly he could not crack. PrimeStar tossed him $1 billion in non-voting shares in return. It was a sad surrender, both for Rupert and for an American public ill-served by the cable monopolies.

It was also a major setback in Rupert's global television strategy. His vision is to make and own every form of television – news, sport, films, entertainment, children's TV – and to beam them to Britain, America and Asia via distribution systems he also owns or controls. The ASkyB débâcle was the biggest set-back to date in his global ambitions: his satellite vision remains an unrealized dream in the richest broadcast market of them all. It had looked as if nothing would block this breathtaking ambition. Now he faces trouble on several fronts.

In Asia, political problems, especially in China and India, have slowed up his ambitions for his Star TV satellite system. In Germany a joint venture for digital TV never got off the ground. Even in Britain, though the established broadcasters offer little threat to him, there are signs that the regulators want to place Sky under a tighter leash.

On 4 June, 1997 a 'private and confidential' fax arrived at Sky from the ITC, the body which regulates commercial TV in Britain, which delivered a serious set-back to Sky's digital ambitions by insisting that BSkyB be dropped from the alliance it had formed with Carlton and Granada to bid for terrestrial digital frequencies in a consortium known as British Digital Broadcasting (BDB). The ITC, reflecting the concerns of the competition authorities in London and Brussels, was worried that if Sky, which was already set to dominate digital satellite TV, was also allowed to be the dominant partner in terrestrial digital then it would enjoy unacceptable monopoly power.

'These competition concerns appear to be so fundamental to the BDB application,' concluded the ITC fax, 'that they may only be addressed effectively by the removal of BSkyB as a shareholder in BDB.'

In a remarkably tough ruling, however, the ITC went even further. Sky would not be allowed to own any shares in BDB but it would have to supply its programmes to it. 'You should note,' the fax continued, 'that it would not be acceptable to the ITC to couple this with the removal of the programme services indicated in the application to be provided by BSkyB.' In other words, Rupert would be banned from owning any share of terrestrial digital; but he would still have to provide his programming to get it off the ground.

In the short term this could work to Rupert's advantage: he will now have to bear none of the capital costs of setting up BDB and will be handsomely paid for the premium programming Sky will provide for it. But there could easily come a time when the owners of BDB may well conclude that they should buy their premium programmes direct from the suppliers rather than use Sky as an intermediary. BSkyB's stock has traded at record highs because it was thought to have a monopoly grip on premium programming – the type for which viewers are prepared to pay a lot of money to watch. The share price slumped in the aftermath of the ITC intervention when it looked as if that monopoly was now in jeopardy.

*

As his seventh decade approaches, 67-year-old Rupert has increasingly given the impression of being an old man in a hurry. His restless energy has built a worldwide media empire and he is still building, despite the occasional set-back. As he grows older he has also set about turning the empire he created into a dynasty: his three children from his second marriage have all been recently seeded into key positions in the company.

At the ripe old age of twenty-five his older son, Lachlan, has been shoehorned into the top job of his Australian empire as executive chairman, which puts him in charge of a host of newspapers and various TV concerns. His 28-year-old daughter, Elisabeth, has been parachuted into multi-billion pound Sky as general manager with responsibility for programming – not bad for somebody who has only ever run two small local stations in California. His younger son, James, has (for the moment) a more peripheral position in New York, looking after music and new media.

These appointments obviously had more to do with genes than merit. Nevertheless Rupert is determined that one of them will be his successor when 'I am carried out of my office in a box' as he puts it. His first choice has always been Lachlan and most effort has gone into grooming him for the succession (he is the only one to sit on the News Corp holding company board). Elisabeth, however, regards herself in the running too and Rupert is happy to go along with that despite his unease with female executives (News Corp's highest levels are a male monopoly). As for James, he worries he is too bohemian for corporate life.

Rupert's dynastic obsession is a recent development. He always hoped that his children would join what he still sees as a family business but the matter has taken on a new urgency now that age has given him intimations of his own mortality. It is an absurd conceit.

All three offspring are intelligent, competent and personable – perfectly normal, in fact, despite their wealthy backgrounds – but none is capable of running or holding together what is Rupert's unique creation, much less continuing his brilliant financial deal-making. Even if one of them were, it would not be a foregone conclusion that they would get the top job: News Corp is now 70 per cent owned by non-Murdoch family investors, which include some of the biggest institutions in the world. They will not automatically vote in a successor just because he or she has Murdoch for a surname.

Their premature presence in key positions has already caused some anguish among shareholders and top managers. Sam Chisholm's departure from Sky was said to be connected with failing health, though he was no more ill than he had been for years. As happens regularly at the Court of the Sun King, Rupert had come to regard this senior courtier as too big for his boots. He particularly resented how Chisholm had dragged his feet over Rupert's plans to take Sky digital. Chisholm, for his part, resented Elisabeth's presence. He did not take kindly to having the boss's daughter on his patch. Significantly, David Chance, the executive expected to succeed Chisholm, surprisingly decided to leave with him: he did not relish the prospect of keeping the seat warm for Elisabeth (those close to Rupert say he is of a mind to have her running Sky in a few years). In Sydney the editor of the *Australian* recently resigned after falling foul of Lachlan's plans to 'brighten up' the broadsheet.

'News Corp today looks a little like the Roman Empire circa AD 350,' says one former Murdoch insider. 'Still imperial but fraying at the edges, full of intrigue and perhaps in danger of decline.' Rupert's penchant for running News Corp as a family store is making share and debt holders increasingly nervous. He recently tried to sell a News Corp debt offering securitized by BSkyB shares. The markets forced him to withdraw it. When BSkyB shares plummetted on Chisholm's departure Rupert opined that they had been 'overvalued' anyway – not quite what he was saying when he offered them as collateral for his debt offer. It is the sort of cavalier behaviour which makes the markets anxious.

When Rupert dies, News Corporation as we have known it almost certainly dies too. Some of its biggest investors are already beginning to think that way. Rupert has always defended the derisory dividends the company pays by promising to deliver long-term capital growth. I'm in for the long haul, he tells investors, you should be too.

In the past the company has delivered that growth in earnings. But Rupert's insatiable appetite for expansion and acquisition is now hindering that growth. In 1990 the debt he accumulated almost brought the company crashing down. Now the huge investment he needs to realize his latest ambitions are hitting the share price.

In recent years investors have had neither decent dividends nor capital growth. Some are beginning to think that they will only ever realize News Corp's true value by unbundling – selling off – its constituent parts. There would indeed be a goldmine in such a strategy for the value of News Corp's various assets, even on the most conservative of calculations, far exceeds the current market capitalization. But News Corp will never be unbundled as long as Rupert is alive.

It is surely not a happy prospect. For all his momentous achievements, which nobody has matched (or is every likely to), there must be something strangely disconcerting about knowing that those who have invested in you are waiting for you to die to make real money out of you. But perhaps it does not bother him: Rupert, after all, has never been sentimental about business.

INTRODUCTION

Guess Who's Coming to Dinner?

THE TELEPHONE RANG in my drawing room: a female voice said my guest was on his way and would arrive any moment. I wandered downstairs to wait; a policeman had already been stationed outside my front door for an hour. It was 29 July 1992. Earlier in the day security men with sniffer dogs had been all over my South Kensington flat, checking for bombs and anything suspicious. Within minutes a dark Daimler followed by a Rover raced down Onslow Gardens and stopped outside my door. A grey-haired man of middling height and build emerged from the back seat and came forward to shake my hand, a friendly smile on his face. The Prime Minister was coming to dinner.

*

I DID NOT KNOW JOHN MAJOR well, having met him only a few times before. My first contact with him was an off-the-record interview in his Treasury office in March 1990, the night after he had delivered his one and only Budget as chancellor of the exchequer. He was affable and in no apparent hurry to end our talk. I had arrived at 7.30 p.m. expecting half an hour or forty-five minutes at most. At 9 p.m. he was pouring me yet another Scotch and I was running out of questions.

Though I was there to talk about the Budget, he spent some time explaining to me how he was an 'Iain Macleod

Tory', meaning he combined a robust attitude to free-market economics with a strong social conscience. The leadership challenge to Margaret Thatcher was still eight months away, though opposition to her was already building up within the Tory Party. Major seemed to be laying down a marker: talk of being an 'Iain Macleod Tory' was calculated to appeal to the editor of *The Sunday Times*.

I asked him when sterling was going to join the European exchange-rate mechanism (ERM), something every economic commentator wanted to know.

'I'm very enthusiastic about the ERM,' he said bluntly, 'and I don't have a shred of doubt we'll go in. The Prime Minister [Margaret Thatcher] knows my position. It's not true that we've had blazing rows about it.' His hope was that ERM membership would allow him to start cutting interest rates at a time when the economic boom of the 1980s was becoming a distant memory.

'If you don't cut interest rates soon,' I said, 'I fear you'll be heading for a very rough recession.'

'Don't worry,' he reassured me. 'We're on course for a soft landing.'

As he dealt with my various concerns about economic policy I was struck by the number of times he used a Latin phrase, *de minimis* (meaning 'of little or no importance'). 'Oh, that's *de minimis*,' he replied several times, waving his hand to sweep my point away. He seemed an unlikely Latin scholar (Major left school at fifteen and never went to university) but he used the phrase with relish, almost as if he had just learned it from one of his Oxbridge-educated civil servants, and wanted to impress me.

It also seemed strange that he had so much time to spend with me. He had been in 'purdah' for months preparing his Budget – a gruelling task. This must have been his first night off for a long time; there was no vote in the House of

Commons and he did not have to be in Westminster at all. 'Why is he not taking his wife out for dinner to celebrate his first Budget?' I thought to myself. Instead, he was alone in his massive, gloomy office overlooking Whitehall, sitting on the sofa with an editor he had never met before. I glanced at my watch: it was 9.30 p.m. and I was already an hour late for a dinner party in Chelsea. I said I had to leave; he looked a little forlorn. I felt like asking him to come with me: one more Scotch and I would have.

I next encountered Major five months later in September 1990 when he came to one of *The Sunday Times* Business section's lunches, which regularly mix businessmen and politicians. It was in a private room at the Savoy, Major was still chancellor and Nigel Broackes of Trafalgar House and Alan Sugar of Amstrad were among our guests from industry. Major disarmed us all with his self-deprecation. 'I've met you before,' he said to my deputy editor, Ivan Fallon, who could not remember the occasion. 'It was when you came to lunch at the Standard Bank,' he continued. 'I took your coat. I was the PR man.' Ivan smiled: though a formidable financial journalist of long standing, it was not every day that a future chancellor had hung up his coat. As we sat down to lunch, however, we quickly discovered that Major was as stubborn as he was charming.

The main topic of conversation was the terrible state of the economy: I was insistent that we were heading for a deep recession and that he had to cut interest rates. I explained how our classified advertising, always a key indicator of how the economy was going, was in freefall; property and jobs were the two worst-hit categories, which did not bode well for future economic activity. The businessmen around the table agreed that we were heading for a bad recession; Broackes said he had just shelved £100 million of investment.

But Major would have none of it. At worst, he said, the economy was heading for a gentle slowdown, repeating his previous reassurance that we were on target for a 'soft landing'. We were exaggerating how bad things were; there was no case for interest-rate cuts – and certainly no reason to make sterling more competitive. The argument became quite heated as I and others pressed the case that we were heading for recession. But Major stuck stubbornly to his Treasury brief: there was nothing to worry about. A month later we discovered why Major had been so adamant that interest rates were fine and sterling was at the right level: he took Britain into the ERM, fixing the pound at D-Mark 2.95 – a disastrously high level.

Two years later in July 1992, the economy unmistakably mired in recession, my dinner party for Major was dominated by the same argument. In the interim, he had replaced Thatcher as prime minister a few months after our Savoy lunch and won the 1992 election. *The Sunday Times* had backed Michael Heseltine for the Tory leadership but the Tory press supported Major because it thought he would remain true to the Thatcher agenda and wanted at all costs to stop Heseltine, Thatcher's assassin, from taking her crown. It was a short-sighted decision which the Tory press soon came to regret. But even I endorsed Major's re-election in 1992 – there was no choice since the alternative was Neil Kinnock's Labour Party – but I struggled to muster any enthusiasm as I wrote the last editorial before polling day advising our readers to 'Vote Tory'.

I visited Major in Downing Street during the campaign, at his request. I told him the Tory campaign was a mess and that it would probably lose him the election. He did not argue: he blamed Tory Central Office and the BBC, whose election coverage he found very hostile to the Tories. He said Downing Street was taking over control of the campaign and that he would take his revenge on the BBC after the election. 'I won't forget what they've done to me,' he said. But, of course, he did forget: a few years after the election the BBC had its Charter renewed on favourable terms for another decade. It was classic Major: talk tough – and do nothing.

At the time I never thought he would have the chance to take it out on the BBC: I reckoned the least likely election outcome was a Tory majority, the most likely a hung parliament with Labour the largest party. Major, however, was in no doubt that he would win. He was right: he won a decent working majority and gave the Tories their fourth consecutive term. But he had been very wrong about the economy: by the time he came to dinner in July 1992 the economy was in the depths of one of the worst recessions since the 1930s – and the Tory Party's natural supporters in Middle Britain – homeowners, small-business folk, white-collar workers, the self-employed – were suffering most of all.

*

I USHERED MAJOR INTO THE drawing room. It was a warm, sunny evening. 'We could have a drink on the terrace,' I said, 'but your security people say I have to keep you indoors.'

'Oh, bollocks!' he replied and headed outside, the rest of us scurrying after him. We sipped our pre-dinner drinks as nervous security men scanned the rooftops and windows looking for potential assassins. I had assembled *The Sunday Times*'s most senior editors in politics and economics: Ivan Fallon (deputy editor), Michael Jones (political editor), John Cassidy (business editor), Jeff Randall (city editor) and Andrew Grice (political correspondent). They were a formidable bunch. The meal, in my dining room just off the terrace, began in friendly fashion; but we were soon jointly complaining that a sense of drift and dither had set in even though the government had won a spectacular re-election victory. Above all, we complained that keeping the pound at an over-valued level within the ERM was crucifying the economy and the Tory Party.

Major would have none of it. He was anxious to convince us that he was a radical leader with his own agenda – and he was frustrated that he was not being given credit for it. 'We're going to privatize coal and the railways,' he said. 'She never did that. We're going to remove a tier of local government and give priority to reforming education. She never did that.' In each case the 'she' was Margaret Thatcher: he seemed anxious to escape her shadow and appear as a prime minister in his own right.

'I'm prepared to take some tough decisions,' he insisted. 'This public-spending round will be much tougher than anyone imagines.' It will have to be, I thought, since you opened the Treasury floodgates to get re-elected. 'We *need* to close one London teaching hospital and we *will* close one,' he insisted. It was almost as if he was looking for unpopular decisions to prove he was made of the right stuff. 'I'm not hung up on being prime minister,' he said. 'It's not the be-all and end-all of life for me.'

Though he had distanced himself from Thatcher's Euroscepticism by saying he wanted Britain to be at the heart of Europe, he was not keen to rush into further European integration with President Mitterrand or Chancellor Kohl, dismissing them as 'two old men in a hurry'. He was particularly critical of Kohl, accusing him of fiddling the books to hide all the money West Germany was having to spend on East Germany, post-unification, and saying that the main effect of his rush to unite Germany was that 'West Germany bought itself twenty-five Liverpools.'

I asked him how he rated John Smith, who had just replaced Neil Kinnock as Labour leader after Kinnock had lost a second general election. 'He's not as good as you chaps in the media think he is,' he replied. I said Labour should have jumped a generation, explaining how, on the weekend Smith had been elected Labour leader, I had put Tony Blair on the cover of *The Sunday Times Magazine* with the cover line: 'The leader Labour missed.'

'Blair,' said Major, 'is the man the Tories need to fear most. I'd have him in the cabinet tomorrow.' An intriguing assessment of Blair's worth now that he is Labour leader (succeeding Smith after his sad death in May 1994). Major added that he would have been happy to have included David Owen in his cabinet too.

The conversation became heated, however, when we turned to the economy and sterling's position in the ERM. We pressed him to cut interest rates and devalue sterling to alleviate the ravages of the recession. He would have none of it. 'I'm absolutely determined to tough it out,' he insisted. 'I need to convince the markets that the government is serious about getting inflation down. The markets don't trust us. They have never believed we really mean it. I want to be remembered as the Prime Minister who really did mean it.

'Your idea of devaluing within the ERM is a non-starter,' he continued, looking at me. I wanted to know why, since the French had originally devalued the frank against the German mark by 31 per cent in a total of six realignments when it first joined the ERM. *The Sunday Times*, which had (in retrospect, mistakenly) supported sterling's membership, had quickly become disillusioned. But even by the summer of 1992 we were not demanding withdrawal from the ERM – just a more sustainable level for our currency. But he sidestepped the point. 'The only way I could contemplate a change in sterling's value within the ERM would be if there was a general revaluation of the other currencies. But I've sounded out all the other prime ministers and finance ministers and I can tell you it is unrealistic, a non-starter. We would be on our own if we tried to devalue sterling – and we'd end up having to put up interest rates.'

He then rounded on *The Sunday Times* for constantly calling for interest-rate cuts. 'The more you call for interest-rate cuts, the more difficult it is for the government to do because the markets think I'm going to buckle under the pressure. So the pound weakens and it becomes impossible. The pressure to cut is actually preventing the cut from happening. What we need is a two-month moratorium on interest-rate speculation from people like you.'

He was also angry about what he called Thatcher's 'constant carping' about the ERM. 'She took us in,' he said bluntly. 'She knew what it involved. I was chancellor at the time: I made it clear that the ERM would not be a magic cure; it would be a long haul and involve some pain.' He did not add that Thatcher had entered the ERM very much against her better judgement, egged on in turn by Major, Nigel Lawson and Geoffrey Howe.

I questioned the competence of his chancellor, Norman Lamont, who had been his campaign manager in the leadership election but was woefully out of his depth as the country's senior economic minister. 'I will not have Norman used as a scapegoat,' he said firmly. 'He's getting a lot of flak simply for carrying out my policy. I took us into the ERM at D-Mark 2.95 – and I was right to do so.'

The argument continued in what diplomatic cables euphemistically call a free and frank exchange of views. 'Andrew,' he said angrily at one stage, 'there is no alternative to what we're doing', echoing the famous words of his predecessor in another context and slamming his palm on the table for effect. His next remarks struck us all dumb.

'Look, I want sterling to replace the D-Mark as Europe's benchmark currency,' he said quietly but firmly. 'I want sterling to be the most trusted currency in Europe. I want Europe's currencies to revolve round the pound rather than the D-Mark.'

We looked at each other in amazement but he continued undaunted. 'Don't talk Britain down,' he said. 'It's not a pipedream. Our productivity is growing faster than Germany's, our wage increases are slowing, our tax rates are lower than America's, we will start growing again soon. We could be Europe's benchmark currency before the decade is out.'

It was an admirable enough ambition in theory, though in practice it was preposterous. It meant Major was prepared to continue crucifying Britain on the double cross of high interest rates and an overvalued exchange rate for the foreseeable future. There was clearly going to be no meeting of minds and it was getting late. I accompanied the Prime Minister to the front door, where he thanked me for a stimulating evening and departed with a cordial handshake. I bounded back upstairs.

'Did he really say what I thought he said?' I asked. Yes, they nodded, he wants sterling to replace the D-Mark. Extraordinary, I thought, either this man is living on a different planet or he knows something we don't.

'Right,' I said, 'nobody leaves until we've reconstructed this dinner while it's still fresh in our memories.' We trooped out to the terrace, opened a bottle of champagne and tried to remember and write down everything the Prime Minister had said. As my editors departed I remember saying: 'I think he's nuts – but at least we have a splash for Sunday.'

'Major aims to make sterling best in Europe', was the front page lead in *The Sunday Times* on 2 August. 'John Major has embarked on an economic strategy designed to see the British pound replace the German mark as the hardest and most-trusted currency in the European Community,' began the story under a joint Michael Jones/Andrew Grice by-line. It went on to report that 'the Prime Minister is determined to resist growing calls to kick-start the economy with a devaluation of the pound and a substantial cut in interest rates'.

The journalists from the daily newspapers who regularly fed off *Sunday Times* stories to help fill the Monday papers thought we had taken leave of our senses. They called Downing Street for a reaction, fully expecting the story to be rubbished. They were dumbfounded when it was confirmed. They ran it again the next day, with their own embellishments.

Seven weeks later, in the third week of September, Major's economic strategy collapsed in ruins, along with his dreams for sterling: a massive run on the pound resulted in its being unceremoniously ejected from the ERM, even though the Bank of England spent billions buying its own currency and even raised interest rates briefly to a crippling 15 per cent in a vain attempt to preserve sterling's value. The Prime Minister's stubborn refusal to countenance devaluing sterling within the ERM and his pig-headed determination to sustain an indefensible value for the pound, whatever the cost, had resulted in sterling being thrown out of the ERM altogether. It was a defining moment for John Major, from which he and his government have never quite recovered.

The Prime Minister called me in my office the Saturday after the ERM débâcle. He wanted to know if there was anything he could say that would help with that week's *Sunday Times* editorial. What followed was less colourful than his telephone conversation earlier in the week with the editor of the *Sun*. 'I hope you won't be too hard on me,' he had said to Kelvin MacKenzie.

'Well, John,' replied Kelvin in his own inimitable fashion, 'let me put it this way: I've got a large bucket of shit lying on my desk and tomorrow morning I'm going to pour it all over your head.'

The Prime Minister laughed weakly, not knowing if Kelvin was serious or joking: 'Oh, Kelvin,' he replied, 'you are a wag.'

Next morning, the said bucket of *Sun* shit duly covered Major from head to toe. Undaunted, Major was now trying his hand for a better press from *The Sunday Times*; but he only made matters worse.

'Where do you go from here, Prime Minister?' I asked. 'You told me only a few weeks ago that there was no alternative to the ERM. You told the Scottish CBI [Confederation of British Industry] that your critics were "quack doctors". You and your chancellor have said repeatedly that inflation and interest rates would have to rise if we left the ERM. What happens now?'

'Oh, Andrew,' he replied with a chuckle, 'as my old father used to say "there's more than one way to skin a cat".'

This flip, off-hand remark destroyed any remaining respect I had for John Major. Here was a man who had inflicted unnecessary hardship on millions in pursuit of an economic strategy to which he had insisted only weeks before there was no alternative. Now that strategy had blown up in his face. But there was no apology, no regrets, no recognition that he had been wrong, that there were other ways of controlling inflation and developing the economy. It was all just a matter of skinning cats.

'Look, Andrew,' he continued, 'I'm a political realist, a pragmatist. The principle of the ERM is sound but the Germans let us down: it's all the fault of Bundesbank [the German central bank]. It was so concerned with its own narrow needs it forgot about Britain. Now we have to start afresh.'

I noted that he was accepting none of the blame for the

biggest disaster in British economic policy since the Labour government was bailed out by the International Monetary Fund in 1976.

'Tell me, Prime Minister,' I asked him, 'as it was all unravelling did you ever think of resigning?'

There was silence for a second at the other end of the phone, then he spoke.

'I'm not going to answer that question,' he said sternly. I took that to be a 'yes'; after all, if resignation had not entered his mind he could easily have said so.

My fury at the manner in which he accepted the collapse of his whole economic strategy was reflected in that week's editorial. I began by outlining the costs of a failed policy Major had been forced to abandon against his will: 'A million more on the dole, more than 100,000 companies gone bust, tens of thousands of homes repossessed, the reignited enterprise of the 1980s superseded by the new bankruptcy of the 1990s. The country will not quickly forgive those responsible for the unnecessary pain of those wasted months. Nor should it.'

I was particularly angered by the absence of any apology:

> Forgiveness might be more forthcoming, of course, if ministers showed any sign of contrition. But, even though the government has just executed the biggest U-turn in modern British history, though billions were thrown at the foreign exchange markets in futile defence of sterling, though interest rates went up and down like a yo-yo, though yesterday's 'betrayal' (devaluation) has become today's official policy, not a single minister or official adviser has offered an apology, much less a resignation.

The editorial also pointed out that Labour and the Liberal Democrats had been just as committed to keeping sterling within the ERM as the Tories: 'Last week's shambles was not just a defeat for the government. It was a defeat for the whole British political establishment. But the government was in charge and must take the blame.'

Four years later, the British people have yet to forgive John Major and his government. Interest rates and inflation have tumbled (contrary to the predictions of Major and Lamont) and job-creating growth has returned to the economy since that infamous Black Wednesday in September 1992; but voters remain reluctant to give Major any credit for it. And why should they? The economy has improved only because a wrenching U-turn was forced on the government against its stiff opposition: the recovery has happened despite the government, not because of it. No wonder we are inclined to give it little credit.

The ERM débâcle destroyed more than the government's reputation. It harmed the many Establishment commentators, such as *The Economist* magazine and Sam Brittan of the *Financial Times* (until Black Wednesday Fleet Street's most respected economic commentator), who were cheerleaders for Major's ERM strategy. Their comments on the economy have lacked a certain authority ever since: they have been tarnished by Major's failure almost as much as Major himself.

The recovery of the economy after Black Wednesday (which we started to call White Wednesday because it had liberated us from the ERM) was a vindication of *The Sunday Times*'s position on the major issue of the day. But we continued to despair at the Prime Minister's inability to exploit the new circumstances to create a British economic miracle and effectively withdrew support from a government whose economic policies the paper had broadly backed for a decade. Two weeks after White Wednesday we feared Major would prove 'an empty vessel, with no firm purpose, no direction, no clear policies to pursue, but vulnerable to the vicissitudes of events and the initiatives of others'. It has proved to be a sadly prescient prediction, one which enhanced the reputation of *The Sunday Times*.

As 1992 ended it was increasingly seen across the political spectrum as a powerful, independent voice which spoke up for economic policies to help the unemployed, householders trapped in negative equity and businessmen struggling to keep their companies alive. It was seen to be in the pocket of no political party, no person or interest was safe from its criticisms and investigations, and nobody could automatically count on its support. The readers seemed to relish it: we were regularly outselling the combined circulation of our two nearest rivals (the *Observer* and the *Sunday Telegraph*) by 150,000.

It was the perfect springboard from which to head towards my tenth anniversary as editor of the world's most famous Sunday newspaper. It was also the beginning of the end of my time as Britain's most controversial editor.

CHAPTER ONE

An Offer I Couldn't Refuse

I HAD BEEN EDITOR for five hours before I received my first death threat. At 7 p.m. on Saturday 1 October 1983, Frank Giles, the outgoing editor, who had just put his last edition of *The Sunday Times* to bed, called me into his office and plonked the keys of his office and drinks' cupboard into my hand and said in his precise, clipped tones: 'This means you're the editor now. I'm off to the country.' With no more ado he was gone.

I savoured my new status alone for a few minutes then called some of the senior editors into my office for a drink and to go over some changes to pep up the front page of the later editions. They were, naturally, eager to please: some on the newsdesk even seemed to relish the prospect of a more hands-on editor in the mould of Harry Evans, who along with Denis Hamilton in the sixties and seventies had developed *The Sunday Times* into one of the world's great newspapers. Frank Giles had taken a more gentlemanly approach during his two-year interregnum as editor: he had regularly departed for the country early on a Saturday evening as soon as the first edition came off the presses, leaving any subsequent changes to his news staff – and strict instructions that he was not to be disturbed except in emergency. I had made it clear I would be staying in the office at least until the last edition was agreed.

Among those who gathered in my office that night was

Brian MacArthur, the paper's deputy editor, a soft-spoken, congenial chain-smoker with the long Fleet Street experience I lacked. Though he had every right to feel disappointed by my appointment – Rupert Murdoch had at one stage indicated that he might well be Giles's successor when he was briefly a Murdoch flavour-of-the-month – he was to become a loyal deputy and good friend, full of sound advice. But not that night.

'There's a farewell party for Magnus Linklater this evening,' said Brian. 'Most of the *Sunday Times* staff will be there. It'll be a good opportunity for you to meet and greet them. You should go.'

I wasn't so sure. Linklater was one of the stars of the Evans era, an influential features editor with the usual once-fashionable, increasingly dated left-wing views that were then ubiquitous among senior *Sunday Times* journalists. He wasn't leaving because of me, though no doubt he would have done: he hated working for a paper owned by Rupert Murdoch and had accepted a senior post at the *Observer* before my appointment was announced. I knew this would be a gathering of the old guard, bemoaning his departure and my arrival. But most of these people were now working for me and I had to get to know them and they me: I agreed to go.

I spent some time in the newsroom overseeing the changes and updates to the front page and a few other pages. Then at around 10.30 p.m. I headed for the Zanzibar, a fashionable Covent Garden watering hole for media types in deprived, pre-Groucho Club days.

When I arrived the party was in full swing. I made my way gingerly to the long bar, where I recognized some faces, even if I could not put names to them. People were curious rather than welcoming: the party was for Linklater but I felt all eyes were on me. Nobody was outrightly hostile – I was their new boss after all – but I have never been comfortable working a room, even if it is full of friends, and this was a strain among strangers.

I spotted Cal McCrystal in the seating area at the end of the bar. Cal was a gentle, friendly Irishman who had made an unhappy transition from accomplished feature writer to deputy foreign editor. I joined his group and spent a pleasant hour in the sort of gossip and story-telling that always happens when journalists gather. By now it was after midnight and I thought I had done enough getting-to-know-you for one night. As I got up to leave, a cocky, wiry character whispered that he wanted to talk about Linda Melvern. I told him that would be inappropriate and continued my goodbyes.

Linda Melvern had come to symbolize, for me, much of what was wrong at *The Sunday Times*. She was an investigative reporter apparently so keen on her work that she had even come to see me at *The Economist* immediately after my appointment as *Sunday Times* editor was announced to discover if investigative journalism would be a priority for me.

'Absolutely,' I assured her. 'I've read and admired *Sunday Times* investigations all my adult life. But I've not seen many significant ones lately. I want to give investigative journalism a new lease of life.'

We agreed that the world-famous Insight team, the core of the paper's investigative efforts, was a shadow of its former self. It had recently broken few stories that were interesting, never mind earth-shattering. She said this was because the paper was no longer committed to expensive, long-term investigations, nor were there enough good reporters assigned to Insight. She poured scorn on the current Insight team and its editor, Chris Hird, a hard-left protégé of Paul Foot, a posh, polemical Trot from a famous left-wing family which included Michael Foot, former (and disastrous) leader of the Labour Party.

I said I wanted to enlist her help in reinvigorating this distinctive *Sunday Times* tradition. 'I'm determined to make it a priority,' I assured her. 'We'll start the moment I arrive in early September.'

'Actually, I won't be there then,' Melvern replied, somewhat sheepishly. She then went on to explain that she had lumped a four-week sabbatical together with her six weeks annual holiday to give herself ten consecutive weeks' fully paid leave to work on a book she was writing, itself a spin-off from a *Sunday Times* investigation. I was taken aback by this generous arrangement though I was later to discover it was pretty normal practice: everybody seemed to be writing a book instead of writing for the paper. *The Sunday Times* had become akin to a feudal estate in which the workers spent all their time working on their own plots of land while the main estate went to rack and ruin. But I refused to be discouraged.

'Well, we'll hit the ground running the moment you return,' I insisted. She said she looked forward to that and departed. I was quite buoyed up by the meeting: at least there are some people there who want change, I mused comfortingly. Perhaps it won't be so bad after all.

Melvern eventually turned up at *The Sunday Times* towards the end of September after I had been there a couple of weeks, waiting to take over from Frank Giles. I called for her immediately. 'Time to get cracking with all these ideas you have for souping up our investigations,' I said enthusiastically. 'I regard you as a key player in any changes we make.'

'Thank you,' she said, staring at the floor. 'But I won't be able to help right away. I'm taking six months off to write another book.'

I was flabbergasted. 'But you've just had ten weeks off!' I exclaimed.

'Yes,' she conceded, 'but you won't have to pay me for the six months – I'll take it as unpaid leave.'

Now I was getting angry. 'You've just returned from ten weeks' paid leave,' I said firmly. 'Now you want another six months off. Yet you came to me in the summer to lobby for a key role in revamping the paper's investigative journalism. That's what I need you to do. It's all hands on deck.'

'But I've already signed the book contract,' she explained plaintively. 'I can't get out of it.'

'Well, you had no right to sign anything without first consulting me,' I responded sharply. I made it clear she did not have my permission to take another six months off and that she should report for regular *Sunday Times* duty. She left almost in tears, clearly aghast at the idea of being made to work for the paper that paid her salary.

After she had gone I began to doubt my own judgement. Was I being unreasonable? Was such outrageous disregard for a journalist's obligations to their paper par for the course at *The Sunday Times* and the rest of Fleet Street? What should I do if she insisted on writing her book?

I called in Brian MacArthur and went through the conversation I'd just had. As he listened to the details and heard the incredulity in my voice an inscrutable smirk crossed his face. 'Welcome to *The Sunday Times*,' he said quietly as he drew long and hard on his cigarette.

'Not *my Sunday Times*, Brian. Go and make it clear to Melvern that if she insists on taking any more time off, she will be deemed to have dismissed herself.'

That had been the week before the Zanzibar party. As I made my way to the exit of the club I continued to be pursued by the insistent character who was still vigorously pressing Melvern's case. I wasn't sure who he was –

husband, boyfriend or colleague – but I had no intention of discussing her. He followed me into the street.

'You don't know who I am,' he said as we stood on the pavement. 'You should realize I'm a big wheel with big connections around here.' I laughed, not sure if he was drunk or joking. He was neither.

'Everything will be fine as long as you let Linda do what she wants,' he continued. 'If not, things will be very unpleasant for you.'

'Look,' I said, exasperated, 'I don't wish to discuss the matter. Now, if you'll forgive me, I have some friends to meet.' I crossed the road and began to open the driving seat of my car. He was right behind me. I tried to get in. He slammed the door shut.

'I don't think you understand,' he continued in his sub-gangster argot. 'I'll have you taken care of unless you do what I want. I have connections. You're going to give Linda her job back and let her do what she wants.'

'No I'm not!' I replied angrily. I opened the car door again but he grabbed it and barred my way. He fixed me with his eyes: 'I don't think you realize how important I am. Your life is in danger unless you do as I say.'

There was menace in his voice and for the first time I was alarmed, not so much by this apparent death threat, which seemed fantastical, but by my predicament. It was clear that forcing my way into the car would involve a fight. I was tempted to thump him, especially since he was smaller than me. But I did not relish 'New *Sunday Times* editor in Covent Garden street brawl' headlines in Monday's papers. I realized I would have to appease him.

'I don't even know who you are,' I said trying to buy time, hoping that a friendly face whose attention I could attract would come out of the Zanzibar. But nobody did; the street was deserted.

'You're going to give Linda her job back,' he repeated. 'Do as I say and you'll be fine. Fire her and you're in big trouble.'

He was about to repeat his big man, big connections routine when I said: 'Tell you what: I'll look into it again on Monday morning.' To my surprise, this seemed to pacify him.

'Yeah, see that you do that,' he said. 'Otherwise, don't forget – I know people . . .' With that he turned round and slithered back to the Zanzibar.

I drove off, angry, frustrated, frightened. I wanted to go home and ponder what had just happened. But some friends from America were waiting for me in a bar in Berkeley Square called Mortons, not a regular haunt but at that time it was one of the few places in London (thanks to our absurd licensing laws) where you could talk over a late-night drink without competition from the thump of disco music. I headed there.

I was disturbed by the incident and could not get it out of my mind. I left the bar after greeting my friends to phone the Zanzibar from Mortons' foyer, asking for Bobby Campbell, a big gruff Scotsman who worked on the newsdesk. 'Did you see that man who followed me out?' I asked.

'Yes, it was David May.'

'Who's he? I've never heard of him.'

Bobby explained that he had once worked at *The Sunday Times* and was now an executive at *Time Out*, the London magazine that mixes entertainment listings with left-wing agitprop. He was also Linda Melvern's lover.

'That explains why he wants me to take her back,' I thought. I told Bobby about my unpleasant experience.

'He's already been boasting about it,' said Bobby. 'He came back in and informed us that he had "just told that new editor of yours what the score is".

'He says you're going to do as he told you. He's just a little squirt,' added Bobby. 'You should have thumped him.'

I explained how that might be construed as conduct unbecoming a *Sunday Times* editor. Bobby gave a Glaswegian grunt and we ended the call.

My friends sensed something was wrong. 'Big man's job getting you down already?' joked one.

'I think it's going to be tougher than I thought,' I replied. 'I need a drink.'

On Monday I gave instructions that on no account was Linda Melvern to be reinstated.†

*

THE IDEA OF BEING EDITOR of *The Sunday Times* had never crossed my mind. My ambition had been to be editor of *The Economist*, ever since its then editor, Alastair Burnet, gave me my first big break in journalism by hiring me as a correspondent in 1973. His career was my inspiration: when I went to work for him he was editor of the most prestigious news magazine in the world and presenter of *Panorama*, the BBC's flagship political programme. It was the ideal

---

† I never heard again from David May. Linda Melvern, who had been embarrassed by his intervention and soon dropped him as her partner, nevertheless sued for unfair dismissal before an industrial tribunal. The lawyers advised me to settle out of court. I refused. Even at the door of the tribunal they were still urging that I buy her off with a severance payment. I still refused. During the tribunal, to which I gave evidence, the trade-union representative on the three-person tribunal was even more flabbergasted by Melvern's behaviour than the businessman or the independent. Melvern lost and left the court (and *The Sunday Times*) without a penny.

combination and I resolved to strive for a similar mix of print and broadcast journalism. But Rupert Murdoch was to make me an offer I couldn't refuse.

By 1983 I had become UK editor of *The Economist* in charge of its British coverage in the days when the magazine mattered in this country and was an influential player in its political and economic debates (it has shown recent signs of recovering this reputation). I do not know if I would ever have become editor of *The Economist* but I already had enough of the 'Burnet dream' to keep me satisfied: I was financially secure, in love with my career, living life to the full.

I look back on my decade at *The Economist* with great affection. It was a satisfying, civilized place to work, if a little unworldly – often more like an Oxbridge college than a news magazine. It was certainly inadequate training for the hornets' nest I was to inherit at *The Sunday Times*. But it prepared me in one important respect: it gave me a broad base of journalistic experience and knowledge on which to draw. When I had to tackle those who tried to thwart the direction in which I wished to take *The Sunday Times*, I knew the arguments to deploy against them.

I had covered the Troubles in Northern Ireland in the early seventies. I had been the magazine's political and lobby correspondent in the House of Commons, then its labour correspondent during the Wilson–Callaghan Labour Government – the dark days of pay policy, strikes and the social contract, when the unions seemed to run the country. I covered the industrial disruption of the 1978–79 Winter of Discontent that was to destroy Jim Callaghan's government – and cast the Labour Party into the wilderness for almost two decades.

At the same time I had built up a dual career in broadcasting, first presenting weekly political shows in my native

Scotland, then on national television. By the late 1970s I had done a major network documentary on North Sea Oil for BBC2, become a presenter on *Tomorrow's World* and helped launch the *Risk Business*, a prime time BBC1 series on industry. I was a regular pundit on BBC's *Nationwide* and Radio 4's *Today* programme. I even had my own late Saturday night show on London Weekend Television called *Look Here*, which covered various media issues.

Above all, I had spent almost three glorious years in America for *The Economist*, covering everything from Wall Street to the White House. I had resisted going to America because of my burgeoning broadcasting career in Britain. But Andrew Knight, who took over from Alastair as editor of *The Economist* in late 1974, convinced me a period in America was essential for my journalistic development. I departed for the United States in the summer of 1979. Though I did not realize it at the time this posting was to prove a crucial move: without my stint in the United States I would never have become editor of *The Sunday Times*.

Two things happened in America which were later to prove vital: I was converted to the virtues of a dynamic market economy; and I became good friends with Irwin Stelzer, one of America's smartest economists and a close friend and adviser of Rupert Murdoch.

I left Britain on Friday 13 July 1979: the superstitious may have hesitated but it was to be lucky for me. My country had been brought to its knees by the brute force of union power; it was one of its darkest peace-time hours and Margaret Thatcher had been elected as a reaction to union excess and Labour impotence. But I had not voted for her: she had yet to discover her radical-right market economics (as had I) and I viewed what she stood for then as an unsavoury amalgam of bourgeois prejudices and simplistic monetarism from the reactionary right. I was glad to be leaving.

Not that America was in great shape under Jimmy Carter. Indeed there was much speculation that under his feeble presidency America was catching a bad case of the British disease. I arrived on the very weekend that President Carter had summoned America's leaders to a special summit to review the country's troubles. The president emerged from his meetings to declare helplessly that America was in a 'malaise'. I began to wonder if I had swapped one declining country for another.

Even in the bad times, however, America is an inspiration: I revelled in its dynamic, can-do culture, the ease with which new technology was introduced and exploited and the free and fast social mobility between the classes. I had left Britain a disillusioned one-nation Tory of an interventionist bent – the sort that Thatcher was later to dismiss as 'wet'. I was to return three years later a free marketeer, convinced that a stiff dose of radical market economics was just the medicine needed to buck up our dozy British Establishment.

I was encouraged in this view by Irwin Stelzer, a lover of Britain in general (despite its collectivist culture) and *The Economist* in particular. He was one of America's foremost experts on deregulation and market economics, an ideological soul mate of *The Economist*'s brilliant and original deputy editor, Norman Macrae. One day I was to hire both as *Sunday Times* columnists.

I had met Irwin on previous visits to America. Brought up in a poor Jewish neighbourhood in New York's Lower East Side, he had built up, with no assets but his own brilliance, National Economic Research Associates (Nera), a leading economic consultancy that he was later to sell for a small fortune. In 1978 he had slipped me the details of Carter's first tentative steps towards a pay policy (something we in Britain then knew plenty about) and I rushed back across the Atlantic to announce this scoop in *The Economist* and on the BBC's *Newsnight* ahead of the American press.

During my posting to America I was to become firm friends with Irwin and Cita, his charming, intelligent wife. He led me to appreciate the radical power of the market, particularly in deregulating industries dominated by a few big businesses. The American airline cartel was in the process of being broken up and I was struck by how the extra competition produced low fares that made it possible for ordinary people to be able to afford to fly. In Britain the people supposedly owned British Airways; but the vast majority could not afford a ticket to travel on it.

I began to apply this approach across the board, even to television. I had gone to America with all the usual prejudices about British TV being the best in the world. Though there was much that was crass and banal on my 35-channel cable set in New York, I was soon impressed by the variety, dynamism and innovation: there were channels devoted to news, films and even the arts. I began to realize that the BBC/ITV duopoly, whatever its past strengths, was not the future.

Irwin and I both speculated that British TV was ready for a multi-channel revolution. When I returned to London in 1982 to become UK editor of *The Economist* we agreed to form a British branch of Nera specifically to promote such a revolution. We set up shop in some smart offices in Victoria, near Buckingham Palace. We had swanky cards and notepaper printed. But we had no customers: nobody in Britain was much interested in extra TV channels, least of all the established broadcasters, who viewed any competition as a threat to their cosy privileges. Since they thought British TV was already the best in the world they could not imagine that viewers might want more channels.

I was missing America and beginning to wonder if I had done the right thing to return to Britain, then deep in Thatcher's first recession. But I busied myself in running *The Economist*'s British coverage. I was now seeing our ills through a strong free-market prism and the Britain section reflected that: there were 'Memos to 10 Downing Street' urging privatization and deregulation and exposés of expensive and debilitating state intervention. There were also some major scoops which Fleet Street rushed to follow: we broke the details of the Downing Street think-tank's report on the future of the welfare state (which, sadly, effectively killed it), published the Peruvian 'peace plan' during the Falklands War and revealed the government's plans for the cabling of Britain. The official history of *The Economist* says it was during this time that the magazine was 'causing more leak inquiries [by the government] than the rest of Fleet Street put together'.

One day I mentioned to Irwin that Rupert Murdoch had bought Sky Channel, a satellite-delivered service that consisted largely of re-runs of dated American shows. It covered Europe though almost nobody in Britain watched it. But it was then almost the only alternative to the established broadcasters. Maybe Murdoch had plans to build on it.

'Why don't you go along and see him,' suggested Irwin on the phone from New York one day in the spring of 1983, 'and try and sell our consultancy services?'

I wasn't that keen. 'There's a general election campaign coming up here,' I replied. 'In any case, I don't know him.'

'I do,' replied Irwin. It was the first time I'd heard him mention Murdoch. 'I'll fix it.'

Contrary to Fleet Street mythology I had never met Rupert Murdoch in America. It was only later that I was to learn that Irwin and Cita were good friends of the Murdoch family. But our paths never crossed until that day in early

May 1983 when I want to his office at Times Newspapers in Gray's Inn Road to talk about what Nera could do for Sky Channel.

Such were my tenuous links with national newspapers that I barely knew where Gray's Inn Road was: those of us who worked in stylish St James's Street never had any real cause for frequenting this seedy, rundown artery between Fleet Street and King's Cross. By sheer coincidence, however, I had been there for the first time the week before. *The Sunday Times* had announced on its front page its intention to publish what were soon discovered to be Hitler's fake diaries, perhaps the paper's lowest moment in its long history, and I was covering the story for the American PBS TV network.

I had stood outside the ugly Times building for a 'piece-to-camera' informing our American viewers that 'Rupert Murdoch in his hour of embarrassment has, not surprisingly, refused to speak to us. He's offered us his PR man [Arthur Brittenden] but we've refused to speak to him. The mood in London is better summed up by a cartoon in tonight's *Evening Standard* than anything he's likely to tell us.' I then held up the cartoon to the camera: it showed Hitler leaning back in a chair, his foot on his desk, scribbling away with a fountain pen jammed between his toes. I read out the caption – 'Ah, so you think we Germans no sense of humour have!' – and signed off, American style: 'This is Andrew Neil of *The Economist* in London for *Inside Edition*.'

This time, thanks to Irwin, Rupert Murdoch had agreed to see me but I thought it prudent not to mention the broadcast or the Hitler Diaries – there was no need to intrude into private grief. I took the lift to the sixth floor of the depressing grey building *The Times* inhabited (*The Sunday Times*' one was even scruffier) and waited in his outer office. Within a few minutes he bounded out to greet me, a smile on his face, faxes in one hand, a handshake with the other. He ushered me on to his sofa, where he joined me, friendly, charming and informal – not at all like the demon of Fleet Street fame.

We talked first about the election: he wanted to be assured that Thatcher would win, which I was able to do. But when we turned to Sky Channel it was clear that he had no great plans for its expansion and therefore not much need for our services. He had taken a stake in it to keep his options open, something I was to discover was a typically Murdoch technique: nothing might come of it, or it might be the basis one day of a huge TV empire.

But he did not want to pour much new investment into it for the moment. 'I've already developed a reputation for taking too many risks,' he confided. 'I don't want to build on that for the moment.' I was surprised that this man whom I had only just met was speaking to me as if I was one of his inner circle. We talked easily; we seemed to be hitting it off.

At his direction, the conversation turned to the Hitler Diaries. 'I still think there's a sixty per cent chance they're real,' he said.

'You'll be lucky,' I thought, since *The Sunday Times* was already pulling out of the serialization.

'What do you think of *The Sunday Times*?' he asked, almost casually.

'I love it,' I replied, instantly.

'Why is that?' he asked, somewhat surprised.

'Well, we publish *The Economist* on a Friday and when *The Sunday Times* comes out two days later it never has anything on the general election that we've not had two days before. In fact, it often re-runs our stories.'

'It's not very good, is it?' he said, almost sadly.

'It could be better,' I replied. 'It used to be great.'

With that the meeting came to an end. He said he would

keep in touch over television developments as I left his office. I called Irwin to report that, though the meeting had been friendly enough, it had been a failure in business terms. 'Not to worry,' he said, 'at least contact has been made.'

To my surprise, several other meetings followed with Rupert in quick succession through May. I soon guessed I was being measured for a major editorial job since we talked more and more about newspapers and less and less about television. But it still did not cross my mind that he was considering me for editor: it would be too big a gamble to give the job to someone who had never even worked for a national newspaper.

I knew by now, however, that he was looking for a new editor. Frank Giles had been promoted from within in 1981 when Murdoch had moved Harry Evans to *The Times*. But he had always regarded Giles as a stopgap, somebody to keep the paper ticking over while he sorted out *The Times*. That was two years ago. Now Rupert was impatient to create a *Sunday Times* more in his own image.

He regarded Frank, a decent man, with a mixture of distaste and derision. He had pushed the Hitler Diaries into *The Sunday Times* without hardly referring the matter to him. He dealt with him politely enough in public; but there was much joking and sarcasm at his expense behind his back. An old-style journalist, with a patrician air and an urbane and congenial manner, if a little stiff, it was hard to imagine an editor less in the Murdoch mould.

Rupert regarded him as a weak and uninspiring editor, presiding over dull news and feature pages and allowing too much free rein in the editorial pages to the left-wing views he detested. The paper has no direction, was Rupert's refrain, and it doesn't stand for anything. It had begun to atrophy, both in sales and reputation. Giles had served his interim purpose, Rupert concluded; now it was time to find a replacement. But who?

Though I did not know it at the time, a number of influential voices were flying the Neil flag. When Rupert mentioned to Irwin that he was looking for a new editor, he immediately suggested me. 'He's got many of the same views as you,' said Irwin, 'and he's young, bright and full of energy.'

Rupert valued Irwin's advice, but not on British journalism. 'Neil doesn't know anything about newspapers,' said Rupert dismissively.

Rupert floated the job in front of Alastair Burnet: he declined, saying he was too old for the challenge. No doubt he was also influenced by his bruising, unhappy experience editing the *Daily Express* in the mid-1970s after he left *The Economist*. 'You should go for the best young journalist of his generation,' advised Alastair.

'Oh, yeah. And who would that be?'

'Andrew Neil of *The Economist*.' It was an inaccurate but typically generous gesture by Alastair.

'He's already come to see me about Sky Channel. Maybe I'd better see him again.'

A third voice also chimed in. My first job after university had been at the Conservative Research Department, where I was the specialist in housing policy. This brought me into regular contact with Peter Walker, then secretary of state for the environment in the Heath government. He became a close friend and staunch supporter of any opportunities to advance my career.

He called Rupert and told him: 'I hear you're looking for a new *Sunday Times* editor. You should hire Andrew Neil.' I don't know if the support of the cabinet's leading anti-Thatcher wet was an asset; but it seemed to do me no harm.

All this was happening without my knowledge. But I

realized something was stirring: in subsequent meetings with Rupert he spent most of the time exploring my views on *The Sunday Times*. This was not something I had thought much about – I was just a casual reader – so I started to give the paper far greater scrutiny.

I told him that *The Sunday Times* was becoming a shadow of its former self, that it was full of too many trivial news stories and that, intellectually, it was stuck in a sixties time-warp. It had to rediscover its confidence for the big stories and features; and shake off its collectivist mind-set to become the champion of a market-led revolution that would shake the British Establishment to its bones and transform the economy and society. He nodded enthusiastically, perhaps surprised to find somebody in Britain who shared so many of his radical-right views. Not that our opinions were an exact match: on many matters Rupert was well to the right of me politically. He was a monetarist; I was not. Nor did I share his conservative social outlook. But we were on enough of the same wavelength for him to feel comfortable with me. This is as it should be between proprietor and editor: the editor should never be a cipher for his owner but ideologically they do have to be on the same planet as each other or it will end in tears.

It still had not dawned on me that I was being sized up for editor. Then one day early in June a call came to my home at 8 a.m. from Rupert's secretary: could I come and see him in an hour? If it's that urgent, I thought, he's going to offer me a job.

The strongest rumour was still that Alastair Burnet was going to be the new *Sunday Times* editor. I concluded that at Alastair's suggestion, Rupert was going to offer me the deputy editorship. Before departing for Gray's Inn Road I called Alastair to say that I would be delighted to be his deputy and looked forward to working for my mentor again.

'Oh no, dear boy,' said Alastair, chuckling. 'He's going to offer *you* the job of editor.' I put the phone down and sat still for a few moments, a mixture of surprise and nervous excitement coursing through me. I wondered if I was up to the challenge; if I had known what was in store for me I would have concluded that I wasn't.

When I arrived at Rupert's office – late as usual – I knew what was on the agenda. But I had to act as if I didn't. Despite his blunt, even brutal, reputation, Rupert can sometimes take a long time to get to the point: this was one of these times. We talked about politics, satellite TV, Fleet Street, even the weather might have merited a mention. Eventually he turned and asked: 'What do you think about being editor of *The Sunday Times*?'

Even though I knew the question was coming I was still taken aback. I rambled on about not really having considered the possibility, about the size of the challenge and other banalities.

'I want you to take the paper in the direction we talked about,' he interrupted, as if this was only the latest in a number of talks we'd had about me becoming editor. 'It must be strongly for democracy and the market economy. I could tolerate it supporting the SDP; but not Labour. There's a lot of dead wood in *The Sunday Times*,' he continued. 'It'll be a tough job to get rid of it. But I'll be behind you and you must consult closely with Pick [Sir Edward Pickering, one of Rupert's most trusted lieutenants]. Would £50,000 be all right?'

It was about double my *Economist* salary but I was already almost doubling it through my broadcasting activities – and they would have to go if I became editor of *The Sunday Times*. So financially it was not a great offer. But money was the last thing I was thinking about: I was being offered the editorship of one of the world's greatest newspapers at the age of thirty-four.

'Yes, £50,000 will be fine,' I replied and we shook hands. He probably realized I would have done it for nothing.

CHAPTER TWO

Into the Hornets' Nest

RUPERT MURDOCH WAS TAKING an enormous risk: I had not even been a reporter on a national newspaper, never mind an editor; I was only thirty-four, my experience in print journalism confined to the rarefied opining of *The Economist*, where we all wrote under a protective anonymity that hid mistakes and diffused responsibility; and we had only just met.

I suspect that he derived a certain satisfaction from bypassing the *Sunday Times* hierarchy (most of whom he detested as lazy and self-important) by appointing a rank outsider. It was a snub to the huge esteem in which they held themselves – a signal that the Murdoch regime had really begun. Rupert is also a man often guided by gut instinct: logic may have told him that it would be foolhardy to make Andrew Neil editor of his most prestigious broadsheet – the flagship of his newspaper empire – but the gambler in him said it was a risk worth taking. I shared many of his views about Britain and he must have felt I had the brains – and brawn – for the challenge. But he must also have been apprehensive about his choice. I was.

Though the deal had been done before mid-June, Rupert wanted to delay any announcement until some time in July: I doubted the secret would keep until then but Rupert, who should know better, has a bizarre belief that you can keep things confidential in the newspaper business – even when he gossips openly about supposed secrets himself – and he still had to square Frank Giles, who did not realize Rupert was in such a hurry to get rid of him as editor. Despite his ruthless reputation, Rupert has little stomach for sacking senior executives; it is a task he prefers to delegate, which inevitably draws out and complicates a process which is inherently difficult anyway.

As the end of June approached, the Fleet Street rumour-mill began to crank up. I was approached by several journalists suggesting I was in the running for the *Sunday Times* editorship. I called Edward Pickering, the deputy chairman of Times Newspapers, who was nearly always a source of wise counsel for me, told him the story was about to break and that I had an obligation to inform Andrew Knight, my editor at *The Economist*, before it did. Pick agreed and promised to speed the process up.

Andrew Knight was out of the office so I called him at home over the weekend. I told him I had been offered and had accepted the editorship of *The Sunday Times*. There was a few seconds' silence then only one word: 'Gulp!' I laughed: it was an appropriate enough response.

Andrew started to offer a few words of caution, mentioned my rosy prospects at *The Economist* then stopped, realizing there was nothing he could say to talk me out of the most prized job in British journalism. He asked when it was to be announced. 'Whenever Times Newspapers get their act together,' I replied.

Events now moved quickly. Rupert finally screwed up his courage to ask somebody to let Frank know his time was up. His pocket was filled with a generous pay-off and his pride assuaged with a meaningless but grand-sounding title: editor emeritus. But, though he must have realized he was always destined to be a caretaker editor, the decision to remove him still rankled. When he called the *Sunday Times* staff together to announce his departure and my arrival he referred to me cryptically as 'a man of whom I know nothing'. His remark was to set the tone for much subsequent comment.

A mixture of astonishment and hostility greeted my appointment. It combined to reinforce my own fears about whether I was up to the job. I had not anticipated a ticker-tape welcome down Fleet Street but I had thought there might be some satisfaction that, at a time when the worry was that Murdoch would drive the paper down-market, he had chosen a serious journalist and editor with a decent track record in political, business and international reporting from the most influential magazine in the world.

But in the eyes of the *Sunday Times* staff – and the rest of Fleet Street – I had two overwhelming shortcomings. I was a Murdoch man (they did not know that I barely knew him) specifically appointed by him (or so they thought) to recast the paper in his image; since most of the journalists deeply resented the fact that they now worked for a Murdoch newspaper and still spoke wistfully of the days when benign old Lord Thomson was the proprietor, the prospect of my arrival filled them with dread.

And, of course, I was an unknown outsider. In reporting my appointment the *Guardian* managed to mention twice in a short story that I had no national newspaper experience and under my picture added the caption: 'Neil: no national experience', just for good measure lest any poor soul had missed my handicap.

I was not surprised by the resentment of my outsider status. Journalists, even the many at *The Sunday Times* who affected a fashionable radicalism in political matters, are a conservative lot when it comes to their own affairs. They fear the unknown because it usually heralds change to a world they regard as already comfortable and in no need of upheaval. In this regard I was their worst nightmare: I had never been a Fleet Street hack, they had never heard of me, I wasn't one of *them*. This could be, they concluded, the end of life as they knew it: time to pull down the shutters and man the barricades against the barbarian intruder.

I was mildly amused, however, by my supposed anonymity within journalism. I had covered most of the biggest British stories over the last decade, from the Ulster Troubles to the Winter of Discontent, alongside journalists from Fleet Street. I had colleagues in the political and industrial lobbies. Though I was hardly a household name and there had been no by-line on my *Economist* work, my television broadcasting had brought a minor celebrity: occasionally people recognized me in restaurants and public places. But I suppose Fleet Street journalists never watched *Tomorrow's World* or *Nationwide*.

In retrospect, I can see that the emphasis on my anonymity was just part of Fleet Street working itself into a lather about the top job going to an outsider. Not only is he not one of us, they lamented, nobody's ever heard of him. He's a complete unknown, a nonentity – probably a plonker. I was part of the Fleet Street demonology even before I had left *The Economist*. The *Sunday Times* staff did not know me – had never even heard of me – but they had already decided to dislike me.

A nasty streak began to run through the several profiles that followed my appointment, fuelled by *Sunday Times* journalists who had never met me. That probably explained the errors that littered them – or perhaps they did not want the facts to get in the way of a good hatchet job.

Even *Tatler*, a magazine which at the time I had never read and to whose journalists I had never spoken, was in on the act. It penned a portrait of me, as ignorant as it appeared intimate, which I did not recognize; but it was even ruder about *The Sunday Times* than it was about me. It claimed that the paper was stuffed with journalists who had written nothing for years but their expenses claims, and unproductive oddballs such as a sports correspondent who allegedly dribbled paper balls up and down the corridor all day.

The article concluded with a warning: unless I took on the 'space barons' – the senior editors who controlled various parts of the paper – I would be unable to effect the changes Murdoch wanted; but if I did take them on I was likely to be eaten alive. As articles go, this was not a morale booster. *Campaign*, the magazine of the advertising industry which was hostile to me from the start, weighed in with a similarly depressing piece; but at least it took the trouble to send somebody to interview me.

Soon unpleasant personal attacks and ignorant tittle-tattle were appearing in diaries all over Fleet Street. The *Observer* developed a strange obsession with the greetings on my answering machine while the *New Statesman* was regularly nasty; but nobody I knew read it, so it didn't matter. They were hardly designed to make my editorship a success. Then came the inevitable *Private Eye* putdown: it established a standard for accuracy which was to become its hallmark whenever it wrote about me in the decade to come. Its tawdry profile was hilariously wrong, reporting that I was teetotal, had only ever had one girlfriend and that my father was a minister (he had been an army officer).

You quickly learn that being attacked by *Private Eye* is an unwritten clause in your *Sunday Times* contract: it goes with the job and you soon begin to miss the weeks when you *don't* merit a mention. You also learn that what it says never matters much: it can be terribly funny but its reputation for inaccuracy is so well-established that nobody is ever sure that what is written about you is true, which is why I never once throughout my editorship bothered to write to the *Eye* correcting the drivel it peddled about me and the paper, much less ever thought of issuing a writ. There was always the hope that they really would go overboard one day with some horrendous libel against me and I would be able to pay the schoolfees of my godchildren on the proceeds; but they never went that far.

For somebody who had never had much publicity, however, it was all a bit unnerving at the time: why were people I'd never met so keen to disseminate untruths? But my friends saw a conspiracy I had not suspected. Their refrain was: 'Son of the manse? No alcohol! No girlfriends! How much are you paying for this new image?'

It was agreed that I would stay at *The Economist* through July, spend August on holiday in America, shadow Frank Giles as editor in September and take over on 1 October. July was to be a busy month: I continued to edit the Britain section of *The Economist* while getting to know my senior-editors-to-be at *The Sunday Times*.

Brian MacArthur came to see me at *The Economist* one sunny night in early July; I took him to dinner at Le Caprice. I had been given the job he had once coveted but he was loyal, helpful and generous from that evening onwards. We became close colleagues and good friends. Brian had been sent to *The Sunday Times* from *The Times* by Rupert to be joint deputy editor with Hugo Young, effectively demoting Young to number three. It was part of Rupert's attempt to reduce Young's liberal-left influence on the paper. Rupert had made clear that if Brian was a success, 'You'll be a candidate for editor.' Gerald Long, then Rupert's mercurial managing director at Times Newspapers, was blunter: 'Bring Frank Giles to his knees and you'll be editor.'

Brian ignored the admonition: brutality is not his style. But he suffered Rupert's wrath for the paper's perceived shortcomings. Since Frank always went home early on Saturday night, Brian was left to take the proprietor's calls, which meant he was regularly at the receiving end of a Rupert rave against the 'bloody pinko Islington liberals' in charge of the paper. In the end, Rupert concluded that Brian was not the man to clean *The Sunday Times*' stables to his liking. That task had now fallen to me. I think Brian was actually relieved.

As he went through the departments and their personnel he made it clear that *The Sunday Times* was in need of radical surgery. The place was full of feature writers, he said, mostly unproductive, many prima donnas past their prime, while the newsroom was short of talent and resources. The news reporters resented their lower status: while so-called 'star' feature writers sucked their thumbs, it was the newsroom that got the paper out. I listened intently, depressed by the magnitude of the task before me.

I had become editor without any great game plan or general strategy. Beyond the broad intention to make it a better paper and recapture its glory days in the sixties and seventies – but attuned to the agenda and climate of the eighties – I had no specific plans at all. I had hoped that any changes could be gradual but as I listened to Brian I began to doubt that a gradualist approach would be sufficient. The paper was in worse shape than I thought.

This was confirmed by a series of dinners that Brian arranged with the senior editors. They were depressing affairs: I was aware that the paper was wallowing in the past; I was not ready for a cast of characters from Madame Tussaud's. *The Sunday Times* was dominated by people stuck in a collectivist mind-set who regarded Margaret Thatcher and what she stood for as a temporary inconvenience: they had nothing but contempt for her and her works. Yet they themselves stood for very little; they had run out of constructive ideas of their own – which is why the paper had become an intellectual desert – and all that motivated them was hatred of Thatcher. Now they had an editor who, though he was no Thatcherite groupie, signed on to the prospect of a market-led revolution.

The two people who stick out most in my mind from these lunches and dinners are Hugo Young, the anti-Thatcherite political editor, and Peter Wilsher, the rotund and voluble foreign editor.

Young was wary and aloof: he clearly resented my appointment – he had harboured hopes of the job for himself – but he kept his distance. With Young you always knew what he was against – usually anything to do with Thatcherism – but it was rarely clear what he was in favour of: he had no alternative agenda to mine, which inhibited his power as an opposition force. He was the high priest of the collectivist consensus that had already brought Britain to its knees, imbued with an Oxbridge disdain for the supposedly crass world of commerce and the market.

Young was the guiding force on the paper's political direction and the staff looked up to him as guardian of its integrity. He must have sensed that he was unlikely to retain such a pivotal role under me and that I was intent on moving in directions he would find distasteful. I realized early on that both of us could not survive at *The Sunday Times*; but I saw no reason to seek confrontation or force a split. I would run *The Sunday Times* the way I wanted to and he could decide if it was enough to his liking to make him feel like staying.

At least Young, an intelligent man, never spoke unless he had something worthwhile to say. Wilsher was determined to contribute even when he had nothing to say. His ramblings were always accompanied by a loud cackle which made many of his comments impossible to decipher. I had come from a magazine which was the epitome of serious comment on foreign affairs. I soon concluded that I would need a new foreign editor even more quickly than I would need a new political guru.

My position was not entirely hopeless. The two senior news executives – Tony Bambridge and Tony Rennell – were encouraged by my talk of beefing up the news coverage. The two Tones – or the Ton Ton Macoutes as they came to be called because they hunted as a pair in the paper's murky internal politics – almost seemed to relish a bit of upheaval. But they were also adept at going with the flow: I sensed that they (and many others) would wait to see if I had the strength to deliver before committing to my editorship.

I was also mildly encouraged by Roger Eglin, the gentle, soft-spoken northerner who edited the business section. He had good contacts with the business community, where he was liked and respected, and seemed willing to strike out in fresh directions – there was much to do to beef up our City coverage, which lagged behind the *Sunday Telegraph*'s.

Another soft-spoken northerner I quickly grew to respect was Don Berry, the features editor. He was a solid Labour man who must have despaired at the political direction in which I was about to take his beloved *Sunday Times*. But he was more a superb technician with words and layout than he was a politically motivated journalist. He was encouraged by my desire to put long, revealing reconstructions of the main stories of the week at the heart of the paper, breaking new ground as we did. That was the sort of serious journalism he revelled in.

I soon realized I had two kinds of senior executive: the hostile and the sceptical. I seemed to have no real allies or natural supporters, other than, potentially, Brian MacArthur – and certainly no ideological soulmates. It was not a promising base from which to mount far-reaching changes. Life at the top was already beginning to look like a rather solitary existence. I needed to cast around to find folk who would rally to my banner. I would, of course, appoint some new executives from outside the paper; but I also needed some allies among the existing staff who knew its strengths and weaknesses. A friend suggested I drive down to his cottage on the banks of the River Test in Hampshire where I would find James Adams, one of my new staff, who was recovering from a serious attack of hepatitis.

I learned later that James had been expecting his new editor to be another version of Frank Giles. So he was surprised when somebody his own age emerged one sunny Sunday in shorts and open-neck shirt from a black convertible BMW with a pretty American girlfriend on one arm and a six-pack of Budweiser under the other. It was not quite the image he had of *Sunday Times* editors. But the radical change in sartorial style boded well for James: he was even more disenchanted with the paper than Brian MacArthur.

Over lunch he explained how the paper was badly run: resources were being squandered, budgetary control was a mess, many posts had become sinecures for people long past their best, there were time-servers everywhere and little new talent was being fostered. He described the mess the foreign department had been in when he took over as foreign managing editor and said most departments were still in a similar state. He was in no doubt that the whole paper needed root-and-branch reform if it was to survive the 1980s as market leader.

Private Eye was later to claim that I had flown to Scotland to meet James on his father's estate, where I had been invited to fish. The idea was to portray me being seduced early on by the landed gentry. An intriguing prospect, except that James's father had died several years before and there was no family estate in Scotland – or anywhere else. But I did spend some of the afternoon being introduced by James to the intricacies of fly-fishing for trout. We waded into the

Test and I cast as best I could. The fish were not biting but I was: here was somebody who would prove a crucial ally in my mission to revamp and modernize *The Sunday Times*. I left Hampshire without any fish: but I had caught somebody who was to become a loyal colleague, a good friend and an invaluable ally throughout my editorship.

*

AUGUST IN AMERICA was the last of the locust days, a carefree, exhilarating time surrounded by good friends and fun in a country I now regarded as my second home. I was going out with a graduate from the University of Colorado, Boulder, a Russian specialist who was as intelligent as she was beautiful. After some days in New York and Los Angeles I flew to Boulder, where I always stayed with a wonderful professor and his wife who had adopted me some years before as their wayward British son.

It was just a normal summer in Colorado: spectacular sunny days in the low eighties with no humidity and cool, clear mountain nights. It is my favourite state in the Union and I was with several of my favourite people. My looming problems with *The Sunday Times* seemed a long way away. I was encouraged by the fact that everybody in Boulder was so delighted that I had been made editor of a paper with an international reputation and so sure I was going to be a great success. They even threw a party for me. Nobody was doing that in London.

I was relaxed and happy in Colorado. But I could not help wondering what was in store for me 6,000 miles away. It was worrying me more than I realized. I began a long, slow return to London with a flight from Denver to New York, during which I had my first ever anxiety attack. As I took my seat on the plane I started to hyperventilate, a knot in my stomach, my heart pounding. One of the flight attendants took pity on me – she must have thought it was fear of flying – and brought me regular glasses of cold water (food was out of the question). But no matter how much I sipped, my mouth remained dry and I struggled for breath. I stared out of the window as the great plains of the Midwest passed below, wondering what was happening to me: their vastness depressed me even more.

The anxiety stayed with me throughout the three-and-a-half-hour flight, which seemed more like three-and-a-half days. Even when I reached the familiar habitat of my New York apartment, my anxious state lingered for another day, until it gradually petered out and I returned to normal.

At the time I refused to admit the attack had been brought on by worries at my prospects at *The Sunday Times*; but clearly it had. I still harboured doubts that I was up to the job, though having met the senior executives I realized you did not have to be a rocket scientist to run *The Sunday Times* passably well. Most of all I feared I was between a rock and a hard place: I would be ground down by a hostile gang of journalists on one side and a demanding proprietor on the other.

I never had any illusions about Rupert Murdoch. I never thought, as other editors had, that I was the one who was going to change him. I knew he was an interventionist proprietor who expected to get his way. Since I was never good at taking orders, I reckoned I would have a six-month honeymoon, if I was lucky, before we would fall out and our relationship deteriorate. I gave myself five years at most. I never thought I would survive for over a decade.

Like everybody else in Fleet Street I had heard numerous 'Dirty Digger' stories about the ruthless Australian proprietor who hired editors to do his bidding, fired them when they didn't (and sometimes even when they did!), who could be charming and supportive one moment, foul-mouthed and tyrannical the next. I did not read the many abusive biographies about him for fear they would only depress me. But Fleet Street was awash with stories about his clashes with Harry Evans soon after he had moved from *The Sunday Times* to be editor of *The Times*; since I admired Harry such rumours made me all the more apprehensive.

I sought solace in the thought that the Murdoch mythology was an over-hyped industry run by bitter people with axes to grind. I consoled myself with the knowledge that, under my contract, it would cost him two years' salary to fire me; if I survived two years in the job, the minimum severance pay rose to three years' salary, a tidy sum on which to embark on a new career. I also concluded that, since he had flouted convention by giving me the job, he had almost as much of a vested interest in making it work as I had. But I never regarded the national directors of Times Newspapers as much of a safeguard should my job security be in jeopardy.

The directors had been appointed at the insistence of Parliament and the previous owners (Thomson) when Murdoch bought Times Newspapers in 1981; their function was to protect the editors from proprietorial interference; in theory, Rupert even needed their permission to hire or fire an editor, though it was usually easy for him to square them in advance. They were not that independent; after all, Rupert had hired them.

But they were a distinguished bunch and even included my friend and mentor, Alastair Burnet. But it was a peculiarly British conceit, doubtful in principle, unworkable in practice: why should the owner not be the ultimate arbiter of what was in his paper? In any case, a proprietor can make life hell for an unwanted editor, as Harry Evans had found. In his struggles the national directors had proved an inadequate, paper-thin shield. I would place no faith in them.

I resolved that I would never outstay my welcome. I would not edit a paper owned by somebody who did not want me. Editor and proprietor have to be a team or they are nothing. They have different, distinct roles but their relationship must be generally harmonious. I think Rupert sensed that I was always ready to go if he wanted rid of me and this made him less worried about having to go through another bruising Evans-style encounter should we fall out.

Before I returned to London, Rupert invited me to join him and his wife for the weekend in their charming English-style country house in old Chatham, upstate New York. It was a relaxed, family affair: he and Anna, his elegant and determined wife, did everything possible to make me feel at ease. I swam in the pool with his children and played tennis with Anna and Rupert. His tennis was only a little better than mine – which meant it was pretty dismal – but he shared one thing with John McEnroe: he challenged every call, even when the ball was clearly out. I suppose you're supposed to indulge your new boss in such situations. But Anna and I ganged up against him and he gave us a sheepish grin every time he tried to insist that he had won a point when he'd obviously lost. It was all good fun.

We barely talked about the paper. But he did explain the importance of producing eighty-page papers for the economics of Times Newspapers: eighty pages was the largest the presses could take at Gray's Inn Road; but even that size – peanuts by today's standards – allowed for enough advertising to make *The Sunday Times* highly profitable when *The Times* looked like being a loss-maker for the foreseeable future. He showed me the famous weekly profit-and-loss printouts for every arm of his empire, which helped him keep tabs on what was happening, and pointed to a new desktop computer which he was planning to master. (He never did.)

Rupert also asked me who would write the editorials when I took over. 'I'll do that,' I replied. I'd written plenty for *The Economist* and unlike the demands of a daily paper, which require a team of editorial writers, I felt sure as a Sunday editor I could manage one a week. He was quite taken by my reply, which strangely struck him as an original idea, so much so that he introduced me to his dinner guests that Saturday night as 'the new editor of *The Sunday Times* – who's going to write the editorials himself'. Maybe the idea appealed because the paper might at last carry an editorial with which he agreed. Whatever the reason I headed back to New York *en route* for London with a spring in my step. I was more confident that I could sustain a working relationship with Rupert and was ready for whatever resistance awaited at Gray's Inn Road. The barricades were already going up.

I returned to Britain in time for my last assignment for *The Economist*: the TUC conference in Blackpool in the first week of September. It was almost five years after the start of the Winter of Discontent and over four years after Mrs Thatcher had begun to tame the unions. The left were in a state of shellshock after the Tory re-election landslide in June 1983; at Blackpool that autumn the moderates had begun the long fight to claw back control from the alliance of Labour left and Communists that had called so many of the shots in recent TUC history and done the Labour Party such catastrophic damage.

My last article for *The Economist* was the lead to the Britain section headlined 'The unions don't know where to go – except down': it predicted a huge loss of power and membership in the eighties. It argued that even the moderates were 'almost as bereft of fresh ideas as the old left' and argued that 'fundamental factors are undermining the power of Britain's unions . . . which would be there even if Margaret Thatcher and Norman Tebbit were not'.

I pointed out that most job losses were in highly unionized industries and most new jobs were being created in small companies and service industries with no unions. The same process in America had seen the unionized share of the labour force decline from a peak of 34 per cent in 1965 to 'under 20 per cent and falling today'. The same was about to happen in Britain.

'The peak of their power has passed,' concluded the article, 'and they must now accommodate themselves to a period of decline.' I finished with a joke: 'Nobody even thought the TUC's deliberations worthy of the annual ritual bomb threat. Now that's a real sign of lost status.' They were the last words I was to write for *The Economist*. The forecast was to prove accurate enough as the eighties unfolded; but I had no idea at the time that I would play a role in the decline of Britain's unions.

My final responsibilities to *The Economist* met, I went straight from Blackpool to Gray's Inn Road on the Thursday morning, 8 September 1983, to begin learning the ropes of editing a national newspaper while Frank Giles completed his last month. I vividly remember entering *The Sunday Times* building for the first time, suitcase in one hand, briefcase in the other, feeling as lost as Paddington Bear. I should have felt exhilarated but a wave of depression hit me as soon as I went through the glass doors.

Could this really be the premises of the world-famous *Sunday Times*? The building was a slum, the worst of modern British brutalist architecture on the outside and a shabby mess inside. The windows were filthy and the floors covered in litter. Print workers milled around, going in no particular direction, slowly. It was a far cry from *The Economist*'s stylish offices in St James's Street, with their stunning views over the Houses of Parliament, St James's Park and Buckingham Palace. This was more like a Dickensian workhouse. I was struck by the sense of decay – an environment almost designed to encourage decline and archaic attitudes. I made my way to the editor's office on the sixth floor: this was spacious enough, on the corner of the building with plenty of light, though with views only up and down scruffy Gray's Inn Road. But the conditions for the journalists were appalling. The newsroom was a particularly dismal place, rundown and shabby. Bad lighting added to the gloom. Metal filing cabinets filled every available space and rubbish – or ancient files (it was hard to tell the difference) – was piled high everywhere. Everybody was still using manual typewriters, which had to be chained and padlocked to green metal desks to stop anybody stealing them; so were the chairs. In fact, almost anything that moved was chained to something substantial. Theft was clearly a major problem.

The feature writers and business and arts staff fared a little better on other floors; some even had their own cubicles. But the whole place was saturated with seediness. I found it hard to imagine how anybody could be creative in such surroundings. No wonder Rupert and his managers camped out in the newer and slightly smarter Times building up the road.

I camped out in Brian MacArthur's office during the three-week transition period. He guided me through the mechanics of producing *The Sunday Times* and introduced me to the middle-ranking executives and some of the writers. I sat in on the editorial conferences, which struck me as tame affairs compared with the intellectual ferment of *The Economist*. I became increasingly convinced that Brian MacArthur was right: too much of the paper's resources were tied up in a bloated features department that was living on past glories and that the newsroom had to be given more prominence and prestige.

I also had to make a quick study of those areas that had never concerned me at *The Economist*. The Look pages, designed primarily for women, had lost their sparkle and seemed suffused with a tired feminism; the coverage of music, books and the arts was competent enough, if jaded and speaking to too narrow an audience for a paper with 3.5 million readers. A gradual programme of rolling change began to develop in my mind; not too radical to provoke widespread resistance but persistent enough to leave nobody in any doubt that things would not stay as they were.

There were also several of Frank's going-away parties to attend. Given the manner of his departure, they were something of a charade. But everyone played their part, not least Frank. At one he joked about his grand new title: ' "E" is from the Latin, meaning "out",' he explained elegantly, 'and "meritus" means "deserves to be".' In a typical distortion by the Fleet Street mischief-makers this was later turned against him by putting the words into Rupert's mouth, which was nonsense, especially since Rupert is no Latin scholar.

Frank behaved properly if coolly towards me throughout the transition. Naturally, he thought the paper was in need of less radical surgery than I. Just some tinkering would suffice. He took me to lunch at Brooks's, his St James's gentlemen's club opposite *The Economist*. As we sat down he informed me that the Archbishop of Canterbury was on the next table. It did not occur to him that this was not necessarily an exciting prospect for a Scottish Presbyterian.

He produced a couple of thin files which meticulously listed the staff and their departments. He named a couple who were not quite up to scratch and identified Henry Porter, a young feature writer, as his prime suspect as the paper's conduit to *Private Eye*. It was the start of a tidy handover which he handled with punctilious courtesy. But I would have wished for more: the paper was clearly not in as good a shape as he thought it was. There was also the problem of his new role.

This had been a sop from Rupert to ease his departure. But his new editor emeritus took it seriously. He had already claimed an office in the Times building to occupy after his departure and was soon planning a number of trips to far-off lands from where he planned to file major features. 'Let him do it then don't use the stuff,' was Rupert's unhelpful advice, though that was, in effect, what happened. Frank's enthusiasm for taking his new post seriously soon waned and he eventually retired without fanfare.

At the time, however, he envisaged a continuing role for himself.

> It seems a rather pompous business to be writing you a memo [he wrote to me during the transition] when I could speak to you direct. But I believe it would be easier for you to reply to a written memo on this particular subject, than if you were to have to answer verbally.
>
> What I want to know is whether or not you would like me to attend editorial meetings . . . It is up to you to say whether you want me or not. Please be absolutely frank on this matter. There is no room for acts of courtesy, deferential gestures, etc., however well motivated . . . I shall accept whatever you decide with good grace . . .

His presence was the last thing I wanted, preferring a clean break with the past, and gently told him so. Relations remained stiff and proper. But it was inevitable that the relationship should become more tense as I started to make changes and had to justify them. A month after I took over I gave the *Guardian* an interview which caused particular offence.

He wrote to tell me it had caused him 'considerable dismay'. References to 'doldrums, sticking in ruts, past indecision and lack of direction', he wrote, were taken as 'a direct and highly critical comment upon his record as editor . . .' and he advised me to dwell on 'the exciting plans for the future and avoid unfair disparagement of the past' for any future public utterances.

He was, of course, right to feel hurt and he was giving me proper advice. But criticism of past ways was implicit in almost every change I made. Nevertheless, I wrote a conciliatory reply, promising to be more careful in future. By then I had enough battles to fight without making an open enemy of my predecessor.

At the start of my first week as editor, on Brian's advice, I addressed a mass meeting of all the staff in the newsroom. I began by saying how proud I was to be editing one of the world's greatest newspapers. It had many enormous strengths, on which I planned to build, and some weaknesses, which I planned to eradicate. Even the best institutions had to adapt to new circumstances to survive and I felt sure that there was a 'constituency for change' among them. I did not want upheaval, I assured them, just a steady programme of improvement.

As I spoke from behind the newsdesk I looked out into a sea of sullen faces, the resentment almost tangible. An unknown stranger was now in command, promising change that was bound to be for the worst. I began to realize that my 'constituency for change' was actually an army of resistance. If I took things too gradually or proceeded in too gentlemanly a fashion they would wear me down in a guerrilla war I was bound to lose. Even as I spoke of gradualism I knew in my heart that the opposition would have to be confronted head on. We were squaring up for a big bang: it was inevitable if I was to survive and succeed.

CHAPTER THREE

Revolution: Year Zero

EVEN THE *GUARDIAN*, no ally in the adventure on which I had embarked, reported that my arrival at *The Sunday Times* had been accompanied by 'miasmas of mischief' (it would have been more accurate to add 'and malevolence'). I resolved to push ahead regardless: my aim was to build up a momentum of change that would sweep everything before it, seeing off any opposition in the process. By choosing to fight on all fronts I risked being overwhelmed by the combined forces of resistance. But I had a greater fear of being ground down in a gruelling war of attrition that would inevitably greet any attempts at piecemeal reform.

Without any great overarching strategy in mind I set about making the most changes where I thought the paper was weakest. Ironically, the first to go was Ronald Butt, the veteran right-wing columnist and the only Tory of influence on the paper – an interesting choice for a new editor supposed to be mounting an ideological purge. I simply felt he was out of touch with the new politics of the eighties. Then I abolished the editorial college that assembled every Friday morning in Frank Giles's office to determine the paper's editorial line. It consisted largely of grand old men from the paper's past plus a few senior editors. I had sat in on their discussions during the transition period and been distinctly unimpressed. I would write the editorials myself and consult senior staff when I thought it appropriate.

Then I summoned Suzanne Lowry, the editor of the Look pages. Brian MacArthur and others had argued that pages which were meant primarily to inform and entertain women had become drab and predictable. I told her I wanted to make a change. She said she had been expecting it and left with good grace and a large cheque in her pocket (as did all those who departed my employ); she subsequently went to Paris and became an acute observer of French life and politics. At Brian's recommendation I brought in Joyce Hopkirk, an experienced women's editor with a lighter touch. I also introduced a People page to help humanize the main section at a time when I wanted to harden the news, and a Scene spread to cover leisure activities. There was much that had to be made more serious elsewhere in the paper.

I had not lost my enthusiasm for investigative journalism, despite the Linda Melvern incident. But *The Sunday Times* had ceased to deliver where once it had been a world-beater. The editor of Insight, the famous unit at the core of the paper's investigative efforts, was Christopher Hird, whose far-left politics at least should have generated some good investigative reporting. But not only had Insight not revealed anything very earth-shattering for some time; there wasn't much in the pipeline either.

I asked Hird to let me see his file of current investigations; he did not need both hands to carry it. It consisted of a few slips of paper summarizing a series of second-rate investigations that were going nowhere and a general disposition to 'look at local government'. Even Don Berry, the sympathetic features editor, had to admit that the cupboard was bare. The state of Insight was symbolic of the state of *The Sunday Times*. I decided on drastic action: I disbanded the Insight team.

Suzanne Lowry's departure had already put the staff on edge. Scrapping Insight caused an outcry. I was reneging on the paper's finest traditions. I had killed investigative reporting at *The Sunday Times*. It was all part of a Murdoch-inspired plan to replace hard-hitting investigations with bland 'lifestyle' features – look at all this People and Scene stuff and the softer Look pages. It was the end of life as they knew it.

Nobody pointed out, of course, that investigative journalism was in intensive care before I arrived at *The Sunday Times*, nor believed that I was beginning a long process designed to revive it. I explained that henceforth various journalists would come together under the Insight logo, depending on the nature of the investigation and the expertise required. My intention was to discover who was best at long-term investigations and build a new Insight team round them. But the staff was determined to believe the worst.

The *New Statesman*, where Chris Hird had friends and which was in the throes of a brutalist-left phase (under an ex-*Sunday Times* journalist) from which it has never quite recovered, began a campaign of weekly sniping and vilification designed to make life difficult. Various mischief-makers on TV's *What the Papers Say* added to the aggravation, including, inevitably, Paul Foot, who was much aggrieved that I had fired his protégé, Hird. *Private Eye* and the *Observer* diary turned up the heat. It felt as if I was working in a goldfish bowl with a microphone hovering above it. Any memo I wrote would be guaranteed to appear in the public prints within days; so would any supposedly private conversation, suitably distorted to put the worst interpretation on my motives. I soon learned there was no such thing as a confidential conversation at *The Sunday Times*. And some strange things started to happen.

My new flat in South Kensington was burgled: whoever it was took only the VCR, even though cash and valuables had been lying around and every drawer and cupboard had been searched. It was hard to avoid the impression that somebody was looking for some dirt on me. I installed better security, including a strong metal door and a new alarm system.

Then rumours started that some confidential files, supposedly belonging to me and potentially embarrassing, had been found in a taxi. One fantasist that *The Sunday Times* employed as a journalist began calling me late at night warning me, for a reason I could never quite discover, to be 'very careful' because 'dark forces' were at work and 'they [!?] knew what I was doing'. It was all quite unnerving. I began to think there might be a co-ordinated attempt to destabilize me. But this was no time to be paranoid; I knew everyone was against me! I pressed on.

At the heart of *The Sunday Times* malaise was an under-resourced, lacklustre newsroom and a bloated team of feature writers who regarded themselves as the paper's élite but many of whom were not always as talented as they thought. The plan was to shift more resources to news and to break down the barriers between news and features, an essentially egalitarian scheme that you might think would appeal to journalists of a leftish nature. It did not.

The great phalanx of well-paid and underworked feature writers felt threatened. A number were right to feel thus: some had written very little but their expenses for months; one staff member had managed 400 words in four years; others were only marginally more productive. There were talented writers who needed to be encouraged; but there were also plenty of prima donnas with an overinflated view of their abilities. The newsroom was more productive though many of the reporters were mediocre. There would have to be a clearout in features and news. But I needed help to do it.

Within weeks of arriving at *The Sunday Times* I had established an inner core of senior lieutenants that I could count on to help me push through the changes. Brian MacArthur was proving to be a solid and resourceful deputy but I needed somebody outside the existing hierarchy, with his ear to the ground, to alert me to problems and give me candid advice. I appointed James Adams as my special assistant.

It was an appointment Rupert was always to resent. 'It's a mistake,' he would periodically mutter. He had no need of such a right-hand man – or so he thought – so why did I? But Rupert was wrong. Throughout the eleven years we worked together James was a constant source of sound advice and good ideas. He was never afraid to tell me when he thought I was wrong and I came to value that quality in him most. The staff realized that he was a reliable conduit to me when there was something to say that I might find unpalatable; and he helped to smooth the rough edges in my sometimes tense relations with various staff members.

In addition to Brian and James, the people I relied on most were Tony Bambridge, Tony Rennell and Bob Campbell, three news executives who relished an enhanced status for the newsroom; Don Berry, who was apprehensive about the political direction I was taking the paper but appreciated my journalistic rigour and commitment to serious analysis of the week's events; and Derrick Collier, the paper's veteran production manager, who rather approved of the upheaval.

Others also played their part in these early days, including Peter Roberts, the managing editor, who looked after the budget and administration. He handled the many redundancies with tact and patience – and a large cheque book – but he was suspicious of James, whom he wrongly suspected of wanting his job, which meant even the inner team was sometimes hindered by office politics.

Together we set about a comprehensive review of news

and features staff. Peter Roberts produced a list of column inches published in recent months alongside each name. Quantity is never the only yardstick by which to judge a journalist but it wasn't a bad place to start. The disparities were huge. Some were prolific, while others were clearly suffering from writer's block, or indolence: two feature writers had managed to produce only two published articles in the previous year.

To this quantitative analysis was added a more subjective appraisal which I gleaned from my own observations and the consensus of the inner team. My notes peppered the margins of the list with comments such as 'lacklustre', 'lame duck', 'lazy, lamish duck' and 'prima donna'. It was not a hit list in the sense that everybody who got a bad report was immediately designated for departure. But it was a guide to action and a yardstick by which to judge future performance.

Thus the clearout and the rejuvenation began. It was an expensive business: one of the frustrations of a Fleet Street editor is that no matter how poorly a journalist performs it is well-nigh impossible to sack them for incompetence or laziness. They have to be induced to leave by waving very large cheques in their faces. 'Shame them into going,' Rupert used to say as he watched the redundancy bill climb. He wanted me to make the lazy or less talented realize the climate had changed and go of their own volition. But some journalists with large salaries and little work are not easily shamed. It was more effective to bribe them into departure.

Several hundred thousand pounds was spent in what was known as 'redundo' in the first six months of my editorship. Thus enriched, a growing diaspora of the aggrieved and dispossessed went off to pour poison into the ears of anybody who would listen about the awfulness of *The Sunday Times* and its new editor. In retrospect, it is interesting to note how few who departed went on to greater things; many seem to have disappeared without trace, confirmation, perhaps, that they were not as good as they thought.

The word spread that everybody who was any good was rushing to take the money and leave *The Sunday Times*. But it was far from a one-way street. We began to hire some bright young reporters and to get the best out of those feature writers whom I wanted to remain. I also set about giving the paper a facelift. I brightened up the front page with a bolder presentation of stories, reinstated Harry Evans' preference for printing good pictures big; and gave priority to detailed reconstructions of the main news stories of the week – what I called the *Time*-magazine function of *The Sunday Times*, at which Don Berry excelled. I also started to take the paper in new directions.

The early eighties were the dawn of the information age; I wanted the paper to be at the cutting edge of its developments. But almost nobody at *The Sunday Times* much cared. Most of its journalists exhibited a traditional liberal-arts distaste for new technology and, since they inhabited the industrial Dark Ages at Gray's Inn Road, knew nothing about it anyway. I hired a new computer correspondent who had the added benefit of being female – I wanted many more women as reporters and executives – and encouraged journalists to take an interest in the information revolution. I even managed to cajole the management into installing half a dozen Atex word processors for the journalists to use. The unions were suspicious but agreed to their use as long as they could re-key every word themselves.

It was ripe for the usual cynical Fleet Street satire. I became known as the computer-loving editor to be ridiculed for his obsession with new technology. A *Private Eye*'s 'Quote of the Week' had an anonymous (of course) staff member saying of me: 'If he can't f—— it or plug it into the wall, he's not interested.' It made me laugh – at least it was an improvement on my previous celibate status – and I had the words framed. Even Charles Wintour, the distinguished former editor of the *London Evening Standard*, who was later to become an admirer, felt it necessary to get in on the offensive. 'The new *Sunday Times* editor,' he opined gravely on television's *What the Papers Say* one night, 'is making many changes – mostly for the worst.' It was unsettling to have such authoritative criticism, even if there was a knee-jerk element to it. But I continued undaunted.

I merged our television, film and video coverage into a new section called Screen, hiring Sue Summers, a television reporter whose husband had produced my *Look Here* show on the media at LWT, to edit the pages. The audio-visual world had been little more than critics' fodder for Sunday journalism, usually written about with a sneering superiority; I wanted to cover it as one of the key business and cultural developments of our day. The *Guardian* and others mocked the attention I was giving to such matters, yet within a few years they all had Screen-type pages of their own (including, of course, the *Guardian*, which years later based its Monday Media pages on the Screen concept).

I also got to grips with *The Sunday Times Magazine*. The only words I had insisted Rupert add to my contract during our talks was a clause that made it clear that I was editor of the newspaper *and* the magazine. This came as something of a shock to Peter Jackson, who recently had been appointed by Rupert to edit the magazine. He flew to New York to complain but the magazine under his editorship had become a lacklustre affair devoted too much to lifestyle and consumerism. Rupert had already lost interest in him and he was given no comfort. I tried to work with him but I wanted more serious magazine journalism than he seemed prepared to deliver. He soon departed, allowing me to appoint Genevieve Cooper as the magazine's first-ever female editor.

My popularity ratings were not helped by my decision to impose some budgetary discipline on the paper. It was a novel concept. In the Thomson era nobody had bothered much with budgets and Harry Evans had been a big spender; in the absence of any sanctions, notional budget ceilings were regularly broken. More stringent financial controls had come with Rupert Murdoch but the prevalent mood was still one of profligacy. I hated meetings on budgets and administration but I insisted on departments sticking to their budgets for one very good reason: I regarded keeping editorial costs within budget as essential to my independence from management in general and Rupert in particular.

The more I stayed within budget the fewer reasons they – or Rupert – would have for interfering. I built up a reputation within the company's bean counters as the editor most likely to stay within budget; throughout my eleven years as editor Rupert never once had cause to complain about major cost overruns. It also meant he rarely became involved in how I was spending the money.

None of this mattered to the journalists at the time. They were disconcerted, even depressed, by the churn of familiar faces departing and new ones arriving; of old departments like Insight disappearing and new ones, like Screen and People, appearing; of a budgetary discipline that did not tolerate too much waste (there has to be some in any creative venture); and of the demand for a higher rigour in news and feature writing.

Widespread resistance to all this never turned into open rebellion. Maybe if the circulation of the paper had been in freefall things would have been different. But as 1983 came to an end, sales were up 50,000 on 1982 and stood at a very healthy 1.338 million. By contrast, the *Observer* was down 39,000 to 769,000 and the *Sunday Telegraph* was down 30,000 to 730,000. It was also generally realized that I had

Murdoch's support for the changes, which made any palace coup daunting to mount. The paper was also starting to break some big stories again, which is always good for the morale of even the most disillusioned journalist.

*

IF THE RAPID STAFF TURNOVER in my first few months was disconcerting enough for the paper's old guard, my determination to establish a distinctive new editorial line for *The Sunday Times* was to cause even greater ructions.

The Sunday Times I inherited in the autumn of 1983 was in a state of ideological decay. The liberal-left collectivist consensus which had inspired and imbued so much of its reporting and analysis in the sixties and seventies – even when the editorials said 'Vote Tory' to keep the proprietor happy – had been thoroughly discredited by the failure of the Wilson–Callaghan government and the disastrous Winter of Discontent in 1978–79. But the overwhelming majority of the paper's journalists were steeped in that tradition and had no taste for the Thatcherite revolution then gathering pace.

There was barely a right-winger among them: they were nearly all various shades of left, from soft to hard. They were the Lost Tribe of the sixties, wandering aimlessly in the alien environment of the eighties. Ideas and events had passed them by but they clung to yesterday, not so much out of a continuing conviction but because it was more comfortable sniping and moaning about current developments than devising and supporting new policies that would meet the challenges of the present and future. I knew from the start that what I wanted *The Sunday Times* to stand for would be anathema to them.

But I felt on firm ground. As a journalist I had always been interested in the ideas and opinions that should determine government policy. My *Economist* pedigree had prepared me. I was as well versed in current issues as anybody on the paper – and better informed than most. My time in New York and Washington had equipped me with fresh thinking and an international perspective *The Sunday Times* old guard lacked. And, unlike those who opposed me, I had a clear idea of the policies I wanted the paper to espouse.

I wanted to commit the paper to turning Britain into a prosperous, dynamic market economy. This meant signing on to much of what Margaret Thatcher was trying to do at the time. But it did not mean becoming a mouthpiece for Tory Central Office or an apologist for the lady and all her works. I wanted to compile a distinctive *Sunday Times* agenda against which to judge government policy. Right from the start I was determined to establish the paper's independence from the government; I did that in my first editorial on 9 October 1983.

It was the eve of the annual Tory Party conference in Blackpool and the news was dominated by the scandal surrounding Cecil Parkinson's messy affair with his former secretary, Sara Keays. We splashed on page one with 'Top Tories tell Thatcher: Sack Parkinson' (not a bad first lead for the new kid on the block) but the editorial, headlined 'Drift, dither and scandal', asserted that the real challenge facing the government was not Parkinson's personal problems but its clear failure to capitalize on its June 1983 general election victory:

> The real worry about Mrs Thatcher's second administration is not the morals of her ministers but that it has already lost its political way . . . Mrs Thatcher needs to husband all her resources if she is to break the mould of corporatist Britain . . .
>
> The sensible course for a radical government seeking to shake Britain out of its torpor and lay the basis for

> prosperity is to move to the right on industrial policy (trust-bust, deregulate, privatize wherever it produces more competition and efficiency) and the centre-left in economic strategy (a few billion extra in capital spending would have little impact on interest rates or inflation but could give a lift to a shaky economic recovery).

This established an original editorial line on economic policy: in microeconomics it placed *The Sunday Times* on the radical right, arguing for more competition, privatization and deregulation than the Thatcher Government was then prepared to contemplate. But on macroeconomics it called for more government investment to get the economy going and reduce unemployment, which aligned us with the demands of Labour and the left against the monetarism and fiscal conservatism of the government. The guiding principle was that if you made the economy more efficient and competitive then the government could afford to pump up demand in the economy to create jobs and growth – it would not all leak away in extra imports.

It was a sophisticated position which crossed party lines – too sophisticated for my critics in and out of the paper, most of whom did not understand the difference between macro- and microeconomics, never mind the complication of each being guided by a different school of economic thought. Even Rupert was a bit nonplussed: 'I'm not sure you're right,' he commented. He would have preferred a paper that was unmistakably monetarist and did not call for an increase in public investment. But he left me to get on with it: at least he now had an editor with whom he could have a conversation about such matters.

I wanted the paper to be in the vanguard of public policy debate. Though the Tory manifesto in 1979 had said nothing about privatization, it was becoming clear by late 1983 that the concept was going to become one of the hallmarks of the

Thatcher years. I wanted to highlight this and explain its significance: I worked with Don Berry to produce a two-page special which was illustrated by a huge billboard on which the word 'Nationalization' was being papered over with a new poster entitled 'Privatization'.

The piece began 'Privatization is to the Thatcher eighties what Nationalization was to the Attlee forties' but was not uncritical of the process. It pointed out that privatization was most likely to work best where state industries were being privatized into competitive markets (such as British Airways) but that privatized monopolies (such as gas and electricity) would need careful regulation. It was a distinction that was to become the consensus as the eighties progressed and I revelled in publishing the sort of pacesetter piece that *The Economist* at its best had excelled at.

As originally filed, of course, the copy had been almost wholly hostile to privatization and what appeared was something of a compromise between myself and the journalists involved. On other issues I felt less inclined to compromise and the strong positions I took provoked a series of clashes.

None more so than the deployment of American Cruise missiles on British soil and the so-called peace movement that opposed it. The Soviet Union had installed hundreds of medium-range nuclear missiles in Eastern Europe for which the West had no equivalent. It had then mounted a major propaganda offensive in the West, finding willing foils among the unilateral nuclear disarmers in Britain and elsewhere, to make it politically impossible for Nato to deploy Cruise missiles to match the Soviet SS-20s. The KGB had informed the Kremlin that the European democracies would face such an outcry from anti-nuclear protesters that they would not be able to deploy land-based Cruise missiles. They were almost proved right.

The battle to deploy Cruise missiles was one of the last

great struggles of the Cold War. I regarded deployment as crucial. Failure to do so would be a famous victory for the unilateral disarmers – who had taken control of the Labour Party in Britain and were a major force in Germany – and allow the hawks in the Kremlin to claim that the West was on the run. But a successful deployment would force the Kremlin to reassess its analysis of Western weakness and encourage it to engage in real talks to cut nuclear arsenals. That was what happened: Cruise was deployed and within a few years both Cruise and the SS-20s were removed from European soil. But at the time those of us who favoured Cruise had a tough and unpopular fight on our hands. I wanted nobody to be in any doubt where *The Sunday Times* stood: foursquare for Cruise and against the Campaign for Nuclear Disarmament (CND).

On 23 October, with the arrival of Cruise imminent, I published an editorial entitled 'Sunset for CND'. It argued that the deployment of Cruise would be an historic defeat not just for the Kremlin but for CND. The anti-Cruise campaign had given CND a new lease of life but the editorial argued that it would prove to be its highwater mark. Successful deployment would bring multilateral disarmament back on to the agenda for it would leave the Kremlin with 'no alternative to large, negotiated nuclear arms reductions on both sides', spelling the end of CND's policy of one-sided disarmament in the process. In retrospect the editorial proved prophetic: Cruise was deployed, the Soviets did come to the bargaining table and CND never recovered its pre-Cruise prominence or influence (even the Labour Party eventually abandoned unilateral disarmament). But at the time the editorial provoked outrage among CND readers, who wrote in droves to complain, and among CND sympathizers on the staff.

Hugo Young was particularly aggrieved, though at the

time he stayed quiet. He was later to say that it was not the pro-Cruise policy that upset him – the paper had always been in favour of Cruise, he claimed – but the harsh words about CND. I had not noticed that Hugo had been in favour of Cruise deployment (but then it was always easier to know what he was against than to see what he was for) and his column on the day of the 'Sunset for CND' leader had been kind to the unilateral disarmers without quite siding with them. I had not touched a word of it – Hugo was always free to write whatever he wanted in his own column – but it was precisely the sort of dissembling on a vital issue of national security that I did not want in a *Sunday Times* editorial.

Within weeks I was offending Hugo and others again. This time the issue was the American invasion of Grenada, a Caribbean island that was in the grip of a Marxist dictatorship which Washington feared was turning the island into another Cuba, enslaving the people and exporting revolution. I was uncertain what the paper's view should be – the invasion was very unpopular in Britain – and consulted several senior editors, including Hugo and David Lipsey, the economics editor: they were all hostile to President Reagan's action (but then they were all anti-Reagan).

I was prepared to go along with them. Then I read an editorial in *The Economist* which gave good if qualified reasons for the intervention and took a call from David Owen, who argued that the non-marxist majority on the island had turned to America for help because the British had ignored their pleas – even though Grenada was a member of the Commonwealth with the Queen as its head of state. But I was most influenced by the on-the-spot file from Will Ellsworth-Jones, our New York correspondent, who had managed to hitch a lift to the island on a fishing boat and was one of the first reporters on the scene. His dispatch made clear that those who had usurped power in Grenada had been well on their way to turning it into another Marxist hellhole and that the islanders were welcoming the Americans as liberators rather than as invaders.

So I wrote an editorial which broadly welcomed the American action while expressing concern about the dangers of any American presence overstaying its welcome. The intervention could only be justified if it restored democracy to Grenada, it argued, even if that resulted in the election of a left-of-centre government. Under the headline 'Great Britain – the lion dismissed' it also attacked Britain for marginalizing itself in a region which had once been a sphere of strong British influence:

> They [Grenada's neighbours, who had joined in the American intervention] turned to America and Britain for help, but found only America interested. Yet a Commonwealth initiative would surely have been preferable to a superpower intervention – certainly a more saleable proposition to international opinion. In the event, Britain had neither the will nor the capacity to give a lead. The superpower had. Grenada is a salutary reminder that Suez, not the Falklands, is the seminal event in the post-war history of British foreign policy.

The first sign of dissent came from David Lipsey, who glared at me angrily when I went down to the composing room that Saturday afternoon to check the front page. Then came a memo from Hugo which, while couched in his customary politeness, made clear his deep opposition to the line I had imposed on the paper and, indeed, the general direction I was taking it.

'Do you intend the leaders to reflect a collective view at all any longer?' he wrote. 'I would like to know – and I should think others would too – whether you reject this method of proceeding, and want to make the leader column into a personal platform, as other editors elsewhere have done before. This certainly seemed to be the basis for your leader on CND which, as far as I know, was completely undiscussed. It also seems to come through today's leader on Grenada, whose pro-Reagan tone hardly reflects the feeling of the general discussion yesterday evening.'

These were honest questions deserving an honest reply. He got one.

> I have no brief on editorial policy [I wrote back] other than my own, which is that we should be tied to no party views, but be surprising, straightforward and state matters strongly.
>
> The problem is, I have inherited a 'collective' which I played no part in creating. If my views are so far out of line with the existing 'collective', then something has to give – otherwise there will be too much fudge and compromise, and the leaders will not have the qualities I listed above.
>
> I have very definite views on the broad editorial stance I want *The Sunday Times* to take: neo-Keynesian in economic policy, radical right in industrial policy, liberal on social matters and European and Atlanticist on foreign policy. Within such broad outlines, there is plenty of scope for debate and disagreement. But you and others may think that these are fundamentally the wrong directions anyway.
>
> I understand the frustrations of having to deal with an outsider who comes in and upsets tried and tested ways of doing things. If I was in your position, I would be just as annoyed, and have sent the same sort of note – though probably a more intemperate one!

My reply was friendly but frank. It went to the nub of the problem but failed to resolve it – because there was no solution. Until my arrival Hugo had been the intellectual guiding spirit of the paper; I was my own guiding spirit. He was high priest of the fashionable centre-left establishment consensus; I was an anti-establishment radical who blamed that consensus for our nation's decline. If I listened to the 'collective' view of the paper, which reflected his opinions, the paper would stand for policies I did not support. If I tried to devise some sort of compromise on editorials each week, it would end up publishing wishy-washy nonsense.

Moreover, I had a proprietor who expected me to take *The Sunday Times* in the policy direction I had indicated when hired. I was prepared to be fired by Rupert for what I believed in; it seemed crazy to risk Rupert's wrath by following an editorial line with which we both disagreed. Something had to give. It was not going to be me.

Hugo did not bring matters to a head immediately. He continued to write his anti-Thatcher columns each week, which I was happy to publish untouched. They were an intelligent leftish critique of early Thatcherism and I wanted the paper to be a broad church in the opinions it printed. But Hugo was clearly miserable at having lost his strong influence over the paper's editorial voice and increasingly wandered around the paper's corridors like a bear with a sore head. Brian MacArthur's departure to launch the *Today* newspaper (see Chapter 4) and Ivan Fallon's arrival as the new deputy gave Hugo his chance to leave with dignity on a point of principle but with a large cheque. In March 1984 the memo I had anticipated for some time eventually arrived.

> It is undoubtedly your prerogative, as editor, to take full and total responsibility for any aspect of the paper including its political direction [Hugo began]. However, this has, in effect, resulted in my being 'redundant'.
>
> Continuing to write the occasional leader and chairing an editorial meeting cannot alter the fundamental situation of my having lost status and influence as political

> editor and my significant involvement, as joint deputy editor, in decision making throughout the paper.
>
> I and Brian MacArthur were joint deputy editors. The appointment of Ivan Fallon as deputy editor replacing Brian MacArthur was the final indication that, in essence, my job on the ST had ceased to exist.

Hugo was using Ivan's arrival as deputy editor to argue that he had been constructively dismissed, thereby qualifying for a substantial redundancy payment. It was true that Hugo was, in theory, joint deputy editor with Brian as well as political editor, though long before I arrived Brian had emerged as the *de facto* number two, editing the paper in the editor's absence, which is always the crucial test of who is second-in-command; Hugo's status as joint deputy had become largely a courtesy title. What Hugo was really complaining about was the demise of his influence on the political direction of *The Sunday Times*, which had once been formidable.

I could understand why Hugo felt miffed. At one stage, pre-Murdoch, he had harboured hopes of becoming editor of *The Sunday Times*. He might have been a very good one (though I wonder if he would have had the populist touch to sustain a readership of almost four million) but that was never going to happen as long as Murdoch was proprietor. Now he had effectively been reduced to its premier (and highest-paid) columnist, writing against the grain of a paper on which he had only recently been its seminal influence. Hugo had determined that it was time for a separation – and that it would not be amicable.

I would have been content for Hugo to continue to write his column and be paid a deputy editor's salary for it. The fact that I eventually replaced him with Peter Jenkins of the *Guardian*, another guru of the centre-left, is proof that I did not want the senior columnist to speak with the same voice as the editorials. But Hugo had always resented Rupert Murdoch's purchase of Times Newspapers; now was his opportunity to depart without hardship.

On 18 March 1984 Hugo wrote his farewell column, 'A press we don't deserve', which was a barely coded attack on Murdoch, full of high principle. But he had a cheque for almost £80,000 in his pocket as he wrote his words from the man he so reviled, even though the BBC, the *Guardian* and book publishers beckoned with alternative, lucrative employment. The money did not assuage his bitterness.

No sooner had he departed than he went into print with a bad-tempered attack on the Murdoch/Neil *Sunday Times* in which he argued that a newspaper that had previously been an objective seeker of truth had been corrupted into a right-wing propaganda sheet that slavishly promoted the Thatcher agenda. His comments on my *Sunday Times* were untrue; and what he had to say about the paper before I arrived was a massive distortion of its recent history. For a start, I was prepared to publish any story I believed to be true, whatever the political fallout. We had just been denounced by Margaret Thatcher in the House of Commons for investigating her son's finances (see Chapter 9). And the idea that *The Sunday Times* had been an impartial recorder of events and issues in the supposedly high-minded Thomson era was a popular myth with the fashionable left that did not bear a moment's scrutiny.

Hugo argued that *The Sunday Times* had a 'detached and objective spirit' until I arrived. Anybody who bothers to scan the back numbers will quickly see that the manner in which it chose to cover the stories and issues of the time was suffused with the liberal-left assumptions of the sixties and seventies. That was what made it such a compelling read: it was an essential part of the *Zeitgeist* of its day, an informed interpreter of its era and a key contributor to it. Stories and analysis were sometimes cleverly written to appear unbiased but the objectivity was bogus; the underlying spirit and inspiration was always liberal-left, just as it still is in the *Guardian*, where Hugo has found true happiness as a columnist and chairman of the *Guardian/Observer* Scott Trust (and imported a little of Murdoch's robust attitudes, judged by the rather brutal manner in which he has recently executed the sacking of some editors).

As evidence of my corrupting ways, he cited the 'derisory coverage of the CND march' which coincided with the deployment of Cruise; the news story, he claimed, had been distorted to fit with the paper's editorial opinion. I checked back: Hugo was talking nonsense. On 23 October 1983 *The Sunday Times* had splashed on its front page with 'Cruise looms as CND march'. A long story which turned to page two reported that CND 'yesterday mounted its biggest ever series of co-ordinated demonstrations in Western Europe' and in a wholly factual way went on to contrast the behind-the-scenes preparations for the imminent deployment of Cruise with the mass rallies against Cruise all across Europe. It quoted leading anti-Cruise campaigners Neil Kinnock and Paddy Ashdown and even published two pictures of CND marchers on the front page. The report was a model of good journalism: the editorial line was hostile to CND but that did not distort the paper's news coverage.

Nor, for all his support for journalism that is 'detached and objective', has he done much to introduce either quality into the *Guardian* and *Observer*, the two papers that come under his remit as chairman of the Scott Trust. I know of no evidence to suggest he has encouraged the editors of either paper to reduce the generous liberal-left spin they put on almost every political story they run; and neither paper has a single right-of-centre political columnist. The *Guardian* is a paper of character and purpose: but it could hardly claim to be an objective journal of record. Hugo did not mind the biases of the old *Sunday Times* because he agreed with them; he probably does not even see the biases of the Scott Trust's papers, because he agrees with them too.

Hugo's original attack on me finished with words that have always stuck in my mind: 'Today's *Sunday Times* may make profits but it no longer makes waves.' These must be the most foolish words that he has written in a long and distinguished career as a commentator. Whatever the shortcomings of my editorship, the one thing *The Sunday Times* consistently did under my direction was make waves – for everybody and anybody, without fear or favour. It was a relief to me that his baleful presence had gone from the paper but his departure was the signal for a further round of Neil bashing and further comment that *The Sunday Times* was going to hell in a handbasket.

*

MY SURVIVAL AT *THE SUNDAY TIMES* in these early years required me to draw on qualities that I had until then been unaware that I possessed, maybe because I had never before needed them: anger, ruthlessness, sometimes a brutal determination to have my way. It was not always a pretty sight.

My decade at *The Economist* had been relatively equable. There had been the odd difference with colleagues and some minor office politics. But it was all reasonably civilized and serious arguments were largely confined to matters of policy and what the magazine should stand for. It was an enjoyable, satisfying environment in which to work, colleagues became good friends and tempers were rarely lost. It was an inadequate preparation for *The Sunday Times*.

Within weeks of arriving at Gray's Inn Road, I had become easily riled and prone to angry outbursts. I never really thought I had a temper until I arrived at *The Sunday*

Times. What caused me to rage most was not outright opposition to my plans: with open confrontation at least you knew what you were up against. I was most frustrated by those who would nod in agreement during meetings then go and do the exact opposite to what had just been agreed. Sometimes the changes I had requested would be carried out for a couple of weeks; then, when they thought my eye was off the ball or I had moved my attention to other matters, they would revert to their old ways.

Nothing was more calculated to arouse my anger. John Whitley, a quiet, intelligent man in charge of our cultural coverage, was a master at it. Time and again we would agree on how to make the visual and performing arts more accessible to readers who were not necessarily passionate about such matters. Time and again I would scan his pages and nod in approval at the changes made. And time and again I would notice before long that the old ways had somehow reasserted themselves. I'm not even sure if this was intentional defiance; I think it was simply inbred. Those who tried this technique soon discovered, however, that I had a good memory: I never forgot what changes I had asked for.

The feeling that I was in hostile territory – and the constant sniping in other publications – made me less effective with the staff than I should have been. I had no patience or skill for massaging bruised egos and no inclination to do so. It is a handicap because being an editor requires the delicate handling of creative people who are often insecure in their careers. I was quick to penalize failure and slow to praise success, not a sensible combination. As a result I made more enemies than was necessary, making my task all the harder.

No doubt a charm offensive in the early weeks would have produced a better acceptance and understanding of what I was trying to do. But invariably when I did open up in a friendly manner to one of the journalists and frankly share my thoughts with them (which hitherto had always been my method of working) I found anything I said quickly recycled – and suitably distorted – in one of the many columns in rival publications that chronicled every event at *The Sunday Times*. The paper was like a secret society, with journalists locked in cabals gossiping madly about the implications of my every word and move. I had never been known to be aloof before but I learned to be guarded and keep my distance, if only to minimize the knocking copy.

One of James Adams's key roles was to act as a buffer between me and the staff. He did what he could to smooth the rough edges and explain to nervous journalists what I was trying to do; in turn, they expressed their concern through him. He had the patience to deal with the insecure journalistic egos that I lacked; and he had a talent for making their concerns more palatable to me than they would have done themselves.

With his help, and the support of others, I slowly rebuilt *The Sunday Times* to my specification. By the summer of 1984 things were beginning to fall into place: the most dissatisfied of the old guard were leaving and new blood was arriving. Some of it was even on the same wavelength as me.

In Ivan Fallon I had an experienced new deputy who broadly supported the paper's new editorial direction. But he was naturally less abrasive and more emollient than me and helped smooth many ruffled feathers. He had been the influential City Editor of the *Sunday Telegraph*, whose business pages were generally reckoned to be the best on Sunday. But we would soon change that.

I had brought in Stephen Milligan from *The Economist*, where he had been a friend and colleague, to be foreign editor. An Oxford Tory I had met in my student days, he had since fled to the Social Democrats. He possessed an enquiring, original intelligence, a wide knowledge of foreign and domestic affairs and he was great fun to work with, his infectious laugh filling our editorial meetings, where he played a major role in redefining the paper's policy positions.

I had promoted the political correspondent, Michael Jones, to the political editorship vacated by Hugo. We did not know each other – indeed in the first few weeks of my editorship Michael had informed Peter Walker that he intended to keep a low profile until the dust settled – but it proved to be the start of an enduring partnership. The relationship between editor and political editor is one of the most crucial in a newspaper and Michael and I struck up a close accord as the months went by.

With these and other fresh appointments I had the beginnings of a new team that would revivify *The Sunday Times*, not least because it was in tune with the tenor of the times. I was not trying to create a paper entirely in my own image; there was no Oxbridge public-school purge as some later claimed. James was an Old Harrovian, Stephen was public school and Oxford, Michael was from Welsh mining stock and had not even gone to university and another who was to become a close colleague and friend, Geordie Greig, was an Old Etonian. But I was determined not to choose on the basis of whatever school, university or college they had gone to; with a more meritocratic approach I hoped a team more in tune with the New Britain would emerge.

That meant, for a start, more female reporters and executives, and a stab at a staff that reflected the country's ethnic diversity, instead of the almost totally male, white, middle-aged group I had inherited. But above all I simply wanted to hire the best people, regardless of background. And with this new spirit came a revival in *The Sunday Times*'s tradition of ground-breaking stories.

In the first year, *The Sunday Times* had revealed the date of the deployment of Cruise missiles, exposed how Mark

Thatcher was depositing his mysterious gains from his business consultancies into a bank account to which his father was a joint signatory and reported the atrocities being carried out in Matabeleland by the prime minister of Zimbabwe, Robert Mugabe. We had also detailed how Thatcher had negotiated away Hong Kong too easily to the Chinese, revealed plans for televising Parliament and showed how the government's 'short, sharp shock' detention policy for young offenders had been a flop.

For a paper which was supposed to have lost its social conscience, we exposed how the 'Care in the Community' policy, which involved the closing of mental institutions, had carelessly dumped helpless outcasts into society; and ran a series of articles on how youngsters were becoming 'Hooked on heroin' – two themes that, after we gave them prominence, were to merit media attention throughout the eighties.

I was proud of the range of ideas now in display. We published extracts from Germaine Greer's *Sex and Destiny*, a revisionist update on her own *Female Eunuch*, Francis Pym's anti-Thatcher memoirs, and a study of the 'Patels of Britain', a celebration of how at least one immigrant community was making it in Britain. We also managed to re-launch *The Sunday Times Magazine*, with a 25 per cent increase in page size and a renewed commitment to the best of photojournalism.

The Sunday Times old guard and their allies in the rest of the media might not have approved of what I was doing but the readers seemed to like it. Readership increased by almost 160,000 in the second half of 1983, while the *Observer*'s slumped by 300,000 and the *Sunday Telegraph*'s fell by 127,000.

All that and the continued confidence of Rupert Murdoch, who had largely left me alone to make the changes I wanted, supporting me only when I needed it. I had spent

New Year in Aspen with him and his family and we were on friendly terms. My prediction of a six-month honeymoon, at most, had proved false. I was almost looking forward to my second year, despite all the criticism and hardship of the first. But the struggle against entrenched journalists, which I looked like winning, was not the only battle I faced. There was an even more entrenched newspaper establishment to deal with, one that made the journalists look like a walkover.

CHAPTER FOUR

A Lesson from the North

'HELLO, MR SHAH. My name is Andrew Neil. You don't know me but I'm the new editor of *The Sunday Times* and thanks to you I won't have a paper this weekend.'

I had never heard of Eddy Shah until a local dispute in the north-west of England in the autumn of 1983 between a tiny group of freesheets and the mighty National Graphical Association (NGA) had flared into a national shutdown. I decided to call him, a small entrepreneur who, unlike the national proprietors, was taking a stand against the domination of his business by the print unions, using the new Tory labour laws to tie them in legal knots and threaten their funds. In fury, they had closed down Fleet Street: there would be no *Sunday Times* or any other national papers on 27 November.

'I'm very sorry about that,' he replied. 'I didn't mean it to happen; things are getting out of hand.' He sounded apologetic, even fearful; but there was a quiet dignity in his voice.

'I'm not calling for an apology,' I told him. 'I would rather lose publication of my newspaper for weeks to come than for you to give in. But now that the dispute has gone national you will come under plenty of pressure to settle. You must do what you think is right, not what those who don't have your interests at heart want you to do.'

I was thinking of Fleet Street's proprietors, who always preferred surrender when the going got tough. Throughout the Shah dispute they never lifted a finger to help him: they regarded him as an inconvenience who was causing trouble that was now disrupting their papers. At one stage Robert Maxwell was to offer him £4 million to shut up shop and go away – even though the business was barely worth £1 million.

'Nobody from London seems much bothered about me. You're the first Fleet Street figure to call me,' said Shah.

'There will be more,' I warned. He went on to tell me how the London establishment had largely shunned him. The local Tory MP had been supportive, he explained, and the Institute of Directors had given him some legal advice. But nobody from the government or the Tory Party hierarchy had been in touch and the regional branch of the Confederation of British Industry wanted nothing to do with him. Under union pressure, advertisers were starting to desert his newspapers. Here was a small northern businessman being left to fight the good fight on his own.

'The unions say you're an advanced guard for Margaret Thatcher,' I told him. 'You've been put up to test the new labour laws.'

'I've only ever met her once,' he replied. 'We shook hands at a cocktail party in Manchester. We must have exchanged no more than ten words. I'm not very interested in politics.' Shah was to tell me later: 'We fought this battle on our own. I was nobody's puppet.'

In my mind's eye I saw an innocent man being hung out to dry by the very people who should have been supporting him. Here was somebody with the guts to take on the print unions, who had never been beaten in a hundred years, and nobody wanted to know about him. We had never met but already my heart went out to him; I felt sorry for his isolation, fearful of his chances of success. He felt he had found a kindred spirit.

'Can I keep in touch with you?' he asked, almost plaintively. I reminded him that I had been editor of a national newspaper for less than two months and was just as much a novice as him. But I promised to help in whatever way I could and we exchanged various telephone numbers.

We talked regularly in the days to come. He told me how his efforts to run an efficient business using the latest technology had been thwarted at every stage by the print unions – and of the depths to which they plumbed once he challenged them. One morning he had woken up to find five coffins in his garden: two large ones for him and his wife, three small ones for his children. It was a particularly cruel piece of malevolence: Shah's wife, Jennifer, suffered from a recurrence of cervical cancer and had been given five months to live; but it was typical of the campaign of threats and harassment against Shah and his staff.

The NGA had been mounting unlawful mass picketing against Shah since the end of October. As the dispute grew violent, Group 4, Britain's second-largest security firm, suddenly and mysteriously withdrew their security cover without notice from his Warrington printing works. They had been his first line of defence against pickets and guarded the empty plant at weekends. But one day a Group 4 van had pulled up outside the factory and the two men were told to leave, without any explanation, leaving Shah defenceless.

The Sunday Times was later to reveal that Group 4 had withdrawn under pressure from Derek Hatton, the hard-left deputy leader of Liverpool City Council, which was then in the grip of Militant Tendency. Hatton called the regional manager of Group 4 to remind him that the company had a contract with Liverpool council worth over £215,000; its contract with Shah was worth only about £1,000. Within an hour Group 4 had called Hatton back to assure him their people had withdrawn from Shah's premises.

'Due to the escalation of the dispute,' explained Group 4, 'we decided to withdraw. We had made it clear that we were not there to intervene in an industrial dispute.' It was an unprincipled decision, prompted by pure expediency – Group 4's Munich; and it left Shah more vulnerable than ever, just as events were about to turn very nasty.

The origins of the dispute lay in Shah's ambition to expand his Messenger Group of freesheets using the latest technology. Shah's first experience with newspapers had been selling advertisements in Manchester freesheets a decade before, just as the idea of free local newspapers financed entirely by advertising was taking off. He had mortgaged his house to launch his own freesheet and by the early eighties he owned a handful of them. They were moderately successful and now was the time for expansion.

But the NGA wanted nothing to do with new technology and made it clear any expansion would only happen on its terms, which meant continuation of the closed shop Shah had agreed with the NGA back in 1980 (Shah had even joined the union himself); increased wages; and all the usual restrictive practices and overmanning.

Shah bought a second-hand press and installed it on an industrial estate in Warrington, where he planned to expand the printing of his freesheets. The press could be comfortably operated by six people. But the NGA told him it would insist on eight and that the other main print union, Sogat, would demand another eight assistants to 'work' alongside them.

In the summer of 1983 Shah had also installed some computer typesetting equipment in his Bury office. By the mid-seventies, advances in technology meant journalists and other staff could type their stories and advertising copy directly into a computer, which would then generate the necessary type. But very little of this technology was used in newspapers because the NGA insisted that only its members could input copy and its monopoly of the keyboard was rigorously maintained throughout Britain. But Shah had started to use the computers himself – and was training two secretaries as well. People were joining him who were comfortable with a computer and had never seen a Linotype machine. This threatened the very *raison d'être* of the NGA, whose skills were fast being made redundant by technological advance. The stage was being set for a major confrontation.

Shah's expansion plans had been held up by the NGA's demand that any new labour be dragooned into its closed shop. So the dispute soon escalated into a struggle about who was in control of the newspaper business. Shah concluded he could not afford to expand if lumbered with the print unions' restrictive practices. He decided to train his own non-union workforce at Bury and Warrington. But he allowed the NGA freedom to recruit these new workers. When they voted unanimously to have nothing to do with the print unions the NGA instructed its members at another Shah facility in Stockport to strike. After three weeks Shah sacked them: the 'Stockport Six' were born.

The print unions affected to make the reinstatement of the Stockport Six the focal point of the dispute. Their real aim was to discipline and punish a small entrepreneur who had started to think he and his business could only grow and prosper without the print unions; and the way they pursued their vendetta against Shah played into his hands.

The NGA resorted to all its usual methods of bringing a rebel employer to heel. It organized the blacking of all work for the Messenger Group. It warned advertisers who continued to advertise with Shah's papers that their copy would be boycotted by the NGA in other papers where its members still ruled the roost. And it began to picket Shah's non-union establishments.

The problem was that these traditional NGA tactics were now largely illegal. The Tories' 1980 labour laws had placed severe restrictions on union blacking and secondary action against people and places not directly involved in a dispute; a new 1982 Act had given these provisions real teeth: it allowed employers to sue unions who broke the 1980 laws and seek substantial damages from union funds. On 17 October Shah was granted an injunction in Manchester against the NGA for its blacking and picketing. If the union ignored the injunction it risked its funds being sequestrated by the court and eventual bankruptcy: it had already been fined £150,000 for ignoring court injunctions against mass picketing and was in danger of having its £11 million of assets seized if it continued to flout the law. It was time to get tough with this northern upstart.

The print unions, led by the NGA, planned a massive picket of Shah's Warrington print works to stop his papers from being distributed and quickly bring him to his knees. Thousands of print workers and their rent-a-mob allies on the hard left, including militant miners and students, descended on his little factory on a Warrington industrial estate. Their aim was to blockade him into submission. It was a lonely, frightening time for Shah and his staff as they stood alone night after night against the might of the mob.

Tuesday, 29 November 1983 was to be a night of shame for Britain's labour movement in general and the print unions in particular, a night when they and their hard-left allies mustered brute force to break a small businessman, who paid good wages and had created jobs in an area of high unemployment, from going about his lawful business – all because he would not bend to their will.

I stayed up late that night at home, anxious for news; but

nobody on London radio or television was giving much attention to the events up north. Then the phone rang just after midnight. It was Eddy: 'They've set fire to the buildings on the next block,' he said, trying hard not to sound hysterical. 'The mob's on the rampage – there's thousands of them. The police lines have been broken. My men have their backs against the corrugated gates trying to keep the pickets from smashing them down. If they get in here we're going to be killed. I have to go. You have to do something.' He hung up before I could ask him: What?

I sat alone in my small television room, over two hundred miles south of the mayhem, in comfortable Onslow Gardens, South Kensington (where, by coincidence, Eddy once had a bedsit) wondering what to do. As part of my induction as editor I had just done the rounds of some cabinet ministers. One of these getting-to-know-you sessions had been with Leon Brittan, the home secretary; at the end of it we had exchanged home telephone numbers. But it was too late to disturb him. I did not know him and it was after 12.30 a.m. What would I say anyway? I put the number away, then pulled it out again: if Eddy Shah was prepared to put his life on the line then the home secretary could have his sleep disturbed.

'I'm sorry to wake you so late at night, Home Secretary,' I began, hesitatingly, 'but I wondered if you were aware about events in Warrington?'

'As far as I know, it's all under control,' he replied, his voice tinged with irritation at being woken up for such a matter.

'I don't think that's right,' I countered. 'Eddy Shah has just been on the phone to me. He says the police lines won't hold. He thinks he and his people are going to be killed. You have to help him.'

'I don't think it's that bad – but what would you have me do?'

'You could authorize the chief constable of Cheshire to deploy the Manchester riot police.' It was clear the local lads needed help, fast, from police trained to deal with serious rioting.

'It's not my job to get involved in operational details,' retorted Brittan, a lawyer who preferred to hide behind legal technicalities rather than take political risks. Now it was my turn to be irritated.

'Fine,' I said angrily, 'but I want you to know that I am now going to make a detailed note of this conversation. If I wake up in the morning to find that Eddy Shah is dead I'll make damn sure that the Prime Minister and the rest of the country is in no doubt who did nothing to stop him being killed.'

That brought the conversation abruptly to an end. I stared at a blank TV screen – these were the days before 24-hour Sky News – wondering what was happening in Warrington. I tried to call Eddy but there was no reply. I feared the worst.

Then at about 2 a.m. the phone rang and I grabbed it. 'I don't know what you did,' shouted Eddy excitedly, 'but it worked. The Manchester riot squad has arrived. We'll be OK.'

I'm not so sure as Eddy that my intervention had been decisive. The Manchester Tactical Aid Group was already on standby in full riot gear, though even when things were getting dangerously out of hand the Cheshire police had been reluctant to deploy it. It had probably done no harm to stiffen Leon Brittan's spine and concentrate his mind. I had been appalled by his apparent indifference to Eddy's fate. I decided that the best way to secure his success was to make sure the Prime Minister was fully briefed – she was likely to be more robust than Brittan.

Margaret Thatcher had been in India during the Battle of Warrington. But next morning, 30 November, I had this confidential letter hand-delivered via her private secretary, Richard Hatfield, to await her return that day. I had already briefed him by phone:

> I thought it might be helpful if I repeated my concerns on paper. I have been in close contact with Eddy Shah, especially throughout the past twenty-four hours. When I spoke to him just after midnight it looked as if the mob was going to break the police lines and his factory door. He is convinced, and I agree with him, that if the mob break into his factory, the lives of his workers will be in jeopardy. We are no longer dealing with a challenge to the government's labour laws, but riotous assembly.
>
> I am most concerned that all necessary resources are being made available to the Cheshire Chief Constable, including help from other police areas, regardless of the cost.
>
> Mr Shah's resolve remains firm (indeed he provides a refreshing contrast to the recent behaviour of most Fleet Street proprietors), but he was clearly shaken by last night's events, which he told me were 'touch and go'.
>
> He will be back in court by Friday. He is determined not to buckle under, and his 150-strong workforce is firmly on his side. It is vital that the government's laws be upheld. It is also vital that Mr Shah not be bullied and intimidated into submission: if a decent and honest entrepreneur like him cannot go about his normal business without violent abuse then there is little hope of the government ever achieving its wider objectives.
>
> I would not want to see either Mr Shah, his factory or the government's laws destroyed because, at a crucial moment, the forces of law and order could not cope.
>
> After Mr Shah's worried call last night I telephoned these concerns to Leon Brittan. Tonight, I understand, the Welsh miners join the picket line.

Hatfield called to thank me for the letter, which he described as most helpful; more important, he said it would be placed at the top of the red box awaiting the Prime Minister's attention.

The cabinet met next morning, Thursday, 1 December. Peter Walker called me after it had finished; he knew of my concern for Eddy. 'I don't think your Mr Shah will have any more worries about his security,' said Peter, chuckling. 'Maggie has just put Brittan in personal charge of it. She said that the police had to be out in full force to protect his business and that the home secretary would be personally responsible for Shah's well-being. The pained look on Leon's face was hilarious.'

It was the beginning of the end for the NGA in its efforts to destroy Eddy Shah. The dispute lingered on but the NGA's mass picketing had failed to stop his papers from being published and Eddy was running circles round them in court. The NGA's funds had been sequestrated by the courts; it had lost control of its finances and risked huge fines for ignoring court orders.

A union that had never known defeat by striking had lost for the first time in living memory – beaten by somebody far removed from the London media Establishment. It was a rare victory over the print unions, worth savouring every moment. But there was no time: my problems with them were just beginning.

*

EDDY SHAH'S STRUGGLE had come to symbolize for me the battle for Britain's future direction: were we to remain a union-dominated society stuck in a collectivist rut or a dynamic market economy made prosperous by the job- and wealth-creating efforts of people like Shah?

After an initial show of solidarity against the national

shutdown, when the NGA had unlawfully stopped all Saturday and Sunday newspapers the weekend before the Battle of Warrington, the Fleet Street proprietors had sought court injunctions against the NGA. There was even talk of only taking the NGA back on management's terms; but most Fleet Street owners, as usual, caved in. By Tuesday the NGA had returned on its own terms and companies like News International, which wanted to teach the NGA a lesson, had to concede they were isolated – and sue for peace. It was the same old Fleet Street story: yesterday's hawks were today's doves. Those papers which conceded first even printed extra copies in the usual shabby attempt to win sales from those still off the streets. While Eddy Shah fought a principled battle for survival in the north of England it was still dog eat dog on Fleet Street. No wonder the print unions treated management with contempt; no wonder Shah referred to Fleet Street as the 'yellow press'.

At least we had a paper to publish on 4 December and Shah was the story of the week. I decided to devote most of our news analysis pages to the events surrounding the Battle of Warrington along with a damning editorial which would spare neither unions nor management.

The editorial was headlined 'A battle for Britain'. 'If decent and industrious entrepreneurs like Eddy Shah cannot survive and prosper in Mrs Thatcher's Britain,' it began, 'then there is little hope for the country, and even less for the government.' (See Appendix to Chapter 4 for full text.) It went on to lambast Fleet Street as 'a microcosm of all that is worst about British industry': pusillanimous management, pig-headed unions, archaic technology. It specifically attacked the NGA's monopoly of keyboard typesetting now that computers had made it possible for journalists and others to key in their own material; but it also laid into management for its predisposition 'to cut and run' in the face of union power. It made Eddy Shah the hero of the hour.

It was not, of course, a foregone conclusion that the unions would print or even typeset such an editorial: indeed, I was warned by Brian MacArthur and others that it was most unlikely and to prepare for problems, especially since our news analysis on the Shah dispute was also pretty hostile to the print unions.

I had instructed Don Berry, now senior features editor, to clear out the four centre pages of the news section to run a Focus Special entitled 'Union at bay'. A team of journalists worked on this: their copy affected to be fair but subtly put the stiletto into Eddy. I edited the copy myself, making sure readers were left in no doubt about the essential fairness of his position, the ordeal he had been through and the disgraceful behaviour of the print unions. It was almost as unpopular a read with our print workers as the editorial.

All Saturday afternoon, as the copy was being carried back and forth between the editorial and production floors, I heard reports of paragraphs being passed around between print workers and discussed in huddled groups. I was told that most were astonished that a national newspaper would even contemplate publishing such an attack on them. But nothing happened.

I was warned to expect trouble when the more militant night shift took over. But production began close to schedule at 7 p.m. and copies poured off the presses and into the distribution system. Then sometime after 8 p.m. a grim-faced Derrick Collier, our production manager and a veteran of *Sunday Times* strikes and go-slows, came into my office: there was a total shutdown of all presses and a delegation of print workers was demanding to see me.

I consulted first with my senior editors, who advised that if I did not see them there would be no *Sunday Times* that weekend. I called Rupert in New York to tell him what was happening; he was remarkably calm at the prospect of losing several million pounds of advertising revenue and said he would back whatever decision I took. I asked Derrick to summon the brothers.

Four fathers of the chapel (leaders of the company union branches) shuffled into my office and sat in a semicircle in front of my desk; Derrick, Brian and some other senior editors sat behind them. I felt somewhat exposed, grateful that there was a desk between me and a delegation that did not seem to have my well-being as its main priority.

A few pleasantries were exchanged and I then asked why they were not printing the paper. 'We are disgusted by your editorial,' piped up an aggressive, rotund little chap in an East End accent.

'What don't you like about it?' I enquired cautiously, wondering whether it was wise to begin a debate with them on its substance. I was flabbergasted by their response.

'For a start, you call him Eddy Shah,' declared the fat one.

'Everyone calls him Eddy Shah,' I replied, somewhat bemused. 'That's his name.'

'No, it's not. His real name is Selim Jehan Shah. That's what you have to call him.'

It took me a second to work out what he was on about. Then it dawned: Eddy was Persian in origin, even vaguely related to the Aga Khan. They wanted to highlight his foreign background and to imply that he was some rich foreign capitalist from the Middle East sent to exploit down-trodden British workers. It was a travesty of the truth for a man born and bred in Britain who had started his working life as a floor manager on *Coronation Street*. It was also racist.

'I didn't know the National Front had taken control of

The Sunday Times print room,' I replied. 'I will not call him Salim Jehan Shah and I will not even debate the matter with you.' I was getting angry. 'If that is why you won't print the paper then we can all go home now. In fact, I'll come and help you turn off the lights – I want to make the late BBC and ITN newscasts about this National Front takeover.'

My spherical adversary was not impressed. 'I fought a war to save this country,' he shouted. 'This editorial is shit.'

'My father fought the war so that people could write what they wanted,' I snapped back.

The other brothers realized they had got off on the wrong tack and began to nitpick at some of the derogatory phrases I had used about them. They wanted them out. I was unhappy about changing a word under such pressure but I also wanted the editorial to be published and read. The changes they were demanding made little difference to the substance or vehemence of my argument; indeed, I was surprised by their modesty.

I looked at Brian and Derrick for guidance. They shrugged their shoulders as if to say, 'Why not, if it means the paper will be printed.' So I agreed to their amendments and they left to re-start the presses. My first confrontation with the print unions was over.

But not my own doubts about whether or not I had done the right thing. To this day I still wonder. I had conceded an important principle: union pressure could change a *Sunday Times* editorial. The changes were minor but it was a dangerous precedent. Maybe I should have sent them packing and made a lot of noise about union censorship. On the other hand I had succeeded in publishing a strongly worded editorial that for the first time in a national newspaper told the truth about the newspaper industry. Charles Wintour, the former distinguished editor of the *Evening Standard*, commented the following week that it was the toughest editorial about Fleet Street ever to appear in a national newspaper.

But it was the brothers who had the last word. The presses restarted all right but they were still in a curmudgeonly mood as they went back to work: the shopfloor did not think their boys had won enough concessions. We had a very bad press run which cost us tens of thousands of copies and late delivery. I learned later that minor sabotage throughout the night – such as flicking cold coffee on the reels of paper spooled through the presses, thereby causing paper breaks and long delays as the paper was slowly re-spooled – had taken a heavy toll. My amended editorial had reached plenty of readers; but not as many as it should. And, without open confrontation, the print unions had subtly shown who was still the real boss in Fleet Street.

*

I FINALLY GOT TO MEET Eddy Shah two months after the Battle of Warrington. He came to London on business in early February 1984 and we met for a cup of tea one afternoon in the Savoy Hotel. He told me his business was prospering.

'What should I do next?' he enquired, clearly ready for a new challenge.

'You should take what you have in Warrington,' I said, 'and repeat it on a national scale. Start a new newspaper, using the latest computer technology and colour presses, but without the print unions. Make it non-union or do a single-union deal with the electricians.'

I was pushing at an open door: he was hungry to know more. I advised him to learn from the technology which had been used to launch *USA Today*, a new colour paper whose journalism was undistinguished but which employed the latest, low-cost cutting-edge technology to become America's first national newspaper. 'Copy their techniques and you'll be able to undercut every newspaper on Fleet Street,' I told him.

Thus was the *Today* newspaper born. I had urged the idea on Eddy not just for his benefit but for my own self-interest. He had shaken off the shackles of the print unions but Fleet Street was still in chains. I yearned to be free too. I wanted the prospect of something like *Today*, a low-cost competitor using the latest technology and colour printing, to frighten the existing proprietors into doing something about their own sorry state. Fleet Street had little incentive to do anything as long as everybody was in the same boat, suffering from the same absurd high-cost, low-tech, union-dominated methods. A new, leaner, fitter kid on the block might just force the old boys into action, if only out of self-preservation.

'Would you be editor?' asked Eddy.

'I'd love to. But I've only just joined *The Sunday Times*. I have a big job to finish there.' His eyes dropped in disappointment.

'Look, I'll do what I can to find you one – and help you in any other way I can.'

Eddy said later that the birth of *Today* could be dated from that meeting. He began working out the finances he would need on the back of a cigar packet as he flew back to Manchester. We had been so engrossed in the idea of a new newspaper that we never got round to ordering the afternoon tea. But after he had departed I began to fear he might be biting off more than he could chew. As his plans gathered pace I pointed him in the direction of Brian MacArthur. I did not want to lose my deputy but I was even more keen that *Today* should be a success and Brian was an experienced, safe pair of hands. He departed to preside over what was to be a troubled launch for Britain's first colour tabloid.

Eddy Shah never made it as a national newspaper proprietor. *Today* never found a distinctive editorial voice and lost its cost and technological advantages in the revolution that swept through all newspapers following News International's move to Wapping in January 1986 (see Chapter 6). He sold *Today* to Tiny Rowland, who subsequently sold it to Rupert Murdoch, who closed it in 1995. Even the great maestro himself could not make it work. But it had served its purpose.

After another failed national newspaper launch, Eddy took to writing thrillers, building up his successful provincial newspaper group, becoming involved in construction in America and leisure facilities in Britain – enough to take him into *The Sunday Times* Richest 500. We never became close friends but I will always retain a strong affection and admiration for him. Almost a decade after the Battle of Warrington he invited me to the launch of his first novel at the Roy Miles art gallery in Mayfair. The party was packed with a selection of the usual London celebrities but when Eddy spoke he said there were two people in the room who mattered more to him that any others: his lovely wife, who had survived her ordeal with cancer, and 'Andrew Neil, the one person I could count on when nobody else wanted to know me.'

It was a generous gesture from a kind-hearted man – but it is Eddy who deserves our gratitude. He had shown that the tyranny of the print unions could be overthrown if you had the guts to take them on – and a strategy for winning. The symbolism of his success should not be underestimated for the move to Wapping might never have happened without him: Shah shamed us into action.

In the immediate aftermath of his victory, however, the prospect of *Today* did not concentrate Fleet Street's finest minds as quickly as I had hoped. Not long after Eddy and I had concocted the idea of a new national newspaper, Rupert came to town and summoned a handful of his senior executives and editors to dinner at his St James's flat. It was a beautiful summer evening in 1984 and we dined overlooking a sunlit Green Park.

'Now that the unions are on the run,' Rupert remarked, 'I hope Mrs Thatcher presses home her advantage. Now is the time to crack down on them hard.' He plunged his right fist into his left palm.

The rest of the diners, myself included, nodded and mumbled in agreement. The purpose of such sessions was usually for Rupert to have reinforced by us what he already thought. But I could not help asking aloud: 'What about us? When are we going to tackle our unions? Thatcher is sorting out the public sector unions. But it's not her job to take on the print unions. It's ours.'

The others studied their plates. Rupert glared at me. 'We can't do it on our own,' he snapped. The rest nodded.

'Eddy Shah did,' I replied. Rupert stared at me again – until somebody helpfully changed the topic of conversation. But within less than a year we were to embark on an adventure that would dwarf even Eddy's great struggle and change the British newspaper industry for ever.

Appendix to Chapter Four

This editorial, headlined 'A battle for Britain', appeared in *The Sunday Times* on 4 December 1983. A framed copy hangs in Eddy Shah's office.

If decent and industrious entrepreneurs cannot survive and prosper in Mrs Thatcher's Britain then there is little hope for the country, and even less for the government. All over the western world the jobs of tomorrow are being created by such people today. In the United States, where the information revolution is most advanced, the dole queues are declining because millions of new jobs are being created by small firms, usually non-union, grasping the potential of the new information technology. In Britain, unemployment is still stuck over three million partly because enterprising spirits who try to do the same are blocked by the job-destroying power of certain unions. Those such as Eddy Shah who dare to challenge the state of affairs risk being threatened by such brute force that minor disputes are turned into a national crisis.

It is no accident that the most serious union challenge so far to the Thatcher government should be in the newspaper business. No industry has been more immune to the Prime Minister's mission to curb union power and encourage management to embrace the new technology. Indeed, Fleet Street and its provincial equivalents are a microcosm of all that is worst about British industry – union fiefdoms where management is not allowed to manage and which, as a result, have become industrial dinosaurs where the microchip and the computer are despised.

Nor is it any accident that the National Graphical Association (NGA) has been taken on by an unknown businessman in a Warrington industrial estate, rather than by the great press lords of Fleet Street. Indeed, when events in Warrington led the NGA to close down Fleet Street last weekend far from standing shoulder to shoulder with Mr Shah, there were enough pusillanimous proprietors desperate to publish to make life impossible for those who wanted to take a tougher stand. It is worth noting that those Tory lords whose newspapers – the *Daily Telegraph* and the *Daily Mail* – are most fond of lecturing government and the rest of British industry about being firm with unreasonable unions were the first to cut and run back into print. Their excuse was that they did not have international resources to sustain a long shutdown. Neither does Mr Shah. And they offered no excuse, of course, for adding to their print run while the rest of Fleet Street stayed out to fight their battle.

But it was ever thus on Fleet Street, which is why the unions still hold the whip hand. Two hundred miles to the north Mr Shah watched the mighty crumble, knowing enough about their ways not to have expected anything better. Undeterred, he has fought on alone. It has not been easy: the inevitable catalogue of obscene phone calls and death threats to him and his family; the loss of his private security because the far-left Liverpool council threatened to end Group 4's security contract with the city if it continued to protect Mr Shah; five coffins delivered late one night to his home, three of them small-sized, presumably to remind him that he has three vulnerable children; and, of course, the baying mob outside his factory. At midnight last Tuesday, when the mob looked like breaching police lines and his factory gate, Mr Shah thought it was all over and that he and his workforce would be lucky to escape with their lives. But the police recovered and his vans got out. This weekend it is the NGA which is on the run.

What has infuriated the NGA and the far-left opportunists who have rallied to its picket lines is that Mr Shah does not fit the Dickensian Identikit employer. He pays decent wages, provides good conditions and has created 150 jobs from scratch in a part of Britain where the dole queues are among the longest. So more subtle smears have been employed to impugn him: call him Selim Jehan, instead of the plain Eddy which everybody else calls him; spread the word that he is being manipulated by far-right activists even though his own views are moderate and his papers somewhat left-of-centre; imply that he is Mrs Thatcher's poodle because he had a ten-second talk with her one hectic afternoon and even though, by and large, the great British Establishment has treated him like an industrial leper; and claim that he is impossible to negotiate with because he changes his ground every time a deal is about to be clinched.

Mr Shah has changed his mind. Unlike his NGA counterparts, he is no professional negotiator and has wandered up several cul-de-sacs, then done several U-turns. More important, he has been shocked by the union attitudes towards his plans to expand his business, use new technology, create new jobs: bloated training levels in an NGA monopoly of the typesetting keyboard, union control of whom he employs and the technology he uses – the litany of Fleet Street's absurd practices were being wished on him. He said 'no thanks' and began to wonder if expansion could only be profitable without union control. Who – especially in Fleet Street – can blame him?

That is the essence of the dispute, which is why it is crucial to the future economic health of the country. It has very little to do with 'Tory' labour laws, whatever Labour politicians would have us believe. There were no such laws on the statute book when a Labour government had to deal with a besieged Grunwick. Mass picketing offends the common law of the land, common sense and even the TUC's own guidelines for picketing. At Warrington there was precious little peaceful picketing and something very close to riotous assembly. The words of supposedly moderate Labour front-bench spokesmen, such as John Smith and Gerald Kaufman, who seek to condemn violence yet blame the government for it, cannot disguise that. It was because three years ago their dignity could no longer stand such dissembling that Labour moderates left to form the Social Democrats. Last week the SDP and the Liberals were forthright in their condemnations of the NGA in marked contrast to the silence of Neil Kinnock, who has failed the first major test of his Labour leadership.

Mr Kinnock wants to give Labour a spruced-up high-tech image. Yet his party supports a union which wants to maintain a monopoly of the computer keyboard in the composing room. If the same had been done with steam in the last century then there would never have been an industrial revolution. The keyboard, the computer and their cable and satellite communications links are the workhorses of the new information society. Everybody needs access to them, just as everybody needs to be able to read and write. A 300-year-old craft union can only perpetuate its monopoly by denying thousands of opportunities to others. It can preserve a handful of hereditary jobs only at the cost of destroying many more for everyone else.

In their hearts, there are many individuals in the NGA who realize this. Indeed, one of them in June 1982 said:

> Unless we are prepared to take on board the full implications of new technology, unless we are prepared to become more flexible in our attitudes, and unless we are

> prepared to cooperate in improving productivity within the industry, we shall be engulfed by a tidal wave of technology which we will not be able to control.
>
> Unless we make the industry more efficient, unless we reduce unit costs of production, unless we become more flexible: what we will undoubtedly get is even more competition from abroad and from instant print shops at home.
>
> If we are not prepared to embrace new technology in a manner which will transform the newspaper industry into a highly competitive one, unless we are prepared to face up to the need to improve efficiency and productivity throughout the whole of the industry, then competitors from alternative sources and technology in this country or from abroad will spell the death knell of the industry as we have known it in the past.
>
> Is it not ironic that in Holland, where they have entered into agreements for single keystroking there is now not a surplus of labour in the printing industry there, but a shortage? Surely there are some lessons to be learned from this.

There are indeed. But Joe Wade, general secretary of the NGA, who spoke those words, has still to learn them himself. He is not alone. Nearly all of Fleet Street – management and men – have not wanted to face up to the truth of Mr Wade's words. Their industry and the country have been diminished as a result. But the logic is irresistible.

CHAPTER FIVE

The Great Escape

THE LAST OF THE SUN still cast its orange glow through my office window on the sixth floor of Gray's Inn Road but the mood inside was grim. It was 7 p.m. on a Saturday evening in early spring 1985, and we were waiting to inspect the fruits of a hard week's work. But the print unions had delayed the start of the paper and were making menacing hints that there might not be a *Sunday Times* that weekend unless their latest demands were met. There was nothing unusual about this: threats, delays and disruption were a weekly feature of life at Gray's Inn Road in those days. I and my senior editors spent many Saturdays wondering if the paper would be published next day. It was becoming almost a weekly occurrence. We were angry and depressed.

Rupert Murdoch poked his head round the door; it was one of the increasingly rare weekends when he was in London. He could see we were miserable. He called me out and the two of us wandered next door into the deputy editor's empty office. 'Look,' he said firmly but quietly, lest anybody should overhear, 'I know this is terrible but we're going to do something about it. I've made up my mind. The key is Wapping: if the unions won't go there on our terms then we'll go without them.' A wave of exhilaration swept through me.

Back in 1979 Rupert had decided to invest £100 million in new printing facilities at Wapping on the edge of

London's Docklands just east of Tower Bridge and at Glasgow's Kinning Park, close to the city centre on the southside of the River Clyde. They had been designed solely to print the two tabloids in his empire, the *Sun* and the *News of the World*; but there was land for expansion and the grand strategy was that one day *The Sunday Times* and *The Times* would print at Wapping too. But not in my lifetime: talks with the unions had dragged on since the early eighties, going nowhere fast. Wapping and Kinning Park lay idle – a folly to newspapers prepared to invest millions as long as the print unions had the whip hand – and the industrial anarchy at Gray's Inn Road continued. Rupert was at the end of his tether – at last.

'The move will take time to plan,' he cautioned, 'and we can't do it until we're ready. The unions must not find out so we have to carry on muddling through as normal. So go back, pour your editors a drink and cheer them up.' I did so with a spring in my step and a smile on my face. Ivan Fallon and Don Berry looked at me curiously: they must have thought I had been given a pay rise. But I had been given something much more valuable: hope of escape from print union tyranny.

*

THOUGH I HAD NEVER WORKED in Fleet Street I knew from my days in the seventies as labour and industrial correspondent for *The Economist* something of the appalling state of industrial relations in the national newspaper industry. If British unions in general were then regarded as the worst in the Western world then the print unions were the worst of the worst. But reporting Fleet Street's industrial troubles had not prepared me for the terrible reality of Gray's Inn Road, which was the worst of the worst of the worst!

Our little difficulty in the spring of 1985 was caused by a

smell that had mysteriously started to appear around 6 p.m. every Saturday night just as the front page of *The Sunday Times* was being prepared to go on the presses. A handful of men in the foundry, where the pages were cast on to metal drums which were then fixed to the presses, said they could not possibly work in such conditions and began to disrupt production. They knew what they were doing: the presses were ready to roll but there was no page one and we could hardly start the print run without it. The mighty *Sunday Times* was being held to ransom by four workers.

It became known as the 'Six O'clock Smell': it was hard for mere mortal noses to detect but the foundry men always found it intolerable at the most crucial stage on a Saturday evening. It was a classic example of the 'Saturday Night Stick Up' which regularly disrupted Sunday newspaper production – and of how a handful of people could bring the whole process to a halt at will at any stage.

The dispute dragged on. Week after week we suffered delayed starts, which meant late finishes, lost copies, missed trains, late deliveries and no page changes to update the news as the night went on. The management spent many thousands of pounds on new ventilation to rid us of this mysterious smell but the printers were not impressed. It was eventually dispersed by waving handfuls of five pound notes in front of their noses.

It was an everyday example of the industrial cancer that then gripped Fleet Street. In my first few months as editor there were two Sundays when we did not publish at all: one in November 1983, when the print unions closed Fleet Street as part of their battle to destroy Eddy Shah (see Chapter 4); and again in January 1984, when Times Newspapers attempted a minor redeployment of personnel in the library. The unions shut us down for having the temerity to think management had any control over the workforce it employed.

Even worse than no paper at all were the countless frustrations encountered every week in the unending struggle to produce a newspaper in the face of print union indifference, intransigence and, at times, hostility. It was as if the production process had been specifically designed to thwart efficiency and create hurdles, made all the worse by the attitude of the men (they were all men) which was invariably surly and unhelpful, despite the huge pay packets they commanded for doing very little.

The company had managed – but only after an eleven-month shutdown of *The Sunday Times* and *Times* – to move from the 100-year-old technology of 'hot metal' typesetting on Linotype machines to computer typesetting. But the NGA still jealously retained its monopoly of the keyboard. Journalists would bash out their stories on ancient typewriters that belonged in a museum – or scrapyard – and NGA members would key them into the computer on modern terminals. The copy was shuffled back and forth between editorial and NGA by surly messengers. The journalists could easily have operated the keyboards themselves and typed in their own stories; but if anybody but an NGA member so much as touched a terminal there would have been a walkout. So the farce of unnecessary, time-consuming 'double-key stroking' was the order of the day. If Britain was on the brink of an information revolution nobody had told Times Newspapers.

The computer generated long galleys of type known as bromides which were cut to length and shape for pasting up on large boards into pages. But the NGA no longer checked its work and the typesetting was always riddled with errors. Journalists, however, were not allowed to correct the bromides even by pen because it was forbidden to touch them:

they had to be photostated, corrections made on the copy and handed back to the NGA for re-inputting. Invariably, new mistakes would appear as old ones were corrected. It was a soul-destroying business, designed to produce ulcers.

We were on very tight deadlines: the huge print run of *The Sunday Times* meant an early start for the presses. But the NGA worked in its own way and at its own pace. Efforts to hurry them up met with uncooperative slowdowns. The atmosphere was always tense in the long composing room on the third floor of Gray's Inn Road, with its rows of paste-up boards under bright lights, where journalists could supervise page make-up but not touch; but the sectioned-off area of computer terminals was an NGA fiefdom where no journalist could wander, much as ancient monks kept the mysteries of the quill pen hidden from plain folk behind monastery walls in the days when they tried to preserve their monopoly on writing.

Sunday Times staff resorted to a forced *bonhomie* to jolly them along. Sometimes it worked, sometimes it didn't. Sue Summers, the Screen editor, told me that wearing a revealing dress on the day her pages were pasted up usually helped matters, though she hated herself for doing it. It was not an option open to all of us, but it was one way of dealing with a male monopoly: all the NGA's jobs could have been done by women. Not a single one was.

The arcane system of typesetting made changing pages to update news and regional editions as the night wore on a painstaking process. But we did not attempt to alter many pages for the presses were always running behind schedule thanks to late starts and bad runs. The trains carrying *The Sunday Times* to Scotland and Manchester were often delayed and sometimes even missed. Readers, whom nobody seemed to care about, were given a spasmodic service.

Once I had agreed the few page changes for the final edition that the system allowed I would often wander down to the press hall late on a Saturday night. The place was always teeming with people but nobody was doing very much. Many huddled in groups talking, some clearly the worse for alcohol. On a good night maybe two or three of the nine presses would be running; on a bad night all would be idle for long periods.

They were being paid up to £130 for one night's work in 1983, big money even now. Many went home after they collected their pay packets; some did not bother to turn up, arranging for somebody else to pick up their money (one man used to send his daughter). Most drifted off as the night went on. The management encouraged this for the print run always picked up after the layabouts had departed, leaving the more conscientious to get on with their work unhindered. Some of the people we employed did not exist at all: the pay packets of these 'ghost workers' were divided up among the rest.

Sabotage was not uncommon, especially if the brothers did not like something in the newspaper, such as an anti-union story or editorial, or if they had failed to get their way in some petty dispute with management. They would flick coffee on the newsprint as it sped through the presses to cause a paper break, which meant the presses had to be stopped and the newsprint re-spooled through the machines, which was never done in a hurry. Even more effective was to urinate on the huge newsprint reels before they went on to the presses. This was a sure way of causing endless paper breaks; but the brothers had to be careful not to pee on colleagues who were lying between the reels: the reel room was a favourite place for those who enjoyed a sleep on the job.

The production manager surveyed this mixture of indolence and indifference from his glass box high above the presses but he was powerless to do anything about it. He was a big, jovial man turned into a nervous wreck by the madhouse below; he died early of a heart attack. Saturday night for him was a giant struggle just to complete the print run and avoid shortfalls. I would often stand with him in his eyrie, not a single press running below, and he would turn to me and say solemnly: 'Sorry. No page changes. We'll be lucky to finish the run tonight.' I would go home with a heavy heart.

Sometimes the first edition would remain unchanged throughout the night which meant Scottish football dominating the sports pages on sale in London; so we had to abandon regional sports editions and stick to a general sports edition which ran unaltered throughout the night. I often wondered what would have happened if the Prime Minister or the Queen had been assassinated around 10 p.m. on a Saturday. It was not a foregone conclusion that our last edition would have carried it.

When the World Summit was in London in the summer of 1984 I was determined that we would show the rest of the world's media how *The Sunday Times* covered such major events. The Insight team, supplemented by the political and economic specialists, did a meticulous four-page reconstruction of all the important negotiations that had taken place. Over a dozen journalists worked round the clock on it. But nobody ever saw it: we had to run all night with the first edition, which had gone to press before the summit had finished.

Producing *The Sunday Times* meant running a weekly gauntlet during which the print unions could torture you at any point; but it had its more ludicrous moments. One Saturday afternoon the foreign editor asked me why it was that wire copy listing the football results was being left on *his* desk; a few moments later the sports editor complained about being inundated with copy from Washington and Moscow. I asked Peter Roberts to investigate.

Ripping wire copy off the telex and delivering it to the relevant desks – something we journalists could just about manage ourselves – was nevertheless the prerogative of an obscure clerical union. That afternoon, Peter discovered, it had sent along two members who could barely read. Even the union was shamed into sending them home. But the system continued: the next week, when we needed a stone-hand to assist in page make-up, Sogat (Society of Graphical and Allied Trades) sent along a worker from a wallpaper factory.

The absurdity of it all made me laugh. But I found the print-union tyranny frustrating and debilitating. I sat through endless management meetings in which Bill Gillespie, the ruddy, white-haired managing director of Times Newspapers, would catalogue in his soft Ulster accent all the breakdowns that had resulted in yet another shortfall the previous Sunday. I would grow angry and demand to know when he was going to do something about it. But it was pointless to complain: Gillespie was powerless to do anything. I grew to have almost as much contempt for the management as the unions.

My naivety was regularly on display in these early days. At one management meeting I announced my intention to produce a tabloid book review section like the one in the Sunday *New York Times*. Gillespie laughed: 'And who's going to print it?'

'We could pre-print it during the week,' I suggested confidently.

'We have no agreement with the unions to do that,' announced Bill, 'and they won't give us one.' The Books section was stillborn.

The farce of Fleet Street affected me more because, coming from outside, I had no first-hand experience of it. Those who had worked in Fleet Street all their life just lived with it; there was nothing that could be done about it. But I refused to accept the *status quo*, taking every opportunity to challenge it, from supporting Eddy Shah to lobbying Rupert that we should also 'do a Shah'. The weight of history and experience was against me: every previous attempt to change Fleet Street had failed (see Appendix to Chapter 5).

*

As 1984 DREW TO a close, it began to dawn on Rupert Murdoch that, as with so many areas of British life, the conventional wisdom about the impossibility of escaping the Fleet Street madhouse might be wrong. Events were conspiring to encourage him to think radical thoughts – with a little prompting from me and others – and to dream that maybe a dash for freedom from print-union tyranny was possible after all.

The previous twelve months had been particularly grim. Another year of talks with the unions to move the *Sun* and the *News of the World* to Wapping had proved fruitless; another year was beginning with both tabloids still stuck in their cramped, archaic Bouverie Street printing hall just off Fleet Street. Plans to expand both titles had been frozen. The same was true at *The Sunday Times*: the presses at Gray's Inn Road could not cope with more than eighty pages. Proposals to expand to 120 pages by using Bouverie Street presses, if and when the tabloids went to Wapping, had been rejected by the print unions. Broadsheets and tabloids were stuck in a print-union rut.

Bruce Matthews is a tough, genial Australian, the permanent worried look on his face concealing an impish sense of humour. He had become Rupert's most senior manager in London in 1984, in charge of all four titles. He was spending Christmas in his beach house in Melbourne when Rupert called him. 'Come via New York on your way back to London,' he said, 'and we can review things for the upcoming year.' A jet-lagged Bruce arrived in the second week of January 1985 at Rupert's charming house in Old Chatham, over an hour's drive north of New York. It was to prove a significant meeting.

'What's happening at Wapping?' asked Rupert.

'Nothing,' replied Bruce. Only one chapel from the *News of the World* – the machine minders – had concluded an agreement to go, and even that had taken almost two years of laborious talks. Negotiations with the other chapels had been 'catastrophic'.

Not that the unions refused point-blank to go – just that they insisted on taking intact all of Fleet Street's restrictive practices and overmanning, such as twice as many men as the new presses needed and the employment of people to press buttons that no longer existed. Negotiations had been deadlocked for two years. During one round of negotiations a union official had tossed a box of matches across the table to a News International manager and said: 'Why don't you just burn the place down? Don't you understand? We're never going to go there!' Another union negotiator advised the company to put a bomb under it. The company eschewed such helpful advice. But six years after its conception, Wapping was still idle.

'How about Glasgow?' asked Rupert, referring to Wapping's sister plant in Scotland.

'Nothing,' said Bruce again. A mixture of anger and despair crossed his boss's face. 'But I have an idea for you,' Bruce added quickly.

The disgraceful state of affairs in Scotland angered Bruce even more than Wapping. The company had installed reconditioned presses in a Glasgow warehouse to print a Scottish edition of the *Sun*.* They had offered the print unions 200 new, well-paid jobs without demanding fresh labour practices in an area of 15-per-cent-plus unemployment. But the Scottish print unions were more interested in protecting the position of the *Sun*'s rival in Scotland, the *Daily Record*, and refused to cooperate: Kinning Park had been idle for three years. 'I was outraged,' says Bruce, who had even made a personal appeal to the Labour Provost [Mayor] of Glasgow, pointing out, to no avail, that the new jobs for his city would not even result in any loss of jobs in London. 'The disgusting situation in Scotland was my main motivation for investigating what the Finns were up to in Wales.' It was time to report his findings to Rupert.

A Finnish company had built a new papermill on the site of an old steel works at Shotton in North Wales. They had negotiated a single-union deal with Sogat, the biggest print union in the paper-making business. But the agreement had been scuppered by Sogat's insistence that it come under the control of its Merseyside branch. The management had previous experience of this militant bunch and wanted

* The story behind these presses provides one of the more amusing examples of Fleet Street's cut-throat competition. They had belonged to Robert Maxwell and he would never have sold them to the *Sun* to compete in Scotland against his *Daily Record*, which dominated the tabloid mass-market north of the border. So the *Sun*'s managers engaged a middle-man, who said he was buying them for India. Maxwell agreed the sale: but what he thought was being crated up for shipping to India was actually heading up the M6 to Glasgow. When he discovered he had been duped he encouraged the Scottish print unions not to sanction their use.

nothing to do with them: it was a deal-breaker. They turned to the EETPU, the electricians' union which had pioneered single-union, no-strike deals in Britain. By the end of 1984, Shotton was an efficient paper plant with excellent industrial relations.

'What's this got to do with us?' asked Rupert.

'Shotton was a greenfield site,' replied Bruce. 'So is Wapping. Nothing is operating there and there are no unions. We could follow the Finns' example and operate it with the electricians, cutting the print unions out altogether.'

'Do you think the electricians would do business with us?' asked Rupert, his quick mind already racing over the possibilities, which were not entirely new to him. I had already been telling him how single-union deals with progressive unions like the electricians and the engineers were being concluded at several greenfield sites, such as new Japanese car plants. I had advised Eddy Shah to seek one with the electricians to produce his new *Today* newspaper (he was to do just that in May 1985). On one of his visits to London in late 1984 Rupert had taken me to lunch to find out more.

Drawing on my experience as labour correspondent for *The Economist*, I explained how, though the electricians branch in Fleet Street was as bad as all the others, nationally the union was carving out a reputation as an American-style union that believed in profits, new technology and labour flexibility. It struck hard bargains – but it kept them. The new general secretary, Eric Hammond, was in the same tough, anti-Communist mould as the outgoing Frank Chapple, which meant he was a pariah with the rest of the TUC, which for years had been in the grip of a Labour Left–Communist coalition. We continued talking in his car on the way back to Gray's Inn Road and stayed in his Mercedes while it was parked outside the *Sunday Times* building.

'Do you think they'd ever do a deal with us?' Rupert had asked me.

'I don't know,' I replied, 'but I could put out some feelers.'

'Don't do anything yet,' he cautioned, 'it's too dangerous. But it's certainly worth thinking about.' By the time of his meeting with Bruce in Old Chatham, he was ready for action.

'I made preliminary contacts with Tom Rice last month,' Bruce told him. 'He's national secretary of the EETPU. Sogat has been trying to poach the electricians' Fleet Street members. There's no love lost between them. I think there's a deal to be done.'

'Great!' exclaimed Rupert. 'I like it. Let's do it.'

Thus, in a silent, snowy retreat in rural New York state, 3,000 miles away from the Fleet Street hothouse, the idea was born for the most audacious plot in newspaper history – a dash for freedom from print-union tyranny, a great escape that would not only free News International's titles but destroy the power of the print unions in Fleet Street and reinvigorate the whole of the British newspaper industry.

The time for audacity was more propitious than most people realized. Eddy Shah had shown during the Battle of Warrington (see Chapter 4) how to use the new Tory labour laws to tie even the powerful print unions in legal knots and threaten their finances to the point of bankruptcy. Nor should the symbolism of his victory over the hitherto invincible print unions be underestimated: it proved they could be beaten if you had the guts to take them on – and the proper strategy for winning.

But it was not just Shah's brave example that gave Rupert cause to act. He had noted how the northern entrepreneur was proceeding steadily towards his dream of a low-cost, high-tech, colour national newspaper which, if it worked, would undercut the lumbering Fleet Street behemoths. This worried Rupert. Though Eddy was hardly an immediate threat he did not like the idea of newcomers competing with all the advantages of the information age that Fleet Street did not have. There was also talk of a new high-tech quality broadsheet to take on *The Times* (it was to materialize in the shape of the *Independent*). As I had hoped, the prospect of external competition to an industry traditionally protected from newcomers might just galvanize one of the established proprietors into action. Rupert Murdoch was always the most likely candidate to pick up the gauntlet.

But it was a daunting project. The recent lesson of the shutdown at Times Newspapers under its previous owners was etched in his mind: the print unions would win any dispute that took the papers off the streets – they had the resources to survive a prolonged closure that even Murdoch could not match. But they might be beaten if the papers continued to come out without them. That was how the *Washington Post* and other American papers had curbed print-union power in the seventies. That was how he was going to do it too.

Rupert Murdoch is an impatient man: when he has decided on a course of action he wants it to happen yesterday, or the day before. The planning for what Bruce and I were to refer to as Operation Armageddon began within days of his meeting with Bruce. Fleet Street would have dubbed it Mission Impossible.

*

ON SUNDAY MORNING, 10 February 1985, only a few weeks after that crucial meeting in Old Chatham, Rupert and a group of senior British executives who had arrived by Concorde that day gathered round the dining table in his luxury apartment in New York's Fifth Avenue, with its stunning view overlooking the reservoir in Central Park. It was there that the plan to print a new newspaper, the *London Post*, a ruse thought up by Rupert himself, was unveiled – and the pretext to make Wapping fully functional devised.

Rupert and Bruce had already discussed the need for a cover story to explain the hive of activity that Wapping was about to become. They concocted the *London Post*, a new evening newspaper supposedly to challenge the *Evening Standard*'s monopoly in the capital. It would be written by journalists using the latest computer technology and printed at Wapping unencumbered by Fleet Street's restrictive practices. If the print unions agreed to these new conditions they could print it; if not it would be done without them. If they disrupted the existing titles in protest all the Murdoch newspapers would be moved to Wapping and Kinning Park and printed by the electricians' union.

The strategy demanded that Wapping be prepared for much more than just the *London Post*: it had to be able to cope with the far more massive demands of the four existing titles if the print unions went on strike, something that it had never been envisaged Wapping would have the capacity to do. That was the fundamental purpose of all the planning that now took place.

The *Post* was a ruse: it was never meant to happen. It was a cover story which would then be turned into a provocation: it would provide the pretext for bringing Wapping up to speed then, when that was done, to goad the print unions into industrial action. Rupert believed that the prospect of another union producing a new paper in Wapping was eventually bound to provoke the print unions to strike on his existing titles: that would give him the excuse to move them all to Wapping. Meanwhile, the pretence of the *Post* had to be convincingly maintained.

'We'll all have to believe,' Rupert told his co-conspirators more than once that Sunday in February. 'We'll *have* to believe it.' It would buy them time: the unions were unlikely to act until the tough terms for printing the *Post* at Wapping were put before them. By that time Wapping would be capable of much more than the *Post* and the unions could do their worst. 'The concept of the *Post* made newspaper sense at the time,' says Bruce Matthews, 'which is why it was such a good cover story. But it was never likely to happen – not unless the print unions behaved in ways we never thought possible.'

'When Rupert asked me to join the team he was putting together,' says Charlie Wilson, the tough, experienced Scot who was then deputy editor of *The Times*, 'it was clear from the very start that we were planning a total revolution. The *Post* was a cover story: Rupert and I knew it was that and no more. I never thought it was going to happen.' Charlie should know: Rupert had made him the *Post*'s launch editor.

The daunting task of implementing this daring plan was assigned to those round Rupert's dining table. In addition to Bruce, who would be Rupert's point man throughout, with particular responsibility for squaring the electricians, and Charlie, who would use his *Post* cover to oversee the introduction of a computerized, editorial text system for all four existing titles, there were a handful of other key figures: Ken Taylor, who had built Wapping and whose job it was somehow to configure the press for tabloid and broadsheet production; Christopher Pole-Carew, a gangling Englishman of the old school who had already done a mini-Wapping at the *Nottingham Evening Post*; and Geoffrey Richards, a smart, bookish lawyer from Farrer & Co., who was there to advise on the legal implications of everything they did. His presence was particularly significant: a vital part of the strategy was to force the unions on to the wrong side of the new labour laws. One of Rupert's first moves was to contact Eddy

Shah's lawyers on tactics, since they had already successfully paved the way.

Within days of the initial meeting in Rupert's New York home, Atex, the Kodak-owned, Boston-based computer company which had provided tried and tested editorial text systems to newspapers across America, had been contacted by Rupert himself at the highest level, sworn to secrecy and given the biggest contract in its history.

By early March a team from Atex, known as Smylie's People after their stocky Texan leader, Barton 'The Human Bulldozer' Smylie, were working fifteen-hour days in a scruffy, anonymous warehouse on an industrial estate near the Thames in Woolwich, which they called The Bunker: this was where, in conditions of great secrecy and security, the computer hardware and systems for all News International's titles were assembled, some of it shipped in via Paris to complicate detection. For months, even Atex's British division knew nothing about what was happening in Woolwich.

Bruce, meanwhile, was building a close relationship with the electricians' Tom Rice. On his return to London they had met for a drink. Bruce explained that they wanted to 'do a Shotton' at Wapping with the electricians. But if the print unions found out they would go berserk. Rice said that one of his closest allies in the EETPU ran the Southampton branch: the company could recruit labour secretly through him from that area. If word got out they would say they were maintenance men making Wapping operational; nobody would know they were being trained to man the presses and operate the new computerized production process.

When Rupert came to London later in February he dined with Eric Hammond at Woodrow Wyatt's house. Wyatt loved to be Rupert's fixer in London – it helped ensure that the *News of the World* would continue to run his slavishly pro-

Tory column – and he had longstanding contacts with the electricians, having helped to expose Communist corruption and ballot-rigging in the union in the 1950s.

Rice had already been whispering in Hammond's ear about what was afoot at Wapping, though Hammond did not know the specifics about the recruitment of his members now underway in Southampton. But he was not averse to a little recruiting of his own: 'We need some stout fellows,' he told his local rugby club, and those interested were pointed in Wapping's direction. At the dinner he told Rupert that his members could commission the plant, get it up and running – and operate it.

'The click in Rupert's brain was audible,' says Hammond. 'Our discussion was based on what had to be done for the *London Post*. But we both knew we were talking about much more than that. Rupert was determined to take a radical step and we were the opportunists ready to help him – there were big openings for us. The print unions were the variable: it was their action which would determine the outcome.'

Hammond left his dinner with Murdoch believing that, if events went the way they expected, his union was heading for a single-union deal at Wapping to print the four existing titles. Just as the EETPU had broken into the paper-making industry at Shotton, so Wapping would make it a major force in the newspaper industry. He would be trampling on other people's turf and be accused of breaching the TUC's no-poaching rules. But the electricians' boss took the view that if the print unions were stupid enough to strike, he would be happy to oblige Rupert. Eric cherished his role as the right-wing maverick of the union movement. He knew it was only a matter of time before his union was kicked out of the TUC anyway.

When he met Rupert in February 1985 the EETPU was already locked in a bitter struggle to take advantage of the new Tory laws which gave unions money to pay for the funding of postal ballots in union elections. The electricians had long elected their leaders by postal ballot and saw no reason why they should not take state money to offset the expense. A majority of the TUC, however, was hostile to the very idea of postal ballots and totally opposed to accepting 'Tory money'.

'We expected to be expelled from the TUC over this issue anyway,' says Hammond. 'You could look on Wapping as a way of getting our retaliation in first.'

Hammond hated Fleet Street almost as much as Murdoch. The wealth of the print unions was used to finance a number of causes supported by a coalition of the Labour Left and the Communist Party known as the 'broad left', to which Hammond was deeply hostile.

'We used Fleet Street as a cesspool,' he says. 'We dumped all our hard-left activists there, where they were happy. And so were we: it got them out of our way.' As a result, the Fleet Street branch of the electricians was almost totally estranged from the EETPU. But it still rankled with Hammond that Sogat had tried to poach his members in the national newspaper industry. There was a score to settle.

*

AT 11 P.M. ON 31 MAY, under cover of darkness, three large trucks drew up outside 'The Bunker'. Inside a row of computer mainframes over 50 yards long had been assembled and tested. They were carefully loaded into the trucks, which had been specially customized to carry their computer cargo, then transported across the river. At dead of night they made their way into a deserted Wapping (the maintenance staff had been sent home); the computers' destination was a secure space on Wapping's fourth floor.

There was much testing still to be done and more

equipment needed: but it had been a remarkable feat to achieve so much in undercover conditions in such a short space of time. Only three months ago Wapping had no facilities for journalists, typesetting, page make-up or plate-making; it was thought to have the capacity to print only two tabloids. Now it was well on its way to being a self-contained publishing centre for four titles and their staff. No wonder Bruce Matthews would later be asked to lecture on logistical planning to the officers of the British Army on the Rhine.

Charlie Wilson played the key editorial role in making Wapping ready for the journalists. He went through the motions of planning the *London Post*, seconding Michael Hoy and Richard Williams from *The Times* and David Banks from the *Sun* to produce layouts and dummies. He even interviewed various journalists for jobs including, ironically, Julie Burchill, then an outspoken left-wing columnist with a penchant for Stalin. None of those who worked with Charlie on the *Post* knew what he was really up to. Even the editor of *The Times*, the patrician Charles Douglas-Home, did not know – nor want to know.

Smylie's People liked Charlie: he was the kind of can-do Brit they did not know existed (and typical of the sort of Scot Rupert liked to gather around him). He did a magnificent job in working with them to turn Wapping into a high-tech editorial centre for four titles. That was not apparent, however, when I first visited Wapping early in July.

The Sunday Times and *Times* had been designated offices in a rum store built by French prisoners during the Napoleonic Wars. It ran alongside the ugly new redbrick print hall for almost a quarter of a mile; Murdoch had originally tried to knock it down when he first acquired the site but it was protected by a preservation order. The walls were four feet thick in places and the basement a series of arched vaults; but the roof had been replaced at some stage with flimsy corrugated iron and as Charlie showed me around I was greeted by a scene of desolation. What was going to be our newsroom was covered in rubble, with water leaking in through the roof. He showed me where my office would be: there was nothing there but the empty corner of a slum. Charlie assured me it would be ready in time; I was sceptical.

We wandered over to the new building housing the presses and distribution areas. It was then that the potential of Wapping dawned on me. The metallic blue presses stood to attention in pristine splendour behind soundproof glass. Friendly technicians who were testing various bits of the machinery smiled and said hello. But it was the huge covered hall where the articulated trucks would be loaded up with papers that impressed me most.

'You could land a jumbo jet in here,' said Charlie, smiling.

'If the print unions could see this,' I replied grimly, 'they'd realize we meant business.'

I did not return to Wapping for several months. The print unions knew what I thought of them: if I had been spotted making regular trips they would certainly have smelled a rat. Rupert asked me to put a trusted lieutenant in charge of preparing Wapping for *The Sunday Times*. I designated James Adams. He shared my enthusiasm for new technology, used a computer to write his books, knew how to get things done and was totally trustworthy. Nobody else on *The Sunday Times* had a clue what was cooking.

I did not even invent a cover story for James, lest some enterprising soul tried to check it. He would simply come into the office at the normal time, hang around for a few minutes to be seen, head down to Wapping for the day and return briefly in the late afternoon. He did this for three months and not one of Britain's most respected journalists ever asked either me or him what he was doing – or even suspected what was going on. They gossiped that he was on some kind of mission for MI5!

James set about with Charlie to turn a derelict rum-store slum into a high-tech office, with desks, computer terminals and telephones for every journalist and offices for senior editors. He also worked with the Atex staff to make sure that the computer software the journalists would use was correctly programmed to handle the specific typefaces, styles and column measures that were unique to *The Sunday Times*.

James was under strict instructions to tell nobody. This led to repeated confrontations between him and Ivan Fallon, my deputy, who guessed that something was up. Eventually I agreed to let Ivan into the loop and, as the demands grew on James, to enlist the help of Tony Bambridge, who was amazed to discover how much had been achieved in such secrecy.

Journalists are always under a particular strain when asked to keep a secret; it is not in our nature. James and I were dying to tell more of our colleagues, at least the ones we knew would be sympathetic. But we had to keep everything bottled up. Towards the end of September we escaped to a remote rented house for a few days on the Greek island of Paxos. James's wife had made some T-shirts with 'Strike-busters! No Man, No Law, No War, Can Stop *The Sunday Times*' emblazoned across the chest. We cavorted around our secluded garden in them but were sensible enough not to wear them in public – which is just as well since on the third night we ran into a left-wing Scottish columnist at the local taverna.

When I next returned to Wapping in early November, the place had been transformed. I knew that the journalists might have to move in difficult circumstances and I had asked James to make our offices as inviting as possible. It was certainly a big improvement on our slum quarters in Gray's Inn Road. Open-plan work stations stretched into the distance, punctuated with potted plants and posters on the wall. Near the entrance was a huge poster of James Dean on the 'Boulevard of Broken Dreams' and another of a big wave – 'The Wave of the Future'. The symbolism was obvious – and it was clear we had the makings of what a modern newsroom of one of the world's great newspapers should look like.

The company's plans for the *London Post* had become public knowledge back in March but the unions still did not suspect what was really in prospect. We had suffered production shortfalls from chapel meetings called to decide their response but nothing dramatic had happened. They waited on management to come forward with its proposals for how the *Post* should be produced and by whom. They did not suspect that the final building blocks of a huge, elaborate strategy to produce all four titles without the print unions were dropping into place – and that they were on the wrong end of a huge swing in the industrial balance of power away from the print unions to management.

The final, crucial piece of the jigsaw was already in place. For over a century national newspapers had been distributed by rail to wholesalers all over the country. But we knew the British Rail unions would black our papers in a dispute. So Rupert had done a deal with TNT, the Australian-owned road hauliers and express parcel service. Its boss, Sir Peter Abeles, was his friend and business partner – they were joint partners in Ansett, the Australian airline – and a contract was signed to distribute our papers by road instead of rail.

The drivers would be Transport Union men from the Midlands who had no love for Fleet Street printers: the EETPU was not the only union to despise them. The original plan had been to deliver directly to Britain's 40,000 newsagents. But it quickly became apparent that Sogat members in the provincial wholesalers had contempt for their fat-cat London brethren. So outside London it was decided to use the existing wholesale network but deliver directly to the 5,000 outlets in the capital (where Sogat was bound to black us) – a less daunting proposition.

When Rupert met the general secretaries of the five main print unions at the Inn on the Park on Monday, 30 September, not only was the machinery and technology beginning to tick over smoothly but the new labour force which had been recruited and trained using the good offices of the Southampton branch of the electricians' union was being bussed in every day and settling down nicely.

The union bosses did not know this, though by now they suspected something was afoot. They should have realized the tables were turning by Rupert's general demeanour. When the meeting began he immediately started reading from a four-page paper. It was clear he was at the end of his tether. Fleet Street was a disgrace to them all, he said, and disputes had come close to 'nearly bringing the whole company down'. He had invested £100 million in Wapping and Glasgow yet union demands for manning levels and work practices meant it would cost the company more money to go there than stay at its existing facilities.

There was a market for the *London Post*, he said, and Wapping would be ready to produce the new paper by the spring. He had decided to go down this route because of 'the announcement of another daily newspaper to be launched by Eddy Shah'. Other people were preparing to move into the market and 'they will be competing with the overwhelming advantages of modern technology and one-union, no-strike agreements'.

'I wish our earlier negotiations had been more fruitful,'

he concluded. 'It is a tragedy for your members that they were not.' He saw no point in 'another series of long, unpleasant and emotionally draining negotiations with so little prospect of success', but if talks over the *Post* made good progress they could be extended to the transfer of the existing tabloids as well. He gave them three months – until Christmas – to agree to a satisfactory deal.

The general secretaries left the meeting thinking there was still all to play for – that talks about the *Post* would now begin and not much had really changed. They gathered differently from next day's *Times*. Though the headline – 'Fleet Street unions agree to talks on printing plant for News International' – and the story were upbeat (it reported both sides had committed themselves to concluding by Christmas a deal to publish the *Post*) there was a shock for the unions beside it: *The Times* printed in full the remarks Rupert had made at the start of the meeting accusing the unions of bad faith, cynicism and much more, from blackmail to the ruination of Fleet Street. It was like a neon sign telling the unions that this time he was playing hardball.

Rupert had been radicalized by the success of his secret strategy at Wapping. Though it was still fraught with risk, he became convinced that there was now no need to do any deal with the print unions; in fact, his unstated aim was now to avoid one at all costs. As the year drew to an end and Wapping reached its peak of readiness he laid down the most stringent of conditions, in the unstated expectation that the unions would be unable to meet them. Rupert was seeking open confrontation that he had become confident he would win. That was by no means a foregone conclusion but the gains to be won from a great escape were too big for him to resist.

Bruce Matthews watched the emergence of Murdoch the Militant with apprehension: Bruce was all for driving the toughest of bargains but Rupert did not want a bargain at all – short of outright union surrender. 'Our master is becoming uncontrollable,' said Bruce to me one day in November. We started referring to Rupert as Rambo.

The unions found out what that meant when talks on the *London Post* started in mid-October. Bill O'Neill, Rupert's gruff Australian industrial relations guru, was flown in from America to tell Sogat that there would be 50 per cent cuts in the machine and distribution areas; and to inform the NGA that there would be direct inputting of copy by editorial and advertising staff. It was made clear these were not matters for negotiation.

All unions would have to agree to legally binding contracts, a no-strike clause (which included compulsory independent arbitration of disputes), no closed shop and management's right to manage. The chapel system would be abolished, the company would fix manning levels and strikers would be sacked. It was all contained in a document marked 'Initial Proposal'.

The unions bosses rejected the package on Tuesday, 10 December. They offered instead agreements to promote labour flexibility and avoid disruptions. Instead of even looking down that path, Rupert hardened his stance. They had no 'God-given right' to go to Wapping, he stated; the company would decide who would go from the existing staff; and nobody would go without a legally binding agreement. The boot was clearly on the other foot.

A week later the union bosses tried to convince Bill O'Neill to withdraw the demand for a legally binding, no-strike clause. O'Neill said that without acceptance of that there was no point in any further talks. The NGA had indicated that in principle they would agree to direct input of copy; the union regarded it as a historic concession, though it was hedged with caveats. O'Neill said the company now took that for granted in Wapping and it was not enough to justify further talks. Something no other Fleet Street management had ever dreamed of achieving had been dismissed almost with contempt by News International. The company had upped the stakes.

The unions upped them even further: just before Christmas, Sogat announced it was after jobs for life and index-linked pay rises – and was prepared to strike for them. It was the last demand from a dinosaur that did not know it was about to become extinct. As Christmas Day 1985 came and went the stage was set for a major confrontation.

Rupert went off to ski in Aspen, Colorado, and I went into hospital to have a painful kidney stone removed. He arrived back in London refreshed, but I returned to work weak – and considerably thinner. I was anxious to be back for the fray, for I knew that *The Sunday Times* was about to move centrestage. On 12 January, the paper announced on its front page that the following week it would carry a fourth section printed at 'News International's spectacular new printing plant in London's Docklands'. The screw was being tightened.

The Wapping presses churned out the pre-print – a twelve-page Innovation Special on the significance of Wapping – and we waited to see if the unions would allow it to be distributed with the rest of our 19 January edition, which was still being produced at Gray's Inn Road. There was much in it to disgust them; it had almost been designed that way. In typical *Sunday Times* fashion it even revealed, in an article filed by our American correspondent entitled 'Drama of Project X', how computers had been installed in Wapping 'in a secret operation that sounds more like an old thriller than a story about high technology'. It also made clear that 'the system would be capable of handling more than the *London Post*'.

The section was dominated by a long, tough interview with Rupert on the 'Future of Fleet Street'. He stressed how continual disruption was undermining the 'habit factor' among newspaper readers and made it clear that if the unions carried out their threat to strike, Wapping would be used to print all four titles 'as best we can'.

The unions had 'no grounds for striking over the *London Post*', said Rupert. 'They have refused to work at Wapping and agreements are still in place at our existing plants.' But even if they voted not to strike there was a warning of unpleasant change to come: as agreements expired at the existing plants, radical new agreements would be sought along Wapping lines.

The toughest message came in the editorial. It was the only one in eleven years that Rupert asked me to submit to him before publication: he wanted to be sure there were no legal hostages to fortune in it, a reasonable request in the circumstances. I sat on the sofa of his office in the Times building as he went through it at his desk. I noticed that he kept putting in 'new paragraph' marks at the start of each sentence, as if it was an editorial for the *Sun*. Tabloid instincts clearly ran deep in him. With one minor change for legal reasons he approved what I had written; I returned to my office, took out his paragraph marks and sent it for typesetting. It should have left the unions in no doubt about the mood we were in.

'Wapping represents the Fleet Street of the future, in which the latest technology goes hand-in-hand with progressive labour practices,' it argued. 'While newspapers have continually lectured the rest of British industry on its inadequacies, Fleet Street itself has remained a microcosm of Britain's industrial malaise at its worst.' It was time to 'put its shameful house in order' in an industry in which 'the arrogance of print union power and the abdication of managerial control have always conspired to keep things as they are'.

'Fleet Street is, in effect, a cartel' – a conspiracy against the consumer in which all newspapers simply passed on their crazy costs to the reader and advertiser. 'Change is coming,' warned the editorial, 'and faster than most people think . . . the question is no longer if this will happen, but only how, and the answer to that lies very much in the hands of the print unions.'

'It will be a painful process of adaptation for some of the country's most conservative unions,' it concluded. 'Their alternative, of course, is to use their industrial muscle to try to keep things as they are. But that way they risk everything.'

The content of the special section and the manner in which it had been printed almost taunted the unions to black it. That was Rupert's purpose. When we met in his office to make final preparations in the event of a strike, his biggest worry was that the unions might not go on strike. Bill O'Neill assured him that they would; Bruce was not so sure. I said I assumed they would because they knew no better. 'I hope you're right,' Rupert said with a chuckle.

In Wapping we had started to 'shadow' the 19 January edition: if they went on strike at Gray's Inn Road we would produce the paper at the new facility. Copy was spirited out of *The Sunday Times* building by James Adams and Peter Roberts, where it was typeset and pasted up by a mixture of *Sunday Times*, *Sun*, American and Australian staff.

The shadow edition was almost needed: Roy 'Ginger' Wilson, the huge Sogat thug who had terrorized *The Sunday Times* press hall for years, had planned to smash the printing plates that night. But Sogat leaders prevailed on him to await the strike ballot. The edition was printed, though cumulative acts of sabotage resulted in a huge shortfall. 'Be my guest, boys,' Wilson had told his men. 'I don't expect you to pay attention to fine detail. We'll do it our way tonight.' Thus was almost half the edition lost. The people in Wapping were disappointed by the anti-climax – but it had been a useful trial run for the real thing the following week. I visited them with a crate of champagne to drink to their efforts – the first of many breaches of Rupert's Wapping anti-drink ban.

On Wednesday, 22 January, the unions announced overwhelming votes in favour of industrial action – 82 per cent of Sogat and 88 per cent of the NGA voted to strike in a ballot which included the ludicrous demand of jobs for life. Armed with this mandate from their members, the union leaders met Murdoch the next day at the Park Lane Hotel, Piccadilly. By now they had sensed that the ground was shifting from under them for they offered concessions inconceivable only a few months before: binding arbitration, ballots before strikes, flexible labour, management's right to manage.

But Rupert was not interested. His attitude to union promises of better behaviour was summed up in a letter he had sent to all staff the previous day: 'The alleged stumbling block was our insistence that any agreement between us should be legally binding on both sides – something that is quite normal in other countries such as the United States and Australia. The unions said: "No, let any agreement be in trust and honour." Can I tell you that between October, when our talks began, and Christmas, Fleet Street newspapers, governed by trust and honour, lost 2,750,000 copies through disruption of production?'

He blew up their olive branch with two bombshells: Wapping was no longer a matter for negotiation – it would proceed without them; and he would soon be seeking Wapping-style manning levels and labour practices at Gray's Inn Road and Bouverie Street. He was prepared to start talks on that now – but Wapping was off the table.

Bruce Matthews sat quietly as Rupert threw every union concession back in their face. He had grown increasingly worried by his boss's hardline tactics as the dispute reached its climax; they had started to argue. I shared some of Bruce's concerns: he and I had agonized with each other on the dangers of Rupert staking out too extreme a position: we feared he was overplaying his hand. He had become too confident, even aggressive: it was becoming too apparent he had no intention of doing a deal. 'My fear was that the unions would smell a rat,' says Bruce, 'and refuse to walk into our trap.'

My worry was different: I had become concerned that print-union tyranny was being replaced by macho-management, hence the warning at the end of my editorial of 12 January against management 'rushes of blood to the head'. As managers sensed Rupert's mood they began to echo it: a gung-ho attitude was taking root. Bill Gillespie said to me as the countdown to the strike began that his biggest worry was having to hire any 'dross and no-users' that crossed the picket lines.

'We should show a basic humanity to anybody prepared to risk their lives for us,' I had snapped back. I wrote in a notebook after our exchange: 'Sometimes I think we're becoming far too callous in our desire to clean this place out.' Bruce was also worried about the decent folk we employed who would inevitably be victims in an all-out strike.

The most significant strike in Fleet Street's long history began on Friday, 24 January 1986. 'We were lucky that they went on strike,' says Bruce. 'If they hadn't, it would have been a sheer bloody disaster for us. But by striking at our existing titles over what was happening at Wapping they put themselves on the wrong side of the law. It would have been far worse for us if they had carried on working but waged a guerrilla war to disrupt production at Gray's Inn Road and Bouverie Street. They knew how to do that in subtle ways not easy to detect. It would have been harder to find good legal grounds for sacking them.'

Charlie Wilson confirmed to me later that at the time Rupert's main concern was that the unions would *not* go on strike, but resort to guerrilla warfare. They did not because they had been told by their left-wing intellectual and media friends that Murdoch's recent purchases in America (he had just bought some expensive television stations which would form the basis of his new Fox TV network and a share in 20th Century Fox) made him especially vulnerable to an all-out strike. The unions were told that if they could cut off his British cash flow he would be unable to service his American debt and be forced into a quick surrender. So they went for a complete shutdown.

It was entirely typical of previous print-union behaviour. Such was the arrogance of their power that they could not even read the writing on the wall. Back in September 1985, the *Morning Star*, the paper of the Communist Party, had got hold of some of our legal documents which left little doubt that we were planning to do more than print the *London Post* in Wapping. Two maverick union activists even infiltrated Wapping and reported to Brenda Dean, the new Sogat leader, that Wapping was being prepared for a Big Bang. But she and the other union leaders studiously refused to believe we could do very much without them. In the end the print unions were brought down by their own hubris.

Rupert's hardline gamble paid off: he got his all-out strike – on his terms. Despite my last-minute reservations his ruthless realism had been right. If he had accepted any union olive branch he would have been mired in further months of negotiations, with no certain outcome. There was nothing in Fleet Street's history to suggest the union leaders could deliver the concessions they were proposing: they would very likely be overruled by the chapels, as had happened before. Even if they did deliver, the printers would quickly have returned to their bad old ways once safely inside Wapping. A clean break was the best way.

The print unions walked into a trap, propelled by their own arrogance. They had a long history of victories in industrial disputes notched on their belts; this would be another one. 'See you in a couple of weeks,' said a father of the chapel to me on the night the strike began. The chapels believed another Fleet Street dispute was about to follow its usual 'hawk-to-dove' course. They did not believe we had the press capacity or the skills to do without them. It was time to tame Murdoch and show him they were still in charge.

A few wiser souls knew better: this would be a very different dispute from those which had preceded it. But for the vast majority of printers it was inconceivable that Murdoch's four titles could be printed and distributed without them. They were about to learn the hard way that they were no longer indispensable – and to be paid back for the years of torture they had inflicted on us.

*

THERE WAS AN EERIE SILENCE on Gray's Inn Road that night as I looked out of my office window. Crush barriers lined the pavements in anticipation of pickets and a few police patrolled the streets; but they were deserted. Inside, there was activity only on the editorial floors. I had instructed the journalists to work normally: they had no need to go to

Wapping at this stage – that would be resolved after the forthcoming edition – and they should carry on producing their stories as they usually did in Gray's Inn Road, even though the copy was being typeset and printed in Wapping. This they did; but they were resentful about being kept in the dark and fearful for the future.

Friday, 24 January, was my last night in Gray's Inn Road. I returned briefly the next morning to ensure the journalists were working normally and the copy was flowing: they were and it was, though the atmosphere was hardly jubilant. I decided to head for Wapping early in the afternoon. But before leaving Gray's Inn Road I wandered down to the third floor where all the computer screens and keyboards the NGA had guarded for their exclusive use lay idle. The room was deserted but for Les Newman, a dedicated overseer who had done his best in impossible circumstances and would join us in Wapping. We speculated on the outcome of the events now underway.

'Before I go, Les, I'm going to do something I've been dying to do since I came here.' I touched a computer keyboard.

'That would have caused a walkout if the NGA was still here,' said Les, laughing.

'I know,' I replied. It was a silly gesture but it underlined the ludicrous position of the NGA: until that moment no journalist in Gray's Inn Road had ever touched one of their keyboards – something today's new generation of journalists must find incomprehensible.

I scooped up all available copy and walked out of Gray's Inn Road for ever, an ITN crew in my wake recording the move. As I drove away I looked back on the old *Sunday Times* building. I had no regrets: for me it had been a temple of torture and frustration. The car turned east at the Embankment and headed for Tower Bridge and Wapping. I did not know what to expect there and I was too concerned about the prospect of a long, dangerous, exhausting dispute to be elated. But I was sure it would be better than what I had left behind.

Appendix to Chapter Five

NIGHTMARE ON FLEET STREET

Fleet Street had long been a microcosm of all the worst symptoms of the British disease: appalling management, pig-headed unions, archaic technology. Three Royal Commissions in thirty years, two investigations by the Prices and Incomes Board and a damning report by the Economist Intelligence Unit (EIU) had left it unscathed, its industrial relations of the madhouse intact.

They had all agreed that drastic change was essential if the newspaper business was to have a future. They all shook their heads in astonishment at the shenanigans of Fleet Street's labour relations jungle. But nothing happened. Everybody had known for decades that Fleet Street's internal affairs were a national disgrace; but everyone with the power to do anything affected to be powerless. Even the chill winds of Thatcherism, which had tamed unions in every other industry by the mid-eighties, had made no impression on Fleet Street.

The EIU's seminal work had been published way back in 1969. Among the shortcomings it highlighted were: a 'small number of highly individualistic proprietors' who took little interest in the efficient running of their newspaper businesses and were more interested in the political power and social status owning a newspaper gave them; the nepotism of the print unions, with sons regularly following fathers into the trade (which made all the best jobs the preserve of white males from East London); and widespread drunkenness 'such as would never be tolerated in other industries'.

The shopfloor was a 'jungle' in which numerous unions determined what rules there were: they supplied the labour –

managers had no discretion over whom they employed – and horse-traded over bloated manning levels. Power lay with the union 'chapels', the union unit on the shopfloor run by 'fathers of the chapel' (FoCs), over which even union branch officials had very little control. About half the national newspaper industry operated at a loss, the EIU concluded, and closures were likely unless it embraced fundamental change.

Fifteen years later, when Harold Wilson set up yet another post-war Royal Commission into the press in 1974, almost nothing had changed. There was, however, a growing realization that things could not continue as they were. The Royal Commission asked the Advisory, Conciliation and Arbitration Service (Acas) to mount a major investigation into industrial relations on its behalf and, even before it had begun, union leaders and publishers formed a Joint Standing Committee 'to oversee technological and manpower changes in the industry and to draw up a framework for discussion at other levels'.

A flurry of reports swept over the industry. The Commission produced an interim report, which stressed the critical cash-flow position of some newspapers and urged higher productivity through reductions in manpower and the introduction of new technology. It even proposed government loans to smooth the path of progress where needed.

Meanwhile the Acas study, 'Industrial Relations in the National Newspaper Industry', published at the end of 1976, picked out the two most salient features shaping Fleet Street's industrial relations.

First, 'the daily production cycle, the intense competition between newspapers and the disproportionately heavy losses that can be incurred as a result of relatively minor disputes encourage fragmented bargaining, short-term attitudes on the part of employers to dispute settlement and impose strains on co-operation between employers'.

Second, the unusual degree of autonomy and power enjoyed by Fleet Street's 360 chapels – 'the nuclear unit of the organization of trade unions in the printing industry' – without whose consent change was impossible. While the power of the publishers had waned through their inability to take a united stand, the power of the chapels had increased; yet they continued to negotiate their multifarious agreements with little consultation and in a manner calculated to cause friction and disputes not just with the bosses but between unions. Many shutdowns were not quarrels with management but inter-union fights.

Publishers and print-union general secretaries were spurred to action: they produced a pamphlet, 'Programme for Action' (published in November 1976), which announced widespread agreement on voluntary redundancy, pensions, decasualization, disputes procedures, new technology and much more. The package was put to the chapels, who immediately reminded everybody of where real power lay in Fleet Street: they rejected the need for change. All the industry's chapels, except those of the National Union of Journalists, voted against the reforms.

When the Royal Commission reported its findings in 1977 it was largely a waste of paper and ink – yet another shopping list for action that everybody knew the chapels would ignore. And why not? They were being paid some of the highest wages in the land for the least work and their power to determine their own conditions was untrammelled. Dictators do not voluntarily cede their absolute power.

The Royal Commission's conclusion was bitter, even despairing:

> It takes an effort of the imagination to picture an industry, in which the vision of some proprietors and most employees extends no further than the end of the next

> week, engaging itself collectively upon the radical transformation of industrial relations.
>
> Habits of weak management bred in the post-war days of easy profits will be hard to break. In the last generation, print workers taught themselves the disastrous lesson that to ask and to threaten was to receive. So 360 separate chapels will be tempted to cling to their individual authority . . .
>
> So far, trade-union general secretaries and senior newspaper executives have been powerless in the face of folly which ignores even the obvious and immediate financial interest of ordinary workers . . . Moreover, at the end of the day, after bitterness and anxiety have soured relationships in the industry, many more jobs will have been lost through closing papers down than would have been sacrificed under the policy expounded in 'Programme for Action'.

The Commission warned starkly of the 'reckless disregard of peril [for the future of the industry]' shown by the chapels, which thought no consequences would ever follow from their 'suicidal' spate of unofficial stoppages. But it allowed itself one flash of humour in an otherwise dismal report. It chose a quotation from Lewis Carroll's *Alice in Wonderland* to head its chapter on industrial relations: 'I don't think they play at all fairly . . . and they all quarrel so dreadfully one can't hear oneself speak – and they don't seem to have any rules in particular: at least, if there are, nobody attends to them.'

Almost a decade later in the mid-eighties, that was still an accurate characterization of the continuing anarchy on Fleet Street. If anything, the power of the chapels to block progress had grown while the disparate proprietors were more disunited and pusillanimous than ever. The print unions had become masters at picking them off one by one.

The bosses got the unions they deserved. The greed and stupidity of many proprietors meant they could rarely resist trying to capitalize when one of their number was in trouble, his titles off the streets. The others would regularly print extra copies of their own papers to steal circulation, thereby forcing any proprietor who was taking a stand to capitulate quickly.

Fleet Street's so-called 'Spanish practices' remained rife. The London branches of the print unions were, in effect, Fleet Street's employment agencies: the management notified them of vacancies and the unions filled them with their members. Everybody operated on the assumption of extra cash for no extra effort and papers were regularly held to ransom by 'pay up or no paper' tactics, often at very short notice. Managerial surrender to buy peace was the norm and occasional flashes of employer defiance were severely penalized.

Ghost workers were everywhere: mythical beings whose pay packets were real enough and shared among the workforce to ensure continuous production. Massive overmanning remained the industry's special hallmark at a time when Thatcherism was forcing the rest of industry to become lean, and systematic non-attendance was tolerated on a grand scale. There was no penalty for not turning up: they were still paid small fortunes. The £1,000-a-week Linotype operator had arrived by the mid-eighties and even if such huge salaries were still confined to a few people earnings of £850 a week for so-called craftsmen were commonplace.

The big money and easy life did not buy co-operation; it encouraged demands for more. Each day brought some fresh skirmish aimed at producing some additional payments. Chapels specialized in calling meetings in the middle of a print run (usually when an edition had to catch a train), a printing press would go mysteriously wrong, a reel of paper would break, a stacker jam. They were all ruses to extort more money – and the management would invariably oblige: the alternative was no paper.

Sunday newspapers were particularly vulnerable. They made more money than the dailies and management hated to lose them; it made them more of a target for print-union extortion. A shotgun was regularly put to Sunday newspapers' heads and a call for ransom made just as the print run was about to start, hence the phrase 'Saturday Night Stick Up'.

Periodically, management would take a stand; as the week progressed their resolve would perceptibly weaken. 'Hawks on Monday, doves by Saturday,' everybody murmured. Even when there was no disruption, management resigned itself to turning a blind eye to the most absurd working practices in British industry.

Most printers and typesetters were expected to work four shifts a week but it had become the norm to turn up for only two, have a mate cover for the other two but still pocket the money for four. This was known as 'working the bingo'. Management not only knew this was widespread: they formally recognized it. So some printers took even greater liberties, turning up for only one shift a week – a 'bingo within the bingo'.

Sometimes those paid for doing a shift at one newspaper were actually doing a shift at another paper up the street. 'Doing a bingo' had become so institutionalized that when a four-shift man retired, the union branches would send along two men to replace him. More than 500 Sogat and NGA men ran the nine presses which printed *The Times* and *Sunday Times*: 40 per cent attendance was regarded as high. The *Sun* paid around 420 men on a normal night; the usual turnout, spread over two shifts, was about 150.

Sunday newspaper staff were paid to work each Saturday,

the crucial day of the week; but they were given at least eight Saturdays off a year rising in one case to an extraordinary 29 – more than one Saturday off in every two. One Sunday-newspaper machine room paid for 52 machine minders to work from 3 p.m. on Saturdays to 7 a.m. on Sunday mornings – ostensibly a 16-hour shift. In practice, 19 men worked from 5 p.m. to midnight and 19 more from midnight to 6:01 a.m. – the extra minute worked allowing them to claim an hour's payment for clean-up time. The remaining 14 notional pay packets were shared out, with £2 a head for chapel funds.

Those who did not report for duty still got paid. Their free time quickly mounted and was put to a variety of leisure and entrepreneurial pursuits. Print workers were famous for the time and money they invested in extra-curricular activities: they owned and ran taxis, mini-cabs, public houses, restaurants and shops. One chapel official had a pilot's licence, ferried VIPs to race meetings in his private plane and hired out his two Rolls Royce motor cars for functions. Another chapel officer regularly invited newspaper executives to shoots on his farm.

Leisure time was well spent. Fleet Street had more than its fair share of first-class golfers. Printers lived as far away as Cornwall and Wales; one reputedly commuted from France. An overseer on a Spanish holiday met a printer from his newspaper he knew should have been at work. He was told unashamedly: 'I'm on a fortnight's bingo.'

Twelve weeks' holiday a year was not uncommon: four from the industry agreement with the National Publishers Association, a week for bank holidays and seven through in-house 'productivity' deals, supposedly granting time off instead of more money (in practice the pay went up too). The closed shop and tight branch control of the labour supply made all this possible. The father of the chapel acted like a managing director in his own domain, deciding how many staff were needed then booking them from the union branches. Managers, in theory, had a choice of candidates for vacancies; in practice they had no say.

Gross overmanning ensured that there were always enough to do the work and that even mass absenteeism did not necessarily hinder production. Chapel officials, particularly in the print and publishing rooms, wielded enormous power and many regularly took kickbacks for placing men in work.

The drunkenness criticized in the EIU report was still prevalent, especially during the Saturday shifts for Sunday newspapers, and theft was widespread, which was why everything that could move in the *Sunday Times* newsroom had to be chained down. In the early eighties *The Sunday Times* press hall was like a bazaar, with everything on sale from anoraks to VCRs (all of which had clearly fallen off the back of a lorry). Petty crime was rife: at one daily newspaper, copies were vanishing in substantial quantities from the despatch area but managers were prevailed upon not to hold an official inquiry or call in the police – if they did, they were warned, production would suffer.

The industrial anarchy at Times Newspapers became so bad that even a soft touch like Thomsons, the Canadian company which owned the group before Murdoch, was provoked into drastic action. Managers wrote to the print unions in April 1978 warning that unless there were radical new agreements on continuous production, new disputes procedures, manning levels and new technology by November of that year the publication of the titles would be suspended.

The unions wanted none of it. At one meeting, Duke Hussey, the company's managing director, lamented the possibility of closure: 'We are a British institution,' he pleaded. The NGA's response was typically terse: 'You're not on, mate.'

The looming shutdown did nothing to concentrate union minds. Unofficial disputes lost the group 9.6 million copies as talks proceeded. A further warning from Hussey in September was ignored. By the deadline, only 18 out of 54 chapels had come to any sort of agreement. A shutdown that was to last eleven months began.

It caused the print unions little pain. They used their power to re-employ their members on other newspapers. No worker was going to be starved back to work in this dispute. But the company was bleeding red ink: it lost £40 million during the closure. The NGA's 'fighting fund', however, reached £1 million within a few weeks – enough for the union's president, the late Les Dixon, to confess: 'We don't know what to do with the money.' Cash flowed in because the chapels 'put the arm' on other newspapers to pay a production surcharge as they rushed to print extra copies of their own papers to mop up the circulation of *The Times* and *Sunday Times*. The unions made them pay for it, using the money to finance the stoppage. This was a dispute Times Newspapers was destined to lose.

Eleven months after it began the company capitulated: both papers reappeared in November 1979. The boldest initiative in Fleet Street's history had been shattered on the solid rock of union resistance. At the time the company put on a brave face, claiming it had won 70 per cent of what it had been after. This was nonsense. Ken Thomson, son of the famous proprietor who had died in 1976, told the truth when he put Times Newspapers up for sale a year later: 'The unions have been impossible to live with. We haven't been able to implement the things we wanted to do to save these papers. We have tried and failed. We have put resources into it but it takes more than resources to make it work. It takes real concern between the staff and management and they have not worked together.'

The last straw for Thomson was a crazy decision by *Times* journalists under the influence of irresponsible, left-wing National Union of Journalists' officials, to strike for a week in the summer of 1980 in pursuit of a pay demand – these were the very journalists the company had just paid to do nothing for a year during the suspension. In the fortnight prior to the announcement that the papers were on the block, disputes lost *The Sunday Times* alone more than 1 million copies and both papers were heading for a combined loss of £15 million. If the unions ever wonder why Thomson sold Times Newspapers to the tender mercies of Rupert Murdoch they have only to look in the mirror.

Nobody rushed in to buy the prestigious *Times* and *Sunday Times* when Ken Thomson unfurled his 'for sale' notice. Some may have coveted the titles but few wanted the unions and the financial losses that went with them. Thomson set a March 1981 deadline for a new owner to take over or publication would cease. Murdoch arrived at the last minute with a £12 million offer and a demand for job cuts to reduce overmanning. He got both: the unions, ironically, saw him as the best guarantee of things continuing largely as they had. And in a few months things were indeed back to what passed for normal at Fleet Street.

Sogat soon walked out without warning and by September, with NGA machine minders demanding more pay and higher manning levels, a dismayed and disgusted Murdoch declared: 'A small group of men are holding the company to ransom and are prepared to close two great newspapers. This is the most serious situation I have ever seen in Fleet Street . . . We have decided to close down if work does not resume properly.'

The dispute was typical for the Street of Shame: an

argument about differentials between NGA and another print union (Natsopa) rather than a fight with the management. Both papers had ceased to publish again and Murdoch realized the concessions he had won as a condition of purchase were worthless. Only the intervention of the general secretary of the TUC broke the deadlock and produced an uneasy peace. Another £1 million was lost in the process.

The troubles of Times Newspapers were worse than most but every major newspaper group was victim of Fleet Street's industrial anarchy. The early eighties saw ugly and costly disputes at the *Observer*, the *Financial Times* and the *Telegraph*.

The *Daily Telegraph* and its Sunday sister were off the streets for ten days in November 1982 at a cost of 7 million copies and £1.5 million – losses the struggling group could ill afford – all because managers wanted to remove one printing press. A festering dispute at the *Financial Times* eventually erupted into a strike in June 1983. It lasted for ten weeks and cost 15 million copies and £10 million – all because the NGA and Sogat could not agree on pay differentials. Nobody was going anywhere fast on new technology. By the mid-eighties the *Guardian* had been trying for two years to use its new computer typesetting equipment without much success – all but its leader page was still set in hot metal.

Printing presses at Express Newspapers, part of a £2 million investment in new equipment, had been 'mothballed' for four years because management could not obtain sensible manning levels. Nobody was surprised: it had taken the *Financial Times* two years to get union agreement merely to replace a worn out Linotype machine with an updated model; the same paper came close to yet another dispute because of some new photocopiers – the unions bickered over who should maintain them, each one threatening to strike if it was not them.

Niggling disputes and major stoppages made British newspaper production the most unreliable in the world: in the twelve months from July 1984 to June 1985 national daily newspapers lost more than 85 million copies through industrial action. There was no prospect of improvement. The conventional wisdom was that nothing could be done about it. The future for those who cared about newspapers and print journalism looked grim.

CHAPTER SIX

Bouquet of Barbed Wire

THERE WERE NO PICKETS as I drove past the security guards at the gate, only a few curious union observers on the main road. Razorwire now topped the high railings around Fortress Wapping, its silent, forbidding exterior masking the frantic activity inside.

I headed first for the main redbrick building, an ugly complex constructed in the new brutalist style of modern British architecture, where David Banks, a big, jolly journalist who had been sent to Wapping from the *Sun* supposedly to work on the *London Post*, was masterminding the typesetting of *The Sunday Times*, a gargantuan task that only somebody with David's capacity for hard graft in Murdoch's service could have organized.

He and a small team of British, Australians and Americans – including an amazing woman from Chicago we called 'the fastest typesetter in the West' – were living in Wapping, catching sleep when they could and frantically inputting *Sunday Times* copy on the Atex computer system all their waking hours. I handed them more articles for typesetting; they groaned then started back at the wordface. I went down to the basement of the rum store below our new offices where the pages were being pasted up. It was chaos.

Rupert Murdoch was striding around in a cardigan, open-necked shirt and casual trousers shouting at everybody to get a move on: he succeeded only in making them more nervous and slowing things down. This was the Ruthless Rupert I had always tried to shield from the journalists, knowing it would only confirm their worst prejudices. But that day brought the handful of dedicated *Sunday Times* journalists who were making Wapping possible face-to-face with him in the worst circumstances; it was not a pretty sight for them, or me.

The journalists and novice stonehands wielded scalpels at galleys of *Sunday Times* print being spewed out of the computer and tried to make it fit the schemes of the page layouts. They were working together in a way unimaginable at Gray's Inn Road but they were inexperienced and barely able to cope. Many articles did not fit because the computer could not quite reproduce our typesize or column width. I remember hacking away at the book reviews, which had no doubt been lovingly written, not much caring where the cuts were being made as long as the type fitted. When the sports copy and results started flowing in late in the afternoon we – and the computer systems – were almost overwhelmed.

The more we slipped behind deadline, the more Rupert raged. Instead of encouraging people with words of support he allowed his fear of failure to overwhelm him. In one memorable confrontation he turned on James Adams because of some delay and began stabbing him repeatedly in the chest with his finger.

'You f——!' he shouted. 'You bastard! Get this f—— newspaper out!'

This was no way to treat somebody who had been working non-stop for forty-eight hours for the cause. But James did not retaliate: he turned away and carried on with his work while Rupert looked for somebody else to hassle and intimidate. I jollied the team along as best I could. Ivan, an even more gentle soul than James, was particularly dismayed by what he saw of Rupert that afternoon. 'He inspires by fear,' he whispered to me, shaking his head.

That is sometimes Rupert's style. But there were very special circumstances that last Saturday afternoon in January 1986. Rupert had every right to be on edge: he was, after all, betting the company on winning his Wapping gamble. If we failed to get the paper out it would only confirm the print-union belief that we could not do without them: Wapping would be over before it started. The consequences of failure were too horrible to contemplate.

The last *Sunday Times* pages were cleared in ragged fashion, not too much behind deadline, and the printing presses plated up. Watched by his managers, Rupert touched the start button just after 8 p.m., late but not disastrously so. The presses slowly gathered speed behind their soundproof glass until they were roaring away, churning out over 50,000 *Sunday Times* an hour. A new era in the British newspaper industry had begun.

I watched the copies climb up from the presses on the conveyor belt into the distribution room, where the new machinery packed them into bundles and sent them down helter-skelters into the huge articulated trucks in the loading bay. I savoured the freedom of being able to walk anywhere in the production area, touch anything and be greeted with a smile by the printers. I could even pick a copy of the paper off the presses myself, an act that would have caused a walkout at Gray's Inn Road.

I took a copy of the new five-section *Sunday Times* to show to the television cameras waiting at the gate. As the trucks roared out laden with papers I held up the front page and announced: 'We've done it. This is the future.' But we were not there yet.

*

I WALKED INTO the dingy basement of the Mount Pleasant Hotel, a crumbling pile in a scruffy area between Gray's Inn Road and King's Cross, at 10.30 a.m. on Monday, 27 January, the morning after the first Wapping *Sunday Times*. The wallpaper was peeling and around 130 *Sunday Times* journalists were sitting in the gloom waiting for me to address them. The venue, which had been chosen by the paper's NUJ chapel, was redolent with everything I was trying to escape. The mood was sullen and apprehensive rather than hostile. I felt their eyes follow me as I made my way to the front, flanked by James and Ivan.

I tried to sound as conciliatory as I could. I thanked them for their help in working normally at Gray's Inn Road even though the production of the paper had shifted to Wapping. But now it was time for them to go there too. The strike had made that inevitable. I was determined to ensure the continuous production of *The Sunday Times*, I told them; I needed them to do it; I wanted them to come to Wapping. I did not add, though it was true, that my private plan was to bring the paper out whether they came or not – a daunting but not impossible task.

Instead I emphasized how much they were needed and that Wapping was where they now belonged. Modern offices with new technology awaited, including computer terminals in which they could type and edit their own copy, free of print union interference. They would be paid an extra £2,000 a year for moving to direct input and they and their families would be given private health insurance. In all other essential respects their existing work contracts would be honoured. At last, I argued, their journalism would be unimpeded by union restrictions: Wapping would be a liberation in which journalists were once again in the driving seat.

They listened silently. The silence continued when I asked for questions. Then Don Berry stood up from the edge of a table on which he had been perched at the front of the hall. But it was not a question; it was a speech – and a prepared one. I knew Don was deeply troubled by the dispute. He was no friend of the print unions – they had regularly mucked around with work in which he took a fierce pride – but he had no love for Murdoch either and wanted no part of what he had come to see as an exercise in union busting. He persisted in the belief that it could all be resolved by negotiation and that the journalists should stay put until it was. It was a principled position; it was also unrealistic and had been overtaken by events.

I had talked privately with Don several times as the strike loomed; I liked him, he was the most respected member of the paper's old guard and I knew he would be a key influence in the journalists' decision. But he had no stomach for a confrontation – few on the moderate left ever did – and thought the management was becoming unreasonable in its demands. I told him that I had favoured an evolutionary rather than a revolutionary approach to change, provided it produced the desired results. I shared with him my unease at some of the hardline attitudes adopted among senior managers as they aped Rupert. But I warned that I sensed a momentum to events that was out of my control or his and that he should be prepared for the worst. He was not excited by the prospect.

I had also made it clear that, in the event of a strike, I would do whatever it took to bring the paper out. I told him that if the unions succeeded in stopping production there would never be a sensible deal – just the usual management surrender. Continuous production was essential to show the unions that this time we would not roll over. Despite the lessons of the eleven-month shutdown of 1978–79, Don said he would rather see the paper off the streets while management and unions resolved their differences. It was a gulf between us that was never bridged.

By that Monday morning Don was now more angry with Rupert and me than he was with the unions. Part of this was professional pride: he and many of the world's finest story-getters were miffed that Wapping had been planned and executed under their noses without them ever discovering what was happening. More important, he genuinely believed – as did many in the room – that the management was treating the journalists with contempt in expecting them meekly to make their way to Wapping at its command.

I had some sympathy with this view, though I could not say so publicly at the time. I felt that Rupert had taken the journalists for granted in assuming they would go to Wapping. He had dealt me a weak hand to play in convincing them the company cared about them: I had wanted more generous terms and at least the semblance of negotiations, if only to assuage their pride. It was the fact that they were being presented with a *fait accompli* that rankled with all but those on the left who were never going to cross a picket line for Murdoch anyway. Since I had been vocal on the airwaves in management's support they now saw me as an apologist for the company rather than an editor who would stand up for their interests.

Don accused the company of waging a 'campaign against the unions' with ruthless deception. The company had provoked the strike and the journalists had been insulted and betrayed, not just by management but by their editor: 'You have treated us with contempt,' he said, staring at me and quivering with emotion. He sat down to an ovation.

His speech emboldened others to ask questions – many of the mundane sort ('How do you get to Wapping?' 'Do I *have* to use a computer?') – but some, inevitably, to grandstand. One journalist from the magazine asked if I really thought she could be bribed to go to Wapping with a 'Tory health scheme'?

'The health insurance is not compulsory,' I replied, 'nor party political.' I was trying hard not to be provoked. James and Ivan sensed the mood could turn ugly at any moment and signalled that it might be time to leave since my further presence would be counter-productive. I left them to debate their future: they did so for the rest of the day. Without strong editorship, *Sunday Times* journalists have never been good at making up their minds quickly.

Peter Roberts called me at 5.30 p.m. with the result of the vote: 68 to 60 in favour of going to Wapping. I was dismayed: it was too close for comfort, though not as tight as the margin suggested, for more than ten executives were already at Wapping and had not bothered to vote. But I had embarked on a crusade with a reluctant army, a fact that would cause a near-fatal breakdown in relations between editor and staff within months.

Next day the majority of staff trudged to Wapping with a heavy heart. They were greeted by Atex specialists to teach them how to operate their new computer keyboards. A company called Bligh Recruitment, which specialized in placing women from Australia and New Zealand in British office jobs, had been used to find folk who could train the journalists on their new computer terminals. They had been interviewed on the other side of the world, not just to check their competence but to make sure they had no family connections in Britain that might spill the beans about their secret mission.

Around twenty had arrived in December and they were supplemented by Atex staff. The *Guardian*, which never lost an opportunity to undermine morale at Wapping or put us in the worst possible light, ridiculed the journalists for having to go back to school – and with foreign teachers who were apocryphally meant to greet us with a 'Hi! I'm Cindy.' It would not be long before *Guardian* journalists – and everybody else in Fleet Street – would have to go on the same training courses, but that did not stop them sneering at the time.

Most of the press was hostile or unhelpful. Robert Maxwell's *Daily Mirror* bleated about Wapping not being the 'British way'. But we had tried the British way and it had not worked. Even the Tory press was sniffy: they wanted the unions to have the bloody nose they did not have the guts to deliver themselves; but they feared the competitive advantage success at Wapping would give Murdoch over them. When we tried to place some full-page ads in other newspapers giving our side of the dispute, they refused to carry them. Nobody was surprised when the *Observer* turned us down: its editor, Donald Trelford, even spiked a book review by Bernard Levin under union pressure because Levin also wrote for *The Times*. Trelford tried to defend his censorship but no weasel words could disguise the fact he had surrendered to union blackmail ('no Levin review or there will be no *Observer*,' they had told him). However, even the Tory *Daily Express* and *Daily Telegraph* refused to carry our ads, putting fear of annoying their print unions above the principle of free speech. I was particularly disappointed that the *Telegraph* editor, Max Hastings, the liberator of Port Stanley, had shown a more robust attitude to the Argentinians than to the NGA.

Yet while scorning what we were doing, our rivals toughened their own demands to the unions, knowing that neither Sogat nor the NGA could afford to open a second front. They were able to negotiate peaceful change because we were in a war they affected to disparage. It was a vintage time for British hypocrisy – and not just from other newspapers.

John Harvey-Jones, then the boss of ICI and one of Britain's best-known managers, opined that barbed wire and mass sackings had no place in British industrial relations. But he had never dealt with the print unions: he had been able to negotiate thousands of redundancies to solve his overmanning and introduce whatever new technology he wanted. Even the softer Tory MPs were queasy about what we had done and, of course, the left was unanimous in its condemnation. The Labour Party said it would not even speak to our journalists. Not surprisingly, Neil Kinnock preferred to pander to the print unions.

The Labour leader said he would not take questions from *Sunday Times* journalists at his weekly lobby briefings in the House of Commons. Chris Moncreif, the splendid chairman of the parliamentary press lobby, stood his ground: this was an intolerable interference in the freedom of the press – if the Labour leader was going to black *The Sunday Times* and other News International titles then there would be no lobby briefings. They were abandoned for the duration of the dispute.

Kinnock instructed Labour MPs not to speak to our journalists. It was a ban more breached than observed. At the height of hostilities between *The Sunday Times* and the Labour leader, Eric Heffer, an independent-minded left-wing MP, walked into Annie's Bar, the discreet watering-hole in the House of Commons where politicians and journalists met to gossip and exchange information on lobby terms, and greeted Michael Jones, our political editor with, 'Hello, scab! What are you having to drink?'

'You are in grave danger of falling foul of your leader,' replied Mike with mock gravity. 'I suggest we communicate through an intermediary.' He then propped up a House of Commons beer mat against a glass and pointed to it.

'Ask the political editor what he would like to drink?' said Heffer, addressing the mat.

'Tell him I'll have a Guinness,' replied Mike.

It illustrated the farcical nature of the Kinnock boycott, which collapsed in futility long before the dispute ended. Our coverage of the Labour Party never suffered. Robin Cook, a member of Kinnock's shadow cabinet, regularly called our political department on Saturdays when he had a story to tell. Tony Blair told me he was happy to meet because 'I hate the print unions even more than you'. Even Peter Mandelson, Kinnock's chief spin doctor, tried to keep contact via various subterranean communications: he knew the political power of the paper. But Mike Jones would not deal with him: he was a key member of Kinnock's kitchen cabinet and Mike bitterly resented the Labour leader's boycott.

Mike was among a number of *Sunday Times* editors and journalists – Ivan Fallon, James Adams, Tony Bambridge, Tony Rennell, Roger Eglin, Chris Navrat, Robin Morgan, Jeff Randall and many key correspondents – who never flinched from defying the unions and making Wapping a success. They daily crossed the picket lines, enduring the taunts and hardships, to spend gruelling days bringing out *The Sunday Times*. Fleet Street folklore has tended to dwell on the stand of the 'refuseniks' – those who would not go to Wapping – and the left has even tried to depict them as heroes. But for me the real heroes of Wapping were those who never wavered in their commitment to *The Sunday Times*, knew what was at stake and changed our industry for the better by their efforts.

For those less enthusiastic about the whole venture, however, things like the Labour boycott all added to the reluctant journalists' sense of isolation. Going east to Wapping was like going to Moscow for most of them: a strange, desolate place far from their usual drinking haunts and friends. Their exile was made much worse because the whole world – and especially their chattering-class friends – seemed to be against them. As a result, minor inconveniences – telephones not working, no dark-room (my 'executive' washroom was converted into one), no newspaper deliveries – which would have been shrugged off had their hearts been in the endeavour, instead served to make them more miserable. Then there were the people they had left behind.

Fewer than thirty of these so-called 'refuseniks' gathered in defiance in Gray's Inn Road and most of them drifted down to Wapping as the days passed. Peter Roberts and Stephen Milligan did sterling conciliation work convincing many to come to Wapping. That was Peter's job as managing editor but Stephen made it a personal mission to bring as many of his colleagues as he could. Though he had written a book called *The Union Barons* in the mid-seventies, which argued that British union power would only be tamed by a series of major confrontations, he found the reality of industrial disputes tougher to stomach. He agonized over lost colleagues and ran himself into the ground trying to 'save' them for Wapping. Those he prevailed upon to come (such as Isobel Hilton and David Blundy, two senior correspondents in the foreign department) soon left when they found alternative, more congenial employment; they had never really wanted to be there in the first place.

In the end, only about half a dozen held out, eventually drifting off to other newspapers. None mattered much for the future of the paper and a few I was glad to see the back of – I would have paid them to leave. But not Don Berry. Despite his damaging speech I wanted him in Wapping for his professional skills and the boost to morale his presence would bring. So did Rupert. I tried to lure him with the promise of a four-month trial period after which, if he did not like it, he could leave with the usual generous pay-off.

At one stage Mike Jones believed he had convinced Don to come. But, in the end, he would not budge: Don had staked out his ground, earned much admiration for his principled stand and could not now be seen to be making special deals. We parted on good terms, with a certain reluctance on his side as well as mine. He would soon become a senior editor at the *Daily Telegraph*, where he helped with the introduction of the new technology which only our fight had made possible and laid out the columns of various right-wing writers far more Tory than *The Sunday Times*. He should have come to Wapping.

*

IT WAS A NEW LIFE for all of us, not least me. On the first Tuesday morning, as the journalists settled in to their new desks and computers, I was assigned a large, bearded bodyguard and a new driver. The company had decided that my appearances on TV attacking the unions and making the case for Wapping – I had become for many the public face of the company in the dispute – had made me a hate figure among the strikers and therefore a potential target. It was a role I relished: I was committed to the fight and, unlike Rupert or Bruce Matthews, had a British accent and plenty of television experience. With the help of a senior figure in the electricians' union and company managers I had compiled a large dossier on the tyranny of the Fleet Street unions. I was on top of the subject and passionate about the cause. But the personal price for such a public profile was high.

There is a certain novelty in having personal security: it makes you feel important. But the novelty quickly wanes to be replaced by irritation at the inconvenience. Though I did not know it at the time, for the next thirteen months a rota of bodyguards would be with me everywhere I went.

I was never in any doubt that the strike would be violent: the print unions would not give up without a bitter struggle and there was a thuggish element prepared to use whatever force was at their disposal, as they had against Eddy Shah. Back in August the company's security advisers had produced a report warning that 'there are among us people who may be regarded as targets for terrorism'. It warned us to avoid regular patterns of behaviour, take different routes to and from work, increase home security and think about keeping a dog. It also gave advice on where to look for car bombs and to screen all parcels.

Christopher Pole-Carew, one of Rupert's original advisers on the venture, was even more apocalyptic. 'The mortars are going to be positioned there and they will come in from over there,' he would say with wild, staring eyes. 'We're going to be under attack and we're all going to die.' By now the rest of the team had concluded that Pole-Carew was not quite the asset Rupert had hoped. He had been increasingly marginalized by the inner core of Wapping planners so that by the time the dispute started he was, says Bruce Matthews, 'in charge of nothing more than ordering the barbed wire'. Nevertheless, it was decided to reinforce the roof of our new office against petrol bombs and for thirteen months I sat behind bullet-proof glass in my office window.

The death threats came thick and fast within days of the dispute beginning. 'We are going to throw acid in your face,' was typical of the messages my office had to cope with, 'and we know where you live'. They probably did: so every night as we approached my home in South Kensington my bodyguard would radio ahead to his colleague outside my house and check if it was safe to proceed. Sometimes we would park round the corner until we got the all-clear. At times of high alert, while I sat in the car outside a security man would search my flat to see if an unfriendly soul was lurking inside waiting for my return.

I grew to hate the phone in the night: it usually meant another death threat. I went to bed every night with a large bit of wood propped up against the wall beside me and a referee's whistle on the bedside table. The wood was my last line of defence but the whistle was not to summon help: it was to blow down the phone whenever some joker wanted to disturb my sleep with another threat. One of the bodyguards gave it to me, testifying to its deterrent value. 'If you blow hard enough,' he advised, 'you'll burst their ear drum.' I'm not sure if I ever managed that but it seemed to work: the late-night threats tailed off.

But not the obscene mail. Typical of the letters passed to me was, 'To the Contemptible Filth, Gillespie, O'Neill, Matthews, The Fuhrer (Murdock [sic]), and the Mickey Mouse Editor A. Neil.' There followed a direct threat to our lives. 'As you the above have terminated us, a small group have put there [sic] monies together and have put out a contract to terminate you. After all, money works both ways, only you slags won't be needing Bupa. As you have put a bullet to our heads, you will find out what it's like to be on the end of one . . . Death to you all, you scum.'

One of the more sinister notes addressed to me had a black border around it and said in flowing handwriting: 'This is to confirm that the anticipated funeral arrangements for Thursday next have hereby been confirmed. And plans will go ahead as anticipated – oak coffin, seven cars plus an escort of pickets. See you up there.' Another followed the night union militants burned down our newsprint warehouse on the banks of the Thames: 'Now we'll burn down you and your house,' was the irenic and anonymous message the next day.

Though I was a major target for such threats I was not the most vulnerable for I had security and I lived far away from the pickets. The ordinary workers who crossed the picket lines were at greater risk. It was not so bad for those bussed in from Southampton; but those who lived in London went in fear.

Many were intimidated and their families threatened. A *Times* journalist who foolishly returned to a Fleet Street drinking haunt had a beer glass smashed in his face. A computer programmer received a typically disturbing threat, 'SCAB, understand the trouble you're in because you're only going to get one warning! I have actually stood outside where you live. I live very close, near the snooker hall. I have planned my escape and have got the necessary equipment. *You have been warned. Stop working at Wapping!*'

Life settled into a routine. Early to work every day, by different routes, bodyguard riding shotgun next to my trusty French driver, Alain, who was apparently trained in evasion techniques, such as reversing at 60 mph. Past the pickets and through the Wapping gates to safety, the car stereo blaring Beethoven to drown out their cries of 'Scab!' Lunch and dinner venues were regularly changed to avoid a predictable pattern; often it was easier just to stay behind the barbed wire. Long days ended around midnight with the usual security checks on my home as we approached.

The bodyguards worked a rota and we became friends. They were all ex-army and looked as if they could take care of themselves, which was reassuring. I felt safe with one in particular, a small, almost slight man, with short dark hair and a moustache. He was ex-SAS and a black-belt karate champion. One day something happened which made me realize the danger I was in: he opened the glove compartment in the Jaguar and a pile of bandages tumbled out. He must have seen me stare. 'It's in case they hit us on the head with a rock,' he explained, somewhat sheepishly, as he stuffed them back in.

Even when the danger is real, constant security quickly becomes claustrophobic. The pickets would follow me to venues that were public knowledge. When I was appearing on a programme at BBC's Television Centre, the studios received a bomb threat. The pickets were waiting at the gates as I left. We never knew when or where they would turn up.

When I appeared on BBC TV's *Question Time*, they smashed some studio windows while we were recording the programme. At one stage the whole studio went dark: it looked like they had managed to cut the power. My security rushed to surround me where I was sitting on the stage. I tried not to look shaken when the recording resumed but it was all a bit unnerving. It was on that *Question Time* that I said the print unions had more in common with organized crime than respectable trade unionism. The BBC's lawyers took fright and, because there was no time to edit it out, insisted the producer dip the sound during the broadcast when I made my offending remarks. Thus I was responsible for the only *Question Time* ever 'edited' between recording and broadcast.

There were lighter moments. One of my journalists often wore a French beret to work, which meant he was regularly met at the Wapping gate with shouts of 'Scab! Oh la la!' At least some of the pickets had a sense of humour. There were other amusing events.

Whenever I took somebody to the cinema I had to buy four tickets. Security insisted we did not enter until the lights went down, lest somebody recognize me and assemble the brothers to await my exit. 'It's really nice being with you tonight,' said a girlfriend one night as we took our seats at the last minute in a Fulham Road cinema, 'you and the two large men sitting in front and behind us.' It was not a time for intimate affairs.

On one occasion I left Wapping late at night and picked up a girlfriend whom I had promised a nightcap at Raffles Club in King's Road, Chelsea. As we headed for the club, security informed me we were being followed. Back-up was summoned. We came to a sudden halt and another car with our security people in it pulled up behind and wedged the one tailing me between us. My bodyguards rushed out, hauled the driver from his car and put him up against a wall. The terrified man denied he had anything to do with the print unions: he was a private detective from Birmingham who had been hired to follow the girl. His story checked out: unknown to me the girl had not quite broken up with her previous boyfriend and he had hired the detective to find out what she was up to. It turned out to be a rather more dangerous assignment than he had bargained for.

Despite the odd chuckle, they were largely tough, lonely times. One of the few people I could count on for regular support was Alastair Burnet. He would often come straight from ITN after presenting *News at Ten* to my house for a night-cap and a morale-boosting talk, in which he would always assure me we were winning. His visits were one of the few highlights of my life in a generally miserable time and I will always be grateful for his support.

Saturdays were particularly long and gruelling. A mass picket of several thousands was mounted every Saturday night to try to stop the trucks getting out; it regularly ended in violence. As evening approached I would watch hundreds of riot police outside my office prepare for the coming battle. They formed up in rows to repel the pickets as they laid siege to our buildings; mounted police waited behind them to be deployed when the pickets turned particularly nasty. The violence was always worse when the pubs closed: we watched the battle between police and pickets raging up on the main road, wondering what would happen to us if the police lines broke. But they never did: before the dispute began Rupert Murdoch had personally visited Margaret Thatcher to seek assurances that enough police would be available to allow us to go about our lawful business. She assured him that there would be – they had a duty to keep the Queen's highways open, she said – and she kept her word. (The absence of such assurances in New York is why Rupert has never tried to 'do a Wapping' at the *New York Post*, which is still bedevilled by old practices: he fears he could not count on the New York police in a violent dispute.)

Those of us who could not escape before 8 p.m. as the advanced guard of pickets arrived were locked in until the early hours of Sunday morning. The mob reached its height after the pubs closed and lingered into the early hours. We had to pile into our cars at around 2 or 3 a.m. and await a convoy of departing trucks – then thunder out with them. We busied ourselves earlier in the evening by updating the news pages and creating regional editions: with no print-union restrictions we were now able to change pages by the score. But on quiet news nights there was not much to do after the last edition had gone around 10.30 p.m.

I alternated between watching television and the skirmishes between police and pickets outside my office. One night a friend bravely volunteered to give me some company. We watched *Escape from New York*, a futuristic movie in which the whole island of Manhattan has been turned into a prison. At one stage there is a breakout. 'They've more chance of escaping,' commented my friend, 'than we have.'

Occasionally I would give my security the slip on Sundays by saying I was staying in all day then joining friends at a local restaurant. Sometimes I wondered if the precautions were really necessary. Mostly I was relieved to have them.

We left Wapping one Saturday night after 2 a.m. There had been a particularly large demonstration that night so we turned right to take the long way home by going east to avoid pickets still milling around the traffic lights at Tower Bridge. We headed straight into hundreds of pickets walking towards us along the main road. I began to panic: I knew if they saw me they would attack the car and try to drag me out. My bodyguard, who was sitting in the passenger seat, reached back, forced me on to the floor with one hand and threw his coat over me with his other. The driver edged slowly through the pickets: I could feel them staring in the windows as I huddled under the coat, hoping it was too dark for them to see. We made it – but only just.

Rupert, who had arrived from New York that day, had said to join him for a nightcap at his St James's flat no matter how late I finished. When I arrived he saw how shaken I was and poured me several large Scotches. We talked long into the night about everything and nothing. At one stage I remember both of us agreeing that the post-war history of Britain would have been very different if the 1945–51 Attlee Labour Government, instead of wasting its time nationalizing coal, steel and the railways, had nationalized the public schools and made them élite grammar schools with entry based solely on ability. It was not a bad idea, since it would have been a body blow to the class system. But Rupert was really talking me down from the shock of a nasty situation: it was a generous gesture, especially since it kept him up most of the night.

Another time I had agreed to give a lunchtime talk to the moderate Institute of Journalists (IOJ). I was apprehensive about the venue – the basement of the Cheshire Cheese pub in Fleet Street, a regular haunt of journalists and print workers – but the IOJ had been supportive over Wapping whereas the left-wingers who ran the NUJ had naturally sided with the print workers. I did not want to snub some of the few friends we had.

The moment I made my way through the crowded pub to the stairs leading to the basement I realized I had made a mistake: somebody was bound to recognize me. They did. Half-way through my speech some print workers appeared at the back of the room and lobbed two smoke bombs into the audience. The meeting broke up in chaos. That familiar feeling of panic ran through me: how was I going to get out? But my security people had already sensed trouble and called for reinforcements. Around half a dozen of them formed a wedge round me and we bulldozed our way up the stairs and back to my waiting car. It had been a narrow escape and a foolish mistake on my part: I had jeopardized not just my own safety but the well-being of those paid to protect me.

The most worried I ever saw them was on the anniversary of the dispute. By then the print unions knew they were beaten and were already negotiating surrender terms. But the militants decided to mount a massive final assault: on the last Saturday of January 1987 almost 10,000 pickets faced 3,000 police, many in full riot gear. It was the bloodiest night of the dispute: mounted police had to be called in to disperse the crowd and snatch-squads of riot police plunged in to pick off the ringleaders. At one stage it looked as if the police were going to be overwhelmed.

Rupert, Bruce and I had once joked that if it all went horribly wrong we would have to be evacuated by helicopter from the roof: visions of the American embassy during the last days of Saigon came to mind. 'I'll have a jumbo waiting for us at Heathrow,' said Rupert, 'and we can all head for New York.' It was a joke which had a grim ring of truth. Those of us most associated with Wapping knew we were finished in London if the print unions won.

Inside Wapping we were all especially nervous that night. I had tried to keep a semblance of normality by going through the motions of updating the paper. In the middle of my editorial conference two security men burst in and said I would have to leave my office immediately and retreat to more secure accommodation. They wanted to activate the 'Doomsday' plan.

We always knew that if the pickets ever breached our defences and made it into Wapping they would go on the rampage: more than just machines would be in danger. The company had devised a series of fallbacks in the event of invasion: if the pickets made it over the fence and across the rings of razorwire, which were meant to inhibit a mass charge, the plan was to retreat to the main building. If that was breached our ultimate sanctuary was behind the steel firedoors at the centre of the building. That was where they now wanted me to go.

'Are we evacuating our building?' I asked.

'At this stage we just want you to leave,' said one. 'You're a prime target if they get in and your office is right by the gate. We can't guarantee your security here.'

I could see they were nervous – which meant I was terrified.

'I won't leave the journalists here,' I replied. 'Either we all go or I stay with them.'

They nodded reluctantly. But I had them check that the underground passages connecting our building with the main facility – and our last line of refuge – were open and clear for a dash to safety. This is the route we would have fled through had the pickets overrun the police lines, the last one closing the steel doors behind him. But it never came to that: the police lines held.

*

In the immediate aftermath of the move to Wapping relations between the editor of *The Sunday Times* and the staff were strained almost to breaking point. I was a true believer in the cause; but many of those I led were a reluctant army that had never wanted to fight in the first place. I regarded the print unions as the evil enemy and Wapping a fresh start without them; they saw themselves as caught in the crossfire between management and unions and dragooned to Wapping against their will. They hated the pickets, the barbed wire, the isolation, the criticisms of their trendier friends, their separation from the refuseniks, the fact that there was no end in sight to the dispute. I grew angry with their reluctance to fight the good fight; they saw me as a management mouthpiece and an editor unsympathetic to their concerns. It came close to divorce.

The strain of being at the centre of a bitter, violent industrial dispute took its toll on me. I resented the complaints of those journalists who moaned about Wapping; I was slow to praise and very quick to criticize. It was not the best way to win hearts and minds. The journalists quickly took to the new technology and appreciated the fact that the print unions were no longer in the way. But they hated the shouts of 'Scab!' every time they came and left Wapping, and their misery about being there was made all the worse by my harsh attitude towards them. A number began to depart for jobs elsewhere, dragging down even further the morale of those left behind. It was not a one-way street: some talented big-name journalists were prepared to join us, including Brian Walden, who wrote to me, 'I don't *need* to write for *The Sunday Times*. I *want* to.' His support was welcome beyond measure but it could not entirely compensate for the drain of established journalists. Matters came to a head with the resignation of Ian Jack.

Jack was the most talented feature writer on the paper, a

Scottish socialist whose left-wing views were tempered by a healthy scepticism for metropolitan political fashion. His beard and scruffy dress made him look like an ageing hippy and he was shambolic when it came to organizing anything. He was not our most productive writer and seemed to disappear for months. For years he had supposedly been writing a book on Indian trains; I don't think it ever materialized.

When he did concentrate his mind on journalism, however, he wrote like a dream. In the aftermath of the Heysel Stadium outrage, when Liverpool football fans had rioted with fatal consequences against Turin supporters, I had asked him to do a long magazine piece on a 'Tale of Two Cities', to contrast the rise of Turin and the fall of Liverpool in the twentieth century and to see if there was something in their history that could explain the violence of the Liverpool fans and the relatively placid Turin supporters. I made it a cover story and Jack won the Magazine Writer of the Year Award for it. Now he was off:

> I wish to resign [he wrote]. I am no great lover of the print unions. I can never forgive them for delivering the paper out of Thomson's hands and into Rupert Murdoch's. I know they have got the management they deserve and that at some stage, as you would say, there has to be blood on the carpet. On the other hand, if I am to walk through the picket lines of the second most bitter dispute in recent British history, I have to be walking towards something I believe in. After a great deal of thought, thumb-sucking as you would say, I have reached the conclusion that I no longer believe in *The Sunday Times*.
>
> I don't take a particularly high-minded view of journalism or of myself. Journalism has always seemed to me a pretty imperfect way of describing the world around us, and I can be as easily compromised as the next man. But

on *The Sunday Times* I have known journalism at its best and I don't think I am prepared to accept it in its present debased form.

The turning point for me was probably your leader [on the Sellafield nuclear reprocessing plant] of two weeks ago. Here Captain Queeg had emerged from his cabin with rattling ball bearings in his hand. Your words were strident to the point of hysteria. Your leader implied that life could and should be reduced to the business of getting and spending. That shouldn't, it seems to me, be the philosophy of an intelligent and civilized newspaper. Like many of your readers, I seem to be a part of your chattering classes. I can do without the poorly framed insults of my own editor.

There is another and perhaps more fundamental thing. One of the parts of journalism that I have always enjoyed most – and perhaps do best – is to talk to 'ordinary' people and write about their concerns, unsentimentally but (I hope) truthfully and sympathetically. It is difficult to be a worker helping to hone the cutting edge of the new capitalism, and at the same time be a journalist who writes about its consequences.

You have certain qualities (beliefs is more accurate) that I respect and even subscribe to. There is a part of me that actually wants to like you; not that being liked is one of your priorities. But your presentation of yourself as a one-dimensional, one-note character with a psyche about as sophisticated as a wolf's has, quite unsurprisingly, won you no friends, no loyalty and little respect.

There was something to his personal criticisms: I had become a harsh, unforgiving editor. I was locked in an exhausting battle: you were either with me, or against me – this was no time for 'thumb-sucking' or equivocation. But his letter also showed that, as one of the old guard from the Thomson era, he hated having Murdoch as his proprietor and working for a newspaper that no longer supported the liberal-left consensus to which he belonged. Given these views he was right to go but his departure was a body blow. I replied more in sorrow than in anger.

> I accept your resignation, though I'm sorry you felt it necessary to deliver it in curt, insulting tones.
>
> As editor I have always tried to act with kindness and respect towards you. Moreover, whatever you may think of the paper's editorial line, you have been given a free hand to write what you like, when you like. So I was saddened by your remarks; but I understand that leaving *The Sunday Times* cannot be an easy decision for you.
>
> I fail to see what is debased about journalism which expresses strong views about, say, Sellafield or the USA and Britain in its leaders, but does not refrain from splashing with the most damaging Sellafield story for two decades or putting the anti-American results of an opinion poll on page one. I hope you find such a rigorous separation of news and opinion elsewhere in Fleet Street. However, I well understand the pain of crossing the barbed wire and picket lines to work for a product you do not believe in, and respect your decision to resign. I am sorry to lose a talented journalist and a pleasant, conscientious colleague; if I could think of a way to change your mind then I would.
>
> I hope you find other work soon, and have no doubt that you will. But if references or any other help is needed, then please don't hesitate to ask.

I signed off with the words 'best wishes for the future'. Ian Jack replied by return of post:

> Thank you for your decent and generous letter. I regret the rancour in mine and I want to apologize for those parts you found insulting. I usually amend everything I put on paper after a night's sleep; either that or my wife

acts as the vital censor. 'No,' she said after reading yesterday's letter, too late, 'that won't do.' But yesterday I felt I had to write it quickly, deliver it and go; otherwise I might have dithered forever and taken on the moaner's role.

I agree; you have always treated me with consideration, you have always allowed me to write what and when I want, you have never interfered with my copy. You have encouraged excellent ideas and got them into print. No journalist, in this sense, could ask for more. I just wish that you had treated other people around me with the same consideration. My anger yesterday didn't come from a sense of personal grievance. It was generated by the distress of seeing good friends and colleagues suffering or leaving.

Your letter affected me. How I wish that more people could see more of this side of you more often. How I wish I had. Perhaps we should have talked more. I am sorry all this has happened to you as well as to me, but it has.

There was nothing more to say. We both had our regrets, we were both to some extent a victim of circumstances, no doubt we would both have liked a second chance to do things differently. But I had no time to dwell on what might have been: Ian Jack's departure provoked the most serious internal crisis of my editorship.

Years later Ian Jack contacted me again, after he had become editor of the *Independent on Sunday*, which he ran as a left-wing paper with more bite and originality than the *Observer*, but with the same lack of commercial success: its sales languished at a fraction of ours even though it had been launched to take on *The Sunday Times*. In his letter he explained that now he was an editor himself he better understood the pressures I had been under; he even offered lunch.

When he turned up at the Savoy Grill they would not let

him in because he was in jeans and a jumper: editorship had not improved his sartorial sense. I had to wait for half-an-hour while he went to change but the lunch was a friendly affair in which he repeated the sentiments in his letter. We parted amicably, promising to stay in touch. Some time later I was being interviewed by the *Guardian* and asked if I deserved my reputation as a tough, even harsh editor. I replied that there were times when you had to be tough – even Ian Jack realized that now. But when the journalist contacted him he denied his friendly overture.

When he resigned from the *Independent on Sunday* he even managed another public sideswipe at me. Perhaps he was angry that his paper had never been the threat to *The Sunday Times* it had vowed to be and was going nowhere with a pittance of a circulation. But it disappointed me that an intelligent, self-made Scot should have resorted to one of the more annoying habits of the English Establishment: attack in public to pander to your constituency, but praise in private so that you remain friends with your victim. Woodrow Wyatt had always done that to me but I expected that of his kind; it was sad to find a fine journalist like Ian Jack in the same category.

His second, more measured letter never became public knowledge. But the tone and broad content of his first did: it quickly spread around the staff that our most talented writer had walked out in disgust with me, making a savage personal attack as he went. The following Sunday the *Observer* ran a page-one story highlighting Jack's departure and linking it with four other recent resignations. It hardly merited front-page billing but had been placed there by our main rival to maximize my discomfort and destabilize my editorship. It succeeded.

The morning the *Observer* published its story I was having breakfast with David Frost and a host of famous faces, including Prince Andrew and Sarah Ferguson, in the huge kitchen of his wife's ancestral home in Arundel, Sussex. I had been invited to join them for dinner the night before but the pickets got in the way of that; I arrived late on Saturday night, went to my room and joined everyone for breakfast next day. It was an informal affair with everybody reading the Sunday newspapers. Nobody said a word about the *Observer* story but it had clearly been devoured along with the bacon and eggs. I sensed an unspoken mood among my fellow guests: 'This editor is clearly on the way out. We won't be seeing him at this sort of event again.' I tried to appear unconcerned and looked for a diversion.

'I see you are being prepared for royal life,' I said to Sarah Ferguson, who was not yet engaged to Prince Andrew.

'Why do you say that?' she shot back.

'I understand you were doing the rounds of Parliament last week,' I replied. By sheer coincidence Michael Jones had happened to spot her being briefed in the Palace of Westminster on how Parliament worked.

'You're very well informed, Mr Neil,' she said with a smile.

David's lovely wife, Carina, had arranged for a guided tour of the historic house, seat of the Duke of Norfolk, her father. I found myself straggling at the back with Prince Andrew.

'I could do with a drink,' he said to me, looking bored.

'So could I,' I replied. 'It's past 11 o'clock.'

We disappeared up a corridor which we reckoned would take us back to the drawing room and the bar. But we got lost and ended up running back into the group being shown round the castle. Like giggling schoolboys we darted up another corridor. This time we found the bar: as we sipped our drinks the butler interrupted: 'The Prince of Wales is on the phone for you, Sir.'

'Please excuse me,' said the prince. 'If he's interrupted talking to his plants to call me it must be important.' I chuckled: though it was fashionable to knock Andrew for being a boor he was certainly easier company than his brother. I wondered if my mini-scoop – Fergie had effectively confirmed her forthcoming engagement to Andrew – would hold for a week. Back in Wapping they had rather more serious matters in mind.

By the middle of the second week in March – six weeks into Wapping – relations between me and the staff had reached rock bottom: the journalists had decided to vote on a motion of no confidence in their editor. I warned Rupert that I had a crisis on my hands. 'Leave it to me,' he said, 'I'll see the chapel committee.'

They met in his office. He listened attentively to their complaints, not just about me but about Wapping. He thanked them for their hard work in difficult times and said they had to understand the huge pressures their editor was under; but he would speak to me about softening my hard edges. He charmed them – but finished with a friendly but clear warning: 'If you pass a motion of no confidence in Andrew,' he said, softly but carefully, 'then you take on the whole company – and you take on me. I am behind Andrew one hundred per cent.'

The very fact that Rupert had agreed to see the journalists and give them a sympathetic ear was crucial in defusing the crisis. But he had also made it clear that they could not expect me to be cast out as a sacrificial lamb – that any fight with me was a fight with him. This encouraged them to draw back from open confrontation. The day had been saved for me by Rupert: I had been able to count on him in a tight spot. His support was to prove equally crucial in difficult times to come.

'You're far too blunt with these people,' he said after the

meeting. 'You have to be a bit more devious. Charlie Wilson [editor of *The Times*] has them eating out of his hands. Just be a bit more two-faced, be a bit more nice to them and then you can do what you want later on. Just try and soft-soap them a little bit.'

It was good advice, though being 'devious' did not come naturally to me; I was often too straightforward for my own good. In my university application back in the sixth form, Paisley Grammar's Rector had written 'forthright' at the start of his personal assessment of me. Under the pressure of Wapping 'forthright' had become 'blunt', even 'brutal'. I was well aware that there were lessons to learn.

'This is clearly a seminal moment in my editorship,' I wrote in an *aide-mémoire* afterwards. 'This is the biggest crisis I've had to face. It looks like Rupert has defused the situation. There's clearly much personal bitterness towards me among the staff (there is also some support) and "What can we do about the editor?" is now the common cry in the newsroom. It's not been a good episode for me. I'm not too happy about Rupert having had to come to my aid, because I feel it has undermined my position: I needed the proprietor to come and save me.' I felt vulnerable: if Rupert could save me he could also break me.

'Clearly there had been a breakdown of appreciation on both sides,' the *aide-mémoire* continued. 'My attitude was: "I've worked my guts out to keep this paper on the road and all they [the journalists] could do is bitch." Their attitude was that they had crossed the picket lines against their conscience and I didn't appreciate them. It is particularly depressing for me that, despite all the new appointments and the promotion of young people, there was such a big element of opposition in the staff of the paper. Rupert said he was surprised that even some of the people I had appointed were alienated from me. It's quite clear that my heavy-handed attitudes and handling of events had produced this. Praise and appreciation must now be the watch-words.'

After the meeting with Rupert I had a long heart-to-heart with Peter Wilby, education correspondent and father of the journalists' chapel. 'Look,' he said, 'we feel guilty about the five thousand people outside. Doing this, raising this issue and seeing Murdoch in person has been a reassertion of our power and our self-respect.'

'I suppose both editor and staff feel they don't appreciate each other,' I replied. 'I have secured the weekly production of the paper, which we could never guarantee before. Salaries had gone up by thirty per cent in two and a half years. I've got you the direct input, so that you control the journalism. I've hired thirty to forty young people, many of them women, and spent £750,000 easing out dead wood to make way for these young people. We have plans for the huge expansion of the paper. I'm afraid, given all that, my mood has too often and easily been "Stop moaning and bitching and get back to work".'

Wilby (who later succeeded Jack at the *Independent on Sunday*) and I parted on good terms, both promising a fresh start. I returned home late that night, feeling tired and low after an exhausting day. I checked the answering machine: 'The Johnstone girls have just cast three votes of confidence for you.' It was a charming message of support from Maureen Johnstone, one of my oldest friends, and her two girls, Sophie and Holly (my god-daughter). I smiled and shed a silent tear as I went to bed.

*

AS THE STAFF and their editor tried to patch things up an even more dangerous divorce was taking place: between *The Sunday Times* and its readers. I had been anxious about sales since the move to Wapping: we had more leftish readers of the sort likely to be anti-Wapping than any other News International title; we had been forced to go from three to five rather flimsy sections because of the limited capacity of the Wapping presses; and the print unions put the most effort into disrupting distribution on a Saturday night. But the circulation department assured me sales were holding up at over 1.2 million – down around 75,000 on the year but respectable given our difficulties. It was an illusion.

At a management meeting in April Bill Gillespie revealed out of the blue that the paper's sales had slumped to 1.16 million – 135,000 down on the year – soon after the dispute had begun. He reckoned they were still falling. I was dumbfounded. 'Why are we only discovering this now?' I asked. 'It's almost three months since the move to Wapping.' Gillespie waffled about the problems of getting a clear picture in the same way he had waffled about production problems in Gray's Inn Road.

Within weeks Gillespie produced another set of figures to show sales were hurtling towards the 1.1 million mark. 'Why are people not buying the paper?' Rupert asked. Gillespie rambled again then came to the point he wanted to make: 'I guess the feeling is that the paper is just not good enough,' he said, avoiding my gaze. 'Thanks a lot, Bill,' I thought.

'Don't turn your back on Gillespie,' Bruce Matthews had warned me recently. His words were coming true quicker than I thought they would. I was about to accuse him of covering up the huge flaws in the distribution of *The Sunday Times* until the audited sales figures meant he could no longer hide them. But Rupert stepped in before I could say a word.

'I think it's a great paper,' he said. 'People haven't yet worked out how to cope with a multi-section product and the distribution is terrible. We have to solve these problems. And I want a promotion campaign to push this paper – it deserves to sell a lot more copies. Let's go for this!' As he said the words he reached into a bag and pulled out a copy of the massive, multi-section Sunday *New York Times*. 'Now we have no union constraints on us let's push for a two hundred-page *Sunday Times*.' The advertising director gulped at the thought of all the extra advertising revenue he would have to find. 'That's what I've always wanted to do,' I replied.

Gillespie's attempts to blame me for the collapse in sales had crashed on take-off. Rupert had once again come to my rescue and placed our problems back in management's corner. It was Rupert the newspaper man at his best. 'Don't worry about the sales,' he said to me afterwards. 'You'll get them back. *The Sunday Times* was a very good paper last week; it deserves to do better.'

I was grateful for Rupert's support – again. But I decided to launch my own investigation. I hired a group of students to visit forty London newsagents on a Sunday morning and find out what was happening. They uncovered a chaotic situation. Many newsagents reported missing sections; those that did turn up were strewn across the floor instead of being inserted together (something the newsagents were paid 2p a section to do); deliveries to the shops were often too late for home delivery; and the company's sales reps were nowhere to be seen. It was a massive management failure – though the management had been happy to blame me and the quality of *The Sunday Times*. 'The newsagents are desperate for contact with News International,' the report concluded, 'so they can pour out their problems, but also so they can know they are loved by us. They feel we are neglecting them.'

I sent a copy of the report to everybody concerned. Nobody challenged it and Rupert commended its contents to those responsible for distribution. But I knew the problem ran deeper than distribution: we were losing the public relations battle and readers were deserting *The Sunday Times* because they disapproved of the whole Wapping venture. The public disliked the way the dispute was dragging on and, though the violence was escalating, thought we were heartless about the five thousand sacked print workers: people forgot that we had sacked them only after they had gone on strike and began to think they were on strike because we had sacked them. It was hard to make Rupert realize that the public mood was turning against us: he was back in Los Angeles and did not understand what all the fuss was about.

It was not just ordinary readers that were turning against us: the Establishment had little sympathy for us either. Bruce returned depressed one night from a black-tie dinner at Claridges of the ultra-exclusive 30 Club, an élite London dining club of big business types. 'They don't like what we're doing at Wapping,' said Bruce. 'The barbed wire, the violence, the refusal to settle the strike – they think it's a very un-British way of doing things. The unions are attracting a lot of sympathy. We have lost the benefit of the audacity of our move.'

I had very little sympathy for these Establishment complaints: they came from those in our society who had made selling out to the unions a way of life and disguised it as sensible compromise. The violent tactics of the print unions had hardened me against anything but victory: as the dispute dragged on through 1986 I told several close colleagues that if any settlement resulted in opening Wapping to the print unions I would resign: it would be a betrayal of the workers who had braved the picket lines and slowly but surely the Fleet Street workers would ease out the electricians and re-establish their old ways. I never wanted to work with them again. Even those colleagues who originally had doubts about Wapping agreed: we had all been hardened by Wapping. But I realized we were losing the PR battle. Charlie

Wilson shared my concern; we drafted a joint memo and sent it to Rupert.

> We need to make more effective use of the violence [we wrote]. It is getting worse and it will undermine the unions' cause. Other Fleet Street papers are unlikely to help. But TV and radio is anxious to do stories about violence and intimidation. We need to initiate such stories: there have been over two hundred attacks on TNT drivers; newsagents and delivery boys are being constantly harassed and our papers destroyed; the verbal abuse and intimidation on the picket line is just as sickening as the violence; one *Sunday Times* journalist [Sally Soames, one of our finest photographers] was verbally assaulted for being Jewish and her family threatened.

We even suggested making posters out of the one *Private Eye* cover that was vaguely favourable to our cause. It showed a photograph of Brenda Dean, the Sogat leader and the sympathetic face of the print unions, saying, 'We want our jobs back so we can go on strike.' But that was just cosmetics: what we wanted was a major initiative to recapture the high ground.

Rupert eventually agreed. Together we concocted something of a public-relations master-stroke: Rupert would offer the TUC, the Labour Party and the print unions our old site at Gray's Inn Road, complete with presses and £15 million in working capital (the amount due to them in statutory redundancy), where they could produce left-of-centre papers to their liking using whatever working practices they wanted. We never expected them to accept though Rupert would have been happy to hand it all over if they had. But the offer took the unions completely by surprise and wrong-footed them. It was the last thing the print unions wanted – they knew they could not keep their old labour practices

Cricket was in the blood of that handsome young chap in the jacket on the front row, second from the right. Unusual for a Scot – but then he always was a bit of a rebel.

This was the Paisley Grammar School 1st XI in 1967. It might have been the start of a great cricketing future but the local newspaper needed somebody to do match reports so I gave up playing for writing – almost certainly a sensible career move. It was my first experience of journalism – an opportunity for me which might have had something to do with the fact that my older brother was editor of the *Paisley Daily Express*. On the other hand, there was nobody on his staff who knew much about cricket – or wanted to spend their Saturday afternoons watching it.

I was delighted to do so, especially since the clubhouse bar was open all day and the tennis club next door was full of pretty girls. It was then it dawned on me that newspapers were prepared to pay you to do what you would do for free anyway. That seemed a pretty reasonable way to spend a life.

Above: My first day at *The Sunday Times*: you can tell how delighted everybody was to see me.

Below: The regular reception committee on the way in to work during the Wapping dispute.

Saturday night's all right for a fight: the mayhem that raged at Wapping's gates while *The Sunday Times* went to press behind riot police and barbed wire.

Above: A reconciliation of sorts: *The Sunday Times* had the rights to her memoirs but after seven years at daggers drawn, Margaret Thatcher was still wary.

Below: No reconciliation at all: Diana authorized the most infamous 'kiss and tell' in history, thereby putting an end to her marriage and the Crown into crisis.

Above: Interviewing the President in the Oval Office. I admired Ronald Reagan: most of the British press never learned not to underestimate him.

Below: My new friends at Sky Television.

Above: 'That's another couple of million just gone up in flames, Rupert.'

Below: Rupert Murdoch hated these extra-curricular activities and so did *The Sunday Times* newsdesk: doing the early morning radio show gave me a daily advantage in spotting the best stories.

My former Indian friend.

Above: Sweet victory in the Pamella Bordes/Peregrine Worsthorne libel case – but only by the skin of my teeth.

Below: Putting the finishing touches to 'Scargill: the Libyan Connection' with Insight's Paul Eddy.

and make a profit – but they had to be careful how they rejected it.

They eventually refused the offer because consultants told them (surprise, surprise) that it was impossible to run a paper profitably at Gray's Inn Road using their methods. For a while it helped us regain the PR initiative. But the violence continued to worsen and there were some Saturday nights when the sheer weight of picketing almost stopped our trucks getting out. If the print unions had realized how close they came to stopping our operations they might have redoubled their efforts.

Bruce and I continued to worry that the company's case was coming over badly to the general public, undermining journalists' morale and newspaper sales. The TUC and moderate print leaders like Sogat's Brenda Dean worried that the violent picketing was giving trade unionism a bad name. Dean, who had been elected by her provincial members and had little love for London Sogat, wanted to bring the dispute to an end with as much face as she could muster. Word reached Bruce that senior Sogat officials believed that, if the right cash offer were made, the dispute would be over. He had already been to see Norman Willis, the TUC general secretary, with company figures for revenues and circulation, to impress on him that the company was financially sound, despite the mass picketing. 'All seems to be going well for you,' Willis was forced to admit. Bruce had also made contact with Dean, who told him how much she hated Tony Dubbins, the hard-line boss of the rival NGA, and how a settlement was possible if Rupert came up with enough money. Bruce passed on this intelligence to Rupert.

'If it's only money that's dividing us,' said Rupert, 'then let's fix it. I'm prepared to deal direct with Dean.'

In the third week of April on a Friday afternoon in conditions of great secrecy, Rupert sent his private jet to

Heathrow, where it picked up Bruce, Brenda Dean and Bill Miles, Sogat's general officer, and flew them to Los Angeles, where Rupert was renting Roger Moore's house in Beverley Hills. They sat around the swimming pool for most of Saturday talking round the sum of money needed to end the strike. Dean and Miles demanded the usual Fleet Street 'going rate' of inflated redundancy payments. Rupert was not prepared to fork out that much – around £100 million – for 5,000 workers. At one stage he went inside out of the sun.

'Look,' said Bruce to Dean and Miles, 'he's never going to agree to £100 million. Settle for £50 million – it's still way above the statutory minimum and he might agree to that.' They thought about it while Bruce found Rupert in Roger Moore's study. There, surrounded by pictures of the James Bond star, Bruce pressed Rupert hard to make a £50 million offer in return for an end to the dispute and no jobs for Sogat or the NGA in Wapping. That night they went out to dinner in Hollywood: eventually Rupert put his £50 million on the table and Dean and Miles agreed to recommend it to their members. The NGA would have to follow suit.

When Bruce returned from Los Angeles he showed me a piece of yellow notepad paper with '£50 million compensation' written in blue ink in Rupert's handwriting. There was a smile on Bruce's face: it looked like the dispute was ending at last. But Dean could not quite steel herself to tell her members that a decent offer was available, never mind endorse it. It took her eight weeks to announce it, by which time the forces of resistance on Fleet Street and the left had got wind that something was afoot and were well-prepared to brand it a sell-out.

'Dean,' says Bruce, 'lacked the guts to sell it. She let me down by failing to give a lead while the militants told the pickets it was a sign of weakness that she had agreed to anything.' They carried the day: not for the first time the London chapels defied their own leadership, voting by 2,000 votes to 1,440 to continue strike action. 'It's very sad,' said Bruce quietly to me when news of the ballot came through on 6 June from the TUC. Kelvin MacKenzie, the *Sun* editor, was chirpier: 'Tell Rupert he's just saved £50 million.' But despite Kelvin's bravado Wapping was gripped by renewed depression: the pickets appeared to be on our doorstep indefinitely and the journalists looked to the future with gloom.

The Sunday Times chapel continued to pass increasingly strongly worded motions which hinted at possible strike action. Their beef was no longer with me but with the company. The manner of the move to Wapping still rankled. They were weary of a dispute which now looked open-ended, they hated working behind barbed wire and crossing picket lines and were unsettled by the critical acclaim which greeted the launch of the *Independent* while their journalistic efforts were still being derided by their peer group. The novelty of the new technology and modern offices had worn off. They felt they had been treated in a cavalier fashion by Rupert Murdoch, whom they thought continued to take them for granted.

I raised these concerns with management but nobody was much interested, largely because Rupert gave no indication that he thought it necessary to assuage the journalists' complaints. He had become increasingly unsympathetic and fractious during his flying visits to London, terrorizing his senior managers and making them too scared to take any decisions on their own. Relations between Bruce and Rupert were deteriorating fast. 'Rambo's running wild,' said Bruce in desperation to me one day, 'upsetting everybody. I wish he would stay away and let us get on with it.' Bruce was liked and trusted by all the Wapping editors and widely admired for his handling of a difficult dispute. But Rupert thought he was getting too big for his boots and resented his independence. He began to insist on approving even minor matters and they began to quarrel regularly.

'Thank God he's gone,' said a weary Bruce with a sigh of relief when Rupert had flown back to America after one of his whirlwind visits. 'He's a very sour man. Nobody can do anything right. He had a go at everybody this week. He even spent twenty minutes on the phone giving Charlie Wilson a bollocking. He gives the impression that he doesn't care about all our difficulties. It'll take me a week to restore everybody's morale. It took me at least that long to put out all the fires after his last visit.'

When Rupert returned Bruce said: 'I hope you won't go around attacking everybody again. A bit of praise would be more useful, especially for Charlie Wilson.' Rupert agreed to be more emollient; but he still insisted on ignoring sensible advice that he had to take special care with the journalists: Bruce had told him that his 3.5 per cent pay offer to the *Sun* was not good enough after all the journalists had been through, but Rupert swept such advice aside, averring that his beloved *Sun* staff would happily accept 3.5 per cent. It was a disastrous miscalculation: the loyal men and women of the *Sun* shouted down their union representative when he put the offer before them and voted for strike action.

Rupert panicked: a strike at the *Sun* was just the fillip the pickets needed. It threatened to undermine his whole position at Wapping. He retreated fast, upping the pay offer to 10 per cent, with no strings. The *Sun* withdrew its threat to strike. Rupert would have more readily dismissed such a rebellion at *The Sunday Times*: broadsheet journalists, he believed, were too prone to behave like a bunch of lazy, intellectual wimps. But if even his loyal *Sun* staff were in rebellious mood then maybe he would realize that it was time to make generous gestures to all Wapping journalists. I immediately faxed him a long memo entitled 'Morale building measures for journalists', explaining in detail what was needed, and trying to confront him with a fundamental truth:

> The manner of our move to Wapping still rankles with many [I wrote]. Whether we like or understand that, it is a fact: the journalists felt, and feel, they were taken for granted. They have been reinforced in their view by a general feeling that the company still takes them for granted. They appreciate they are being well paid. But they reckon they deserve that, given the pickets, the barbed wire and the very unusual circumstances they are being asked to work in. Not enough has been done to make them feel loved – to make them feel they are wanted and appreciated.

Rupert indicated to me he was in a mood to make concessions: events at the *Sun* had knocked his confidence. But *Sunday Times* journalists were close to a strike ballot. I called a mass meeting of all the staff.

'Let me share a few thoughts with you,' I said. 'There's no end in sight for the dispute, I have to be honest with you. It's not a matter of money any more. The only way to settle the dispute is if we let them into Wapping and give them jobs here, and I will not be a party to that. If that happens I will resign. We've got a lot of crisis management here and the result is that editorial has taken a back seat. We need a positive management to make the editorial needs a priority. Last night I sent Rupert a long list of things to be done. I think there is a change coming.'

I told the journalists what I had asked for and what Rupert had promised. 'There will be a 10 per cent pay rise with no strings. There will be the progressive removal of the barbed wire. I've been promised a healthclub and swimming pool; a proper darkroom and the library are now coming. We have new journalists joining and there will be more. Compensation was offered to the refuseniks but they would not take it. I will not sign blanket guarantees of re-instatement, nor will I operate a black list.'

The refuseniks, though much diminished in number, were still a tricky problem. The management and its lawyers had been pressing me for months to sack them. I had no intention of taking them back but I did not want to antagonize the staff by dismissing them outright. I wanted them to be paid off as part of an overall settlement of the dispute.

'We are expanding papers, the productions system now works,' I continued. 'We have people who are faithful, pleasant and industrious working the presses for us. If you strike now you let the paper down, you let me down when loyalty does matter. You let those that we work with down.'

I concluded with a warning: 'You'll be joining the pickets outside. You'll be throwing *The Sunday Times* into another crisis.'

The chapel voted not to strike. Rupert had saved me when the journalists wanted rid of their editor; now I had helped prevent a potentially disastrous strike among *Sunday Times* journalists. The swimming pool and the health club, however, never materialized. Perhaps this was confirmation of Kelvin MacKenzie's long held view that Rupert has little regard for journalists and will give them as little as he can get away with.

With the journalists squared, it became only a matter of time before the pickets realized their cause was futile. Brenda Dean was desperate for a settlement. In mid-January 1987, as the strike reached its first anniversary, she called Bill O'Neill in New York and said they had to meet. Bill said she would have to come to New York. She arrived on the Air

France Concorde via Paris. They met at the Hilton Hotel at JFK Airport and she had an astonishing proposal.

'Sue us into submission,' she said to Bill. 'I have a Sogat conference motion which says union funds must not be jeopardized. If renewed legal action by you were to threaten us with bankruptcy that conference motion would give me the pretext for a settlement, whatever the pickets think.'

'The danger is,' said Bill cautiously, 'that once we go down this road in the courts we might not be able to stop it. You could lose all your funds.'

'That's a risk I'm prepared to take to end this dispute,' replied Dean.

As they spoke, a woman sat near to them and picked up the phone: 'The dispute is close to being settled,' she reported. Dean and O'Neill froze. They thought they had been rumbled. But it turned out the woman was a reporter covering a strike on the Long Island Railroad.

Two weeks later and thirteen months into the dispute, with News International pursuing even tougher action in the courts as Dean had requested, the unions reluctantly accepted a lump-sum redundancy settlement no more generous than the £50 million offered to Brenda Dean in Hollywood nine months before. Not a single striker was given a job in Wapping. It had been one of the longest and most violent strikes in British industrial history yet News International had only ever lost one Saturday edition of *The Times* and *Sun*, during the first weekend of the dispute – a remarkable achievement. It ended in the total defeat of print unions which had once regarded themselves as invincible. The rest of Fleet Street was soon able to negotiate with them the sort of labour practices and new technology that they had refused us. The power of the print unions was broken for ever.

Victory, as usual, had many fathers. 'What a wonderful victory,' Robert Maxwell called to say on 7 February 1987, the day the dispute ended. 'Well done. I trust there will be no brutes outside your gates tonight.' Not unless you paid them, I thought to myself as I accepted his congratulations. Donald Trelford, the *Observer* editor, was another surprising supporter of our struggle. 'I much admire what you and Rupert have done,' he said. 'It has brought great benefits to our industry.'

'Thanks, Donald,' I replied. 'But I'd never have guessed it from your coverage of our struggle.'

It was also a defeat from which the career of Brenda Dean never quite recovered. Until Wapping she had been seen as the coming woman in the Labour Party. Some even spoke of her as 'Labour's Thatcher': smart, modern, tough, popular. It was thought that after a successful stint as the new face of progressive unionism a career beckoned in the Labour Party, with who knows what limit. But her failure to bring an early settlement at Wapping and the decline of the print unions post-Wapping left her a diminished figure in Labour circles and her undoubted potential was left unexploited. She was eventually given a life peerage (Labour knows how to look after its own, just like the Tories) and places on the quangos of the good and the great. But they all seemed a consolation prize for what might have been.

The morning after the strike ended I walked from my office to the main gates. Two policemen were there just in case any rebel printers still wanted to carry on the fight. But there were no pickets, no demonstrations, no riot police. I stood at the entrance and savoured my new freedom: for the first time since the move to Wapping thirteen months before it was safe to walk through the gates to my office.

*

WAPPING CAST ITS SHADOW long after the dispute was over. Years after my bodyguards had departed, I remained careful about personal security, avoiding anywhere, such as bars in the East End of London, where print workers might gather. Every now and then the Battle of Wapping would return to haunt me. One night in May 1987, on returning home after a late dinner with the American ambassador, the phone went. 'I'm going to get you,' said a Scottish accent. 'I know where you live. I'm going to get you. You broke up my family – you and that bastard Murdoch.'

'Thanks for your call,' I replied, hanging up and trying not to sound unnerved. But I was.

In the autumn of 1988, over a year after the pickets had gone, I was walking through Glasgow Airport to catch the shuttle back to London. My heart was heavy and my head was down: I had been visiting my father, who was dying. That morning I had kissed him goodbye on the forehead: he was so ill I doubt if he even knew I was there. I realized it was the last time I would see him.

I was shaken out of my sad thoughts as I headed for the shuttle gate by loud cursing and swearing from a group of people to my right. I looked up to see who or what it was they were shouting at: it was me – I had walked into a group of Sogat activists returning from a conference in Glasgow.

They rushed up and followed me on the long walk to the gate, howling obscenities every step of the way. People were wondering what was going on but sensibly kept their distance; there were, of course, no police around.

I checked in at the gate. As I turned round with my boarding pass one particularly obnoxious little man started spitting four-letter abuse in my face. I was already at a low enough ebb having just left my dying father. I did not need the attentions of this odious character. He was small enough to hit. I put my bag down and placed my boarding card in my left hand. As I pulled back my right fist, Gerry Malone appeared from nowhere, grabbed it and hustled me off on to the plane. He shoved me in a window seat in a crowded part of the aircraft so that my Sogat admirers had no room to join me, took the centre seat beside me and ordered two stiff drinks on take-off. It was sheer coincidence that he was returning to London on the same plane and I will always be grateful for his intervention. Two days later my brother called me at 6 a.m. to say that our father had died.

CHAPTER SEVEN

At the Court of the Sun King

WHEN YOU WORK FOR Rupert Murdoch you do not work for a company chairman or chief executive: you work for a Sun King. You are not a director or a manager or an editor: you are a courtier at the court of the Sun King – rewarded with money and status by a grateful King as long as you serve his purpose, dismissed outright or demoted to a remote corner of the empire when you have ceased to please him or outlived your usefulness.

All life revolves around the Sun King: all authority comes from him. He is the only one to whom allegiance must be owed and he expects his remit to run everywhere, his word to be final. There are no other references but him. He is the only benchmark and anybody of importance reports direct to him. Normal management structures – all the traditional lines of authority, communication and decision-taking in the modern business corporation – do not matter. The Sun King is all that matters.

Other courtiers who believe they are your boss may try to tell you what to do; but unless they have the ear of the Sun King on the particular matter at issue, you can safely ignore them if you wish. All courtiers are created equal because all have access to the King, though from time to time some are more equal than others. Even Sun Kings have a flavour of the month – though those who enjoy that privileged post at the Murdoch court must remember that a month is not a very long time.

The Sun King is everywhere, even when he is nowhere. He rules over great distances through authority, loyalty, example and fear. He can be benign or ruthless, depending on his mood or the requirements of his empire. You never know which: the element of surprise is part of the means by which he makes his presence felt in every corner of his domain. He may intervene in matters great or small: you never know when or where, which is what keeps you on your toes and the King constantly on your mind. 'I wonder how the King is today?' is the first question that springs to a good courtier's mind when he wakes up every day.

Even when the Sun King has not expressed an interest or shown any desire to become involved, or you think his attention is absorbed in another part of his vast empire, such is his omnipresence that you strive to keep in mind whatever you think his wishes are. The knack of second-guessing the Sun King is essential for the successful courtier; anticipation of his attitudes is the court's biggest industry. It is fatal ever to make the mistake of taking him for granted.

All Sun Kings have a weakness for courtiers who are fawning or obsequious. But the wisest – among whom we must number Rupert Murdoch – know they also need courtiers with brains, originality and a free spirit, especially in the creative media business. But independence has its limits: Sun Kings are also control freaks – and they are used to getting their way.

No matter how senior or talented or independent-minded, courtiers must always remember two things vital to survival: they must never dare to outshine the Sun King; and they must always show regular obeisance to him to prove beyond peradventure that, no matter how powerful or important they are, they know who is boss.

My problem was that I was not very good at either of these courtly virtues. I was too inclined to become a public personality in my own right; and I am not by nature deferential – to call anybody 'boss' sticks in the throat. Looking back, it is remarkable I survived so long at the court of King Rupert and enjoyed it so much – a decade-long rollercoaster ride with the man who runs the world's greatest media empire.

*

THE BIGGEST PLUS ABOUT HAVING Rupert Murdoch as your proprietor is that he has no great social aspirations in Britain. He does not seek the approval of the Establishment nor is he interested in their baubles, having turned down a knighthood and a peerage. This is a huge advantage for an editor out to make waves: when various parts of the Establishment objected to our coverage of the Thatcher government or the Royal Family or whatever powerful interest we had most recently upset, they often tried to work through Rupert to put pressure on me. He invariably resisted their blandishments.

I grew to learn that you could count on Rupert in a tight spot, even when he did not agree with what you had done. Our exposé of Denis Thatcher's bank account (see Chapter 9) brought down on us the wrath of Margaret, his heroine, but Rupert never criticized me for running the story: the most he ever said was that maybe we had given it too much prominence (and, in retrospect, he was probably right). When a constitutional crisis flared round our story of the Queen falling out with Mrs Thatcher (see Chapter 8) and there were calls for my head, Rupert was as solid as a rock. Even when he disagreed with my attack on the Royal Family during the Gulf War, and its supporters were baying for my blood, he never gave them any joy.

It helps, of course, that Rupert is a closet republican. He

does not want his papers openly to espouse republicanism because he believes that would be bad for sales. When tackled about his views he always obfuscates and dissembles, saying it is up to the British people, as he did when William Shawcross interviewed him for his recent biography, *Murdoch*. In private, he leaves you in no doubt he would sweep them away tomorrow if he had the chance: he regards them as the apex of a class system that has held Britain back – and slighted him on numerous occasions. He is enthusiastic about proposals to replace the Queen as head of state in Australia with a president.

He could be robust with complaining advertisers. Mohamed Al-Fayed, the owner of Harrods, called me one night in the mid-eighties to complain about a story we had run criticizing the way he was renovating the house in Paris once occupied by the Duke and Duchess of Windsor. I offered him space to put his point of view. He demanded a retraction and an apology. I refused. He threatened to withdraw all Harrods' advertising from Times Newspapers.

'You can't do that,' I said.

'Why not?' he asked. 'It's my advertising.'

'Because as of this moment,' I replied, 'you are banned from advertising in *The Sunday Times*.'

He hung up, somewhat mystified. A little later the phone rang again. It was John King, the chairman of British Airways. He sought to intercede on Mohamed's behalf. 'Look, John,' I said firmly, 'I've just banned Britain's biggest department store; I'm happy to ban Britain's biggest airline too.' I was clearly in a bad mood.

'I think I'll just stay out of this,' said John.

'Good idea,' I replied.

A half hour later the phone went again. It was Rupert, calling from New York. This, I thought, could be a tough one.

'I hear you've just banned our biggest advertiser,' he said.

'Yes,' I replied, explaining the circumstances.

'How much do Harrods spend with us?' he enquired.

'About £3 million,' I said nervously. There was silence at the other end of the line. I contemplated whether it would be better to back down or resign and become an unlikely hero of the chattering classes.

'F—— him if he thinks we can be bought for £3 million,' he said, and hung up.

Years later I visited the Windsor house in Paris. It seemed to me Mohamed had done a magnificent job of restoring the house, which was almost exactly as the Windsors had left it. But I did not regret my stance: once one advertiser knows you are a soft touch they all do and editing a paper free of commercial pressure becomes an impossibility. Anyway, Harrods had come back to *The Sunday Times* when it discovered no other paper could rival its upmarket advertising clout.

Relations with Rupert remained cordial for a lot longer than they might partly because he was not living over the shop. It was tough enough for him to keep tabs on everything when he was based in New York, but at least New York is on the same information network as London. When he moved to Los Angeles, which is on another planet as far as the news agenda is concerned, he found himself becoming increasingly out of touch. When he called from LA one day I remember saying enthusiastically, 'We've a great story for Sunday.'

'Great story?' he repeated. 'They wouldn't recognize one in LA if it came round the corner and hit them.' For all the power and glamour of owning a major motion-picture studio and an American television network, he still hankers for Fleet Street. He regards British newspapers as the best in the world; for all he believes that the future is with television, he will never give newspapers up: they are his first and last love.

*

THERE IS A COMMON MYTH among those who think Rupert Murdoch has too much power and influence that he controls every aspect of his newspapers on three continents, dictating an editorial before breakfast, writing headlines over lunch and deciding which politician to discredit over dinner. He has been known to do all three. But he does not generally work like that: his control is far more subtle.

For a start he picks as his editors people like me who are generally on the same wavelength as him: we started from a set of common assumptions about politics and society, even if we did not see eye to eye on every issue and have very different styles. Then he largely left me to get on with it.

But you always have to take Rupert into account: he is too smart to ignore. The snobbery of his British enemies has meant they have constantly underestimated him: they have regarded him as something of a colonial hick because of his 'Dirty Digger' image and strong Australian accent. His competition has had to learn the hard way he is one of the smartest men in business with a restless, ruthless brain that is more than a match for any British competition, in newspapers or broadcasting. With a mind that is always buzzing, always up on the issues and always original, it means his editors have to be on their toes if they are to keep up with him.

When I took the job of *Sunday Times* editor I imagined a short honeymoon before I would feel his wrath. In fact, he left me alone for most of the decade, keeping a wary eye on my progress from a distance, intervening only when he felt strongly about something. He would more often than not call me as the paper was going to press on a Saturday (though there were weeks, sometimes months, when I would not hear from him at all) to find out what was on the front page and share political gossip, which is Rupert's stock-in-trade – give him some good inside information and he will go away happy, even if you haven't a very good paper to tell him about.

He never barked orders to change what I was planning for the front page; he was invariably complimentary about our story list and would usually finish his calls with his customary courtesy by thanking me for all my hard work and saying he looked forward to reading the paper. He only once ever directly tried (and failed) to influence the paper's editorial line when, in the 1990 Tory leadership contest, I decided to back Michael Heseltine's attempt to oust Margaret Thatcher (see Chapter 9). On no other occasion did he ever discuss an editorial with me (bar the one for the special Wapping supplement in 1986), either before or after publication. Nor did he ever try to tell me what – or what not – to put on the front page. He kept to the letter of his promises to Parliament of editorial independence when he bought Times Newspapers in 1981.

Editorial freedom, however, has its limits: Rupert has an uncanny knack of being there even when he is not. When I did not hear from him and I knew his attention was elsewhere, he was still uppermost in my mind. When we did talk he would always let me know what he liked and what he did not, where he stood on an issue of the time and what he thought of a politician in the news. Such is the force of his personality that you feel obliged to take such views carefully into account. And why not? He is, after all, the proprietor.

Rupert is a highly political animal: even meetings about some technical matter to do with colour printing or pagination would invariably begin with an exchange of views on the current political scene in America or Britain. Business and politics are his only two passions: art, music, hobbies, poetry, theatre, fiction, even sport (sailing may be an exception) have no interest for him. He is fascinated by politics for its own sake – but also because politics affects the business environment in which he operates.

Rupert expects his papers to stand broadly for what he believes: a combination of right-wing Republicanism from America mixed with undiluted Thatcherism from Britain and stirred with some anti-British Establishment sentiments as befits his colonial heritage. The resulting potage is a radical-right dose of free-market economics, the social agenda of the Christian Moral Majority and hardline conservative views on subjects like drugs, abortion, law and order, and defence.

He is much more right-wing than is generally thought but will curb his ideology for commercial reasons (thankfully, he realized that a *Sunday Times* which entirely reflected his hard-right politics, especially on social issues, would lose readers). In the 1988 American presidential election his favourite for the Republican nomination was Pat Robertson, the far-right religious fanatic who claims to speak in tongues, has direct access to God, takes credit for having convinced the Lord for sparing America from Hurricane Gloria and believes in a 'Jewish money conspiracy'. 'You can say what you like,' Rupert said to me during the Republican primary campaign, 'he's right on all the issues.' During the Thatcher years he regularly sought assurances that, should the lady fall under a bus, Norman Tebbit would be her successor as British prime minister.

His instincts on many political issues come from the gut. One time when we were talking about the need for the radical reform of welfare I remarked that we still had to make sure there was a basic provision – a safety net – for everybody. 'Yeah, yeah, maybe,' he growled, 'but it should be very low.' On another occasion he called to find out what was in one of Nigel Lawson's budgets. I started to go through the details. He quickly interrupted: 'But has he cut government, will government be smaller as a result of this budget?' Judged by this fundamental light, I had to admit, the budget was a failure.

Since the demise of Reagan and Thatcher, Rupert has found nobody to replace them in his affections on either side of the Atlantic. He supported Robert Dole in the 1996 presidential campaign without enthusiasm and because he loathes Bill Clinton; but Dole is far too moderate a conservative for his tastes. So was George Bush: in 1992 he voted for Ross Perot. He detests John Major with a vehemence few outside Rupert's own circle have appreciated. After Thatcher was removed all his papers (except *The Sunday Times*) backed Major to stop Heseltine becoming Tory leader. But Rupert quickly grew disillusioned with Major, whom he regards as a weak, indecisive man, not up to the job.

He is less absorbed by British politics these days, which is good news for his editors, and now has no right-wing favourite in Britain: he regularly urged the virtues of Michael Portillo on me, though backed off when I argued he was too voter-unfriendly. He is determined, however, to stop Chris Patten ever becoming prime minister: he thinks him too 'wet' and bears a grudge against the Hong Kong governor's tough line with Beijing, which has not been good for Rupert's business in China, where his Hong Kong based Star satellite-TV service is trying to gain a foothold. 'It may be just my wallet talking,' he said to me in 1993, 'but I think Patten is making a hash of it. He's trying to make a name for himself back in Britain; but he's a lightweight who's screwing everything up.'

Where political principle and business expediency clash,

you can be pretty sure expediency will win. When his business interests force him into an expedient solution which goes against his political grain, a convoluted thought process then takes place to justify his position.

When I informed him in 1987 that I had secured serialization rights to Tom Bower's highly critical biography of Robert Maxwell, his great rival, he was delighted. Rupert believed Maxwell was a crook and a KGB agent. 'I hope it takes the lid off him,' he said.

Serialization was set for February 1988. As the New Year began I started to get calls from Rupert questioning why we were doing it. 'There's an unwritten agreement that proprietor does not attack proprietor,' he said. 'I hear the book's not very good anyway – and nobody's interested in Maxwell.'

The pressure to pull the serialization grew; I resisted – we were publicly committed and could not renege without suspicious questions being raised – but I also wondered what had changed Rupert's mind. I discovered that he had begun talks with his great rival for Maxwell's newspapers to use the News International distribution system, at huge savings to both newspaper groups.

Instead of *The Sunday Times* 'lifting the lid' on Maxwell he wanted to do nothing to upset him. Maxwell was trying to injunct the Bower book and leaning on Rupert to pull the serialization. Hence the increasingly bad-tempered calls to me.

I was angered by the pressure and refused to budge: editor and proprietor were at a stand off. 'Do you really have to publish all the dirt about his business dealings?' asked Rupert. 'That's what's really worrying him.' I said that parts of the book were very dense and that Maxwell's complex business dealings would probably make only one extract. 'Good,' said Rupert, 'I'll tell him.' He then moaned again about why we were bothering with it all: it was clear he was itching to tell me to withdraw it, but feared my reaction.

I was in America when my deputy, Ivan Fallon, called from London to tell me Maxwell had just issued a statement as part of his campaign to have the Bower book banned, saying Murdoch had personally assured him that *The Sunday Times* would not be touching the book. If that was true, I felt a resignation coming on.

I was due to see Rupert in his *New York Post* office that afternoon. I stormed in, clutching a piece of wire copy, and thrust it at him. 'This makes my position untenable,' I said in despair. 'It means either *The Sunday Times* publishes Bower or you're looking for a new editor.'

Rupert read the wire copy. 'Stupid bastard,' he said, referring to Maxwell. 'I never told him that – I only told him you'd keep his business affairs to one extract. And I never told him to go public. The bastard can't keep his mouth shut. Dot! [Rupert's faithful PA] get that shit Maxwell on the phone!'

There followed a transatlantic telephone call dominated by expletives at the end of which Rupert turned and said angrily: 'Publish what you want!' I had won – but only because Maxwell had overplayed his hand.

In the eighties Rupert insisted on the hardest of lines against the 'evil empire' of the Soviet Union, as befits a right-wing hawk. At one stage he tried to convince Ian Chapman, chairman of Collins (the book publishers in which Rupert had a substantial stake but not yet complete control), not to publish the memoirs of Mikhail Gorbachev, the Soviet leader, when he was at the height of his reforming phase. Chapman thought it a great publishing coup and I had agreed to buy the British serialization rights. But Rupert hated the idea.

'He's still a Communist, you know,' he snapped at Chapman over the phone.

'I realize that,' replied the Collins boss, 'but he's also a historic figure and we'll be publishing his memoirs while he's still in power.'

Further argument ensued. When Rupert saw he was getting nowhere he finished with a frustrated flourish: 'Well, Ian, if you're content to be an arm of Soviet propaganda, go ahead and publish.'

Chapman did not rise to the bait, the conversation ended and Collins published the book.

Yet Rupert has cosied up to China, another evil Communist empire, in the nineties.

This has required a wrenching U-turn in attitudes towards China since the mid-eighties, when Thatcher was negotiating with Beijing over the future of Hong Kong. Rupert wanted his papers to take a tough line to stiffen her resolve against China. 'She should hold out,' he told me one day, 'make no concessions and tell the Chinese that there's a Trident submarine off their coast: if the Red Army moves into Hong Kong they should be left in no doubt that we'll nuke Beijing . . . though I suppose we could fire a warning nuke into a desert first,' he added, after a moment's thought.

I think I'll leave this one for the *Sun*, I thought to myself, trying to change the subject.

There is no mystery as to why Rupert has changed his tune: he will always moderate his political fundamentalism if it suits his business strategy. He had no business interests in the Soviet Union in the eighties; he is selling satellite TV to the Chinese in the nineties.

Despite being one of nature's conservatives, he found it expedient to support Australia's Labour Party in the days when their right-wing opponents had no chance of winning; for the same reasons, and partly out of sheer disgust with

Major's failure to push the Thatcher revolution to its conclusion, he is now toying with supporting Tony Blair's New Labour in Britain. If the Tories were certain to win a fifth term, he would have less time for Blair.

Rupert met Blair for the first time over dinner at a private room at Mosimann's, the fancy private restaurant club in a former Belgravia church, on Thursday 15 September 1994, when Blair had been Labour leader for only a few months. The dinner was arranged by Gus Fischer, then Rupert's senior man in London. Gus had been lobbying the Labour Party on News International's behalf on such issues as cross-media ownership and Sky TV's control of satellite scrambling systems. He had made contact with Chris Smith and Mo Mowlam, two media spokespersons on the Blair frontbench, and even lured them to lunch at Wapping, quite an achievement since much of Labour still regards the place as the devil's furnace, after what happened to the print unions there in 1986.

Gus had also struck up a relationship with Blair and urged Rupert to meet him on the grounds that the company 'could not talk only to the Tories'. Rupert was happy to oblige since he regarded Major as a lost cause; Blair was odds-on to be the next prime minister and he was intrigued to see at first hand this new acceptable face of Labour – a party Rupert loathes, despite his support for it until the 1979 general election. Besides, both Rupert and Gus had something important on which to sound Blair out: they were worried about a growing sentiment in favour of union recognition among the Wapping workforce and feared a Labour government would change the law to make it easier for unions to organize.

The dinner went very well. Blair discovered Rupert was not the ogre his party had painted and Rupert found what Blair had to say a refreshing change from the usual Labour nostrums. Both revelled in being self-styled radicals, impatient with the old Britain. Blair indicated that media ownership rules would not be onerous under Labour, Rupert that his newspapers were not wedded to the Tories. The union issue was not resolved: Labour remains committed to giving workers the legal right to collective bargaining if over 50 per cent of any workforce votes for union recognition. But at least the lobbying – and Rupert's charm offensive – had begun.

'Well, he certainly says all the right things,' remarked Rupert after Blair had departed. 'But we're not letting our pants down just yet.' They met again – and Blair was invited to address a high-level conference of Rupert's most senior executives on Hayman Island, Australia, in the summer of 1995.

Blair began to think that at least the hostility of the Murdoch papers to Labour could be neutralized – and that one or two might even support him in a general election. His Australian speech was specifically designed to appeal to Murdoch and his henchmen. Jonathan Powell had become Blair's chief of staff in 1995. The diplomat brother of Sir Charles Powell, Thatcher's chief foreign policy adviser in Downing Street, he had a clear understanding of the political importance of the popular media, especially after a stint in the British Embassy in Washington when he had closely followed press coverage of Clinton's 1992 presidential campaign.

Powell consulted several News International executives to try and discover a theme that would sell well. Blair wrote much of the speech himself, with Powell's guidance, on the long plane journey to Australia. The result was a speech in which Blair, though he stood his centre-left ground on many issues, described himself as the natural successor to the Thatcher revolution. Rupert was impressed: he started telling his confidants that Blair would indeed get his support. Almost immediately, stories started appearing in the *Sun* and the *News of the World* praising New Labour and attacking the tired Tories. Irwin Stelzer, Rupert's long-time confidant and a formidable policy analyst in his own right, began meeting with Blair regularly, at the Labour leader's instigation, to discuss various important issues privately.

By the end of 1995 Rupert's editors were in little doubt that Blair was his man. But as 1996 progressed the signals became more blurred. Blair was still popular with Rupert but he started getting cold feet about the prospect of a Labour government, particularly as its pro-Europe stance became more apparent. The final outcome of the dalliance between Murdoch and Blair has yet to be seen. Whatever happens it will be a clever calculation on Rupert's part, perhaps some of his papers supporting Blair, others sticking with the Tories, none savaging Labour the way the *Sun* did in 1983, 1987 and 1992. Having voted for Perot in America in 1992, he might even be tempted to throw one or two papers behind Britain's maverick third-party leader, Sir James Goldsmith, and his anti-Europe Referendum Party. But there is time for subtle deals to be done with the mainstream parties before it comes to that. Says Gus Fischer, who has seen him operate at close quarters, 'I've never seen anybody more astute at manipulating politicians to his advantage than Rupert.'

*

I AGREED WHOLEHEARTEDLY only with the free-market part of Rupert's policy agenda, though like him I was also something of a Cold War warrior – the combination was enough to keep him satisfied about our editorial line for most of the time. I had little time for his social agenda, especially that part inspired by America's Christian right, to which he became more devoted as the eighties progressed. He never struck me as a religious man – for Rupert's religion is an extension of politics – and I believe he liked the Christian right for political rather than religious reasons.

But he is also under the influence of Anna, his strong-willed wife who is a staunch Catholic. He took up a fundamentalist anti-abortion position. Late one night he told me he was considering turning Catholic. 'Since we both come from the same Scottish Presbyterian stock you can hardly expect me to be over the moon at that prospect,' I replied, surprised at my own bluntness. He never raised the subject again – nor did he turn Catholic. I still suspect his Christian fundamentalism owes more to political expediency than religious conviction.

There were occasions when *The Sunday Times* reflected very little of what its owner thought; but it did so enough of the time for us not to fall out. I was able regularly to criticize Margaret Thatcher, even though he adored her. Criticizing Ronald Reagan was a more risky business: Reagan was Rupert's first love.

I admired Reagan's economic and foreign policies too, so there was not much friction between us. But I felt it impossible to support the President's Iran-Contra shenanigans: Rupert suffered our attacks on his hero in sullen silence because he knew Reagan had screwed up. But he regarded Oliver North, Reagan's wayward White House assistant, as a national hero: 'He sold weapons to the Iranians, freed hostages and used Middle East money to finance the Contras,' he once said to me admiringly. 'The man deserves the Congressional Medal of Honour.'

He did not expect to see his particular views immediately reflected in the next edition of *The Sunday Times* after one of our many talks, though he would not have objected if they had been. But he had a quiet, remorseless, sometimes threatening way of laying down the parameters within which you were expected to operate. Editors whose sole purpose is survival have to become adept at reading Rupert Murdoch: stray too far too often from his general outlook and you will be looking for a new job. It can be strangely oppressive, even when you agree with him: the man is never far from your mind. Rupert dominates the lives of all his senior executives. One who parted company from him fifteen years ago confessed to me that he had only recently stopped dreaming about him. He still pops up from time to time in mine.

His first love is tabloid journalism (witness his willingness to sustain open-ended losses at the *New York Post* because of the enjoyment the paper gives him); it is what gets his juices going and he has a brilliant populist sense for it. The wall of his office at Twentieth Century Fox in Los Angeles is covered with front pages from the *Sun* and the *News of the World*; there is nothing from *The Sunday Times* or *Times*. Despite his privileged upper-middle-class background he sees himself as an anti-Establishment man of the people (which he once wincingly described on BBC TV's *Wogan Show* as the 'common people') and believes his tabloids speak for their concerns, even though he has never had any real contact with Britain's 'common people' and mingles largely with Establishment types when he is in Britain. As his empire in America has expanded he has grown out of touch with Britain. The popular hatred for the poll tax, for example, remained a mystery to him, though he was quite content for me to oppose it.

He has a less certain touch for broadsheets. It has taken him almost two decades to make a circulation success of *The Times* – and then only by spending tens of millions on price-cutting, which means it is still accumulating substantial losses. At one stage in the eighties he dragged it too far downmarket, creating a gap at the top end which the

Independent filled and which has cost Rupert dear to rectify. Though it would grieve him to think so, he has become an old-fashioned *Times* proprietor of the type he used to sneer at, keeping the paper going at a loss for years because of the power and prestige it brings its owner.

We were always broadly in agreement about the general direction of *The Sunday Times*, especially its development into a multi-section giant. Any pressure he did exert, however, was in a downmarket direction: he complained regularly that there was too much politics in the paper, that it was too issue-driven and that it needed more human interest stories and personality pieces. Sometimes the best reaction was to nod in agreement then do nothing in the hope he would forget; it usually worked. A close aide once explained to me that Rupert sometimes counted on his best people *not* to do his bidding – it allowed him to make broad attacks, which he enjoys. He once instructed me to redesign *The Sunday Times* so that it looked exactly like *The Times*. I saw no reason to revamp the paper to make it look like one with a third of our circulation. A few months later he asked angrily why I had not done the redesign; I explained again why I thought it would be a mistake. He insisted on doing it. I did nothing. He forgot or perhaps even deferred; the matter was never raised again.

There were times when you thought you had the most wonderful proprietor on earth. I remember flying to New York in 1987 to impress on him the case for a *Sunday Times* tabloid Books section. The move to Wapping had made it technically possible to pre-print such a section and I thought it would bolster our position among the liberal-left when some of the paper's politics were putting them off. But there was no money in it since, unlike their American counterparts, Britain's publishers are an uncommercial bunch who do not think they need to advertise.

Rupert agreed that a Books section would widen the paper's appeal even if it was a loss-maker; he backed it against a resistant advertising department which lacked the sophistication to win what advertising there was from publishers. Better than that, as we sat in his New York apartment he began folding bits of paper together to work out the press configuration which would allow us to wrap a broadsheet Travel section round a tabloid Books, which was how the *Washington Post* did it. I had gone to argue for one section and left with two: I walked back down Park Avenue to my apartment feeling ten feet tall. When I returned to London and unveiled my plans for two new sections the Wapping management said it could not be done. 'Rupert says it can,' I replied. It was.

Rupert gives his broadsheet editors far more latitude than his tabloid ones. If you want to know what Rupert Murdoch really thinks then read the *Sun* and the *New York Post*. His name is above the editorial of the *Post* as 'Editor-in-Chief'; there are no names on the editorial page of the *Sun* but his is written in invisible ink – the *Sun* reflects what Rupert thinks on every major issue. He dislikes Europe, for example, and barely even visits it as a tourist. He despises the idea of the European Union: hence the *Sun*'s strident anti-European line. If the paper backs Tony Blair at the next election you can be sure it is because Rupert Murdoch has so decreed it; if it doesn't, it will be because he fears New Labour is too pro-Brussels.

Though he loves his tabloids and affects an inverted snobbery of disdain towards his broadsheets – he once sneered at me in a management meeting for working at the 'unpopular' end of the market – he is far more brutal with his tabloid editors, who live in fear of his calls. I only ever had a few harsh words with Rupert on the phone in eleven years; he nearly always treated me with respect, courtesy and sometimes even kindness. Others were not so lucky.

Kelvin MacKenzie of the *Sun* endured almost daily 'bollockings' from the man he always referred to as 'the boss' – a steady stream of transatlantic vituperation and four-letter words was his regular diet for over twelve years, even though he ran a paper which netted his proprietor £70–90 million a year. 'He treats the tabloid editors like dirt,' confirms John Dux, who was managing director at Wapping in the early nineties. 'Kelvin used to go into great depressions after Rupert's onslaughts. When you run the most successful tabloid in the world it is not nice being regularly told you're a f—— idiot by your proprietor.'

The abuse did not get better with time. A depressed Kelvin called me in February 1992. 'I've just had the worst ever four-letter tongue-lashing from Rupert,' he informed me. 'I came very close to resigning last night. I've told Gus Fischer that I can't take any more from that Australian bastard.

'Monty [David Montgomery, then editor of *Today*] has also been lambasted. In effect, Rupert said to him, "I don't like your f—— paper, and I don't like you!" John Dux has been thumped as well.'

Aren't I the lucky one, I thought. I've not heard from Rupert for two weeks and all he wanted to talk about was the state of the British recession and the effect it might have on his UK revenues. He hasn't even called to complain about my editorial on the royals and the Gulf War (see Chapter 8).

In the summer of 1993 Kelvin finally snapped: in the middle of a particularly bruising face-to-face encounter with Rupert in his office, Kelvin simply stood up, put on his jacket and walked out. His resignation followed within hours, by fax from home. He refused to take Rupert's calls or answer his faxes. 'I've gone too far this time,' Rupert confessed to Gus Fischer. 'Will you intercede on my behalf?' It took Gus several days to talk Kelvin round to returning, with Rupert even promising, 'I'll change.'

Rupert got his way and treated Kelvin with more respect after that. But things were never quite the same again: the whipping-boy had finally stood up to the boss – and the boss was unsettled by it. Kelvin was soon moved from his beloved *Sun* to Sky Television early in 1994. My belief is that Kelvin's revolt in 1993 led directly to that unhappy and short-lived transfer, which, given the obvious fact that Kelvin and Sky's boss, the cantankerous Sam Chisholm, were bound to fall out, could easily be construed as a disguised firing.

Kelvin was not the only Wapping editor to experience regular 'bollockings'. Wendy Henry and Patsy Chapman used to live in fear and trembling of his calls when they were editors of the *News of the World*; they would call me almost every Saturday afternoon to ask if I knew where Rupert was, if he had called – and what kind of mood he was in. Patsy found it particularly tough to cope with Rupert's telephone terrorism: she suffered a nervous breakdown from the pressure and had to resign. Rupert made sure the company picked up the medical bills. Even somebody as tough as David Montgomery was once reduced to trembling silence when he was editor of *Today* by a call dressing him down for daring in an editorial to support Nigel Lawson in his economic battles with Margaret Thatcher.

There was an element of the bully in this: Rupert ranted at Kelvin and others because he knew he could get away with it – they were prepared to put up with it. I think Rupert sensed that I would be out of the door before he finished uhis sentence if he talked to me in the same way; he never did. I always made it clear that if he was unhappy with my editorship I would not fight him to keep it – I would walk whenever he wanted, provided the pay-off was right. But I would not take being scolded like a schoolboy. Telephone terrorism is his weapon of choice to make sure his influence extends throughout his worldwide empire. He was often grumpy with me on the phone for no particular reason – and sometimes downright curmudgeonly, especially when the jetlag was bad. His global flying schedule regularly added to his bad-tempered calls. He takes sleeping pills to help cope with the time-zone changes, prescribed by a friendly doctor in Wapping. Gus Fischer used to deliver regular supplies to him in America but Rupert's trusty personal assistant, Dot, was always worried that he would become too dependent on them. 'I'll take these,' Dot would say when Gus arrived, so she could ration their use. But if they helped him to sleep on planes they did not make him any more cordial when he hit the phone on arrival. These were the calls I came to dread, not because I feared their consequences but because they were unpleasant and pointless. It was never quite clear why he was in such a bad mood – whether I or Kelvin or some other editor was the cause of it or whether it was because he was dog-tired from his perpetual globetrotting. There were simply times when he relished giving his underlings a bad time. You sensed the bleak atmosphere the moment you lifted the phone.

There was nothing you could say on such occasions to cheer him up or please him: he would quarrel with every remark you made, no matter how trivial, and nitpick the previous Sunday's paper while praising the weakest stories of our rivals. He was determined to be miserable. If I had said, 'Rupert, I've discovered a billion dollars in gold bars in the basement at Wapping. I'm shipping them to you today,' he would have replied, 'Why didn't you find two billion?'

He punctuated such calls with long silences – traps inviting you to say something else with which he could disagree.

You'd say something innocuous to keep the conversation going like, 'Thatcher's doing better these days,' and he'd snap back, 'It won't last.' Or I'd say, 'The *Sunday Telegraph* was pretty weak,' and he'd reply, 'They had better page-one stories than you.'

These calls were not designed to build morale; they left me angry and depressed. But over time I learned how to deal with them: when his 'silent routine' began – I decided to say nothing. It worked. I remember one call when he seemed to have nothing to say – certainly nothing nice – and I just let the silence run. It became a test of wills, with the cost of a transatlantic call running up as neither of us said anything. I could have gone and made a cup of tea. Just as I was about to crack he finally said, 'Are you still there?'

'Yes, Rupert,' I replied.

'Sorry, I have to go now,' he said. 'Thanks for everything.' And off he went. I never got the silent treatment again.

There is a Jekyll and Hyde quality to Rupert Murdoch: despite the bad-tempered calls, there were many times when he was courteous, even charming. Almost every time he called he began by asking if he was not interrupting something important; of course, there is nothing more important to a courtier than a call from the Sun King. One Friday, when he was in London and I was behind with the editorial, I put a 'Do Not Disturb' notice on my office door. I learned later that he had come across to see me, looked at the notice and gone for a chat with the deputy editor, who advised him that the notice was not meant for him. 'No,' said Rupert, 'it means Andrew's busy. I'll leave him alone.'

Some of our frostiest times were over something I had said publicly about his tabloids. Though I did not share the usual snobbery about them, I was always uneasy about working for a group that included the *News of the World* and

Sun. One of the drawbacks of the move to Wapping was that we were thrown together cheek by jowl. Our many enemies on the other broadsheets sneered by referring to the *News of the World* and *Sun* as our 'sister' papers and *The Sunday Times* was often contaminated by their antics through corporate association with them. To distance our own journalism from them and because I believe certain journalistic standards are universal regardless of the shape of the paper I felt it necessary sometimes to be critical. Several times in public I was less than complimentary about their sleazier journalism and underhand methods; in the 1980s I feared their excesses would give politicians the pretext to shackle us all with legal curbs. Nothing was more calculated to infuriate Rupert.

Rupert is very defensive about the *Sun* and the *News of the World*, perhaps because everybody else attacks them. The slightest in-house criticism was certain to provoke his wrath. One night I gave a speech at a press dinner. When it came to questions Roger Bolton, the producer of the infamous ITV *Death on the Rock* documentary (which tried to make out the SAS had operated a shoot-to-kill policy when it shot dead three IRA bombers in Gibraltar), mischievously asked if I was 'always happy with the standards of the *Sun*'.

'No,' I replied, and sat down, realizing this was a minefield it was unwise to enter. Next evening my car phone rang as we crawled along the Embankment. It was Rupert from New York: 'I hear you've been beating up on the *Sun* again,' he said loudly, his Australian accent always stronger when he was angry. I explained the limited nature of my criticism but this only provoked a tirade about how the tabloids wrote better, tighter English than the broadsheets, went to far greater lengths to check their stories and worked much harder than us limp-wristed lot at the quality end of the market.

I was on the wrong side of several such conversations. Over time he succeeded in intimidating me into curbing my tongue about the tabloids; by the late 1980s I had stifled my criticisms – it made for a quieter life at News International. Rupert also had his revenge: during my Pamella Bordes libel case against Peregrine Worsthorne in 1990 (see Chapter 10) there was much embarrassing testimony; Rupert gave Kelvin the green light to go to town in the *Sun*.

Its coverage was so personally unpleasant that during the trial Michael Jones, my political editor, complained to Rupert about it while he was in my office one Saturday. 'Andrew's been rude about the *Sun*,' Rupert snapped back. 'He deserves all he gets.' I later poured Michael a drink and explained the background to this score-settling. He was astonished.

Every Saturday evening, after the first edition was away but before we started work on the later editions, I shared a glass of champagne with my senior editors. It was a weekly ritual. But not when Rupert was in town: he had decreed that Wapping had to be 'dry' and I thought it best to maintain this pretence. There was one ludicrous Saturday evening when he came over to celebrate my fortieth birthday. He must have guessed that I had bottles of champagne stashed away and he would not have objected to a glass. But I did not know when it would be used against me; we toasted my birthday in mineral water and Diet Coke, before he departed for dinner. When he left Wapping (we had a system for letting us know when he was arriving or leaving the premises) the corks popped.

Those weekends when he was in London (which became increasingly infrequent as his American interests expanded) had everybody on their toes. He would spend Saturdays going through budgets or administration with his managers then wander across to my office as the first edition came off the presses. He would lay the paper on the lectern then noisily turn each page, stabbing his finger at various stories or circling them with his pen. He had the unerring knack of zooming in on the paper's weaknesses – ones you had sensed as the paper was going to press but hoped nobody else would notice. Rupert always did.

Sometimes he would leave you wondering if you had done anything right; it cast a cloud over your whole life. Other times, when he liked the paper, you felt you could walk on water, not just because the boss was happy but because Rupert's newspaper judgement is unrivalled. It was part of his management style that he could leave you in deep depression or on top of the world. I grew to resent that one man could have so much effect on me.

*

IN THE EARLY YEARS we had been quite close. He liked what I was doing with *The Sunday Times* and my interest in all things American. In the mid-1980s I spent several Christmas Days in Aspen, Colorado with the Murdoch family, who always made me feel welcome. Christmas Day dinner was a delightful, low-key affair with only the immediate family present; I felt privileged to be there. The children – Elisabeth, Lachlan and James – never behaved like spoiled rich kids and were always fun to be with. Anna, Rupert's wife, brought them up in a no-nonsense fashion, as befits her Scottish roots. But it was a competitive household. When we played charades after dinner, the most obscure phrases – some in Latin! – were acted out. The same competitive instincts emerged on the ski slopes.

Both Rupert and I are enthusiastic if clumsy skiers. He had an obsession with finding the most difficult route down a slope which meant going from one black run to another. Once, he took a gang of his executives from Australia down a particularly challenging run; though most could barely ski none said so for fear of loss of face in front of the boss. I slipped away and took a fast, easy route to the bottom. When I looked up it was like the Battle of the Somme: bodies and skis everywhere on the slope, with Rupert at the bottom shouting at them all to get a move on.

On another occasion we took a snowcat and went in search of powder off-piste on the back of Aspen Mountain: we spent most of the day on our backs, struggling to stay upright in the soft, champagne snow. I made it down to the bottom of one slope which had a small river at the bottom obscured by a recent flurry. Rupert came hurtling down after me. I waved frantically to warn him: 'There's a river here!' I yelled.

'What?' he shouted, shooting past me, flying over the river and landing flat on his face with a thump in the snow as he came to a sudden halt when the tips of his skis dug into the far bank. It was like a scene from a Tom and Jerry cartoon and I collapsed in uncontrollable laughter. I then pulled myself together and rushed to dig him out before he suffocated.

For Rupert, everything in life is a competition. Gus Fischer told me of the time Rupert took him sailing round Sardinia in his huge new yacht. They had dropped anchor and taken the dinghy to a beach for a swim. Then it was time to return for dinner: Gus suggested they swim back to the yacht. 'It was a joke,' says Gus. 'The boat was over a mile away on the horizon and the tide was coming in. But Rupert immediately replied, "Let's do it", and started swimming out to sea. We made it: but there were times when I thought we were both going to drown.'

The boat was Rupert's latest executive toy, but also the culmination of an Australian's dream: sunshine and water. He had agonized over the huge expense of building it.

'Maybe I should wait before buying,' he said to me, 'it's hard to justify the cost.'

'You work hard, Rupert,' I replied. 'Why not enjoy the fruits of your success now?'

He thought for a moment. 'You're right,' he said, 'why should I wait till I'm too old to enjoy it?' His high-tech floating palace was built in Italy, providing long-term employment for an entire village. But by the time it was delivered I was no longer flavour of the month and never sailed in it.

Such examples of conspicuous consumption are rare for Rupert, who is his mother's son in this regard. His Scottish Presbyterian background makes him reserved about spending too much on the baubles of billionaires. He has beautiful houses on three continents but he actually lives quite modestly, eating simply and drinking moderately, even preferring taxis to limousines. For a Sun King, his immediate entourage is very small. There is no kitchen cabinet that follows him around the world: he travels alone; but then he is a loner.

It took him ages to acquire his own executive jet, despite his endless globe-trotting. He finally decided it was time when we arrived by commercial jet in Aspen one morning only to find that Barry Diller, the boss of Twentieth Century Fox (a recent acquisition of Rupert's) had already arrived in his own jet. I could see the bubble coming out of Rupert's head with the words, 'It's time I had one of these.' Within weeks, he had.

Even when I worked closely with Rupert I knew it would not last: Rupert does not allow himself to make lasting friendships. 'Don't fall in love with Rupert,' Bruce Matthews had warned me in 1987, when Rupert and I were very close. 'He turns on lovers and chops them off.' The only people who are really close to him are his wife, his children, his sister, Helen, and his mother. He has no real friends. He does not allow himself to become intimate with anybody else for he never knows when he will have to turn on them: it is always more painful to sack your best friend, whereas courtiers are disposable. When Gus Fischer, who had worked closely with him, departed on less-than-friendly terms, Rupert's mother, Elisabeth, sent a letter to Gus (with whom she had been friendly) in which she wrote sadly about 'business relationships changing and friendship becoming endangered'. But that is to assume that friendship was involved in the first place. 'He cannot afford friends,' says Gus. 'He has built his empire by using people then discarding them when they have passed their sell-by date. It is not the sort of management style which lends itself to lasting friendships.'

*

'THE MANAGEMENT STYLE of News Corporation,' said Richard Searby, at a company seminar in Aspen which I had helped organize in the late 1980s, 'is one of extreme devolution punctuated by periods of episodic autocracy. Most company boards meet to take decisions. Ours meets to ratify yours.' Searby was Rupert's Australian chairman and one of his longest-serving lieutenants (though that did not save him when Rupert decided it was time to sack him, which he did by fax despite an association which went back to their schooldays) and he knew Rupert's style well.

For much of the time, you don't hear from Rupert. Then, all of a sudden, he descends like a thunderbolt from Hell to slash and burn all before him. Since nobody is ever sure when the next autocratic intervention will take place (or on what subject), they live in fear of it and try to second-guess what he would want, even in the most unimportant of matters. It is a clever way of keeping his executives off balance: they live in a perpetual state of insecurity.

Everybody in the company is obsessed with him, he is the main topic of conversation, even among executives who have not heard from him for months; everybody is desperate for any titbit of information about him, especially if it sheds light on what his latest thoughts and movements are.

'Calculated terror' is how one of his most senior associates has best described Rupert's management style – that and a simple but superb weekly financial reporting system combined with an eerie grasp of numbers explains why his remit runs everywhere and he is able to keep tabs on almost all that is happening. It is a combination which provides the backdrop to his many telephone calls and it has its advantages: quick unbureaucratic decision-making (providing you can get his ear), a daring corporate ethos and a continuous adrenalin flow that keeps everybody excited and on their toes. But it also has its drawbacks: senior managers are easily demoralized and undermined by Rupert's cavalier behaviour, which encourages sometimes irrational and unpredictable decisions.

Nobody in the company other than Rupert knows the whole picture. He relishes keeping even his most senior executives in the dark: a divide-and-rule approach which leaves them all feeling vulnerable. I knew many senior executives who spent far more time trying to second-guess Rupert than run the company. Kelvin MacKenzie once said, only half in jest, that the only real decision senior executives at Wapping ever took was to toss a coin to decide who was going to call Rupert in New York to find out what they should do. This makes for weak management – but then Rupert is surrounded by weak managers. Those who behave otherwise do not last long.

One of my duller chores as editor was to attend the monthly Wapping management meeting. This was supposed to be a gathering of top Murdoch executives where problems would be resolved and policies agreed. But the meetings were a complete waste of time: no decision of any importance was ever taken unless Rupert was present. So I delegated them to James Adams who, after a year of diligent attendance, realized that not a single decision had been taken over the twelve months – and delegated the meetings to his deputy.

It is not just managers Rupert regards as second-class citizens. He has little time for shareholders or board directors. Shareholders are a potential threat to his control of a global company he has built from scratch. He recognizes their interests only with reluctance. His view is that News Corporation shareholders should have no interest in current earnings or dividends; they should leave it to him to build long-term capital values – and anybody who buys the company's shares should realize this. His boards are full of placemen who will do his bidding; he rarely consults them and only nominally seeks their approval. Gus Fischer told me of the time Rupert called to say he had just spent $550 million for 64 per cent of the Asian Star satellite system. 'Could you call a couple of the directors and tell them?' asked Rupert.

'He had not bothered to seek board approval,' says Gus, amazed to this day. The Murdoch family-holding in News Corporation is down to only 30 per cent; he once told me he would be nervous if it fell below 40 per cent; but he still runs it as his personal fiefdom. As long as he delivers, non-family shareholders, which now include important financial institutions, will remain quiet.

Those who survive longest at the court of the Sun King are a group of unthreatening Australians who have been with him for years. They are totally loyal to their master and he is comfortable and relaxed in their company, though they will suffer the rough side of his tongue when he feels like it. This they take without complaint. They have no choice: they are unemployable elsewhere at anything like the salaries and status they enjoy with Rupert.

They are the consummate 'yes' men, their purpose to reinforce his judgement in decisions the Sun King has already taken, to nudge him in directions he has already decided to go and to present no challenge to him. It always amazed me how the company prospered with such people in key posts. But they are the time-servers whose job is to keep the show on the road. They are regularly supplemented by more talented folk whom Rupert hires temporarily for specific jobs he needs done. They might not last long and Rupert invariably falls out with them at some stage; but they serve their purpose at the time.

Their intermittent presence is easy to accommodate in the company because there is no hierarchical management structure at News Corporation. If there is a structure at all it is a circle of courtiers, with the Sun King sitting at the centre. This allows him to intervene anywhere at will, facilitating his over-weening presence. Though he cannot be everywhere all the time, he is in a mysterious way ubiquitous.

His restless energy makes him prone to micro-management. When I once complained about the food in the Wapping canteen he spent part of a week sorting it out; another time he wanted to be involved in the deployment of various secretaries on the executive floor. He regularly calls distribution or sales managers himself for the latest circulation figures and other information, so that when he calls his top men he will know more than them.

The flaw in all this is that Rupert is actually not a very good manager; he does not have the patience for it. He is at his best as a consummate deal-maker, maybe the most formidable in the world for spotting an asset with potential then acquiring it with the most imaginative financing methods. It is the excitement of the deal that attracts him. It awakens the gambler in him. It suits his short attention span. It makes him one of the world's greatest business predators. But these very qualities make him an erratic manager.

'In fact, Rupert is a lousy manager,' says Gus bluntly. 'He terrorizes those under him when he makes one of his flying visits: it takes weeks to restore their morale. He provides no leadership to inspire. He wants to take all the decisions himself – so he won't delegate power. He wouldn't even agree who should report to me. He prefers the tension between executives which his episodic intervention creates.'

John Dux agrees: 'Rupert is the world's worst manager. During his visits to Wapping he should have inspired and encouraged his lieutenants. Instead he left them miserable and demoralized with his autocratic style and raging temper. It used to take weeks to restore morale after he had gone.'

Imitating the Sun King is always a great temptation even for minor courtiers: it was something too many of Rupert's managers found impossible to resist. He was brutal with them; so they were brutal in turn with their underlings. This method of management filtered all the way down to a group of middle managers who made life miserable for the shop-floor. Thus was the promise of Wapping thrown away.

*

THE SENSE OF COMMON PURPOSE and direction started to dissipate from Wapping almost as soon as the pickets departed. With no enemy at the gates to unite workers and management, the place soon degenerated into the sort of rule by management diktat that I had feared. The rough tactics of a group of middle managers, apeing Rupert's style, began to sour relations with the shopfloor. 'They were terrorizing the workforce,' says John Dux, who was later brought in to pacify the situation; and the workers had no electricians' union to protect them. Only a few months after the move to Wapping Bruce Matthews had warned me in 1986 that there was the potential for a lot of blue-collar unhappiness in the plant. 'We have a tender situation here,' he said, 'because the management has no idea how to deal with a non-union environment.'

Eric Hammond, the leader of the electricians' union (EETPU), had always assumed that Rupert – as a quid pro quo for his union's invaluable help during the Wapping dispute – would grant him collective bargaining rights in the production of his newspapers. When the dispute ended in February 1987, Hammond was forbidden by the TUC, on pain of expulsion, from doing a deal to represent the workers in Wapping.

'I explained to Rupert,' says Hammond, 'that we regarded our members in Wapping as a bridgehead. We would have to abandon them for the moment but when circumstances allowed we would come back and expect a deal. Rupert seemed to understand this.' But, ever the opportunist, Rupert saw his chance to keep Wapping entirely non-union.

Bruce Matthews says he first realized Rupert had no intention of doing a deal with Hammond when the three of them lunched together at Duke's Hotel in St James's in October 1986. The Wapping dispute was still running its course but it was clear by then that Rupert would win. Hammond made a number of complimentary remarks about how it had been a pleasure to deal with Bruce in plotting the move to Wapping and keeping the presses running during the worst of the picketing. Hammond said he looked forward to a fruitful long-term relationship between company and union. But Rupert only muttered something about waiting to see the situation when the dispute was over and then changed the subject.

'I realized then,' says Bruce, 'that Rupert was going to renege on the arrangement.' Other Australian voices, such as John Cowley, brother of Rupert's top man in Australia and the dour, uncommunicative general manager of Wapping, were already urging Rupert to forget about the electricians. This was what he wanted to hear and Bruce, who had already outstayed his welcome by becoming too much of a chief executive in his own right, was not improving his chances of survival by arguing the opposite. He departed at Christmas, before the dispute in which he had been so pivotal was resolved.

When the EETPU was thrown out of the TUC in 1988 for accumulated misdemeanours, thereby releasing it from TUC constraints, Hammond naturally came knocking on Rupert's door to collect his just desserts. But Rupert no longer needed Hammond or his union – they were history. He had used Hammond to go from print unions to electricians; now he seized the opportunity to go from electricians' union to no union. He refused to do a deal.

From early 1989, Hammond bombarded Rupert with letters pressing his case for a deal; Rupert stonewalled. By June of that year Hammond was so frustrated that he wrote to Rupert again saying he now regarded News International as 'bad debt' and that he felt 'like advising our members to join Sogat, for it is clear that your local management and Sogat need, if not deserve, each other'. But Rupert would not budge: in a letter to Hammond dated 6 June 1989 he said it would be too 'dangerous for us to have any communication, direct or indirect'. Hammond had outlived his usefulness.

Eighteen months later, in January 1991, Hammond tried again, warning Rupert of 'the steady growth of union membership at Wapping', pointing out the 'number of dismissals of individuals involved in union organization' and calling for a 'fresh start' with his union. But Rupert wanted nothing to do with Hammond or his union. He declined to meet him and in a letter from New York dated 31 January 1991 insisted 'the matter should end here'. As a final indignity, he told the man who had made Wapping possible that 'should there be need for future correspondence' to send it to John Dux, the Wapping managing director. He had the grace (or guilt), however, to finish with a personal sweetener: 'I am very seldom in Britain these days,' he concluded, 'but would love to meet you socially if you ever come to this side of the Atlantic.' Not surprisingly, Eric was too miffed to take up the offer.

Rupert was free of all union involvement at Wapping and he had no intention of voluntarily inviting one back, even one as progressive as the EETPU. He showed 'no spark of gratitude', Eric wrote bitterly in his memoirs, 'even though he couldn't have succeeded without us'. But it was not long before Rupert and his managers realized that running a non-union company is a lot tougher than running a unionized one. The harmonious atmosphere we had worked so hard to create at Wapping quickly gave way to trench warfare; it was management's fault.

One of the ironies of the move to Wapping was that, though it revolutionized attitudes on the shopfloor, it left management largely untouched. It was the managers who brought Fleet Street with them to Wapping, not the workers. Many executives were simply not up to the job: they had been no more than glorified industrial relations fixers in Fleet Street and could not cope with the more sophisticated demands of running a non-union company; others had played second fiddle to union bosses for so long that they saw Wapping as their chance to rule the roost at last.

Just how badly industrial relations deteriorated at Wapping has never been revealed. Shopfloor resentment grew so strong that at one stage in the late eighties there were demonstrations outside the office of the production manager. In one incident his office was attacked with firehoses; in another, walls were covered in pictures from homosexual magazines, his face superimposed on the bodies. Matters were not helped when 700 of the workforce were laid off during the company's global credit crunch in 1990.

The printers began to sabotage production, just like the bad old days in Fleet Street. There were a suspiciously high number of web breaks and the newspapers experienced regular late runs and shortfalls. I was furious that managerial incompetence once again threatened the smooth production of *The Sunday Times*. Bill O'Neill had to be brought back from America to help with the firefighting: after a preliminary investigation he reported to Rupert that over 70 per cent of the workforce would vote for union recognition.

The mood had been made uglier by the rush to install colour presses. Rupert had always argued that newspapers did not need colour. Then Robert Maxwell produced a colour *Daily Mirror*: Rupert panicked and decided that the *Sun* and *News of the World* would have to have colour too: over £700 million was spent on 26 brand-new presses at Wapping, Knowsley (on Merryside) and Glasgow. They were running in record time: but conditions in Wapping were cramped, the workers were not properly trained and the software did not work. The tensions spilled on to the shopfloor, encouraging further unrest. 'The whole place was a shambles,' says Gus Fischer, who was brought in to help sort it out in 1989. 'And the situation on the shopfloor was a disaster.'

It took several years to get the colour presses to work tolerably well. Even when I left for America in the summer of 1994, there were continuing production problems and Wapping could hardly be described as a happy place. A number of 'troublemakers' had been fired and efforts were made to institute a more benign management regime. The demand for union recognition receded: Rupert realized it would be expedient to create a better working environment before a Labour government more sympathetic to demands for union recognition came to power. Even so, management estimates privately that if a ballot were held in Wapping today over 50 per cent would vote for the right to union representation. The spirit of Wapping – a model of harmonious industrial relations, with everybody pulling together because they were treated generously and with respect – has gone for ever.

The move to Wapping had put *The Sunday Times* in the vanguard of newspaper technology but over the years its lead has been squandered. Today's *Sunday Times* journalists still use the same (now dated) Atex terminals that were installed in 1985. Other newspapers have leaped ahead but at Wapping the latest desktop personal computers, e-mail, the internet and access to the latest on-line libraries – all the developments that are transforming communications – have yet to arrive because the investment has not been made. The whole place has started to look very dated.

One reason why Wapping soured was that Rupert never trusted anybody else to run it: nobody ever met his expectations, and if they looked like doing so, his expectations changed. Bruce Matthews was ousted because he thought he should run the place. Rupert parted company with Andrew Knight because he came to regard him as too laid back and semi-detached. Gus Fischer, being a logical Swiss-German, tried to steer a middle course between Matthews and Knight, becoming fully involved in running Wapping but always consulting Rupert and deferring to him. He departed early in 1995 when Rupert tried to sideline him.

Gus, who secured a generous financial settlement, is still

not sure what he did wrong: 'He simply called out of the blue to say he wanted to make some changes. After all I had done for this guy, it's outrageous to finish a relationship like that.' Gus had been one of the team which had saved the company when it was on the brink of bankruptcy. He called suppliers and pleaded with them not to demand payment for outstanding bills. They were reassured by the sight and sound of a conservative Swiss-German businessman in such a crucial post in a buccaneering company. At one stage he managed to talk the owner of Ferag, suppliers of printing equipment, to delay a £60 million demand for a year.

None of this matters when you are past your sell-by date: Rupert does not allow past favours to accumulate in his favour bank. He had decided Gus had become too much of an 'empire builder' and wanted him out. 'I think he's happiest,' says Gus ruefully, 'when he has someone in London who will call him on everything, even if it's just to go to the bathroom.' Perhaps that is why he has been happiest with acquiescent Australians nominally in charge, from the grumpy John Cowley to the affable Les Hinton, currently sitting in the London hot seat.

The only time Rupert seriously tried to hand over power in London was when he appointed Andrew Knight, my former editor at *The Economist*, who had gone on to run Telegraph Newspapers. When Rupert consulted me about hiring him, I was all for it. I saw Andrew as a perfect ambassador for the company in building bridges with the Establishment. 'We've won the battle of Wapping,' I told Rupert, 'and our papers are prospering. It's time to make some friends.' I envisaged Andrew taking over the role Sir Edward Pickering had played so well over the years, keeping a wary eye on the papers and smoothing ruffled feathers in the corridors of power.

So I was delighted when Rupert called me over to his

office in July 1989 to say 'I've done a deal with Andrew Knight. He won't be coming here for a while [in fact it was March 1990 before he arrived officially] but once he has prised himself away from Conrad [Black, the owner of Telegraph Newspapers] he's ours.'

'That's good, Rupert,' I replied. 'I'm sure we'll get on very well together. I'll give him all the help I can.'

I was flabbergasted, however, when Rupert added, 'He'll be moving into this office.'

'What do you mean?' I asked, incredulous.

'Look, I can't run this place any more,' he said. 'I've got to have somebody here to do it. I'll only come over maybe twice a year. You and I will still talk about the paper. But in general I now want you and everybody else to work through Andrew Knight.' To give symbolic significance to this seismic shift, Andrew was to occupy Rupert's massive office – while he would move (he implied) into a broom cupboard down the corridor.

I was stunned. I had never envisaged Andrew Knight becoming chief executive. He was an accomplished courtier to the rich and powerful, especially outsiders who needed help with the British Establishment (Conrad Black and Tiny Rowland had both at various stages fallen under his suave spell) and, though very different characters, we had worked reasonably well together at *The Economist*, where he nudged me several times in sensible career directions. But I never saw him as chief executive material (nor did he: he once confessed to me that he was 'not a very good manager, more a strategist') – and especially not a Murdoch chief executive. Though both had antipodean backgrounds they were very different: Andrew was the sophisticated New Zealander who felt at home with the British Establishment, Rupert the self-styled rough-and-tumble Australian who wanted to stay outside it. This was never a marriage made in heaven, I mused.

Nor did they stay married long, though the honeymoon was sweet. For a while Andrew stroked Rupert's ego and Rupert regarded him as a genius: he would make a point of deferring exaggeratedly to him in meetings. When investors in News Corporation grumbled that Rupert had no heir apparent, Andrew was wheeled before the *Financial Times* as his natural successor. In fact, Andrew never even got to run Wapping, for he was temperamentally unsuited to the hard slog that would have been required and all Rupert's talk about relinquishing power was just so much hot air – something everyone but Rupert and Andrew were pretty sure about from day one.

Andrew Knight's experience underlines a fundamental weakness of News Corporation. Outside of Rupert, there is no real management. During the eleven years I was editor, Rupert fired or eased out every chief executive of real talent or independent mind-set. As a result, there is no historic memory at the top, and the organization has poor mechanisms for promoting from within. There are no serious annual reviews of staff performance, no process whereby talented people can move around from one part of the media empire to another – unless it is on Rupert's whim – and little thought given to providing people with a career within the organization. The talented either leave of their own volition or are fired.

This reflects Rupert's general disdain for individuals. He has never expressed regret about those he has axed and has repeatedly said that every individual can be replaced. That is, of course, true but there is a real price to be paid in the underlying strength of the company when it comes to its long-term future. When Rupert dies, there will be no management team in place ready to fill the breach and few managers with any real experience of taking important decisions.

My mistake was to play the game in this haphazard executive environment: as requested I worked through Andrew Knight, who was always courteous, helpful and largely left me alone. But a courtier is at his most vulnerable when he does not have the Sun King's ear, for rival courtiers can do him down. This is a particular danger at the Murdoch court for Rupert is highly susceptible to poison being poured in his ear about someone. I have seen him turn against a previously treasured executive because some new darling of the moment has whispered something bad about him. Such invective is most effective when Rupert has already started to go off you. This was the position I found myself in by 1990. When Rupert heard criticisms he was already inclined to think badly of me and our relations deteriorated accordingly. Whenever anything went wrong I was automatically blamed for not being there enough. The Business section made a host of horrendous mistakes in a controversial feature comparing company performance with managerial rewards. It was so serious that I asked for the business editor's resignation, which he reluctantly gave. Andrew Knight was acting as intermediary with Rupert over this crisis and suggested to me that I should also offer my resignation to Rupert.

'He won't accept it,' explained Andrew, 'but it would let him know how seriously you take the matter.'

'I see no reason why I should resign,' I replied. 'But if I ever do offer my resignation it will never be on the basis that it won't be accepted. When I resign, I'll mean it – and I'll be off.' This is one piece of advice from a fellow courtier that I think I'll ignore, I mused after our conversation.

I could tell my position was being eroded from the gossip that was drifting back to me. Wapping executives from Gus Fischer downwards had started characterizing me as a semi-detached editor who was losing interest in the paper and looking elsewhere for other work. They were merely mouthing what Rupert was saying and reinforcing his view. Word reached me that at one meeting Gus had said, 'Andrew's a great editor when he's engaged, but he's not always engaged – and you can tell from the paper when he's not there.' He was only repeating what Rupert was saying.

Nobody sought to correct him – to tell him, for example, that with the Iraqi invasion of the Gulf I was working harder than ever before and driving my staff as never before. On Saturdays we would start early and work into the small hours of Sunday morning updating editions through the night as news came in from the Gulf. Morale on the paper was high, our Gulf coverage superb and everybody was working flat out (see Chapter 13).

After the first edition was on the presses and we had approved changes for the second I would take some of my senior editors to a nearby Italian restaurant for a break. We would review the week's work and plan the next week; we were in regular touch with the office by phone and fax and no more than ten minutes away should a major development break. These dinners became a regular Saturday night event, they were fun, next week's coverage was planned and everybody enjoyed them. But word reached me that Rupert regarded them as an unnecessary extravagance – and that 'living it up on a Saturday night at his expense' was just another example of how semi-detached I was becoming. I resented this ignorant long-distance carping and grew furious with the disinformation and innuendo being plied into Rupert's receptive ear. I confronted him in his office on one of his London visits.

'I hear you're not happy with me,' I said bluntly. 'What's the problem?'

'You don't seem that involved with the paper,' he said,

almost embarrassed. Rupert does not like confrontations unless he provokes them, which he rarely does.

'That's rubbish,' I snapped back. 'It's poison being poured in your ear. I'm more involved in the paper than ever before. Yes, I'm doing other things [I had started broadcasting on LBC, the London talk radio station] but they complement what I'm doing at the paper, which remains my first priority. I'm not married, haven't got a family, I live to work. Anyway, you should judge me not by the input but by the output of the paper; everybody thinks the paper's going gangbusters, our Gulf War coverage is great and sales are soaring.' He was somewhat taken aback by this blast. But I was angry.

'Yeah, yeah,' he recovered, 'but everybody says you're going to head up an ITV franchise bid.'

'I've heard that rumour too; it's not true. If you were worried about it why didn't you pick up the phone and ask me?'

'Maybe I should have,' he replied sheepishly.

The meeting cleared the air. I learned my lesson and started dealing directly with Rupert again, as all successful courtiers must; for no courtier can ever really trust another at the Court of the Sun King. For a while I had the best of all possible worlds: a disengaged, even remote proprietor from whom I heard less and less and a chief executive on the ground whom I hardly ever saw. The early nineties were the years when I hardly had a boss. I exploited this unprecedented independence to the hilt – I knew it would not last for ever. At some stage, Rupert would inevitably seek to cage, remove or destroy this monster he had unleashed.

CHAPTER EIGHT

The Queen and I

'HAVE YOU GOT A MINUTE?' asked Michael Jones, peeking his head round the editor's office door. 'I think we might have a big one here.'

It was late on a Friday night in July 1986, I was struggling with the editorial and did not relish the interruption. But Michael Jones is one of the most cautious and reliable political editors in the business. When he thinks it's 'a big one' it is time to junk everything and listen.

'I've just been reading Simon Freeman's Focus article on the Queen and the Commonwealth,' he said. 'It's dynamite. If we turned it into a news story it would give us one hell of a splash.' Thus began one of the great constitutional rows of modern times, involving the two most powerful women in the country.

Freeman was an experienced news and features writer who had been assigned to investigate an apparent growing rift between Buckingham Palace and Downing Street over the Commonwealth. A number of stories had appeared claiming that the Queen, known to take her position as head of the Commonwealth very seriously even though it was only a nominal title, was worried that Margaret Thatcher was alienating the rest of the Commonwealth with her uncompromising opposition to wide-ranging sanctions against the apartheid regime in South Africa. The Queen, it was said, did not like Britain being in a minority of one;

Thatcher's refusal to go along with sanctions had particularly infuriated the Commonwealth's black African leaders, to whom the Queen was especially attached.

Freeman had been told to establish if the rift between the Queen and the Prime Minister over the Commonwealth was real. If the rumours were true then it was a major story: splits between head of state and head of government that spill into the public arena are rare in modern British history. He discovered that the disagreement went far wider than sanctions against South Africa: the Queen was unhappy with the whole thrust of Thatcherism. It was an unprecedented insight into a ruling monarch's political views.

I read Freeman's Focus article in rough draft: it listed everything from the American bombing of Libya to the coal-miners' strike as a source of contention between monarch and prime minister. This was indeed 'dynamite' for it is a long-standing convention of Britain's constitutional monarchy that the sovereign stays out of politics, so much so that we have rarely ever known the Queen's private thoughts on any major issue. Now, it seemed, we were being briefed on a whole range of them – and they were very different from the policies of her elected government.

'Who's the source for this?' I asked Freeman, sceptical that we could have any hard knowledge on the Queen's politics.

'I've spoken to several people close to the Queen, including one in particular,' he replied. 'They all say the same thing.'

'Who's the main source?' I enquired. Freeman shuffled, unhappy about revealing the name.

'If I don't know, the piece doesn't run,' I added.

'It's Michael Shea,' he said softly. 'He spoke off the

record [meaning Freeman could use the material but not name him] and he gave me detailed guidance.'

'The Queen's own press secretary,' I said, surprised. 'He's said all this?' Freeman nodded. 'Will he stick by the story if we run it?' I asked.

'I've been reading it back to him,' said Freeman. 'He's happy with what we're saying. In fact, he's corrected some points and filled in a few more details. Other royal sources have confirmed the thrust of what he's saying.'

I was flabbergasted. I looked at Mike. He shrugged his shoulders: 'Sounds like a page-one story to me,' he said, matter-of-factly. I agreed.

'We'll still run the full Focus,' I said, 'under Simon's by-line. Mike, you'll do a page-one news story picking out the most dramatic parts. We'll source it to the Palace.'

On 20 July 1986, under the page-one banner headline 'Queen dismayed by "uncaring" Thatcher', we reported that 'Sources close to the Queen let it be known to *The Sunday Times* yesterday that she is dismayed by many of Mrs Thatcher's policies. This dismay goes well beyond the current crisis in the Commonwealth over South Africa.

'In an unprecedented disclosure of the monarch's political views, it was said that the Queen considers the Prime Minister's approach often to be uncaring, confrontational and socially divisive.'

The story went on to explain how *The Sunday Times* had been given this information 'in several briefings by the Queen's advisers, who were fully aware it would be published and who were in no doubt about the dramatic impact it would have. Specifically, it was said by Her Majesty's close advisers that:

> The Queen believes that the Thatcher government lacks compassion and should be more 'caring' towards the less privileged in British society.
>
> The Queen feared during the year-long miners' strike of 1984–85 that long-term damage was being done to the country's social fabric.
>
> Her Majesty has misgivings about Thatcher's decision to allow American bombers to use airbases in Britain for their raid on Libya last April.

Freeman's Focus appeared as 'The African Queen'. It explained the background to the dispute and fleshed out the details. The timing could not have been better: the Commonwealth Games had just begun in Edinburgh and were being boycotted by Black Africa; and the Commonwealth Summit was due to begin in London in two weeks, at the start of August.

The balloon went up within hours of our first edition reaching other media. ITN was first off the mark: when they came to interview me early on Saturday evening, as the first copies were coming off the presses, the reporter told me they had contacted the Buckingham Palace press office and there had been no denial. 'How could they?' I thought to myself. 'The Palace is the source.'

But I had underestimated the Palace's ability to speak with forked tongue: by 9 p.m. the Palace was running a mile from the story. It was, said the Palace press office, 'entirely without foundation'. I told the newsdesk not to print this denial in our later editions, probably a mistake (since newspapers should always give both sides of a dispute) but I was furious that Michael Shea, the very person who had fed us the story, was now instructing his office to rubbish it: I saw no reason why I should print what I believed to be a lie. Why should I allow him to plant his bomb then print his denial of any responsibility for the explosion?

The row that followed publication dominated the headlines for days, in Britain and around the world. The American television networks were particularly interested in a story which involved the Queen and Margaret Thatcher and so were many Commonwealth countries. There was a certain satisfaction in seeing *The Sunday Times* at the centre of a major international storm. But it had its dangers: the story had put many powerful noses in royal and political circles out of joint. They had formed a lynch mob and were baying for blood – mine. Various worthies were wheeled out to rubbish the story and condemn me, as did the most royalist parts of the press. I was accused of having a reckless disregard for the truth and attempting to undermine the monarchy and the government (for what motive it was never made quite clear: I was not a republican and I was broadly sympathetic to the Thatcher government). I rushed from studio to studio to defend myself and the paper.

On the Tuesday after publication I went to ITN to pre-record an interview for *News at Ten*. David Nicholas, the editor of ITN, asked me to join him and Alastair Burnet for a drink in his office to watch the newscast. It was the eve of Prince Andrew's wedding to Sarah Ferguson but the continuing storm over *The Sunday Times*'s story led *News at Ten*. 'That's amazing,' said Alastair, turning to me with a smile on his face and a whisky in his hand, 'I never thought I'd be sharing a drink with the man who knocked the royal wedding into second place on the news. Congratulations!'

We repaired to Pontevecchio in Kensington for a late supper: with so many powerful folk after my blood it was good to be among friends and unwind. Alastair had to leave early: he was doing the wedding commentary for ITV next day. David and I stayed into the small hours and drank too much Sicilian wine. The waiters eventually prevailed on us to leave. 'I'm going to have a walk down the Mall to see if folk are already gathering for the wedding,' David announced. 'I always do that the night before a big state event just to check that everything is all right for the live broadcast.'

'I'm going home to bed,' I replied. 'I haven't slept much since Sunday and I'm knackered.'

*

I WAS WAKENED by the sound of a helicopter. I looked at my alarm clock: it was early afternoon. I rushed to the window: it was a royal helicopter taking off from Chelsea old folks' home, which the newly wed couple had visited after the ceremony. Now they were off on their honeymoon. I had managed to sleep through the royal wedding! But while I slept, behind-the-scenes moves were being made to have me sacked.

Some of the more Establishment-minded national directors of Times Newspapers, whose appointment had been sanctioned by Parliament to protect my editorial independence, had started to lobby Rupert Murdoch for my removal. One even mooted a deal: if I was fired, he said, the Palace had indicated they would be prepared to sacrifice Michael Shea. When that got nowhere an even more elaborate trade-off was suggested: if Freeman and I were forced to resign then perhaps the Palace would be prepared to orchestrate the resignations of Michael Shea and Sir William Heseltine, the Queen's private secretary and most senior courtier. It seemed that our story had done so much damage that only a blood sacrifice would cleanse the stain – but I did not want my blood to be part of the process. 'At least they think I'm worth more than a bloody press secretary,' I thought.

Lord Drogheda, a well-connected figure in the Palace and

the press, and Lord Dacre, better known as Hugh Trevor-Roper, the distinguished Oxford historian whose reputation never quite recovered from his 'authentication' of the fake Hitler Diaries, were the two national directors of Times Newspapers most anxious to be rid of me. They had held a cabal on the top floor of *The Economist* in St James's Street, where Drogheda was a director and had an office, and invited Alastair Burnet, another national director, to attend.

They explained their plan for the national directors to petition Rupert Murdoch for my removal. Alastair, an old friend and mentor, said immediately that he had been summoned under false pretences: 'I don't see why Andrew should resign,' he said, 'for publishing a story that was true.' He said he wanted nothing to do with a plot to oust me and left to square enough of the other directors to his way of thinking and out-vote these two. But discontent among some directors continued to rumble until Rupert Murdoch was forced to take them to lunch to remind them that their job was to safeguard the independence of the editor, not to seek his sacking. Rupert had been inundated with complaints about the story from politicians and the Palace. A friend who breakfasted with him at the Connaught Hotel the day after the story broke told me later that Rupert was constantly being dragged off to the phone about it. But he never wavered. All he ever did was warn me to be wary of tangling with the Establishment which would 'lie and cheat'.

This was one of several crucial times when I had cause to be grateful that Rupert Murdoch was my proprietor. It had been somewhat ambitious to cross the monarchy and the Tory Party at the same time. Both were furious with our story: the Royal Family hated being dragged so openly into politics because they knew it could undermine them in the long run; the Tories knew it would do Thatcher no good to be seen to have a sovereign as respected as the Queen ranged against her policies – in the immediate aftermath of the story the Tories' ratings in the polls slumped nine points.

But Rupert never wavered: since he wanted nothing from either the Royal or Tory Establishments he could afford to ignore them. A British proprietor with greater anxieties about his social standing in London would have been more easily nobbled. I had told him about our story just before we went to press. 'Are you sure it is true?' he asked. I told him the background. 'It doesn't surprise me,' he said. 'The Establishment hates Thatcher and you can't get more Establishment than the Royal Family. But they're crazy to bad-mouth her like this; it'll backfire on them.'

It was not just the nobs in London who were upset. Letters poured in from angry readers demanding my resignation and threatening never to buy the paper again: since most Tories are royalists (at least they were in 1986) they felt doubly aggrieved; and, since around 70 per cent of our readers were Tory-leaning, it was obviously not a popular story with the bulk of them. Right-wing commentators like Paul Johnson and Woodrow Wyatt piled in against me. Johnson and Wyatt had recently praised me for my stance over Wapping but consistency has never been their hallmark. I had offended their favourite lady (Thatcher) *and* the Queen so it was time for the inevitable dose of vitriol.

My darkest hour came on Monday, 28 July, eight days after we had published the original story. Charles Wilson, the editor of *The Times*, had rung me the night before. 'The big one has arrived,' he informed me. He went on to explain that Monday's *Times* would be carrying a long letter from the Queen's private secretary, attacking me and defending Michael Shea. 'It's an unprecedented intervention by such a senior courtier,' added Charlie. But under the house rules governing letters to *The Times* I was not able to reply until the letter had been published. I went to bed knowing that there was an Exocet heading my way in the morning.

Next day it duly exploded. I rose early and listened to the 6 a.m. news on LBC, the London talk station. The Heseltine letter (see Appendix 1 to Chapter 8) was the lead and LBC's royal correspondent reported how it was a dramatic, unheard of intervention, that it could only have been written with the Queen's permission, that it dismissed our story as 'preposterous' and that it was difficult to see how the editor of *The Sunday Times* could now survive. I switched over to the BBC: more of the same. I dressed slowly, feeling depressed for the first time since the row began.

My telephone started ringing with calls from the media demanding a response. Since I had not worked one out I let the answering machine handle them. Around 8 a.m. I heard Mike Jones's voice and picked up the phone. 'I think we have a fight on our hands,' he said. I told him I was feeling depressed and beleaguered. 'Maybe the Establishment will have its ritual sacrifice after all,' I said.

'Don't throw in the towel just yet,' said Mike. 'I'm off for a walk in the woods with the dog. I always do my best thinking there. I'll call you on my return.'

About an hour later he was back on the line: 'I think we should come out with all guns blazing and blow this guy out of the water,' he said.

My morale was lifted by Mike's attitude. Together we set about drafting a robust reply for the next day's *Times* which accused the Palace of 'playing with fire' and 'lacking the wit to blow it out before it burned them'. (See Appendix 2 to Chapter 8.)

Curiously, this reply all but ended the crisis for me. Perhaps the Palace was surprised that I had not rolled over and surrendered; perhaps it was taken aback by the uncompromising tone of my reply and did not relish a prolonged public fight; maybe it was afraid of being dragged further into murky waters it would prefer to avoid. Whatever the reason the story died down almost as quickly as it flared up. But as time went by and more facts came out, most people came to realize that a serious rift between sovereign and prime minister had indeed developed in the summer of 1986. I believe it was more than that: I now realize what we had uncovered was a conspiracy by a faction within Buckingham Palace to distance the Royal Family from the policies of Margaret Thatcher and undermine her government in the process.

Our story was the culmination of a Palace whispering campaign against Thatcher that had been going on for months. One of its first manifestations was a long profile of Prince Charles in *The Economist*, which analysed his views and painted him as a cross between a 'one-nation' Tory paternalist and a moderate Social Democrat – the very antithesis of a Thatcherite. What *The Economist* never revealed was that it was able to write with authority about this because of a long, off-the-record interview with the prince in which he ranged high and wide on some of the major issues of the day. 'It was the manifesto of an SDP King,' says Simon Jenkins, who conducted the off-the-record interview (he was then political editor of *The Economist*) and wrote the profile. 'He was raving about David Owen and clearly regarded the Social Democrats as the saviours of Britain.' By disguising its source, *The Economist* had managed to distance the heir to the throne from Thatcherism while hiding the prince's own fingerprints.

Then stories began to appear in the press hinting at a rift between the Queen and Prime Minister over South African sanctions. Their thrust was that the Queen feared Thatcher's strong opposition to sanctions could lead to the break-up of the Commonwealth; she wanted the Prime Minister to reach some sort of compromise. The most explicit story along these lines appeared in the *Today* newspaper on Saturday, 7 June, headlined 'The Queen warns Thatcher'. It reported that the Queen had urged Thatcher to agree sanctions against South Africa: 'She fears Britain's stand on trade sanctions could lead to the break-up of the Commonwealth. The Queen gave the Prime Minister a discreet warning during a private audience at Buckingham Palace.'

The main source for the story was Michael Shea. He had fed the story to the newspaper as a reward for apologizing – something tabloids are not inclined to do – for a false piece it had run claiming Princess Diana was pregnant. But *Today*'s scoop was largely ignored: the Saturday edition of a struggling tabloid with no clout among opinion formers is not the place to make an impact. But another story distancing the Royal Family from the Thatcher government had made it into the public prints and the cuttings files. The Palace never issued a denial nor sought to correct the story in any way. It was time to give it greater, more credible currency.

Shea had first ventured opinions about the Queen's political views to Freeman in a discussion about *The Economist*'s article on the Prince of Wales. The information for the bulk of the Focus article came in two long phone calls with Shea on the Friday before publication. Freeman spoke to Shea five times. 'The African Queen' was read to Shea before it went to press. In his letter to *The Times*, Heseltine acknowledged this but claimed Freeman had omitted 'crucial parts'. He was wrong.

When Shea called me at home on the Monday after publication to see if there was anything that could be done to dampen down the row he made no complaint about being read less than the full text by Freeman. Since we were making great play of the fact that Shea had known the contents of the Focus in advance and had approved them, he would surely have been anxious to remonstrate with me if he felt he had been duped by Freeman. But all he said was: 'I knew Simon was writing the Focus and, yes, he read out large chunks to me.'

In fact, Shea had suggested a number of textual changes to Freeman to make the Focus a more accurate reflection of the monarch's views. We accepted them all but forgot to make one: the Focus said the Queen was 'furious' that Thatcher had allowed American bombers to take off from Britain for their raid on Libya in spring 1986; Shea had preferred the word 'misgivings' which duly appeared on the page-one story but not the Focus. The claim that not all the Focus had been read to him was invented by the Palace later in the week as part of its frantic damage limitation efforts.

Shea had a different complaint: 'I raised no objection to the Focus,' Shea told me but the 'conclusions' in the front-page news story were 'very different' from the Focus. Much was also subsequently made of the fact that, though we had read back the Focus to Shea, we had not read back the page-one story. But by trying to draw a distinction between the Focus and the news story Shea was once again tap-dancing round the truth.

Every fact and opinion attributed to the Queen in the news story was drawn from the Focus. It was what is known in Fleet Street as a 'write off': you take the best bits from a long feature and turn them into a hard news story. But there was one difference: whereas the sourcing in the Focus was somewhat elliptical (as all previous press stories on the rift had been) the page-one story pinned down the 'Queen's advisers' as the source. This was our real crime: Shea and his allies had been happy to see stories about a rift between the Queen and Thatcher provided it was distanced from them. But *The Sunday Times* had not played the game: the origin of the news story was unequivocal and the Palace was rumbled. It had overplayed its hand, its fingerprints were all over the story and it rushed for cover, rewriting history as it did so.

Nor was the news story an unknown quantity to the Palace. Michael Jones had called Bernard Ingham, Thatcher's press secretary, on the Saturday and read the news story over to him for a Downing Street reaction. An angry Ingham informed Thatcher's private secretary who called William Heseltine and told him the contents of the story. Heseltine then consulted Shea. So hours before publication the Palace and Downing Street, at the highest levels, knew the details of our story. But nobody sought to deny it or dissuade us from running it. Somebody in the Palace wanted this story out.

I have never discovered if the Queen was aware of what was being done in her name. I am certain Shea was too cautious a man to act on his own, a rogue courtier. He must have felt that his controversial briefings had the approval of at least part of the Royal Family and courtiers in the Palace at least as senior as him. As an ex-diplomat he was too careful not to believe he had higher authority. I was told later by a senior cabinet minister that the Palace had been encouraged to distance itself from Thatcher by some Tory grandees who hated the Prime Minister. Willie Whitelaw, the Deputy Prime Minister, had referred to a potential rift between Palace and Downing Street in a briefing to lobby journalists the week before we published our story. The aristocratic Whitelaw, with close links to the grandees and the Palace, was later assigned by Thatcher's people to tell the Palace to ignore the dissident Tory toffs and behave itself. By then all concerned were anxious to cool it.

The irony is that a staunch monarchist like Thatcher – who always curtsied in an exaggerated display of deference to her sovereign – should have been the target of royalist efforts to discredit her. A clash between monarch and a left-wing prime minister with republican leanings had always been regarded as a possibility. Nobody predicted a rift between the Queen and a Tory prime minister.

But the Thatcher revolution had unsettled the Royal Family. The monarchy has a vested interest in social harmony, continuity and consensus. Thatcher threatened all of these. Her willingness to accept high unemployment as a painful part of making British industry more efficient and her determination to tame the unions sharpened social divisions which the Royal Family feared could eventually rebound on them. The violence and class rhetoric of the coal-miners' strike in 1984/85 particularly worried the royals: they were more comfortable with previous Labour and Tory governments which had bought industrial peace by kowtowing to union demands.

Similarly, Thatcher's uncompromising opposition to South African sanctions conflicted with the Queen's interest in heading a united Commonwealth. The Queen had come to take her position as head of the Commonwealth as seriously as her position as Queen of the United Kingdom. Her grandfather, after all, had been sovereign of the greatest empire the world had ever seen: the Commonwealth was a means by which the House of Windsor held on to some of its former global glory despite Britain's diminished international status.

Thus did a government of the radical right – with its questioning of hierarchy, deference and the collectivist consensus at home and abroad – come to be seen by Buckingham Palace as almost as big a threat as a government of republican Socialists. Our exposé of the Palace's whispering campaign damaged Thatcher in the short run but in the longer run we had done her a favour: the Palace took fright and the bad-mouthing ceased. Even the Foreign Office saw a silver lining: its private view was that the Queen's rift with

Thatcher had rallied the black leaders of the Commonwealth to the Queen and encouraged them not to leave it.

After a decent interval Shea was quietly dropped as Palace press secretary – without ceremony or the usual gongs by way of thanks – and went off to write books and articles about spin-doctoring, for which he is eminently qualified. As the row receded, it became widely accepted that Shea had spoken for more than himself. Previously sceptical newspapers and commentators accepted there had indeed been a rift. Over three years later, in October 1989, I was lunching at the Ritz with Norman St John-Stevas (now Lord St John of Fawsley), an old friend who had always taken a helpful interest in my career. A loyal monarchist with close ties to Princess Margaret and other royals, he had publicly gone in to bat against me during the Queen vs. Thatcher débâcle.

'Why did you attack me, Norman,' I asked, 'when you must have known the story was true?'

He looked hard at me: 'Yes, Andrew, it was true – which is precisely why I had to deny it.' Then he added with a smile: 'It was more true, Andrew, than you'll ever know.'

In her memoirs, Thatcher glosses over the issue. But she does not deny the rift with the Palace in the summer of 1986. Her real inner feelings were revealed when Brian Walden went to interview her for *The Sunday Times* some time after the row. Brian, an ex-Labour MP turned Thatcherite, had become friendly with her. He noticed that she was a bit sniffy that he was there for *The Sunday Times*.

'Does that "Queen vs. Thatcher" story still rankle?' he enquired.

'Yes, it does, Brian,' she replied firmly. 'It hurt me very badly at the time.'

'But you know it was true,' said Brian. 'The Palace was out to undermine you.'

Thatcher hesitated for a moment, then took off her glasses and pinched her nose, bowed her head and said sadly: 'I know, Brian, I know. The problem is the Queen is the kind of woman who could vote SDP.'

*

MY FIRST CONTACT WITH ROYALTY came about six months into my editorship when I was invited to lunch at Kensington Palace with Charles and Diana, along with Charles Douglas-Home, the editor of *The Times*, early in 1984. It was a reasonably intimate affair, with only the four of us, the food was somewhat strange (the starter, main course and pudding were all the same brown colour and tasted virtually indistinguishable) and, though newspapers were still peddling fairytales about their marriage, it was clear the royal couple had very little in common.

Charles roamed far and wide on the issues of the day: he was particularly keen that Britain's armed forces developed a rapid-reaction out-of-Nato-area capability to respond to threats to our interests outside Europe, a sensible view with which I concurred. Diana played little part in the conversation, talked about a rock concert she had been to the night before and piped up when President Reagan's imminent visit to London was mentioned.

She said Reagan was 'Horlicks' – apparently a Sloane Ranger expression for boring old folk – and claimed Nancy Reagan was only coming so she could have her photograph taken with the royal couple and the children. She was determined not to oblige the First Lady. She seemed to have the typical English upper-class distaste for supposedly vulgar Americans. Other than that she stayed pretty quiet, especially when issues of substance were being discussed; Charles made no attempt to involve her.

The Diana I met for lunch ten years later in February

1994, after she was separated from her husband, was a far more confident, independent-minded woman. Instead of being flighty, she employed a bitter humour. She told me that the royal family did not like her driving an Audi, a German car, in which she had come on her own to lunch: 'I don't know why they're complaining,' she said, 'after all, I married a German.'

She asked me what I thought of the 'show in the snow'. I didn't know what she was talking about. 'Charles, skiing with the children in Klosters,' she explained. 'It's only for a few days and it's all for show. I'll give them a proper ski holiday later.'

The princess, who had shown no interest in current affairs a decade ago, now wanted to be a goodwill ambassador for Britain. But her husband was blocking it. 'John Major has been very sympathetic,' she said, 'but the moment the newspapers wrote about it he [Charles] gave an interview to the *Financial Times* saying he wanted to be an ambassador for Britain too. It's pathetic – but it's stopped me getting the role I want.'

I asked her what she intended to do: she did not know. I found myself staring at her face while, over coffee, she chatted to other guests. Beneath the soft skin was a defiance mixed with sadness. 'We need to find her something to do,' said our host to me, 'or she will deteriorate rapidly.' Two years later, still with no proper role, she does indeed seem to be deteriorating.

My only contact with the Queen was when she paid a visit to Gray's Inn Road on the 200th anniversary of *The Times* in 1985; it was pretty fleeting. I stood in line with other Times Newspaper senior executives, she shook my hand, smiled weakly and quickly moved on. That was before we had written anything to offend the royals but maybe she sensed even then that I was trouble in the making.

In these early days we wrote very little about the Royal Family, unless it involved an issue of importance, such as Charles's views on architecture or education, which we supported. I refused to carry the sort of run-of-the-mill royal pictures – such as one of the Windsors opening a fête or going to a gala night – that *The Times* was so fond of; we were neither hostile nor fawning, just neutral. I was only interested in the Royal Family insofar as it was a source of news. When I was summoned to Buckingham Palace in 1986 along with other Fleet Street editors so that the press office could plead with the newspapers to behave themselves in the run-up to Prince Andrew's wedding, then take tea with the Queen, I declined to go, saying we had no plans to do very much to cover the wedding.

It was the only invitation to Buckingham Palace I received in eleven years as editor. I rather blotted my copybook with the Queen vs. Thatcher story and I must have been taken off the royal garden and official dinner party list that some editors rather relish. I am not sure if I was ever on it in the first place. Diana told me many years later that she had argued with the Queen and Prince Philip that they should make friendly overtures to those like me they suspected of being hostile; but they took no notice. I did not mind: social climbing is not one of my many weaknesses and not being on any official royal lists rather enhanced my 'outsider' status, which I did not mind cultivating.

But I had no hidden republican agenda. Unlike Rupert, I am not a closet republican, though as the past decade has unfolded I wondered sometimes if the House of Windsor, by its behaviour, was determined to make republicans of us all. Far from seeking a fight with the royals *The Sunday Times* gave Charles solid support for most of his passions: we backed his attacks on the brutalism of modern British architecture (even serializing his book on the subject, at great expense, and writing an editorial in September 1989 – 'The Prince's perfect vision' – praising it) and supported his efforts to restore the proper teaching of English grammar and literature in our schools. At one stage he even penned me a handwritten note – asking me to excuse the shaky writing, he was in a helicopter at the time – to thank me for our support.

Then, in the summer of 1991, came the events surrounding Diana's thirtieth birthday. There had been growing speculation in the newspapers that all was not well with the marriage but there was more gossip than hard fact. Diana's birthday celebrations – or lack of them – produced a torrent of stories suggesting the couple were fast becoming estranged. One paper reported that Diana was unhappy because Charles was not throwing a proper birthday party for her. Another responded that Charles had offered to organize a dinner but Diana had refused. Then came the retort that she had said no because Charles was going to invite only his 'Highgrove clique' of stuffy friends. Whatever the truth Diana spent the night of her thirtieth birthday (1 July) alone in London while Charles stayed in Gloucestershire.

The growing and increasingly transparent rivalry between the prince and his wife was documented by Andrew Morton in *The Sunday Times* in May. By Diana's birthday it had become a remarkably public spat, fought out in the tabloids for all to see, and orchestrated, we discovered, by competing factions belonging to each side in the marital divide: so-called 'friends' of Charles and Diana were involved in competitive briefings so that each side got their case across. It added to the deterioration in public respect for the royals that had been underway for several years, particularly since the disastrous *It's a Royal Knockout* show on BBC, which showed several younger royals cavorting around like upper-class buffoons. On 7 July Andrew Morton wrote another major Focus about the troubled royal relationship, optimistically called 'Truce', which detailed the efforts to patch things up.

The Sunday Times got caught up in the public-relations offensive which followed. We were sponsoring a special performance of Verdi's *Requiem* at the Albert Hall to commemorate Diana's thirtieth birthday on 8 July. The elaborate preparations for this event had gone on for months on the understanding that only the princess would attend. But a few days before, the Palace called me to say how much the princess *and* the prince were looking forward to the evening.

'The prince?' I said, surprised. 'I didn't know he was coming.' Oh yes, the woman from the Palace press office assured me, he had always planned to be there. 'Fine,' I said. There was no point in arguing but the Palace was once again being economical with the truth. Charles was a last-minute addition to the guest list, whatever the Palace liked to maintain.

I sat in the royal box with them during the performance: it was clear the reconciliation would not last. The body language was revealing: though they sat together, both spent the whole *Requiem* turned away from each other. At the end, when the applause died down, the audience rose as the royal couple left the auditorium. Diana turned round and waved to the audience: a huge roar went up. Charles stormed out, looking miserable.

At the party afterwards, I stayed out of their way as they were ushered round to meet the various VIP guests. Diana seemed in no hurry to leave but Charles was ready to go by 10.30 p.m. As they headed for the door Diana saw me standing at the corner and came rushing over. 'Now, Mr Neil,' she said with mock seriousness, 'I hope you are not going to run away and spend all that money we've raised for charity tonight.'

'Oh, no,' I replied, 'I've deposited it with the BCCI [a Middle Eastern bank which had just gone bust in a welter of corruption and money laundering].'

'You'd better not,' she said with a laugh, and headed for the door.

Morton's articles for *The Sunday Times* led directly to his devastating book. They identified him among Diana's circle as a writer sympathetic to the princess, someone who could perhaps be trusted with her story. Diana had been upset by two elements of the coverage surrounding her birthday: her continued portrayal as an essentially frivolous person still requiring the guidance of her husband; and the new consensus that, though the fairytale was over, they were still an amicable couple who had learned to live with their differences.

Morton was to learn the truth, as Diana saw it, in the rather unlikely setting of a north London working men's café, where one of the princess's circle briefed him over bacon and eggs on the real story of her life inside Kensington Palace. Nine months later, in the spring of 1992, his publisher, Michael O'Mara, was in my office trying to sell me the serial rights to his book *Diana: Her True Story.*

O'Mara said this was the most explosive book that had ever been written about the Royal Family. He indicated that it had effectively been authorized by Diana, that some of her closest friends had collaborated with Morton, and that the book revealed a marriage that had deteriorated beyond saving. In particular, it claimed that the emotional stress of her relationship with Charles had made Diana bulimic and driven her to several suicide attempts.

I told O'Mara that, frankly, I did not believe it. It all seemed too fantastical. I was not sure what bulimia was at the time but I was pretty certain that a woman like Diana, who put so much effort into her appearance, would not do anything to harm or mutilate herself. 'It all sounds a bit far-fetched to me,' I told O'Mara rather sniffily. 'I think it would be better off in a tabloid.'

Rupert had got wind in New York that there was a supposedly sensational royal book on offer and called to find out about it. I expressed my reservations. 'If you have any doubts about it,' he said, 'then you should not touch it.' He put me under no pressure to buy the rights: he was happy to leave the decision to me and I had decided to pass on it.

Then Andrew Morton came to see me. He spoke with a quiet authority, stressing that, unlike most royal books which quote anonymous sources (using vague formula such as 'friends of the Royal Family' or 'those close to royal circles'), he was naming his sources and attributing quotes to them. They were all close to Diana and, he assured me, they would never have spoken to him without her approval. In particular, James Gilbey and Carolyn Bartholomew, two of Diana's best friends, were quoted as verifying the suicide bids and the bulimia.

I was intrigued but still doubtful about the authenticity of the book's central claims. I told Morton that *The Sunday Times* would have to check them out itself and speak to some of his sources. He assured me he had taped interviews and documents to back up everything that was in the book. 'In fact,' he said, 'I know a lot more than I've put in the book. I've taken no risks.'

I assigned Sue Douglas, our resourceful and thorough executive editor, to put together a small team to authenticate the book. I called Rupert in New York: 'I'm having second thoughts about the Morton book,' I told him. 'It might be a runner after all.'

'I'll back whatever decision you take,' said Rupert. It was

one of those times when he came close to being the perfect proprietor.

As we mounted our own investigation, I was reassured by something Andrew Morton had said to me. I had asked him if there was much in the book about Prince Andrew and Fergie. 'No,' he said, 'but they'll be separated before the book is out.' Ten days later their separation was announced. 'This man knows what he's talking about,' I thought.

We were able to verify most of what was in the Morton book. I learned that the text of the book had been read by a confidant of Diana's (I suspect she saw it herself) who had approved it. I enlisted the help of Andrew Knight, who had his own royal sources: they corroborated what Morton was saying. Since Andrew is a cautious chap not prone to taking tilts at the Establishment, his support for publication was important. But I was most impressed by the fact that Morton was able to produce signed statements from his major sources confirming what they had told him for publication. I wanted more: I asked that they assent to the context within which their quotes appeared. I wanted none of them to wriggle out. They all agreed.

I wanted belt and braces because, if the book crumbled to dust on serialization, I would have to resign: you cannot publish material which is untrue claiming that the wife of the heir to the throne is so unhappy in her marriage that she is suffering from bulimia and has made several suicide bids and hope to keep your job. There was always – until Diana confirmed them herself in her famous *Panorama* interview for BBC TV in 1995 – a small doubt in my mind about the suicide bids; but we had on-the-record testimony from Gilbey to back up the claim.

I clinched the serialization rights for £250,000. Our main competitor was the *Daily Mail* whose then editor, David English, later congratulated me on my negotiating skills for securing a world-class scoop for a relatively modest sum. I was happy to accept the plaudit from a veteran Fleet Street editor but I believe the bidding was not allowed to get fierce because Diana always wanted the book to be serialized in *The Sunday Times*: she wanted her story to be given the more authoritative provenance of a broadsheet so that it could not be dismissed as just more tabloid tittle-tattle.

There was a crazy feeding frenzy by the other newspapers in the run-up to serialization: they were desperate for any titbits and had an amazing ability to concoct long stories out of the tiniest morsels. In one pre-serialization interview with Sky News I happened to mention in passing that Diana thought she would never be Queen: next day it was the splash in the *Sun*, filling two pages.

The world came to Wapping on the first weekend of June 1992 when we began the Diana serialization with the first extract and a page-one story headlined 'Diana driven to five suicide bids by "uncaring" Charles'; underneath was the subhead: 'Marriage collapse led to illness; Princess says she will not be Queen'. There was intense global interest in the story – more so than any other I ever published – and in twenty-four hours I gave the same number of TV interviews; crews from America to South Korea (and almost everywhere in between) queued up to film the printing of the paper, to talk to me about its contents and grab the first edition coming off the presses.

The revelation that the wife of the heir to the throne was so unhappy in her marriage that she had made five attempts to take her life – albeit in a half-hearted 'cry for help' manner – was an astounding story by any standards and one of the great scoops of modern journalism (Morton was later to win Granada TV's Scoop of the Year Award). But many did not see it that way, at least not at the time. A week before publication Rupert had warned me to beware the wrath of the Establishment: 'They will try to destroy you,' he said on the phone from New York. 'Be careful: they are not nice people and you are about to become their number one enemy.' He was not exaggerating.

At the time I shrugged his remarks off. I realized some staunch royalists were angry at what I was doing; but I was not prepared for the outpouring of bile which followed. Even before publication it was clear many were going to be offended. On the day the serialization began (7 June) I was a guest of Dunhill at their prestigious annual polo match in Windsor Park, which is always attended by the Queen and various courtiers. I called their PR woman that morning to say it might be a good idea if I did not appear. She agreed: 'Some young Guards officer might try to make a name for himself by challenging you to a duel,' she joked. I'm not so sure it was such a far-fetched idea.

Emotions against the serialization ran highest among the Establishment bovver boys of the Tory press – notably Paul Johnson, Peregrine Worsthorne and Charles Moore (the *Telegraph/Spectator* stable was particularly outraged); they dipped their pens in vitriol to denounce me. What seemed to rile them most was that I was not susceptible to the usual constraints that might stop an editor from publishing this sort of material: deference to the royals, a desire not to rock the boat, fear of being a social pariah, a sense of solidarity with the Establishment, the hope of baubles and gongs in return for good behaviour – the sort of attitudes and aspirations, in other words, that had kept editors in line (and the public largely ignorant) during the great abdication crisis in 1936.

Some of the criticism was redolent with snobbery: the very fact that Morton came from Leeds (of all places!) was cited as somehow discrediting him; I, of course, was socially beyond the pale. I had expected them to come after me but I was taken aback by the personal vituperation they aimed at me: there was clearly some score settling after my victory over Worsthorne in the libel courts (see Chapter 10). Alastair Burnet said they had to descend to personal abuse because they were losing the arguments on the substance of the serialization.

But it was an unpleasant time nevertheless. They had lost control of events, their beloved monarchy was under attack – and with it the solidity of a social system that guaranteed their status and privileges – so they decided to take it out on me, rather than deal with the serious issues the serialization raised. Charles Moore, however, soon destroyed his credibility when, in the course of debating the Morton book with me on BBC TV's *Newsnight*, announced that journalists should use 'hypocrisy and concealment' when writing about the Royal Family. Jeremy Paxman looked incredulous; I went for the jugular, saying we had obviously come into journalism for very different reasons and that I did not think my job was to be a propagandist for the Establishment.

Moore, who had replaced Worsthorne as *Sunday Telegraph* editor, was easy meat in such debates: he is a more lucid writer than he is debater; people began to wonder why he volunteered to be regularly savaged by me in various TV and radio studios. But even Max Hastings, then editor of the *Daily Telegraph*, was less than formidable when we clashed on Radio 4's *Today* programme the Monday morning after our first extract appeared. Hastings denounced Morton as unfit 'to play the piano in a bordello' and dismissed our first extract as a 'deluge of rubbish and a farrago of invention'. It lacked a 'single reliable fact'.

I was riled by his remarks, which I knew to be based on ignorance, but repressed my natural inclination to savage him verbally. Instead, I calmly asked him what parts were an invention. Did he believe, for example, that Diana's bulimia was untrue, even though Caroline Bartholomew, one of her closest friends, was on the record confirming it?

'I don't know if it's true or not,' said Hastings dismissively, about to start another tirade.

'Then,' I interrupted, 'you are not qualified to describe it as a deluge of rubbish.'

'I hear you destroyed Hastings on the BBC this morning,' said Rupert on the phone from New York later. I had certainly taken the wind out of his sails. But this was an issue in which facts or good arguments counted for nothing. I went to ITN to debate the matter live on air with Norman St John-Stevas, who could always be counted on to take the royal line. He was equally dismissive of the contents of Morton's book.

Just before the newscast Morton had given me a further statement from James Gilbey, the source of Diana's suicide bids, which I proceeded to read out on air:

> I can confirm [said Gilbey's statement] that I was interviewed by Andrew Morton when he was researching his book, *Diana: Her True Story*. My interviews are represented fairly and accurately in the book. I did not receive nor ask for any payment. I can confirm that the princess discussed with me, on numerous occasions, her attempted suicides, as she has done with other close friends. Her friends have given interviews freely in the knowledge that the information would be treated in a responsible manner. I have no further comment to make.

That seemed a pretty definitive statement to me but Norman dismissed it with a cliché: 'With friends like that,' he spluttered, 'you don't need enemies.' The remark made no sense, for Gilbey had not betrayed the princess: he had spoken to Morton only with Diana's full approval.

I was encouraged by Gilbey's robust words, for my fear

was that those who had confided in Morton would come under huge pressure to renounce their remarks. Gilbey's statement suggested that at least he was holding up. My biggest worry, however, was that Diana would crack. I feared that the full weight of the Royal Family would bear down on her, forcing her, against her will, to denounce the contents of the book as untrue and to distance herself from those who had spoken to Morton. If she does that, I thought, I'm finished. Late on the Monday afternoon, following the first extract's appearance, I thought I was.

Diana was on a visit to Merseyside. As she greeted the crowds a woman well-wisher said something. The princess broke down: the tears were very public and unstoppable. I heard the news on the car radio. 'Oh, no,' I groaned to my driver, 'I'm going to go down in history as the editor who made a princess cry.'

But the tears were not my doing. Diana was feeling the strain of the huge Palace pressure being brought to bear to force her to repudiate the book. But she did not buckle. Two days later she made her famous and mysteriously well-trailed visit to the house of Carolyn Bartholomew where she hugged her on the doorstep in front of a bevy of Fleet Street photographers. I breathed a huge sigh of relief: if Diana had felt betrayed by a friend like Bartholomew, one of Morton's two main sources, she would hardly have indulged in such a public display of affection. It was Diana's way of letting it be known that they had spoken to Morton with her approval. I learned later Diana had been reluctant to do it. Her friends had prevailed on her: people don't believe we spoke to Morton with your approval, they said to her, you have to support us now.

By now, most intelligent critics must have realized that this was a royal book like no other. Deep down, as good monarchists, they felt betrayed by Charles and Diana: their collapsing marriage was hardly good news for the future of the Crown. But they were too loyal to attack royalty: they lashed out at me instead. One knight of the realm said I should be horse-whipped – and he was a fellow journalist. A politician wanted me to be incarcerated in the Tower of London. Government ministers threatened new laws to curb the press.

The critics resorted to desperate arguments to attack our serialization. We were accused of giving only one side of the story. But the book was called *Diana: Her True Story* – it *was* her side of the story. When we published extracts from General Schwarzkopf's memoirs on the Gulf War, they did not include any considered case in favour of Saddam Hussein's invasion of Kuwait. It is in the nature of book serializations that they are somewhat one-sided. But our journalism was not: while we were still running the Diana extracts we published a long news story and Focus on 28 June entitled 'The case for Charles', which was pieced together from numerous conversations with the prince's various friends and allies and gave his version of the events in the Morton book; and in the autumn of 1994 *The Sunday Times* serialized Jonathan Dimbleby's official biography of Charles, which confirmed all the major events in the Morton book but gave them a very different interpretation.

It was my successor, John Witherow, who clinched that contract. But before departing for my secondment to America in the summer of 1994 I talked to Dimbleby about his book. He told me Charles was not keen to see it serialized in *The Sunday Times*; he was still annoyed about the Morton book. I told him that it was precisely because we had carried the Morton book that Charles should now give his side of the story to our readers. Dimbleby agreed.

It was also argued that, even if accurate, the book was an unwarranted intrusion into the personal lives of members of the Royal Family that *The Sunday Times* should have resisted. This point was given force by a rambling statement by Lord McGregor, chairman of the Press Complaints Commission, who spoke of 'intrusive and speculative' royal reporting and of 'journalists dabbling their fingers in the stuff of other people's souls'. At the time, this was taken as an attack on *The Sunday Times*; in fact he later confirmed he had in mind the Fleet Street feeding frenzy of those newspapers which had sought to steal, spoil and sensationalize our serialization.

The Morton book was hardly an intrusion when it had been authorized by Diana. Moreover, the Royal Family had been quite happy for the press to 'intrude', on its terms, when it had been peddling a fairytale about the Charles–Diana marriage. Now that Morton had uncovered the truth, it seemed to me the press had a duty to put the record straight. Above all, if the marriage had collapsed in the manner described by Morton, there were serious consequences for the monarchy.

McGregor's statement added to my discomfort at the time. He had made his remarks after he had been assured by senior Palace officials that Diana had played no part, direct or indirect, in the compilation of the book. These same officials were later to apologize to Lord McGregor for misleading him; he was forced to admit that both Charles and Diana had done much to orchestrate the press coverage themselves.

That retraction came much later: at the time, it was open season on me and *The Sunday Times*. Even one of the royals got in on the act. As the row over the Morton book raged, I found myself in line outside the Lanesborough Hotel at Hyde Park Corner waiting for the arrival of Prince Michael of Kent (he's the minor royal who looks like the last Russian tsar): he had been invited months before to present the awards at the annual *Sunday Times*/Royal Fine Arts Commission ceremony to announce the best new buildings of the year. The competition had been thought up by Norman St John-Stevas and me to encourage higher standards in modern British architecture. Norman loved to use the occasion to invite his royal chums. I was surprised Prince Michael had not cancelled.

But there was a purpose to him keeping his commitment. As he approached me on the greeting line he delivered a well-rehearsed royal rebuke: 'I think these awards are wonderful, Mr Neil,' he said solemnly, 'but I think what you're doing to members of my family is quite disgraceful.'

'It's nothing compared to what they're doing to themselves,' I muttered back furiously. But the prince did not wait for a reply: he had already moved on, no doubt content he had done his bit for the honour of the House of Windsor. Throughout the ceremony (where we shared the platform) and the lunch that followed (where he sat opposite me) he made a point of studiously ignoring me. At one point we were left sitting on the stage alone: he quickly turned the other way and said nothing. I did not mind – he had just made a speech of mind-boggling banality and there was very little I wanted to say to him – but it was uncomfortable nevertheless.

I was so furious with Prince Michael's remark that I sent him a handwritten letter of protest on 24 June. 'I did not reply to the remark you made because I felt it was neither the time nor the place,' it began, '[but] I resent your claim that what I am supposed to be doing to members of your family is "disgraceful" . . . As today's *Evening Standard* concludes: "Not even the most loyal palace courtiers pretend any more that she [Diana] had nothing to do with the book." . . . I understand your anger . . . but it would be better to confront the message rather than blame the messenger.' I never received a reply.

Far more serious than the barbs of minor royals, however, was the fact that the serialization had provoked a haemorrhage of readers. Sales had soared to over 1.45 million on the first week of the serialization – the highest of my editorship – as non-*Sunday Times* readers flocked to find out what was in the Morton book. But circulation soon fell from that peak and by the end of the extracts had declined to below its pre-serialization level. Some of Middle Britain was deserting *The Sunday Times* in protest, some because they did not believe the book, others because they did not want to believe it – the content offended too many royalist myths about the monarchy and many would have preferred not to know.

They wrote in their hundreds to complain, to say they were cancelling the paper and to demand my sacking, resignation – or worse. It was an unsettling time but I was determined not to be intimidated by readers any more than by the Establishment's faithful scribes in rival newspapers. I drafted a firm reply and sent a signed letter to everybody who wrote to protest.

As developments vindicated the paper's stance, readers who had deserted us returned to the fold: by late autumn, sales were actually above their pre-Morton level. When the official split was announced I wrote again to all those who had complained in the summer, saying I hoped they now viewed my actions with a little more understanding and inviting them back to the paper. Some responded positively (a few even apologized!), some still wanted to blame me for everything that had gone wrong with the royals, most never replied.

Four years after the fuss of serializing the most famous ever 'kiss and tell', I feel exonerated by events. In her BBC interview Diana admitted she had encouraged her friends to help Morton and that her deteriorating marriage had driven her to bulimia and attempted suicide – all facts widely denied by our critics at the time. Charles and Diana have now divorced and the monarchy has faced greater public criticism than it has since the middle of the last century. Speculation about its future is rife: those who said there were no constitutional implications in Andrew Morton's book have been proved as wrong as they were about its factual content.

But it was never my critics in the rest of the media that worried me most. The call I really feared came within days of the serialization beginning: it was my mother.

'I see you're in trouble again,' she said, a weary resignation in her voice. I waited for the bollocking from this staunch royalist to begin. 'It's all the Queen's fault,' she continued.

'Excuse me, Mother?' This was not the line I had expected.

'It's all the Queen's fault,' she repeated. She then proceeded to tell the story of the day long ago when a four-year-old Charles ('you were four too') was waiting on the runway at London Airport in a little double-breasted coat with lots of buttons and a velvet collar ('you had a coat like that too') for his mother's return from a long tour of the Commonwealth. The plane taxied to a halt and the Queen came down the gangway to be greeted by her waiting child.

'And do you know what the Queen did?' she asked.

'No, Mother,' I replied.

'She shook his hand. She had not seen her four-year-old boy for weeks but all she did was shake his hand. No cuddles. Not a hug. No kisses. They can say what they like about Diana: she shows her children plenty of love and affection, which will help them to grow up well-adjusted. Charles never really knew he was loved by his parents. No wonder he does not know how to love his wife.'

*

'THIS COUNTRY IS AT WAR,' thundered *The Sunday Times* as the Gulf War raged in February 1991, 'though you would hardly believe it from the shenanigans of some of Her Majesty's clan. As usual, it is not the most important members of the Royal Family whose behaviour has been less than we have a right to expect, though the performance of even the inner circle since hostilities broke out has hardly been faultless. It is the exploits and public demeanour of the minor royals and nearly royals which cause most offence.'

The editorial went on to excoriate Lord Linley for disappearing to the Caribbean (after featuring in the *Sun* with red lipstick, fancy dress and some drag queens), the Duchess of York for maintaining her endless social round of skiing and nightlife, Prince Edward for doing nothing (despite his £100,000 a year from the civil list) and Lord Althorp for his 'recent adulterous fling in Paris'. Even Prince Andrew, who had 'served bravely in the Falklands' was playing golf in Spain.

The editorial caused a massive outcry. Monday's newspapers were universally abusive, and hostile mail poured in. Even Rupert Murdoch had been furious, though he said nothing to me at the time: 'You don't attack the Royal Family when the country is at war,' he fumed to one associate.

As the week went on, however, the public began to rally behind *The Sunday Times*: many others had been just as outraged by some royal behaviour, while the best of Britain risked its life in the Gulf, as I had. Some commentators spoke up in favour of the editorial, and the *Daily Mail* conducted an opinion poll: it showed a majority agreeing with many of the sentiments *The Sunday Times* had expressed. The week had begun with Fleet Street loyally rushing to the monarchy's defence; it ended with a *Daily Mail* banner headline: 'Queen in crisis'.

Rupert was forced to reappraise his opinion: 'I still think he was wrong to do it,' he confided to the editor of the *Sun* about me, 'but he has his finger on the pulse of this country more than I have.' The Royal Family quickly came into line too: news reports were full of royal visits to various military installations and royal partying was curbed.

The fundamental problem was that the new generation of Windsors seemed anxious to enjoy all the privileges of royalty without meeting the responsibilities that went with them. As the eighties ended the paper had warned that too many royals were behaving as if they were in a soap opera, with the inevitable consequence that the media would increasingly treat the Royal Family *like* a soap opera. It was exactly what happened.

The Sunday Times was regularly dismissed as a 'republican' newspaper and it was often fierce in its criticism of the House of Windsor. But rather than call for its abolition the paper urged an agenda to make the monarchy fit for the twenty-first century. In an editorial in January 1988 ('Modernize the monarchy') it had called for an end to the male line of supremacy and the continued exclusion of Catholics from the throne which, if it happened, would automatically disestablish the Church of England. 'By the time of Charles III,' the editorial argued, 'Britain is unlikely to want religious and sexual discrimination enshrined at the apex of its national life.'

In subsequent editorials and features *The Sunday Times* argued that the fact that the Queen did not pay income tax was indefensible (she subsequently paid some). It devised plans for opening Buckingham Palace to the public (it was opened for a few weeks in August – when the Queen was in

Scotland). Above all it called for a scaled-down monarchy more suited to Britain's present than its imperial past – and one which was not class-based: in other words, not the top of the aristocracy but an institution with close links to all classes. That meant clearing out the old-school courtiers with which the House of Windsor still likes to surround itself and creating a court which was far more representative of the multi-racial meritocracy that Britain was becoming.

But the Royal Family has moved only grudgingly in this direction, too little, too late. 'The Royal Family is not streetwise,' Diana explained to me in 1994. 'They have no strategy and do no thinking ahead. They just blunder from day to day.'

In August 1996, however, it was revealed that the Queen had formed a strategy committee of close family and senior advisers called 'The Way Forward', which had met twice a year since 1993 to consider proposals to modernize the monarchy, including abolishing male supremacy, ending the ban on Catholics and downsizing the Royal Family to an effective hardcore. All of a sudden, *The Sunday Times* had the support of the Queen, the Duke of Edinburgh, the Prince of Wales and the most senior Palace courtiers for its supposedly 'republican' agenda.

Appendix 1 to Chapter Eight

WILLIAM HESELTINE'S LETTER

Sir, In the debate about the supposed revelations of the Queen's opinions about government policies, I take three points to be axiomatic:

1. The Sovereign has the right – indeed a duty – to counsel, encourage and warn her government. She is thus entitled to have opinions on government policy and to express them to her chief minister.

2. Whatever personal opinions the Sovereign may hold or may have expressed to her government, she is bound to accept and act on the advice of her ministers.

3. The Sovereign is obliged to treat her communications with the Prime Minister as entirely confidential between the two of them. This was central to the statement issued by the Buckingham Palace press office on 19 July, as soon as the original *Sunday Times* articles appeared.

After thirty-four years of unvarying adherence to these constitutional principles, it is preposterous to suggest that Her Majesty might suddenly depart from them. No sensible person would give a moment's credence to such a proposition.

It is equally preposterous to suggest that any member of the Queen's Household, even supposing that he or she knew what Her Majesty's opinions on government policy might be (and the press secretary certainly does not), would reveal them to the press.

It is the business of the press secretary and other members of his office to deal with press enquiries to the Palace;

and in the process to comment on, or refuse to comment on, propositions put to them by journalists. There is *nothing* in any way improper about that and there is no secret about it either.

I am assured that, in the several exchanges between the press secretary and Mr Simon Freeman before *The Sunday Times* articles were published, the press secretary said nothing which could reasonably bear the interpretation put upon it by the writers of the article on the front page in the edition of 20 July.

Although parts of the feature article 'The African Queen' were read over to the press secretary, other crucial parts were not; and no warning was given directly by *The Sunday Times* to the Palace of the article on the front page or of the impact which *The Sunday Times* expected the articles to cause. At no point did the editor himself attempt to contact anyone at Buckingham Palace in order to check what was said in the articles.

The Sunday Times today makes much of the fact that from lunch-time on Saturday the Prime Minister's private secretary and I both knew that articles were likely to be published on Sunday and yet did nothing to stop them. It is not difficult to imagine the reaction to a request that the articles should be withdrawn: suffice it to draw attention to the sub-heading to today's Focus article in *The Sunday Times*, 'The story they could not kill', and the editor's refusal to publish last Saturday's Buckingham Palace statement on the grounds that he found it 'completely unacceptable'.

The publication of the original articles was clearly bound to call in question the constitutional relationship between the Sovereign and the Prime Minister, and this without any attributable source and without any attempt by the editor himself to verify the story. The subsequent claim that the unnamed sources were 'within the Palace and at the highest level' constitutes a totally unjustified slur on the impartiality and discretion of senior members of the royal household.

In short, I repeat what the Buckingham Palace press office said on the night the original story was published, and which the editor of *The Sunday Times* refused to print:

As with all previous prime ministers, the Queen enjoys a relationship of the closest confidentiality with Mrs Thatcher, and reports purporting to be the Queen's opinion of government policies are entirely without foundation.

Yours faithfully,

WILLIAM HESELTINE,

Palace of Holyroodhouse.

27 July.

Appendix 2 to Chapter Eight

ANDREW NEIL'S REPLY TO HESELTINE

THE SUNDAY TIMES AND THE PALACE

From the Editor of *The Sunday Times*

Sir, Sir William Heseltine's letter from Holyroodhouse today admits but then seeks to obscure a number of essential points to which *The Sunday Times* drew attention yesterday in its report of the events leading to the publication of two articles on 20 July on the Queen's alarm at government policies.

It is now officially admitted for the first time that Mr Michael Shea, the Queen's press secretary, was sufficiently involved with the preparation of our 20 July feature article for us to read the article back to him. We have said from the start that all of it was read, Sir William now says only parts of it. But when Mr Shea contacted me the day after publication he made no complaint that he had been duped in the reading back of the feature story. His complaint was that we had taken the contents of the feature story and made unwarranted conclusions from them in the page-one story. Of course we reject that too, but it is a quite different allegation from the one Sir William now makes eight days later.

Sir William does not say which part we are supposed to have missed out. Certainly not the section on the US raid on Libya. The feature article said the Queen was 'furious' about it. Mr Shea told us that was too strong. It was the only one of Mr Shea's several suggestions about wording that we forgot to make. But we did correct it on the page one story, which said the Queen had 'misgivings'. I give this example because I want nobody to be in any doubt about the extent to which a senior figure in the Palace was involved in the preparation of the article.

Sir William accepts that he and the Prime Minister's secretary knew from lunchtime on 19 July the main elements of our front-page article based on the feature, but did nothing to try to prevent publication.

Sir William's explanation is the astonishing and unwarranted assertion that we would have ignored any representation the Palace might have made to us. He has absolutely no basis for saying that: We have never met and have never had any professional dealings. On the only occasion when the Palace has asked me to change something prior to publication – an interview with Prince Charles – I complied. If Sir William or Mr Shea had made representations to me let nobody be in any doubt that, given the crucial nature of the subject, I would have responded positively. But they chose not to. By Sir William's own admission, the charge of negligence now lies firmly with the Palace.

Mr Shea was in no doubt of the impact our front-page story would have and contributed to it as late as 11 a.m. Saturday morning. This, and the Palace's failure to make representations throughout the afternoon, was the reason we refused to publish the Palace denial of our story issued at 9.30 p.m. that night. At no time did Mr Shea make even private representations to us once the Prime Minister's private secretary had expressed Downing Street's concern at our intended publication of views attributed to sources close to the Queen. Sir William's quotation of a subsidiary headline, 'The story they could not kill', in our 27 July issue as evidence of our attitude is patently absurd. How can he use a headline which had not even been published to justify his inaction that Saturday afternoon?

The events prior to publication on 20 July are what

matter. Why did we bother to read anything back to the Palace if we were contemptuous of its views and mindless of our reputation? Would we have bothered to seek Palace approval for only part of the feature article, knowing the Palace would then immediately deny the front-page story it had foreknowledge of based on the whole article? Furthermore, had we been as devious as Sir William implies, would we have alerted Downing Street to the contents – all the contents – of the front-page article seven hours before publication, knowing that the Prime Minister's office was likely to contact Buckingham Palace well in time to influence our decision whether or not to publish?

At no time has *The Sunday Times* inferred that Her Majesty was party to or aware of any of the attitudes being attributed to her. Nor did we claim there was a constitutional crisis; we said the opposite and gave warning against it in the editorial column.

For some time, however, unattributable briefings and guidance have been given to various journalists by the Palace which clearly distance the attitudes of the Royal Family from the Thatcher government. Articles reporting that have appeared in publications as varied as *The Economist* and *Today*. But the sourcing of this information has always been left suitably vague. At *The Sunday Times* we thought it more honest to be more specific about our sources: that seems to have been our crime.

Sir William claims that Mr Shea is not in a position to know the Queen's opinions on government policy. In that case why was Mr Shea briefing us at all? He knew we were preparing an article purely political in its scope. Mr Shea is the official voice of the Queen and newspapers have always worked on the premiss that he speaks authoritatively about her.

It is difficult to avoid the conclusion that those in the

Palace who knew about *The Sunday Times* articles before their publication, who provided guidance for them and who failed to use the ample opportunity they had to undo the damage were playing with fire and did not have the wit to blow it out before it burned them, and, more grievously, reflected upon Her Majesty's constitutional position.

The original Palace denial of the story as being 'entirely without foundation' can no longer be sustained, even on Sir William's own testimony.

Yours faithfully,
ANDREW NEIL,
Editor, *The Sunday Times*,
PO Box 481,
Virginia Street, E1.
28 July.

CHAPTER NINE

The Other Queen and I

THE HOUSE OF COMMONS fell silent as Margaret Thatcher rose to her feet. It was 6 March 1984 and she had just been asked a pointed question about a Barclays Bank account, used by her son Mark to deposit the proceeds of his various business activities.

'Arrangements affecting that bank account are perfectly proper,' she boomed, 'and not in any sense a public matter. What should be a matter of public concern is that methods of impersonation and deception were used to obtain details about a private bank account which were subsequently used in a national newspaper.'

The newspaper in question was *The Sunday Times* and it deserved to be in the dock, she made clear, rather than her son. It was one of the most savage attacks by a prime minister on a newspaper in modern times and the rest of the media was soon beating a path to my door to demand a response: it was the first time in my editorship that the role of *The Sunday Times* had become as big news as the story it was covering.

'Denis shares Mark's Oman account' was the headline stripped across eight columns on the top of *The Sunday Times* front page on 4 March. There had been much speculation in the press that Mark Thatcher had been using his mother's name to further his own business interests, especially in the Middle East. There was particular interest in Mark's role in the efforts of Cementation, a British construction company, to win a large university building contract in Oman, where Mrs Thatcher had recently paid an official visit. The *Observer* had implied in several stories that the Prime Minister may even have helped her son to do business in Oman, though it never had the facts to prove it.

Our story, however, scooped the *Observer* and put Downing Street in the frame. We discovered that Mark's substantial commission from Cementation for whatever he was doing in Oman had been paid into the London bank account of his company, Monteagle Marketing, on which the Prime Minister's husband, Denis, was a co-signatory. There was nothing necessarily corrupt about this – and we claimed no corruption at the time – but given the controversy surrounding Mark's 'middle-man' activities in the Middle East it was somewhat reckless, even stupid, to pay his gains into an account to which Denis had access, especially since he was not a director of Monteagle.

The story was bound to cause a row and we had to be certain it was true. So as part of the verification process two reporters paid £25 in cash in a false name into the relevant Barclays Bank account at a branch in the Strand. They asked the teller to make sure it was the right account: she obligingly turned her screen round and our reporters could see that both the Thatcher names were on it. It was a minor, if imaginative, piece of subterfuge to check an important fact that we could not afford to get wrong. But it offended Thatcher and many other powerful voices. In a statement obviously co-ordinated with 10 Downing Street, Barclays announced it was taking *The Sunday Times* to the Press Council for 'deliberate deception'.

This was what interested the rest of the media; how Mark had earned his cash and what he had done with it took second place. A band of television crews began to besiege my flat, then a small penthouse on the edge of Onslow Gardens, late into the night. It was my first taste of being at the centre of a major controversy; I rather enjoyed it.

Breakfast television was in its infancy in Britain and they saw this as a good overnight story. Well after midnight, when I thought the interviews were over, I was enjoying a drink on my balcony with Gerry Malone, who had been elected Tory MP for Aberdeen South in the 1983 general election. I was exhausted but in high spirits, especially since nobody had challenged the authenticity of the story. We spotted yet another TV crew wending its way towards us on the pavement below.

'He's not coming down!' Gerry shouted from on high. 'You'll have to come and get him!' The crew looked up, somewhat bemused: they did not know if we were joking or if *The Sunday Times* editor was breaking under the strain. We let them in anyway: they were from BBC *Breakfast Time*. While they set up their camera and lights in the main room a reporter from Radio 4's *Today* programme arrived. As he was interviewing me out on the balcony I noticed Malone was sitting in front of the BBC camera and the reporter was about to interview him. I stopped the Radio 4 interview so I could listen.

'What do you say to the Prime Minister's complaint that your paper used deception and impersonation?' asked the BBC reporter sternly.

'I've got nothing to say,' said Malone.

'Why not?'

'Because it's a question you should be putting to Andrew Neil. That's him sitting outside.'

Clearly I was not yet a household face for the BBC's breakfast show.

'You should have done the interview,' I said to Malone when they had all gone. 'You could have said something like "the stupid old bag should be more careful where her son puts his money"; they would probably have run it.'

'Yes,' replied Malone, 'and that would have been the early end of a promising political career in the Tory Party.'

Many readers did not find the row so funny: they objected to the way we had managed to discover the details of a private bank account, perhaps fearing that if it could happen to the Thatcher family then plain folks' accounts must be even more vulnerable. Barclays was furious because it illustrated that its security was easily penetrated. At the time one of its rivals, the Midland Bank, had as its advertising slogan: 'The Listening Bank'. People soon began referring to Barclays as 'The Talking Bank'.

We published our defence in a long article the Sunday after the original story entitled 'Gutter press or a newspaper just doing its job?' Various readers and luminaries also had their say: Harry Evans supported our techniques as legitimate investigative journalism in the public interest; William Rees Mogg, a former editor of *The Times*, did not.

Thatcher's outburst helped to counter all the criticism from the growing diaspora of *The Sunday Times* old guard that the paper was becoming nothing but a Tory propaganda sheet. On the night of publication Bobby Campbell, the gruff Glaswegian news executive, held back in my office after our regular meeting to decide the last edition: 'I just wanted to congratulate you,' he said, a little embarrassed, 'on running this story.'

'Thanks, Bobby,' I replied, 'but you don't really know me if you thought I would ever have stifled it for political reasons once I knew it to be accurate.' An editorial the following week called 'The virtues of disclosure' summed up my attitude to the separation of news and views: 'As a paper which sympathizes with many of Mrs Thatcher's efforts to build a more prosperous, dynamic Britain, *The*

Sunday Times is hardly likely to be part of a politically inspired campaign to discredit the Prime Minister. But equally, as an independent paper, we are not prepared to suppress or ignore information just because it may embarrass Mrs Thatcher, or her government.'

This was to be my *modus operandi* throughout the Thatcher years; it was an approach the lady could never quite understand. She was used to papers, like the *Sun*, *Mail* and *Express*, that were slavish in editorial support for her in their opinion, news and features pages; and she accepted that some papers, like the *Mirror*, *Guardian* and *Observer*, were downright hostile to her. What she found hard to cope with was a paper which gave her such strong intellectual support in its editorials yet regularly published news stories which were harmful to her cause. Perhaps she felt that because they came from a paper with a broadly Thatcherite agenda they did her all the more harm.

Five months after the Mark Thatcher/Oman story the Press Council cleared *The Sunday Times* by rejecting Barclays complaint (echoed by Thatcher) of 'improper deception'. *The Sunday Times* had 'acted within permissible limits' said the Press Council and was 'justified in the public interest' in the manner in which it had verified its story. But I was now *persona non grata* in Downing Street.

Though I was to be editor for another ten years I was never invited to Downing Street after that story, granted an interview or included in the Prime Minister's many official social functions. Thatcher has always been over-protective of her wayward son, perhaps out of a sense of guilt for not paying him enough attention while he was growing up and she was immersed in her political career. Our story had upset her mightily. The new editor of *The Sunday Times* on whom she had pinned such high hopes had let her down; from now on he would be regarded by the Prime Minister as a non-person.

*

I NEVER MINDED being dispatched to the Thatcherite gulag: I rather relished it. Too many editors and other senior journalists became so involved in the Thatcher magic circle in the 1980s that it compromised their journalism. The peerages and knighthoods handed out to various media Thatcherites symbolized the incestuous relationship between Thatcherism and the Tory press. I always thought that editors and politicians should keep their distance – and that it was even more important to be at arm's length if the paper was broadly supporting the government of the day. The only senior politician I had ever become good friends with was Peter Walker and I had known him before I became a journalist.

I had first met Mrs Thatcher when I was active in student politics in the early 1970s and she was education secretary. I was invited to lunch in her Flood Street house in Chelsea along with several other Tory students. It was all very informal: she did the cooking and the serving and we all helped with the washing up. The conversation ranged far beyond education: she gave us a little lecture on the virtues of a property-owning democracy.

'So why don't you just give every council house away to the current tenants?' I asked. 'You would take the state out of housing and create a real property-owning democracy overnight.'

'Oh, no, Andrew,' she replied, 'we could never do that. It would do nothing for *our* people – and they wouldn't wear it.'

Her remark has always stuck in my mind. By 'our' people she meant the middle class who had already bought their own homes or were planning to do so and would rather resent millions of the working class getting their homes for virtually nothing. I was struck by the class-based nature of her comment: the Tory Party existed in her view, or so it seemed, to further the interests of the bourgeoisie.

When she became leader of the Tory Party in 1975 and Peter Walker resigned from the shadow cabinet in fear that the Tories were heading for the 'bunkers and boltholes' of middle-class politics, I concurred with his remarks and kept my distance from the Thatcher Tory Party. But when we next lunched together, in 10 Downing Street early in 1982, along with other senior editors of *The Economist*, she was already well along her transformation from Tory bourgeois lady to leader of the radical right – and I had been to America and learned to love the market. There was much more of a meeting of minds.

At one stage, she gave a little lecture on the virtues of competition. 'So why is your Trade Department going to deny British Midland a licence to compete with British Airways on the London–Scotland routes?' I interjected when she stopped to draw breath.

'I didn't know it was going to do that,' she said, glancing at Bernard Ingham, her trusty press secretary. He indicated that he knew nothing about it.

'Well, it is,' I continued. 'They've swallowed all BA's nonsense about not being able to afford to continue with their Glasgow and Edinburgh shuttle service if they're forced to compete with an airline which will undercut BA's extortionate fares.'

She got up from the table, asked to be put through to some poor chap in her private office and barked: 'Please get a message to John Biffen [the trade secretary] that I want to see the papers on the British Midland application first thing on Monday – and he's to take no decision until he's heard from me.' Some time later British Midland won its licence to compete with BA's Scottish services (and council houses were being sold to sitting tenants at giveaway prices!).

That was the Thatcher I warmed to: bold and decisive in taking on vested interests. But the lunch was most memorable for the presence of Denis: it was a Saturday and he was miffed to be stuck in Downing Street with a gang of journalists instead of playing golf (I noticed his clubs were stacked behind the door as we entered No. 10). He said little, except for a couple of characteristic interventions.

The train drivers, traditionally a troublesome bunch, were disrupting rail services with a complicated dispute over something called 'flexible rostering', which threatened a few of their many restrictive practices. Over the main course we had a long discussion on how to end it. Then Denis piped up: 'Give them £20,000 apiece and tell them to sod off.' That seemed to end the matter.

Over coffee an official handed the Prime Minister a note. Her brow furrowed: 'I'm sorry,' she said, 'I have to go: the hijacked Tanzanian jet has just landed at Stansted Airport.' As she departed for the Cabinet Office emergency room Denis shouted: 'Send in the SAS – best in the bloody world!'

'I'd pay a fortune for a tape of their pillow talk,' I thought to myself.

I next encountered Denis when I was invited to afternoon tea with Mrs Thatcher on becoming editor. The Prime Minister was clearly encouraged that Rupert Murdoch had appointed a Tory-leaning editor to *The Sunday Times* and she was hoping for a better press from it. At the end of my tête-à-tête with the Prime Minister (a casual talk in which she revealed nothing) we bumped into Denis as I was leaving.

'This is Andrew Neil,' she said, introducing me to her

husband, 'the new editor of *The Sunday Times*. He's planning big changes at the paper.'

'You couldn't make it any worse,' said Denis sniffily, clearly no fan of the paper's politics to date. I fear I was to disappoint him. I never talked to Thatcher again after our cosy chat until after she had ceased to be Prime Minister. I blotted my copy book with the Barclays Bank story then compounded matters with the 'Queen vs. Thatcher' exposé (see Chapter 8).

This arm's-length relationship suited me well. It allowed me to establish *The Sunday Times*'s credentials as an independent paper, sympathetic to the Thatcher revolution but free to criticize it on its own terms and to judge her progress against its own agenda. I remained to some extent on the inside track, at one remove, because there were others on *The Sunday Times* who continued to cultivate their close connections to the Thatcher camp.

Brian Walden, who had joined *The Sunday Times* as senior columnist not long after we moved to Wapping when others were fleeing for the door, kept in close touch with the Prime Minister and reported to me regularly; Ivan Fallon, the deputy editor, had excellent contacts with a number of Tory ministers and senior Thatcherite businessmen; and Michael Jones, the political editor, was close to Bernard Ingham, the PM's press secretary and close confidant. With this intelligence network to draw on I never felt excluded from Thatcher's thoughts which, because of the confidential manner in which the information was passed, I was not always able to put in the newspaper.

In early 1987, for example, I learned that it was her intention to fight at least two more general elections (she was already certain to win the one later that year). If she was ever faced with a hung parliament her strategy would have been to divide the Liberal–SDP Alliance, enticing the harder-headed SDP leader, David Owen, from his softer partner, David Steel, the Liberal leader, to keep in power.

She even confided to Brian Walden at one stage that, despite all the grief *The Sunday Times* was causing her, she still preferred it to the more Tory *Sunday Telegraph*, edited by Peregrine Worsthorne: 'Perry doesn't really understand the changes that are going on in society, *The Sunday Times* does,' she explained (though it did not stop her handing him a knighthood). 'The future of the Tory Party depends on attracting the votes of the old pro-Labour working class, not all these yuppies that are flocking to the Alliance.' She asked Brian, a working-class Labour lad turned Thatcherite, if he would like a seat in the House of Lords, where she was appalled at the lack of support for her policies, even among Tories. But Brian was still enjoying his transition from Labour MP to well-paid journalist: he declined.

After she was elected for a third time in 1987 Thatcher still saw no immediate successor in the Tory Party. She had grown disillusioned with arch-Thatcherite Norman Tebbit's performance as party chairman during the election campaign. Rupert Murdoch saw Tebbit as Thatcher's natural successor but, said the Prime Minister, 'I couldn't get him elected as leader of the Tory Party even if I wanted to – nor would the country elect him if he was.'

She was even more critical of some of her other cabinet colleagues. She regarded Ken Baker as 'smarmy' – but then he was a Heathite-turned-Thatcherite – and John Moore, the Kennedyesque face of Thatcherism whom she had promoted above his abilities, was 'one of my greatest disappointments'; the problem is, she said, 'he's dominated by his wife'. But she always had great admiration for David Owen and no regard whatsoever for her Labour opponent, Neil Kinnock: she counted herself lucky that he was Labour leader, regarded him as a lightweight and believed the

British people would never elect him. But her worst bile was reserved for Michael Heseltine, long before his leadership challenge. She hated him. 'If you knew what I know about him . . .' she confided to several of my associates. But she never firmed up on what she thought she knew that was so damaging.

Even as far back as 1987 she had identified John Major as her heir apparent. At the time he was only a junior minister – 'young and inexperienced' – and it would be many years, in her view, before he was ready. She did not throw her weight behind Major in the second ballot of the 1990 Tory leadership contest (after she had withdrawn) simply because he was not Michael Heseltine; he had been her chosen one for several years. That probably explains her bitterness when she discovered that Major in power was not the 'one of us' she had long assumed. Her choice of the then unknown Major in 1987, long before her leadership became an issue, also illustrates that it was her intention to stay in power for a very long time.

Some Tory grandees had different ideas. Willie Whitelaw, who positioned himself as Thatcher's candid friend, made it clear as Thatcher's star started to wane that he would not fight to save her. 'If Maggie has to go,' he told me over dinner, 'I want Geoffrey Howe [thank God Whitelaw never got his way: Howe would have been a disastrous Tory leader]. He'd win the support of a majority of Tory MPs. And if she loses a general election then I won't hesitate to tell her she has to go – even if it's only a hung parliament, she'll have to go.'

Thatcher would have moved heaven and earth to stop Howe succeeding her. Almost three years before his resignation from her government she was describing him privately as 'a once comfortable slipper that has become an unpleasant old boot'. I happened to mention this to Rupert, making clear it was private. 'Don't worry, I won't tell anyone,' he assured me. But he couldn't resist telling Kelvin MacKenzie. Next day the *Sun* went to town on a 'Thatcher says Howe is an old boot' story. I was furious, since I had been told it on a strictly confidential basis. Political gossip was a currency that kept Rupert happy; but he was not always a secure recipient. I became more careful what information I traded with my proprietor.

The Sunday Times seemed to have the knack of upsetting the Prime Minster even when it did not mean to. Almost a year after the Barclays' Bank débâcle, in January 1985, we splashed on page one with 'Thatcher ready to let £1 = $1'. We did so in good faith: after all, we had it from no less an authority than Thatcher's own trusty press officer, Bernard Ingham, that the pound would be left to find its own level, even if it meant parity with the dollar. Thatcher awoke on Sunday morning, 13 January, to hear BBC radio news repeat and confirm our story. 'They're talking down sterling,' she fumed. In fact, it was worse than that: in the Far East exchange markets the pound was about to go into freefall. The government, through *The Sunday Times*, had given the impression that it was indifferent to the level of sterling: selling it became a one-way bet.

To make matters worse, different parts of the government were giving out conflicting signals. The Treasury had briefed the *Observer* that the policy of leaving the pound to float would have to be abandoned at the same time Ingham was telling us the opposite. The *Observer* splashed with 'Thatcher in U-turn to save pound'. It was proved right more quickly than it could ever have realized. As the pound slumped in the Far East in response to our story and fell to $1.10 by Monday ministers panicked: they rushed to increase interest rates by 1.5 per cent and throw official reserves at sterling to stabilize its exchange rate. Official spin doctors told anybody who would listen that the government really did care about the currency, whatever *The Sunday Times* had reported.

Though we had done no more than repeat the official line from Downing Street – this was never denied – it was another black mark for *The Sunday Times* in the Thatcher book. The fault lay with the failure of Downing Street and the Treasury to co-ordinate their own policies, but somehow it was us she was furious with. She certainly did not blame her beloved Bernard.

At an official reception later in the week, as speculation about Ingham's future mounted, she strode up to him and in front of a group of journalists cooed loudly: 'Isn't he brilliant?' This was in marked contrast to the way she greeted me later in the year at a spetacular bash at Hampton Court to celebrate the 200th anniversay of *The Times*. As she made her way through the post-dinner drinks party, greeting and chatting with the many distinguished guests, she looked up to discover I was next in line to meet her. The lady who once famously said she was *not* for turning did just that: she glared at me for a split second, swivelled on her heels and set off in a different direction.

*

THOUGH DIRECT RELATIONS between us were now non-existent and she had many grounds for resenting *The Sunday Times*, I will always be grateful for her invaluable help in saving my old school from the educational barbarians in the Labour-dominated Strathclyde Regional Authority. In 1987 I learned from my brother that the authority was planning to close Paisley Grammar, a sixteenth-century foundation whose main crime seemed to be that it remained a centre of educational excellence in an age of comprehensive mediocrity.

Its high educational standards had been somewhat diluted since my day, when it was a selective grammar school that even charged modest fees (the princely sum of 18 guineas a year in 1960) to ensure the parents were committed enough to their children's education to make a small extra contribution. But in difficult circumstances the rector, Robert Corbett, a teacher of the old school who believed in discipline and standards, along with his dedicated staff, had done their utmost to retain its best traditions: it remained a 'magnet' school for the area and one of Paisley's biggest assets – everybody still wears school uniform and much of the sixth form goes to university.

The Labour Neanderthals who dominated education policy in Strathclyde resented the school's success – even the fact that it was still called a grammar school, though it had been effectively comprehensive since the early 1970s. Its 900 places were regularly oversubscribed and the school was bursting at the seams with pupils; but Strathclyde decided to close it and move everybody to an undersubscribed 1960s comprehensive facility that few wanted. It was a calculated act of vindictive educational vandalism.

I buttonholed Malcolm Rifkind, who was then secretary of state for Scotland, during the annual *Sunday Times* cocktail party at the 1987 Tory Party conference: 'I hope you're going to do something to save my old school, Malcolm. It's just the sort of school the Tories should be encouraging.'

'I couldn't agree more, Andrew,' he replied stiffly. 'But I have only limited powers of intervention and I'm not sure there's much I can do.' This was the voice of the privately educated Edinburgh mandarin. The fact was Rifkind did not care enough about a school like Paisley Grammar to intervene.

'Let me tell you this, Malcolm,' I replied angrily. 'If you're not prepared to lift a finger to save the school then I will appeal over your head directly to the Prime Minister: I think she knows she's presided over the death of quite enough grammar schools.' Rifkind shrugged his shoulders (I think he thought I was bluffing) and we parted company. I knew there would be no joy there.

I launched a campaign to save the school in the Scottish edition of *The Sunday Times*; it shed embarrassing light on Strathclyde's plans but I knew they could not be shamed into changing their minds. Labour's biggest Scottish fiefdom, effectively a one-party state, had long been impervious to public opinion. I had no idea if Thatcher would be interested in saving the school and she certainly owed me no favours, especially since relations with her were at a very low ebb: that summer I had published *Spycatcher* (see Chapter 12) and she was so angry that the government was seeking to put me in gaol. It was not the best time to ask for help. But I knew she felt guilty that she had allowed so many grammar schools to close when she had been education secretary in the early 1970s. Here was an opportunity for her to make a small amends.

Back in London I contacted Brian Griffiths, the head of Thatcher's policy unit in 10 Downing Street. A former Welsh grammar-school-boy, he grasped immediately what was at stake and shared my outrage. 'Rifkind is in the pocket of the Scottish Office,' he said, 'and there are not many Tories there. I will bring the matter to the Prime Minister's attention. But you must arrange for the rector to write requesting the school be saved backed with a petition of the parents.'

Both were with Downing Street within days. 'We have served the community of Paisley since 1586,' wrote the Rector to the Prime Minister, 'without a break. In the year in which the town of Paisley is celebrating 500 years of continuous growth Strathclyde Regional Council is bent on closing an education unit which has brought fame to the town.'

Griffiths soon reported back that Thatcher had been outraged by Strathclyde's plans and Rifkind's indifference. She had instructed him to issue a new regulation giving the Scottish Office powers to save schools where 80 per cent of parents disagreed with a local authority's closure plans.

The school was saved and the largely left-leaning Scottish media and local Labour politicians were furious. Paisley's Labour MP accused me of 'deceit and connivance', which was strange since I was so proud of saving my old school that I was happy for the world to know exactly what I'd done. The left-wing press, especially the *Glasgow Herald* and *The Scotsman*, were spitting blood. I was accused of that most heinous of crimes – 'using my contacts' – to stop the school from being closed. But the pupils and parents of Paisley Grammar were delighted. They invited me to a victory rally in the school assembly hall. It was one of the most rewarding nights of my life.

'I have been accused by the Labour MP of this town of using my contacts to save my old school,' I began to a packed hall from the stage where I had once operated the lights for the school play. 'But what kind of former pupil would I be if I didn't move heaven and earth to save a school that did so much for me?' The audience cheered.

'This is not so much a victory celebration,' I continued, 'but more of a thanksgiving. Throughout my life I have always been grateful for two things: first, my parents and the loving family home they gave me; and second, my education, first, here at Paisley Grammar and then at the University of Glasgow – two ancient centres of learning which gave me a world-class education. The foundation was laid in these very buildings: I learned discipline, hard work, a healthy interest in academic enquiry and a belief in opportunity for all, regardless of background. It is a tribute to the tenacity of the parents, the pupils, the former pupils, the rector and his staff that future generations will be able to enjoy the same benefits as I, from a school that has served this town well for four hundred years.

'In every American city now they are trying to establish magnet schools like Paisley Grammar. It is because Japan and Germany have so many more schools like it that they are so much more prosperous than we are. I cannot think of any other country in the world that would even dream of closing a school like Paisley Grammar. I salute your victory.'

I sat down to a standing ovation, with people cheering and a few even crying, feeling as if I had just been nominated for president. It was heady stuff. Back in London Thatcher was making the same points in her own way. Peter Walker, who knew I had enlisted her help in Paisley, approached the Prime Minister before a cabinet dinner: 'You know, Margaret,' he said, 'though we've had many disagreements we've both always agreed that the destruction of the grammar schools was a disaster.'

'It was a huge mistake, Peter,' she replied, then hesitated. 'Where's Malcolm?' She looked round and beckoned to her Scottish secretary to join her. He scurried over. 'You must always remember, Malcolm,' she said to him sternly, 'that it's your job to save good schools, not preside over their closure.' And with that Britain's future foreign secretary was sent on his way, tail firmly between his legs.

The battle for Paisley Grammar was a parochial example of *The Sunday Times* and Margaret Thatcher being at one. But on many of the biggest struggles of her decade in power *The Sunday Times* also stood shoulder to shoulder with her: the need for outright victory in the miners' strike (when even Tory voices were counselling compromise); the controversial deployment of cruise missiles; the unpopular American air-raid on Tripoli launched from British bases (when even the Tory Press turned against her), the privatization programme, the radical cuts in marginal income-tax rates, the host of measures taken to make Britain a more competitive market economy – on these and more, Thatcher's battles were our battles.

*

THE THATCHER REVOLUTION, however, began to run out of steam and lose its way after her landslide victory in 1987. The economic miracle her supply-side reforms had been designed to achieve turned instead to familiar British stagflation: there was a resurgence of high inflation and a return to recession. By March 1990 a *Sunday Times* editorial was saying that 'Thatcher's administration is clearly entering a night of the soul even darker than the bleak days of 1981 . . . that famous "Thatcher factor" may now be working against the Tories. Once she could add five points to her party's poll performance; could she now be taking five points off it?'

The worse things got, the more imperious the Prime Minister became, and impervious to good advice. It grew difficult to reason with her: former loyal Thatcherites – such as Tebbit, Lawson and Howe – fell by the wayside. 'Mrs Thatcher's appeal lay in public admiration for her grit and her success,' commented the paper. 'The admiration is wearing thin. The grit is hackneyed – the stuff of television satire – and the success dented.'

I did not quarrel with the fact that some economic downturn was inevitable after the boom of the mid-eighties; nor could I claim to be any more perceptive than the government in anticipating the overheating of the economy in 1987/88. But, just as her obsession with narrow monetary targets had made the recession of the early eighties unnecessarily deep, so her total reliance in the late eighties on high interest rates to squeeze inflation out of the economy risked the very economic renaissance of Britain she had struggled so hard to achieve.

'Interest rise puts Britain on brink of recession' warned a *Sunday Times* page-one splash in early October 1989 as base rates reached 15 per cent. For the next year *The Sunday Times* told anybody who would listen that a bad recession was looming. But Thatcher and her ministers would hear none of it. When, in the autumn of 1990, *The Sunday Times* Business section devoted most of its front page to a 'Britain hits recession' special report, Downing Street dismissed it as 'hysterical' and Thatcher attacked *The Sunday Times* in a speech in Wales for 'doom-mongering' and talking Britain down. But she had more to worry about than the fact that she was wrong about the course of the economy.

The decline in the government's fortunes was symbolized by the disastrous poll tax, her worst mistake in a decade in power. It dawned on me just how indefensible it was when I discovered that my daily cleaner would be paying more poll tax than me – and I had just had my top rate of income tax cut to 40 per cent. *The Sunday Times* did more than argue against the poll tax in its editorials: it campaigned against it in its news and feature pages. Back in April 1988 we had called for this 'wholly misguided reform' to be 'consigned to the dustbin'. But Thatcher would not budge.

Through 1989 and into 1990 I began to feel it was time for a change of leader: with Thatcher still at the helm the Tories would likely lose the next general election, yet Labour was still not fit for power. Most senior editors on the paper thought the same. Though he was no Thatcherite, I had always admired the dash and leadership qualities of Michael Heseltine; after walking out of the cabinet over the Westland crisis in 1986, he had developed a distinctive radical agenda of his own. I warmed to the idea that he was the man to win the next election, consolidate the Thatcher achievements of the 1980s and build on them in the 1990s. As 1990 progressed and Thatcher's position deteriorated further I resolved to back Heseltine in any Tory leadership contest. We barely knew each other (nor were we ever to become close) but he seemed to me to be a fitting successor to Thatcher; since I had never been part of Thatcher's inner circle of admiring editors and journalists, it was easier for me to make the break. But would Rupert Murdoch let me do it?

Efforts to dissuade me from putting *The Sunday Times* behind Heseltine if he challenged Thatcher for the Tory leadership began early in 1990, eight months before the Heseltine challenge materialized. Rupert was beginning to sense my mind was moving towards a change of prime minister and began a series of calls and not-so-subtle lobbying to leave me in no doubt where he stood, which was solidly behind Thatcher. Relations had already started to sour between Rupert and me in my final months at Sky Television (see Chapter 11). My support for Heseltine was not calculated to improve them.

Early in March, as Tory sentiment was beginning to turn against Thatcher, he called to discuss the political situation. I told him I was beginning to doubt that the Tories could win a fourth election with Thatcher still at the helm. He did not demur: 'It may just be my cheque book talking,' he said, 'but this country cannot afford a Labour government. If Thatcher can't win then Heseltine should have his chance.' We seemed to be on the same wavelength.

At the end of March, however, he was already changing his tune. He called from Sky, where he had been watching Thatcher speak on Sky News to the Tory faithful at its annual mini-conference in Cheltenham. 'Isn't she marvellous?' he enthused. 'We can't have her replaced by somebody like

Heseltine. If there is any chance she can still win we must keep her.' I offered no reply: it was not an argument I needed to have at this stage. Rupert had been polite, if insistent; already I sensed we were drifting apart.

A week later his anti-Heseltine line had hardened. He called on a Friday night as I was writing the editorial, with no other purpose than to rail against Heseltine.

'I don't want him,' said Rupert firmly. 'He won't preserve the Thatcher revolution. I can think of at least three or four other alternatives to Thatcher who would be better than him.' Again, I said nothing: since one of the 'alternatives' he mentioned was David Waddington, an old-school cabinet right-winger who was soon to disappear from politics without trace (to become, in a fine example of the Establishment looking after its own, governor of Bermuda). It was clear there was not going to be a meeting of minds. But the conversation depressed me. I was growing less tolerant of my proprietor's heavy-handed political leaning. After we finished talking I wrote an editorial calling for the return of Heseltine to the cabinet. It made me feel better.

Leadership speculation abated during the summer and so did Rupert's lobbying. But the Tory position continued to deteriorate, the poll tax hanging like an albatross around its neck. I dined with Michael Heseltine at his request at the Stafford Hotel towards the end of July.

'Are you going to run in the autumn?' I asked him bluntly. He obfuscated at first (he did not really know me well enough to take me into his confidence) but later, as we lingered over several brandies past midnight, he said: 'I am of a mind to do it. But I have only one bullet in my gun. I can't afford to miss.' He then asked me, just as bluntly: 'Can I count on the support of *The Sunday Times*? Would Murdoch let you abandon Thatcher?'

'I don't know,' I replied. 'He's made it pretty clear he

wants Thatcher to stay. But it will be my decision, unless he sacks me over supporting you – and that will cause a bigger row than if he grudgingly lets me do it.' Heseltine seemed encouraged by this, and by the autumn rumours were rife again that he – or some stalking-horse – would mount a leadership challenge.

I next heard from him towards the end of October. He had been doing a round of lunches and dinners in the City: 'There is absolute vilification for her in the City,' he said. 'They nearly all think she must go. So do many in the Tory constituencies, though publicly they profess loyalty. There is a lot of unease in the parliamentary party too.' It was clear he was working himself up to a challenge: 'But the joker in the pack is the Gulf [Saddam Hussein had invaded Kuwait in the summer of 1990 and British forces were gathering in the Gulf, making a change of prime minister more difficult].'

Geoffrey Howe, the deputy prime minister, fell out with Thatcher over Europe and resigned on 1 November. Coming on top of Nigel Lawson's resignation as chancellor, it was a sign that things were slipping away from the Prime Minister. Leadership speculation had reached fever pitch when Heseltine called me on Saturday, 10 November. We discussed the frenetic political situation. I was more convinced than ever that Thatcher had to go, he seemed more eager than ever to run. But he was still vacillating. I told him our page-one splash for the next day was 'Heseltine poised to take on Thatcher'.

'That's pushing me,' he complained, then after a pause added, 'but I can live with it.

'If I knew I could count on *The Sunday Times*,' he said slowly, 'it would be a major influence on my decision.'

I thought for a moment, realizing it was important to give a straight answer. 'I can guarantee that there will be no rubbishing of you in any way,' I said slowly, 'which there might be in the other Murdoch papers. In fact, we're likely to be very sympathetic.' I added with a laugh, 'But you have to declare first!'

'I understand,' he said, satisfied with my reply. Though I was pretty clear in my own mind I would back him against Thatcher I was not yet sure I could fend off Rupert. No sooner had I put the phone down than my proprietor was on the line. He launched into another attack on the man to whom I had just been speaking.

'Heseltine would be a disastrous prime minister,' said Rupert firmly. 'He was pretty hopeless as a minister and he would be just as useless as PM.'

I said nothing: I saw no point in having an argument until Heseltine had declared himself. But my silence clearly communicated disagreement with what I was hearing. Rupert rang off in something of a huff.

As a leadership contest became increasingly certain, 10 Downing Street got in on the act. John Whittingdale, Thatcher's political secretary, called Gerry Malone, my oldest friend since university days. He had lost his Aberdeen South seat in the 1987 general election but was to return to the House of Commons for Winchester in 1992. He was known to be a close friend and colleague, having helped me launch the Scottish section of *The Sunday Times*.

'Rupert Murdoch's papers have always been very helpful to the Prime Minister,' said Whittingdale, 'except for *The Sunday Times*. The PM has asked me to speak to Mr Murdoch about it. Its editorial line has become very hostile and she has not forgotten the damage done by the Queen vs. Thatcher story – she's still angry about that, even more than the publishing of *Spycatcher* or the Barclays Bank business.'

Malone duly passed these words on to me: I suspect they were meant to intimidate me – a warning that Downing

Street was prepared to go over my head to Rupert unless I toed the line.

I do not know if Whittingdale ever did speak to Rupert. Not that there was much need: he was already placing quite enough pressure on me to stick with Thatcher. At the time, however, Whittingdale got little joy from Malone.

'What would you like me to do, John?' asked Malone, jokingly. 'Spike Andrew's copy before it gets in the paper? And, if that fails, would you like me to spike his coffee?'

Whittingdale tried another tack. He collared Michael Jones, the political editor. 'We hear *The Sunday Times* is thinking about endorsing Michael Heseltine. That would be very damaging. Can you do anything about it?'

'No,' said Jones bluntly. 'But don't worry: the editorial is in the second section – I'm sure not many people will notice it!' Whittingdale did not seem reassured.

Geoffrey Howe made his resignation speech in the House of Commons on Tuesday, 13 November. For a man whose verbal attacks on opponents had previously been best dismissed by Denis Healey as the equivalent of being 'savaged by a dead sheep' it was a devastating indictment of Thatcher and underlined how isolated she was becoming: if she could no longer tolerate even those like Howe and Lawson who had once been in the Thatcherite vanguard it was clearly a crisis for the Prime Minister. She was now highly vulnerable: Heseltine threw his hat in the ring at last.

The pressure on me not to support him intensified. Andrew Knight, whom Rupert had taken to referring to privately, with perhaps a hint of sarcasm, as his 'viceroy' in London, called me on 15 November, three days before our crucial editorial endorsement in the Tory leadership contest was due to appear. The call was undoubtedly at Rupert's instigation.

'Who will *The Sunday Times* support?' he enquired.

'Ivan [Fallon, the deputy editor] is for Michael Heseltine,' I replied, not yet wishing to show my full hand.

'That's stupid,' he replied.

'That's the way my mind is going too.'

'Heseltine would make a disastrous prime minister.'

I noted the use of the same derogatory adjective as Rupert.

'I wouldn't want *The Sunday Times* [by which he meant News International!] to play any part in Thatcher's downfall,' he continued. 'If she's badly wounded in this leadership contest she will go of her own volition.'

I was being invited to let events take their course, without *The Sunday Times* contributing to her demise. I declined to take that option. A polite argument ensued. Andrew sounded worried when he realized he was getting nowhere. He had been bombarding me with handwritten memos on the need to stick with Thatcher since early November.

Soon Rupert was back on the telephone. No doubt the transatlantic lines had been humming. 'I hear you're going to come out for Heseltine,' he said quietly. I confirmed that was the way my mind was going.

'It's your decision,' he continued, resignation rather than rancour in his voice: I think he realized by now I would not budge. 'But the paper will be seen to have turned tail when the going got rough. Heseltine would be disastrous [that word again!]. We owe Thatcher a lot as a company. Don't go overboard in your attacks on her.'

I assured him I would not but pointed out this was no overnight conversion. The paper had been going in this direction for some time. 'I'll speak to you later,' he said, hanging up. It had been a civilized exchange.

Ivan returned from a lunch with Thatcher supporters. 'The only thing on everybody's mind,' he reported back, 'is *The Sunday Times*. They think its decision is the only one that matters. Everybody is waiting for it. They think we're going for Heseltine – but they believe if we now came out for Thatcher it would be such a surprise that it might clinch the contest for her. That's why they want our support.'

I began writing the editorial on Friday afternoon, 16 November. Andrew Knight was back on the phone, with a new tack: 'I just wanted to stress,' he said, 'how very wrong it would be to remove a prime minister in this way.' I replied that I was more concerned about getting the government back on the rails again and in a fit state to stop Neil Kinnock from becoming prime minister.

Now it was time for Woodrow Wyatt to get into the act. As a confidant of both Thatcher and Murdoch he had a double reason for wanting to bring *The Sunday Times* to heel. He had already approached Irwin Stelzer, my friend and Rupert's closest adviser, asking him if there was anything he could do to change my mind. 'No, there's not,' said Irwin, who did not approve of my decision to support Heseltine but was content to leave the editorial line of *The Sunday Times* to its editor.

At 5.30 p.m. my secretary announced that Woodrow Wyatt was on the line. 'Tell him I'll call him back,' I said. 'If I don't put a stop to this lobbying the editorial will never get written.' I never did get back to him.

Rupert rang again on Saturday morning; since the editorial was in the pre-printed News Review, which was already coming off the presses, it was too late to change anything. 'I'm sorry I've taken a line of which you disapprove, Rupert,' I said, 'but I've been covering British politics for almost twenty years and I had to write what I felt.'

'It's your privilege,' he said. It was a perfectly amicable exchange. Though the pressure from him and others had been relentless, we had never exchanged cross words on the matter. A major issue of policy had been decided by the editor, just as Rupert had promised Parliament it would when he bought Times Newspapers.

On 18 November, *The Sunday Times* published 'A reluctant goodbye', one of the most important editorials of my editorship. 'This newspaper has long maintained that the best result in the next general election would be for Margaret Thatcher to lead the Tories to a fourth victory,' it began. 'Sadly, the course of events has conspired to make that unlikely. Crippling interest rates, soaring inflation and deepening recession have combined to deprive the government of its reputation for economic competence (once its most valuable electoral asset). It now presides over an economy mired in stagflation. The poll tax – the conception of which was a mistake, its birth a mess and its infancy an expensive embarrassment – has proved the most unpopular tax in modern British history. All the perfumes in the government's boudoir cannot make it smell sweet.'

The editorial was polite but firm about Thatcher: 'possibly the greatest peacetime Prime Minister of this century, but now also, if the polls are to be believed, one of the most unpopular. The public, rightly or wrongly, is jaded with her and tired of her ways to an extent that has made her an electoral liability . . . the poll tax is Mrs Thatcher's tax: that precludes doing much about it as long as she is in charge . . . That brings us to the rather painful matter of Mrs Thatcher's future . . .'

The editorial went on to press the case for Heseltine. It commended his support for strong defence, privatization, workfare and low taxes and his proposals to reform the poll tax, introduce directly elected mayors and free schools from local authority control – 'that reads like an agenda for the 1990s that *The Sunday Times* could support'. We parted company with him on his enthusiasm for 'industrial policy' if it meant greater state intervention in industry but looked forward 'to a constructive dialogue with him on such matters. That has become well-nigh impossible with Mrs Thatcher, perhaps the inevitable consequence of being in power for eleven years.'

The editorial's conclusion was clear: 'The issue before Tory MPs this weekend is not the re-election of Margaret Thatcher, it is the defeat of Neil Kinnock. That requires saying a reluctant goodbye to Mrs Thatcher and the endorsement of Michael Heseltine.'

Looking back, I still believe it was right to remove Mrs Thatcher in 1990; it is a pity she did not step down gracefully on her tenth anniversary as prime minister, when her reputation was higher. If she had led the Tories into the next election with the poll tax intact I believe they would have been defeated. But the record of her successor makes me less sure now that it was right to get rid of her than I was six years ago; but then I was not responsible for choosing John Major.

There is one judgement in that editorial which I now believe to be wrong. It attacked 'the fundamentalist manner' in which Thatcher was approaching Europe, which had 'needlessly divided the Tory Party . . . creating the damaging impression of a party as disunited as Labour was a decade ago'. It also attacked her growing anti-Brussels rhetoric as 'misplaced chauvinism'. But the Tories are even more disunited under the emollient John Major and the British people are increasingly Thatcherite in their attitude to the federalist schemes of our European partners. On Europe, Thatcher was ahead of her time.

Thatcher failed to win a big enough majority by the Tories' complicated voting system in the first ballot on Tuesday, 20 November, against Heseltine. I learned later that Thatcher thought *The Sunday Times* played a crucial part in her downfall: she needed only two more votes to survive and believed *The Sunday Times* editorial swung at least that number of Tory MPs against her. Though she vowed to 'fight on' it was clear she was mortally wounded. Rupert called me next day: 'I've already spoken to Downing Street urging her to continue fighting,' he said, 'but I've warned her not to anoint Hurd if she feels she has to stand down.' Rupert had a special distaste for Douglas Hurd, who as foreign secretary encapsulated everything he hated about the Foreign Office.

'Would you prefer Heseltine to Hurd in a second ballot?' he wanted to know. I said yes.

'Would you prefer Heseltine to Major?'

'I haven't thought that one through, Rupert. But my instinct is to stick with Heseltine. By the way, it looks very bad for Mrs T.' He agreed and hung up.

Next morning she withdrew from the contest. Heseltine called soon after.

'What you've done for me!' was his opening sentence.

'What you've done for yourself,' I replied.

'Will you still be with me in the second round?'

'Yes, but we'll be nice to John Major and Douglas Hurd.'

'I'd keep both in their current positions [as chancellor and foreign secretary].'

'How does it look?'

'Some of the right are coming our way. I expect five or six vocal right-wingers to declare for me shortly. But it's too early to say if I can win an overall majority in the second ballot. I've inevitably lost some support to Hurd.'

He called again later that day. 'Howe, Lawson and Carrington are all coming over to me. Even Neil Hamilton [a maverick right-winger]. We're now well ahead of Major, but probably not yet by enough to win on the second ballot – unless Hurd's votes crumble to us; I already have most of his second preferences in a third ballot.'

As I was writing the editorial backing Heseltine in the

second ballot, Rupert called me to say he was now 'unequivocally for Major'. The other four Wapping titles, having backed Thatcher in the first round, now backed Major in the second. But Rupert put no pressure on me to switch: he realized that would have made us look contrary; besides it was useful to him to have at least one of his papers support someone who could be the next prime minister.

The Heseltine camp certainly thought it was going their way. Peter Walker called me on the Saturday to report that Heseltine could count on 162 firm pledges to Major's 140. 'People are being put off by Major's TV appearances,' he said. 'The backbenchers are also revolting against the idea of a cabinet cabal designed to keep Michael out.'

But my own journalists were telling a different story. Ivan Fallon and Michael Jones reported a strong swing to Major as part of a concerted 'stop Heseltine' campaign. Even the lady was campaigning against him: she had just harangued David Hunt (the Welsh secretary) for supporting Heseltine. By the time our edition of 25 November went to press I realized that Major had it in the bag but backed Heseltine nevertheless.

Two days later Major polled 185 votes, Heseltine 131 and Hurd 56. Though it was not the necessary majority by Tory rules, Major's vote was enough to force the withdrawal of the other two. Heseltine immediately strode out of his Belgravia front door to announce gracefully to the waiting press pack that he was bowing out. As he walked back in the phone was ringing: it was Major. 'Thanks, Michael,' said our new prime minister. 'You'll have a job in my government.'

Heseltine called me the next afternoon.

'I failed you!' he said apologetically.

'You fought the good fight,' I replied, seeing no reason why he had any need to apologize to me. 'What job are you getting?'

'Environment,' he said, which meant he would have to sort out the poll tax mess. Then he added prophetically: 'Mark my words – Major is not a Thatcherite.' It seemed an odd remark at the time, since the whole basis of Major's leadership campaign had been his claim to be Thatcher's natural heir. Even the lady had thought so. But Michael was to be proved sadly right.

*

THERE WERE NO IMMEDIATE recriminations from Rupert, at least not on the surface. But it probably hastened my departure from his inner circle of confidants and contributed to the growing distance between us. Several News International executives certainly saw it as a turning-point. 'He saw it as an act of defiance,' says John Dux, 'and it contributed to his feeling that he was losing control of *The Sunday Times*. It was also a black mark for Andrew Knight: he was meant to control you – or so Rupert thought – and he had failed.'

Rupert was later to claim, no doubt based on Andrew Knight's testimony, that the only reason the 'dump Thatcher' editorial had been gentle on the lady was because of Knight's intervention. I had to remind Rupert of our own conversation on the matter – and of my total agreement that in backing Heseltine we should not beat up Thatcher.

If my support for Heseltine was a significant milestone on the long road to divorce with Rupert, it eventually led to a reconciliation of sorts with Thatcher. She began work on her memoirs and sold the publishing rights to Rupert's HarperCollins publishers in a multi-million pound deal, which meant we got the British newspaper serialization rights. I had played no part in the negotiation, though £750,000 was taken out of *The Sunday Times*' budget and passed to HarperCollins for the cost of serialization.

Thatcher had originally balked at extracts of her book

appearing in *The Sunday Times* because of past enmity, but she realized it was an essential part of her lucrative deal with HarperCollins. She insisted, however, on a contract which gave her approval over every change we made to the text, no matter how minor, headlines, pictures and even picture captions. There was clearly a lack of trust on her part that we would play fair.

In fact, she never had any need to worry. My only concern was to extract the best bits from a long, dense book so that we would have a return on our costly investment. I edited the extracts myself, choosing the most interesting episodes in her career then subbing them down to read more tightly than the book. There were never any complaints from her about the editing or condensing: later she told me she had been delighted and impressed by the professional manner in which we had handled the serialization.

I wanted to begin the serialization on the eve of the October 1993 Tory Party conference, for maximum impact. For the same reason – she did not want to be seen to be trying to dominate the conference with her comments on various leading Tories, including her successor – Thatcher insisted it begin the Sunday after the Tories' annual jamboree. The extracts were prepared in great secrecy. Eddie Bell, the London boss of HarperCollins, even delivered the page proofs of the book to me in a locked briefcase, complete with handcuffs. I was assured that every book was under lock and key and that the warehouses in Britain and America had special twenty-four-hour security. But the *Daily Mirror* still managed to procure a copy.

David Banks had come a long way from the days when he had keyed *Sunday Times* copy into the computer during that first hectic weekend at Wapping and I had brought him and his team a crate of champagne in gratitude for their sterling efforts (see Chapter 6). Now he was editor of the *Daily*

Mirror and hosting a drinks party for the head of the Opposition at the Labour Party conference in Brighton. A team of his journalists had been scouring Britain and America, offering a bounty to anybody who could supply them with an advance copy of Thatcher's memoirs. Not exactly investigative journalism, more like bribery – and they came away empty-handed. As Banks chatted to the Labour bigwigs his mobile phone rang. It was his London office: an anonymous man had just offered the *Mirror* night newsdesk the Thatcher book for £10,000. What should they do? 'Get it,' barked Banks.

The men from the *Mirror* met their anonymous caller in a London pub the following night. He had what they had so far failed to get by fair means or foul. The £10,000 was handed over in used banknotes and the journalists scurried back to the office with the book. As the Tories gathered in Blackpool for their conference the *Mirror* began publishing some of the juiciest bits. I was furious. They were in receipt of stolen goods and in breach of Thatcher's copyright – and our legal right to exclusive serialization. We rushed into court, certain the judge would tell them to desist.

To my anger and amazement the judge upheld their right to publish stories based on the content of the book on the bizarre grounds that it was in the public interest that they came out while the Tories were in conference, which seemed an overtly political decision for a judge to make. We appealed immediately: incredibly the appeal court upheld the decision. It was the last of many bizarre judgements that the courts delivered during my editorship: they had stopped me from serializing *Spycatcher*, which the government was trying to suppress, against the public interest, and to which *The Sunday Times* owned the serialization rights. But they were prepared to allow the *Mirror* to publish stolen property, which was legitimately about to be published in a few days' time, trampling over the author's copyright in the process. Some began to conclude this was the revenge of the judges against Thatcher for daring to try to reform the legal system.

The *Mirror* continued to publish more stories based on text from the book and I learned that the *Mail on Sunday*, which now also had access to the book, planned to do its own extracts to coincide with our serialization. I have always relished the cut and thrust of Fleet Street competition but the courts had just handed its more disreputable elements a thieves' charter. They had replaced the laws of fair competition, confidentiality and copyright with the law of the jungle. It was a crazy decision, reversed in May 1994 in the *Mail on Sunday* case at huge cost (over £600,000 in costs and damages) to that paper when we sued both papers for punitive damages (the *Mirror* case is still pending).

It seemed to me the judges had gone collectively bonkers, but then I had never found Britain's courts reliable on freedom of the press issues. Their rulings went far beyond our little local difficulty: unless they were reversed it meant nobody's intellectual property rights were safe from piracy. Why negotiate exclusive serialization rights in good faith when others could plunder and pillage them at will? Why bother to pay for these rights when the law would not lift a finger to stop others from stealing them? The judges had given a green light for theft and bribery on a massive scale.

I watched these events unfold with a mixture of depression, helplessness and anger from my Blackpool hotel. I knew this would be the last major serialization of my editorship and it was being picked clean by other papers, with the sanction of the law. Others said not to worry, it would only heighten interest when the real thing appeared on the coming Sunday. There was some truth in that but the thrill of revealing the book's most dramatic revelations for the first time had gone. Under its previous ownership (Robert Maxwell) the Mirror Group had stolen people's pension money; now it was stealing other people's books. I joked in one interview that you couldn't let a *Mirror* journalist into your home unless everything was nailed down: it was an attempt to put on a brave public face to mask my sorrow. The grey skies and the windswept rain coming off the North Sea and battering my hotel room window were a more accurate reflection of my real mood.

Then on Friday morning, as I was packing to return to London, the phone by my hotel bed rang: it was Margaret Thatcher. 'Now, Andrew, don't be depressed,' she said firmly, in her best morale-building voice. 'You're a good editor. You're an honourable man. You're a gentleman. You've taken that paper and you've improved it beyond measure. Don't let them get you down. We'll beat them. You have behaved exactly as you said you would, they are the ones who are not gentlemen.'

They were generous, uplifting words to an editor who had caused her so much aggravation during her premiership.

CHAPTER TEN

A Tart in Tramp

'I'M SORRY,' I said to my companion as the curtain came down for the interval, 'I can't concentrate on this. I have to go back to the office.' It was very unusual for me to be at the theatre on a Saturday night but some tickets had come my way. I had dashed to the West End to join a female friend after agreeing changes to the first edition; we took our seats just as the house lights at the Apollo Theatre on the Strand dimmed.

It was 19 March 1988, the afternoon two off-duty soldiers in Ulster, after running by mistake into an IRA funeral, had been dragged out of their car, brutally beaten then murdered. Television had been running footage all afternoon of the men trying to escape, firing a gun in the air to no effect, then being surrounded by the mob and taken away to their terrible fate. I could not get the images of these two young men out of my mind and I shuddered to think what had been done to them before they were shot, out of sight of the cameras. The events we were watching on stage – it was a rather convoluted play about George Bernard Shaw – seemed an irrelevance to the real events on the streets of Belfast.

I should never have gone in the first place; it was always risky to plan anything on a Saturday night, which was why I rarely did it. I was desperate to return to Wapping. My friend offered to accompany me. We dashed back to my office where I busied myself supervising page changes and updating the story. It helped me deal with my distress at the gruesome death of the soldiers. I asked the picture editor why we had no stills of the ringleaders of the mob. He explained that the IRA had made the photographers hand over their film. 'Somebody must have got away with pictures of these murdering bastards,' I said angrily. 'Scour Belfast: I want them for next week.'

The picture editor delivered. He discovered that one brave photographer had managed to escape with a roll of film stuck down the side of his shoe. When it was developed it showed exactly who had been in the forefront of the murderous assault. By the following Sunday we had identified the ringleader and some of his accomplices: we splashed with 'Caught in the act: the IRA man who led the attack', under a picture of the besieged car with several key faces in the mob clearly visible. The story gave details we had uncovered of their terrorist past. It was a classic *Sunday Times* scoop, a product of the bravery and diligence of the Insight team and our Ulster correspondents, which contributed towards the gaoling of the killers.

That was in the week to come. By 11 p.m. on the night of the incident there was not much more to do but lock up the final edition and leave the night editor to monitor any breaking news. 'I'm sorry to have screwed up your Saturday night,' I said to my friend, who had been waiting patiently in my office watching television. 'I'll take you for a nightcap to Tramp, if you like.'

'It's the least you can do,' she said with a smile. It is a pity she did not feel as exhausted as I did and just wanted to go home – for it was the night I met Pamella Bordes.

*

CONTRARY TO FLEET STREET mythology I hardly ever went on a Saturday night to Tramp, the fashionable St James's nightclub and haunt of royalty and rock stars, film celebrities and TV folk, posh people and second-hand car dealers. It was the social variety of the place and its easy-going ambience which attracted me to it. But I was nearly always too tired on a Saturday, and Tramp is in a basement where my mobile phone didn't work, which meant the office couldn't get hold of me. If I went out at all on Saturdays after work, my preference was for a quiet supper somewhere in easy reach of the office should a major news story break.

Tramp was packed with people I did not know that night for Saturday is not an evening most members go. But they gave us the table of Johnny Gold, the generous, popular owner, who was having a rare night off. The table was at the entrance to the restaurant, where the disco music is in the distance and you can hear yourself talk. It was not long before I was locked in argument with some friends over the events of the day (I always seemed to get dragged into deep political discussions at Tramp); at one stage we were joined by Lady 'Bubbles' Rothermere, the eccentric wife of the owner of the *Daily Mail*, and her entourage of young men. Even a singer from the Drifters joined in. The conversation continued; I was getting a second wind.

Around 1 a.m. I called the office on the club phone to see if there were any developments from Belfast but the story was not moving. When I returned a beautiful young woman in elegant designer clothes had joined the table and was talking to Lady Rothermere. I asked her what she did: she said she was doing courses on cordon bleu cooking and flower arranging at Moyses Stevens, the up-market Mayfair flower shop, as a prelude to starting a business that would provide up-market home catering and flower arrangements.

'I do little dinner parties to practise,' she said. 'You and your friend should come over for dinner to my place in

Belgravia,' she continued, writing down her telephone number. 'You can be my guinea pigs for the night.'

A beautiful, single, well-dressed woman who cooks and lives in Belgravia, I thought to myself as I put the scrap of paper in my pocket, this could indeed be worth a follow-up call. I was single with no regular girlfriend at the time and she had pulled a face affecting disappointment when I said we would have to leave. She seemed keen enough but I was in no hurry: I had not been swept off my feet, though I was intrigued.

We met for Sunday lunch in Pontevecchio three weeks later, after I returned from a trip to Aspen. As we talked I felt she seemed a little harder than I had remembered her; there was a bitter edge to her voice which was not endearing. But she softened as the afternoon went on and, as we walked in St James's Park in the spring sunshine, she told me her family were landowners in India. Her father, now dead, had been a senior officer in the Indian Army killed in the Indo-Pakistan war in 1965 and she lived off a generous allowance from her mother. That must explain the fancy clothes, I thought.

We started seeing more of each other and by the end of April she was regularly staying overnight at Onslow Gardens. It began as a perfectly normal relationship, she could be good company and in private she looked much more the pretty, young girl than the designer-clad society vamp she often appeared in public. But as we grew closer I noticed she was prone to dark moods and flashes of temper. There were times when we delighted in each other's company but she could be sullen and withdrawn, which did not endear her to my friends, who generally did not like her, or to me. She grew increasingly possessive and suspicious of what I was up to when not with her, though she had no cause for concern. It had become a full-time relationship and the rest of my time was taken up with work.

I took her to many of the glamorous social events – cocktail parties, opera, opening nights – to which an editor of *The Sunday Times* gets invited; in public she always behaved as correctly as she dressed. If the evening was glitzy then she could certainly look the part; but she also knew when to dress soberly. I took her one night, with a little trepidation, to a private dinner at the house of the Chief Rabbi. She turned up in an ankle-length skirt and a blouse that buttoned to the neck. As I engaged in deep conversation with the Chief Rabbi and his guests, who included Lord Sainsbury, during what was a warm, engrossing dinner party, she spoke only when she felt she had something worthwhile to say. By the end of the night she had charmed everybody.

But in private she was sulky and demanding, prone to pick a fight on the flimsiest of pretexts. I learned when the affair was long over that she suffered from bulimia, which must have contributed to her violent mood swings (I have some sympathy for Prince Charles in this matter since Diana has suffered from the same eating disorder, which does not make for placid relationships). We began to row regularly, which was unusual for me since previous relationships had always been fairly even-keeled affairs – at least until their dying days. I began to find it all pretty exhausting.

In late May, after we had been seeing each other regularly for about a month, she called me from Onslow Gardens in high dudgeon on my mobile phone while I was on my way to lunch. She was almost hysterical about something I was supposed to have done, but I could not fathom what; so I quit lunch early and rushed back home, where I had left her that morning. She rushed past me out the door just as I arrived, her face red with tears and anger. I had no idea what the trouble was but clearly something had upset her. She had scrawled obscenities on both drawing-room mirrors and an empty whisky decanter lay in the sink, its contents having disappeared down the drain. My heart sank. What other damage had she done – and why? I was soon to find out when I went to the bedroom: she had taken the scissors to half a dozen business suits and some shirts.

She had not, as *Private Eye* and everybody else was later to relate, cut out the crotches of the trousers, though it made for a better story with more fitting symbolism to say that she had. Her handiwork was more mundane: she had slashed the sleeves of the jackets and some shirts. I rushed around the flat frantically looking for more damage, but fortunately there was none.

I was furious with what she had done – nothing remotely like this had ever happened to me before – and it was only much later that I realized that even in her anger she had been quite calculating: her 'messages' were on easily washed mirrors, not the wallpaper; the crystal decanter was not smashed; plenty of business suits and shirts had been untouched (though she had cut up one I was particularly fond of). Her anger had been controlled, the damage limited, despite her supposedly fraught state. She had not decided to walk away – just throw a tantrum.

I locked up the house and returned to the office, bemused and worried by the whole episode. Late that afternoon she called, accusing me of betraying her by seeing somebody else; I did not know what she was talking about. I must have sounded convincing since it happened to be true – as the whole world was later to discover, the secret in our relationship was not that I was the one who was seeing other people. But she would not be placated. I told her that it did not matter if she did not believe me because after that day's little episode I did not wish to see her again.

I was still puzzled by what had made her fly off the handle. It was only much later, long after she had disappeared from my life, that I learned that she had played back the messages on my answering machine. It was an out-of-date tape and there were some messages over a year old at the very end which had never been wiped: on the very last one she heard me tell Gerry Malone, my close friend, that I could not have lunch with him that day because I was lunching with a female friend. Maybe she did not realize it was a year old, though the messages preceding it should have alerted her since they dealt with matters that were obviously history; anyway, it turned out to be the reason for the explosion. I have always immediately wiped my message tape ever since.

She began to bombard me with telephone calls, which changed from haranguing to pleading with me to take her back. I let the answering machine handle them: my mother had come down from Scotland to stay for a long weekend and I did not want any nonsense from Ms Bordes to spoil it. My anger was further fuelled when a garbled account of the incident appeared in *Private Eye* about me having to cancel my wedding (!) because my 'fiancée' had walked out on me: though she denied it at the time, she had called the magazine with the story, posing as the housekeeper, as part of her revenge on me. She knew I hated that sort of publicity.

She continued with her charm offensive. One night as I was leaving the house I found her waiting on the steps. She handed me six expensive Turnbull & Asser sea-island cotton shirts with six silk ties and matching hankies and said she had made arrangements with a Savile Row tailor to make me some new suits if I would go for a fitting. I told her I was still very angry. But I took the shirts and ties (I *am* Scottish, after all!). She asked if I would at least have breakfast with her one morning. I agreed. 'If I didn't love you,' she explained,

'I wouldn't have done it.' I was not entirely convinced. But by mid-June we were back together again. It was a big mistake.

It was not long before the rows started again, worse than before and increasingly unpredictable. We would return home from a perfectly pleasant evening out and she would immediately fly into a rage about something that had supposedly upset her. I began to realize that I had a Jekyll and Hyde character on my hands, a charming, beautiful, interesting woman one moment, who could transform in seconds into a foul-mouthed, ranting monster. There was not just a dark but an evil side to her which frightened me and made me realize the relationship would have to end.

'Look,' I said in exasperation to her one day, 'I haven't got the time or the energy for all these fights. I've never had such a fractious relationship. I can't continue with it and do my job properly – it's too draining.'

'I need help,' she said, 'I think I'm schizophrenic.'

She talked about how she had fallen out with her mother after she had become Miss India in 1982, how she had briefly married a homosexual Frenchman while living in Paris to get a European passport, how she needed to settle down and gain some stability in her life. She suggested that she move in with me. But I could not cope with that; ever since the clothes-cutting incident I had refused even to leave her in the house alone. I was very attracted to her but some inner sense of self-preservation told me this was not a woman to fall in love with.

'Let's see how things develop between us,' I told her. 'If we're going strong at the end of the year then we can think about living together.' In the meantime I promised to help find her a new flat (she was living on the ground floor of a friend's mews house in Belgravia at the time) and to assist her with her plans to start a home and office catering/flower business by placing some ads in a couple of society magazines. She also wanted to improve her accent: there was a harshness to her voice which could sound ugly. I arranged for her to see a voice coach.

She never asked for money (which she did not seem to be short of anyway) or expect expensive presents (the only thing I ever bought her was a food mixer to help with her cooking – romantic that I am!). But she thought little of any kindness or consideration shown to her and did not have the commitment to build a business, perhaps because (as we were all to find out) she was making money in less arduous ways. Nor would she seek medical help. The tantrums escalated.

Going out with her during the summer of 1988 was like a roller-coaster ride: exciting but exhausting and sometimes frightening – you never knew when she would erupt or what you would be accused of. One night she walked out of a restaurant in the middle of dinner because an attractive woman had waved to me from another table. A friend from America who was with us said as she disappeared: 'She's very pretty, but she's trouble.' He was right. I decided she was too much to handle and that I had to get out of the relationship, which was now punctuated by rows which lasted longer than the calm. But I sensed that it was not going to be easy.

My opportunity to disengage came when I discovered that she had made a secret trip to Paris in early August while telling me she was with friends in the country. I had no idea why she had gone to Paris, though the fact she had lied about it was suspicious. I confronted her when she returned. At first she denied she had been in Paris, then admitted it, saying she had just gone to a party with some friends. It was later revealed that she had gone to the Plaza Athénée Hotel to meet a 'friend' who was a senior figure in Libyan intelligence and a cousin of Gadaffi. I told her I felt I could not trust her, that it was best to wind the relationship up. But she was not going to get out of my life without a fight.

'You will never be able to give me up,' she said one day. 'You are addicted to me. You will come crawling back.'

'We'll see about that,' I thought, more determined than ever to escape this woman. The more I refused to see her, the more bitter and threatening she became. I found myself with the starring role in the sequel to *Fatal Attraction*. It began with abusive phone calls, then threats, first of all to destroy me, then kill me. The Mr Hyde in Ms Bordes was on the loose. She took to throwing stones at my front windows; since I was on the first floor she did not usually have the strength to hurl anything big enough to break them. But she managed to shatter two panes in a week; and there were greater dangers than that.

My caretaker told me one day that a woman had been sitting on my doorstep all night; he had noticed a bread knife in her bag. She had waited until about 7 a.m. then gone. I shuddered: fortunately I had been out of town that night. Who knows what might have happened if I had staggered home in the early hours of the morning. Her campaign of terror convinced me I was right to want no more to do with this woman; but it also frightened me. I had a dangerous stalker on my hands: I took to parking my private car well away from the house (to avoid its expensive mutilation) and to approaching my front door very carefully. I began to feel like a hunted rabbit, but it only made me more determined to rid myself of her. Then, when all else failed in her various efforts to woo me back, she reached for what she thought was her atom bomb: Donald Trelford.

*

THE EDITOR OF the *Observer* had been on the margins of our relationship ever since I had introduced her to him at a performance of *Swan Lake* in the Royal Opera House at the end of April. I noticed his little eyes stand out on stalks the moment we walked into the private room being used for drinks by our corporate hosts as he came bounding over to say hello to me while he stared at her. After the performance, they were seated together at dinner on the other side of the table while I had the estimable Mrs Trelford on my left. He barely took his eyes off my date throughout the meal and was engrossed in conversation with her most of the time. I was a little embarrassed for his wife but she is a strong woman and did not seem to mind; perhaps she was used to it. But I was not best pleased.

In fact, I was both amused and irritated: amused by his obvious attraction for her and irritated that she seemed to be encouraging him, no doubt for my benefit. Afterwards she told me he had offered her a job writing about horseracing, which she affected to know about having once dated Steve Cauthen, the jockey. 'How pathetic,' I replied, moodily. 'What do you want me to do about it? Make you our science correspondent?' But I was not too worried about Trelford: he was a married man with children; it would surely be playing with fire for him to get into a competition for the girlfriend of a single man who edited the *Observer*'s biggest rival.

I heard no more about Trelford for a while. Then one night I was sitting in the new flat she had just moved to in Pimlico when the letter box opened and there was a thud on the floor. She retrieved a parcel from the hall and proceeded to open it: out fell a gold Cartier pen and white gold Cartier bracelet.

'Who's that from?' I asked suspiciously.

'It must be Donald Trelford,' she replied. 'He's always sending me presents.'

'Oh, yeah?' I replied, thinking she was winding me up. 'How do you know it's from him?' There was no card.

'I told you,' she said. 'He's always sending me things. Come into the kitchen if you don't believe me.'

The kitchen looked like a greenhouse: it was covered in bouquets of flowers. 'There's still no evidence that all this came from Trelford,' I said, refusing to believe that the editor of the *Observer* could be so foolish.

She then produced two books written by Trelford, one on chess, the other on snooker. Inside one was the handwritten message: 'To Pamella, a Queen among pawns'; the other was inscribed 'To Pamella, who has snookered us all'. Both were signed 'Donald'. I recognized his handwriting immediately. I was flabbergasted. Not because Trelford fancied her – I had realized that on the night of the ballet – but because he was actively wooing her, which seemed to me an incredible folly for, just as on Sunday mornings on the newsstands, it was a competition with me he could not hope to win.

She already believed herself to be deeply in love with me: the best Trelford could hope for was to have a walk-on part as a pawn, used by her whenever she felt she thought she needed to make me jealous. In the unlikely event that he did succeed in winning her away, he would then be very vulnerable to whatever revenge the scorned single man chose to wreak against his married rival; and since the single chap just happened to be editor of *The Sunday Times* the scope for mischief was clearly massive. In fact, I would most likely have done nothing; but he was not to know that.

'What should I do with them?' she said, pointing to the Cartier presents. 'I'm not interested in them – or him. He's such a little pixie.' I told her that if she wanted to have an affair with Trelford then I would clear the field. 'I compete with the man on the newsstands every Sunday morning,' I said. 'I'm not competing with him for a girlfriend too.' She burst into tears: 'I told you,' she sobbed, 'I don't want anything to do with him. Please don't go.'

'Then the proper thing to do is to return them,' I said. 'Maybe then he'll get the message – if that is the message you want to deliver.' I was naturally suspicious that she was encouraging Trelford, if only to upset me when she felt she needed to. We agreed that my driver would discreetly drop them off at the *Observer* office the next day. She seemed quite relieved that I made no more of the matter. My biggest fear was the potential publicity that could erupt about two rival editors chasing the same girl as a result of his reckless behaviour. I consoled myself with the thought that that would be a bigger problem for him than for me.

She called me the next night: 'He's sent them back,' she said, sounding a little concerned. 'What should I do now?' I was incredulous: did this man's stupidity know no bounds?

'You've done all you need to do as far as I'm concerned,' I replied, 'you can do whatever you want with them.'

'I'll sell them,' she said, 'and the money can go towards that holiday in Aspen you promised me.'

All this had occurred earlier, when we were still an 'item'. Now it was August and I was in the rather wearysome process of trying to split with her. As her guerrilla war to get me back only succeeded in having the opposite effect, I sensed that it was only a matter of time before Trelford would be dragged centre stage. Sure enough, as the end of August approached word reached me that they had been seen out together. I thought it was time to have a chat with Trelford on the phone.

'Who you see is none of my business,' I began, 'but I think it's in both our interests for you to know that she is using you to try to get back at me. I've been trying to make her realize for weeks now that it's over between us but she thinks I'll be so infuriated by thoughts of her seeing you that I'll take her back.'

'I'm not after your girlfriend,' said Trelford.

'Well, you could have fooled me, Donald!'

'Oh, you mean those baubles and bangles?'

'If that's what you want to call them, yes. It seemed bizarre behaviour.'

'Oh, Andrew,' he replied, 'that's just my way.'

'It's a pretty strange way, but it's of no significance now. I'm not calling about that. I'm calling to warn you that you're being used to get at me and to give you some advice: I'm a single man and I've found this woman too hot to handle; if you fancy an affair with her you'd better be prepared to see your marriage blown apart.'

'I'm not taking her out,' he replied, 'and I don't propose to. She's the same age as my oldest daughter! I regard you as tough enough competition professionally and have no desire to take you on personally as well. I have not seen her since the night of *Swan Lake*, though I admit I've made contact with her.'

This was true. Though in the story she later sold to the *Daily Mail* she tried to make out that she was seeing us both at once, and playing one off against the other, this was a product of her febrile imagination – and, of course, it made for a better story. But Trelford did not assume more than a walk-on role until I had made it clear to her I was departing from the scene. A dalliance with him was meant to entice me back in a jealous rage.

'I've been keeping in touch with her,' Trelford continued, 'because she said her family had close connections with the Swami [a very dubious religious guru]. I think she worked for him at one stage. The Swami has had dealings with the Sultan of Brunei – and you know his connections with Harrods, which obsesses my proprietor [Tiny Rowland, who thought Harrods had been stolen from under his nose]. I hoped she could lead me to the Swami.'

He must have heard the disbelief in my voice that this was his only motive.

'I'm not out to have an affair with her,' he repeated. 'She's clearly besotted with you: it must be very flattering to have a beautiful woman want you so much.'

'No, Donald, it's a bloody nightmare which I want to end. Frankly, I'm calling you more out of self-interest than from any concern for you. I don't want stories surfacing about two rival editors supposedly chasing the same girl. I think we could both do without that sort of publicity – and I suggest you have more to lose than me.'

'Absolutely,' he replied emphatically. 'Don't you worry: I see the dangers for us both. You can rely on me to do the right thing.'

'By the way, Donald,' I enquired before hanging up, 'why did you send the Cartier stuff back to her?'

'Because your driver returned the presents and I hadn't sent them to you. I'd sent them to her.'

This is a man, I thought, who doesn't recognize a warning when it's staring him in the face. I would never have had the effrontery to send them in the first place, never mind send them *back*.

A few days later I heard that they had both been seen in Tramp together. 'Bloody fool,' I thought, 'but at least if she's seeing him she won't be bugging me.'

But I was wrong. The failure of her Trelford strategy roused her to even more rage. She waited outside the gym I regularly used in the Fulham Road, appearing from nowhere to slap my face then scurry off. Then I made the mistake of picking up the phone early one Sunday morning to receive a verbal volley of four-letter words, which ended with the triumphant claim that she was pregnant by Trelford. It was, of course, nonsense. When I calmly congratulated her, offered them both my best wishes for a happy life together and politely hung up, I think she got the message that Trelford was not quite the weapon she had hoped.

That night the doorbell rang. I looked at the screen on the video entry phone, which had become a regular habit, but there was nobody there. I made my way tentatively to the front door: there was an envelope with my name on it in the letter basket. I opened it gingerly: inside was a large piece of dog excrement. That was it. I had had enough of being harassed and hounded by this bloody woman! I called my lawyer to say that unless he could secure a voluntary agreement through her lawyer that she would stay away from me, I wanted to go to court to seek a restraining order. He warned me it would attract a lot of publicity; I told him I did not care – I had done nothing wrong and wanted her off my back.

When my lawyer contacted her she denied that she knew anybody called Andrew Neil, maintained she was happily married, lived with her French husband and, furthermore, she was pregnant. The distinction between fact and fantasy was never clear in her mind; as the *Daily Mail* was to find to its anguish when it bought her story, she was an accomplished liar. But eventually she agreed, on threat of court action, through her lawyers, to a 'restraining order' in which she bound herself 'during our joint lives . . . not to have or seek to have any contact whatsoever with Mr Neil' anywhere in the world, nor to come within 100 metres of me or any of my residences or places of work. That seemed comprehensive enough – and she even paid my legal costs. To my surprise, she kept to the agreement. I think involving lawyers frightened her: she was never quite sure what her legal right to residence in Britain was.

Trelford faded into the background, having ceased to be of any more use to her. 'It's funny,' she was later to tell the *Daily Mail*. 'When Donald and I meet we do nothing but talk about Andrew. We're both obsessed with him.'

She had stopped bothering me by November, a merciful end to a tumultuous affair which had begun in late April. I did not hear from her again until Boxing Day. I was screening calls on the answering machine and heard her voice come over its speaker: 'I hope you won't report me for breaking the ban on contacting you,' she said, 'just because I'm calling to wish you a Merry Christmas. I'm now working as a researcher in the House of Commons. You should be proud of me.'

I did not pick up the phone, nor return her call. She seemed an unlikely political researcher but if some stability had entered her life I was happy for her – as long as she was out of my life. As far as I was concerned she was history – or so I thought.

*

'SORRY TO DRAG YOU out of your meeting,' said Rupert on the phone from New York, 'but I need to have a word with you about a story the *News of the World* has got.' It was 6.30 p.m. on a Friday night, 10 March 1989, and I was just starting my regular news conference to review the possibilities for page one that weekend; I had left it to take the call in the outer office.

'It seems that one of your former girlfriends is a call-girl,' he continued, somewhat embarrassed by the information he was imparting.

'Who is it?' I asked, a tightness forming in my stomach,

my brain racing to think who on earth it could be. No name came to mind.

'Pamella Bordes,' he replied. 'But don't worry. The story doesn't involve you. Just keep your head down and it'll all blow over in a couple of days.' For once, his tabloid instincts had deserted him – or perhaps he was just trying to comfort me. I was incredulous. I had realized not long after we had first met that she was in some ways an accident waiting to happen. But not this!

'Are they sure about this?' I asked Rupert, my spirits sinking.

'Pretty sure. They set a trap for her and she walked into it. But I'll have Patsy [Chapman, *News of the World* editor] call and go over it with you.'

I thanked Rupert for the early warning and wandered, dazed, back into the news conference to race through the news list, my mind unable to concentrate. As the office emptied Patsy came on the line: she was apologetic, saying she wished they did not have the story.

'Are you certain she's actually on the game?' I enquired anxiously. 'She's a pretty screwed-up lady and I think she might mix with some dodgy, rich characters. But I would be astounded if she did it for money herself.'

'I'll send you over the evidence and you can judge for yourself. Don't worry: we won't mention you in the story.'

'Oh yes you will,' I replied adamantly, ' – if it's true. I don't think I deserve top billing but if you don't say somewhere that I'm a former boyfriend it will encourage claims of special treatment – and in the end more publicity.'

As I waited for Patsy's evidence to arrive I wondered what she had been up to. There is a phenomenon in London (no doubt common to other international cities too) which *The Sunday Times* was to dub 'peripheral prostitution'. Dinner parties are held in expensive restaurants or large houses for rich men from the Middle East, America, India and Europe and attractive young women who are well-spoken, designer-dressed and able to hold a conversation. The men cannot take it for granted that any of these women will be prepared to sleep with them – though those girls who refuse too regularly will quietly be disinvited from the dinners.

Those who do acquiesce to male advances, which will be subtle and polite, are unlikely to be rewarded in anything as crass as cash. Instead of crisp £50 notes wedged under the bedside lamp they are more likely to be taken on a shopping trip down Bond Street, have that large bill for unpaid rent settled for them, be given a car, a credit card or taken on holidays to private houses in St Tropez. A 'Boat', as a *Sunday Times* columnist once called this kind of woman (for Bordering on a Tart), is rarely cash rich but despite having no visible means of support is always well-turned out and seems to live the good life. Invariably, and you might think unnecessarily for somebody who does not seem to do very much, she rarely goes anywhere without a mobile phone: you just never know when that nice rich prince from Jeddah will next land in London. When you ask them what they do they say they are 'in jewellery' or 'public relations' or something else suitably vague.

I concluded that Pamella must have got involved in something along these lines. She knew plenty of well-off international men and as our relationship ended I was told she had started organizing dinner parties for rich visiting Indian businessmen and politicians. That must be it, I thought; after all, she knew lots of pretty girls who did not seem to do very much. I still refused to accept that she would be involved in taking money for sex herself.

But when the transcripts of various conversations taped by the *News of the World* arrived the truth was inescapable:

Pamella was a prostitute. As I pored over the papers, my heart sank: I felt disgust, betrayal, anger. At the core of the evidence was a taped call between her and another prostitute in which Pamella agreed to meet a businessman from Hong Kong at the London Hilton to have dinner – and sex for £500. On the night the 'businessman', much to her surprise, turned out to be a *News of the World* reporter.

'Looks like you've got her bang to rights,' I said to Patsy.

'I don't think there's any doubt,' she replied. 'I'm very sorry, Andrew.'

'Don't worry about it,' I said. At no stage did I try to dissuade her from running the story. It would have surfaced in another tabloid anyway, perhaps even as 'The story Andrew Neil tried to suppress', which would have taken me from what I hoped would be the periphery of the story to centre stage.

'It's embarrassing,' I continued, already thinking through my defence, 'but I have done nothing wrong and have nothing to hide, though others may. I'm a single guy who dated a single woman in the summer of 1988 who, unbeknown to me, turns out to be a prostitute. Sad but true. End of story as far as I'm concerned.' Patsy agreed. But we were both too experienced as journalists to know it would be as clean-cut as that.

The whole story was bound to be given a substantial extra lift by the fact that she had been working as a part-time researcher in the House of Commons for David Shaw, Tory MP for Dover. She had taken this unlikely work for my benefit. After the failure of her campaign to terrorize me into going back out with her, she was now involved in a long-term strategy to impress me with her seriousness of purpose and desire for respectability. She was even doing research into the Net Book Agreement, which forbade price competition between book publishers and which *The Sunday Times* had long campaigned to abolish. Shaw was preparing a private member's bill to do just that. She had mentioned this in her Boxing Day message, no doubt thinking I would approve.

But by March 1989 she was just a bad but fading memory for me: even if she had been made Speaker of the House I would not have had her back. She must have cut an unlikely figure in the House of Commons in her designer clothes and there is little evidence she did much work; but no doubt she brightened up the corridors of a place dominated by boring, grey men. She had got the job by striking up a friendship with Marc Burca, then owner of *Boardroom Magazine*, after we had split. He had borne an old grudge against me (we're now friends) and enjoyed plotting with her about how she could, alternatively, gain revenge or restore our friendship. He had contacts among some young Thatcherites on the Tory backbenches and had helped arrange her job with Shaw. Instead of causing a change of heart in me it was to be her own undoing.

A couple of weeks before the *News of the World* story broke she had accompanied Colin Moynihan, the minister for sport, to a Tory fund-raising ball. A picture of the Tory minister arriving at the ball with what was dubbed an 'exotic mystery woman' made the front page of London's *Evening Standard*. But for one woman there was no mystery: another call-girl recognized Pamella immediately as one of the prostitutes she worked with; they had gone to meet clients together. Now she was with a Tory minister; her fellow call-girl saw the chance to make some money at Pamella's expense. The *News of the World* was contacted. Within weeks Bordes had walked into a trap her prostitute friend and the newspaper had carefully laid together.

She caught me on the car phone as I drove to work on the Saturday morning before publication. The *News of the World* was already staking out the flat where she lived with a new boyfriend and she was hysterical: 'You've got to stop this story being published,' she shouted, 'it's all nonsense!'

'There's nothing I can do about it,' I replied. 'If it's untrue you can sue and make a lot of money. But from what I've seen, they have the evidence to back it up.' She became quiet, then tearful, explaining how she had put me behind her, given up her House of Commons job and planned to marry the new man in her life; they had even decided on a honeymoon in Bali.

'I was prepared to believe a lot of things about you, Pamella,' I continued, 'but not this. Yet I always had a feeling you'd come back and haunt me. Now I'll be tainted by association – but it's my own stupidity for ever getting involved with you in the first place.'

She began to remonstrate again that the story wasn't true.

'Look, Pamella,' I snapped, 'they even know how much you charge.'

'You're kidding . . .' she replied, her flabbergasted voice trailing off.

'If you want my advice,' I continued, 'the best thing you can do is disappear, leave the country until it all dies down – otherwise you'll be at the centre of a tabloid-feeding frenzy.'

She thought that was a good idea and said she would go to Paris that day, then maybe get further away. These were the last words we ever spoke. I was relieved: her departure might dampen things down a bit.

I hid behind my answering machine on the Sunday morning (12 March) when the *News of the World* story broke, expecting to be inundated with calls. But most of them came from well-wishers, including David Frost and John Birt, saying how sorry they were, but to tough it out because I had done nothing wrong. The media was more concerned about the potential for political scandal. A new film about the

Profumo affair called *Scandal* had just been released. It revived the infamous story of Christine Keeler, the call-girl who had slept with the then war secretary, John Profumo, and a Soviet naval attaché who was also (inevitably) an officer in the KGB. It was the biggest British political sex scandal of the century which had rocked Harold Macmillan's Tory government in 1963, contributing to its demise the following year.

The media were licking their lips at the prospect of another government-destroying sex-and-security scandal involving prostitutes and politicians. At my own Tuesday morning editoral conference I instructed the features editor to plan a Focus on the subject – it was too big a story to ignore. But I thought it best to keep my head down and retain a rigid silence while the tabloids scoured Westminster for any politicians she might have compromised. I had nothing to say anyway, bar the fact that I had been astounded and dismayed to learn she was a prostitute. I was running Sky TV and *The Sunday Times* and had plenty to get on with. Silence was the best policy, I concluded, and it looked like working. But Trelford could not keep his mouth shut.

On the Thursday after the story surfaced, with the press still thankfully awarding me no more than a walk-on role, the editor of the *Observer*, speaking at a trade-union-sponsored conference on the media, hit out at what he called 'a crude abuse of power' by News International papers, notably the *Sun*, for linking him with Bordes and delving further into their relationship. He claimed that coverage had concentrated on him to steer attention away from my own involvement with her. It was another sign, he told his audience, that News International was 'too big for its boots'.

It was Trelford tosh. After all, the story had been broken by a News International paper, which had named me and not mentioned him at all. The fact that she had been my girlfriend was widely known to everybody in the media; we had been photographed together at many public events. But I had not seen her since the previous September, whereas Trelford had continued to meet her at least up to Christmas, when they had exchanged gifts (he gave her another Cartier 'bauble'). David Shaw, in trying to justify why he had taken her on as a researcher, had explained that he had first met Bordes 'in the company of a distinguished editor'. Most folk assumed it was me but I had been long off the scene by the time of this encounter: I made him clarify that it had been Donald Trelford. Moreover, Trelford was the married man with children: unlike my relationship with her, which had been out in the open, nobody knew exactly the status of his links. It was inevitable that the media would, at least for the moment, be more intrigued by him than me.

His attack, however, brought me fully into the frame. The media, even the BBC, rushed to me for a reaction. The fear I had always had about 'Two editors chasing the same girl' stories had materialized. I was furious and cursed Trelford: because of his pointless grandstanding about News International before a left-wing audience he had moved us both on to centre stage. But anything I said would merely fuel the flames. I bit my bottom lip and kept quiet.

The Bordes story would not die. Every day brought fresh tabloid revelations of famous names supposedly associated with her, though none of Profumo-like standing. Indeed, given the propensity of middle-aged male politicians to fall for a pretty face which shows any interest in them, it is quite remarkable that she did not do any political damage at all: no politicians were compromised by her brief career in the House of Commons and the government emerged unscathed – a lucky escape, for this girl had the potential to cause chaos.

Fleet Street, which was still scouring the globe for her (a

manager from the *Sun* eventually stumbled across her by accident in Bali), had to be content with a string of minor celebrities and rich foreigners who had supposedly been her clients. The possibility of a scandal of Profumo proportions briefly flickered into life when the story broke about her Libyan connection. Labour MPs, out to embarrass the government, demanded an inquiry into how she had obtained a House of Commons pass and speculated about what national secrets she might have passed on to Tripoli. But unless Gadaffi was anxious to learn the intricacies of the Net Book Agreement it was never clear what she knew that could have been of the remotest interest to him. As Fleet Street's hope of a security scandal faded attention turned back to titbits about Trelford and me.

Stories began to surface that she had in her possession certain tapes of mine which would supposedly do me great damage. I told enquirers that there were no tapes. Then I remembered that in my first six months at *The Sunday Times* I had tried to keep an audio diary of my experiences at the paper, using a pocket Dictaphone.

They were personal reminiscences of the early resistance to my editorship, of little interest to anybody outside the paper, but I thought they might be useful if I ever came to write a book about my *Sunday Times* years. I had neither the discipline nor the energy to keep this taped diary going for long: the Dictaphone and cassettes had long been undisturbed in a bottom drawer by the bed. Or so I thought. I rushed upstairs: they were gone, taken by Bordes, I was to discover later, on the day of her clothes-cutting, with a mind to further revenge.

I was angry, not because there was anything on the tapes that could cause embarrassment or was top secret, but because a record of some very personal thoughts had been stolen from me. I learned later that she had taken the tapes to

Trelford after I had refused to see her again: not only had he listened to them with her, he had transcripts made of them. Even the dog-eat-dog world of Fleet Street would question if these were the actions of an honourable man. He must have known this was stolen property she had brought him and the proper course of action would have been to return them to me forthwith. But he did not.

He told me later that there was nothing of an embarrassing personal nature on them and the 'interesting commercial information' they contained was several years out of date. He said he had instructed Bordes to remove the tapes and transcripts from his office: no doubt he did not want to be caught in possession of stolen goods. He also had the gall to tell me, 'I couldn't use them, we're not that sort of paper.' So why did he ever listen to them in the first place? Had there been anything damaging about me on the tapes, I'm in no doubt he would have found some way of recycling the material.

I instructed my solicitor to tell the lawyers of Trelford and Bordes that I wanted the tapes and transcripts returned or I would report the matter to the police. He reported back to me that their lawyers said if I dropped the threat to call in the police they would co-operate fully. Bordes' boyfriend then confessed that, on her instructions, he had burnt the tapes and transcripts, which she had stored in a large brown envelope, a few days after the story about her being a prostitute had broken. She had called him from Paris on Thursday, 16 March, and told him to burn the envelope: she had been so worried about being caught with stolen property that she had even called him back to make sure he had done it. A little part of my life had gone up in flames with those tapes. This woman was destined to cast a long shadow over me, especially since. Another rival editor had decided to capitalize on my involvement with Bordes.

*

A WEEK AFTER THE *News of the World* story broke, the *Sunday Telegraph* carried an editorial by Peregrine Worsthorne entitled 'Editors as playboys'. It took a couple of swipes at Trelford but the main target was me. It argued that I was obviously unfit to be the editor of a serious quality newspaper by consorting with a woman like Bordes. Since I had been a single man dating a single woman it seemed to me logical that his strictures were only valid if I had knowingly gone out with a prostitute, something the editorial, plus accompanying feature article ('Dangerous liaisons') and cartoon (showing me with a streetwalker), seemed to imply and certainly did not rule out. It was a typical piece of Worsthorne humbug and I would have been wise to have treated it as such and ignore it. But at the time I regarded it as a serious attack on my personal integrity and professional reputation. I asked for a clarification to be published the following week making it clear that I had known nothing of Bordes's nocturnal activities. It was refused. All other efforts to secure a correction or clarification were dismissed with cavalier disregard. No doubt Worsthorne was enjoying himself. I'll take the smile off his face, I thought: a writ for libel was issued. The lawyers assured me I had a very strong case. They were right: I had. But it was still a big mistake.

The case should never have come to trial. I never imagined that it would, since I was not seeking an abject apology or massive damages: just some words which recognized that I had not known Bordes was a prostitute when I had dated her. Then *Sunday Telegraph* readers could better make up their minds whether or not I was unfit to be an editor. But, though Worsthorne was later to claim that he had never thought I knew her profession, he refused to budge, even returning one request for a clarification with a rebuke.

There was nobody at his company to tell him to do otherwise.

Telegraph Newspapers was somewhat rudderless as 1989 progressed: Andrew Knight, its chief executive, was being wooed by Rupert Murdoch (see Chapter 7) and relations between Knight and Conrad Black, the *Telegraph* proprietor, were strained. There was nobody in charge to urge conciliation or point out it was in neither of our interests to go to trial. Worsthorne wanted to tough it out, regarding even the smallest concession to me as unconscionable. With no management to bring him to his senses, the libel case opened in the High Court in London on 23 January 1990.

The Bordes business had long died down, but the court proceedings brought it back on to the front page. The original story had caused much mirth and sniggering at my expense among my many Fleet Street enemies; the trial gave them front-row seats at the sequel. But to back out would have required total surrender on my part, which I was not prepared to do. Worsthorne and I were locked into a very public confrontation – like two 'great steam engines' in a head-on collision, as the presiding judge was to say.

The trial lasted for six days. The problem with libel cases is that anything, no matter how extraneous to the dispute, can be brought to bear on the case. The defence, led by Patrick Milmo QC, succeeded in convincing the judge that all the newspaper cuttings mentioning me which followed the *News of the World* story could be included as evidence. When I took the stand, he went through every one. It gave me a chance to refute most of the nonsense that had been written but it also meant it was all repeated in the press the next day.

The cross-examination in the witness box caused me little pain. Anybody who goes into a libel battle should be sure they have nothing to hide for there is every chance it will be dragged into the case, no matter how irrelevant. The defence had been scouring around for dirt on me but came up with nothing: no sordid affairs, no record of relations with unsavoury types, just a series of normal and respectable girlfriends, of which I had wrongly assumed Bordes was one. Milmo insisted that there had been no insinuation in the article that I had known she was a prostitute which meant he was reduced to justifying the editorial's claim that I was unfit for my job by saying that 'editors should not expose themselves to circumstances that bring themselves into disrepute' – in other words I devalued the position I held by frequenting a nightclub.

At one stage he repeated Worsthorne's point that editors of serious newspapers should spend their time at 'Oxbridge high tables' rather than nightclubs. I replied that, though I was always happy to visit Oxford or Cambridge, those of us who were the product of the ancient Scottish universities had a less high regard for Oxbridge than was common in London.

When Worsthorne took the stand he had a rather tough time of it from my QC, Richard Rampton. He conceded that I had done a 'superb job editing a very fine newspaper' and that it had never crossed his mind that I might have known she was a call-girl when I dated her; however, a man in my position should not go to nightclubs – it was 'frivolous behaviour' for somebody who should be an '*homme sérieux*'. I should resign and if I did not I deserved to be fired. 'Frivolity was the real charge' that disqualified me, he said, because my past connection with Bordes had made me look 'faintly ridiculous'.

No doubt much of Fleet Street agreed – indeed they probably relished the sight. But our defence was that for a bachelor to visit a perfectly respectable nightclub hardly meant he was unfit to be editor of *The Sunday Times* and that the only thing that could justify Worsthorne's harsh judgement was that I had knowingly gone out with a prostitute. Rampton pointed out that, unlike nearly all the tabloid coverage of the affair, the *Sunday Telegraph* had nowhere in its extensive coverage pointed out that I was a bachelor and that I neither knew Bordes was a call-girl nor had any reason to know. The whole tone of its articles had been to 'cast me into the gutter', he said, then trample on me.

He rather demolished Worsthorne's defence that my real error had been to expose myself to the danger of meeting such women in a nightclub when Worsthorne was forced to admit that he had written his editorial without knowing where I had first met Bordes; he had learned that it was Tramp from our coverage in *The Sunday Times*, after his own article had been published. Rampton easily portrayed Worsthorne as somebody in no position to give moral lectures to anybody. They had managed to dig up no embarrassing dirt about me; but there was plenty of juicy stuff from the past behaviour of my adversary.

Worsthorne had the distinction of being the first person to use the F-word live on television – and at family viewing time – when in 1973 he said that he thought most British people rightly did not 'give a f——' that Lord Lambton, then a Tory minister, had been seeing a call-girl. In other words, said Rampton, Worsthorne did not care that a cabinet minister had knowingly slept with a prostitute but when I had unknowingly dated one it was a matter for dismissal. Worsthorne squirmed. He did so again when Rampton moved on to quote from Worsthorne's own memoirs a passage in which he had almost boasted about being seduced on the sofa by George Melly, the jazz musician, while they were both at Stowe public school.

There was one piece of information that further undermined Worsthorne's authority to judge other editors' behaviour: it was well-known among senior Fleet Street folk that he had been having a long affair during his marriage with another woman, whose name was also known by many of his colleagues. This seemed a rather more serious transgression for a self-appointed moral arbiter than a bachelor frequenting a nightclub. But Worsthorne's wife (now deceased – he has since married again, to the delightfully eccentric Lucinda Lambton) had been sitting loyally beside him every day in court. To bring his affair up so publicly in front of her seemed unnecessarily cruel. I asked my lawyers if we had not already done enough to undermine him and demonstrate he was a ludicrous figure, unqualified to give moral lectures. They said we probably had; I replied that we should not therefore pursue the matter of his mistress. I am glad we did not; I might not feel the same if I had lost.

The jury of seven men and five women retired around 11 a.m. on 30 January. During the trial I had hosted sandwich lunches at the Howard Hotel, near the High Court, for my senior editors so that I could continue to edit the paper despite the time-consuming trial. But that day I wanted to be alone – and I certainly was not hungry.

I had my driver drop me off at the RAC on Pall Mall, where I sat in a quiet corner and fretted, a knot in my stomach the size of a balloon and a mouth that insisted on staying bone dry no matter how much mineral water I sipped. I was contemplating the consequences of defeat.

In a fit of reckless independence I had told Rupert Murdoch, who had hated the publicity surrounding the trial (his wife, Anna, hated it even more) and had complained to me about Times Newspapers having to foot the legal bill, that this was my fight and I would pick up the costs, running into hundreds of thousands of pounds, should I lose. But I also realized that defeat would mean open season on me from the rest of Fleet Street, where my many enemies were already sharpening their knives in anticipation of a field day at my expense. It was bound to undermine my ability to edit *The Sunday Times*. Even worse, defeat would mean that a jury had effectively backed the Worsthorne verdict – I was unfit to edit one of the world's great newspapers – and my judgement in bringing the case would have been shown to have been fatally flawed. As I pondered such matters alone in the RAC I resolved that if I lost I would have to resign.

In retrospect, it was crazy to risk financial ruin *and* professional humiliation on the throw of the dice – the outcome of modern libel cases is as much a gamble as the spin of a roulette wheel – and all because I wanted to correct the meanderings of a pompous old fool in an editorial most people had long forgotten. My heart thumped faster and louder and I found it hard to swallow the water. It was one of the most miserable, loneliest two hours in my life. But there was no turning back now: I had to prepare myself to face the jury's decision. As I headed back to court I told myself I would win only because the consequences of defeat were too horrendous to contemplate.

The jury returned at 3.30 that afternoon. It seemed to take an age for them to troop in and take their places; the judge, who had clearly enjoyed the proceedings, seemed in no hurry either. Eventually the young foreman of the jury stood up to announce that they had unanimously found in my favour; but my relief and joy was tempered by the damages they awarded: only £1,000. Better than the traditionally derisory penny, which would have been tantamount to defeat, and I was always aware that no jury was going to award a substantial amount to an editor (nor did I seek it). But £10,000 would have been a more convincing victory than £1,000. I had won by the skin of my teeth.

But it was a victory nevertheless. The *Sunday Telegraph* had libelled me and thanks to the jury's decision its libel could not now be drawn from the cuttings file and endlessly repeated in every article about me. I was also awarded full legal costs which meant that, when all the bills were in, Telegraph Newspapers would have no change from £250,000.

As I left the High Court a throng of reporters, photographers and TV crews gathered round me. 'What did it all mean?' shouted a journalist. I had prepared some remarks in the event of defeat but nothing for winning. 'It's a victory for the New Britain,' I heard myself saying. It was an off-the-cuff response which was to set the tone for much of the subsequent commentary.

British newspapers love nothing more than a clash of the classes and my remark gave them their cue. The libel case was presented as a clash of the Old Britain, stuffy, snobbish, established, pseudo-aristocratic, High Tory, versus the New Britain, brash, upwardly mobile, meritocratic, Thatcherite (though for the story to work best Worsthorne's up-market roots had to be enhanced, his Belgian roots buried and my proletarian background exaggerated). No matter: there was more than a kernel of truth in making this the division between us. It was to earn me the enduring enmity of what was known as 'Worsthorne College', the small coterie of fogeyish right-wing journalists who worked at the *Telegraph* stable. They took their revenge when I serialized Andrew Morton's book on Princess Diana two years later (see Chapter 8).

Looking back, I'm not sure that either of us won. I had scored the technical victory but our main achievement had been jointly to provide the rest of the media (and maybe even the country at large) with an amusing diversion at our expense. Faced with the prospect again I would probably decide it was not worth the candle: a reputation is important to preserve but if the libel process results in it being further besmirched, even when you win, then it can be self-defeating to resort to the courts.

As for Pamella Bordes, she kept to the terms of our exclusion agreement: I have not heard or seen her since the day she fled to Paris, nor do I wish to. But, strangely, I am not sorry that I met her: she was an interesting experience, a close shave that could have led to disaster but did not, and certainly added to the excitement and intrigue of life. It also led to racist remarks about 'Asian Babes' and some people talked as if she had been the love of my life, which was nonsense – though I had come very close to falling in love with her. If her behaviour had not been so erratic after the first few weeks of dating her, I probably would have.

The whole episode, despite the embarrassment and even anguish, gave me a fresh currency, even a new cachet. Women were intrigued and men curious, even jealous, about our association. It made me more suspicious of women than I had been before, especially ones who had no visible means of support but who seem to live well (and always clutched mobile phones!). But it did me no long-term damage. Maybe every man should have one notorious affair in his life.

Donald Trelford did not even manage that, at least not with Bordes. During the court case he had been the ghost at the feast: much mentioned without ever making an appearance. He had to suffer in silence as his role in the Bordes affair was revealed but I did not feel sorry for him. If he had acted more sensibly I would never have been given such a starring role in the Bordes story and Worsthorne would not have been able to write such a high-minded 'two editors' editorial.

One day when it was all over I spotted Trelford coming towards me as I walked through the Savoy Hotel. He saw me in the distance, hesitated but saw there was no escape. 'I warned you, Donald,' I said more in sorrow than in anger as we approached each other. 'I warned you.'

'Yes, you did, Andrew,' he admitted. 'But vanity got the better of me.' He was right: it had. But it might be a fitting epitaph for *all* the editors involved in the Bordes saga.

CHAPTER ELEVEN

Sky High

IT WAS A GLORIOUSLY SUNNY but bitterly cold Monday in mid-November 1988, and I found myself spending my day off from *The Sunday Times* shooting a piece to camera by the moat of a ruined castle in Sussex for a BBC documentary series I was presenting on finance and investment. It had been a pleasant assignment: I had already used some holiday time from the paper to film in the Bahamas and New York; now we were finishing off in Britain. I stood by a large treasure chest, with the castle as a sunlit backdrop, to explain how the way modern governments raised and borrowed money was only a more sophisticated version of the techniques used by medieval monarchs. During a break in the shooting I rushed back to my car for some heat. The phone rang: it was Rupert Murdoch.

I had been expecting to hear from him. It was only 6 a.m. in New York, but I thought I knew what was on his mind that was making him hit the phone so early. Word had reached me that he was looking for a new editor for *The Times* and that I was his favoured candidate. The idea did not appeal to me: I did not regard moving from Britain's biggest-selling, most profitable, most influential broadsheet to a loss-making daily with a third of *The Sunday Times*'s circulation as a promotion or a major career advance, despite the social prestige being editor of *The Times* confers. I was also worried that Rupert had never settled on a proper strategy for *The Times* and that dealing with him on a daily basis, with uncertain goals, would lead to friction between us: our relationship had thrived on limited but constructive and amicable contact. I had a little speech prepared to turn the offer down. But Rupert had a bigger priority on his mind.

'I need you to go and run Sky Television,' he said, after a few pleasantries. 'It's vital that we launch the new four-channel service on time in February [1989] ahead of BSB [the rival satellite service]. The people running it at the moment are just not up to the challenge and the way they're going they'll miss the launch date, which would be disastrous for us. I need your drive and energy to get it back on schedule. There's no time to lose: I'd be grateful if you could start right away.'

He explained that there was no question of me having to give up *The Sunday Times* to do it. 'You'll stay as editor and be on secondment to Sky,' he suggested. 'You should still take all the big decisions at *The Sunday Times* but leave the day-to-day running to Ivan [my deputy] and the other executives. You'll be doing both jobs but I need Sky to be your priority for at least the next six months.'

I gulped. Rupert had said nothing before to indicate this was on his mind, though I had heard that Sky was struggling to meet its launch deadline. He had caught me off guard, my thoughts on turning down *The Times* now rather redundant. But I was excited by what was on offer and, without really knowing what was involved, accepted at once. This was what made working for Rupert Murdoch so exhilarating – and full of surprising opportunities. Besides, I had been in the vanguard of advocating multi-channel television since my return from America in 1982, often clashing with the British broadcasting establishment in the process: here was a chance to show I could bring multi-channel TV to Britain, not just write about it.

*

DURING THE 1980s I had come to regard British television as a cosy cartel – a classic duopoly run for the benefit of those who worked in the BBC and ITV rather than the viewers who paid their salaries and financed their programmes, which too often were made to satisfy the producers' own interests rather than meet what viewers wanted to see. I had gone to America in 1979 for *The Economist* with the usual British belief that our television was the best in the world. I was gradually disabused of that complacent notion as I became familiar with the bewildering variety of channels available on my Manhattan cable system.

I was dismayed by the trashy and crass commercialism which makes up much of American TV; but I was also increasingly impressed by the huge choice on offer: there were separate channels for news, films, documentaries, sport, the arts, even the weather. It was a choice denied British viewers because of the stranglehold of the BBC and ITV and the inertia of the government in encouraging new ways of distributing TV channels. I still believed that, at its best, British television *was* the best in the world: but I wanted to graft the wide variety of choice of channels available in America on to what was best about British public-service broadcasting. These thoughts went through my mind in America as a viewer: it never occurred to me that in less than a decade I would have the chance to do it.

While working in British TV in the 1970s I also had first-hand experience of its wasteful, debilitating, restrictive practices and overmanning, which inflated production costs and hindered the introduction of new technology. When presenting LWT's *Look Here*, a weekly programme about broadcasting, during the winter of 1978–79 I had gone to Thames TV to interview Verity Lambert, the doyenne of ITV drama producers. I had trekked across town from the South Bank to Thames TV's Euston studios with the usual panoply of folk who made up a travelling TV crew in those days: cameraman, assistant cameraman, electrician, sound man, director, producer, producer's assistant, researcher – and me – all for one interview.

The nine of us were met at the Thames entrance by the station's shop steward for ACTT, the TV technicians' union, who barred our way. 'You can't film in here,' he announced, 'unless the crew is all-union.'

'It's an LWT staff crew, so they're all union members,' replied Rod Allen, my producer.

But that was not good enough. He demanded to see their union cards then went off to call ACTT headquarters to check that their dues were fully paid up. He returned to tell us we were still barred: one of the crew was a month in arrears.

'Who's running this place?' I said loudly to Rod. 'Where's the management?' But there was no Thames executive in sight: they were all keeping their heads below the parapet. Rod, an amiable chap who was finding his left-wing views sorely tested by this piece of union intransigence, wanted to avoid a confrontation: he paid the arrears (I've often wondered if ACTT ever saw the money). We started through the entrance.

'You still can't come in,' said the shop steward, standing in our way. 'You have only one sound man. The house agreement requires Thames crews to have two – and you'll need two if you want to film in here.'

A reluctant Rod said he would send back to LWT for another sound man. But I was having none of it.

'You can do that if you want,' I said to Rod furiously. 'But

I am not doing the interview. I'm going back to LWT: if you want me to interview Verity she'll have to come there.' And that's what happened.

The incident was a minor example of the sort of absurdities that dominated British television in those days. In the space of a few decades TV had managed to create a video version of Fleet Street's industrial madhouse that it had taken newspapers a century to achieve. It allowed a few highly unionized workers to live very well by doing very little – and at everybody's expense. It added hugely to production costs: some ITV companies agreed to first-class travel for crews flying over 1,000 miles (which meant most could rarely afford to film in America) and on location crews became surly unless they were entertained for dinner in the best restaurants, where they regularly ordered whatever was most expensive on the menu (lobster thermidor was a particular favourite). Worst of all, their restrictions meant British TV was slipping behind in the use of new technology.

When I arrived in America in 1979 all the network newscasts had just started using Qantel, a computer device which, among other things, allows you to key in sharp pictures and artwork behind the shoulder of the newscaster and animate them into all manner of shapes. It had been invented in Newbury and I had featured it in a *Tomorrow's World* report; updated variations of it now dominate the visual presentation of TV news in Europe and America. But at the time no British broadcaster was using it because nobody could get union agreement on who would operate it. There were other signs that British TV was slipping in the technology stakes. While covering the American presidential election in 1980 I never had any difficulty spotting the BBC or ITN crews: they were the only ones still using film for newsgathering instead of the new video cameras.

I returned to Britain as UK editor of *The Economist* in

1982 with a mission to expose the inefficiencies of British television and argue the case for adding multi-channel choice to our public-service tradition. Though I became the *bête noire* of the established broadcasters, who saw me as a threat to their comfortable, settled ways, I regarded what I was proposing as the only way to ensure a successful future for British broadcasting. I did not want British television to go the way of the car or shipbuilding industries, which ceased to be world-beaters through managerial complacency, union restrictions, a failure to invest in the latest technology – and a smug belief that they were the best in the world.

My move to *The Sunday Times* gave me a far more powerful platform from which to argue my case. I never campaigned for the abolition of the licence fee or the destruction of the BBC (though other News International titles did) because I always regarded public-service broadcasting as essential to the variety and quality of a multi-channel system. But I did urge the BBC to end its imperial mission to do everything (born of the days when it was the only British broadcaster), by shedding its local radio stations, privatizing or taking commercials on Radios 1 and 2 and concentrating its resources on what it did best, especially the sort of programming the market might not deliver.

My biggest beef with the mandarins of the BBC and ITV, however, was their resistance to any changes which allowed new competitors to enter the market and provide alternative channels to theirs, unless it was on their terms. It is classic cartel behaviour to seek to exclude or control newcomers and the BBC/ITV duopoly had become pretty adept at it. In the 1960s, when the government decided on a third national channel, it went to the BBC. In the early 1980s a fourth network (Channel 4) was tied to ITV. Even Britain's first step into satellite TV, which failed miserably, was given to a BBC/ITV consortium. This cosy club needed a stiff dose of competition, to enhance viewer choice and force them to tackle their restrictive practices.

The investigative skills of *The Sunday Times* were deployed to reveal the expensive industrial shambles behind British broadcasting, while feature articles explained the exciting proliferation of channels in America (instead of the usual knee-jerk trashing of all American broadcasting then dominant in every other broadsheet) and the sort of fare that could be on offer to British viewers if more channels were available.

The move to Wapping in 1986 allowed us to write about broadcasting with rather more authority: we had at last cleansed our own stables and now had a more convincing basis on which to challenge television to do the same. I brought in Jonathan Miller (no relation to the Hampstead polymath) as media editor. I had first met Miller when he was producing a new media newsletter for *The Economist* out of Washington, DC and liked his bare-knuckle approach to American broadcasters. I thought it might stir things up to turn him loose on the British ones. I needed to do something: for all our efforts, they were proving hard to shake out of their indolence.

Faced with the stiffening breeze of Thatcherism some tentative steps had been made to put television's house in order but there was still a long way to go – and a dogged refusal to recognize just how bad things really were. I remember lunching with Paul Fox, then the much-admired head of Yorkshire TV, who assured me that his station was now a beacon of efficiency. The next Sunday we revealed the wheeze of Yorkshire sound engineers who claimed overnight allowances and special payments for mythical trips to production-facility houses in London.

In systematically challenging every aspect of the broadcasting duopoly, *The Sunday Times* re-invented media journalism in newspapers, whose media correspondents tended to be in the pockets of the broadcasting Establishment. It was later claimed, largely by those embarrassed by our stories, that *The Sunday Times* was doing Murdoch's work for him by paving the way for Sky's expansion. But it would have been most in his interest for the BBC and ITV to remain their cumbersome, inefficient selves: that they were leaner and fitter by the time Sky came along was to their benefit, and in part thanks to the prodding of *The Sunday Times*.

The crucial story – the one that crystallized our campaign and caused public and political outrage – was the Zeebrugge ferry disaster. Some time after that tragedy, I was tipped off that a technician for TV-am, the commercial breakfast station, had managed to chalk up an entitlement to massive payments for the two weeks' work he had done in the aftermath of the tragic sinking of the *Herald of Free Enterprise* in March 1987. When we checked it out we discovered that he was able to claim an incredible £92,000 for fourteen days' work because of TV-am's crazy overtime and special-allowance bonuses. I put the story on the front page in June.

It provoked a huge outcry. At first TV-am denied our story – on the spurious grounds that it had not actually paid the money – then had to confess that the man was entitled to that sum, but had settled for under £30,000, still a huge amount even if he had been working round the clock. It confirmed the worst suspicions of the woman in Downing Street, who had been carefully following our broadcasting coverage. In September Margaret Thatcher summoned the great panjandrums of British broadcasting to a seminar in 10 Downing Street in which she denounced their industry as 'the last bastion of restrictive practices – except for Covent

Garden [the Royal Opera House]', and called for greater competition to force greater efficiency and choice.

It was a severe dressing-down from the Prime Minister but not much changed in its aftermath. She had been as concerned at the seminar to stop the violence and pornography that might come into people's homes with extra choice as she was about increasing competition. The sad fact was that the government had no idea how to break the BBC/ITV cartel and expand choice: it was an aspiration without a policy to realize it. The American cable revolution which I had been so enthusiastic about importing at the start of the 1980s remained stillborn in Britain as the decade drew to a close, with only a fraction of the country cabled and few cable channels worth watching. An earlier British sortie into satellite broadcasting had bombed and it was hardly worth the expense of a dish to watch a single Sky Channel of old American repeats.

The established broadcasters argued that the only reason cable had expanded in America was because terrestrial reception was so bad. They claimed that the quality and variety on the existing four British channels was so good that hardly anybody would be prepared to pay for more. They sounded like the nineteenth-century postmaster-general who said that Britain had no need of the telephone being developed in America because 'we have plenty of messenger boys'. But multi-channel television was still not happening in Britain – and even I was beginning to doubt that it ever would. Then Rupert Murdoch decided to do something about it.

In July 1988 he announced in London the mother of all TV launches: a new four-channel Sky service to be transmitted via a new medium-powered satellite system called Astra based in Luxembourg. Its footprint covered all of Europe but its signal was strong enough to be received with a satellite dish no bigger than a dustbin lid, though viewers also needed a black-box decoder to convert the signal into pictures for their televisions. The multi-channel revolution was underway at last.

Rupert had chosen the Astra route because he had been excluded from the government-approved and licensed British Satellite Broadcasting (BSB), a consortium which just a few months earlier had been given what it imagined would be a British satellite monopoly by the Independent Broadcasting Authority (IBA). BSB had strong links with the established broadcasters (Granada was a major shareholder, as were Pearson and Reed, two other blue-chip British media companies) and boasted that it was the second-biggest private-sector start-up (after the Eurotunnel) in British business history. But the concept was fatally flawed from the start.

BSB intended to launch its own high-powered satellite (plus a back-up), at a cost of well over £200 million. Its powerful footprint would be pinpointed on Britain and it planned to pioneer its own satellite receiver technology, a Brussels-approved sound and picture system called D-Mac, which added enormously to the technological challenge. The signal from its satellite would be picked up by a small device known as a squarial – but that had to be developed too and was more complicated than a simple dish. Most fatally of all for the future, the BSB satellite had capacity for only five channels, which meant it did not have the capacity to expand as the multi-channel revolution gathered pace. These flaws were Rupert's opportunity.

Sky avoided the huge upfront capital cost of building and launching its own satellite by leasing four transponders from Astra for ten years for a relatively modest £54 million. Sky would use PAL, the tried and tested picture system already used by the existing terrestrial networks, and the European-wide Astra system had the capacity to expand to at least 48 channels as demand developed. Since it was based in Luxembourg, Rupert did not need a British licence to operate on it – and, in a typically audacious piece of Murdoch entrepreneurial risk-taking, his plan was to pour resources into Sky so that it would be on-air before BSB, which had been conceived and financed on the complacent assumption that it would be the only British satellite provider on offer.

The so-called smart money was still on BSB. It had the backing of the British broadcasting Establishment, especially a partisan IBA which had licensed it and regarded BSB as its baby and passport to a regulatory future in the satellite age; its technology was regarded as superior (though untried or tested); and Sky was dismissed as a low-tech buccaneer destined to fail.

But by the autumn of 1988 neither satellite system was faring well. Miller reported to me that BSB's D-Mac chip was in trouble (so was its squarial) but that Sky was likely to miss its ambitious launch date: indeed, the industry was beginning to think it might not launch at all. Rupert's call for help came not long after.

*

SKY WAS A SHAMBLES when I became its executive chairman in November 1988, forty-eight hours after my car-phone conversation with Rupert. The people who had presided over the little-watched Sky Channel, with its diet of ancient American repeats, were out of their depth trying to launch a sophisticated four-channel satellite service, with channels devoted to films, entertainment, sport and news. It was a massive undertaking. It had taken Britain sixty years to develop its four-channel terrestrial broadcasting: we were attempting to double the number of channels in only six months.

The Sky staff were still stuck in slum offices in Foley Street in London's West End because the new Sky Broadcast Centre in an industrial estate in Isleworth in west London (chosen by Rupert for its cheapness) was not ready. When I went there for the first time I discovered a construction site in the middle of a mud field – and we were due to launch in two months. It was a daunting task and, at the time, I doubted that we could make it. But I would do my best: I began a punishing schedule, rising at 6 a.m. every morning to begin a day which often did not finish until 2 a.m. the following morning. I concentrated on Sky for most of the week then, as the weekend approached, spent more time at *The Sunday Times* to shape that week's paper: I was determined to remain in control there, even if I had to delegate much of the work. I was fortunate in having Ivan Fallon and a first-class team at the newspaper to take some of the burden from me; the same could not be said for Sky. There was no leadership, no sense of direction, not even any urgency despite the looming deadline.

I soon realized that Rupert had been desperate when he called me. To my astonishment I discovered that he had chosen to launch a multi-million pound venture with a handful of Australian TV cronies he had known for years – and not much else. Some, like the amiable, laconic managing director, Jim Styles, welcomed my arrival: I might save the day for them and if not it would be me who would carry the can. Others, such as Sir James Carruthers, a long-serving Murdoch courtier from Australia with no obvious talent for the task at hand, resented my presence. Styles was soon to return to Australia with no hard feelings. Carruthers stayed to criticize from the sidelines and get in the way.

'Who is this Carruthers?' I asked one of his fellow Australians, David Hill, the immensely talented sports producer, after several run-ins with him.

'Imagine somebody who is the station manager of the lowest-rated station in Boise, Idaho,' he replied. 'Then you'll have his measure.' It was not quite the calibre Sky needed, given the scale of its ambitions. But Carruthers did provide amusement. During one discussion about the launch of the Astra satellite he came up with the bright idea of having the astronauts wear Sky logos as 'they threw the satellite into space'. I had someone gently point out to him later that the rocket would be unmanned. But there was Australian talent at hand too: Hill (who had already revived the broadcasting of Australian cricket, was to do the same for British soccer on Sky and went on to mastermind Fox's successful American football coverage) was a huge asset. Where he was flamboyant and original, John O'Loan, the Australian head of the planned twenty-four-hour news channel, was quiet and determined. Both were to become key allies in rescuing Sky's chances. Along with Stewart Till, a tough Englishman charged with launching the film channel, Peter Smith, our technical whiz-kid and Jonathan Miller, whom I brought with me from *The Sunday Times*, they formed Sky's praetorian guard.

My job was to galvanize the staff into action by providing a sense of leadership, drive and direction: there were times when I had to be harsh, even ruthless, but it did not require the brutality of my *Sunday Times* initiation: unlike then, I was not working with people set in their ways and determined to thwart me. I had a young team which made up for what it sometimes lacked in talent or experience with energy and enthusiasm.

Miller put up a huge sign with the number of days to the launch, which he updated every morning, to concentrate minds. I started almost every day with an 8 a.m. executive meeting in the middle of the construction site at Isleworth. Tough targets were agreed and regularly monitored at subsequent meetings. The toughest were set for the men from Sony UK, who were providing most of the sophisticated broadcast equipment. With a mixture of threats and cajoling they met their deadlines in the most difficult of circumstances, installing equipment that required clean, tender care while plasterers, carpenters and dust swirled around them.

With the reliable John O'Loan I set about formulating the schedules for the 24-hour news channel, on which most of our original (as opposed to bought-in) programming would appear. He had devised a format which involved a half-hour of news on every hour followed by a documentary or current affairs programme on almost every back half-hour. Since the plan was to give the headlines during the breaks in this back half-hour, viewers would never be more than a few moments from the latest news, a distinct improvement on Cable News Network (CNN), the American pioneer in twenty-four-hours news.

I insisted we take some of the programme formats of CNN and give them a British spin: they had already invented the wheel and I had no time to reinvent it. We took their popular *Crossfire*, a political debate show, and turned it into our *Target,* and CNN's *Larry King Show*, a talk/phone-in programme, and made it our *Frank Bough Show.* I also copied ABC's *Nightline* and called it *Newsline*. Formats that would have taken the BBC or ITV months or even years to launch were being piloted within weeks. I knew Sky News would lose money and never command a large audience. But it was the channel the opinion-formers would watch, it was a genuine addition to British broadcasting and it could win us favourable publicity while others were criticizing the largely American programming of the entertainment and film channels.

I impressed on Sky News that above all it had to have the ability to cover breaking news live (which is how CNN was making a name for itself) and never be afraid to scrap its planned schedules to do so. It was easier said than done: live-news coverage of breaking events in Britain requires microwave links to send pictures to the broadcast centre, which are then uplinked to the satellite. But the necessary frequencies were allocated by an Industry Department committee in the grip of the BBC and ITV – and they were in no hurry to allocate them to a new arrival. I investigated the possibility of the news crews linking up direct to the satellite from their location: but that was fraught with regulatory problems as well. I went to see David Young, the industry secretary, to say that if the government believed in competition in broadcasting it had a funny way of going about it. He promised to see what he could do: but the rules to allow Sky News in were changed only slowly and grudgingly.

Then there were the problems of Rupert's own making. To save money he had agreed that Sky's sports channel would be Eurosport, a consortium of European public-service broadcasters which pooled some of their sporting rights and planned to broadcast the commentaries in four languages. Sky operated but did not own Eurosport: those who controlled it were European state broadcasters who liked long meetings in some of Europe's most fashionable cities to decide very little. I argued for a specifically British sports channel since I did not believe there were many sporting events that crossed European borders. But we had neither the time nor the resources to get one ready for the Sky launch and had to go to air with characterless Eurosport (a real Sky Sports, however, was to emerge and win some of the biggest sporting rights once Sky was up and running).

Disney was an even bigger problem. To off-load the huge costs of launching Sky, which looked like it could cost at least £500 million before it began making an operating profit, Rupert had done a complicated deal with Disney in

Hollywood which effectively made them fifty–fifty partners in a joint venture. Disney would share half the huge costs of acquiring Hollywood film rights, contribute its own Touchstone studio output (just as Rupert was making Twentieth Century Fox films available) and launch the Disney Channel as Sky's fifth channel. But a merger between Disney's cautious corporate culture and the buccaneering Murdoch was not likely to be a marriage made in heaven.

I realized it would never last when I went to Hollywood to finalize some of the film deals. BSB had already bid up the price of film rights to a ridiculous level in an effort to deny Sky movies that were essential to its success: Hollywood could not believe its luck that there were these Brits in town prepared to throw their shareholders' money around like confetti. Michael Eisner, the Disney boss, understandably balked at paying such sums and the people at Disney wanted endless meetings to decide what to do. But Rupert rightly realized that it was first-run movies that would move the dishes and that we had no choice but to bid against BSB.

BSB, however, had taken out advertisements in the Hollywood trade press depicting Sky as an unreliable fly-by-night operation. Some of the big studios thought it safer to stick with BSB. I remember sitting in Rupert's office in Los Angeles in December as we tried to clinch a deal with Paramount. 'I have a cheque for $300 million in my pocket,' he said on the phone to Paramount's boss. 'Andrew and I are ready to come over with it now.' But though it was more than BSB had offered, Paramount reckoned it was safer to go with our rivals.

Disney was not used to doing business in this cavalier way. Its caution became an impediment in our rush to air. So did its refusal to commit any senior management to the cause. It sent over one young man from Burbank to 'help' us and prepare the launch of the Disney Channel. He was a lost soul, asking me one day before he flew from London to Scotland, where he was going to visit our subscriber management facility, if he was going to a different time zone – and would he need a passport! Disney executives bombarded me with phone calls from Los Angeles at all times of day and night: they wanted to micro-manage everything we were doing from a distance but were unwilling to roll up their sleeves and pitch in themselves.

In one memorable phone call, John Cooke, the president of the Disney Channel, flew off the handle when I told him I had concluded a deal with the cable companies to take our channels. This apparently urbane and civilized man started swearing and cursing at me. I was working eighteen-hour days and was in no mood to take this long-distance lambasting: 'If you hadn't sent over a boy to do a man's job,' I shouted back, 'I wouldn't have to do everything myself! We need what cable viewers there are to give us a half-decent audience for the launch. If you think you can do better, come over and do it your bloody self.' He never did.

Rupert told me to sideline Disney as best I could: 'Ignore them whenever you can,' he told me, 'but keep them in play. We need to get their money – and we don't want them defecting to BSB.' Disney conferred an element of respectability on Sky and it would have been a major blow to have lost their channel to the other side. But it was not easy to satisfy them. Rupert had agreed a ludicrous deal with Disney and they were intent on sticking to its every detail. It was symbolic of Rupert's approach to deal-making: sign up to whatever it takes to clinch agreement then re-negotiate it in the implementation. But the nitpickers at Disney were wise to that and the partnership was bound to unravel. It ended with both companies suing each other for several billion dollars.

I flew to Los Angeles to brief our lawyers when hostilities

broke out, expecting to be less than popular for what I was saying about one of that town's icons. I told the American press that, having been reared on Disney's cuddly cartoon characters, I had been surprised and dismayed to discover how nasty, mean, even brutal Disney's management could be. To my surprise I was briefly the toast of the town: everybody in the industry seemed to hate Disney and there was general delight that somebody was attacking them publicly. 'You can have the best table in any restaurant in LA tonight,' said one senior Warner executive, shaking my hand, '– at my expense.'

Hollywood is another planet, obsessed with its own politics, personalities and narrow concerns. Conversation is dominated by what is happening in the entertainment industry, especially the rivalries between the various studio executives, all of whom are paid enormous salaries. It was a strange new world to me and I knew nothing of its internal dynamics. I discovered later, for example, that personal animosity between Paramount's bosses and Barry Diller, the brilliant head of the Fox studio and TV network, had made them less inclined to deal with us – and that Diller and Eisner were less than best friends either.

Rupert is intrigued, but not seduced, by the glamour of Hollywood and he enjoys the power and prestige that accrues from owning a major motion-picture studio. But he is never entirely comfortable there and regularly hankers for New York: Hollywood's extravagance offends his Presbyterian instincts and its obsession with its own navel can bore him. What happens in the outside world rarely impinges.

I happened to be in LA on a programme-buying spree when news broke that the Chinese army had started its brutal clear-up of the demonstrators in Tiananmen Square. It was one of these huge news events that rarely happen on a Saturday and I regretted not being back in London at *The Sunday*

Times. I called the office for an update and to discover what our plans were to cover it then asked my LA hosts if I could switch the TV from the baseball to CNN, which was broadcasting live from Beijing. They agreed reluctantly but I felt sure they would be captivated once they saw the dramatic footage. In fact, they could not have cared less, drifting off to gossip about who was up and down in the various studios and returning periodically to catch the baseball score. This is not a town for journalists, I thought, and when Rupert asked me to launch an American TV news show five years later my first stipulation was that it had to be based in New York, not Los Angeles: there was no argument.

Disney and Sky eventually settled their dispute out of court and the joint venture was wound up. Disney did not defect to BSB: they got cold feet and walked away from British satellite TV altogether, but not before agreeing that Sky could retain the rights to its Touchstone films, then the most successful studio in the world. It left Rupert to bear the burden of Sky's burgeoning costs on his own. But he had the last laugh on Michael Eisner: instead of sharing in the huge profits that Sky was eventually to make, Disney crept on to Astra in 1995, belatedly negotiating its channel on to the Sky subscription system where it became just one new channel among many by then on offer. But that was in the future: when our civil war with Disney began we did not even have the satellite in place.

The Astra satellite was due to be launched into space by the European Ariane rocket from French Guiana on 9 December 1988, but take-off was postponed because of bad weather and technical problems. Next day was a Saturday and I waited for news while preparing the next edition of *The Sunday Times*. The phone rang as I made it home around 11 p.m.; it was Rupert from New York, anxious to know if the launch had gone ahead yet. I told him I expected to hear any moment. He called back again but there was nothing new to report. It was unlike him to be so jittery.

'You sound a bit nervous,' I said to him.

'Andrew,' he replied quietly, 'I'm betting the whole company on this.'

Around midnight Miller called me from Guiana. 'It's a beautiful launch,' he reported, describing the rocket arcing over the equator, its motors carrying the Astra to its final parking space in geostationary orbit, 22,300 miles above the earth. I called Rupert immediately.

'Thank God,' he said, clearly relieved. 'I'm going to pour myself a large drink.' Just how big a risk he was taking was graphically illustrated in June 1996 when a new-generation Ariane rocket malfunctioned on take-off and had to be blown up. If that had happened to the rocket carrying the Astra satellite there would almost certainly have been no Sky TV.

There was no time for celebration in London. We were still struggling to prepare our four channels for broadcast, there were no satellite dishes yet available and we had not developed the scrambling system for the decoder box which would allow us to charge a subscription for the film channel, the means by which we would make most of our money. Alan Sugar, the prickly boss of Amstrad, had been contracted to produce the dishes and decoder, while a company based in Israel was working on the sophisticated scrambling system.

Sugar had been reluctant to produce the dishes and decoder until he knew the satellite was in place and the Sky launch would go ahead. He was not an easy man to prod and he feared he would be lumbered with huge stocks of unsold dishes. But we were less than two months from the launch, scheduled for 5 February, the decoders were being shipped from the Far East and it was clear we would not have enough of them on time. I was relatively relaxed about this since I did not believe the dishes would sell until the four channels were up and running. I knew we would begin with only a small audience and pointed out that when BBC TV had begun its first broadcasts in the 1930s only a few hundred homes had TV sets. We would be beaming Sky, via cable and dishes, to several hundred thousand homes. My main aim was to ensure that there were enough dishes in the aftermath of the launch to satisfy demand – and after a few hiccups Sugar did indeed deliver.

But the so-called dish shortage was used by our many vociferous critics as one of several sticks with which to beat us. The rest of media, print and broadcast, was obsessed with the launch of Sky. Rarely have so many supposedly well-informed journalists been so wrong: few gave us any chance of success and most (since they hated Murdoch and had little interest in multi-channel TV) were willing us to fail. I will not embarrass them by repeating the drivel they wrote at the time. I came to regard media correspondents as lower than crime reporters in Fleet Street's hierarchy: they were certainly less reliable. To muddy the Sky proposition even further, BSB had mounted a massive propaganda campaign urging people to wait for their squarial.

We struggled as best we could against a mountain of scepticism and bad press, which overwhelmed the positive reporting in the *Sun* and other News International titles (but not *The Sunday Times*, where I had effectively banned reporting of Sky so that there would be no conflict of interest). I took whatever opportunities there were to put forward our case but nobody really believed it: at the time Rupert was delighted to have an articulate and informed public advocate of his case but the wide exposure it gave me was later to rankle with him. Meanwhile, the rest of the media sharpened its knives: the established broadcasters dismissed us as 'trash TV', and media correspondents in the *Independent* and *Guardian* sniped regularly from the chattering-class sidelines, keeping up a cacophony of criticism. Even Ray Snoddy of the *Financial Times*, the normally level-headed doyen of media reporters, opined that we were trying to do too much too quickly, and likely to fail.

It was a gruelling time. I left Foley Street at 10 p.m. one night to be reminded by my driver that it was Christmas Eve. I had cancelled a skiing holiday to work through Christmas. London had already emptied out and there was nothing to do but go home, where there was only some Stilton cheese and a bottle of port to consume. I saw in Christmas 1988 partaking of both, watching a film on television. When I awoke on Christmas morning I was still on the couch.

By January there was a real momentum behind Sky and I was able to report to Rupert (with fingers crossed) that we would indeed be ready to launch on time. The team had been strengthened by two arrivals from Fox in New York: Gary Davey, a creative programmer (now running Rupert's Star TV in Asia) and Pat Mastandrea, who knew about selling advertising in a competitive environment. It is one of the strengths of Rupert's diverse empire that when in trouble or launching a new venture he can call on talent from its four corners.

The building site at Isleworth was now beginning to resemble a TV centre and the programming for each of the channels was settled – though because the scrambling device for the film channel was not yet ready Hollywood would not let us use the films for which we had paid so much: we had to rely mainly on Fox and Disney product. I was still unhappy with Eurosport and thought Sky One (the renamed Sky Channel) depended too much on American imports; but at least they were no longer ancient repeats. We were ready to provide a perfectly respectable four-channel service which would improve with time.

Some extra free publicity had come from an unexpected quarter: the leader of the Labour Party. I had hired the ex-Tory minister, Norman Tebbit, and broadcaster-turned-Labour MP, Austin Mitchell, to present *Target*, our answer to CNN's *Crossfire*. Mitchell was a junior spokesman in Kinnock's team and his leader said, in effect, that he had to choose between working for Murdoch and him. Mitchell chose Murdoch and Kinnock fired him, causing a delicious row and masses of publicity for Sky.

Rupert and I decided on a low-key launch: it had been a rush and we were not really sure it would all work on the day: even as guests turned up for the launch, workers were still painting and fixing wires. Some facilities were not ready and we had to hire trucks with the necessary editing and broadcasting equipment and hide them round the back of the building. Nor was there much point in launching with a fanfare when the political and broadcasting establishment was of a mind to shun us anyway (John Birt, then deputy director-general of the BBC, being an honourable exception: he came to the launch and wished Sky well). The only senior Tory to attend was Tebbit, and he was on the payroll.

A few minutes before 6 p.m. on 5 February 1989 Rupert and I stood on a platform in front of a modest audience of largely News International employees, a few well-wishers and the assembled press. We both thanked everybody for their efforts then I got slightly carried away, beginning a New Year-style countdown to 6 p.m., with everybody joining in. As we counted down the last few seconds Rupert and I looked at each other, fear in both our faces. If nothing happened or there was a hitch, we would look total plonkers and the rest of the media would destroy us. But at precisely 6 p.m. all four channels – Sky One, Sky News, Sky Movies and Eurosport – illuminated the terminals around us, with bright, clear pictures and strong sound. A new era in British broadcasting had begun.

*

WE HAD DEFIED THE CARPERS and critics who thought we would never launch. But we still had to prove we could turn Sky into a successful business. The priority now was to drive the dishes into people's homes. There were two fundamental problems: a shortage of dishes and a reluctance among the public to buy them. Now that we were up and running Sugar pulled out the stops to increase Amstrad's dish/decoder production. But people were still wary about buying satellite TV. The rest of the media was giving it a bad press, dismissing the programming as rubbish, predicting it would not last and speculating on how long Murdoch could afford to keep it going when it was costing about £2 million a week to run and taking in almost no revenues. The *Daily Express* even managed to splash on its front page a piece of nonsense about Sky dishes melting in the sun.

Worst of all was the way BSB did its best to muddy the waters. Between them, Sky and BSB had managed to recreate the VHS/Betamax dilemma consumers faced when video recorders were first launched. Like the two different video systems, the Sky/BSB technologies were not compatible. People were not sure which one to buy lest, like Betamax owners in the end, it turned out to be the wrong one. So most bought neither, waiting to see which emerged as the dominant standard.

But we wanted to get Sky into as many homes as possible before BSB got off the ground. We were helped when BSB failed to meet its autumn 1989 launch date – as we had always predicted it would – because of problems with its D-Mac chip and squarial. I promptly ordered a full-page advertisement to be placed in the *Financial Times*, whose owners, Pearson, were a big stakeholder in BSB. It had a picture of a Sky dish captioned 'On Air' and one of a BSB squarial with the caption 'Hot Air'. It dented BSB's credibility though the press were still remarkably kind about its failure: if Sky had failed to meet its deadline they would have destroyed us. But there was still huge consumer resistance to spending hard-earned cash on a Sky dish in case BSB turned out to be better (which all fashionable opinion still insisted it would).

I decided to learn from the experience of VCRs: they had spread faster in Britain than anywhere else in the world in the 1970s because people could rent them; if their rented video became obsolete they could simply swap it for another one. That was the way Sky had to go. I sold the idea to Rupert and put Davey and Mastandrea in charge of Project X, code-name for our rental proposition plans.

By early autumn 1989, as BSB failed to materialize, we were ready to offer Sky to the consumer for a modest monthly rental, with no capital cost up-front. If they did not like it we would take it away: but we had enough confidence in our programming to believe that the more people who saw it, the more would want it. The market in dishes immediately took off: by September over 40,000 dishes a month were being installed, in the run-up to Christmas over 20,000 a week – they were moving far faster than colour TVs, VCRs or CDs at the same stage in their introduction – and a backlog of demand was building up.

Gradually the sneering stopped as the media Establishment realized there was a market for more channels and pay-TV. While Sky dishes proliferated BSB was still struggling to get on-air and did not make it until March 1990, thirteen months behind Sky, by which time it was too far behind to catch up. Being first had given us a crucial head-

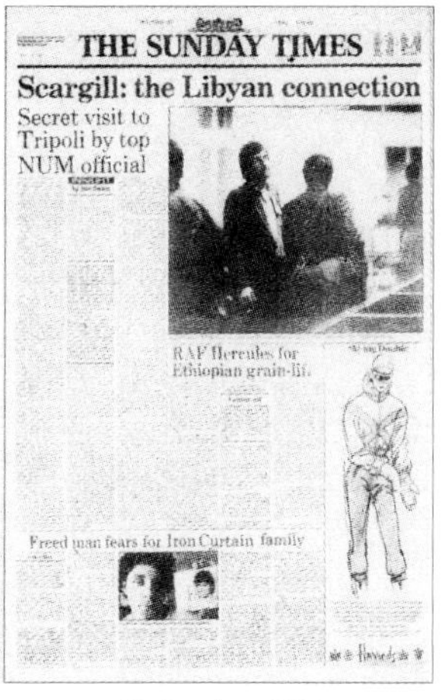

THE SUNDAY TIMES

Scargill: the Libyan connection

Secret visit to Tripoli by top NUM official

RAF Hercules for Ethiopian grain-lift

Freed man fears for Iron Curtain family

28 October 1984

THE SUNDAY TIMES

132 die as plane is 'blown' down

Gerry Adams takes over as IRA chief

Why BBC banned interview

Wartime hide-out ordeal filmed by Jews

Legal aid shock for test family

Labour plans in disarray

4 August 1985

THE SUNDAY TIMES

Tina dead in her mother's flat

Mitterrand aide agreed secret fund

Scandal of the 97 dirty hospitals

Mexico's leader says 'We'll renew our will to live'

Kinnock set to veto NUM bid

Exclusive: how The Sunday Times raised the Titanic

22 September 1985

THE SUNDAY TIMES

Queen dismayed by 'uncaring' Thatcher

High-powered Howe faces Botha snub

HARRODS SALE

Chaos at games as more join the boycott list

Stalker: 40 RUC men face charges

20 July 1986

THE SUNDAY TIMES

ROYAL WEDDING

DEATH IN HOLLYWOOD

Top officials were informed of the revelations but nothing was done

Queen's aides knew of anti-Thatcher leak

Secret price of Labour government

HARRODS SALE

Carnage as train hits van on rails

Rally set to fight Thatcher

Andrew and Sarah sink press armada in the Azores war

27 July 1986

THE SUNDAY TIMES

Revealed: the secrets of Israel's nuclear arsenal

Thatcher to fly to Reagan talks

Nunn steps down at RSC

BA bars terrorist

5 October 1986

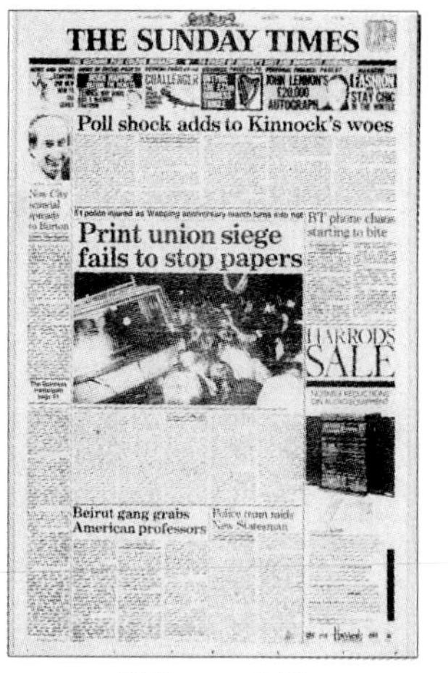
THE SUNDAY TIMES

CHALLENGER

JOHN LENNON'S £20,000 AUTOGRAPH

FASHION

STAY CHIC

Poll shock adds to Kinnock's woes

Print union siege fails to stop papers

BT phone chaos starting to bite

HARRODS SALE

Beirut gang grabs American professors

Police team raids New Statesman

25 January 1987

THE SUNDAY TIMES

LIFE PLAN

Experts agree water came in the bow ● Lorries may not have been chained down

Ferry disaster: the open doors that drowned 135

The survivors come home

SPAIN

THE NEW STYLE

Britain swept by blizzards

Curb left now, warn Labour's moderates

NEWS DIGEST

Harrods

8 March 1987

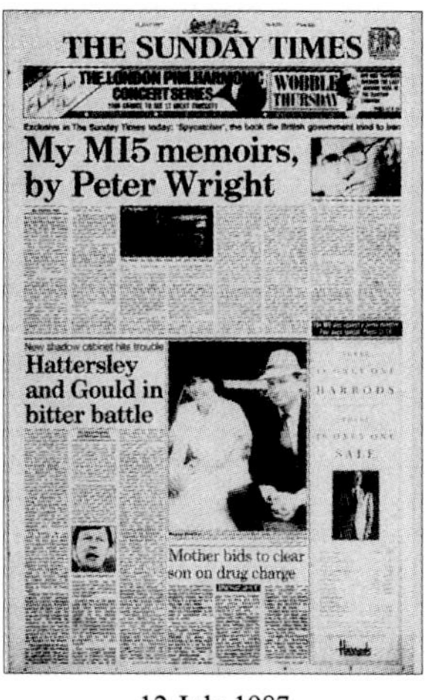
THE SUNDAY TIMES

THE LONDON PHILHARMONIC CONCERT SERIES

WOBBLE THURSDAY

My MI5 memoirs, by Peter Wright

Hattersley and Gould in bitter battle

Mother bids to clear son on drug charge

12 July 1987

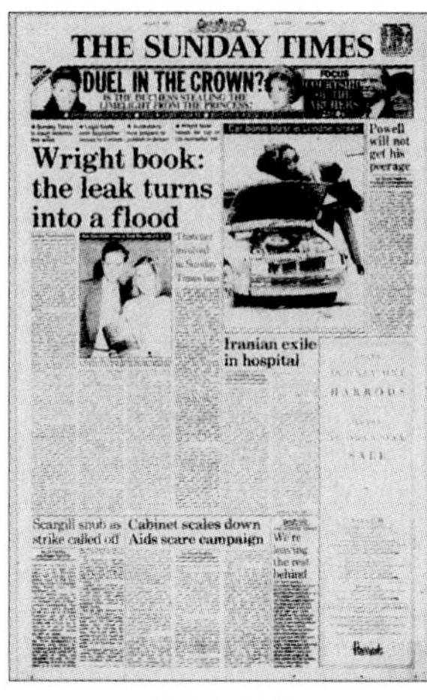
THE SUNDAY TIMES

DUEL IN THE CROWN?

Wright book: the leak turns into a flood

Powell will not get his peerage

Iranian exile in hospital

Scargill snub as strike called off

Cabinet scales down Aids scare campaign

We're leaving the rest behind

19 July 1987

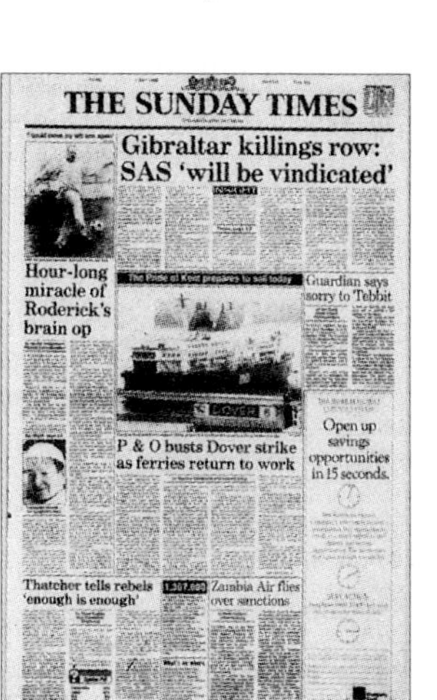
THE SUNDAY TIMES

Gibraltar killings row: SAS 'will be vindicated'

Hour-long miracle of Roderick's brain op

Guardian says sorry to Tebbit

P & O busts Dover strike as ferries return to work

Open up savings opportunities in 15 seconds.

Thatcher tells rebels 'enough is enough'

Zambia Air flies over sanctions

1 May 1988

THE SUNDAY TIMES

Pan Am bombers identified

Race to find brain disease blood donors

Tories regain a 4-point lead

Row over speech by Bishop of Durham

Telegraph chief moves in on Express

26 March 1989

THE SUNDAY TIMES

HAROLD MACMILLAN'S SECRET DIARIES PROFUMO AFFAIR

THE DUKE AND THE DUCHESS

CRY FREEDOM

COMMUNISM IN CRISIS SPECIAL REPORT

Fear grips China as reign of terror begins

Budget battle looming over 8.5% inflation

Good doctor guide ends medical secrecy

Tories plot to dump Heath

Japan's bloody recipe for sharks' fin soup

11 June 1989

THE SUNDAY TIMES

14 LONDON CONCERTS FOR £25

BIGGER THAN BOND

Revealed: the Lockerbie plot

The paymaster, the bomber and the bungling Germans

THE TANGLED TRAIL

Thatcher says next election is her last

KRENZMAN

Schools that top the exam class

Fly Continental To The States And Save A Kings Ransom

5 November 1989

THE SUNDAY TIMES

FORTISSIMO THE BEAUTY OF BEING 40

PAVAROTTI LARGER THAN LIFE

THE LIAR OF KNIGHTSBRIDGE

Centre court battle: Wimbledon may fall to ITV

Thatcher must go, says one in four Tory MPs

Harrods fibbers won't spoil our day out

Revealed: how Militant has re-entered Labour

Centre-right surge in East German election

Free flights *to* the States.
Free flights *in* the States.

CONTINENTAL AIRLINES

11 March 1990

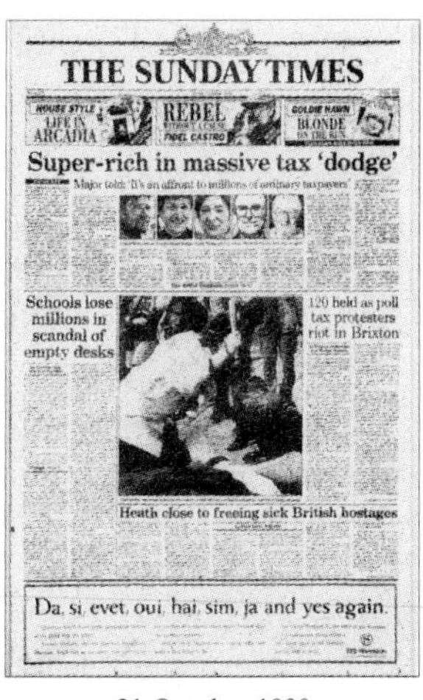

THE SUNDAY TIMES

LIFE IN ARCADIA

REBEL FIDEL CASTRO

GOLDIE HAWN BLONDE

Super-rich in massive tax 'dodge'

Major told: 'It's an affront to millions of ordinary taxpayers'

Schools lose millions in scandal of empty desks

120 held as poll tax protesters riot in Brixton

Heath close to freeing sick British hostages

Da, si, evet, oui, hai, sim, ja and yes again.

21 October 1990

THE SUNDAY TIMES

WINTER 90 PARTY FASHION

MATCH GOOCH'S ASHES XI TO WIN £2,000

FILMS TAKE CENTRE STAGE

Howe and Lawson back Heseltine; Thatcher to quit as MP if he wins

Hurd trails as Major aides say 'It's a two-horse race'

She will vote for Major in second ballot on Tuesday

Major rivals Heseltine as election winner

Polls forecast a clean sweep for the Tories

CHRISTMAS STOCK HORROR!

25 November 1990

THE SUNDAY TIMES

HARD MAN AT No10

DENIS COMPTON'S ASHES XI

MEN'S FASHION WINTER TACKS A PUNCH

Minister helped British firms to arm Saddam

'Allo, 'allo. Welcome to France, monsieur

Britain is no longer an island; Our man first through the hole

Revealed: Ingham's role as a leftist Tory basher

Alarm over Iraq agenda for talks

SAVOY TAYLORS SALE

2 December 1990

THE SUNDAY TIMES

Allies face long and bloody war; Bombing to last ten more days

US steps up B-52 attack on Iraq's elite guards

Israel agrees to hold fire

Overwhelming public support for British role in attack on Iraq

WAR

MORE EXOTIC...LESS EXPENSIVE

KUONI

20 January 1991

THE SUNDAY TIMES

2AM: LAND WAR BEGINS

Allies mount assault on six fronts; Desert Rats to lead Kuwait attack

Large number of Iraqi troops surrendering

Saddam 'lets loose execution squads'

Which company would you buy your pension from?

24 February 1991

THE SUNDAY TIMES

THE GANDER DYNASTY LIVES ON

VOGUE'S

Banks hammer customers with penal rates as bankruptcies soar

Firms pay up to 18% for loans

Bank chief to pocket another £150,000

MPs vote themselves tax-free £26,000 golden handshake deal

Gunfire in capital as Ethiopia teeters on brink of collapse

Do ~~not~~ disturb.

26 May 1991

THE SUNDAY TIMES

LIZ

INGLES! ARE WE REALLY THAT BAD?

IS THE FRINGE TOO SILLY?

No more money for evil regimes of Third World

Scandal over Britain's high food prices

'I stand by my forecast' – Lamont

Modest mayor ends an era as Cannes goes for a cover-up

"You'll never know until

18 August 1991

THE SUNDAY TIMES

Gorbachev destroys Communist party in new Russian revolution

Yeltsin frees Baltic nations as the Ukraine votes for independence

R.I.P.

Raisa taken ill after ordeal in dacha

RAISA SPEAKS

IF YOU WANT TO IMPROVE YOUR BOTTOM LINE, READ OURS.

25 August 1991

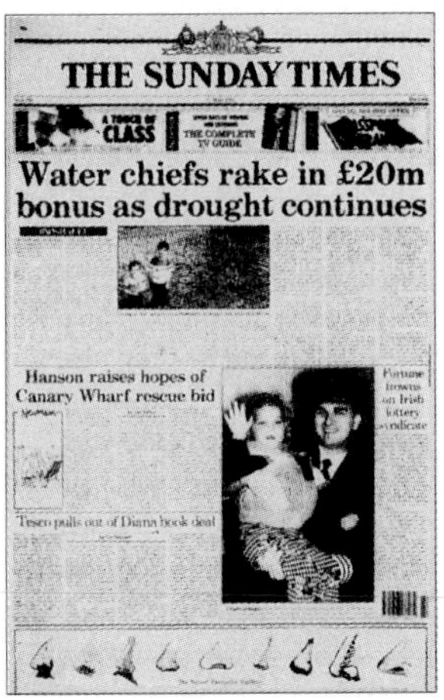

THE SUNDAY TIMES

A TOUCH OF CLASS

THE COMPLETE TV GUIDE

Water chiefs rake in £20m bonus as drought continues

Hanson raises hopes of Canary Wharf rescue bid

Fortune frowns on Irish lottery syndicate

Tesco pulls out of Diana book deal

31 May 1992

THE SUNDAY TIMES

Diana driven to five suicide bids by 'uncaring' Charles

Government to bail out Maxwell pension victims

Maastricht poll: three out of four call for referendum

Gadaffi to hand over IRA secrets to Britain

Bodega Language

7 June 1992

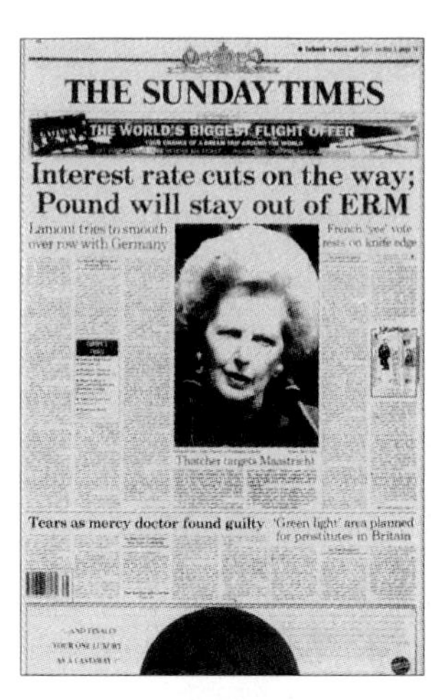
THE SUNDAY TIMES

THE WORLD'S BIGGEST FLIGHT OFFER

Interest rate cuts on the way; Pound will stay out of ERM

Lamont tries to smooth over row with Germany

French 'yes' vote rests on knife edge

Thatcher targets Maastricht

Tears as mercy doctor found guilty

'Green light' area planned for prostitutes in Britain

20 September 1992

THE SUNDAY TIMES

Major's popularity rating dives to new low as economic crisis deepens

Treasury warns public borrowing set to soar

Kohl snubs Major over El Alamein

Foreign patients cheat NHS out of £40m

Rainforest will be gone in 50 years, warns UN report

4 October 1992

THE SUNDAY TIMES

Recession turns into Depression; 200,000 jobs to go by Christmas

Top Tories to tell Major: back down over pit closures

Business predicts a bleak future

TUC calls for mass action as power protest grows

Hard-up Britain joins poor man's club

18 October 1992

THE SUNDAY TIMES

Massive IRA bomb was meant for lord mayor's parade

MI6 secret files reveal scale of Iraqi arms trade

Council tax sparks new Tory uprising

Intelligence documents show size of Iraqi shopping list for British arms

Dubcek memoirs tell of kidnap by Russians

15 November 1992

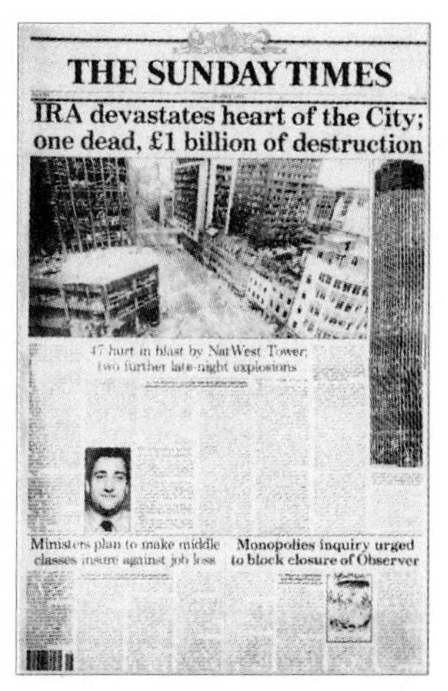

THE SUNDAY TIMES

IRA devastates heart of the City; one dead, £1 billion of destruction

47 hurt in blast by NatWest Tower; two further late-night explosions

Ministers plan to make middle classes insure against job loss

Monopolies inquiry urged to block closure of Observer

25 April 1993

THE SUNDAY TIMES

WIMBLEDON

Nadir donated stolen money to the Tories

Clarke considers phasing out mortgage relief

Courts fail to prosecute thousands of criminals

Ozone layer hole does not cause skin cancer

20 June 1993

THE SUNDAY TIMES

Tories took huge sums from arms dealer, fraudsters and tax evaders

Revealed: fugitive car boss gave £1m

Mates the minister was also a director

MP abused Commons rules to help Guardian

Major plans purge of right-wing critics

27 June 1993

start and, realizing it was losing the battle in the market-place, BSB sought regulatory relief from the politicians, demanding cross-ownership rules to stop Murdoch from using his newspapers to promote Sky and to force him to divest one or the other. BSB exploited its Establishment contacts to the full and gained a receptive hearing among Labour and Tory politicians.

We mounted our own PR campaign but Sky had suddenly gone from loss-making irrelevance to a threat to life as the broadcasters knew it. In July 1989 I faxed Rupert a serious warning: 'The tide is running strongly against us on the cross-ownership issue, even on the Tory side.' We had to make contingency plans to safeguard what we were winning in the market-place from being taken away by the politicians.

Jonathan Miller and I flew discreetly to Luxembourg to have dinner with the Prime Minister, Jacques Santer, now president of the European commission. We were in danger of being closed down in Britain, we told him. If this happened, could we move our operations to Luxembourg and continue broadcasting to Britain from there? Santer, recalling the history of his country as a successful base for 'offshore' broadcasting operations, readily agreed. In the end BSB's campaign failed and it never came to that: but had we been forced to move to Luxembourg the main casualty would have been Sky News, the most British of all our services. We could continue to beam films and entertainment from offshore but we could hardly do a twenty-four-hour news channel without being based in Britain.

I tried to make BSB see that competing on two incompatible satellite systems was bad for both of us and our viewers. At a cocktail party in the Savoy Hotel I cornered Frank Barlow, managing director of Pearson, a major BSB shareholder. 'I know you think I'm biased,' I began, 'but you're on the wrong satellite. You have no ability to expand. Dump it and bring your channels on to the Astra satellite. Then we can compete with each other on programming and channels, not different technologies.'

But I got nowhere, and did no better with Anthony Simmonds-Gooding, the big-spending, complacent chief executive of BSB, whose background was in brewing and advertising and who knew very little about television. 'It will all be decided by the technology,' he told me airily at a media conference, 'and ours is better than yours.' 'You fool,' I thought, 'it will be decided by what viewers want to see and Astra will have a far better mix than you.'

Even if technology had been the ultimate arbiter, BSB would have been in trouble: its famous squarial had become a troublesome, expensive gimmick. While BSB was spreading lies about our own technology – claiming, for example, that when it rained Sky's pictures broke up – it was having serious problems with its squarial.

A month after our launch Sky was contacted by John Collins, the man to whom BSB had entrusted the development of its squarial: he offered to defect to our side, saying BSB was run by 'idiots'. It would have been an attractive propaganda coup to 'steal' BSB's much-touted squarial but we were not sure it worked or, even if it did, whether it was worth the extra expense compared with Sky's cheaper, simpler 'dustbin-lid' dishes.

I dispatched Jonathan Miller and Peter Smith, Sky's technical genius, to a secret research laboratory in Leatherhead where Collins laid on a demonstration. Smith remained unimpressed, arguing that the squarial was too complicated and expensive to become a mass consumer item. But we opened negotiations with Collins nevertheless. Our talks had a surreal, James Bond quality about them.

Collins was terrified that BSB would rumble what he was

up to and insisted on clandestine meetings in various West London hotels. In the end he decided that his contract with BSB was too hard to break and we ended our talks amazed that BSB should place so much faith for such a crucial part of its plans in this one man, who did not engender confidence.

They poured money in his direction – even paying him a large loyalty bonus to keep him sweet – yet when BSB eventually launched the squarial it was not the one designed by Collins: it had been forced to buy in an earlier squarial from Comsat, an American telecoms company. Nor was the D-Mac technology turning out to be all it was cracked up to be: there had been huge problems and delays developing the microchip and some wits in the business started saying MAC stood for Major Catastrophe. In the end it failed to deliver significantly better picture or sound quality.

BSB should have taken up my offer to come on board the Astra satellite: it might still be around today if it had. Instead, within only five months of its launch, it had become the biggest lemon in British corporate history, a textbook case of a fatally flawed business start-up run by flashy lightweights with superior airs whose biggest talent was squandering their shareholders' money. Even as the whole gigantic venture headed for self-destruction, those in charge of it presided over a culture of excess, an appalling legacy and supreme self-delusion: by its end, BSB had spent £1 billion and sold just over 100,000 squarials – which worked out at £10,000 per household.

It has always been a mystery to me why its shareholders – blue-chip media companies like Granada, Reed and Pearson – allowed the people running BSB to throw so much of their money into a black hole for so long. But businessmen often suspend their usual rigorous judgement when confronted with alluring media opportunities and, of course, they were being urged on by some of the most respectable voices in the business.

Nor did there seem to be many penalties for their profligacy. When the whole operation collapsed those responsible disappeared to other jobs, many with large pay-offs in their pockets. 'Next time you ask me to do something,' I joked with Rupert, 'I'm going to make sure I fail.'

'Why's that?' he asked, bemused.

'Because Simmonds-Gooding has made a lot more money from BSB bombing than I have from making a success of Sky,' I said pointedly. Rupert was not inclined to see the joke.

Sky's approach had been positively parsimonious compared with BSB's extravagance, perhaps best epitomized by the fact that whereas I had banned company cars at Sky everybody at BSB seemed to be swanning around in leased BMWs (and eating Prue Leith's fancy food at BSB events, while we served sausage rolls). Sky cut corners where it could, which was why we were in an industrial estate in darkest west London while BSB was in a brand-new pile by Battersea Bridge. But even with tight housekeeping Sky was an enormous risk investment which was beginning to take its toll on its parent company at a time when the rest of Rupert's empire was struggling to service the huge debts he had incurred by launching Sky and expanding into films and TV in America.

In late 1990 News Corporation's over-borrowing and BSB's failure to make much headway in the market had thrown both satellite systems into a forced marriage. It was presented as a merger but in reality it was a Sky takeover of BSB, whose channels were either ditched or merged with Sky's on the Astra satellite, with Sky in charge of operations. It was only after Sky got its hands on BSB's books that we saw the full extent of its profligacy: Simmonds-Goodings's 'fastburn' strategy of throwing hundreds of millions of pounds into an all-out plan to beat Sky to the draw had been a disaster. 'I'm having the greatest fun spending other people's money,' he told a City media analyst. But the money was rarely spent wisely: almost a quarter of a million pounds, for example, was squandered paying for BSB executives to fly to Florida to see the launch of its satellite. One senior BSB executive had *three* company cars: one each for him, his wife and his mother-in-law. 'I've taken over companies where executives got cars for themselves and their wives,' said Rupert, shaking his head. 'Even one where the mistress got a car. But never the mother-in-law!'

All that was after I had returned full-time to *The Sunday Times*. I had launched Sky on time and hit the target of 1.15 million homes by February 1990, a month ahead of schedule. The company was still spending over £2 million a week more than its revenues but it was an investment in the future that would reap rich rewards. Today Sky is the biggest and most profitable television company in Europe, with weekly profits of over £5 million. It has gone from being a loss-making no-hoper in the eyes of the established broadcasters to a rich and powerful satellite service which has revolutionized British television and is now feared as a threat. Senior British broadcasters who less than a decade ago had dismissed Murdoch's broadcasting ambitions are now mesmerized by his achievements. Like rabbits caught in the headlights they are unable to act and afraid to compete; like BSB before them they are looking to the politicians to provide some regulatory relief from his power rather than show the same entrepreneurial, competitive spirit he has.

At least it is now possible to argue with conviction that British television is indeed the best in the world. We certainly seem to have the best of all possible worlds: the traditional quality and strengths of public-service broadcasting *and* the diversity of multi-channel television, provided by an industry which is now leaner, fitter and using all the latest technology. No country can now rival Britain for the quality and choice of its television, not even America. A decade ago I thought it inconceivable that I would ever be able to write that.

*

RUPERT ALREADY FELT CONFIDENT enough about Sky's success to accept an invitation to give the keynote address to the Edinburgh Television Festival in late August 1989, an annual pilgrimage north of the border for the broadcasting Establishment. He had taken a close interest in his speech, though I did most of the drafting, helped by Jonathan Miller and Irwin Stelzer. I made sure the final draft pulled no punches: 'Much of what is claimed to be quality television in Britain is no more than the parading of the prejudices and interests of like-minded people who currently control it,' he said in his hour-long lecture. Too many programmes are 'obsessed with class, dominated by anti-commercial attitudes and a tendency to hark back to the past' and too much drama was 'run by the costume department'. He concluded: 'The freeing of broadcasting in this country is very much part of the democratic revolution and an essential step forward into the Information Age.'

I was delighted that Rupert was prepared to deliver these words. But I feared how he would withstand the onslaught that would follow during question time. But his audience was stunned into silence by his frank, bold puncturing of their pretensions. The speech was regarded as a triumph, even by his enemies, and when he returned to his hotel Rupert called me in London to thank me profusely. At the time I did not realize it was the last time we were ever to work closely together.

I had done what Rupert required of me – and more – in helping lay the foundations for Sky's future success. But, ironically, it was my success at Sky which marked the beginning of the end of our relationship. He had largely left me alone during the tough launch period but once Sky was up and running he wanted a more hands-on role. It was his toy train, he was paying for it and he had every right to play with it when he wanted. But he strangely resented the publicity and credit I had received during my tenure at Sky and began to resist my further involvement in his television plans. Though we had originally agreed that at the end of my secondment I could have the choice of Sky or *The Sunday Times* full-time, it was clear he had no further use for me at Sky.

He began coming to London to chair more meetings at Isleworth, taking over Project X and demanding a bigger say in programming. We were not on the same wavelength. I argued that Sky One had to invest in more British programming for the future if it was ever to become a threat to the terrestrial networks; Rupert thought nearly all American programming superior to British fare and wanted to schedule Sky One almost wholly with American imports. Since the film channel was inevitably overwhelmingly American I thought this shortsighted.

I tried to explain to him that there was a simple rule of thumb in British entertainment: we went to the cinema to watch American films but stayed at home to watch British television. There are usually no British films in the top fifty British box office just as there are hardly ever any American programmes in the most popular fifty TV shows. I urged him to begin the development of a British soap and sitcom and to start planning some quality drama. But he did not want to know, mumbling that I knew nothing about programming. Six years later good British programming is still hard to find on Sky One and nearly all its programme budget goes on expensive American imports and sport.

His increasing involvement in Sky also brought far greater contact with him, something I had always tried to avoid. I had been right to do so: the more he saw of me at Sky, the more he resented my presence. When I finally left Sky in March 1990, Rupert did not even bother to turn up for the farewell drinks, which he had decreed should be a low-profile affair (unlike the huge goodbye dinner given to Jim Styles, which he had made a point of attending). In my notebook in April I wrote the following: 'Rupert and I are moving apart. We are now on the homeward stretch of our relationship. I'm less tolerant of him, he's more remote with me. Sky, in retrospect, could turn out to be the beginning of the end. I suppose I always knew that if we worked too closely together we were bound to fall out.'

I was happy to return full-time to my beloved *Sunday Times*. But success at Sky had started to sour our relationship: the grounds for divorce had been laid.

CHAPTER TWELVE

Ruining the Sunday Breakfasts of the Rich and Powerful

'IT'S IN THE BAG,' whispered the man across the table in a New York restaurant, 'but don't open it here.' I felt a nudge on my left knee, looked round to see if anybody was watching and put a hand down to take a plastic bag from him. At last I had the book that every British journalist had been seeking: Peter Wright's *Spycatcher*. But the possession of this property was to place *The Sunday Times* at the centre of one of the longest and most bitter battles between press and government in modern times.

Securing the British serial rights had been fraught with problems long before these events under the table of a Manhattan steak house in early July 1987. The memoirs of Peter Wright's life as an MI5 agent first came to international prominence when the British government began a foolish and doomed attempt to ban publication in Australia. News Corporation had tried to buy worldwide serialization rights from his Australian publishers but negotiations had broken down. I stepped in and clinched the British rights for *The Sunday Times*.

But there was a problem. Because the British government's case was still wending its way through the Australian courts, there were legal constraints which forbade the publishers from letting me have a copy of the manuscript. I had agreed a six-figure sum for a book they could not give me. The solution was in America, where the British government had been correctly advised that any legal efforts to stop publication of *Spycatcher* would be futile because of the American constitution's rigorous first-amendment rights guaranteeing free speech. Wright's American publishers, Viking Penguin Inc., were a subsidiary of Pearson, the British media company which owned the *Financial Times*. Margaret Thatcher had prevailed on Lord Blakenham, the blue-blooded chairman of Pearson, to postpone American publication until after the 1987 British general election, to avoid any political embarrassment its contents might cause. But Blakenham would not agree to abandon publication altogether. It was set for late summer, a suitable time after Thatcher's re-election; I planned our serialization to coincide with US publication.

The Sunday Times had already revealed details of the most explosive claim in Wright's book in November 1986 when it splashed with 'How MI5 plotted to topple Wilson', which reported Wright's claim that elements within the British intelligence services had tried to undermine Harold Wilson's Labour government in the 1970s. Other newspapers were also carrying stories based on *Spycatcher*'s contents, the British government's discomfort in the Australian courts was generating huge publicity and I felt the story slipping away from me. Though I had negotiated the rights in total secrecy – nobody else at *The Sunday Times* knew we had them – by late June the rumour mill was working overtime and speculation was growing that *The Sunday Times* had something very big up its sleeve.

I feared that the British government would go to court to insist on an undertaking that we would desist from publishing or, even worse, that one of our rivals would secure a copy of the book (Fleet Street was scouring Australia and

America for one) and gut its contents. I called my contact at Viking in New York at the beginning of July to relay my worries: he had been inundated by British enquiries for the book and was feeling the strain. He agreed to bring forward publication and to make a set of page proofs available to me immediately. I caught the 7 p.m. Concorde to New York on Tuesday, 7 July, after telling my colleagues I had to go to Scotland on a family matter. Before departing I took Antony Whittaker, one of the paper's two excellent in-house lawyers, into my confidence: I told him that I intended to publish extracts from *Spycatcher* the following weekend and wanted him to have established our legal position by my return from America. He gulped.

My Viking contact had agreed to meet me at Smith & Wollensky, a steak house in midtown Manhattan at the corner of Third Avenue and 49th Street, only half a block from my apartment. He would be waiting for me at the bar, carrying a Viking Penguin plastic bag. I arrived in New York in the early evening, dumped my bags at the flat and walked the couple of hundred yards to the restaurant, watching all the time to see if I was being followed.

The man from Viking was bemused, exhausted and more than a little worried by the huge fuss surrounding the book he was about to publish. Over dinner, he told me that he knew there was nothing the British government could do to stop American publication but he was being pestered endlessly by British journalists and Labour MPs for a copy, or even an inkling of its contents, and was uneasy about being caught up in the murky world of British espionage.

I walked back warily to my flat about 11 p.m. clutching the plastic bag and its contents, made some coffee and began to gut the book for its best passages. My original intention had been to stay in New York and fax back the extracts before returning to London, so that there was no danger of the book being impounded by Customs at Heathrow. But I had been advised that the fax was not secure enough: electronic eavesdropping, perhaps by satellite, might detect that *Spycatcher* was being digitally transmitted across the Atlantic. I decided to risk returning with the book.

After working into the night doing as much as I could before falling asleep exhausted I caught the Concorde back to London next day, sitting among the empty seats at the back so I could continue editing the extracts undetected. My heart sank when I recognized a man who had been on the same flight the night before; I wondered if he was following me and I half expected to be stopped by Customs at Heathrow and my hot property confiscated. But I sailed through.

Back in London the legal news was good. Though there were already injunctions against two other papers from publishing any material from *Spycatcher*, Anthony Lester QC, our leading counsel and a veteran of freedom-of-the-press battles, advised that we would not be in contempt of court because these injunctions did not apply to us: indeed, a distinguished judge had just ruled that an injunction against one paper did not mean that every paper was injuncted. This was being challenged by the government but it was a legal window of opportunity for *The Sunday Times*.

It was time to take more of *The Sunday Times* into my confidence. I explained to my deputy, Ivan Fallon, what I was planning and that he should quietly take control of the rest of the paper that week while I concentrated on *Spycatcher*, codenamed 'Operation Eagle'. I sat in the sun on my terrace just off my office continuing to select and edit the extracts from what was a dense book, which were then keyed into a secure file in the computer by my two secretaries. A small, hand-picked team, led by Brian MacArthur, took a suite at the nearby Tower Hotel, overlooking Tower Bridge, to sub-edit the copy and design the layouts. Nobody else at

The Sunday Times knew what was happening. It is not that I did not trust my staff: but journalists as a species cannot help themselves from gossiping and dropping hints to rivals that they are in the know. There was also a solid legal reason for secrecy. I feared that if the government got wind of what we were up to it would rush to court to seek – and almost certainly obtain – an injunction. Rumours at the *Observer* were rife that we were about to publish *Spycatcher*. In its usual helpful way, our rival even tipped off the treasury solicitor, a senior government legal officer, of its suspicions. As a result he faxed every newspaper office on the Friday, warning that any newspaper which published material emanating from *Spycatcher* risked being named in contempt of court proceedings. We noted his legal advice but, crucially, he did not ask us for an undertaking not to publish any of Wright's book. Amusingly, he did demand such an undertaking from the *Observer*, whom he must have suspected of laying a false trail to *The Sunday Times*.

By Saturday, 11 July, Operation Eagle had moved back to Wapping to some offices at the far end of *The Times*, which were always deserted on a Saturday. By 5.40 p.m. the four pages of extracts were complete along with a page-one splash. The first edition started on the presses at 6.03 p.m. – but it contained nothing from *Spycatcher*. This was the edition that would be sent abroad, go on Saturday night street sales, be delivered to our rivals and, most important of all, to the duty press officer in government departments. After 76,000 copies of this edition were printed the presses were stopped and replated. By 7.08 p.m., with security guards stationed all over the print hall to make sure nobody left with an illicit copy, the first of 1.4 million copies of our special 'Spycatcher' edition were pouring off the presses. As they departed Wapping securely bundled for overnight distribution, officials of the British government, having seen there was nothing to worry about in our first edition, went off to dinner or their country homes, satisfied that the world was still safe for their idea of democracy.

On Sunday, 12 July, readers of *The Sunday Times* woke up to a page-one banner headline: 'My MI5 memoirs by Peter Wright'. Inside, a special four-page pull-out contained Wright's allegations of an MI5 plot against the Wilson Labour government, how Wright and other agents had 'bugged and burgled' their way round London, infiltrated the British Communist Party and even eavesdropped on the French delegation during negotiations about Britain's membership of the Common Market.

It was fascinating stuff, full of serious allegations about a security service out of control, riven by internal factions and fear of Communist infiltration. Our defence for publishing it was clear: the book was about to be published in America, making its contents available to the world. The British people had a right to know what was in it: it was, after all, about our security services. Was the government seriously saying that what a member of the KGB could buy in a Fifth Avenue bookstore could still not be seen by the British people, in whose name MI5 and MI6 were operating? Actually, yes, it was.

By Sunday mid-morning the Attorney-General, Sir Patrick Mayhew, was already preparing his retaliation: he announced that he would be seeking an undertaking from *The Sunday Times* to desist from publishing further extracts and would commence proceedings for criminal contempt against me and the newspaper. Whittaker, our in-house lawyer, called me from Oxford: 'Are we in trouble?' I asked him. 'We certainly are,' he replied. 'The penalty for criminal contempt is gaol.'

We gathered at the offices of Theodore Goddard on the Wednesday after publication to plan our defence. At 2 p.m. a call came through from the Treasury Solicitor to Martin Kramer, who was acting for *The Sunday Times*. 'As soon as she [the Prime Minister] becomes free,' he told Kramer, 'I anticipate being told to ask you for an undertaking not to publish any more.' It was a crucial revelation, indicating that Thatcher herself was orchestrating the campaign to gag Wright and ban his book. The public fiction all along had been that the government's lawyers were acting independently of political control. Michael Havers, the previous Attorney-General, was later to confirm privately to a colleague that Thatcher's fingerprints were all over the legal action. 'We were meant to cease legal action after Australia,' he explained. 'We knew the game was up in America. But we were overruled by Thatcher. She wanted this book banned in Britain.'

The Treasury Solicitor called back two hours later, giving us until 5.30 p.m. to promise to publish no more extracts. I refused to comply: I did not think it was the Prime Minister's job to decide what could appear in *The Sunday Times*. I issued a defiant statement: 'I have been advised that the government is not entitled to stop *The Sunday Times* from publishing further extracts. The book is out in America, it is not secret or confidential any more and insofar as it involves official iniquity and wrongdoing it is recognized by the European Convention on Human Rights that where there is a "pressing social need" to publish the workings of government, the press are justified in doing so. It is now time to let the courts decide. The time has passed for judgements to be made about this book behind closed doors. On what possible basis can the government justify not publishing this book in Britain when it has done nothing about it in America nor instructed British Customs to stop the book coming in?' Next day the attorney-general was granted an interim injunction stopping *The Sunday Times* from publishing any further extracts. *The Sunday Times* counter-sued the government, seeking damages because it was preventing us from exercising our civil rights.

Thus began a *tour d'horizon* of the upper echelons of the British legal system. It was not an edifying experience, at least not for those of us who had been brought up to believe that the country had an independent judiciary dedicated to the defence of our freedoms. Nor was it a comforting one for me personally, since the official papers always began with the government's request to the courts that I 'be detained at Her Majesty's pleasure' in some suitable place of incarceration. I did not relish the prospect of gaol, even in the defence of press freedom.

We opposed the interim injunction in the High Court on 22 July. We won. The government went to the Court of Appeal two days later. We lost. On 13 August we took the matter before five law lords in the House of Lords, the ultimate British arbiter. Their lordships wore no robes or wigs but sat beneath huge paintings of Moses bringing down the tablets of law and the judgement of Daniel to the side. It did not inspire them to think kindly of press freedom. We lost.

Now we had to begin the legal battle all over again to stop the government's interim injunction becoming permanent, which would mean never being able to publish *Spycatcher* in Britain. We won in the High Court on 21 December. The government went to the Appeal Court on 21 February 1987, eight months into the saga and *Spycatcher* becoming staler by the week. We won again. The government, like a terrier whose bite on an old slipper tightened the more you tried to shake it free, appealed again to the House of Lords. We won for the third time. It looked like a famous victory: but not when you read the judgements of their lordships, whose ruling was grudging and mean-spirited.

At no stage did the majority opinion recognize that a free press had a public duty to expose official wrongdoing. Lord Keith, the senior of the five law lords, said he was lifting the injunction not because of any considerations of press freedom but simply because the cat was out of the bag. Foreign publication of *Spycatcher* meant its contents had become widely known in Britain. The injunction served no useful purpose, he conceded. But he made it clear that if he could have thought of any way of stuffing the cat back in the bag then he would have. He attacked *The Sunday Times* for its 'sneaky methods', said we would have to account for any profits we had made from serializing *Spycatcher* and affirmed that a gagging order would and should have been issued had the courts discovered in advance our plans to publish. Lord Brightman spoke in much the same vein, saying *The Sunday Times* was a 'proven wrongdoer' and part of a 'deceit to hoodwink the government'. He had wanted to ban *The Sunday Times* from ever being able to write about MI5 again but his fellow judges would not go quite that far. Lord Griffiths said we were 'tainted with Peter Wright's breach of confidence' and that the proper course of action if any potential wrongdoing had come to our attention would have been to have taken it to 'the responsible cabinet minister'. He seemed to think newspapers should be an arm of the government.

The most charitable comment that can be made about their lordships' judgements is that the whole *Spycatcher* saga went through so many judges that we ran out of ones who could think for themselves by the time we got the final House of Lords verdict. But it was hardly the ringing endorsement of our actions or of press freedom in general for which I had fought this long and expensive legal battle. I was determined not to leave the matter there but to refer it to the European Court in Strasbourg. Our case was eventually heard in November 1991: we won hands down by 24 votes to 0 that the British had unnecessarily violated free speech. The European Court ruled that the British government had breached free speech as guaranteed by Article 10 of the European Convention on Human Rights (the 'pressing social need' clause) in seeking to ban the publication of *Spycatcher*. Our serialization had been justified in the public interest as fulfilling the press's duty to expose official wrongdoing. The judgement was an expensive humiliation for the government: we were awarded all our costs and the British taxpayer was £2 million the poorer because of the government's pig-headed determination to stifle what, in an age of international communication, could not be suppressed.

Peter Wright died in Tasmania in May 1995. His case revealed to me many disquieting features about British justice, from the ease with which judges are prepared to grant gagging orders to stop material from being published (almost unheard of in the United States) to the dangers of having a judiciary which at times can be more executive-minded than the executive. I also had a sense of dismay that we had been forced to go to Europe to establish the principles of press freedom. But under the editorship of Harry Evans the paper had also been forced to go to Europe to establish its right to publish during the Thalidomide scandal. In a country in which basic freedoms have been established for as long as they have in Britain, it is sad that press freedom is now better understood in Strasbourg than the courts of London.

As for Wright's allegations, their essence – that the British intelligence service had been running amok, that elements of it had tried to destabilize a democratically elected British government and the whole service had been riddled with KGB agents – amounts to the most serious set of accusations that anybody could make against the secret service of a democracy. They demanded to be published so that they could be scrutinized in the full light of public debate and enquiry. The national security was not threatened in any way by their publication. Even if Wright had been only partly correct, the national interest was most at risk if his revelations were covered up.

It has become fashionable to dismiss *Spycatcher* as fantasy. Certainly Wright – bitter, zealous, prone to conspiracy theories – was not the most credible of whistleblowers. His most dramatic contention that Sir Roger Hollis, once head of MI5, was a Soviet agent remains unproven, and is probably untrue. The extent of the anti-Wilson activities of our own spies has been exaggerated, though there does seem to have been a faction within MI5 which wanted to bring down Wilson and that it was led by Wright himself (something he did not reveal in *Spycatcher*). But the case for publishing something is not always because it is certain to be true: it is sometimes a means of discovering whether it is true.

Eight years after *The Sunday Times* serialization of *Spycatcher*, there can be little doubt that Wright's portrait of an inefficient, infiltrated and unaccountable security service was largely correct. Wright's ruthless hunting down of moles was far preferable to the Establishment cover-ups of Philby, Burgess, Maclean and Blunt. Perhaps we will never know the full extent of Soviet penetration of our security services; we now know that it was far greater than the authorities wanted us to believe.

Wright's revelations strengthened the case for the public to have at least some idea of what the security services were doing in our name. *Spycatcher* hastened government legislation to place MI5, MI6 and GCHQ on a statutory basis. A decade ago government ministers would not even acknowledge that MI6 existed. It ended the convenient fiction (convenient, that is, for the governing classes) that there was an irreconcilable conflict between the demand for public accountability of the intelligence services and their obvious need for secrecy. There is now a parliamentary committee to oversee their activities; its powers are weak but it is a start.

These developments are full and final justification for the publication of *Spycatcher* and an instructive example of the proper role of a free press. Many of our readers were appalled that I had serialized *Spycatcher*, believing we were aiding and abetting a traitor. They wrote to tell me so in far larger numbers that those who expressed support for our press freedom stand. But sometimes an editor has to offend his own readers in pursuit of a principle and I have no regrets: I would do it again tomorrow. The Thatcher government, for its part, emerges with no credit whatsoever. As Lord Bridge wrote during the book's suppression in a judgement dissenting from the majority: 'Their wafer-thin victory in this litigation has been gained at a price which no government committed to upholding the values of a free society can afford to pay.'

*

SUNDAY NEWSPAPERS CANNOT LIVE by news alone. You need a regular diet of *Spycatcher*s to spice things up. Saturdays are traditionally slow news days. During my decade as editor of *The Sunday Times* only a handful of major news events – the Harrods and Warrington bombs, the Hillsborough and Bradford stadium disasters, Tiananmen Square – broke on a Saturday. The only news a Sunday paper can count on is sport and it has its own pages; you cannot hope to fill the news pages by depending solely on the events of the previous twenty-four hours. So successful Sunday newspapers have to make their own news through scoops, investigations and campaigns. They are what gives a Sunday paper its character and personality, which readers can identify with or react against. They are also what can differentiate a newspaper in Britain's crowded, competitive Sunday market.

Exclusives, campaigns and investigations are in turn dictated by the agenda and interests of the editor and senior colleagues. An editor has to hope that what interests, intrigues or infuriates him or her will also capture the interest and imagination of the readers. The selection of news stories is not a matter of objective choice. There are, of course, some stories that select themselves because of the importance of the event; and no newspaper should ever refuse to publish a significant story simply because it does not fit in with its view of the world – I never once killed a good story for that reason – for then it becomes no more than a propaganda sheet for its beliefs.

But what an editor chooses to put on the front page of a Sunday paper often reflects that editor's agenda. It is a consequence of his subjective interests, what he has decided to devote journalistic resources to uncover, what he considers important or interesting. That is what attracts readers to a newspaper – and repels others. But even readers who did not share *The Sunday Times*'s outlook on issues and events often felt they had to read it because it was making a significant contribution to matters of public interest and debate. Every successful newspaper in Britain has always had a clear identity, which in turn has generally reflected the character of a strong editor. Between 1983 and 1994 the attitudes and interests of *The Sunday Times* were very much a reflection of my own.

*

SCOOPS AND INVESTIGATIONS are the lifeblood of good

Sunday newspapers. They can be expensive to produce, you have to be prepared for a high wastage rate and they are risky: when you get things wrong you can be forced into abject apologies and costly out-of-court settlements, as *The Sunday Times* sometimes was under my editorship, for example with a company called Control Risks and a northern millionaire businessman called Owen Oysten. I also made the huge mistake of using David Irving, the Nazi apologist historian, to translate the Goebbels' Diaries. He was the only expert able to read Goebbels' writing and all the excerpts we published rather refuted Irving's views on Nazi history. But many were understandably appalled we were having anything to do with him and it did the paper damage – a good illustration of the maxim that if you lie down with dogs you get fleas. There were plenty of other mistakes and misjudgements, often caused by pushing stories too far, too fast. But the exhilaration of revelation makes the risk worthwhile, provided the failure rate is low.

There is much to be said for the simple maxim that good journalism is publishing what powerful people do not want to be published – all the rest is just public relations. That may overstate the case for exclusives and investigative reporting but the Saturday nights I was happiest leaving my office, usually sometime after 10 p.m., was when I knew the copy of *The Sunday Times* tucked under my arm was going to cause some important person to splutter over his or her Sunday breakfast.

It was fashionable to claim in the 1980s that investigative reporting was dead in Fleet Street, that a new breed of commercially minded proprietors was not prepared to finance its huge costs, that television had usurped the newspapers' traditional monopoly of investigative journalism. This complaint was most often heard from those who had been investigative reporters in the sixties and seventies and now found themselves sidelined by a new generation of journalists. As far as *The Sunday Times* was concerned, it was nonsense, though that did not stop it being oft repeated. Throughout the eighties and nineties, *The Sunday Times* broke scoop after scoop and published important investigations that rocked governments and politicians, businessmen and trade unionists, crooks and terrorists. It has been a heyday for investigative, campaigning journalism, in the best traditions of Denis Hamilton and Harry Evans, who started it all. You can tell that by the number of breakfasts *The Sunday Times* managed to ruin.

*

THE SUNDAY TIMES INSIGHT TEAM, the core of the paper's investigative efforts, was rejuvenated in the 1980s after some years in the doldrums, breaking major story after major story. It consisted of a regular team of up to four journalists, often among the most talented and determined on the paper, who called on the expertise of our specialist correspondents as and when it was needed. If the Insight logo was on a story then readers could be sure it contained some dramatic revelations and nobody in the world seemed safe from its ability to cast the investigative light of a free, enquiring press in dark corners powerful people would have preferred to have kept hidden.

In September 1985, in the aftermath of the blowing up of Greenpeace's *Rainbow Warrior* in New Zealand by French secret agents, Insight reported that the scandal went to the very top of the French government. The report revealed that the money to finance the bombing had been authorized by one of President Mitterrand's closest aides, his personal military chief of staff. The French Prime Minister, Laurent Fabius, was also implicated: the £300,000 released for the operation to destroy the boat that was protesting against

French nuclear tests in the Pacific had come from a secret fund administered by his office. A few months later Insight had another French scoop when it revealed that a Member of the European Parliament for the French far-right party, the National Front, was actually an agent for the Romanian secret police. The spy had paid Jean-Marie Le Pen for his seat, though the National Front leader had not known he was in receipt of Communist money. The French media, which has no investigative tradition, wondered aloud why such scoops were appearing in a British newspaper.

The Prime Minister of the Bahamas, Sir Lynden Pindling, also found himself at the centre of Insight's unwelcome attentions in the autumn of 1985. A special edition of *The Sunday Times Magazine* was devoted to an exhaustive Insight investigation entitled 'Paradise Lost', which reported how the islands were sinking in a sea of crime and corruption because they had become a major distribution point for drugs from Latin America on their way to the United States. Insight revealed how some of the Prime Minister's closest aides and associates were implicated in the drugs trade and how Pindling himself enjoyed a lifestyle which could not have been financed by his modest PM's salary. I had timed the story to run just two weeks before the Queen was due to arrive in the Royal Yacht for the Commonwealth Conference for maximum international impact. The brave editor of the local Nassau paper reprinted the Insight report and opposition parties sold 5,000 copies of our Magazine on the islands at $5 a time. Our report hung like a dark cloud over Pindling during the conference but he survived, which is more than can be said for one of Insight's main sources, a Kojak-looking character who had personally briefed me in a Washington hotel: he was murdered shortly afterwards.

When Pan Am 103 was blown up over Lockerbie, Scotland, on 21 December 1988, I had been dining with Rupert

Murdoch at the Savoy Grill, reviewing our plans for the launch of Sky Television (see Chapter 11). We both lamented the fact that there would be no *Sunday Times* that week because Christmas Day fell on a Sunday. But Insight, supplemented by a number of the paper's specialist correspondents at home and abroad, began its investigations immediately. By March 1989 the paper was reporting that American intelligence had identified the bombers as a Palestinian splinter group, the Popular Front for the Liberation of Palestine General Command (PFLP-GC), led by a Damascus-based renegade from the PLO opposed to Yasser Arafat. The group had been paid $10 million by Iran to carry out the attack, in revenge for the accidental downing of an Iranian Airbus in the Persian Gulf by the US Navy.

As Insight delved deeper into the story it was able to piece together a detailed account of what had happened from sources in British, German and American intelligence and the Scottish police. By the end of 1989 some remarkable investigative work by two Insight reporters, David Leppard and Nick Rufford, allowed *The Sunday Times* to name the PFLP-GC terrorists operating in Germany who had originally been tasked with the bombing (PA 103 started its journey in Frankfurt) and revealed that because the terrorist cell had been compromised by the German police the job was handed over to the Libyans, who were responsible for placing a suitcase with the bomb on to an Air Malta flight from Malta to Frankfurt. The bomb was then interlined on to the Pan Am flight. When the British Foreign Office and the US State Department later tried to blame the Libyans alone for reasons of political expediency (the Gulf War was underway, the Arabs were our allies and it suited Britain and America to make pro-Saddam Libya the lone pariah) *The Sunday Times* was able to point out that Libya had only been the last link in a dastardly deed which involved Iran, Syria and hardline Palestinians.

Insight was also active on the domestic front, much to the British government's embarrassment. In December 1990, as British troops mustered in the Saudi desert to take on the might of Saddam Hussein's army, *The Sunday Times* splashed with 'Minister helped British firms to arm Saddam'. It was an Insight investigation into how a government minister and senior civil servants had helped British firms export military equipment to Iraq, contrary to the government's own guidelines.

Drawing on dozens of confidential commercial documents and extensive interviews with businessmen at the centre of the arms trade, Insight reconstructed the events which allowed British companies to export arms to Iraq with government approval. Two years before Iraq's invasion of Kuwait, when Britain was supposed to be operating an arms embargo against both sides in the Iran–Iraq War, Insight revealed that a government minister had given some British businessmen some helpful hints on how to fill in their export licence applications to disguise the fact that their machine tools were being bought by the Iraqis to make munitions.

'The intended use of the machines,' Insight quoted the minister, drawing on the minutes of the meeting, 'should be couched in such a manner as to emphasize the peaceful aspect to which they will be put. Applications should stress the record of "general engineering" usage of machine tools.' The minister was Alan Clark, then at the Department of Trade and Industry, and among the businessmen present were executives of Matrix Churchill, who were to be arrested and tried for breaking the government's Iraqi arms embargo even though they had done so, as one of them put it, because 'the minister was giving us a nod and a wink'. Thus began the great arms-to-Iraq scandal which was to cause various ministers so much pain and embarrassment, culminating in the publication of the Scott Inquiry in 1995.

Clark at first denied our story then changed his tune and admitted it was true. He confirmed it again during his testimony to the Matrix Churchill trial, thereby blowing out of the water the government's case against the businessmen: if they had breached the guidelines it was with ministerial encouragement. The trial was abandoned and the men acquitted. Meanwhile, Insight was still digging. Two years after that first seminal story it reported in November 1992 ('MI6 secret files reveal scale of Iraqi arms trade') that confidential documents, compiled by the British intelligence services, showed beyond doubt that the government had known for at least five years that Saddam was buying a huge range of sophisticated military equipment to modernize and enhance his war machine.

Insight revealed that Saddam had been shopping in Britain for centrifuge equipment essential to uranium enrichment plants and the development of nuclear weapons; technology to upgrade his Scud missiles so that they could reach Israel; vital parts for his 'supergun' project; and machine tools to manufacture mortar and artillery shells. It was a formidable shopping list that somewhat belied the government's claims to be operating a strict arms embargo. But, as Insight also revealed, in December 1988, as the Iran–Iraq War came to an end, ministers had secretly relaxed their own official guidelines while publicly maintaining that the status quo still operated.

The Sunday Times was also busy exposing the murkier side of the private sector. In June 1990 the paper splashed on another Insight exclusive: 'Car park giant planted woman spy in rival firm' which revealed that for two years National Car Parks (NCP), Europe's biggest car parking company, had planned and financed a major industrial espionage campaign against its main British rival, Europarks. NCP had enjoyed a virtual monopoly of prime car parking sites in Britain since the end of the Second World War and suddenly felt threatened when an upstart company called Europarks, run by a young man who had once been a clerk with Manchester City Council, started winning lucrative parking rights that NCP regarded as its own.

The final straw came in 1986 when Europarks broke NCP's grip on airport parking by winning a multi-million-pound contract at Heathrow. NCP decided it needed to know a lot more about its new rival: it hired a shadowy company to infiltrate Europarks to uncover information from senior managers and obtain confidential documents; it even managed to plant a female spy in the post of personal assistant to Europarks' chairman. In what Insight described as 'the most extensive espionage operation in British industrial history' the spies also tried to collect dirt on the private lives of Europarks' executives.

The NCP operation was being orchestrated from a very senior level in the company but Insight had not implicated its chairman, Sir Donald Gosling, self-made multi-millionaire, charity fundraiser and friend of royalty. I did not know Gosling but by coincidence he had invited me to a charity ball in the presence of Prince Charles on board HMS *Invincible* while she was berthed at Greenwich. The Insight story appeared a few days before and I called Gosling's office to say that I had no wish to cause any embarrassment and offering quietly to disinvite myself. But I was assured that Gosling would be delighted to see me and my guest. I did not know what he looked like but as we were piped on board I spotted him immediately: he had seen me and started to look very nervous. I felt uncomfortable too and tried to keep matters friendly with a few pleasantries before moving on.

Every time I looked round, however, I could see him

staring at me. I think he feared we were out to destroy his company but there was no vendetta, just a splendid piece of investigative journalism which resulted in a number of people being arrested and charged. In the end, however, they were acquitted and NCP resolved its problems with its rival by mounting a successful takeover bid, a sale in which the government acquiesced. So much for the Tory desire to foster competition.

There were other dirty tricks to unravel. In the early hours of a cold morning in March 1992 a white transit van pulled up outside a house in a quiet suburb of west London. The driver rushed up the front path, dragged three refuse bags back to the van and sped away. The man, a private investigator, had no idea for whom he was working or from whom he had stolen the bags. The voice on his answering machine had simply given him the address, told him to collect the bags and wait for another phone call. The next day he was to meet his contact at a night-time rendezvous by a flyover on London's Edgware Road, where he passed a package of documents taken from the rubbish. Two days after that he was arrested and charged with theft: a neighbour had spotted him and taken down his van's registration. By then the documents had been passed on to an ex-London policeman who had organized the burglary. He, in turn, was working for a man who was a senior security consultant to British Airways. The rubbish belonged to Roger Eglin, business editor of *The Sunday Times* and an authority on the airline business.

In November 1991 *The Sunday Times* had carried a report containing allegations that BA had mounted a series of unfair tactics against its smaller rival Virgin Atlantic, aimed specifically at discrediting Virgin's owner, Richard Branson. The claims were repeated in a television documentary the following January. BA was furious and authorized private investigators to spy on airline staff and journalists to discover who was leaking sensitive company information. Hence the early morning raid on Eglin's rubbish – and the story on page one of *The Sunday Times* on 30 August 1992: 'Revealed: how BA spied in dirty tricks campaign'. Five months later, in January 1993, Insight revealed the extent of BA's underhand activities against Virgin, which included obtaining confidential computer information about Virgin passengers and flights, instructing BA staff to impersonate Virgin representatives and mounting a counter-espionage operation – code-named Covent Garden – because BA feared Branson was spying on them. BA was later to admit in court that it had undertaken 'regrettable' activities to undermine Virgin and discredit Branson. But Eglin never got his rubbish back.

The rich are always with us and *The Sunday Times* had nothing against them, especially if their wealth was the product of their own hard efforts; indeed, one of our themes was that the whole country was benefiting from the new breed of wealth-creators and that they should not be overtaxed and driven away. But we thought they should pay whatever taxes they were legally required to pay, wherever they came from. Insight discovered this was not always the case.

In June 1988, under the page-one headline 'How Arab billionaires avoid tax in Britain', *The Sunday Times* reported that the Kuwait Investment Office (KIO), with a £15 billion portfolio of British shares and bonds making annual returns of at least £1 billion, did not pay a penny of tax. Insight estimated that the KIO could be avoiding an annual tax bill of around £500 million because of something called 'sovereign immunity', a shadowy concept based on a nineteenth-century convention that allowed tax exemption to sovereigns and their governments in certain foreign territories. Insight speculated that the British investments of the

Sultan of Brunei and the Saudi royal family must also be tax free but it was unable to establish how 'sovereign immunity' actually worked: all questions to the Inland Revenue, the Treasury, and the Bank of England were met with a blank refusal to discuss the matter, yet another example of the 'Secret Britain' mentality I was to encounter again and again during my editorship. Despite the publicity we brought to the matter, 'sovereign immunity' still exists. I invite New Labour, which is always promising to close all tax loopholes, to look very closely at the matter if and when it becomes the government.

But it was not just rich foreigners that attracted our attention. In October 1990, under the page-one splash 'Super-rich in massive tax "dodge" ', we exposed a tax loophole which was costing the Treasury up to £1 billion in lost capital gains revenues. A special Insight investigation into tax avoidance named a number of prominent rich British people, including top businessmen and politicians, who had transferred money, shares, property and other assets to offshore trusts, thereby escaping capital gains. The loophole had been unintentionally opened by the 1981 Finance Act and remained unreported until the Insight story. Accountants and lawyers had become adept at offering rich folk special offshore trust 'packages' to exploit it to the full.

Alerted by *The Sunday Times*, John Smith, then shadow chancellor, wrote to John Major, then chancellor, demanding a crackdown: 'I hope you appreciate the sense of outrage felt by millions of taxpayers in this country', he said in a letter, 'who pay the full amount of taxes owed by them, that others who are much better placed financially are able to easily and effectively reduce their tax liability by huge amounts.' Tory MPs also clamoured for the loophole to be closed and the government was moved to tighten the rules somewhat in a subsequent Budget.

The Tory Party was not so keen on another of our investigations. For some time we had been sniffing around the Tories' secretive sources of funds. A young left-wing reporter had done some preliminary work and made some interesting discoveries about a series of companies that the Tories had set up, named after various rivers, to channel major donations to the party. But it was felt we had not quite cracked the story: she assumed we were refusing to run her findings for reasons of Tory bias, resigned in a huff and took her story off to the *Independent*, which promptly ran it. This only served to make Tory Central Office even more secretive about its funding and the shutters came down. But we persevered and our big breakthrough came in September 1991 when Jeff Randall, our superbly connected and resourceful City editor, was able to report that a secret £2 million gift had been made to the Tories by a Greek shipping billionaire to help the party over a cash crisis.

'Greek tycoon gives secret £2 million to Tory Party' ran the headline across the top of page one. Randall revealed that John Latsis, a mysterious Greek shipping, banking and oil tycoon with close ties to the Saudis and an estimated fortune of £3 billion, had made what was probably the largest ever single donation to a British political party to help reduce the Tories' £12 million overdraft. Outside Tory Central Office there was general outrage that the governing party was being bankrolled by secret foreign donations.

The Sunday Times turned up the pressure by revealing that a second overseas tycoon, Li Ka-shing, whose £1.5 billion business empire stretches from South-East Asia to Britain, had also made a substantial donation to the Tories. John Major had even visited Li in his private club in Hong Kong while on an official visit of only two days to dine with him and other Hong Kong businessmen, some of whom were also suspected of being generous to the Tories. We kept up the drumbeat of revelation two weeks later by reporting that a second prominent Hong Kong billionaire, Sir Yue-Kong Pao, had secretly contributed £1 million to the Tories.

The Tories were furious that some of their richest confidential donors were being exposed, but *The Sunday Times* took the view that who financed our political parties should be a matter of public record. There was even a strong case for making any foreign donations, secret or public, illegal, as in America. But as the paper delved deeper into Tory finances it became clear that there were also question marks over its domestic sources of money.

For much of 1992 Insight worked on a massive investigation into Tory funds, unearthing 4,000 donations by 711 companies since 1982. When *The Sunday Times* published the results on its front page in September 1992 it revealed a clear correlation between donations to the party and the awarding of honours. The heads of big companies had a 50 per cent greater chance of being honoured if their firms had donated to Tory funds: regular payments of around £50,000 a year were almost certain to guarantee a knighthood but those hankering for a peerage had to shell out much more. The top ten corporate contributors to the Tories counted ten peers on their boards; companies of an equivalent size which made no donations to the Tories had no peers on their boards. Unlike private donations, company contributions are a matter of public record. But Insight also revealed the ten biggest British private donors: nearly all of them had been honoured by the Tories. Central Office squirmed. But much worse was to come.

In September 1990 *The Sunday Times* had revealed that the Serious Fraud Office was studying evidence that suggested that millions of pounds had been used illegally by Polly Peck, an eighties go-go stock that had soared under the control of its Turkish-Cypriot owner, Asil Nadir, to buy its own shares, thereby artificially ramping up the price. Insight's own investigations had uncovered a Polly Peck share-buying operation involving £7 million of the company's own money designed to boost by illegal means the value of Polly Peck stock. It was, said the report, a share scandal likely to be 'bigger than Guinness'.

Nadir fled to Cyprus, where he is still a fugitive, after jumping £3.5 million bail and before he could face a British court. But he became an acute embarrassment for the Tory Party when in June 1993 *The Sunday Times* revealed that he had made six confidential contributions to the Tories totalling £365,000 which had been paid out of secret offshore accounts through which Nadir had illegally siphoned over £370 million belonging to Polly Peck shareholders. In other words the governing party of Great Britain was in receipt of stolen money.

By now our coverage of Tory Party funds had become something of a campaign. We took the view that all donations over a certain amount, say £5,000, should be a matter of public record, that those who want our votes have a duty to tell us who is financing them, and that the private right to make a confidential contribution to the political party of your choice was outweighed by the public right to know who was bankrolling our parties. A week after our revelations about Nadir, *The Sunday Times* reported that yet another suspected foreign fraudster and fugitive from British justice had poured money into Tory coffers: Octav Botnar, disgraced former chief of Nissan UK, was revealed as the party's second biggest foreign donor, after Latsis. He gave £1 million from offshore accounts over a number of years in the late 1970s and early 1980s, during which time the authorities suspect him of defrauding the British government of almost £100 million in unpaid company taxes.

This drip-drip of damning revelation led Tory Party

bosses to claim that *The Sunday Times* had a vendetta against their party and to some extent they were right: my aim was to try to shame the Tories into coming clean about the source of their finances and to establish more transparency in political party donations. But the Tory Party is not easily shamed and, despite our many dramatic revelations, it still refuses to publish the names of its major private donors. It continues to be embarrassed by periodic revelations – in the summer of 1996 *The Sunday Times* reported it had accepted funds from a foreign businessman with close connections to the regime of the Bosnian Serbs – but the secrecy of its private funding remains intact and it has still to hand back any of the tainted money it took from Botnar and Nadir. Until it does come clean the newspapers should continue to expose the source of its funding at every opportunity.

It was not uncommon for scoops to lead to campaigns – and vice versa. In a bitterly cold January in 1985 *The Sunday Times* reported that 1,000 old people were being treated for hypothermia because they could not afford to heat their homes properly. The special payments intended to help them out with heating bills during cold spells were confusing and inadequate and some were dying in their homes from the cold: 'Our winter harvest of death among the old and lonely' was how the page-one headline summed it up.

Two years later brought another freezing January and no improvement for the country's 'old and cold'. Indeed, we discovered that the new scheme devised by a junior social security minister which was supposed to make payments easier actually made them more difficult. Our investigations suggested that the new scheme had been rigged to avoid triggering payments except in abnormally cold weather. Using the new formula we calculated that only one £5 payment would have been made to old folk in London if it had been in operation since 1979. We mounted an 'Old and Cold' campaign to highlight this absurdity.

But our junior social security minister denied there was any need for a rethink. 'I see no crisis for the old and cold,' he told the paper. 'Hypothermia is not a problem.' His boss saw things differently. Margaret Thatcher read our coverage and sensed looming political embarrassment as old folk died because of a mean-minded scheme of cold weather payments: she overruled her minister and ordered a more generous formula. The minister, we commented in an editorial on the week the government changed its mind, 'is said to have had an uncomfortable time of it and is now no lover of *The Sunday Times*. But why did he devise a scheme designed not to pay anything in four years out of five? It lacked only the condition that there had to be no "r" in the month to make it complete.' The junior minister in question was an obscure chap called John Major. It was our first encounter with him – but not the only time, as he rose to prominence, that he was to show a stubborn and foolish determination to defend the indefensible in the face of the facts.

His worst mistake was to make the recession of the early 1990s far deeper by persisting to defend an overvalued pound within the European exchange-rate mechanism (ERM). Sterling's membership of the ERM eventually went the same way as Mr Major's cold-weather payments scheme though not before huge economic misery had been caused unnecessarily. But John Major was not the only culprit. Britain's major clearing banks made matters worse for borrowers and business folk already suffering from the ravages of the recession. *The Sunday Times* highlighted their plight in May 1991 with a huge page-one story headed 'Banks hammer customers with penal rates as bankruptcies soar'.

The paper reported that our major banks were driving

firms out of business by charging penal interest rates of up to 18 per cent, even though base rates had fallen to 11.5 per cent. There was widespread evidence that the banks were not passing on the benefits of the falling rates but increasing their own profit margins instead. Many small businesses were paying more for their loans and overdrafts than a year before, when base rates had been far higher. A page-one editorial accused the banks of 'taking shameless advantage of falling interest rates to fleece their more helpless customers'. It argued that the banks were rebuilding their balance sheets after losing billions in loans to the Third World and costly ventures into stockbroking at the expense of small businesses in Britain, which were being forced into record bankruptcies.

The story produced an avalanche of mail from aggrieved bank customers and we highlighted several case studies of appalling behaviour by the high street banks: they reeled under the worst publicity they had ever endured. *The Sunday Times* presented a dossier of small-business complaints to the Office of Fair Trading and called for an inquiry by the Monopolies Commission because we believed the banks to be colluding to keep lending rates high. The powerful Treasury Select Committee of the House of Commons announced its own inquiry as a result of our articles but the chancellor of the exchequer, Norman Lamont, did no more than invite the bosses of the banks round for afternoon tea and a friendly chat. There was no reference to the Monopolies Commission and it was only the continuing bad publicity in *The Sunday Times* and other newspapers which picked up our campaign which shamed them into better ways.

Later in 1991 we turned our attention to the high prices supermarkets were charging for food, revealing that British shoppers were paying up to twice as much for basic foods as consumers in other Western countries. A special investigation by *The Sunday Times* discovered that, even when allowing for different purchasing powers, British shoppers were having to pay a great deal more for food than their equivalents in America or Germany; food prices were rising far faster in Britain than elsewhere; and British mark-ups were much greater, at an average of 60 per cent. Sainsburys was so outraged by our stories that it took out a full page advertisement to refute them, making several mistakes about its own prices in the process. It was the first time a *Sunday Times* campaign had actually generated revenue for the paper.

There were no similar financial benefits when in February 1989 Insight named the chairmen of the major British companies (which we dubbed the 'water rats') that were polluting Britain's rivers at a faster rate than at any time since national records began; or when we printed on the front page the pictures of the bosses of those water companies that were still allowing untreated sewage to pour into the rivers (March 1989); or when we revealed, in the very week when it had just won an international award for conservation, that British Petroleum was bulldozing and burning thousands of acres of rain forest in a supposedly protected Brazilian national park (June 1989). But at least our readers knew that they had a campaigning newspaper on their side big enough to take on some very powerful interests, from the country's strongest union to the British and Israeli governments, the influential Aids Establishment – and even the IRA.

*

JON SWAIN WAS MORE used to the killing fields of Cambodia than the murky backwaters of Britain's National Union of Mineworkers (NUM) but it was *The Sunday Times*'s dashing war correspondent who got the crucial tip-off that Arthur Scargill, the Marxist leader of the NUM, was up to no good.

It was the autumn of 1984 and the coal-miners strike, one of the longest and most violent in British industrial history, was in its sixth month. What Scargill had told his members would be a quick, glorious victory was turning into a long war of attrition that the previously invincible miners looked like losing.

The ostensible cause of the strike had been the National Coal Board's desire to close uneconomic pits. Many, including *The Sunday Times*, saw it as an extra-parliamentary effort by Scargill and his hard-left allies to challenge and if possible overthrow an elected Tory government. But Margaret Thatcher was better prepared than previous prime ministers, all of whom had been forced to back down before the might of the NUM. New labour laws had played havoc with the NUM's funds, severely limiting its ability to finance a long strike, the police were being deployed in huge force against mass picketing which was attempting to intimidate working miners and close the power stations and – most crucially of all – the moderate Nottingham miners refused to strike because Scargill would not call a strike ballot of all miners, as the NUM's constitution demanded.

Six months into the strike and coal stocks were high, there was little prospect of power cuts, Nottingham was continuing to churn out plenty of coal and a trickle of strikers was starting to drift back to work. Scargill was getting desperate: above all, he needed money to keep the strike going through the winter, when he thought coal stocks would run down as electricity demand rose. *The Sunday Times* was to reveal the lengths to which he was prepared to go to replenish his depleted funds.

Swain was contacted by a friend who worked in Paris at the headquarters of the CGT, France's Communist-run trade union federation. He told him that Scargill and one of his sidekicks, Roger Windsor, the chief executive officer of the

NUM, had paid a visit to the CGT's offices on 8 October. There was nothing unusual in that: the Communist CGT was a natural source of support and solidarity for Scargill. But the NUM leader had also held a long meeting with a top-ranking Libyan named Salim Ibrahim.

Swain was dispatched to Paris immediately and soon discovered that something suspicious was afoot. Scargill had flown to Paris under an assumed name ('Smith') from Manchester; and Salim Ibrahim was well-known to the French intelligence services as 'Gadaffi's bagman', the paymaster who negotiated and arranged financial payments to the Libyan leader's favourite causes, including European terrorist groups. Were the British miners after Libyan money? If so, it was an explosive story. But we had to prove it.

Swain, aided by the Insight investigative team, established that Ibrahim had stayed at the Hilton International, near the Eiffel Tower; we managed to obtain a record of the telephone calls he had made during his stay. He had called only two numbers: one was his home in Tripoli, the other was in Doncaster. This was a crucial clue: we discovered that he had been calling an expatriate Pakistani called Mumtaz Abbasi, who lived in South Yorkshire, Scargill's heartland. He was, on the face of it, a run-of-the-mill shopkeeper; in reality he was a radical activist pledged to overthrow the regime of General Zia in Pakistan. He had worked with the Libyans before in plotting Zia's downfall and had been sentenced to twenty-five years by a Karachi court for treason. He was released after a Libyan-backed group hijacked a Pakistani airliner to Kabul in Afghanistan and demanded the freeing of Abbasi and others.

From Doncaster he had continued to maintain links with various radicals and revolutionaries, particularly an anti-Zia group backed by the Libyans. It was becoming clear that he was the middle man who had put Scargill in touch with Libya. Things were moving fast: while Swain continued his investigations, we got word that Windsor was on the move again. We had him covered: on 22 October he flew to Frankfurt, where he met up with Abbasi; together they flew to Tripoli for another meeting with Salim Ibrahim. It was during this visit that Windsor was granted an audience with Colonel Gadaffi. It was later presented by Libya's official news agency as nothing more than a goodwill visit; in fact, Windsor was scrounging for funds.

I was doing some checking of my own: this was a story we could not afford to get wrong. I informed Peter Walker, the energy secretary in the forefront of the government's battle against the miners, that we were working on a story that Scargill was seeking money from Libya. I asked him to see what he could find out. We met in the lounge of the Waldorf Hotel late one morning but as we began talking we noticed we were being closely observed by a tall man. We decided to leave; the man followed us. As we began walking round the Aldwych, past the offices of the BBC World Service, we made it clear we knew we were being followed. The mystery man held back and we did not see him again.

As we continued on our walk Peter indicated that British intelligence also had reason to believe Scargill might be after Libyan money, though they did not seem to know as much as *The Sunday Times*. I suspect the intelligence services were bugging the phones of Scargill and other leading NUM figures, because the government had come to regard the strike as more an insurrection than an industrial dispute. It gave me further confirmation that we were on the right lines.

Gadaffi later told Marie Colvin, *The Sunday Times*'s resourceful Middle East specialist, that Windsor had asked for so-called 'humanitarian aid' during his Tripoli visit. He had come with a sob story claiming that 'when the children of the miners died, they could not be buried because their parents had no money to pay for their graves', said Gadaffi. The NUM's financial position was becoming daily more desperate: while Windsor was in Tripoli the High Court in London ordered the sequestration of the union's assets.

Windsor had also come armed with a propaganda video which was supposed to show police violence against picketing miners. 'The video was very dramatic,' said one of Gadaffi's henchmen. 'We could see the hoofs of the [police] horses striking the people. Windsor quoted figures like seven thousand gaoled, two thousand injured and a few deaths.' None of this was remotely true; but the Libyans liked the idea of helping the internal enemies of the Thatcher government. 'I asked the General Producers' Union of Libyan Workers to provide some help to the miners,' confirmed Gadaffi. Windsor's trip to Tripoli had been co-ordinated by the head of this government-controlled union.

At the time we did not know how much money passed hands but Colvin later established that Gadaffi authorized $200,000 for the NUM, worth £163,000 at 1984 exchange rates. The money was taken to Britain by Abbasi in three instalments. *The Sunday Times* was unable to get anybody into Tripoli during the Windsor/Abbasi visit. The only way we could establish beyond doubt that they had been there was to catch them coming off a plane from the Libyan capital. But Windsor had not taken a direct flight from London to Tripoli because he knew he could have attracted the attention of British intelligence, which monitored who travelled to Tripoli, especially since Britain had cut off diplomatic ties with Libya because of its terrorist activities. We could not be sure what route Windsor would take for his return: so we staked out with reporters and photographers the several European airports he and Abbasi could fly to for a connection back to Britain: they were caught together in Frankfurt coming off a plane from Tripoli *en route* to Manchester on Friday, 26 October.

'Scargill: the Libyan connection' was our eight-column splash on 28 October 1984, under a joint Insight/Jon Swain by-line. 'Secret visit to Tripoli by top NUM official' ran the sub-head beside a picture of Windsor and Abbasi at Frankfurt airport. It was a dramatic story which caused a huge public outcry and widespread disgust: many ordinary NUM members were ashamed to learn that Scargill had been touting for terrorist money and for most Britons at the time it would have been hard to imagine a more tainted source. Only a few months previously a young British policewoman, WPC Yvonne Fletcher, had been shot and killed from a vantage point inside the Libyan Peoples' Bureau in St James's Square, London, while on duty at an anti-Gadaffi demonstration in the street outside. Gadaffi's regime was also well-known as a supporter of the IRA, providing it with money, weapons and explosives. The Labour Party, the TUC and even members of the NUM executive rushed to distance themselves from Scargill's actions.

When we approached various NUM figures for a reaction hours before publication, we got a mixture of bluster and denials. Most leading NUM figures had not known about Scargill's Libyan initiative. When we tried to approach the NUM leader during a miners' march in Scotland on the Saturday afternoon prior to publication Scargill walked on in sour silence when asked about his Libyan connections while Mick McGahey, his gravel-mouthed Communist deputy, told our reporter 'to get the hell off the road'. He was bundled away by Scargill's bodyguards.

Iain MacGregor, the Scottish-American chairman of the National Coal Board, said to me later that the story had been a significant turning-point in the strike. Peter Walker agreed.

It badly discredited Scargill in the eyes of his own members and ordinary British workers in other unions. But the man was incorrigible: the following week we caught him making a surreptitious visit to the Soviet embassy in London. The strike was to continue for another six months but the return to work gathered pace and Scargill's reputation never quite recovered from the revelation that he had been prepared to take money from Gadaffi.

The whole episode, however, helped re-establish the credentials of *The Sunday Times* as the country's leading investigative newspaper. In February 1985 Jon Swain was awarded Granada TV's Scoop of the Year Award. His story, said the judges, had been a 'meticulously documented revelation' written in 'classic Insight style' which had been 'morale-shattering for miners'.

*

THE SENIOR EDITORS of *The Sunday Times* filled the L-shaped sofa in front of my desk. It was Saturday morning, 4 October 1986, and we had a big decision to take. 'So, do we run with it or not?' I asked, trying to bring the discussion to a conclusion. But there was no consensus. The editors and journalists who had worked on the story were naturally keen to go with it. But others counselled against publication. Peter Jenkins, our senior political columnist and a man who put great store by his own judgement, was adamant that the story was untrue, probably a hoax. 'The reputation of the paper will be seriously impaired,' he intoned gravely. Others nodded. Their case was strengthened by the fact that our only source had mysteriously disappeared and all efforts to trace him had drawn a blank.

I looked at the executives as they argued among themselves. It was clear there would be no agreement. 'OK,' I interrupted, 'we go with it. Clear page one and all of pages four and five.' They shuffled out, some of them clearly dismayed by my decision: 'This will be Andrew's Hitler Diaries,' Peter Roberts, the managing editor, was heard to mumble as he returned to his office. But you cannot run a newspaper as a democracy and decide important matters by a vote. An editor should consult his colleagues but he or she is paid to take the final decision and accept the responsibility for it. I had decided to go with my instincts and my faith in those who had checked the story out.

Next day the front page was dominated by a massive headline: 'Revealed: the secrets of Israel's nuclear arsenal'. With the imprimatur of the paper's famous Insight team logo, the story revealed in remarkable detail Israel's clandestine nuclear arms programme. It had long been suspected that Israel had managed to build a few nuclear bombs but it had never been publicly proved. The Insight story not only confirmed that Israel was manufacturing nuclear weapons in a subterranean facility at Dimona in the Negev desert but revealed that it possessed a sophisticated plutonium extraction plant which had allowed it to build hundreds of nuclear bombs.

Without telling anybody, even its own people, Israel had become the world's sixth nuclear power, after America, the Soviet Union, Britain, France and China, in a totally different league from countries like India, Iraq or Pakistan which were suspected of developing a very limited nuclear capacity. There was crucial evidence to suggest that Israel even had the technology to manufacture thermo-nuclear weapons, the most powerful of all.

It was a major global scoop, backed up not just by a long and detailed text but by photographs and diagrams of what was happening underground in Dimona, accompanied by a huge 3-D graphic to illustrate the purpose of each of its six subterranean floors. The rest of the world's media, impressed by the evidence and authority of the story, rushed to follow it up. But not Fleet Street: since Israel would neither confirm nor deny the story they were not sure how to react. Our rivals were always quick to repeat any official rubbishing of *Sunday Times* exclusives, as they had over Mark Thatcher's Barclays bank account (see Chapter 9) and the Queen and Mrs Thatcher (see Chapter 8). But since Israel would neither confirm nor deny the story it could only be followed up by sourcing it to and crediting *The Sunday Times*. They decided to ignore it, except for a churlish piece in Monday's *Daily Telegraph* from its Tel Aviv correspondent largely dismissing our revelations as nonsense. But events were to confirm the veracity and importance of our exclusive in a manner that even Fleet Street could not ignore.

Five weeks before the story appeared, a mercurial Colombian named Oscar Guerrero had bumped into Jon Swain in Madrid. He showed him a few colour snapshots of what he said was an Israeli neutron bomb which he claimed had come from a top Israeli scientist called Mordechai Vanunu, whom he had helped to defect. They had been chased by Mossad, the Israeli secret service, but managed to escape undetected to Sydney, Australia. He was on his way to sell the story to an American news magazine. Swain, while suspicious of much of his story, convinced him of the merits of *The Sunday Times* instead.

Investigations in Australia quickly established that 31-year-old Vanunu was not a top scientist but a nuclear technician, that he had not defected nor was he on the run from Mossad. He had worked at the Israeli Atomic Energy Commission in Dimona, where he claimed to have been involved in the production of nuclear weapons. By now we realized Guerrero was a slippery character (he turned out to be a con man with criminal convictions – he had even been associated with one of the Hitler Diary hoaxers, which made me particularly nervous); but Vanunu seemed genuine enough. He had grown increasingly disillusioned with his work at Dimona, dabbled in radical politics, ended up in Sydney after he had been made redundant and become a Christian. His story merited closer examination: I dispatched Peter Hounam, a dogged, determined investigative reporter with a background in nuclear physics, to Sydney as the start of a major Insight effort to establish if what Vanunu claimed was true.

Hounam discovered that Vanunu had taken careful notes of everything he had seen, and had shot several rolls of film deep inside Dimona as he had begun to rebel against his country's secret nuclear strategy. His testimony was relayed to London and placed before a leading nuclear expert, who was impressed. What he told us about his life in Israel also checked out there. It was time to bring him to London for further interrogation. We still did not know if we had a genuine source on our hands, a hoaxer, a Mossad plant or an Arab-inspired plot to discredit Israel.

In London he was interrogated for two days by our nuclear expert and his pictures and diagrams subjected to specialist scrutiny. He impressed everybody because he did not claim to know any more than what a relatively junior technician would know. The results of his interrogation and the pictures were sent to senior scientists involved with the British nuclear weapons programme, who authenticated them in strictest secrecy and on condition they were never named. Still I was not satisfied: I wanted American corroboration as well. Insight took its evidence to Washington to place it before one of America's leading nuclear weapons experts. He confirmed what his British colleagues had already told us: it looked as if Israel did indeed have a far more sophisticated nuclear weapons capability than had ever been publicly suspected. We also checked with our sources in British and American intelligence: they confirmed that what Vanunu was claiming was what they believed to be happening in Israel.

All this took time and Vanunu was getting restless. From my end of the newsroom I watched this young olive-skinned man – slight, serious, edgy, gentle – undergo further cross-examination. It was agreed I would not meet him until all the evidence was in and I could make the final judgement. But I never did get to meet him.

The Sunday before we were due to publish, the *Sunday Mirror* went to press with a story exposing Guerrero as a con man and implying Vanunu's story was a hoax. The Colombian, with whom we had stopped dealing, had gone to the *Mirror* to try to sell his story there. They had turned him over instead. But they also published a picture of Vanunu and this made him very nervous: he feared that Mossad would now catch up with him. It was a legitimate fear: given the strong pro-Israeli sympathies of Robert Maxwell, the owner of Mirror Group Newspapers, it is perfectly possible that everything they had about him had already been passed on to the Israeli authorities.

'Take him on a Wallace Arnold bus tour of the north of Scotland,' I instructed Insight, 'and bring him back at the end of the week so I can see him before we publish.' But it was too late. Vanunu contacted Insight to say he was going abroad; he would contact them later. They pleaded with him not to go but he was determined to disappear, thinking that after the *Sunday Mirror* rubbishing of his story we were unlikely to proceed with it, whatever our assurances. Insight never saw him again. But in the months after publication of his story they were able to piece together what had happened to him.

Mordechai Vanunu was kidnapped by Mossad on the direct instructions of Shimon Peres, then Israel's Prime

Minister. His only caveat was that they must do it in a way that 'did not embarrass Margaret Thatcher', whom Israel saw as a prime minister who supported their interests against the pro-Arab proclivities of the British Foreign Office. Peres had taken a special interest in Vanunu from the moment he knew we had his story: almost two weeks before publication he had summoned Israel's editors to his office and warned them that if *The Sunday Times* revealed Israel's nuclear secrets they could not repeat them. To their credit they ignored him: *The Sunday Times* scoop was headline news in almost every Israeli newspaper.

Peres knew what was coming because on 28 September *The Sunday Times* had taken its findings based on Vanunu's testimony to the Israeli embassy in London for an official reaction. We were following proper journalistic practice. No helpful response was forthcoming: but it was the day Mossad went into action.

Israeli agents disguised as TV crews covering the Wapping dispute began staking out *The Sunday Times* offices to try to catch Vanunu coming and going. They were linked by radio to motorcyclists on the main road, ready to follow him the moment the bogus TV crews spotted him. Insight had been moving him between various safe houses and hotels but a Mossad agent on a motorcycle had eventually succeeded in following him with his Insight 'minders' to the last hotel where he stayed. From then on he was a marked man, especially since he was beginning to bridle at his confinement.

He insisted on seeking out the bright lights of London, anxious for female company. On the day after we had gone over our findings with the Israeli embassy he was befriended by a young blonde, who called herself Cindy, in Leicester Square. She claimed to be a trainee beautician from Florida: in fact, she was an American-born Mossad agent, the wife of a major in Israeli military intelligence. Insight warned Vanunu to be careful but he insisted on seeing her: they kept an eye on him from a discreet distance.

'Cindy' seized her chance when the *Sunday Mirror* ran its foolish story. She warned Vanunu that it was now dangerous for him to stay in London: he would be easily recognized, above all by Mossad. She offered to go abroad with him, even producing two business-class tickets to Rome, where her sister had a flat. There was the added lure of sex: she had spurned Vanunu's advances in London but she indicated that things might be different in Rome, where she would feel more relaxed.

Vanunu was reluctant to leave London but eventually succumbed. He checked out of his hotel on the morning of 30 September and caught a British Airways flight to Rome with 'Cindy'. She hailed what he thought to be a taxi at Rome airport but was in fact a Mossad car; it took him to a flat where he was drugged by two Mossad agents and taken in chains back to Israel in the hold of a cargo ship. He did not even know *The Sunday Times* had published his story until one day his interrogator slapped a copy of the newspaper on the table in front of him shouting: 'Look at the damage you have done!' Vanunu was tried in camera for treason and espionage and sentenced to eighteen years. He was placed in solitary confinement and not allowed to communicate with other prisoners.

As Insight unravelled the details of Vanunu's fate there was an international outcry. Kidnapping Vanunu had been a flagrant breach of international law and a disgraceful abuse of his human rights. Everybody now accepted that his revelations about Dimona were true (indeed the week after the original story the former head of France's nuclear programme admitted to Insight that the French had played a major role in building Dimona) and most commentators agreed that they needed to be made public. But not in Israel, where government and people saw him simply as a traitor. *The Sunday Times* paid much of Vanunu's legal costs and worked behind the scenes for clemency. I did not want to join the international brouhaha because I feared boxing Israel into a corner would make her even more intransigent.

We argued in a series of private letters and entreaties to the authorities that Vanunu was not a spy or a traitor but a young man who felt strongly about what his country was doing. He had not taken his information to the Arabs or sold it for personal gain. Nor had he jeopardized the security of his country: Israel's friends and enemies had long known something was going on at Dimona. Revealing Israel's huge nuclear strength made it less likely that anybody would want to attack or invade the country. In my correspondence I did not argue that Israel should not be a nuclear power – just that in a democracy it was a decision that should not be taken secretly but in open, public debate. I thought it right that Britain should be a nuclear power but I would have exposed any British government that tried to do it without the people's permission.

I had hoped that reasoned private argument, rather than stirring things up in public, might help Vanunu's appeal. But in June 1990, as he stood in court in manacles and leg chains, the Israeli Supreme Court abruptly dismissed in five minutes over one hundred legal arguments from his lawyers appealing against his sentence. They returned him to solitary confinement, where he still languishes. I was provoked into publishing an open letter to Chaim Herzog, the president of Israel, arguing that Vanunu was paying an 'inhuman price for doing no more than telling the world that Israel has a nuclear capability – something the world, and the Israeli people, have a right to know . . . Israel has become the first Western democratic state to punish someone as a traitor for leaking information to a newspaper . . . We ask you to pardon or at the very least commute the sentence . . . By pardoning Vanunu you would demonstrate that Israel is capable of reconciliation, humanity and mercy. At the very least, it would be an act of simple humanity to end his solitary confinement.'

This and subsequent appeals have fallen on deaf ears. Mordechai Vanunu has now spent a decade in solitary confinement in a cell measuring three metres by two metres. A cubicle in one corner contains a shower whose drain doubles as a lavatory. He also has a small table, a bed and a chair. If he stands on it he can just see other prisoners in the yard below, through a small window. But he is not allowed to communicate with them in any way. He will not be released until 2004, a lonely, almost forgotten prisoner of conscience, to Israel's lasting shame.

*

'ANDREW NEIL IS CONDEMNING thousands of young heterosexual men and women to death,' intoned Jerry Hayes, Tory MP for Harlow and vice-chairman of the all-party British Parliamentary Group on Aids on ITV's *Frost Programme* in May 1993. The studio audience – dominated by activists from the National Aids Trust, the Terrence Higgins Trust, Aids Care, Education and Training (Acet) and the plethora of other well-financed lobbies that make up the formidable Aids Lobby – nodded enthusiastically in agreement. 'For the first time,' continued Mr Hayes, 'we are now seeing that heterosexuals are seriously at risk.'

Among the many criticisms made during my eleven-year editorship of *The Sunday Times* this was the only time I was to be publicly branded a mass murderer. Mr Hayes is a politician whom few take seriously, even in his own party, but he was merely mouthing the mantra of the most respected medical experts of our age. A year before Dr Patrick Dixon, the boss of Acet, had written to *The Sunday Times* to protest that 'the scientific evidence is so overwhelming that HIV is a great danger to heterosexuals that it is hard to see how different conclusions can be drawn'.

Medical authorities like the Royal College of Nurses in Britain and public figures like Ms Oprah Winfrey in America predicted that millions on both sides of the Atlantic would soon die of Aids. The most respected voices the medical profession could muster spoke of a new Black Death sweeping the Western world (concern about Africa was to come later). Most of the media slavishly reflected what the medical establishment had to say. All manner of opinion, on the right and the left, was taken in.

I remember Sir James Goldsmith hosting a dinner for me in Paris in the mid-1980s in which he had assembled various luminaries from French politics and the media. Over dinner we talked about Europe, the Cold War and French politics; but as the coffee was being poured Goldsmith leaned back and as he lit his cigar opined that these were all yesterday's topics: Aids was now the greatest scourge facing mankind and it was time policy-makers gave it a far greater priority. At the time it was a consensus to which *The Sunday Times* wholly subscribed. On 2 November 1986 we ran a full-page Focus with a picture of a typical white, middle-class married couple with two children beside a massive headline: 'At risk'. The article explained how everybody – even normal, happy families like the one illustrated – were all 'potential victims' of Aids and went on to predict that Britain was about to see an explosion of the fatal disease that would infect heterosexuals and homosexuals alike. The following week our senior columnist, Peter Jenkins, weighed in with a piece saying that he had spoken to a senior government minister and that 'nothing' now caused him 'more loss of sleep'. The week after that an editorial claimed that it 'does now seem clear that the virus can easily spread from male to female and from female to male through normal vaginal intercourse'. It went on to predict that within a decade, according to 'authoritative forecasts', 20,000 a year could be dying of Aids in Britain.

Much coverage in a similar vein followed. I was determined that the paper take its responsibilities seriously. I instructed the editor of the *Sunday Times Magazine* to prepare a special edition entirely devoted to Aids and it duly appeared on 21 June 1987 with a dramatic coverline which filled the front page: 'Aids: the crisis that threatens us all'. The advertisers hated being associated with such a gloomy edition of the Magazine and many threatened not to pay when they saw it. But I did not care: we had a duty to our readers to alert them in the most dramatic manner we saw fit – and to urge the government to do more.

In 1985, while public money and attention was concentrated on those at risk from Aids through sexual activity or drug abuse, *The Sunday Times* had highlighted the plight of a particularly tragic set of sufferers: haemophiliacs who had become HIV-positive from contaminated blood. They were the forgotten victims in the great Aids scare of the 1980s for they lacked the numbers and finances of the homosexual lobby and they were also uniquely innocent: after all, as word spread about how you could contract the virus it was possible for heterosexuals and homosexuals to minimize the risk of catching it by altering their behaviour. But haemophiliacs had been infected by the very blood transfusions essential to keep them alive. Several years later we discovered that the government was still refusing to pay them or their families any compensation. So in October 1989 we began a major *Sunday Times* campaign: 'The Forgotten Victims'.

Week after week, in a series of page-one articles, features and editorials we argued the case for compensation. They had been contaminated by an infected clotting agent in their blood transfusions, Factor 8, imported from the United States by the National Health Service. We uncovered that though the government had been well aware of the dangers of importing blood products from America, where blood donors, because they were paid, were often poor people and drug abusers most at risk from infection, it had instituted insufficient safeguards to make sure the blood was clean. The whole system of blood collection and processing in the NHS had become obsolete and over 1,200 haemophiliacs had become HIV-positive as a result. But the government steadfastly refused to pay compensation, insisting that if they really felt aggrieved they should sue in the courts for negligence. Several hundred had begun proceedings to do just that; but it would be a long and expensive legal battle during which many of the victims might die before justice was done.

The Sunday Times campaigned for a generous out-of-court, no-fault settlement. We orchestrated public opinion, which was outraged by the government's meanness, and scores of Tory MPs joined with Labour in parliament clamouring for action. It was an encouraging indication of the power of the paper to highlight a clear wrong that seven weeks into our campaign the government felt forced to act. Kenneth Clarke, the health secretary, announced a lump-sum compensation of £20,000 per victim. But it was presented on a take-it-or-leave-it basis, the victims and their families did not think it was enough and *The Sunday Times* agreed. The campaign continued.

Within a year the government was running out of the few allies it had. In September 1990 the High Court judge who was presiding over the legal challenge to the government called on ministers to put an end to the legal wrangling and stump up the cash before any more victims died. The following month the NHS Health Authorities, which had been fighting the case on the government's side, jumped ship and indicated it was time to settle. *The Sunday Times* weighed in with another powerful editorial: 'There is no single issue on which the government, throughout its eleven years in office, has become more morally isolated than the case of the 1,200 haemophiliacs infected by the Aids virus from blood transfusions received through the NHS. More than two-thirds of MPs, across political boundaries, have written to support *The Sunday Times* in its campaign for a just settlement to the tragedy. They have pursued the case in parliament, with massive public support. But the government has remained stubborn, grudging, mean . . . [it] must now abandon its stance while a few shreds of honour can still be salvaged. Mr Clarke should shut up – and stump up.'

The pressure eventually paid off. Belatedly, it was forced to double its original offer and make around £40 million available to the 'forgotten victims' and their families. One night as I was flying to Scotland, I bumped into Tam Dalyell, the independent-minded Labour MP, who had fought for the haemophiliacs in the House of Commons. He was travelling with one of their leading campaigners. 'This is the man who did it,' said Tam to his companion. 'Without *The Sunday Times* the government would never have paid up.' Tam was exaggerating: thousands had fought the good fight, our approach had just been a bit more high-profile than most. But I was proud that *The Sunday Times* had done its bit.

While we battled for justice for haemophiliacs, however, I began to have far more controversial thoughts about Aids which were eventually to bring down the wrath of the Aids Establishment on me and *The Sunday Times*. As the 1980s ended and a new decade began, there was still no sign of the heterosexual epidemic that had been so confidently predicted from the mid-1980s onwards. Part of my growing scepticism was born out of personal experience: though a single man with an active social life, I knew of no heterosexuals who were HIV-positive, never mind victims of full-blown Aids. Neither did anybody else I questioned. But we all knew of several homosexuals who were suffering from the disease, including a much-loved colleague at *The Sunday Times Magazine* who was eventually to die of it. The more I looked at the matter the more elusive the heterosexual threat seemed to be; and no matter how the Aids Establishment dressed up the figures there seemed to be very few HIV-positive cases as a result of heterosexual sex. The overwhelming majority were homosexuals or needle-injecting drug abusers.

The Sunday Times first dipped its toes into these contentious waters in November 1989 with a Focus headline 'Fears versus the facts', which looked at the evidence for and against a heterosexual epidemic. It was tentative stuff.

We reported that the government had just admitted in a parliamentary answer that it had discovered only one heterosexual man in the country with full-blown Aids as a result of having had sex with a woman who was not a prostitute; and revealed the private advice of a former president of the Royal College of Surgeons to the Prime Minister, who had told her that the caption under the 'handsome young woman' in the latest heterosexual Aids campaign should have read: 'Fortunately this young woman is unlikely to develop Aids unless she becomes a drug addict or allows herself to be buggered.' But over half the article was given over to the counter-views of the medical mainstream, with leading Aids experts assuring us that a heterosexual epidemic was on the way. The Cambridge professor of public health said the number of heterosexual cases was 'accelerating rapidly' while a doctor who dealt daily with Aids patients concluded: 'I don't know how doctors who claim there is no heterosexual risk of contracting the Aids virus can sleep at night.'

But the evidence was still hard to come by. To stimulate the debate further I serialized excerpts from a controversial American book by Michael Fumento called *The Myth of Heterosexual Aids*. Fumento had trouble finding a publisher in America, where it is still regarded as politically incorrect to challenge the Aids orthodoxy, and no major British publisher wanted to know either. Since newspapers should always be ready to give space to dissenting views, this was reason enough to serialize it. The reaction was astounding: instead of confronting Fumento's arguments and figures, the Aids Lobby resorted to abusing him for daring to write such a book and *The Sunday Times* for having the temerity to air his views. I began to think that maybe all this bluster was to hide the truth: there was no heterosexual epidemic.

It is profoundly depressing for an editor when you have to confront the fact that a line you have been supporting for years has turned out to be wrong. The temptation in journalism is to gloss over such a development and turn to other matters. But lives were at stake with Aids and if we were wrong in the past at least we could set the matter straight now. From 1990 onwards the tone of *The Sunday Times* became increasingly hostile to the idea that there was a heterosexual epidemic, or ever likely to be one. I do not regret the cautious line we took in the early days when Aids was surrounded by ignorance and it was better to be safe than sorry. But, in retrospect, I think we can be criticized for not changing our tune quickly enough: we continued to peddle the orthodox line long after it was clearly false.

But at least after 1990 our coverage started to reflect reality. Most of the rest of Fleet Street was still stuck in an Aids time-warp, determined to ignore the facts. The writings of Steve Connor, then the *Independent*'s medical correspondent who could usually be counted on to toe the Aids Lobby line, were typical of the consensus of the broadsheets. In the early 1990s he and many others were still writing stories about 'Heterosexual HIV epidemic predicted' and 'The truth about growing menace of heterosexual Aids' long after there were no figures to substantiate such views. On the BBC it was for a long time almost impossible for any other opinion to get a hearing.

In April 1993 the science correspondent of *The Sunday Times*, Neville Hodgkinson, produced a major scoop which effectively settled the debate, though it was another three years before the Aids Establishment would admit it and even the authorities at the time tried to put a different spin on their own figures. Under the headline 'Experts confounded on Aids as grim reaper fails to strike' Hodgkinson reported that figures compiled by the government's own experts showed that out of a total of almost 7,000 Aids cases in the previous decade only sixty-three were heterosexuals who had no established contact with the main risk groups. Even among homosexuals the spread of Aids had ceased to be rampant.

Three years after Hodgkinson wrote that story the figures are even more convincing. Of the 12,565 people in Britain who have developed Aids since the disease was first diagnosed in 1982, a mere 161 have been heterosexuals not exposed to a high-risk category, such as drug abusers or bisexual men. Even that tiny number is probably an exaggeration: just because the authorities have been unable to establish exposure does not mean some of the 161 did not also catch Aids from well-known risks. The fact is that the number of people who have caught Aids through normal vaginal sex is infinitesimal – so small as to be almost impossible to identify.

We now know that there are two overwhelming ways in

which Aids is transmitted: one is to stick an infected needle in the skin; the other is to stick a penis into an anus. Heterosexuals who indulge in anal sex, especially women with bisexual men, are just as much at risk as homosexuals. Aids is not exclusive to a sexual proclivity, it is closely associated to a very specific sexual practice. And if, as is often the case, regular anal sex is accompanied by copious amounts of recreational drug-taking, then the immune system is in even more danger.

I do not feel so much vindicated as angry by the course of events. If Aids had been accompanied by more plain speaking and honest opinion right from the start then many thousands of lives would probably have been saved. Instead a Tory government in the pocket of the Aids Lobby spent millions of pounds of taxpayers' money on advertising campaigns telling young, white, affluent middle-class heterosexuals – a category at almost no risk at all – that they were in just as much danger as anybody else.

The history of Aids is one of the great scandals of our time. Aids had become an industry, a job-creation scheme for the caring classes: at one stage there were three times as many Aids counsellors as Aids victims. The efforts of the Aids Establishment to suppress the facts and rubbish any contrary views outside its mainstream have resulted in a scandalous misappropriation of scarce medical resources. Hundreds of millions of pounds – over £1.5 billion has been allocated to Aids in Britain alone since 1987 – that could have been spent on far greater risks to life, such as breast cancer, from which more die every year than have died of Aids in fourteen years, was siphoned off and squandered by fashionable Aids activists. Money that should have been targeted at the real risk groups was spread uselessly across the population instead. By the summer of 1996 homosexual groups were at last calling for money to be concentrated on those still at greatest risk, something *The Sunday Times* had been arguing for years.

Hodgkinson's success in debunking the threat of a heterosexual epidemic encouraged him to look more closely at other tenets of the Aids Establishment. He was helped by Gordon Stewart, emeritus professor of public health at the University of Glasgow, who had warned from the early 1980s that Aids was a threat only to specific high-risk groups and was either derided or ignored for his pains. Hodgkinson soon discovered that there was a group of distinguished dissident scientists, including a Nobel Prize winner, who challenged much of what the public had been taught about Aids. But their views were ignored in the popular prints and stifled in the specialist medical journals. From early 1992 onwards *The Sunday Times* set out to give them an airing. We did not endorse them but we thought they deserved publication to encourage debate – and they did reveal things the Aids Lobby would have preferred to keep quiet.

In April 1992 Hodgkinson reported on our front page that a group of distinguished scientists had concluded that HIV was *not* the exclusive cause of Aids. At one extreme was Peter Duesberg, professor of molecular and cell biology at the University of California, Berkeley, who claimed that HIV actually had nothing to do with Aids: the destruction of the immune system was being caused in many cases by the explosion in the use of recreational drugs and even the use of AZT, a powerful drug which was meant to thwart the onset of Aids. A more mainstream view was presented by Luc Montagnier, the French professor who first discovered HIV in 1983: he now believed that HIV alone was not a killer but needed several complicated 'co-factors' to become fatal.

These were promising lines of enquiry and in the months

ahead Hodgkinson investigated them further and the paper published critical correspondence from the Aids Establishment in response. In the process, and in concert with several dissident gay groups, we raised serious questions about the efficacy of the much-trumpeted AZT drug, presenting evidence that in some cases it might actually be undermining the immune system of those who were HIV-positive but healthy. One scientist described it as 'Aids by prescription'.

Hodgkinson also went to Africa to investigate what was really happening there; he returned with a very different perspective from the Aids Establishment's constant references to an African Aids epidemic. He reported that HIV had spread into the heterosexual community in African countries because anal sex was widespread (often used as a form of birth control) and so was venereal disease, on which HIV piggy-backed and became more easily transmitted. He discovered that many children diagnosed as HIV-positive were being denied medical treatment because the West had taught the world that HIV was a death sentence and African doctors had decided not to waste scarce resources on them. They went down as Aids deaths when in fact they had died of the many diseases that Africans had always died of. Many HIV-positive children who were being well looked after continued to live healthy lives.

Hodgkinson's ground-breaking reports put a new perspective on the Aids pandemic supposedly sweeping the Third World. But it only further alienated the scientific establishment from *The Sunday Times*. Its anger culminated in an astonishing outburst towards the end of 1993 by *Nature* magazine, the bible of the international scientific community, which savaged the paper for airing dissident views and called for it to be boycotted.

But I wanted *The Sunday Times* to be open to all opinions. So on 12 December 1993 I reprinted the whole of the *Nature* editorial attacking us, along with an article by Hodgkinson summarizing all the reasons why the 'HIV equals Aids' hypothesis could not be taken as gospel. It is an argument on which the jury is still out. *The Sunday Times* never endorsed the Duesberg view, though Hodgkinson has largely come to believe it. More pertinent is the fact that, despite the billions of dollars that have been thrown at Aids research for over a decade, we still do not know the exact cause of Aids. Its pathogenesis (how HIV causes the immune system to deteriorate) remains a mystery. In such circumstances it seemed only right for a serious newspaper to give space to rival interpretations and to help counter the popular view that to be HIV-positive is a certain death sentence. At the very least it helps to reduce the stigma placed on those who are HIV-positive (many of whom, having adopted healthy lifestyles, continue to live long and normal lives) and suggests hope where previously there was none.

In a previous decade under Harry Evans *The Sunday Times* had taken on the medical establishment when it had revealed that the thalidomide drug was responsible for various malformations during pregnancy. It was a tradition I was proud to continue with the paper's Aids coverage.

*

IT WAS VERY EARLY in the morning and I was still in bed in my New York apartment when I heard the phone ring in the other room. When the answering machine picked up I heard the voice of Sir Edward Pickering, long-standing confidant of Rupert Murdoch and a formidable newspaper man in his own right. He was calling from London and anxious to get hold of me. I picked up the phone in my bedroom.

He wanted to talk to me about an article published in *The Sunday Times* alleging that a number of men were involved in fundraising for the IRA, claims that these men vigorously disputed.

'We need to talk about this pending case,' he began. 'I think you should settle.'

The problem was that our lawyers' advice was clear: 'Libel litigation is a dangerous game; it is always wise to try to settle', and the management at News International, fearing heavy legal fees, was running scared of the risk.

'Are you aware of the other risk,' I asked slowly, 'that if we were to settle, the money might find its way to the IRA?'

'No, I see that risk,' replied Pick.

'Then I am not prepared to do it,' I interrupted. 'If the Courts force us to make a payment, then that is one thing: I suppose we have to obey the law. But I will not be a party to volunteering a payment that might end up being used to kill British people and soldiers. I would rather resign than agree to that.' It was the only time in over a decade I was to refuse to take his generally wise counsel.

Our problems were that our intelligence sources were not anxious to come forward and support us in Court; although many wanted to do so, the Northern Ireland Office was concerned that they might betray intelligence sources, even though the senior civil servants and military personnel from whom we wanted help only had access to information, not sensitive sources.

The Northern Ireland Office almost seemed to relish the prospect of our defeat in Court. As one senior government lawyer put it: journalists never defend the national interest so why should we defend them? The official word came down from on high: do not help *The Sunday Times*.

We wrote to Tom King, former secretary of state for Ulster who had become defence secretary, for help. We also alerted the Prime Minister through an intermediary. Though relations with Margaret Thatcher were not friendly she was outraged by the official attitude. But the system beat them both. At King's prompting, two government lawyers arrived at my office on 3 November; one from the Attorney-General's Office (who had fought against *The Sunday Times* in the *Spycatcher* case), the other from the Home Office. In polite Oxbridge tones straight out of the BBC's *Yes, Minister*, they both expressed sympathy with our plight, but said that there was nothing they could do about it. A few days later they washed their hands of the matter. King fumed with frustration, Thatcher continued to be concerned, but some of our witnesses remained barred to us.

Not everyone tried to abandon us, several courageous people in the Irish Customs and Gardai (Irish police) who had evidence that might help agreed to testify on our behalf.The Irish Authorities did nothing to stop them coming forward. A brave Irish MP, Brendon McGahon, whose constituency was nearby, also agreed to give evidence, as did a former commander of the British Parachute Regiment who had extensive knowledge of the situation on the ground. This Irish bravery of testifying on our behalf was remarkable. In the wake of his courageous stand in our defence, McGahon received over 400 letters from constituents, only two of which were critical.

The problem no doubt haunts my successor; the case is ongoing following an Order for a retrial. Our story was typical of *The Sunday Times*' robust coverage of Irish afffairs. In other stories we had named first Martin McGuinness then Gerry Adams as chief of staff of the IRA. When two off-duty soldiers were pulled out of their cars and brutally murdered by a republican mob we published the photographs of those 'caught in the act' (see Chapter 10), identifying two as IRA terrorists and inviting people to identify the rest. When Thames TV broadcast a documentary implying that the SAS had employed a shoot-to-kill policy when it had intercepted three IRA terrorists preparing to bomb Gibraltar we cast grave doubts on the veracity and accuracy of Thames's witnesses, much to the fury of the UK broadcasters.

In a series of articles amounting to 16,000 words we amassed evidence to show that if the SAS had killed these bombers in cold blood Thames TV was very far from proving it.

*

LATE ON THE AFTERNOON of 24 February 1994 my secretary buzzed through to say that there was a senior Special Branch officer on the phone and that he wanted to come and see me right away. He needs to see you on a 'confidential matter of some urgency and importance', she said. 'Better tell him to come on round then,' I replied. He arrived at 6.30 p.m.

'We have recently arrested some people in connection with IRA terrorist activities on the British mainland,' he began. He was referring to those who were arrested, charged and later convicted of IRA bombings in the north of England.

'We found what looked very much like a death list on two of the people we apprehended,' he continued. 'Your name was on it.' I felt a shudder down my spine.

'Can you give me any reason why your name would be on an IRA hit list?' he asked. 'You were the only non-political name on the list; all the others were well known politicians.'

'I can think of lots of reasons,' I replied, explaining our coverage of Ulster and the IRA over the years.

'Was there anything about me on the list?' I enquired. 'Did they have an address?'

'No address,' he replied, 'but they had written beside your name "no wife" and "son of an army major".'

'They probably got these details from my entry in *Who's*

Who,' I replied. 'Tell me: how seriously should I take this threat?'

'We would assess it as an above-average threat,' he said quietly. 'Not category one – but definitely above a general threat.'

'So what should I do?'

'We can advise you on a number of steps to take to improve your personal security,' he replied. 'We'll send a specialist round to advise on improving home security. In the meantime, here's a pamphlet and a video with some helpful personal security tips.' Somehow, they seemed an inadequate defence against the IRA.

A week later another man from Special Branch surveyed my house and compiled a report on all manner of extra security precautions. 'I don't think it's worth bothering with bullet-proof glass,' he advised, adding helpfully, 'it doesn't really work against high-velocity bullets. But we can cover the windows with a special film which will reduce the danger of flying glass in the event of a bomb.' I was not enormously reassured.

My housekeeper and I were equipped with special clip-on panic buttons, a bit like pagers, so that police help could be immediately summoned wherever we were in the house and the car was fitted with special sensors to detect if anybody had opened the doors or attached explosives to the engine or chassis. These were sensible precautions but it was hard not to conclude that if the IRA was determined to get you they would. When Rupert Murdoch raised the prospect of going to America a few weeks later (see Chapter 14) it seemed not a bad time to be leaving the country.

CHAPTER THIRTEEN

Manifesto of a Modern Meritocrat

NEWSPAPERS SHOULD STAND for something: they should hold forthright opinions and express them strongly. They should not seek to suppress alternative views; indeed they should prove a forum for all manner of opinions, as *The Sunday Times* did with its mix of left and right columnists, and writers of no fixed ideological abode. But readers should be left in no doubt what their newspaper believes on the major issues of the day and its attitude to current events should, in turn, be determined by a broad set of principles which guide its outlook on life.

Meritocracy, social mobility and the market economy were the constant refrains of *The Sunday Times*, perhaps its dominant leitmotiv, during my editorship. This reflected my own strong view that Britain was still too hidebound by class division and privilege and that it had been failed by a post-war Establishment which preferred what it was calling privately by the late 1970s the 'civilized management of decline' to the hard slog of pushing through the policies that would produce a British economic and social renaissance. In my later years at grammar school and then university I had developed a dislike for the peculiar combination of snobbery and incompetence which characterizes the English Establishment, its automatic assumption of its right to rule, its failure to do so wisely. It was not that it was holding me back: thanks to caring parents, education, luck and opportunity the world seemed to be my oyster. But it was certainly holding my country back.

My main reason for championing a dynamic market economy was not to reward a few successful entrepreneurs or even to revive the fortunes of British business, worthwhile as that would be. It was the radical potential of market economics to produce a social revolution that interested me most: after the failure of the collectivist consensus to make Britain a success, I had concluded – influenced above all by my time in America – that the market stood a better chance of sweeping away the social rigidities of British society and its debilitating class system, reversing our economic decline in the process, than the broadly social democratic approach to which mainstream opinion on the left and right had subscribed in post-war Britain. It was an analysis the newspaper broadly shared with Margaret Thatcher – though *The Sunday Times* was to take it much further and apply it to cherished institutions which she, as a Conservative, found unpalatable.

The Sunday Times promoted a radical agenda which unsettled and sometimes even appalled the High Tory Right as much as the Old Labour Left – and often left the Thatcherites gasping too. Margaret Thatcher had taught the country to judge the country's institutions by how much they helped or hindered the creation of a prosperous market economy. She had in mind the unions, the nationalized industries, the sclerotic management of much of big business and the anti-market attitudes which dominated so many centres of power and opinion, including the civil service, academia and the media.

But *The Sunday Times* applied the same test to our social system in general and to some very traditional institutions, including the Monarchy, the House of Lords, the Established Church, the middle-class professions (especially in law, education and medicine), the Welfare State and the continuing power of inherited wealth and privilege – and found them all wanting by the Thatcher test. It was an anti-Establishment prospectus which incurred the wrath of the most respectable elements of British society – and much of the rest of the media, including publications as diverse as the *Daily* and *Sunday Telegraphs*, which liked our support for market economics but hated our social agenda, and the *New Statesman*, which hated our economic agenda but once commented that on several social matters *The Sunday Times* was to the left of the Labour Party. I liked that.

*

THE MERITOCRATIC OUTLOOK of *The Sunday Times* was very much a result of my own background and experience. I was the product of an open education system – a fine sixteenth-century Scottish grammar school (Paisley) and an ancient Scottish university (Glasgow) – which had a long tradition of giving opportunity to those who showed ability and effort regardless of background. In many ways, given the quality of the institutions, I had enjoyed a privileged education – but it was a privilege open to the many, regardless of social background or parental income.

A Scottish Presbyterian upbringing had further instilled a meritocratic outlook in me. I remember, when I was about ten, asking my mother why Father was not coming to church with us one Sunday morning. She explained that our minister was retiring and that, as an 'elder of the Kirk', my father had gone with some of the other elders to listen to the preaching of another minister at a nearby church; if they liked his sermon they would recommend him to the congregation to be our new minister. For some reason this explanation stuck in my mind and as I grew older I warmed to the idea of a church in which the people chose their priest and power came from the bottom up, rather than the more hierarchical systems of the Anglican and Roman Catholic Churches, in which appointments were made from the top down.

Though I was to lose its religious influence in my teens (when I was ten my mother was convinced I was going to be a minister because I did well at Bible studies!), the cultural influence of Presbyterianism has stayed with me all my life: democratic in outlook, suspicious of social hierarchy, hostile to deference that is not earned, disposed to judge people by their abilities and achievements rather than their privileged position, a premium put on hard work and effort, a belief that success should belong to those who strive, a reverence for education as the prerequisite of success and social mobility, even a basic egalitarianism in the sense that every human has a certain worth regardless of background or achievement.

My parents reflected many of these attitudes and encouraged me to take every educational opportunity open to me as the route to a better chance in life than they had enjoyed. They instilled in me a sense that anything was possible if I worked hard at school and maybe even made it to university. They were plain, decent folk. My mother, Mary, had taken a job in Paisley's cotton mills while my father had gone off to fight Hitler: it was the only way she could support herself and my brother, who was born ten years before me in 1939, just a few months before war broke out.

My father, Jim, rose through the ranks, seeing active service with Montgomery's Eighth Army in North Africa; he was then based in Cairo after Rommel's panzer divisions had been defeated. He ended the war a captain and was made a major when in peacetime he took over the administration of the Territorial Army in the Paisley area. It was not a well paid job and there were few opportunities for advancement; but my father was not the ambitious sort – he was too gentle

– and it was secure employment, at least until Denis Healey's defence cuts in the late 1960s made him redundant and he was forced to become a clerk in the town and country planning department of our local government, where he saw out his working life. Both my parents worked hard for everything they had, which was not very much. I have often wondered why they never quite progressed into the middle class, especially given my father's success in the army. Perhaps they were too content with what little they had, perhaps ambition skipped a Neil generation, perhaps rewards in mid-twentieth-century Britain still bore too little relationship to effort. Whatever the reason, it was something that never concerned them.

My father's move to local government ended what had been a long family connection with the British Army. My mother's father had been a regimental sergeant-major and a piper in the Argyll and Sutherland Highlanders, one of her brothers had died in the 1920s on duty with the British cavalry in India (he is buried in Lucknow and I was named after him) and her other brother was caretaker of the Paisley TA drill hall, where my father worked and everybody referred to him as 'Major Neil'. But he was the most non-militaristic of army officers – he rarely talked about his war experiences and often expressed the hope that his two sons would never have to fight in one – and he certainly did not put me under any pressure to follow in his footsteps, though he gave me an affection and admiration for the British armed forces that has never left me.

My parents were independent-minded, patriotic people who believed that everybody should try to stand on their own two feet – but that society should provide for those who needed help. These were attitudes I was to inherit – as well as, for a while, their politics, which were moderate, mainstream Tory. I also took a sense of the theatrical from my mother, who was regularly disposed to turn any crisis into a drama; and a sense of proportion from my father, whose views were always thoughtful and considered. Drama and proportion are good qualities for popular journalism.

My parents were the generation that had come through the Great Depression and the Second World War and took nothing for granted: the modest prosperity they enjoyed in the 1950s, when we moved from a rented inner-city tenement to a semi-detached council house on one of the new estates then springing up on the edge of most British towns in Harold Macmillan's Britain, was enough to satisfy their own ambitions. My brother and I shared a bedroom – which must have been tough for him when I was five and he was fifteen, though he was always very tolerant of me, having inherited our father's good nature – until he got married in his early twenties (he became a journalist too, though there was no history of this occupation in our family) and I had a happy, uncomplicated childhood, being well grounded in the basics of education at our local primary school and spending the long summer holidays with friends roaming the wild hills that bordered our council estate.

It was said much later, when I was locked in hand-to-hand combat with various parts of the Establishment, that I had a chip on my shoulder because of this background. But I never felt deprived or denied opportunity and it would have been quite easy to slip into the Establishment fold. The British Establishment has enjoyed longevity because it does not totally exclude outsiders: it identifies some of the up and coming and, provided they are prepared to obey the rules (which is a very major proviso), welcomes them on board. That way it replenishes its brainpower and stops the resentment of too many outsiders from building up. It was a route I could well have taken: I was certainly obtaining the necessary credentials to be accepted.

At Paisley Grammar I was receiving a high-quality education, for the equivalent of which many English parents had to pay several thousand pounds a year in public school fees. Rugby and cricket were the main sports, in the best private-school tradition, and I won my school colours for playing cricket, which meant I could proudly wear some fancy braid round the navy blue jacket of my uniform. Discipline was tight but you were encouraged to speak your mind: the school had a debating society where I could indulge my passion for political argument and current events. I do not know where this passion came from but I can remember even as young as seven or eight pleading with my parents to be allowed to stay up to watch some documentary on television. I still recall one about the Ku Klux Klan, complete with fiery crosses in the night and men in white robes in the woods, which scared me out of my wits for weeks.

Teachers also encouraged political debate. When I was fourteen I discovered that my English teacher was a great Labour supporter so every day I stuck some article from the *Daily Express* on the blackboard attacking the latest failures of the Wilson government. 'If you want to debate politics with me,' he said, 'you'll have to read a better paper than that. Why not try the *Guardian*?' I subscribed to *The Times* instead (there was a 50 per cent rebate for pupils and students) and took the *Spectator* for good measure too. I watched the news avidly on television and wrote an essay about the 1964 American political conventions which pleased my English teacher so much he read it out to the class – perhaps the first signs of a talent for political journalism.

I had enough qualifications to make the University of Glasgow after fifth year but enjoyed school so much I stayed on for a sixth. I took some A and S levels from the English examination boards because it had crossed my mind that maybe I should try for Oxford or Cambridge. 'Why do you want to go there?' my French teacher asked sniffily one day. 'Glasgow is as old as most of the Oxbridge colleges and you want to do economics; Glasgow is where Adam Smith wrote the *Wealth of Nations*.' Another teacher even counselled me against going to Edinburgh University, where I had also been accepted, because it was not as old or distinguished as Glasgow. Nearly all my teachers had been to Glasgow University, which made them somewhat *parti pris*, but it seemed the natural place for me to go to anyway. Nobody I knew was going to Oxbridge and very few were even going to other Scottish universities: all the brightest kids were going to the University of Glasgow, which meant standards were high because there was no 'creaming off' to Oxbridge. No doubt it was a very parochial view. We were being given an inflated picture of how good Glasgow was and it involved a Scottish version of the educational snobbery that I was later to rail against in England. But, rightly or wrongly, it had been drummed into all of us that we were privileged to be going to a very superior seat of higher learning. The question of feeling inferior to Oxbridge never arose.

Nor did it throughout my four years at university (1967–71), where I took an MA in politics and economics and developed a love of American history as my 'additional' subject (Scottish universities try to give a broad education). The only time we came across Oxford or Cambridge was when Glasgow regularly beat them in the *Observer* Mace national debating competition. Glasgow University Union was the most formidable debating student chamber in the country: it won the Mace so often that the *Observer* gave it to the Union and had a new one made. I could not have wished for a better training ground in which to hone my verbal skills and build confidence in public – training that was to stand me in good stead for all the scrapes I was to find myself in at *The Sunday Times*.

I plunged into Glasgow University's varied extra-curricular life, becoming a Union board member, editor of the *Glasgow University Guardian* newspaper and president of the Tory Club. I carried Tony Benn's bags to his car after he addressed the Union as minister of technology, got thrown out of a rally for Tariq Ali, the Marxist revolutionary, for asking why a Pakistani aristocrat like him thought he could lecture someone like me about the British working class – and watched Edward Boyle, the liberal Tory, being hit by a pork pie in the middle of his address, which was interesting since whoever threw it had forgotten to take his fork out. My year as president of the Tory Club allowed me to attend various national conferences of the Federation of Conservative Students (FCS), in the days when it was a serious student organization, and in the spring of 1971 I won the election to be national chairman of FCS, beating off Neil Hamilton (who became a Tory MP and government minister) and Tom Spencer (who now leads the Tory MEPs in Strasbourg). The Tory Party gave me a job at the Conservative Research Department for £1,500 a year so that I could fulfil my FCS duties in London after I graduated in the summer of 1971. I was also expected to perform all the duties of a research officer which, in my case, meant briefing Tory MPs on housing policy.

My dreams were being fulfilled: straight out of university and I was in the thick of politics, with an office in Westminster within the sound of Big Ben, a pass to take me into the Houses of Parliament and a job which allowed me to mingle with all those famous political faces. I was on the fast track for a political career and, with vowels a little more Anglicized and some pinstripe suits, no doubt membership of the Establishment beckoned, as one of the up-and-coming outsiders they periodically allowed in. But the more I saw of the Establishment the less I wanted to join it.

I have nothing against élites, especially if they are open to all the talents and do a good job. If I had been in a position to join the ruling élite of America, Germany, Japan or even France, or any other governing group that had made a success of their country, then I would have queued up to join. But the British Establishment seemed to be presiding over the decline of my country, which offended the patriotism my parents had instilled in me.

Worse, it seemed lazy and complacent, almost giving up the struggle to reverse our national decline. One of my jobs at the Conservative Research Department was to take the minutes of the Scottish Tory MPs' backbench committee: they were an almost entirely Anglicized bunch, educated at English public schools and Oxbridge and represented much of what I was coming to hate about the Old Britain. In the week that the Heath Government announced the closure of Upper Clyde Shipbuilders (in 1971), with huge consequences for the Clydeside economy (including massive job losses), they spent an hour agreeing to complain to British Airways because it had just removed the first-class seats from its Scottish flights.

Joining *The Economist* in 1973 gave me a front seat on the continuing decline of the country, which gathered pace as the seventies proceeded, and on the inability of the ruling groups of the left or right to halt it. I slowly started to realize that Britain would have to break out of the failed post-war consensus which dominated official thinking, a view which was reinforced when I was posted to the United States in 1979 and I saw at first hand the dynamism and wealth-creation of a socially mobile, meritocratic market economy. I was radicalized by my stint in the United States. I returned with views calculated to annoy mainstream opinion on the left and the right. I saw the British Establishment as something to antagonize or even destroy, not curry favour with. Such were the thoughts uppermost in my mind when I became responsible for the editorial line of *The Sunday Times*.

*

IN THE SUMMER OF 1988 John Lloyd, one of the most perceptive left-of-centre commentators of the eighties, wrote three lengthy articles in the *Financial Times* which argued that 'Britain is no longer run by an Establishment. In its place is a Disestablishment, comprising men and women whose values, assumptions and habits are those of outsiders . . . They have successfully dethroned much, though not all, of the old Establishment, and in many crucial centres of power have taken its place.' Lloyd went on to describe *The Sunday Times* as 'an important Disestablishment organ'.

I regarded his description as an accolade to be worn with pride and shared some of his analysis. The Thatcher years had brought a refreshing and long-overdue changing of the guard to Britain in which old Establishment values (amateurish, paternalistic, disdainful of money unless it was inherited, keen on sticking to rules it had devised for its own benefit) were giving way to a new Disestablishment (efficient, populist, materialistic, mobile, rule-breaking). At the top of some important institutions and in various walks of life, inheritance, social class and snobbery were giving way to the talented meritocracy and I believed that to be one of the chief reasons for the country's economic resurgence. What intrigued a left-of-centre columnist like Lloyd was that this social sea-change was happening under a right-of-centre government. It illustrated the power of the market to open up Britain in a way that the old collectivist approach had not.

But I felt that he had exaggerated the extent to which the old Establishment was in a retreat.

In an editorial on 24 July 1988 *The Sunday Times* expressed itself dissatisfied with the progress that had been made. It pointed out that 'there are too many areas in which it [the old Establishment] is still firmly entrenched' and went on to make a statement of its own guiding philosophy for the sort of society it wanted to see: 'A safety net through which nobody should be allowed to fall and a ladder up which everybody should be allowed to climb as high as their abilities will take them. Judged by that ideal even the new Britain remains something of a disappointment. Though the government spends upwards of £50 billion [by 1996 it was close to £100 billion] on social welfare, our cities remain scarred by deep pockets of poverty . . . at the other end of the economic scale too many important positions remain the preserve of privilege and inheritance. Britain may be more meritocratic than ever; but it is still a long way from being a meritocracy.'

The editorial celebrated the fact that entrepreneurs from nowhere (like Alan Sugar and Richard Branson) could take on big business and win; that a Liverpool grammar school boy (John Birt) could become director-general of the BBC; that a grocer's daughter from Grantham could become prime minister. But 'these are the exceptions rather than the rule'. Mrs Thatcher's cabinet was still overwhelmingly public school and Oxbridge, so was the Foreign Office and, though the East End had made it on to the trading floors, 'the old school tie still has a stranglehold on City boardrooms . . . [and] The top of the legal profession remains a high-security zone of social exclusivity. Indeed most of the professions have been able to brush off the advances of the Disestablishment without too much disruption to their restrictive-practice ways . . . The Disestablishment still has many more fortresses to storm before it can ever dream of seeing off the

Establishment.' This was radical stuff for many of our readers, especially those who were doing rather nicely out of the white-collar professions that had remained untouched by the bracing winds of Thatcherism.

Contrary to what has often been written, I have never been against people just because they were products of public school and Oxbridge, which would have been a stupid and self-defeating reverse snobbery. But I felt strongly that those who had benefited from such institutions did not have an automatic right to power and privilege in our society. They should have to prove their worth, in open and fair competition with everybody else, and be judged on their merits. I regard these as unexceptional sentiments that most folk would support; but it is a sign of the entrenched power and privilege that remains in Britain that they were seen by many Establishment types as a direct threat to their own status in society. They could hardly attack the principles without sounding reactionary: so they attacked me instead, for 'chippiness', lack of 'social grace and confidence' and other dreadful misdemeanours in the eyes of polite society. These were slights I could live with.

My general outlook guided my own hiring policies at *The Sunday Times*: I never once refused to hire anybody because they were public school/Oxbridge types, but nor was I ever over-awed by such credentials. Geordie Greig, now the newspaper's literary editor and a good friend, once said to me that I was the only editor who had ever interviewed him about a job who did not ask what school or university he had gone to; they had been especially interested in this at the *Mail* and *Telegraph*, he added.

'I was more interested in your cuttings book,' I said. 'By the way, where were you educated?'

'Eton and Oxford,' he replied.

'You're fired,' I said. (I later relented when he agreed to

take me out to dinner.) When Geordie, who was to become one of my closest colleagues on the paper, was made editor of the Books section in 1995 we both had a good laugh at the London *Evening Standard* diary, which remarked that appointing a 'toff' to such a post would never have happened in Neil's day.

The House of Lords was a regular target, not because it had much power but because it had social symbolism and in Britain such symbols matter. 'What kind of parliamentary democracy is it,' asked an editorial in May 1988, 'that still depends on an unelected, unrepresentative second chamber whose members enjoy permanent membership, allowances which can reach nearly £100 a day and a social status more akin to the Middle Ages than a society desperately in need of an end to stupid social distinctions and class obsessions? Gowned prelates apart, the Lords is packed with titles mostly rooted in other ages – 4 peers of the royal blood, 25 dukes, 28 marquesses, 157 earls and countesses, 103 viscounts and 494 hereditary barons and baronesses.' The paper was not impressed with the system of appointed life peers either: they may 'add a thin veneer to this feudal mass' but they were largely 'placemen and women who have served their time doing what their party whips wanted in another place'.

The Sunday Times called for a 'renewed drive to sweep this ermine pile into the history books'. It favoured a second chamber elected by proportional representation from regional constituencies, with distinct, limited powers, especially over issues concerning individual and constitutional rights; but it feared that 'since our political system seems incapable of reforming the Lords it might be easier simply to abolish it' and adopt a Bill of Rights (perhaps by incorporating the European Convention on Human Rights into British law) 'against which all legislation could be tested in the courts'. That, the paper concluded, would be a 'far greater defence of the liberties of the people than the current House of Lords'.

The newspaper never lost an opportunity to drive its meritocratic message home. An annual opening was given when we began publishing every year a list of the richest people in Britain. This was a massive exercise because wealthy British people go to great lengths to cover up their money. American publications which do similar exercises are regularly berated by those on their lists for underestimating their wealth. But rich Brits always complained to me that we had overestimated theirs. Indeed, the only person ever to complain that he was worth more, and provided his accountant's records to back it up, was David Sullivan, the porn merchant (which no doubt only confirms the worst suspicions of old money about the self-made). The Sainsbury family would write every year to ask to be excluded from the list on the grounds that it made them kidnap targets. 'Anybody that does not already know the Sainsburys are stinking rich,' I said, 'is too stupid to be a kidnapper.'

An editorial ('Old money vs. new values') on 2 April 1989, which coincided with our first list of the country's richest two hundred, lamented that the 'old Britain – of Eton, Oxbridge, the land and the Guards – is still secure in its privileges and wallowing in its (inherited) wealth.' It pointed out that over half the folk on the list had inherited their money: 57 were landowners, 55 had gone to the same school (Eton), 25 even served in the same regiment (Brigade of Guards) and there were 11 dukes, 6 marquesses, 14 earls and 9 viscounts. It argued that 'there were precious few jobs in simply passing wealth on from one generation to another and the only industry involved is in avoiding taxation', contrasting the way the Saatchi brothers had made their £35 million (by building the world's biggest advertising agency) and the £35 million that the Earl of Seafield, 'Ginger' to his pals, had inherited from his mum and done nothing very much with since. The entrepreneurial drive of the Reagan years had created nineteen million new jobs in America; in the same decade Thatcherism had managed an increase of fewer than one million. Establishment attitudes were still holding us back.

By the early 1990s the newspaper began to fear that the meritocracy was already in retreat: 'High Tories and the chattering-class left are creating a social atmosphere in which it is once more becoming unfashionable to be self-made,' concluded an editorial. 'Once again paternalism is being praised, meritocracy derided . . . the country looks condemned to remain a second-class power.' But changing social attitudes were not the only reason the meritocratic revolution was under threat: the collapse of standards and reverence for excellence in our state schools was even more of a worry for those of us anxious to promote the widest possible opportunity.

*

I REMEMBER MY FIRST DAY at school vividly. It was in a long, narrow wooden hut because the new primary school being built in the middle of our housing estate was not yet finished. About forty of us sat at individual desks while a rather fierce-looking woman called Mrs MacGregor, in a grey suit and hair pulled back severely from her forehead, stood at the front, drew a large apple on the blackboard and had us all repeat: 'A is for apple.' Thus were the five-year-olds of Glenburn housing estate in the south side of Paisley inducted into the mysteries of the alphabet. We were given little sandtrays to practise writing letters and numerals: reading, spelling and mental arithmetic were standard features of our class work from the start.

The teaching methods remained just as old-fashioned when we moved into our newly built school. A BBC TV *Panorama* programme reported from Taiwan in the spring of 1996 that primary school children there sat in rows in large classes, everyone dressed in school uniform, and were taught the basics of reading, writing and arithmetic as a whole class, using traditional methods and subject to strong discipline. The educational results were excellent. The reporter wondered if such an alien system could ever work in Britain. There is nothing foreign about that, I thought: that's exactly how I was taught in the 1950s, until the system was destroyed by so-called progressive teaching methods in the 1960s.

We were all working-class children but the vast majority of us came from stable, two-parent families, and we had a great reverence for our teachers, who dressed smartly, seemed to know everything, were dedicated to their profession and had great authority with pupils and parents. Discipline was rarely a problem: those of us who did occasionally get badly out of line were brought back to better behaviour with a few quick blows to the palm of the hand with a leather tawse known as 'the strap'. It was used sparingly, but with great effect.

We were regularly tested on the basics of English and arithmetic, with history, geography and religious studies thrown in. Everything was building up to the 11-plus, which would decide many of our futures. Those of us who did well would go on to grammar or senior secondary schools; the rest would go to secondary moderns. I remember my growing nerves as this crucial exam approached, barely able to sleep the night before. My parents told me it would probably be the most important exam I would ever take. It was too brutal a watershed, too early in young lives. Whatever admiration I was to retain for traditional teaching methods and the quality of grammar schools later needlessly destroyed – and though I came to regard comprehensives as a disastrous, failed experiment – I never called for the return of the 11-plus as the sole method of selection when it came to determining the education policy of *The Sunday Times*.

Paisley Grammar was my passport to an excellent education and social mobility. A majority of fellow pupils came from middle-class backgrounds but there were plenty from the council estates like me. Nobody ever really bothered what your background was: we all conformed to the same rigid uniform code (which meant those from better-off families could not flaunt their superior clothes), we all spoke pretty much the same and we were all anxious to do well. The school charged fees – a modest 18 guineas a year – even though it was a state school, to help pay for sports and various extra equipment. It was mixed, with equal numbers of girls and boys, just as my primary school had been. So from the age of five onwards I was used to females doing at least as well, and often better, than boys. It was entirely natural to have girls around and by our teens to have girls as friends as well as girlfriends. It is why I have always felt at ease in female company – and at *The Sunday Times* saw nothing unusual in promoting women journalists to executive positions; nor, in broadcasting, have I ever had a problem with female bosses. The single-sex English public school system may be good academically for females but it does not always produce well-adjusted males.

Grammar schools had a superior status in Scotland to their English counterparts. Years later people in London used to say to me: 'You've done very well for a grammar school boy'; in Scotland they would say: 'You've done well – but then you went to grammar school.' There are very few Scottish public schools and those that exist, such as Fettes, Gordonstoun and Loretto, are really English public schools based in Scotland. The best schools in Scotland were either state or direct-grant schools and a handful of private day schools. It was not easy to discern much difference between them. When we played rugby and cricket against Glasgow High and Royal High we did not know they were grammar schools, nor that our games with Glasgow Academy and Edinburgh Academy were against private schools. But we knew we all belonged to élite schools, with the best grammar schools at least as good as the best private or direct-grant schools. My first girlfriend had been taken out of Paisley Grammar and sent to an exclusive private girls' school because her father regarded the Grammar as 'academically too tough'. Many of today's young parents, unable to afford private school fees and struggling to find a decent state school for their children, might be amazed to know that this country once had state schools that were as good as anything money could buy – and that they were destroyed by successive Labour governments, with the acquiesence of the Tories.

By the mid-1980s it was clear to me that standards in our state schools, to which over 90 per cent of our children go and the only ones about which I was ever concerned during my editorship (despite the high percentage of *Sunday Times* parents who used private schools), were in freefall. The comprehensive experiment the country had embarked on with such high hopes in the late 1960s was failing the very people it should have been helping, as were so-called progressive teaching methods. But a massive cover-up was being masterminded by the teaching unions, academics specializing in education and bureaucrats in local and central government to hide the sorry reality of what was happening in what a Labour prime minister had called education's 'secret garden', which its guardians regarded as out of bounds for mere mortals.

In February 1986 a long *Sunday Times* Focus called 'It's

trendy to be trad' highlighted how a return to traditional teaching methods under governments of the left and right in France and Germany was producing far better school standards than in Britain. In April of that year, as schools were being threatened by industrial action by teaching unions, an editorial attacked the late-1960s intake of left-wing militants into the teaching profession: they were now calling the shots in the teaching unions and the teacher-training colleges, where they inducted subsequent generations of teachers into their progressive ways. Mrs Thatcher had once described this to me in the early 1980s as the '*trahison des clercs*' – the treason of those meant to guide us – though her government was slow to do much about it. *The Sunday Times* called for teaching performance to be regularly assessed, an end to annual pay rises regardless of results and a purge on those who preferred strife to schooling. All of this, of course, was anathema to the teaching unions, as was a page-one exclusive in November 1986 which reported that Kenneth Baker, then education secretary, was planning a series of reforms that would allow schools to break out of local authority control and be funded directly by central government, and would provide a variety of schools within the state system. Action at last – but it was slow in coming.

The Sunday Times continued its efforts to expose how the education system was failing the nation. Early in October 1988 the paper conducted its own survey, using reputable pollsters, which showed that one in six of the adult population could not identify Britain on a map, half did not know how to read a railway time-table and two-thirds could not spell 'embarrass', 'harassment' or 'satellite'. About 12 per cent did not know the difference between Nigel Lawson (then chancellor of the exchequer) and Nelson Mandela (then languishing in a South African gaol) – which was deeply worrying for Mr Mandela; and 2 per cent thought Ronald Reagan was leader of the Opposition – which was even more worrying for Neil Kinnock. Two weeks later we carried out a similar survey among teachers and discovered they were not much better informed than the country at large – and in some cases they were worse.

Three-quarters failed the same easy spelling tests that two-thirds of the general population had failed; a surprising number of maths and science teachers could not manage simple calculations (What's 15 per cent of £10?; 16 per cent of teachers got it wrong, including 13 per cent of maths teachers!); less than half could name the capitals of West Germany, Poland and Afghanistan; but 95 per cent knew who Mandela was – as all good left-wingers did in those days. 'The results,' concluded the paper, 'suggest that many teachers should spend their free periods detained in one another's classrooms.' Less than a year later we turned our attention to university graduates and undergraduates.

Drawing on the experience of employers recruiting from the universities we discovered that most graduates made elementary spelling mistakes and were unable to do simple sums. 'In some cases they are not actually literate or numerate when put to the test,' complained British Petroleum's recruitment manager. 'We've even had people who could not spell their own names correctly on an application form.' Under pressure from employers many universities and polytechnics were introducing remedial lessons for undergraduates to brush up on written English, mathematics and computer studies – the three basic building blocks of education in the Information Age.

By February 1990 a *Sunday Times* editorial ('Our blackboard jungle') argued that Britain's rising generations were 'unable to cope with the subjects that matter most in the modern world: English, mathematics, science, modern languages and technology'. Drawing on a damning report by the chief inspector of schools, which identified serious problems of low and under-achievement, poor teaching and inadequate facilities, it pointed out that it was now officially admitted that at least 30 per cent of our schools failed to match up to basic requirements; many others were barely adequate and far too many state-school pupils were 'getting a raw deal'.

The Tory government did not escape its share of the blame for this sad state of affairs: 'Why should a Tory cabinet,' the editorial asked rhetorically, 'which almost to a man (and woman) has sent its children to private schools, care too deeply about standards in state education? If you drink vintage champagne, nicely chilled, you don't worry too much about the taste of lukewarm bitter. Of course, ministers are concerned about state schools as a matter of policy . . . but they do not have the consuming interest or passionate concern that grows out of being a consumer of the system – of being a parent whose children are actually going to schools, two-thirds of which are officially deemed to have unsuitable accommodation, many of them suffering shortages of equipment and a scandalous lack of textbooks for the seven- to nine-year-olds.'

I believed passionately that the Tories would never have allowed the deterioration in state schools to happen if their children had been going to them; if Labour had attempted to close the public schools with the same vandalistic fervour that it shut the grammar schools, Tory resistance would have been far greater. It was a point that I put again and again to Tory ministers throughout the 1980s: they shrugged their shoulders, denied it and changed the subject. Their reaction convinced me all the more: 'The Tories have got to care enough about state education to end the stranglehold of local authorities and teaching unions,' the editorial concluded, 'interested in preserving only their monopoly of state education and their special privileges, and devise a school system which gives parents genuine choice and encourages competition for excellence *within* the state system . . . After almost a decade in power it is a disgrace that the Thatcher government has done almost none of the above. But then such radical reforms could only be contemplated by a government which really cared about state schools.'

Towards the end of the Thatcher years the government moved in the direction *The Sunday Times* was advocating and the Major government has continued the process of reform. But it has been half-hearted, piecemeal, insufficiently radical for the problems at hand. In October 1991 the paper got hold of a confidential report which showed just how bad things were. Under the page-one splash headline 'Scandal in our schools: one in three can't count' we reported that the government's first tests for seven-year-olds had revealed that less than one in seven could do simple multiplications (such as five times five) and up to a quarter were unable to spell simple words like 'car', 'man' and 'hot'. The tests revealed nationwide ignorance about the basics of learning. An editorial ('The writing on the wall') said there was 'increasing evidence that we are breeding a nation of illiterates' with hundreds of thousands of British schoolchildren subject to a sharply downward trend in reading ability at seven and eight – a downturn unprecedented in modern educational history. 'The writing is on the wall for our schools,' it concluded, 'if we do not act now there might soon be nobody able to read it.'

At least the cover-up was unravelling. The teaching unions and other parts of the educational establishment had fought national testing and performance league tables of schools because they did not want their inadequacies to be rumbled. But the tests confirmed just how bad some teachers and their schools really were. The teaching unions and Tory ministers pointed to the rising pass rates in GCSEs and A levels to claim that standards were rising but it was easy to show they had been diluted to produce more passes. We took some GCSE papers to those parts of Africa where poor black children still sat the old O levels they had replaced: they hooted with laughter at how easy they were. We looked at A level exam results in Hong Kong, where children were still sitting old-style A levels: they sailed through the British A levels, scoring far higher marks than they did in their own. A Tory government which had promised never to debase the A level 'gold standard' had done just that to make the results look better. We reported on those British universities which were giving remedial courses to first-year students – even those with top-grade A levels – before they could begin their university degrees.

In September 1993 I was asked to give the keynote address to the Headmasters Conference at Oxford University, the annual gathering of the heads of the country's top public schools. I agreed, seeing it as a chance to pull together the educational themes I had been developing in *The Sunday Times* for almost a decade. Over dinner in a college dining room before my lecture I found myself sitting next to the head of Manchester Grammar, a superb direct-grant school which had gone private when a Labour government had taken away the state funding on which it partially depended. He told me his school was still attaining wonderful results.

'So it should,' I remarked, 'given how they've diluted the A levels to get more passes in the state system.' To my surprise he agreed.

'I'm afraid you're right,' he said. 'We've had the same entrance exam for years and we get about the same results every year. But our A level results are far better than they ever were two decades ago, by a huge margin. I'd like to claim our teaching had improved or that the boys were brighter. But the simple fact is that the A levels are easier.'

I gave my talk in a lecture hall, the cream of Britain's headmasters sitting in steep rows in front of me. If only my old teachers could see me now, I thought. My theme was that the culture of mediocrity that had taken root in the state system had to be replaced with a competition for excellence. It was no good educating the élite to a high standard and forgetting about the rest. That may have been fine for the Industrial Age and its need for unskilled assembly-line fodder but countries that wanted to succeed in the Information Age, in which almost everybody would be a brain-worker, had to educate all the people in depth. We had to make the quality and choice for the few in private schools available to the many in state schools. The best way to do that was to abolish the dead hand of local education authority control, which presided over a comprehensive monopoly, and fund every school direct from central government, depending on the number of pupils they could attract. Successful schools that had parents queuing up to enrol their children would prosper and expand; those that failed would be closed, their children moving to better schools. The idea was to replace today's levelling down with a constant pressure for levelling up. Sophisticated league tables would let parents know what each school excelled at, and where it was weak.

I related my visit the previous March to Baverstock, a school which had recently opted out of Birmingham local education authority control. It was based on a bleak council estate to the south of the city and was surrounded by tower blocks, from where it took most of its intake. It had a reputation for being a sink school but its performance had been transformed since opting out: discipline was restored, school uniform was mandatory and exam passes had soared. On the night I presented the prizes so many parents turned up that they had to open an overspill hall. The children behaved immaculately during a long prize-giving and there were poetry readings, rock music and a madrigal group. An inspiring headmaster was looking to start a sixth form and some middle-class parents from nearby were trying to enrol their children.

Failing schools can be turned round, I argued, with the right teaching ethos and proper funding. But we needed to do more. The comprehensive monopolies had to be replaced with a wide variety of state schools catering to different needs and aptitudes. Some would become centres of excellence in particular disciplines; above all we needed to create a new range of high-quality technology schools with the same status as the best grammar schools, as the 1944 Butler Education Act had envisaged (the idea was killed by Oxbridge arts graduates in the Department of Education). It meant selection, but not a return to the old, brutal 11-plus. Schools would need to devise various methods of selecting, depending on what they were offering, and at various stages in a pupil's career.

With this diversity and a competition for excellence the best state schools would rival the best the private sector had to offer. Some private schools might want to opt into the state system, partially or completely, to take advantage of state funds. As a result, it would become hard to know where the state system ended and the private one began, thereby softening the rigid educational apartheid that has been so socially destructive for Britain, keeping class divisions alive and opportunities restricted.

It was not a blueprint that had many takers at the Headmasters' Conference. When it came to questions they were largely hostile. They did not have much interest in improving the state system – it might reduce the number of parents who wanted to go private – nor in breaking down the barriers between state and private sectors. The prospectus I had unveiled was too radical for them: they would have preferred a talk on how the private sector could retain its distinction and privileges.

Britain's schools are caught in a limbo-land of indifference and special interests. The Tory government continues to say the right things but move with aching slowness in the right direction. The voluntary opt-out movement has run out of steam, but ministers show no inclination to make it compulsory and no desire to close bad schools and open good new ones. The education Establishment continues its relentless guerrilla war to halt all progress, with plenty of allies in the Labour Party. The cost could be catastrophic for Britain early in the new century. The lack of progress in bringing excellence back to the state system means that the age of the meritocrat – the flowering of those who left school in the 1950s and 1960s, and came to prominence in the 1970s and 1980s – may already be over. In order to secure the same quality of education they enjoyed in the state system they have nearly all been forced to send their own children to private schools. As the millennium approaches, we could be on the brink of the return of the dominance of the public-school pupil.

The other prospect is even more dire: the failure of so many of our schools to provide even the basics of an education is contributing to the emergence of something at the lower end of the social scale that the country has never seen before but which has the makings of a social disaster: the creation of an underclass.

*

MARGARET THATCHER insisted there was no such thing as an underclass in Britain: everybody could participate in her market economy provided they were prepared to make the effort. The social commentators and sociologists, overwhelmingly of the left, also denied the existence of a British underclass. America might have one, they said, but that was because it was a racist society. We did not: we had very poor working-class communities that would be fine if only the government gave them more welfare and found them a job. It took the arrival of a mild-mannered American academic to establish that Britain did indeed have an underclass. Even more shocking, it was largely white.

I brought Charles Murray over to Britain in 1989. I had read 'Common Ground', his seminal, radical-right assault on the American welfare state consensus, and been impressed by the clarity of his thoughts on the welfare dependency culture and how so much of existing social spending helped to perpetuate poverty rather than alleviate it. Though he was widely attacked by mainstream American social policymakers at the time his analysis and ideas were eventually to form the basis of the speech-making welfare reforms passed by a Republican Congress and signed by a Democratic president in the summer of 1996. I wanted to turn his radical searchlight on Britain, where nobody in the 1980s – not even the Thatcherites – was much interested in welfare reform, to see what he could find. His discoveries confirmed my worst suspicions.

Having been brought up in a largely working-class community, I was vaguely aware that things were changing. The more prosperous working-class folk were buying their own homes and even investing in the newly privatized industries; some were starting their own businesses and becoming self-employed, while their children headed for university or college. But a substantial minority of the old working class seemed to be sliding into a morass of despair and decay. Previously clean, safe and respectable working-class areas, like the council estate where I had spent my childhood, were becoming tatty and dangerous, increasingly stalked by a violent yobbery which was once confined only to the very roughest parts of town. It was clear that one of the problems was a lack of blue-collar jobs for young males whose fathers had worked in heavy industries that had now disappeared. But that was not the whole explanation by any means.

The emergence of large pockets of social decay and unsocial behaviour in some working-class areas also seemed to be accompanied by a collapse in traditional family structures. In the 1950s almost everybody with whom I had gone to primary school had come from two-parent families; a few had lost a parent through death but I cannot remember a single classmate whose parents were divorced. A few boys were the product of tough 'problem' families and they became more unruly as they grew older – and more threatening to boys like me who were academically inclined. But the vast majority of those I grew up around were well behaved and shared much the same values and aspirations as the middle-class children in the bigger, owner-occupied houses down the road, even if we did not enjoy their level of affluence. The gap grew, however, as the disintegration of our estate began. By the early 1970s, after I had gone to London, my parents moved to a flat near the town centre, lamenting what had happened to an estate they had once regarded as peaceful and safe. By the standards of some, however, it was still a relatively pleasant place. Other estates built in the 1950s and 60s were becoming almost no-go areas.

In an editorial in July 1988 ('Morals for the majority') I made a tentative effort to come to terms with why there was a 'social rot that has gone deeper than the industrial decay of the 1960s and 1970s – and which cannot be cut out with the simple, crude strokes which proved so effective on the economy . . . But where to begin? With the family: nothing can be done without a conscious revival of parent power and family cohesion. The old, extended families . . . were powerful organisms and bulwarks of social order. Family hierarchy and respect for one's elders was matched by hierarchies and a sense of purpose and order elsewhere – in the school, in the churches, public life at local and national level.' This was fine as far as it went but I was in uncertain territory, still unsure of what was really happening. A year later Charles Murray crystallized it for me.

On 26 November 1989 I devoted the bulk of *The Sunday Times Magazine* to his study of the British underclass. It taught us that the underclass was not the poorest of the poor, indeed it was not a degree of poverty at all but a type. It was made up of people increasingly cut adrift from society and outside its social norms, existing on welfare, the black economy and crime (a combination which meant some of the underclass had plenty of cash), and usually shunning conventional work even when it was available. The most controversial part of Murray's analysis was that the most reliable predictor of an underclass was the illegitimacy rate; young males growing up in single-parent families with no worthwhile male role models – indeed with precious few such models in the whole community – were the foot-soldiers of the underclass.

It was not a generalized attack on single mothers, as some tried to portray it, but the identification of a very specific kind of single mother whose increase had created the conditions for an underclass to take root: young, unmarried teenage girls who had children whose fathers quickly disappeared or were unknown in the first place. Murray pointed out that the illegitimacy rate in some of Britain's worst 'sink' estates was coming close to the 60 per cent rate in America's black ghettos (where it is now over 80 per cent). The difference in Britain was that the emerging underclass was white.

Collapsing family structure rather than race determined who the members of the underclass would be.

In an accompanying editorial, the newspaper spoke of a 'social tragedy of Dickensian proportions', an underclass 'characterized by drugs, casual violence, petty crime, illegitimate children, homelessness, work avoidance and contempt for conventional values . . . the underclass spawns illegitimate children without a care for tomorrow and feeds on a crime rate which rivals the United States in property offences. Its able-bodied youth see no point in working and feel no compulsion either. They reject society while feeding off it: they are a lost generation giving the cycle of deprivation a new spin.'

Murray, it seemed to me, had hit the nail on the head with his emphasis on illegitimacy and young males growing up without a father figure. The working class had been far poorer in the Great Depression but there was very little unsocial underclass behaviour because children were being brought up in stable, two-parent families. Today's underclass was far better off than the vast majority of working-class folk in the 1930s – but the collapse of the family placed it outside mainstream society and made it far more disruptive for the rest of us.

Exactly the same sorts who had originally attacked Murray in America did so in Britain. But, as on the other side of the Atlantic, the force of his analysis began to take root. By February 1993 *The Sunday Times* was able to publish an editorial entitled 'Return of the family' which began: 'The family has not been fashionable for at least a generation . . . yet, suddenly, the family is back in fashion.' The reason was simple: 'the disintegration of the nuclear family is the principal source of so much social unrest and misery. The creation of an urban underclass . . . is directly linked to the rapid rise in illegitimacy . . . What is not widely understood is that this is a new phenomenon: fifteen years ago the illegitimacy rate was considerably less. Of course, illegitimacy has increased among all social groups; but the biggest increase has been overwhelmingly among the poorer, the unskilled, the unemployed. As a result, they have gone from being merely poor to becoming an underclass . . . in which the dominant family structure is the single-parent mother on welfare whose male offspring are already immersed in a criminal culture by the time they are teenagers and whose daughters are destined to follow in the family tradition of unmarried teenage mothers.'

By now Murray had some allies on the British left. Two Socialist academics from Newcastle penned a pamphlet echoing his analysis. The introduction was written by Professor A. H. Halsey, a great guru of left-wing social policy, who told the *Guardian* bluntly: 'We're talking about a situation where the man never *arrives*, never mind leaves. There is a growing proportion of children born into single-parent families where the father has never participated as a father . . . and from the missing father flows the missing community ethic.' This was strong stuff for fragile leftish souls who had been taught to deride the family as a form of bourgeois repression and there are many fashionable folk who still resist Murray's logic and evidence. But the welfare debate is underway in Britain at last and both Tory and Labour politicians are using Murray's language when they talk about reforms to encourage people back into the labour market, discourage illegitimacy and turn welfare into a limited hand-up rather than an open-ended hand-out. That is progress indeed but little cause for celebration. The harsh fact is that we may now know what causes an underclass but we have very little idea if there are any effective policies to eradicate an underclass once it has taken root. The underclass looks like being with us for the foreseeable future. One thing is for sure: it is not eliminated by a general rise in economic prosperity.

*

THE ECONOMIC REGENERATION of Britain was the consuming passion of *The Sunday Times*: I wrote more editorials about it than any other subject, positioning the newspaper on the radical, supply-side, privatizing, deregulating, trust-busting, pro-competition wing of contemporary economic arguments. I was urging a market revolution more complete than even Margaret Thatcher was contemplating; but then my own views had undergone some revolutionary changes.

I had developed an interest in economics as a teenager because so much political argument required a certain economic expertise. At university I was inculcated in the mainstream economic thought of the day. My professors and lecturers were not the mad academic lefties of right-wing mythology: they were moderate folk steeped in the centre-left, collectivist post-war tradition. They believed that the market needed regular doses of state intervention to make it work to everybody's benefit and that government should be omnipresent. They were not that keen on nationalization but they did not think the private sector should be largely left to its own devices – and the privatization of state industries was too absurd an idea even to merit discussion.

I swallowed this centre-left consensus without resistance. My main speciality was 'Government in the economy', the paper in which I scored the highest marks in my finals. I knew all about French indicative planning, incomes and regional policies and the efforts of Tory and Labour post-war governments to bring more planning to the economy. An economics lecturer of Tory leanings once recommended a pamphlet to read by the Institute of Economic Affairs (IEA), then a tiny pro-market think-tank, which argued it had been a mistake to nationalize the coal industry; he wanted us to read it just to get an idea of old-fashioned, nineteenth-century thinking, then discard it. Its views were regarded as beyond the pale. It never crossed our minds that within a decade the IEA would be the most influential economic research group in the country.

Yet even by the turn of the 1960s there was a sense that the collectivist consensus was failing to deliver. I remember one professor giving an inspiring lecture on the theory of indicative planning but finishing with the words, 'Well, that was what was meant to happen but of course it never worked out like that in practice under Harold Wilson – the National Plan and most of the state intervention that went with it were largely a waste of time.' But I did not notice the warning signs. In the Federation of Conservative Students the 'enemy' was the free-market 'nuts' that had taken over the St Andrews University Tory club; I was always making speeches attacking them (it did them no harm: they went on to form the nucleus of the Adam Smith Society in London and the Heritage Foundation in Washington and have a strong influence on Thatcher and Reagan). In the only speech I ever made to a Tory Party conference, in 1970, I pressed the case for incomes *and* regional policies. The Tory faithful in those days had no problem with any of this. Robin Day, in his live commentary, remarked that I was a young man clearly heading for Parliament.

The failure of interventionist Tory and Labour governments in the 1970s was the start of my conversion to market economics. Much of modern British politics has been concerned with the challenge of the Labour left and their allies in the unions. The Bennite tendency had to be beaten but it was largely a diversion from something more fundamental: the fact that moderate, centre-left social democracy had been tried and failed in the 1970s, collapsing ignominiously in the

1978–79 Winter of Discontent. At the very least it needed major revision or even replacement – but with what? If state Socialism was out of the question, as all experience from the Communist bloc suggested it should be, that left only the market economics we had been taught to dismiss at university. Maybe there was something to it after all.

Norman Macrae, deputy editor of *The Economist* while I was there during the 1970s, certainly thought so and his writings – he was the first to explain how many town-hall services could be put out to competitive tender – had a huge influence on me. So did Irwin Stelzer, the brilliant American economist who specialized in market competition and who was to become a good friend. I watched the early days of the Reagan revolution firsthand in Washington and became impressed by the power of markets to create prosperity and facilitate change. The more intelligent on the American left also saw the radical potential of the market and it was the Democrats who played the leading role in the deregulation of the airlines and the trucking industry, which created fresh competition and benefited consumers. This was the new economic baggage I took with me to *The Sunday Times*.

The first signed article I wrote for *The Sunday Times*, published on 18 September 1983, was called 'Permanent faulty line'. I complained (from personal experience) about how useless the state-owned BT monopoly was and finished with the words 'God speed privatization'. Such attitudes were quickly applied across the board. *The Sunday Times* came to stand for deregulating huge chunks of British life from busting the cartelized airline industry (a conspiracy against passengers to keep air fares high), to scrapping the country's ludicrous licensing laws to making it legal to shop on Sundays. We began campaigns to achieve the deregulation of all three: big business and the unions bleated, so I knew it had to be in the interests of ordinary consumers. 'Let the people fly', 'The right to shop on Sunday' and 'Drinking round the clock' became regular campaign logos in the paper. So did calls for a tax system that would encourage enterprise.

Tax reform was a constant theme of *Sunday Times* editorials and columns. Early in 1984 I had Brian Reading, former economics editor of *The Economist* and an original mind, write one of the first newspaper columns arguing the case for a flat-rate 15 per cent income tax, a proposal which is now much talked about in America. It was an idea to which we regularly returned, notably in February 1988 ('Towards a flat-rate tax'), when we proposed taking most low-income earners out of tax altogether and taxing everybody else at the same flat rate, but with no deductions of any sort. That was our long-term goal. In the meantime we pressed the government to cut the high marginal rates of tax at every opportunity.

Such tax-cutting zeal flew in the face of the centre-left consensus, which still regarded high taxes as a virility symbol of its belief in 'justice' and 'fairness'. What was fair about taxing poor people, taking away huge chunks of the hard-earned income of the moderately affluent and allowing the very rich to exploit complicated loopholes and pay almost no tax at all escaped me. 'High taxes . . . frequently afford a smaller revenue to government,' Adam Smith had written in his *Wealth of Nations*, 'than what might be drawn from more moderate taxes.' In a seminal editorial on 19 October 1986 *The Sunday Times* revealed the modern truth of that.

Headlined 'Who's selling the snake oil?' it challenged the view that high marginal rates brought in more revenue from the rich by revealing that in 1978/79, the last year of Labour government, when the highest marginal tax rates were between 83 per cent and 98 per cent, the top 5 per cent of income earners had paid 24 per cent of total income tax receipts; by 1985/86, when the highest rate had been cut to 60 per cent, the richest 5 per cent were now accounting for 26.7 per cent of income tax receipts. Why did a lower marginal rate result in rich folk paying a bigger share of tax? Because when faced with ridiculous penal rates of up to 98 per cent the rich naturally used the best lawyers and accountants to place their money in tax shelters or paid themselves hard-to-tax perks or left the country or simply stopped working – all of which left the tax collectors poorer. The 60 per cent rate had made high-earners less inclined to avoid tax. We urged the chancellor to try a top rate of 40 per cent.

We were a nagging thorn in the government's side, constantly urging it to be more radical. In the autumn of 1985 the paper said there was a 'dead-in-the-water feel about the government' and complained that, despite six years of Thatcherism, there were still far too many distorting tax privileges for homeowners, wasteful subsidies to farmers and job-destroying regulations still in place. A year later we taunted the prime minister by claiming she was 'running out of ideas and reforming zeal': instead of Reagan-style tax cuts, in which many rich people would pay tax for the first time and poor people would pay no tax at all, she had delivered only 'piddling tax cuts', some tinkering with the tax code and no reduction in the high marginal rates (after the initial reduction to 60 per cent in 1979). 'The government looks tired and so does Mrs Thatcher,' concluded the editorial. 'The economic decline of Britain continues apace. She needs to listen to people she does not want to hear.'

The campaign for a top 40 per cent rate, in which we had precious few allies (even in the Tory press), also involved harrying and badgering Nigel Lawson, the chancellor. He did not take kindly to it: one Sunday morning, after another editorial which annoyed him, he dashed off a handwritten note to me, obviously written in a bit of a temper, telling me to desist from making simplistic calls for the Thatcher government to follow in Reagan's tax-cutting footsteps. At least we were being read in the right quarters; and in his Budget of 1988 Lawson at last obliged: the top rate was cut to 40 per cent and *The Sunday Times* expressed a 'special satisfaction'.

Five years later, in November 1993, an editorial ('Tax truths') looked at the consequences of cutting high marginal tax rates. The evidence from both sides of the Atlantic made uncomfortable reading for the liberal-left for it blew out of the water two of its long-held premisses – that when you cut high marginal rates the rich pay less tax; and when you increase them they pay more. In America the top 1 per cent of earners had contributed 17.6 per cent of income tax revenues in 1981, when marginal rates were high; by 1991 they were paying 24.6 per cent of all income taxes, even though the marginal rates had been slashed. The same was true in Britain: the share of income tax paid by the top 1 per cent of earners had risen from 11 per cent in 1979 (when top rates were penal) to 17 per cent in 1993, when the top rate was 40 per cent. Ditto for the top 5 per cent and 10 per cent of income earners: they all paid a bigger percentage of tax receipts. Indeed the top 10 per cent accounted for 45 per cent of all income tax receipts.

'A tax regime which results in the richest 10 per cent being responsible for £1 out of every £2 raised in income tax,' commented the paper, 'should warm the hearts of even the most egalitarian of redistributionists. But Britain's liberal-left is so determined to make the better-off pay higher marginal rates – because it accords with its outdated, illogical notions of justice – that it does not seem to mind if the higher rates result in the rich actually paying less tax overall.' It is a tax lesson many politicians and pundits are still determined to ignore.

There were some central economic issues on which *The Sunday Times* was to the left of the Thatcher government: we were never mesmerized by monetarist alchemy and I had remained enough of a Keynesian to realize that public spending still had a vital role to play in macroeconomic policy. Back in 1985 the paper was urging Lawson to 'go for growth' with a reflationary Budget of tax cuts and increased public investment to cut unemployment. But these were the days when fiscal conservatism was all the rage, there was no 'Budget for Jobs' and unemployment continued to rise. A year later we were drawing attention to the 'million-strong army of the long-term unemployed' festering in the country and calling for the government to take millions of poor people out of tax altogether and send in joint public/private development corporations to revive our worst inner cities.

The taming of the unions, the deregulation of business, the privatization of state industries, an incentive-based tax system – all these developments encouraged *The Sunday Times* to believe that Britain had at last turned the corner: 'Plain folk,' said an editorial ('The true view from afar') in May 1988, 'sense they no longer live in a country in economic decline.' It went on to quote the approving comments of prestigious publications from Germany, France and America about the country's economic resurgence: 'Britain has not had economic reviews like this for over a century.'

But the joy was short-lived. By July 1988 the paper reported that 'Britain's economy has started to overheat' and chronicled the regular rise in interest rates that was to end the Lawson boom and usher in the recession. *The Sunday Times* urged the chancellor to take direct credit controls in the housing market to 'douse the credit boom' and not rely entirely on interest-rate increases, which could see the 'new

Britain' return to the 'old stop-go'. But for the rest of 1988 and 1989 interest rates were the only weapon the government deployed in its efforts to turn an economic surge into a more sustainable canter. Instead, it tilted the economy into a full-scale recession.

The Sunday Times was as slow as the government to see the dangers of overheating. We were so delighted that the British economy had shaken off its long-term decline that we did not notice the short-term dangers. Nor did we get it right by advocating sterling's membership of the European exchange-rate mechanism (ERM), an idea the paper had first proposed back in January 1986, lamenting the fact that Mrs Thatcher was 'implacably opposed'. By 1989–90 we were again pushing the government to sign up sterling to the ERM, on the grounds that the pound was at a very competitive rate against the German mark and, because sterling would have the full support of the ERM behind it, interest rates could be cut without the currency collapsing. In other words, ERM membership would help us pull out of the recession.

But it was a mistake. Against Thatcher's best instincts, John Major, as chancellor, eventually took sterling into the ERM in October 1990; but it was at too high a rate, he refused to budge from it, even when he became Prime Minister and the recession deepened, and it only made the economy worse. I regret *The Sunday Times* ever supported sterling's membership of the ERM, but at least we learned quickly from our mistakes and turned against it. John Major stuck doggedly to it: until the currency markets blew his economic policy to smithereens in the autumn of 1992 (see the Introduction).

The Sunday Times was to become John Major's fiercest critic as the recession deepened and the government appeared oblivious to the pain its inaction was causing. Our first target was Norman Lamont, who ran Major's leadership campaign but was not up to the job of chancellor: every time he spotted 'the green shoots of recovery', the economy took another dive. An editorial in August 1991 detailed eleven forecasts he had made which had proved wide of the mark and commented that the chancellor was 'reminiscent of a racing tipster whose selections are invariably consigned to the knacker's yard . . . His policy of modest interest-rate cuts has kept the economy mired in recession . . . It must now be dawning on John Major that he needs a new chancellor.'

The occupant of 11 Downing Street was livid and penned a long defence, which I was happy to publish the following week. But it did not convince: the campaign to force the government to take the ravages of the recession more seriously and rescue the economic gains of the 1980s continued. By October 1992, with sterling at last free of its ERM straitjacket, *The Sunday Times* called for a 'New Deal for Britain'. John Major has 'built a Maginot Line against inflation', it warned, 'but the real enemy is now deflation and its blitzkrieg threatens to bring the country to its knees . . . the prospect is for prolonged stagnation.' The day that editorial ran (18 October) I devoted the whole of the front page of the paper to the state of the economy with the double-decker headline across eight columns 'Recession turns into Depression; 200,000 jobs to go by Christmas'. I put a thick black border round the whole page for good measure to highlight the gravity of the situation.

The editorial attacked a 'do-nothing government which refuses to countenance new thinking'. We offered some: a substantial cut in interest rates, a lower pound, a major programme of pump-priming capital spending in infrastructure (including the Jubilee line to London's Docklands) and a conscious strategy to turn Britain into the 'low-cost, high productivity Hong Kong of northern Europe'. Major had 'lost his way', the editorial concluded. 'He needs to tear up the script and start again, casting himself as the Franklin Roosevelt of the decade. At present he is destined to be its Ramsay MacDonald.'

Relations between *The Sunday Times* and 10 Downing Street hit an all-time low. The Prime Minister began to ignore my presence whenever our paths crossed at public events; our cosy chats in Downing Street ended. I did not mind: I had nothing to say to him that I had not already written in *The Sunday Times*. But Michael Jones, our trusty political editor, was summoned to see Tony Newton, the Leader of the House, and Murdo McLean, the government's chief behind-the-scenes fixer in Westminster, the conduit politicians refer to as the 'usual channels'. Mike knew it was going to be a tough meeting because relations between paper and government were deteriorating fast: the Chief Whip had just refused to meet with Andrew Grice, our political correspondent. Newton and McLean made clear the government's general displeasure at *The Sunday Times*: 'It has its own agenda,' complained one, 'and it's always shitty to the government.' They then subjected him to a volley of abuse, McLean calling Mike a 'c——' four times. My political editor saw no reason why he had to listen to this and beat a hasty retreat. 'It was,' he told me later, 'the most extraordinary meeting I've ever attended in over two decades of covering Westminster.'

Meanwhile, Lamont was being more public with his vituperation. When asked on BBC TV's *Question Time* about *Sunday Times* criticisms of his handling of the economy he dismissed us as a 'pretty squalid newspaper'. Coming from him, I regarded this as a badge of honour. I asked one of our political staff to check with 10 Downing Street to see if they agreed with the chancellor's words. But the Prime Minister's people had no desire to mix it so publicly. They dissociated the PM from his remarks, saying the chancellor had allowed personal irritation to get the better of his political judgment: 'Downing Street disowns Lamont over "squalid" *Sunday Times*' ran a cheeky page-one story the following week. Lamont was eventually fired in May 1993.

Our assault on the Major government did not let up. A long editorial in 1993, 'Aboard the *Marie Celeste*', talked of the 'awesome' decline in the Prime Minister's popularity ratings, from most popular PM since Churchill during the Gulf War to most unpopular since polling began. Even more worrying was 'the absence of any sign from the Prime Minister or his entourage that they have the slightest idea how to reverse this decline'. This was a 'tired, second-division government'. The newspaper tried once again to give the Prime Minister a 'vision to articulate and a strategy to follow: the PM should state, as boldly as he can, that it is his government's intention to turn Britain into the Hong Kong of Western Europe – a low-cost, high-productivity, low-tax, high-tech offshore island whose growth and dynamism would be in marked contrast to the recession and sclerosis of the other major European economies.'

Major has since made some faltering steps in this direction but half-heartedly, too little and too late, as is his way. He has shown little appetite for the kind of radical reform of tax, welfare and education that *The Sunday Times* was advocating in the early 1990s. But there were other potential takers: Tony Blair, the Labour leader, was becoming interested in some of our ideas, even if he could not always admit it.

*

THEY BEGAN AS THREE BLACK SPOTS moving across a deep blue sky. As I peered at them from my perch on a metal box wedged between captain and navigator in the cockpit of a VC10 refuelling tanker, they edged closer to reveal themselves as two Tornados and a Buccaneer. It was February 1991 and we were 12,000 feet above the Saudi desert on the Olive trail, the route that Allied planes took to bomb Baghdad.

As our fuel supply lines extended backwards from each wing, the Tornados approached the nozzles to lock on and drink from our fuel tanks, which filled the fuselage where seats in this former BOAC passenger plane had once been. I could see their undersides laden with bombs and counted the little black bombs painted beneath the cockpit: this was their thirty-seventh sortie. The sun glinted on the crews' helmets and one of the pilots waved over; another took a picture of me taking a picture of him. Suddenly the screen above the control panel began to flash and bleep.

'What's that?' I asked. The captain must have heard the concern in my voice.

'We're being "painted" by the radar of an Iraqi surface-to-air missile battery,' he explained. 'But don't worry: they have to lock on before they can fire and we're almost certainly out of range.' I did not find this entirely reassuring.

'What would we do if they did fire a Sam at us?' I enquired nervously.

'Turn tail and fly due south at full throttle,' he replied.

'What's our maximum speed?'

'About five hundred and fifty miles an hour.'

'And the speed of a Sam?'

'About two thousand miles an hour.' He paused for a moment: 'You do know that these tankers are nicknamed the "flying coffins"?' I did not answer: the blood was too busy draining from my face.

By the time we were fifty miles from the Iraqi border our RAF crew had refuelled four Tornados and two Buccaneers:

they had peeled off to continue their bombing mission and we were flying east along the Chinaberry trail, just south of Iraq, waiting to off-load what fuel we had left into another tanker. In the great expanse of red desert below I could see the Allied troops moving into position for the land war to come, the roads choked with supplies. My eyes darted skywards again, however, when I noticed the huge bulk of another tanker appear from nowhere and pull silently in front of us, only 70 feet away. The sight of two giants joined together high in the sky by an umbilical cord was striking enough even for our unflappable captain to hand over to his young co-pilot while he videoed the scene.

As the other tanker waited for the fighter-bombers to return, we headed back to the huge King Fahd Airport in Riyadh, where the British forces were using an unfinished terminal as a base, complete with row after row of hospital beds in the basement awaiting casualties and hermetically-sealed operating tents so that surgeons could carry on operating in the middle of a gas attack. Later, we bumped into the crew of the other tanker. Yes, they said, all six RAF planes had made it back. Our captain smiled: 'Thank God,' he said. 'Last week we waited at the same spot for four Tornados to return. Only three did.'

It was seven months since Saddam Hussein had invaded Kuwait and several weeks since the Allied air offensive had begun to soften up Iraqi forces before the land attack. *The Sunday Times* had taken a hawkish position from the start. In a forthright editorial towards the end of August 1990 called 'War aims' the paper set out in uncompromising terms what they should be: 'First, the defence and long-term security of Saudi Arabia and the Gulf states. Second, the liberation of Kuwait. Third, the toppling of Saddam Hussein and the destruction of Iraq's ability to develop and deploy chemical and nuclear weapons. If the military might being assembled in the Gulf fails to realize all three of these war aims then America and its allies will have lost the war, no matter the short-term victories it may score.' Six years later, with Kuwait free but Saddam still presiding over a reign of terror in Iraq, that prediction proved to be sadly accurate.

I was well aware that the third war aim was the most controversial; but I also regarded it as the most important. The editorial argued that 'Saddam must be removed because he is a tyrant with expansionist ambitions to spread his tyranny across the Middle East . . . any resolution of the Gulf crisis which leaves him in power and his military machine intact would leave the Gulf at his mercy [and] America and its allies will have made a mistake of historic proportions'.

I wanted the West to realize the evil it was up against so *The Sunday Times* began serializing the *Republic of Fear*. This book by an Iraqi dissident academic catalogued as never before the hellhole of repression, savagery and brutality of Saddam's Iraq, whose secret police and torturers were reminiscent of the Gestapo in Nazi Germany. As the weeks went by and the allied build-up began, *The Sunday Times* broke scoop after scoop, partly because James Adams, our defence correspondent, seemed to have a hotline to the Joint Chiefs of Staff in Washington. Thanks to his contacts and the work of our other specialists, *The Sunday Times* reported ahead of its rivals (including the American newspapers and networks) that America was planning to deploy a half-million-strong force and B52 and Stealth bombers; and that Cruise missiles would be used and targeted at key installations, including where Saddam was thought to be. We made some mistakes, notably that Saddam had deployed and would use chemical weapons (we had fallen for Iraqi disinformation) but we also revealed President Bush's private letter warning Saddam of the terrible consequences that would follow if he did resort to chemical weapons.

By the end of 1990, however, the paper was getting frustrated with what seemed like drift and delay in the desert. I began to fear that President Bush was dragging his feet and looking for a way out that did not involve the eviction of Saddam from Kuwait. An editorial in early December ('America, Bush and Munich') commented that though the President continued to talk tough, 'he grows less convincing as the weeks go by and the mood music coming out of Washington increasingly sounds like peace in our time . . . we must take seriously the appalling prospect that Christmas 1990 could go down in history as America's Munich'. The momentum was now with the American peace-movement, the paper feared, drawing on false analogies with Vietnam, and there were too many powerful Democratic voices in Congress 'as supine in the face of aggression today as the British Establishment in the 1930s'. The suspicion was that some sort of face-saving deal, for America and Iraq, was on the cards and *The Sunday Times* was appalled at the prospect: American resolve would have been found wanting and its allies would never trust it again, President Saddam would be the undisputed leader of the pan-Arab world, throwing his weight around in Opec, maybe even preparing for a pan-Arab assault on Israel and it would be a 'signal to all dictators with territorial ambitions and an easy prey to take what they can with impunity'.

The editorial was meant to stiffen American resolve (British opinion was already strongly for war) and I was delighted when the *New York Daily News* asked for permission to reprint it on pages two and three of its news section. In the end a fudge was avoided by Saddam's inexplicable refusal to do any kind of deal that involved the withdrawal of his invasion forces from Kuwait. The Allied air offensive began in January as a prelude to a land attack. It was the biggest military offensive for Western forces since the Second World War, the biggest story during my time as editor, and *Sunday Times* journalists were risking their lives to cover it: for all these reasons I thought it was time to see things for myself.

The day after our tanker trip in the sky I set out with John Witherow, then foreign editor, and Richard Ellis, our war correspondent in Saudi Arabia, on a freelance foray to the front line that we had observed from the air the day before. We had tried to talk the American and British forces into taking us but with the land war imminent they had better things to do: indeed they now frowned on journalists operating outside the official pools and warned that if we went on our own we risked arrest and deportation. So we headed the four hundred miles north to the Egyptian segment of the front line hoping we could bluff our way through by wearing khaki, placing a helmet on the dashboard and approaching every checkpoint as if we had a right to pass through. Our progress was delayed by sandstorms but the Saudi guards waved us through the roadblocks; some even saluted and the children we passed smiled and made Churchillian victory signs.

Huge convoys of tanks, armour and ammunition which stretched for miles slowed us down; the allies were clearly preparing for a massive war. But north of Hafr al-Batin, past the football ground covered in tents awaiting Iraqi prisoners and the road sign pointing to Kuwait, an eerie silence gradually took over and I began to feel we were alone and exposed. A US attack helicopter buzzed us at one stage and an Egyptian jeep with a mounted machine-gun came for a look but both allowed us to continue unhindered. The scene became ever more desolate. Ahead we could make out Ruqi, the border town where a CBS TV crew had recently been taken prisoner by the Iraqis. We were very close to the front line.

I was gripped by a mixture of fear and fascination. Fear that with the Iraqis only a few miles away this was not exactly the safest place to be; but fascinated to be at the very heart of where the eyes of the world were watching and history about to be made. There was a curious peace about the place, like some remote flatlands in the very north of Scotland – clearly the lull before the storm.

About a mile from Ruqi our progress was finally halted by a roadblock of three Egyptian guards. They were friendly enough but as Richard began to negotiate our way past there were explosions in the distance and smoke rising from the far side of town. An Egyptian commander came on the field phone to say the Iraqis were shelling the place and it was too dangerous to enter. As I listened to the rumble of bombs and artillery and watched smoke billowing to the sky, I saw no reason to challenge his assessment. We set off instead along the road which runs parallel to the Saudi–Kuwaiti border to observe the huge sand berms the Saudis had constructed after the Kuwaiti invasion. This was where four Iraqi deserters had recently given themselves up to a British journalist but we saw only the sky blackening to the north and felt the ground trembling beneath us as the Allied planes continued to pummel Iraqi forces a few miles away.

Back in Hafr al-Batin we bumped into Dave in a scruffy hotel lobby where soldiers and journalists mingled. Dave was in town to make what he reckoned would be his last phone call before battle commenced: he was with the British 1st Armoured Division, the famous Desert Rats, strung along the Iraqi border thirty miles to the west of Hafr, the junction of the two main supply routes to the front. Soldiers from Britain, America, France, Syria and Egypt, all armed and in full battledress, milled about as huge articulated trucks carrying tanks and guns splashed through the flooded streets, the town's sewage system having long given up the challenge of the increase in population.

Dave rested his rifle on a chair and told us he was from Manchester. He said he and his mates were anxious to get on with it. They had waited long enough in the desert, done all the training they could, tested their equipment again and again. He hoped they would go head-to-head with the élite Republican Guard rather than the 'beer-belly brigade' of Iraq's conscript army. He shook hands with us, slowly and firmly, as he picked up his rifle to head back to the desert. 'Keep your head down,' I shouted as he disappeared. 'See you in Baghdad,' he replied, with a wave.

The land war began twenty-four hours later. Dave never made it to Baghdad though the allies scored a speedy, crushing defeat over the Iraqis. It might not have been necessary to go all the way to the Iraqi capital to topple Saddam, though our correspondent there reported that the road was wide open and that the allies would have been welcomed by the population. Wiping out or rounding up more of his Republican Guard, which kept him in power, would probably have been enough to encourage a popular uprising. But President Bush stopped the Allied offensive after one hundred hours: Kuwait had been liberated and he feared public opinion would turn against the war because of the Iraqi carnage on the road to Basra.

Maybe so. But the consequence of his premature halt to hostilities was that Saddam was able to visit carnage instead on the Kurds to the north and the Shi'ites in the south – and he was still strong enough to smash any other internal opposition. Moreover, those most vociferous in wanting to stop the fighting were those who had never wanted to fight in the first place and whose predictions about the Gulf War had been proved famously wrong by events.

On 3 March 1991, with Iraq evicted from Kuwait with minimum loss of life on the Allied side, *The Sunday Times* listed some of the Jeremiahs who had counselled appeasement and now had to eat their words: Edward Heath ('The world will lose up to fifty per cent of its oil supplies and it is going to take years to get them back again . . . It will be the Third World War'); Arthur Schlesinger ('The war most likely will be bloody and protracted'); Denis Healey ('This nation is sleepwalking to disaster with its eyes open and its mind closed . . . [there will be] mutual catastrophe on a devastating scale . . . a war will push the price of oil up to $65 a barrel, produce a collapse in the American banking system and a world recession'); Tony Benn ('It would be the greatest catastrophe since the atom bombs at Hiroshima and Nagasaki'); and the *Guardian* (quotes too numerous to mention: it was to the Gulf War what *The Times* was to Munich).

In fact, it had been a famous victory for the allies. But Saddam was to survive the peace because the allies lacked the will to finish the job: Iraq is still his Republic of Fear and one day he could again threaten his neighbours.

*

The Sunday Times established its credentials as a hawk abroad right from the start of my editorship; a position which was to cause much discomfort to the old guard of the paper and lead some of them to depart. By putting the newspaper behind the American liberation of Grenada and the deployment of Cruise missiles, and strongly against the one-sided disarmament of the Campaign for Nuclear Disarmament (see Chapter 3) I was backing the more assertive American policy that had been heralded by the presidency of Ronald Reagan.

This was very much a minority view in Britain but I did

not share the general British and European tendency to sneer at President Reagan and scorn his simple verities. I had lived in America during the final phase of the Jimmy Carter years, when America seemed to retreat before Soviet expansionism, and began to fear that, economically, it had entered a long period of British-style decline. Reagan offered America a fresh start – 'Glad, confident morning, again' – with his determination to rebuild America's defences, reassert its power and reinvigorate its economy with a series of supply-side reforms.

In April 1986 an American army sergeant was killed when Libyan-backed terrorists exploded a bomb in a Berlin disco frequented by US forces, the latest in a series of Libyan-financed or inspired outrages. On 14 April, President Reagan authorized a military strike on the Libyan capital, using F1-11 bombers based in Britain. Western Europe was appalled by Reagan's firm response, and, in Britain, Thatcher was condemned even by the Tory press and her own party for allowing the bombers to take off from British soil. There was even talk that the 'sacrifice' she had made to keep the Atlantic Alliance together by acquiescing to Reagan's request would cost her the next election. I was in New York on holiday when the raid took place but I sensed that the senior colleagues I had left in charge of *The Sunday Times* were caught up in the anti-American furore and preparing to write an editorial attacking the raid. I interrupted my vacation to inform them that I would write the editorial myself – and that it would back Reagan.

'I don't think you understand the depth of feeling,' protested Ivan Fallon, my deputy, who was editing the paper that week. 'We've done a poll which shows that seven out of ten Brits disapprove of the raid and Thatcher's complicity in it. The mood is even stronger in the rest of Europe. And

James [Adams, my personal assistant, a close friend and an expert in terrorism] thinks it was a big mistake too.'

'Fine,' I replied, 'put the poll on the front page and let James write the main piece on the leader page putting his views. But *The Sunday Times* will be backing Reagan: the editorial will be waiting for you when you arrive in the morning. Fax me back a proof.'

'Just what sort of allies has America been defending in Europe these past forty years?' I fumed to myself as I put the phone down. I stayed up half the night writing the editorial, after absorbing the coverage of the raid in the US media and speaking to some contacts in Washington. 'It is as well to remember what Sergeant Ford [the murdered black soldier] was doing in West Berlin in the first place,' began the editorial. 'He was one of more than three hundred thousand Americans stationed on this side of the Atlantic to defend the democracies of Western Europe. Yet his death, the latest atrocity in a wave of terrorism which has swept Europe with increasing intensity in the past eighteen months, was greeted in Europe with nothing like the outrage which was directed at the Americans for bombing those in Libya responsible for his death.' It went on to speak of the 'shame' of Europe's reaction, quoting Second World War veteran, Senator Bob Dole, saying he had not remembered the French complaining about American bombers flying over France in 1944 (Paris had refused the Americans permission to use French air space *en route* to Tripoli).

I called the editorial 'Alone but right', which was meant to endorse the Reagan–Thatcher position, but 'alone' also described the position of *The Sunday Times*. All manner of respectable opinion wrote to tell me how wrong the paper had been to back the Americans, with the usual crop of readers promising never to buy *The Sunday Times* again. The typical reaction was that Reagan's robust response would only provoke the Libyans to further terrorist retaliation. In fact, Colonel Gadaffi had been scared out of his wits by the attack, which almost killed him, and he retreated before this new assertive America. By August I was able to write an editorial ('The raid did work') pointing out that Gadaffi had become a 'diminished figure' since his capital had been bombed, that there was 'no new wave of Tripoli-inspired terror' and that Europe's anti-terrorist intelligence forces were now working closer together with the Americans. James Adams had the grace to admit that he had been wrong to criticize the raid at the time, a retraction I particularly valued. It began to dawn on me that being a lone British voice in favour of Reagan was likely to make *The Sunday Times* more often right than wrong, but not necessarily popular.

I had doubts, however, about 'Star Wars' when Reagan announced his 'High Frontier' defence system, designed to stop a mass attack of incoming missiles. In Moscow the Soviets had given me their reasons why it was a bad idea – it would undermine the existing anti-ballistic-missile treaty, destabilize the East–West nuclear 'balance of terror' and the Kremlin would refuse to negotiate mutual cuts in missiles if Washington proceeded down the Star Wars route – and Peter Jenkins, our senior columnist in the mid-1980s, had written some sniffy pieces about Reagan's vision of space-based defence, though he was barely qualified to opine on the matter. Thatcher was not that enamoured by Star Wars either: indeed all European opinion was fairly hostile to it. I asked my contacts in Washington if they would brief me on the subject: they agreed, provided it was kept confidential.

I flew to New York by Concorde one morning, telling my colleagues I had to see Rupert Murdoch on business, and caught the shuttle to Washington. I went straight to the White House, where I was taken to the situation room in the basement, greeted by the deputy head of the National Security Council, and briefed by him and two colleagues. I emerged over an hour later still unsure if Reagan's High Frontier was anything more than a dream but certain of one thing that nobody in the West had talked much about: it was a dream the Soviets shared. I was shown classified satellite photographs of several sites where the Kremlin was developing its own Star Wars programme. In some of the advanced physics required for such weaponry the Americans thought that the Russians were ahead of them. But they were way behind in developing the sophisticated computer systems, capable of taking billions of decisions per second, that were essential to any operational space-based defence. That was one reason why the Soviet consulate in San Francisco was as big as the Soviet embassy in Washington: the KGB had mounted a massive industrial espionage operation in Silicon Valley to steal the computer technology they needed.

It was fascinating stuff, though under the terms of my briefing I could not use it. But what I had been told made me less inclined to join in the general European rubbishing of Reagan's Star Wars plans. At the very least they were concentrating Soviet minds on the need to negotiate: the Kremlin, thanks to the Reagan arms build-up, had at last abandoned all thoughts of outspending America on defence. Indeed the Kremlin's defence costs were crippling the Soviet economy; now Reagan was committing America to a high-tech defensive system which the Soviets lacked the computer expertise to follow. Mikhail Gorbachev has been given much of the credit for ending the Cold War; but it was Reagan's hardline policies which produced the more emollient Gorbachev in the first place when the Kremlin hawks realized they were losing the arms race – and Reagan, like Thatcher before him, recognized that this was a man with whom he could do business. Both men agreed first to rid Europe of all medium-range missiles – which would never have happened if Cruise had not been deployed in the first place – then began to cut their bloated long-range nuclear arsenals. The newspaper welcomed Gorbachev's drive for *perestroika* and *glasnost*, though it believed he had no alternative: 'Marxist-Leninism is a busted flush, as is its brother, state Socialism. Command economies are in tatters all over the world . . . far from the future belonging to Communism or even Socialism (as the intelligentsia approvingly foretold in the 1950s and 1960s) they were no more than temporary twentieth-century phenomena.' A few years after this was written the Berlin Wall was dismantled and Soviet Communism collapsed. But I never shared the enthusiasm of the West in general, and the State Department and the Foreign Office in particular, for Gorbachev. I recognized he was a humane, decent man – a huge improvement on what had gone before – but he wanted to reform Communism, give it a more human face, like a latter-day Dubček, rather than abolish it. I always regarded Boris Yeltsin as the more authentic voice of the new Russia.

I had dined with Yeltsin in the Reform Club in London's Pall Mall when we serialized his memoirs and he came to London to promote them. He had fallen out with Gorbachev and left the Kremlin's inner circles. He told me that Thatcher had refused to see him during his visit: the Foreign Office had told her it would upset Gorbachev.

'She'll have to see me on my next trip,' he said through an interpreter.

'Why is that?' I asked.

'Because by then I will be President of Russia,' he replied, staring at me hard, his brow furrowing. 'Tell me,' he continued, 'about the Queen's role in the Commonwealth.' I explained how she was regarded as the nominal head of the Commonwealth, a position of status and regard among the members but of no real power.

'That's what Gorbachev can be!' he said with a smile. 'He can be the head of a new loose-knit Russian Commonwealth of independent states. But I will be President of Russia.'

We talked long into the night. He sipped wine; there was no bingeing on vodka and he remained coherent throughout. No doubt he drinks too much; but I have always suspected that some of the stories about his alcoholic excesses were put about in the early days by his enemies in the Kremlin – and the pro-Gorbachev foreign ministries of the West. At the end of the meal we all signed a napkin for him. There were a number of Russian aristocratic *émigrés* at the dinner and I noticed the grand titles they had written down. 'Build a democracy, not an aristocracy,' I wrote on the napkin, signed it and passed it back to him. He peered at it and asked his translator what it said. As the translation was whispered in his ear, he looked at me, smiled and nodded slowly.

At a lunch with British intelligence soon afterwards the conversation turned to Russia. Our official line was still wedded to Gorbachev and the people at lunch were anxious for the West to do all they could to keep him in power. I told them that I thought Yeltsin was the up-and-coming man. I recounted how I had been in a bar in Moscow when the latest increase in food prices had come on the television screen, followed by a picture of Gorbachev. Everybody started shouting and swearing at him. 'Gorbachev is loved abroad and hated at home,' I argued. 'His halfway house will not hold. Yeltsin is the authentic voice of Russia: he travels to work by tube and his wife stands in line at the supermarket with everybody else. With plain folk suffering such hardship, these symbols matter.'

I explained how Yeltsin had told me in Moscow that, as

the Soviet's East European satellites had abandoned Communism, there was a huge debate in the Politburo about 'who was losing Eastern Europe'. Some voices, he had told me, had argued for tougher Soviet intervention to hold the line. But Yeltsin had argued that the East European nations deserved their freedom. He wanted to dismember the Soviet Union and run Russia – and he believed in a mixed, market economy. 'He told me he thought the state was a bit too big in Sweden,' I finished, with a smile.

Those around the table confessed that British intelligence had no links to the Yeltsin camp; all the emphasis was on Gorbachev. 'You should get alongside some of his aides and build bridges. I promise you: he is the coming man.' I was no expert on Russia and there was no reason why British intelligence should take any notice of a newspaper editor. Much of what I said had already been stated in *The Sunday Times*. But I learned later that they had contacted their people in Moscow and told them it was time to get to know Boris better.

It was also time to say goodbye to Ronald Reagan. As he stepped down after his two-term presidency to make way for George Bush an editorial in January 1989 ('Farewell to the chief') took stock of his achievements and attacked British attitudes to the 'perpetually confused puppet in *Spitting Image* or the dangerous war-mongering halfwit that always raised an easy laugh in supposedly smart social and political circles . . . Just once, as we look at the Reagan record and the world he leaves behind, we should have the grace to feel ashamed of themselves.' In Grenada, Nicaragua, Libya and in its rearmament programme, Reagan's America had sent a message which got through to its enemies, if not its friends: 'The United States was not going to be pushed around any more. It had rebuilt its arsenal and was ready to hit back . . . Future generations may come to bless him as the danger of nuclear war recedes ever further.' And there was now what Reagan called 'a satisfying new closeness' between America and Russia: 'That the Cold War is no longer with us in the menacing form it was owes much to Mr Reagan's perceptions of the way East–West relations should be.'

The Cold War Warriors had won – and without a shot being fired between the superpowers. My father had told me from an early age that the best guarantor of peace was a strong defence and spoke of the disastrous consequences for Europe when Britain had forgotten this when faced with the dictators of the 1930s. The least warlike of men, he nevertheless saw it was essential for the democracies to be fully armed when faced with evil and aggression and that those who preached most about peace – like CND – were really spouting policies that were more likely to lead to war.

My reading of inter-war history at school and university confirmed the accuracy of his simple analysis. Reagan was later to be criticized for the huge burden of debt that his defence spending would bequeath to future generations. But better that they be confronted with paying off past bills than facing the continual threat of nuclear holocaust.

*

'THIS IS EUROPE'S HOUR,' the jumped-up foreign minister for Luxembourg had boasted when Brussels dispatched him in 1991 to the former Yugoslavia to sort out its problems. But nobody noticed him when he arrived there, the killing continued and European efforts to affect events in its own backyard proved futile – a defining failure, for me, in what had becoming a growing disillusion with the European dream.

I have not been a lifelong Eurosceptic. As a Tory student leader I joined with my Labour and Liberal equivalents to form 'Students for a United Europe', an all-party group which marched on Downing Street one night in the early 1970s, a brass band at the head, to deliver a letter which claimed that students of all political persuasions should back entry to the Common Market. I had the privilege of handing it in. We went on expenses-paid trips to student conferences in Stockholm and Verona to bond with our European counterparts, a gravy-train that many of the young politicians who travelled with me were never to leave. It was great fun, but fun with a mission: we were the new young Europeans, or so we thought. It was at one of these jamborees that I became friends with Carl Bildt, a young, staunchly pro-European Swedish conservative who was briefly to become his country's prime minister. When I see him now on television as the powerless representative of the European Union in Bosnia, my disillusion with the European dream becomes more acute.

But back in the early seventies, all bright, young people in London were pro-European: it was the only politically correct thing to be – and look at who opposed it: the worst elements in the Labour and Tory Parties, the Communists, the National Front, for goodness' sake! Conservative Research Department (my first job) was pro-Europe, so was *The Economist* (my next job) and when Harold Wilson called his referendum in 1975 to decide Britain's European future we rallied to the cause to keep Britain in, working out of the European Movement's offices in Whitehall, which were full of pretty young girls and earnest young men. I even edited a magazine called *The Federalist* which, in the full flush of youthful idealism, attacked our own pro-European politicians for their emphasis on mundane bread-and-butter issues and urged them to raise their horizons to the case for a United States of Europe.

Federalist dreams had dissipated by the time I arrived at *The Sunday Times* but not a general disposition to be pro-

European. This was reflected in editorials throughout the 1980s including various ones which urged Thatcher to listen to her senior ministers and take sterling into the European exchange-rate mechanism (ERM). An editorial in June 1989 ('Adieu to Little England') warned Thatcher not to play the anti-European card: 'We are no longer a nation of Little Englanders . . . we are all Europeans now.' But we liked Thatcher's Bruges speech the year before and the Gaullist vision of a 'Europe *des patries*' in which Europe cooperated as nation-states across a range of policies, including defence and foreign affairs, rather than any federalist vision. However, when *The Sunday Times* parted company with Thatcher in the 1990 Tory leadership election, her increasingly strident anti-Brussels stance was one of the things which put us off. In retrospect, Thatcher was right and *The Sunday Times* was wrong.

Europe began to sour for *The Sunday Times* not long after Thatcher's departure. By November 1991 an editorial entitled 'Eurolunacies' marked a major shift in policy.

> It was not meant to be like this [it began] . . . it was never envisaged that we would increasingly be ruled by Brussels, that the European Commission would attempt to intrude into the minutiae of everyday life on bogus grounds of 'harmonization' and that the Treaty of Rome would be perverted to operate in the interests of producers' cartels, from farming to computers. The great European experiment has gone sour.
>
> Such a statement is doubly sad for a pro-European newspaper such as *The Sunday Times* . . . [but] the cause of the disillusion is easy to find: the European Community has become obsessed with interfering in areas which are none of its business while its response to the big issues that face Europe has generally been pathetic . . . Attempts to build a united European front

> when the interests of all its members are threatened have been lamentable. If Saddam Hussein's invasion of Kuwait had been left to the European Community to resolve, the Iraqi dictator would still be in Kuwait. As Dubrovnik, a priceless European asset, is being bombarded by Serbian guns, the Community sits on its hands devoting its energies to the flavour of crisps and the size of condoms.

The editorial marked the start of an increasingly Eurosceptical *Sunday Times*. Failure to reform the absurdities of the Common Agricultural Policy, the propensity of the Brussels Commission to spew out directives like an awesome Euro-nanny state, the huge Euro-fraud and corruption (which Insight exposed), the inability of Europe to act when it mattered – all these encouraged that tendency. But there was something deeper at work.

One of the attractions of Europe in the sixties and seventies was that it seemed to conduct its affairs so much better than we did. I remember as a fourteen-year-old watching Labour Party political broadcasts during the 1964 election which showed how Britain was slipping behind its European competitors. It offended my patriotism but there clearly seemed to be so much to learn from Europe if we wanted to be a successful social democracy. By the seventies I was one of a number of print and broadcast journalists who went regularly to Sweden, West Germany, France and even Italy in search of stories which would teach the Brits how to make better cars and run a better telephone system. Being at the heart of Europe, to use a phrase once popular with John Major, seemed essential to the reversing of our economic decline.

By the 1990s, however, particularly as Britain emerged from the recession with its supply-side reforms intact and the fundamentals of its economy very strong, Europe seemed to have few lessons to teach. European social democracy was in crisis as unemployment soared, France and Germany were crippled by huge welfare costs and European business struggled to compete in global markets. Now it seemed that Britain was the teacher: the Thatcher reforms of the 1980s meant Britain had tackled the crisis in social democracy ahead of everybody else. But European politicians, Christian and Social Democrat alike, were not keen to learn. They struggled to make the old ways work better rather than discard them altogether; they wanted us to join them, but that meant reneging on the gains of the eighties.

I do not want Britain to leave the European Union though I would be happier to have a more arm's-length relationship with it. Nobody should wish to be at the heart of something which is fundamentally rotten. Until Europe faces up to and makes the same tough choices that Britain made in the 1980s – and which New Labour has no intention of reversing, which is true testimony to their fundamental rightness – then it will make sense to keep our distance. It is a measure of the progress the country has made since 1979, despite the Major government's best efforts to throw it all away, that Old Europe is no longer good enough for New Britain.

CHAPTER FOURTEEN

Decapitating the Blossom

'THE INTERESTING THING about having Andrew Neil as an editor,' said Rupert Murdoch, 'is that you never know which president, prime minister or company chairman is going to call you on a Sunday morning to complain about what he's done to them in the paper that day.'

The audience laughed. Rupert was speaking at a lavish dinner he had thrown for me in October 1993 in a private suite at the Dorchester Hotel to celebrate my tenth anniversary as editor of *The Sunday Times*. It was a gathering of senior colleagues from the paper plus old friends and luminaries from politics and the media, including Kenneth Clarke, Cecil Parkinson, Alastair Burnet, David Frost and John Birt. It was a splendid evening during which Rupert paid tribute to my editorship. But it was also something of a watershed for us both.

We had been drifting apart since the end of my secondment to Sky TV at the start of 1990; even by the summer of that year I was able to write in a private note that I was 'now out of the Rupert Murdoch/News Corporation loop'. Placing *The Sunday Times* at the centre of so many controversies had given me a certain celebrity, not to say notoriety, in Britain. Rupert was beginning to find the constant controversy, which he would sometimes get dragged into even though he had played no part in generating it, a little wearing. More importantly, going in to bat for the newspaper in countless television and radio broadcasts had made me a public figure in my own right; so had my efforts to launch Sky. Rupert resented it.

At first I could not believe my public profile was a problem for him. How could the billionaire owner of the world's most powerful media empire, a man fêted by presidents, prime ministers and captains of industry wherever he went in the world, be jealous of my minor fame in Britain? It sounded too ridiculous even to consider. But I learned that it was the major reason behind his growing disillusion with me.

'Do not underestimate how much Rupert resents you becoming a public figure in your own right,' I was warned early in 1994 by one of his closest confidants, as our relationship deteriorated. 'He hates the fact that you are better known, more regularly recognized than he is in Britain. He resents the way people talk about "your" *Sunday Times*. He *hates* it when you refer to "my" paper. He thinks your social life is a whirlwind of glamorous women and expensive restaurants. He does not like being upstaged like that. There is room for only one superstar at News International.'

'He used to get very annoyed when you got more or better publicity than him,' confirmed Gus Fischer three years later. 'He couldn't stand it. "One day he'll get too big for his boots!" he used to fume.'

I discovered that he had started to bridle every time word reached him in America that I had been on television or radio. He was even angry about a perfectly innocuous 'At Home' feature in London's *Evening Standard*. It consisted of a pleasant picture of me sitting on my Onslow Gardens terrace with some anodyne words about my flat. 'Why did he have to do that?' Rupert moaned. 'He's his own worst enemy. He'll go too far!'

These were petty matters to bother the world's most powerful media baron; but little things did seem to annoy him. I remember dining with him after taking him to the Last Night at the Proms. During the meal, two women approached and asked if I was Andrew Neil. Yes, I replied, immediately introducing Rupert as the owner of *The Sunday Times*. But they wanted to talk about some broadcast I had just done. Rupert seethed.

Ian Chapman, then chief executive of HarperCollins, mentioned to Rupert at a party that he must be very pleased to have such a professional broadcaster (me!) representing the paper. 'He should keep his energies for *The Sunday Times*,' Rupert snapped back.

There was more to it, however, than just a resentment of my supposed celebrity. My extra-curricular activities were giving me a growing economic independence. I was not dependent solely on my *Sunday Times* salary, which I was able to supplement substantially with other work, mostly broadcasting and public speaking. This financial independence put me in a more autonomous frame of mind. I was seen increasingly (even by enemies) as my own man, not a Murdoch editor in the pocket of his proprietor. Rupert grew to disapprove of these other activities as improper diversions from *The Sunday Times*; I thought they enhanced my job and the paper's profile. He had an all-or-nothing attitude towards those who worked for him, the better to control them; I did not want News International to own me lock, stock and barrel.

The more I spread my wings the more effort I put into *The Sunday Times* so that nobody could accurately say I was neglecting it. While on a skiing break in Aspen, Colorado over Thanksgiving 1993, I had my office pipe the radio broadcast of Kenneth Clarke's first Budget over the telephone so I could listen to it live; I then had all the relevant commentaries faxed over next day, consulted with my senior editors in London then sat down and wrote the Budget editorial. I regarded it as too important a commentary to be written by anybody else but the editor, even though I was supposed to be on holiday 6,000 miles away.

When Robin Morgan, the *Sunday Times Magazine* editor, said Madonna had agreed to a three-hour exclusive interview with *The Sunday Times* provided I did it, I left for Los Angeles early on a Sunday morning after a late night at the office, read the cuttings on her during the long flight, interviewed her on Monday afternoon, caught a flight back to London that night and was at the Labour Party conference in Blackpool by late Tuesday afternoon. From Beverly Hills to Blackpool in less than twenty-four hours was an interesting culture shock! But I thrived on such variety.

When I presented the early morning news show on LBC, the London talk station, I would go straight into the office, already fully briefed on what was happening in the world. It made life hell for the newsdesk but it put me on top of the news as never before – and produced some scoops. As a result of an aside I picked up during an interview I was able to direct the Insight team to the European Community's £400 million of subsidies to tobacco growers (mainly in Greece) while it was trying to ban cigarette advertising in member countries. But there was more than hypocrisy to expose: the tobacco so generously subsidized by Brussels was thought too dangerous to sell in Europe, so it was dumped in the Third World. Insight revealed the scandal in a page-one investigation.

I was firing on all cylinders and my multi-media existence gave my editorship a new lease of life. But Rupert was determined to see it differently. My extra activities were deemed as evidence of neglect of *The Sunday Times*. 'It's a great paper,' he started telling his Wapping executives, 'but you can sure as hell tell when Andrew is not giving it his full attention.' His loyal Wapping courtiers were soon repeating this mantra. Even Gus Fischer, who had nothing to do with editorial matters, began to claim that he could tell which editions of the newspaper I had been fully engaged in editing, and those where my attention was supposedly elsewhere.

There were always a few helpful Wapping souls anxious to tell Rupert what he wanted to hear. One of them told him that I had gone to interview Madonna for LBC; he added that to his list of grievances. In fact, I had gone for *The Sunday Times* because I had been told she wanted a serious discussion about popular culture, because I thought it would be interesting to meet the second most famous woman in the world (after our own Diana), because I thought it was the sort of unusual thing I was entitled to do after ten years of editorship if that was where my fancy took me – and I was bored with interviewing politicians.

I had gone armed with the page proofs of Michael Medved's *Hollywood v. America*, a seminal study which *The Sunday Times* was to serialize, about how the American entertainment industry was debasing popular culture. Madonna's new album was called *Erotica*, she had just produced a controversial picture book full of sado-masochistic illustrations and was starring in an explicit new film; she seemed the perfect superstar to challenge with Medved's views.

I arrived at the massive gates of her house in Hollywood Hills with Sue Ellicott, our talented Los Angeles correspondent. They swung open when I revealed my identity to the electronic security box. A little lady in a black combat outfit, boots, no make up and scruffy dyed blond hair, the dark roots clearly coming through, opened the door. 'I'm here to see Madonna,' I said, thinking it was the housekeeper/cleaner. 'I'm Madonna,' she replied, gingerly shaking hands and beckoning me into a tasteful lounge with stunning views over Los Angeles.

I was offered a sofa to myself and a mineral water; Madonna spread out on the chaise-longue opposite; Sue Ellicott, an experienced journalist in her own right, was offered the chance to go shopping: she was female and attractive and Madonna had automatically assumed she must be a secretary or assistant. It seemed a strangely sexist response from a rock star who projects an image of independent womanhood. 'Don't worry,' said Sue to me, laughing it off. 'I'll come back for you in a couple of hours.'

I spent the next three hours alone with Madonna, grilling her on what motivated her to do what she did. It was a gruelling experience for me as well as her. Getting answers was like getting blood out of a stone: she had indicated she wanted to engage in serious discussion of her work but she had not thought beyond glib defences of what she was doing. She was restless and at times tetchy. At one stage I thought she was going to cry when I suggested the flamboyant lifestyle, lipstick lesbianism, sado-masochism and all the rest of it were just a cover for the fact she was a rather lonely woman in her thirties who wanted a baby.

'When are you going to ask me about my music – or my panties?' she asked coyly, trying to change the subject. 'I'm not,' I replied and threw another Medved quote at her for a response.

Her publicity people said later she regarded it as the toughest interview she had ever given. She refused a rematch when she was in London in 1996 shooting *Evita*. *The Sunday Times* added 60,000 in sales on the week it made the cover of the Magazine and it was syndicated throughout the world. The exercise had been an interesting diversion for me, something of a minor success for the paper and a bit of a disaster for Madonna – some say her career never recovered from it! Rupert even hired Medved as his film critic for the *New York Post*. But nothing would placate him about me: though he never raised the matter directly I knew it rankled with him.

'Editors should be anonymous,' he said to me out of the blue on the phone one day. 'Your profile is too high and it's generated too many enemies.'

'I gained many of them defending your interests,' I retorted. I did not remember him complaining about my TV exposure when I was the only one publicly defending the move to Wapping or the promise of Sky.

'I know that, but you've become a public figure,' he continued. 'You're great on TV defending the paper and keeping it in the public eye but for many people you've also become the one to like or hate: they divide into for and against Andrew Neil. I don't think it helps the paper.'

It was certainly true that in many people's minds I had come to personify *The Sunday Times*, which is probably what Rupert really objected to. No doubt I did put some people off buying the paper. But it was hardly suffering in the market-place from my supposed over-exposure in the media: indeed, *The Sunday Times* had never been more dominant. But that was not enough to placate Rupert. In fact, it only served to exacerbate matters: I was getting the credit for the paper's success, which made the Sun King surly; and he had his way of dealing with uppity courtiers acting above their station.

Barry Diller, the brilliant boss of the Fox motion-picture studio and TV network, had departed soon after Rupert moved to Los Angeles to be more hands on with Fox. The semi-autonomous nature of Diller's Fox empire – almost a state within a state – had infuriated Rupert for some time. He itched to get his hands on it. Once he was based in LA,

Rupert made it clear the town was not big enough for both of them. Kelvin MacKenzie had departed from the *Sun* not long after he stood up to Rupert to an unhappy and short-lived time at Sky. Andrew Knight's brief period basking in the Sun King's warm glow was over. Gus Fischer and John Dux would not be with the company much longer. Other more minor figures who had shown flair or independence had also been fired or sidelined. Even a compliant, faithful and long-standing company chairman like Richard Searby, who never caused Rupert any trouble, had been unceremoniously ousted because Rupert decided he wanted to be chairman *and* chief executive.

'Murdoch and News Corporation are like nature in the raw,' a lawyer who had worked closely with Rupert once said. 'When a flower reaches full bloom it's decapitated.' It was only a matter of time before I was the next to be guillotined.

*

The Sunday Times was certainly in full blossom when it happened. By early 1994 it was regularly selling over 150,000 more copies every week than the *combined* circulation of the *Sunday Telegraph* and *Observer*, our two nearest rivals, and making almost £1 million a week on average sales of around 1.25 million. The only contest in the Sunday broadsheet market was for second place; nobody was within striking distance of *The Sunday Times*.

We had seen off the challenge of two new quality Sundays (the *Independent on Sunday* and the short-lived *Sunday Correspondent*), weathered numerous re-launches of the *Observer* and *Sunday Telegraph*, coped with the huge expansion of Saturday broadsheets and dealt with the aggressive, well-financed *Mail on Sunday*, which had been nibbling away at the bottom end of our market. The competition had thrown everything they could at us but *The Sunday Times* had emerged from the most competitive period in the history of Sunday newspapers stronger than ever, the undisputed leader in the Sunday broadsheet market and Britain's biggest selling, most profitable quality newspaper. It was a testament to our efficiency that we were producing a ten-section newspaper with roughly the same number of journalists it had once taken to produce three.

The *Independent on Sunday* and the *Sunday Correspondent* had been launched in the newspaper boom that followed our triumph at Wapping with the idea that there was a gap in the Sunday broadsheet market – that the existing quality Sundays were failing to satisfy readers. It was a false premiss based on a wrong reading of the figures. David Lipsey, former economics editor of *The Sunday Times* and one of those behind the launch of the *Sunday Correspondent*, produced figures to show that by 1988 sales of Sunday broadsheets were almost 500,000 down on the start of the decade. But he had made a cardinal error, especially for an economist: he had taken the wrong base year.

When *The Sunday Times* was on strike in 1978–9 sales of the *Observer* and *Sunday Telegraph* soared. When *The Sunday Times* returned after the eleven-month stoppage its circulation shot straight back to its old level; but sales of its rivals did not plummet immediately. Through 1980 and into 1981 there was an unprecedented amount of double and treble buying of all three quality Sundays, which gave the broadsheet market an artificial, temporary boost. If Lipsey had taken 1978 as his base year – a more reliable yardstick when all three Sunday broadsheets were in what passed for normal production in these days – he would have discovered that sales a decade later were only about 175,000 down. Most of that modest amount had been lost to the *Mail on Sunday*, which had eaten into the lower end of the Sunday broadsheets. There was no gap in the market, as the *Sunday Correspondent* found to its cost in its short life before disappearing without trace.

The *Independent on Sunday* was looking for more than a gap: it was launched with the specific intention of knocking *The Sunday Times* off its pedestal. *The Times* had vacated the top end of the daily market in the 1980s, under Rupert's mistaken guidance; the *Independent* had spotted the gap and successfully filled it – so much so that it was soon breathing down the neck of *The Times*, in sales as well as critical acclaim. Many thought it only a matter of time before it overtook *The Times*. It aimed to repeat the trick on a Sunday. The *Independent on Sunday* was launched to the cheers of the chattering classes and the plaudits of the critics: even someone as shrewd as Richard Branson opined that it would soon topple the market leader. The view among senior managers at Wapping (including Rupert) was that we would be lucky to be above 1.1 million after the launch, a loss of 150,000. But *The Sunday Times* was a far tougher nut to crack than *The Times*.

The *Independent on Sunday* made much of its supposed slim sophistication, in contrast with the bulk of *The Sunday Times*. It was launched with a commercial showing a man at the counter of some dingy East European bank, handing over a $100 bill and being given thousands of worthless bank notes in return. The *Sunday Telegraph* had also run television commercials attacking our size, with an arrow piercing through a multi-section newspaper like *The Sunday Times* and viewers urged to 'shoot through the bumf' to get to the more compact *Sunday Telegraph*. The *Observer* tried a similar appeal.

All our rivals attacked the bulk of *The Sunday Times* because it was the conventional wisdom that British readers did not like multi-section newspapers; almost every media pundit predicted that the burgeoning *Sunday Times* was turning readers off with its *Sunday New York Times*-style sections and that we were vulnerable to slimmer rivals. As usual, the media pundits were wrong. There was some initial resistance to sections because readers found the concept unfamiliar. So we ran generic commercials showing a typical *Sunday Times* extended family lounging around the house, its various members all reading different bits of the paper. The public soon grasped the point that you did not have to read every section, just those that interested you – and they liked the value for money a multi-section paper represented. Above all, it never dawned on our critics and the competition what a powerful tool a multi-section paper could be in the right hands. '*The Sunday Times* is *the* Sunday papers' was more than just a marketing slogan: it was the key to success in our war with the opposition.

I had complete faith in the multi-section proposition to see off whatever the competition could throw at us. I devised each section with specific rivals and threats in mind. The Books and Culture sections, for example, were developed to appeal to the *Independent/Observer/Guardian* market. *The Funday Times* was invented to encourage children to nag their parents to buy the paper for the cartoons. The Style section was designed with *Mail on Sunday* readers in mind, especially women.

The Sunday Times had never had to cope with an aggressive middle-market tabloid with broadsheet pretensions. Throughout the 1960s and 1970s it could safely ignore the *Sunday Express*, then a middle-market broadsheet which, under the dead hand of John Junor, the last of Fleet Street's dinosaur editors, was haemorrhaging circulation and no threat to anybody. But the *Mail on Sunday*, whose talented editor, Stewart Steven, was rather obsessed with *The Sunday Times* and never missed a chance to snipe at it (or me), was a more formidable competitor: the Style section plus the revamping of the Magazine to make it more female friendly was our successful response.

The Culture was a new departure for national journalism and drew on the approach of a small-circulation tabloid magazine, the *Modern Review*. It aimed to analyse the significance of arts and entertainment for our culture, to take *Eastenders* as seriously for its impact on our culture as *Hamlet* (but not to grant it the same worth or artistic value!) and above all to break away from an arts journalism that was review-based, with reviews of concerts or plays often written with only a few hundred of the arts *cognoscenti* in mind. I wanted longer essays on all manner of cultural developments. The approach was based on Harry Evans' guiding principle that *The Sunday Times*, as a quality paper that reached beyond the normal broadsheet market, should deal with serious matters in a popular way, and popular matters in a serious way.

The Culture became a formidable addition to our armoury to deal with the upmarket competition just as Style protected our middle-market flank. The beauty of a multi-section newspaper is that you can go up- and down-market at the same time, simultaneously dealing with tabloid and broadsheet threats. This bamboozled the opposition which thought in terms of very specific niches in the market-place, which is why their sales lagged far behind ours: they were up against a newspaper which covered the waterfront, from the *Daily Mail* all the way through to the *Financial Times*. Though they sneered at the time, all Sunday broadsheets have now gone the multi-section route, but none has ever managed to reproduce the logic and distinct identity of each *Sunday Times* section: it remains by far the most powerful package in British journalism.

After a strong start, the challenge of the *Independent on*

Sunday petered out. A paper with pretensions to take on *The Sunday Times* never managed more than a third of our circulation, before slipping back and becoming no threat at all. Its launch editor, Stephen Glover, having failed in his mission, went off to write snooty yet strangely compelling columns advising rather more successful editors than he had been how to run their newspapers.

Meanwhile the *Observer* was in freefall. When I took over *The Sunday Times* in 1983 it was still regarded as our main challenger, with sales close to 800,000. It was the paper we all grabbed when the first editions arrived early on a Saturday evening to see what stories it had that we did not. A decade later, under the leisurely, complacent editorship of Donald Trelford, it was slumping towards 500,000, a catastrophic fall of 40 per cent (the decline has still not ended, despite three editors in the same number of years: it was slipping to 450,000 at the latest count even though it is now in the tender care of the *Guardian*) and its journalism could be safely ignored, bar one or two surprises a year. *The Sunday Times* deserved better competition than Trelford's *Observer*, which was even overtaken by the *Sunday Telegraph*, for second place in the circulation ratings.

But it was a very distant second. It had carved out a distinctive niche as a sort of High Tory *Sunday Spectator*, but, as its owner, Conrad Black, admitted to me, it lacked the broad appeal ever to be in a position to challenge *The Sunday Times*. So by 1994 we had very little effective competition on a Sunday; certainly none of our rivals could be said to be challenging us in terms of sales or editorial content. It was a satisfying position to be in for an editor whose survival the *Guardian* and others had put at only six months a decade before. But it was also dangerous: newspapers need strong competition to keep them on their toes. The absence of it in America explains why its big-city monopoly newspapers are so dull. I urged my senior editors not to become complacent: we needed to create our own competition, I told them, to keep improving the paper.

We gathered in a London hotel towards the end of February 1994 for one of our periodic day-long strategy sessions to take stock and plot the next stage in the paper's development. Paul Wolfenden, head of our promotion and marketing, who, along with Graham King, a marketing genius, had done a wonderful job, positioning and promoting the paper, unveiled his latest readership study. It was very positive.

In the previous twelve months, we had gained new readers among women, 35–44 year olds and what the advertising industry calls ABC1s, the most educated and affluent in society and the group advertisers crave for. We were doing especially well among well-educated Bs in full-time employment. Our losses had been among C2DEs, 55+s and the less educated – some of which had gone to the *Sunday Telegraph*. So much for the constant refrain of critics that I had taken *The Sunday Times* downmarket. The image of the paper among readers and potential readers was also very encouraging: we were growing in strength and authority in our readers' eyes, seen to be very successful and record numbers of non-readers were now prepared to consider buying us (which in the months ahead they proceeded to do). Even the resistance to size and sections had gone: 95 per cent liked the variety they offered.

It was all very satisfying. But I did not want anybody to think we could rest on our laurels: I had seen the way even a famous, long-established franchise like the *Observer* could atrophy through neglect. We agreed that the main competition now was not the Sunday but the Saturday edition of the *Telegraph*. The Saturday *Telegraph* was the only broadsheet with a circulation anywhere near ours, it had built itself into a multi-section clone of *The Sunday Times* and competed hard for the same advertising market.

We discussed plans to produce a new Home section, printed on newsprint and stitched and trimmed like the Style and Culture sections, to take on the Saturday *Telegraph* in those areas of 'service journalism' – leisure, travel, cooking, cars, interior design, gardening – where it outpunched us, in editorial and advertising.

We also decided to develop a regional section for the north-west of England. Our separate Scottish section had proved to be a great success and so had our distinct and substantial Irish edition: sales of *The Sunday Times* were strong in both countries. Indeed, the Scottish section had helped us to contain the challenge of *Scotland on Sunday*, a new Edinburgh-based broadsheet edited by Andrew Jaspan who, years before with Gerry Malone, had helped me launch *The Sunday Times*'s Scottish section. In Ireland our sales were booming. It was time to see if the same formula would work in an English region and I began devising plans for a North-West section, based in Manchester, to boost our sales there and scoop up local advertising. If it worked the plan was to develop separate sections for every English region.

We emerged from our strategy session with plans for new Home and North-West sections, the expansion of our Irish edition and some thoughts on how to beef up the Magazine. We finished the day with something of a celebration dinner for about forty of the senior and section editors: after a decade I had assembled a brilliant team around me, many of whom had become friends as well as colleagues, quite a contrast with my early days. It had been a good session and the mood was buoyant: we knew we were a success story but we planned to do better still.

When I outlined our latest plans to Rupert at a subsequent budget meeting, however, he did not want to know: No! to the Home section, No! to any English regional sections, No! to any new development whatsoever. He had embarked on a costly price war to increase sales of *The Times*, his latest, most expensive attempt to make it a success, and he was in no mood to spend anything on *The Sunday Times*, even though we were the moneymaker. But there was more to it than that.

Rupert felt he had lost control of *The Sunday Times*. Though he had been involved in some of the earlier innovations, such as Books, as we grew into a multi-section monster, the paper had developed without much input from him. He had played no part in devising the Style or Culture sections, or launching a separate Sports section, or turning News Review into an eclectic mix of opinion and analysis. 'He did not recognize it as his paper any more,' says John Dux, whose support had been vital in developing the new sections, 'and he didn't like that.'

I had not sought to exclude him: but the more he was based in Los Angeles, the less close his interest seemed to be and I had gone ahead and developed the paper as I saw fit. With his rejection of our latest plans, he was also sending me a signal to remind me that I had only a leasehold on the paper: he was the freeholder and he would determine any further developments if he chose to. I had always been aware of my leaseholder status and made it clear I was ready to relinquish it whenever required. From very different directions we were both moving to the conclusion that it was time to let the lease expire.

I was beginning to weary of Wapping, which I had grown to dislike as a place of work, and to find *The Sunday Times* a constriction on other things I wanted to do. I had forced myself to keep up the momentum of change, to keep driving forward, to fight complacency setting in. But the job no longer excited me the way it had: my enthusiasm was waning. I even stopped looking forward to Saturdays. I resented Rupert's intermittent and unpredictable interventions. If, for whatever reason, he was now intent on stifling further developments, then I would be left just to keep things ticking over, a prospect which bored me. When editors start to think such thoughts it is time to move on. I began to think more about life after *The Sunday Times*.

I was attracted to the idea of quitting while I was ahead, of 'declaring victory and going home', as a friend put it. Too many editors stay beyond their sell-by date, building up a newspaper then presiding over its subsequent decline. Newspapers are a creative business that constantly need to be replenished with fresh talent, even at the top. After ten years it was time to bow out. But to what? What job could possibly rival *The Sunday Times* in terms of prestige, interest, influence and excitement? I had not yet answered that question when Rupert was to resolve the matter for me.

*

'IT'S THE GREAT ANDREW Neil,' Rupert bellowed down the phone one afternoon in mid-March 1994. 'Not content with taking on one f——g prime minister you have to take on two.' He was referring to the fact that *The Sunday Times* was at war with the British and Malaysian prime ministers.

Along with other British broadsheets, *The Sunday Times* had been investigating the links between the £234 million of British aid to Malaysia to build the Pergau hydro-electric dam and a £1.3 billion contract from Malaysia to buy British arms. The government had always denied there was any link between aid and arms, which would have been illegal under its own rules, even though the dam project had been condemned as an 'unequivocally bad buy' by its own most senior aid-official and very few people were prepared to justify it as a proper use of our overseas aid budget.

Why the British government wanted to pump so much money – against official advice – into a dam which would raise electricity prices and destroy a chunk of the rainforest remained a mystery, unless it was linked to the lucrative arms deal. On 23 January 1994 *The Sunday Times* revealed that many of the British companies involved in the controversial dam project would also benefit from the Malaysian military contract. Douglas Hurd, the foreign secretary, was forced to admit that aid and arms had indeed become 'entangled' in Malaysia, which was as honest as the Foreign Office was ever likely to get to admitting the linkage.

The increasing evidence that British overseas aid, meant to help the poorest in the world, had been used as a sweetener to build a dam only a few rich Malaysians wanted in order to clinch an arms contract encouraged us to widen our investigations. On 20 February *The Sunday Times* reported that Wimpey, the British construction company, had made arrangements for 'special payments' to be paid to the Malaysian Prime Minister, Mahathir Mohamed, and other senior political figures in the country's ruling party, in return for a contract to build an aluminium smelter. Confidential company documents which had come our way while investigating an unrelated matter (Wimpey's activities in Liverpool and its links with Derek Hatton, once that city's hard-left leader) showed that Wimpey had approved an initial payment of $50,000 to a Malaysian middle man who in turn was expected to pay it into nominated Swiss bank accounts for a team of Malaysian politicians who were helping Wimpey win the £600 million contract, among them the country's prime minister, who had 'stated his personal commitment to the project and agreed that it should come to Wimpey'. The $50,000 was just a down-payment: millions more were expected to follow.

The article was careful not to claim that Mahathir had

actually requested or received any money, just that Wimpey had been willing to recommend and approve payments to a middle man, in the belief that they would be going to Malaysian politicians, including the Prime Minister. But the very suggestion that bribes were on offer to clinch Malaysian contracts sent Mahathir, an authoritarian leader with an anti-British colonial chip on his shoulder, into a spin. He had already been fuming at the British press for its investigations into Pergau. The Wimpey story was the last straw: he announced a ban on any more Malaysian government contracts for British firms.

The Sunday Times was blamed for the potential loss of British jobs and profits by the British government and big business in a volley of attacks from the Malaysian Prime Minister and his acolytes for supposedly smearing their good names. British ministers and businessmen also protested loudly. We hit back, firing on all sides. We told the British government to 'stop grovelling and retaliate' against the ban by withholding further funds for the Pergau project, we refused to apologize to Mahathir and warned him we would not be intimidated by his threats. We widened the attack against the British and Malaysian governments by showing that there was a well established pattern of using our overseas aid budget to clinch arms deals, despite the many official denials that the two ever went hand in hand; and by showing that money from the Pergau dam had been used to enhance the share price of the electricity company that operated it, prior to its privatization, we made it clear that there were plenty of rich snouts in a trough that was meant to feed the world's poorest. Shares in the electricity company were being parcelled out to cronies of the Malaysian Prime Minister and his ruling party, who had cashed in on huge windfall gains, courtesy of the British taxpayer. It was all good stuff in classic whistleblowing *Sunday Times* tradition. Then Rupert called.

I was taken aback by his onslaught but there was no alternative but to defend what I was doing. 'We're under attack from the British and Malaysian governments, Rupert,' I replied, trying to sound beleaguered and win some sympathy, 'as well as big business. The paper has to defend itself.'

'But you're boring people!' he shouted. 'You're doing far too much on Malaysia. Page after page of it, which nobody can understand. Malaysia doesn't merit all this coverage. They're all corrupt in that part of the world. Everybody knows Mahathir is corrupt – but you can find examples like him everywhere.'

'The only time we've spoken about this,' I replied, 'you said it was great to see the paper at the centre of another controversy.'

'But it's become a battle between *you*,' he said bitterly, 'and the Malaysian Prime Minister. Even *The Sunday Times* is not part of it. You've turned it into a personal campaign. You're *always* on television.'

I wondered if that was the real reason he was angry but this was no time for private thoughts: Rupert was still ranting: 'It's my fault,' he continued. 'I've been letting you get on with it. But it's too much. It has to stop.' With that he brought to an end the most bad-tempered call I ever had from him.

After he had hung up I pondered what was really riling him. It could hardly be the extent of our Malaysian coverage, unless he was more out of touch with events in Britain than I had realized: it was the biggest story in town and we were at the centre of it. Was it all the publicity I was getting from the television interviews, I wondered? I knew by now that he resented the minor celebrity status that regular appearances on television and radio had given me. Or was it his satellite television interests in the Far East he was worried about? I had always known that Rupert does not like anything to get in the way of business: he had just thrown BBC World, the BBC's answer to CNN, off his Asian Star satellite system because the Chinese had objected to a critical BBC documentary. Mahathir had widened his attacks against *The Sunday Times* to include Rupert Murdoch, making it clear that Star's chances of being allowed into Malaysia had hardly been helped by our stories. This was the first time there might be a clear conflict between *The Sunday Times* and his business interests.

He was back on the phone exactly twenty-four hours later. 'Look,' he said, 'I want no more public statements from you on this Malaysian business.' He had obviously read my robust response to an attack from the Malaysian Prime Minister in the morning papers. I had tried to cool things down with a conciliatory letter in *The Times* but the Malaysian PM threw it back in my face; I went back on the offensive. 'I'm getting lots of letters from people asking, "Who does Mr Neil think he is, taking on a prime minister?" And you're *boring* people,' he added, harking back to yesterday's theme. 'The paper needs a public spokesman – but it shouldn't be the editor. Get Jane Reed [News International's head of corporate affairs] to do it.'

It was an absurd proposition. Jane is a wonderful, underappreciated (above all by Rupert) spokesperson for the company but she did not know the intricacies and nuances of a complicated story. Anyway I was the established public face of the paper and if I were suddenly to hide behind Jane everybody would think we were in retreat. But it was pointless to argue the case. I decided it was best to placate him until I worked out what was happening. I told him the row was dying down and that we planned no more editorials or analysis, though we were still working on a fresh news angle. 'Thanks,' he said, grumpily. It had been a quick call, not as bellicose as the day before's; but I clearly had an unhappy proprietor on my hands – disgruntled enough to start thinking it was time he had a new, less troublesome editor at *The Sunday Times*.

I did not hear from him again until early April. I braced myself for another broadside but it was a good-natured call: he was coming to London the following week, he had a very hectic schedule but he wondered if I was possibly free for dinner, just the two of us, at his St James's Place flat on Wednesday, 13 April. I sensed immediately that something was brewing. My suspicions were confirmed when Gus Fischer called to ask if I was free for lunch. The softening up process had begun. I realized that I was in my final days at *The Sunday Times* but, strangely, I was not perturbed by the thought. I was ready to go, provided the exit was graceful and financially advantageous.

Gus took me to lunch at Le Pont de la Tour across the Thames from Wapping overlooking Tower Bridge. It was an affable occasion in which we talked about everything and nothing. He came to the point over coffee, explaining that News Corporation was a big company with plenty of opportunities for somebody like me. 'I know you feel under-rewarded for what you've done at *The Sunday Times* and Sky,' he said. 'There could be a chance for you to make big money in the United States.'

He did not elaborate what they could be and I remained noncommittal in my replies: Gus was on an errand for Rupert, a fishing expedition to sound me out. I saw no reason to be too open with my thoughts at this stage, except to make it clear I was always open to lucrative alternatives. I had already learned from other sources that Rupert was of a mind to make me some offer to do with a new show for Fox to compete with CBS's *60 Minutes*, American television's most established and highest-rated weekly news magazine. But I did not raise it with Gus: this was a conversation I wanted to have direct with Rupert.

Two days before I was due to dine with Rupert I took the train to Leeds on my day off from *The Sunday Times* to record ITV's *Through the Keyhole* with David Frost, who had asked me to be on the panel for two shows – precisely the sort of 'celebrity' appearance certain to infuriate Rupert. The whole Frost clan was in Yorkshire that day and after the show we repaired by hired mini-bus to a local renowned fish and chip shop. It was great family fun, especially with David's delightful wife and children, but my mind was elsewhere. When I returned to my gloomy hotel room in Leeds city centre I lay in bed contemplating my options. Suddenly, I had become very wary of what was before me.

I could stay as editor of *The Sunday Times*. But I was beginning to realize that Rupert wanted me out, I was already thinking of life after the newspaper and I had always made it clear that I would never outstay my welcome. I did not know if Rupert wanted me to go badly enough that he would attempt to force me out; but if he did I had no intention of resisting. So the second option was to depart on agreed terms, a clean break and a substantial pay-off. Then there was this vague American TV option, which no doubt I would hear more about over dinner. But there might also be a fourth option, a sort of hybrid: go to America on secondment (much as I had gone to Sky), staying as editor, then review the alternatives at the end of, say, a six-month experimental period.

As these thoughts went through my mind I felt a mixture of apprehension and elation: I had a fear of the future because it seemed uncertain; but I was excited at the prospect of moving on to what looked like being the post-Murdoch phase of my life. I had a rough idea of what he had in mind in America but I already felt it was likely to be only a transition rather than the start of a new American TV career. I slept fitfully and caught an early train back to London next morning.

On the night I was to dine with Rupert I was also hosting a cocktail party for *The Sunday Times Magazine* at Daphne's, the fashionable Chelsea restaurant. It was a glamorous event for friends, colleagues and celebrities featured in the recently relaunched Magazine. Everybody seemed to be enjoying themselves and I had to tear myself away, with the sad thought at the back of my mind that I would not be hosting many more nights like this.

Rupert was in his shirtsleeves when I arrived at his fifth-floor flat looking west over Green Park. He had flown in from New York and looked tired and drawn. But he was in a good mood, having just agreed a deal with a Bombay businessman, who passed me on the way out, to expand his satellite TV interests in India. As the two of us dined at a large round table on asparagus and flounder, served by a butler, he was at his most charming. This is also when he is at his most dangerous.

We talked about the newspaper: I gave several examples of how well it was doing, both in sales and stories. He agreed: 'You've done a great job with the paper,' he said. 'It's a *great* paper. If I have one criticism, it's your tendency not to take any prisoners in a controversy. But that's OK. That's you.'

We moved on to politics, discussing the relative merits of Michael Portillo and Michael Heseltine to take over from John Major, whom he was anxious to see replaced. I told him that Heseltine's day had probably come and gone (which brought him some relief) but that his right-wing favourite, Portillo, was too voter-unfriendly to be a credible Tory leader. 'The problem is,' I said, 'there is no natural heir apparent to Major and that's what will keep him in Downing Street.' He nodded in agreement, unable to think of a worthy successor. It was only when we adjourned to the sofas at the other end of the long room to sip camomile tea that the conversation turned to me.

'We've talked about the paper and politics,' he said hesitatingly. 'Let's talk about you. I've the feeling that you want to get back to America and earn some real money.' In fact, I had never expressed a desire to return to America but I did not contradict him. This was a time to listen and I had no objection to working in America again if the job attracted me.

He talked about how his Fox TV network had concluded a multi-million-dollar deal to secure the rights to live games in the National Football League (NFL) on a Sunday. Many folk thought he had paid too much to steal the NFL from CBS, which had broadcast the games for years, but he regarded the Sunday afternoon rights to American football, the country's most popular spectator sport, as an essential part of his ambition to turn Fox into a fully fledged network. He then explained how CBS had followed its NFL broadcasts with *60 Minutes*, its popular and prestigious news magazine show, at 7 p.m. every Sunday. That helped give it a lock on the Sunday-night ratings; it then did a substantial amount of on-air promotion before this big audience to preview shows it had coming up during the week. In its heyday, it was part of the strategy which had made CBS America's number-one network. Rupert wanted Fox to develop its own version of *60 Minutes* to follow the football and similarly build Fox's ratings. This is where I came in.

'I think we'll need an American host for the show,' he said, 'if we need a host at all [in *60 Minutes* the reporters shared the presenting] but I see you as the senior of four reporters: you do the big international stories, the interviews with people like Clinton, the major investigations. I see you as the Mike Wallace figure in the show [Wallace is the senior, most respected reporter in *60 Minutes*].' There was no word about me also being executive editor of the programme, which I had heard was also on his mind. I was not totally enthused by the prospect of going from editor of one of the world's great newspapers to being a reporter on America's fourth-rated network.

'I think *60 Minutes* could be really vulnerable,' he continued, 'now that it's lost its inheritance from the football, whereas a Fox news magazine could be heavily promoted during the NFL games and, over time, start to challenge it.'

'Do you want a new editor, Rupert?' I asked him calmly.

'No,' he said emphatically, his eyes looking away. 'I just thought it might appeal to you. Take your time and think about it.' It was 10.30 p.m. and his jet lag was now taking its toll: I thought it best to leave without committing myself to anything. We parted with a friendly handshake.

I rushed home to ponder what was afoot. Did he want me out of *The Sunday Times* and was he offering the Fox job as a lure to facilitate his objective? Or did he need me so badly at Fox that he was prepared to take me away from the paper? The latter would have been flattering but against all logic; and what I knew about Rupert's simmering resentment towards my increasingly independent status pointed strongly to the conclusion that his primary concern was to get me out of *The Sunday Times*. I reconsidered my options.

The Fox offer was unacceptable, at least on the terms he was suggesting. That left staying as editor, with the danger of our relationship becoming increasingly rancorous; or departing his employ on generous terms, now or after a decent interval in the near future. Early next morning I consulted a couple of friends whose advice I valued and

I knew could keep a secret. One warned me to volunteer to do nothing: 'Murdoch's the one pushing for a change; let him resolve it. Remember: if you volunteer to resign you are technically entitled to no pay-off.' My other confidant was blunter.

'It's a f——g insult,' he said angrily. 'You're one of the most successful editors in the world and all he can offer you is a reporter's job in America! Why should you walk the plank? Don't volunteer to go. If he wants you to go he'll have to do a lot better than that. Just say no thanks and put the ball firmly back in his court.' Steeled by such sensible, robust advice that was what I decided to do. But Rupert was already racing ahead.

At the previous night's dinner we had speculated who might succeed me if I went to Fox. He had mentioned some American right-wingers he was thinking of bringing over. My heart sank: I saw a decade's work about to be destroyed by one of Rupert's ideological soulmates who knew nothing of British nuances. I argued strongly that there were suitable internal candidates, notably John Witherow, the senior news executive, and Sue Douglas, the executive editor. I did not press the case for my deputy, Ivan Fallon, much as I valued him: I knew Rupert had already discounted him. Rupert was worried that John was 'not driven enough' and that Sue had 'no political touch'. But he agreed they would be on any shortlist. Now, only twelve hours after our dinner, he was on the phone asking me to arrange for them to have lunch with him the next day. 'You come too,' he added.

'No,' I replied firmly. 'They'll be inhibited by my presence. If you really want to assess them fairly I shouldn't be there. I'll ask Jeff Randall [the City editor] and Andy Grice [political correspondent] to join you as well. That'll give you cover as you get the measure of John and Sue.'

'Good idea,' he replied enthusiastically. 'Can you come

and see me beforehand so we can continue our discussions? Say 10 a.m. tomorrow, my office?' So much for taking my time, I thought: there was now no doubt in my mind Rupert wanted me out. My priority now was to do it on my terms, not his. I was well prepared when I took a seat in front of his desk that Friday morning.

'It's the most surprising offer I've had since you made me editor of *The Sunday Times*,' I began, 'and I thank you for it. I don't rule out going to America if the terms are right. Nor do I wish to overstay my welcome here. But being one of four reporters on a TV show is not enough.'

'OK,' he interrupted before I could give my reasons. 'How about managing editor and chief reporter?' There was no rancour in his voice, no sense he felt he was being pushed too far. In any case, the only time you can lean hard on Rupert is when he wants something from you. His offer over dinner had clearly been just his opening shot. But his latest one was still not enough.

I revealed to him that in 1987 the BBC had made me a very attractive offer: John Birt (then the deputy-director general) had wanted to rebuild its prestigious daily news programme, *Newsnight*, around me: I would be the editor in charge of the content of the programme *and* present it five nights a week. It was tempting but I felt there was unfinished business at *The Sunday Times*.

'If you're prepared to make me executive editor and chief reporter,' I said, 'then we might have a deal. I don't mind if there's also a senior producer to handle all the technicalities of television. But I would have to have editorial control of the content.'

'That's certainly worth considering,' he replied, 'but I'd need to clinch a deal with Roone Arledge first.' He explained that he was trying to woo Arledge, the man who had made the ABC network, historically America's third network, into the major force in news and sport. He wanted him to do the same for Fox and felt he could not make an appointment as senior as mine without his approval. I admired Arledge, almost a legend in American TV: but this was an unnecessary complication. (In the event Arledge resisted Rupert's charm offensive.)

'Look, Rupert,' I said, my voice rising for the first time, 'do you want me in America because you really need me for your new show? Or because you want a change at *The Sunday Times*?'

'I really need you,' he replied quietly. 'I'm not in any hurry to get rid of you,' he obfuscated. 'Maybe you could try it for six months, get it through the launch. We'll have an acting editor here. Then if it works, stay; if not, come back as editor.'

Now it was my turn to say 'It's worth considering', but it was time to be blunt: after all, it was my future.

'We both know that the chances of me returning to *The Sunday Times* if the show fails, or it doesn't work out for me, is less than fifty–fifty,' I said firmly. He made a face as if to disagree but I pressed on: 'If I had to walk away from Fox and *The Sunday Times* I'd want to agree the departure terms in advance – before I went to America.'

He saw no problems with that. 'I'm glad we're on the same wavelength,' he said, ushering me out of the office, 'and that we understand each other.' It had been a relaxed, friendly affair but my understanding was clearly less than his. I had agreed nothing; and we had not even talked terms yet.

I next saw Rupert when he came over to my office early Saturday evening, 16 April, only three nights after our dinner. I was reading an interview with Prince Charles by Roy Hattersley in the first edition of the next day's *Mail on*

Sunday, failing to find anything newsworthy in it for our later editions, when Rupert walked in.

'I've spoken to Les Hinton [a senior Fox executive],' he said, clearly in a mood to clinch a deal. 'There's no problem: you can be editor of the show. I suggest you're paid $500,000 for a six-month trial period, then move to a salary of $1.5 million a year if it all works out and you stay. I've decided to go with Witherow as acting editor. I want you in New York in a couple of weeks.'

'I'm sorry, Rupert,' I replied, angrily, 'I won't be railroaded into such a fundamental change in my career like this. The prospect of dropping everything that quickly depresses me. We haven't even agreed a contract.'

'Well,' he said, retreating, 'don't plan to start in New York until mid-May and you can come back and forth on Concorde after that – and take that holiday in the South of France with your godchildren you were talking about. But we've got to get started – I'm still aiming to launch in August while *60 Minutes* is still in summer repeats.'

He left agreeing to have breakfast with John Witherow on Monday to offer him the acting editorship and that we would meet that afternoon to agree my contract. I was being swept along by Rupert's desire to move fast: when Rupert has made up his mind everybody else is expected to fall in line without delay.

He was in such a rush that it was left to me to break the bad news to my deputy that he would not be my successor. I tracked him down in South Africa, where he was on assignment, ignorant of the stirring events back home. When I told him John Witherow was to be acting editor he was clearly very disappointed but I think he knew in his heart of hearts that Rupert regarded him as too gentle and Establishment-minded to be editor.

'It's an interesting choice,' he said very quietly. 'I don't object.'

I thought I owed it to him to give him some good advice. 'When I leave on 1 June for New York,' I said, 'the least likely option is that I will return to *The Sunday Times*. I think it would be a mistake for you to hang around as deputy to John. I advise you to insist from Rupert that since he's passed you over, he makes you a generous pay-off and gives you a good contract to carry on writing your column in the Business section. I'm arranging a similar parachute for myself.' I'm glad to say Ivan did just that – then Tony O'Reilly lured him away to run his extensive newspaper operations in South Africa.

I always took it as a compliment that so many other media moguls wanted my executives and writers: Conrad Black hired Max Hastings from me to edit the *Daily Telegraph*; Roy Greenslade became editor of the *Daily Mirror* (until he fell out with Bob Maxwell); Andrew Jaspan edited the *Scotland on Sunday*, *The Scotsman* and the *Observer*; the *Sunday Express* had first Robin Morgan and now Sue Douglas; and Ian Jack was followed by Peter Wilby as editor of the *Independent on Sunday* – though I'm not sure they would wish to be regarded as part of the 'Neil Diaspora'!

Rupert had asked me to dine with him and his wife, Anna, that Saturday night, requesting me to select a restaurant they would not normally go to. It was all part of the wooing process. I chose Daphne's, where the owner and staff knew me and would give good service.

Over dinner he lamented being in Los Angeles and wished he could spend more time in New York, 'the capital of the world'. He talked about moving back. Anna did not want to know: she had settled into their beautiful Spanish-style house overlooking Beverly Hills and hated the grime and crime of New York. For the first time ever, they began to argue in front of me. 'You're a perpetual motion machine,' she said to Rupert. 'I've had enough of keeping pace with you. I'm staying in LA.'

Their exchange confirmed what I had already heard: Rupert had become increasingly unpredictable, even whimsical, moving people about for no very good reason ('spinning wheels' was how one executive put it), except to satisfy his latest wheeze. He was even doing it to himself. Now over sixty, with intimations of mortality but still so much to do, he had become even more of a man in a hurry. He was moving senior executives around like pieces on a chessboard to suit whatever ephemeral purpose obsessed him at that particular moment; regardless of the disruption in their lives they were expected to fit in, even if fundamental decisions risked being reversed only weeks after they were taken. I was the latest victim: I was only prepared to go along provided I got everything I wanted.

There are only two times when Rupert is generous to those who work for him: one is when he wants you, the other is when he wants rid of you. Since I was in both positions at once in the spring of 1994 I decided to exploit the situation to the full. After that Saturday dinner, I called a council of war among a small group of confidants to draft my demands for going to America. We met in Onslow Gardens on Sunday morning and agreed I should hold out for a substantial severance payment should things not work out at Fox and I did not wish to return to *The Sunday Times*. I also wanted a column in the paper – it would form a base for a new freelance life.

I was right about Rupert's time-sensitive generosity. When we met late on Monday morning he agreed to everything without bargaining, which only underlined how anxious he was for a new editor. Maybe I should have demanded more. After all, Andrew Knight, after a rather less arduous time with Conrad Black and then Rupert Murdoch, had managed to accumulate a staggering £33 million for his efforts (£26 million of it in News Corporation shares), which he had placed in a trust, before departing Rupert's employ. A lot of it had come from share options with Black but Rupert had been so anxious to woo him that he had agreed to underwrite his arrangements with Black – and then add some incentives of his own. As I said: the time to get what you want from Rupert is when he wants you. Perhaps I undersold myself.

But I was content with my parachute, which gave me a sense of security in what were about to become uncertain times. Under my original contract I was entitled to nothing if I walked away from *The Sunday Times*; I only qualified for a severance payment if Rupert wanted rid of me. Now I could trigger a severance package worth almost £1 million. Since *The Sunday Times* was making £1 million a week I did not consider it an unreasonable severance amount for over a decade's work.

I tried one more time to make sure the American part of the deal was not just a charade to get me out of *The Sunday Times* without having to admit it.

'The parachute is all I really want, Rupert,' I said. 'You've agreed to a substantial payment and a column. I'm happy to walk away from *The Sunday Times* now with absolutely no hard feelings on my part whatsoever: I'm happy to part publicly and privately on the best of terms. There is no need to go through with America if it's just a ruse to get me out of the paper.'

'Andrew,' he said, fixing me with his gaze, 'I *need* you in New York. I hope we'll do great things together in America.'

*

TO THIS DAY I STILL DO not know if Rupert meant it. I am in no doubt that he wanted me out of *The Sunday Times* and that it was our Malaysian coverage that had finally brought matters to a head. But the exit door he was indicating was one I was inclined to go through anyway. Whether the American venture was just a ruse or a lure to facilitate the smooth departure of a high-profile editor I do not know. I am not even sure if Rupert knew at the time either.

Rupert has always been prepared to pay a lot to keep his options open. He had had enough of me at *The Sunday Times* but he had yet to decide if he was finished with me altogether. Moving me to America dispensed with an immediate cause of aggravation for him and placed me in alien territory where I had no power base and could be more easily controlled. If the American TV venture worked out well, it would be on his terms; if not, then he would deal with my future come the time. For the moment he had achieved his priority: he had rid himself of his troublesome editor. That was worth a great deal to him.

It was only later that I discovered what had really happened over Malaysia, though I suspected something like it at the time. It was more than just the culmination of a series of *Sunday Times* controversies of which he had finally tired. He had seen our row with Malaysia as a potentially disastrous threat to his Far East business interests. Though Mahathir had never allowed Star TV to be viewed in Malaysia (he saw it as too Western), Rupert regarded this prosperous, fast-growing tiger economy as an ideal target market from which, thanks to *The Sunday Times*, he looked like being excluded for the foreseeable future. There was also the danger that *The Sunday Times* might turn its investigative attentions to other countries, such as India or China, which were crucial to Star's success but where corruption was also rife: he gulped when I told him after the Malaysia story broke that I was off to Delhi to interview the Indian Prime Minister. Though no harm to Rupert came from that particular trip,

Malaysia was a warning of potentially far greater damage to come. Rupert had also come under direct pressure from a number of big business interests in Britain who contacted him personally demanding he do something about me.

Events were to vindicate our Malaysian coverage, though never in Rupert's eyes. The courts in London ruled that the government had acted improperly in using the overseas aid budget to fund the Pergau dam project. Wimpey never denied the accuracy of our story: the senior executive involved in trying to secure the deal effectively confirmed it: 'When you have people on the ground in Malaysia trying to win a contract,' he explained elliptically, 'you have to play ball with them to a certain stage to try to keep in the race. If you understand what I'm saying then you will understand why I did what I did at the time.'

The Malaysian government dropped its ban on British companies soon after it realized it was doing Malaysia's international reputation as a reliable business more damage than it was British industry. Indeed, during the ban for the first time our balance of trade with Malaysia moved into surplus instead of the usual deficits: the *Guardian* even named me Britain's new 'secret weapon' in the country's export drive! But the whole episode had frightened Rupert: he wanted to placate Mahathir and send a signal to the rest of Asia that *The Sunday Times* was not a loose cannon that would soon be exposing business practices they would rather keep hidden. Murdoch and Mahathir came to an understanding.

In the autumn of 1995 a British minister dined with our High Commissioner while on a trade mission to Kuala Lumpur. He asked our man in KL if there was still any residual animosity to British business since the ban provoked by *The Sunday Times*. 'Not since Murdoch fixed it with Mahathir,' replied the High Commissioner. 'The

Malaysian Prime Minister made it clear that Murdoch would never do business in his country as long as Andrew Neil was editor of *The Sunday Times*,' he continued. Neil had to go: Murdoch obliged.

Another British minister was told the same by Mahathir himself. The Malaysian Prime Minister boasted that he had demanded my head on a plate from Murdoch, who had contacted Mahathir to explain that he had a 'rogue editor' on his hands but that the matter was being 'sorted out'. I had been seconded to Fox TV in America and would not be returning to *The Sunday Times*. Later in 1994 Rupert met Mahathir in KL to patch matters up. The combination of his charm and my departure clearly worked: at News Corporation's grand bash for senior executives on Hayman Island, Australia, in the summer of 1995 (the one addressed by Tony Blair) the deputy prime minister of Malaysia appeared as Rupert's guest of honour.

As I prepared to depart for America in the summer of 1994 I was unaware of any deals between Murdoch and Mahathir. But I knew that the story had struck a bitter note with him and brought long-simmering matters concerning my editorship to a head. Though we both publicly maintained that it was only a secondment to New York and that I still had the option to return to *The Sunday Times* after six months, we both knew that was a fiction. It was the last thing Rupert wanted; and it no longer interested me either. As I left for America there was no doubt in my mind that, regardless of events in New York, I was leaving *The Sunday Times* for good.

Before departing I spent a last weekend in my house in France, surrounded by close friends and their children. I rose at 5 a.m. on 1 June and crept out of the house before anybody was awake to catch the first plane from Nice airport to Paris, in plenty of time for the Concorde to New York and my new American TV career. I left with a heavy heart, not just because of who and what I was leaving behind but because of apprehension at the unknown trials and tribulations that might lie ahead. I was sure Rupert's latest scheme for me would be fraught with difficulty and that my chances of success were slim. I still wondered if I was doing the right thing, whether it would not have been best just to walk away altogether, without going through a potential charade in America. But I would give it my best shot: at the very least it was a convenient way out of *The Sunday Times* for us both. I would regard my American TV adventure as a rite of passage to secure a lucrative transition to a post-Murdoch life. I kept my spirits up by remembering that, whatever happened in the next six months, freedom and financial independence would be the prize at the end of it all.

POSTSCRIPT

Postcard from Gotham

I ARRIVED IN NEW YORK to discover that somebody already had my new job – and Rupert had not quite mustered the courage to tell him that I was coming to take over. David Corvo had been executive producer of *Front Page*, Fox TV's previous attempt at a news magazine show, a sort of yuppie *60 Minutes* which had been produced in Los Angeles and cancelled after a season of being ignored by critics and viewers alike. Corvo had returned to New York expecting to be the boss of the new, more grown-up show Rupert was now supposed to be determined to launch.

Rupert had hinted to me in London that there might be a 'two popes' situation waiting for me in New York, though he had promised to resolve it before I got there: in fact, he had told Corvo (or anybody else at Fox for that matter) next to nothing about the purpose of my secondment – another example of his desire to avoid tough conversations when he can, since he knew his plans for me would be opposed by most of those at Fox.

Corvo and I lunched with Rupert in his private dining room on the day I arrived. We were joined by Judith Regan, whom Rupert had hired from Simon & Schuster with the promise of having her own book label within his HarperCollins empire and of being a television star for his Fox TV network: he had only really wanted her publishing skills but lured her away with the prospect of a TV career.

A small, tidy woman in her thirties, Regan had impressed Rupert with her mix of intelligence and tabloid instincts. She was briefly to be one of Rupert's flavours of the month because she had just made a fortune for Simon & Schuster by publishing a book by Howard Stern, one of America's controversial radio 'shock jocks', and another by Rush Limbaugh, the radio host who was a darling of the Republican Right. She was smart and original but she had no background in serious journalism, no experience in front of camera and possessed a somewhat uncertain judgement.

The four of us brainstormed about the kind of show we should produce, with Regan pleasing Rupert with her tabloid attitudes. I was beginning to feel a little depressed about how down-market this show was going to be and wondering what I was doing there when Corvo asked a crucial question: 'Who's going to anchor this show?'

'You're looking at them,' replied Rupert, nodding his head at Regan and me.

'Ah aah,' was all Corvo could muster. But you could see what he was thinking: 'An unknown Brit with a non-American accent and an unknown American with no television experience. The man must be out of his mind.'

Corvo, a small, dark Italian-American with a quiet, thoughtful air, was the latest TV executive Rupert had hired from an established network to give Fox a credible news presence. None ever got anywhere because Rupert never gave them enough backing, changed his plans or changed his mind about them. Corvo was to be no different: always uncomfortable with the way Fox's direction was dictated by Rupert's latest unpredictable whim, he eventually returned to the more stable corporate structure of a traditional American network. Meanwhile, Rupert had thrown us together: I decided to make the best of it; after all Corvo had a far longer track record in American TV news than me.

After lunch we wandered round our new offices on the second floor of News Corporation's US headquarters on Sixth Avenue in midtown Manhattan, wires hanging from the roof and builders drilling and hammering everywhere. It reminded me of the early days at Sky.

'I know we've both been asked to do the same job,' I began. 'It's the sort of infuriating thing Rupert does. So let's divide it between us. You concentrate on the television side, I'll concentrate on the journalism. We'll have offices the same size beside each other, with a connecting door which will always be open, and we must be careful not to let anybody divide us. You remain executive producer, I'll be executive editor, but the staff must see us as equal: we'll decide things together and if there is a major disagreement we'll refer it to Rupert to resolve.'

That was pretty much the way it was in the crazy months ahead. I resented the cavalier way that Rupert had thrown us together but I was in alien territory, uncertain about the prospects for the venture on which I had embarked and thought it wise to avoid unnecessary conflict: it seemed sensible to sue for peace with my new partner. In the event, Corvo and I never fell out on anything important, even as we were buffeted around by Rupert's constant changes of mind.

Time was not on our side: Rupert, as usual, wanted everything done yesterday. He had originally urged me to get the show ready for a launch in August, while *60 Minutes* was still showing summer repeats. It was a ludicrous proposition, an impossibility. During brunch on my first Sunday in New York I told him that we had neither the staff nor the stories in preparation to be ready to air in only two months: even our production facilities were still being built.

He agreed instead to a late September launch, when Fox would be running its football games and we hoped to inherit the audience. Then he suggested in the first of a series of changes of mind, that, instead of following the football, the show should begin with a weekday time slot then move up against *60 Minutes* on a Sunday night when it had found its feet. Since he hinted that we might follow *Melrose Place*, one of Fox's highest-rated shows, I had no great objections, though the ease with which supposedly firm plans were discarded unnerved me. His great scheme for a Sunday night news show was already unravelling.

Worse was to come: at our next meeting he began to think aloud about the wisdom of doing a weekly magazine at all, arguing that a late-night daily news show might be more distinctive. The conversation ended with the matter unresolved. I wandered back to my flat feeling depressed. There was obviously no settled plan in his mind, despite his certainties in London. I had come to New York well aware it would be a high-risk venture: I began to wonder if I had been brought over on a false prospectus and if I had made a mistake in bothering with the American secondment at all. I consoled myself with the money I was earning, which would help ensure my future financial independence. But feeling fulfilled in my work was as important to me as money and that was not going to be easy in the glitzy, superficial world of American network news, especially not with a boss who could not make up his mind what he wanted.

In contrast with Rupert's confusion, I had a clear concept of the kind of weekly news magazine I wanted to run. Despite the huge number of competing television news services in America, there is a depressing monotone to most of the output. The newscasts and magazine shows broadcast by the three main networks (CBS, NBC and ABC) are all produced and presented by journalists who generally share the same liberal-left attitudes and agenda of the East Coast media establishment. Since that same outlook and agenda also dominates the leading big-city newspapers (the *New*

York Times, *Washington Post* and *Los Angeles Times*) and the main weekly news magazines (*Time* and *Newsweek*) it means that news in America, despite the variety of outlets, is something of a one-party state.

The *Independent* newspaper had wondered as I left London what I would do without an Establishment to lock horns with, for 'there is no Establishment in America'. It was wrong: there is a media establishment in America and I wanted the Fox news magazine to run counter to it, challenging its assumptions and values with stories and issues from which it shied away. American radio was then in the process of being revolutionized by several talk-show hosts of a distinctly conservative bent who ran counter to the liberal values of most American broadcasters and were winning huge ratings, since they were more in tune with most Americans' views. I did not want to produce a 'right-wing' news magazine but I wanted one that was different and distinctive from the many news magazines already on air – one that was not automatically hostile to the new ideas that were sweeping America from the right of the political spectrum.

I also wanted the Fox news magazine to be on top of important breaking news. Many of the current shows seemed to exist in their own world, pursuing often trivial stories without regard to what was making the headlines. Along with Corvo, I devised a four-item format: we would begin with an in-depth look at the news story of the week; then take an unconventional look at a major issue; follow that with an investigative report that would break new ground; and finish with a celebrity profile. It was not an inflexible format: I reserved the right to do only two subjects or even devote the whole hour to a single subject if it was strong enough. But it was a template which helped guide the sort of stories we should be looking to deliver each week. We began with the working title *On Assignment* but that sounded too worthy, like something you'd expect on America's small audience, non-commercial Public Broadcasting System. We eventually settled for *Full Disclosure*.

I outlined my plans to a mass meeting of my new staff, many of whom had just arrived from Los Angeles, not a city renowned for taking news seriously. They were happy enough with the format but wary of my desire to be outside the liberal-left consensus to which most of them belonged. 'I want to do news stories that cause controversy,' I explained, 'that challenge the assumptions of the other networks, that tackle subjects they would not dare, that are not afraid to be regarded as politically incorrect. We'll know we're succeeding,' I added with a smile, 'if there are a number of very powerful interests and lobbies mounting picket lines and demonstrations against us out on Sixth Avenue.'

They were a pleasant enough bunch of young folk – most had come from the failed *Front Page* show – but they lacked the journalistic ability or experience to do what I was asking. They seemed a bit perplexed, even dumbfounded. The only decent question came from one young chap: if demonstrators are going to be throwing bricks at us, he asked, would it not be safer to be on a higher floor? Good point, I said, we'll measure our progress by the speed with which we're moved from the second to the fiftieth floor. Such British humour probably confused them even more. I finished the meeting by asking for story ideas.

It was a big mistake: they came flooding in afterwards but most were unusable, more like worthy college essays than stories fit to broadcast. I was attempting a grown-up show with a team still wet behind the ears. Corvo and I agreed that we would have to fire many of them and start hiring a more experienced crew. We began to lay off the weakest and employ journalists with more experience; but it was hard to find people of quality who were enthusiastic about developing a distinctive agenda – or, because of previous false starts, who trusted Fox's commitment to news. I yearned for journalists with the flair and experience of the people I had left behind at *The Sunday Times*.

Corvo had good contacts among New York broadcast journalists and we lured several over to Fox with promises that this was to be a proper, grown-up news show. It helped that I had been editor of *The Sunday Times*: that was seen as evidence of serious intent. But it was a laborious process: in American broadcast journalism almost everybody has an agent – even production assistants – and we had to negotiate through them. American broadcasters cannot quite make up their minds if they are serious journalists or showbiz personalities.

A major addition to the team was Emily Rooney, a tough, no-nonsense journalist (and daughter of Andy Rooney of *60 Minutes* fame) who joined us from ABC News. She immediately saw what I was trying to do and started using the word 'contrarian' to describe it, which seemed to be less controversial with the staff than 'politically incorrect'. Some bright young sparks from the other networks also took a risk and joined our venture. As the summer progressed I felt we had the beginnings of a team that could deliver.

It was a strange time for me. I was happy to be back in America, where I had a strong social support system of old friends – and soon made plenty of new ones. It was fun to spend long weekends again in the Hamptons or fly out to Los Angeles to watch the World Cup final. I was relieved to be free of the responsibilities of *The Sunday Times* which, though I was nominally still editor, I left almost entirely to the acting editor. I enjoyed being back on the road again as a journalist, flying off to Moscow to tape a piece on the Russian mafia (we even went along with some special forces on a raid), opening a money-laundering bank account in Antigua as part of a story on drugs and going to the University of Michigan to interview a leading dissident professor on Aids.

I also learned a lot about American television and the news magazine format, which barely exists on British television, where news programmes tend to be issue-driven. As a result, British current affairs programmes are made in a way that gives them limited appeal. The more populist American broadcasters are weak on issues – they think viewers don't have the attention span or interest to follow anything in depth – but they are consummate story-tellers and know how to deal with issues through personalities and story-telling. These are not skills to be sneered at – indeed British television could learn from them – for it means you can bring important matters before a massive audience, instead of just a small elite, as is too often the case in Britain. CBS's *60 Minutes* is regularly in the top ten rated shows – there are years when it has been the country's top-rated show – and British television has nothing to rival it among its most-watched shows, which are nearly all soaps. Perhaps the difference reflects our contrasting social systems: British broadcasters still regard issues as a matter for the elite to decide; American broadcasters want to reach the widest audience and don't mind being populist.

My stint in New York was instructive and gave me a better understanding of television on both sides of the Atlantic. But it was also an unsatisfying time, however carefree and enjoyable. All my apprehensions that I was on an essentially futile exercise were being confirmed as the weeks passed. Every time I tried to pin Rupert down for a specific launch date for *Full Disclosure*, he either obfuscated or took a decision which was changed twenty-four hours later. I felt I was going through the motions of preparing a news show rather than fulfilling a concrete plan. I knew there were plenty of people in Fox who had no interest in news and doing their best to sideline the whole venture. I was never sure if the show would launch and, even if it did, if Fox was committed to making it a success. Our only ally seemed to be Rupert – and given his uncertainties I was not even sure we could count on him. Les Hinton, then one of Rupert's senior Fox executives, now the man who looks after Wapping for him, would regularly come to my office and wonder why we were not getting the green light. But even he could not get a decision out of Rupert.

All American television networks are riven by something close to civil war between their news and entertainment divisions: they are both competing for the same scarce resource – airtime, especially prime time – and the conflict is sharpened by the fact that news is based in New York, entertainment in Los Angeles, two cities with very different agendas and priorities. In the traditional networks it tends to be a war of equals, for the news divisions of ABC, NBC and CBS are massive fiefdoms in their own right and they bring their networks prestige, a public face through their presenters and good ratings.

But in Fox there was no news division: we were all there was and we were no match for the mighty entertainment division, which had been responsible for Fox's success, unless we could count on Rupert. He was our atomic bomb: with him on our side we could overcome the resistance of the vastly more powerful entertainment bosses; without him we were lost. It was the arrival of a new president of the Fox network called John Matoian that disarmed us of our only weapon. He was to talk Rupert out of doing a news magazine, or any other kind of network news, for that matter. With his appointment, our defeat was only a matter of time.

There was another factor at work. Rupert has a less certain touch with television programming than he does with newspapers. He lacks the confidence to bet on his hunches or to take the risks in television he would think nothing of in newspapers. He believes, with good reason, his instincts are infallible when it comes to print, but in television he is more inclined to defer to whatever seasoned executives are currently in favour. He had taken a huge risk in appointing me editor of *The Sunday Times* in 1983, at the tender, inexperienced age of thirty-four; but it was a newspaper and he trusted his instincts. He was taking at least as big a risk asking me to launch a prime-time American news magazine; but it was television and he could be more easily talked out of his gut feeling.

Neither of my appointments would ever have been made in a traditional corporation, only one run by the individual hunches and flair of Rupert Murdoch. But, strangely, Rupert's remit did not run at Fox as fully as it did through the rest of his company. It was a matter of course that what Rupert wanted to happen anywhere in his global empire usually did happen; that was the Sun King's right. But not at Fox: it seemed to resist his determination, even after he moved to LA, to be more hands on. I always got the impression that the Fox people worked for the Hollywood entertainment industry rather than for Rupert. They were creative folk who could easily find other lucrative employment in the industry should Rupert ride them too hard – and he could not afford to lose too many. Several times Rupert expressed his frustration to me at not being able to get a grip on Fox. He blamed Barry Diller, who had run Fox and kept Rupert at a distance in the early days, for building a 'state within a state'. But Barry was long gone and still Rupert was not master in the house that Barry built. It was another reason he was so easily thwarted in his desire to have a news magazine.

The rest of the American media, however, was fascinated by what we were up to. Who was this Brit who had come over to show the Americans how to do television news? And had Murdoch at last begun the process of building a network news division for Fox? It seemed sensible to use this interest to raise Fox's news profile (which until now had been invisible), impress journalists we wanted to hire with the seriousness of our intent and gain useful pre-launch publicity for *Full Disclosure*.

I gave a long interview to Howard Kurtz, the *Washington Post*'s highly respected media commentator; it resulted in a largely positive piece which led the paper's well-read Style section. The *Full Disclosure* staff were delighted and morale rose: the fact that the mighty *Washington Post* was treating their efforts seriously and prominently made them feel good – and raised my stock in their eyes. But Rupert was furious.

'Why can't you stay away from the press?' he moaned.

'I thought it was good publicity,' I replied. 'It's the first time Fox News has been treated seriously.' He did not answer but I sensed immediately what the problem was: he had hated the publicity and controversy I had generated back in Britain; now he feared the same monster had arrived to haunt him in his own backyard.

'You've let everybody at Fox know that one of our shows will fail!' he complained. It took me a minute to work out what he was talking about. Then it dawned: I had explained to the *Post* that we would not be ready in time for the launch of the autumn schedules but that we would be ready to replace whatever was faltering in the ratings by mid-season.

'You'll be lucky if only one show fails,' I countered curtly. In the voracious, ratings-obsessed world of American TV, shows were always falling off the schedules. His complaint was a pathetic attempt to mask what was really bugging him and I was in no mood to succumb to it. 'I've got a team to motivate,' I continued. 'There have been plenty of snide bits in the trade press speculating that the show won't run at all. The *Post* piece has lifted everybody up. They now feel they're being led by somebody other journalists take seriously – and that Fox might actually deliver for them.' I surprised myself by my robust response: I suspect the financial parachute I had negotiated back in London made me bolder. But Rupert was back on the phone a few days later.

'I hear you've allowed the *New Yorker* into the offices,' he said angrily. I explained how Tina Brown, who had just become editor of the magazine, had asked for a reporter to be a fly-on-the-wall while we developed the show, with the aim of running a major piece on the eve of its launch. Everybody had been impressed that a publication as prestigious as the *New Yorker* was taking Fox's efforts so seriously.

'Don't you realize Tina hates us?' he thundered. 'They all hate us – Tina, Harry [Evans, Tina's husband and former *Sunday Times* editor], all of them.' I didn't quite have the guts to tell him that Tina and Harry might hate him, but they didn't hate me. I argued instead that even if the eventual piece was hostile, it would still be good free publicity. 'It's your funeral,' he sulked, then rang off. A year later Rupert invited a *New Yorker* writer to be a fly-on-the-wall as he went about his business for a major profile of himself.

Without a definite launch date, the staff were all uneasy – and operating in something of a vacuum. But the story list was hardening up and our contrarian look at issues was coming along nicely: stories were being shot claiming that many sexual harassment cases were bogus (that would outrage the feminist lobby) and costing business unnecessary billions; questioning the effectiveness on the war on drugs and raising the issue of liberalization; revealing that there was effectively no heterosexual Aids in America; attacking black groups for not allowing black orphans to be adopted by white parents; and arguing that the American Civil Liberties Union had gone from defending the underdog to protecting the dangerous.

We had several strong investigations underway too and Judith Regan was building up a reasonable portfolio of celebrity profiles. But we still had no launch date – or clear guidance from Rupert on the format he wanted. I was happy to share the studio presentation with the other reporters introducing their own stories, as happened on *60 Minutes*, and Rupert would probably have preferred that too, since it reduced my role. But Corvo and Rooney were adamant that the reporters were not strong enough to have a studio presence: the show had to be co-hosted by Neil and Regan, as Rupert had originally suggested.

We recorded the pilot on 1 and 2 September. The set looked good, the opening titles strong, the direction excellent and the stories perfectly respectable for a pilot: one by me on drug-money laundering, the attack on the ACLU, a murder story with a message and a profile by Regan. We would never have wanted to broadcast this pilot but some of its contents could have been reworked for broadcast and it gave an indication of what we were capable of. As we flew to the West Coast to show it to Rupert, we also hoped it would concentrate minds at Fox.

*

RUPERT VIEWED THE PILOT in his office in Los Angeles on 23 September 1994, making notes as he watched. We waited anxiously for his verdict as the closing credits rolled.

'Congratulations,' he said, 'this show is further along than any other similar show I've seen at this stage. I like the stories – of course, they'll be better by the time you're ready to broadcast, and the reporters still need to hone their storytelling skills.'

'What did you think of Judith?' asked David, who had always been against her co-anchoring the show.

'I agree she's not up to it,' said Rupert. 'We'll have to find an alternative. She can continue as a reporter.' Then he turned to me: 'But I've got no problem with you or the British accent. You could even anchor the show yourself until we find a Judith replacement.' It seemed a strong endorsement of my role as executive editor and lead presenter. But he then added a crucial caveat.

'When this show goes out I don't want people to divide for and against Andrew Neil,' he said, averting his eyes from me. 'I don't want you doing a story then spending five days defending it, with you justifying what you've done in a great controversy. Just do the stories and move on. Hire a publicist to say, "We stand by our story" – and nothing else. You [his eyes finally alighted on me again] don't get involved.'

'Why not?' piped up a perplexed Emily Rooney. 'If we can generate that sort of controversy shouldn't we try to milk it for all it's worth?'

'Let's just leave it to the publicist,' he growled. Emily looked at me and shrugged her shoulders in disbelief. I explained the problem later.

'You should be spending sixty to seventy per cent of your time,' he said, turning to me again, 'doing your job as executive editor and only about thirty per cent being bothered with being on-air.'

'That's the way it's working out,' I assured him, seeing no point in pursuing an old argument in front of everybody else.

'There's too much of the reporters in the pieces,' he continued, 'and not enough story-telling.' I think he had my role in the drug story particularly in mind. I explained that our reporters did not have strong story-telling skills: either we had to give them time to develop these, or replace them with reporters who had – and there were few top-notch ones prepared to come over to Fox. One of the strengths of *60 Minutes*, I argued, was that the viewers saw reporters they trusted going in to bat for them. We had to build up the same trust and respect for our reporters.

'We must be careful not to be seen to be too conservative or controversial,' he said, changing tack. 'We're aiming for respectability here, not forever rocking the boat. We have to behave like a proper network.' It was a revealing remark: every time I had sent Rupert an updated story list, he would make it clear he was less keen on controversy in America than he had been in London. He did not like being an outsider in America: he wanted to be in the club. He loved collecting awards at various media and charity dinners in New York and Los Angles. Rupert had at last found an establishment he wanted to join.

'Can you be ready to get on-air by mid-October?' he asked, still showing every enthusiasm about the pilot despite his fears about me becoming a celebrity in America. 'Because if you can't you'll run into the November sweeps [the period when the networks run their most popular shows to boost their ratings and set their advertising rates as high as possible for the year ahead] and have to wait until December.'

'That would be too close to Christmas,' I replied. 'We can be ready to air by mid-October. David [Corvo] and I will programme the first six shows and send you a schedule.'

'Great. Let's shoot for mid-October then – and let's go up against *60 Minutes*.' Now he was almost rushing us on air and there seemed to be genuine enthusiasm in his voice. He was even back to the original Sunday night spot following the football. 'Thank you *very* much for all your efforts,' he said as we left the office. 'I appreciate all the hard work you've put in.'

David and Emily were cockahoop as we walked out in the

sunny Fox lot. But for some reason I still felt uncertain about the show's prospects and counselled caution: 'Rupert has already changed his mind several times,' I warned. 'He could do so again. We don't yet have a definite air date, the time slot could shift again – and there are plenty of powerful folk in here who don't want this show to happen at all.'

'So what should we do?' asked Emily.

'Return to New York and tell everybody we've been told to prepare for a mid-October launch. What else can we do?'

I returned to New York to programme the first six shows, working on the basis of a 23 October launch. I was pleasantly surprised by the quality of the stories we could offer and knew it would improve dramatically once we were on air. But events were already moving against us in the Fox hierarchy.

Rupert had just fired Lucy Salhany as president of the Fox network. The woman whom a year ago he had described as 'the best female executive in American television' was already history. This was a body blow to our efforts. Not that she had been an ally. Like nearly all entertainment people in LA she had no interest in television news: throughout *Front Page*'s run she had allocated it just one network promotion spot, which was a subtle way of killing it.

But the man who replaced her was even less interested in news: John Matoian had been a senior executive in the CBS entertainment division, where he had developed the successful 'movie of the week' slot. Rupert had poached him to breathe new life into Fox's flagging entertainment programming. He had no interest in journalism and the last thing he wanted screwing up his schedules was a news magazine. The timing of his arrival could not have been worse for us: since he was the new kid on the block that Rupert had lured at great expense and wanted to keep, he felt he had to defer to him, in the exaggerated way he had once done to Andrew Knight.

Rupert has a habit of allowing new recruits to overrule his own wishes, for a while: it makes them think they will have real power at News Corporation and helps them feel at home. Matoian, who by 1996 was measured to be no longer a Murdoch flavour of the month, used his honeymoon with Rupert to kill off any network news ambitions for Fox.

The undermining of *Full Disclosure* began almost the moment Rupert gave us our marching orders to prepare for an October launch. Matoian and his men bombarded him with two messages: a news magazine would rate badly on Fox, especially one in which I was the main on-air presence. It reinforced Rupert's preference for me to have no on-screen role at all so that I would have none of the public visibility that so annoyed him in London. The man who only a few days before was saying I could anchor the show on my own was now agreeing privately with his Fox executives that my role should be confined to executive editor. His problem was that he feared I would quit when he told me that. His executives' problem was that they had achieved only half their objective: they had turned him against me – now they wanted to turn him against the whole idea of a news magazine.

They had already talked him out of October. On 29 September, only six days after he had given me the go-ahead for a mid-October launch, Rupert called me in New York to say that perhaps it was a mistake to rush on-air, that mid-October was maybe a bit ambitious, that December might be more sensible.

'I've geared everybody up for 23 October, Rupert,' I said, exasperated. 'They're rushing off all over the place to complete stories. Are you telling me to stand them down?'

'No, no,' said Rupert, 'just take a bit longer to get it right. Build up your story bank and let me see it again.'

'It's a bit strange to launch a news show just a few weeks before Christmas, Rupert,' I said. 'Surely we'll have to come off air right away for holiday specials.'

'No, that won't matter,' he assured me. 'But we could always postpone the launch to January. Anyway, just keep everybody at it.'

I put the phone down, deeply depressed, my lack of euphoria the week before amply vindicated. The feeling of foreboding that I had felt about this project ever since I had arrived in New York looked like being justified. It's all beginning to unravel, I thought. I made a couple of calls to find out what was really going on.

I discovered that Rupert was saying I'd make 'a brilliant executive editor, but he's too combative for American TV'. So why did he bring me over in the first place? My supposed aggressive instincts were hardly news to him. But I also learned Rupert was fighting a rearguard action to save the very concept of a Fox news magazine. I headed to London for a long weekend. It was then I took the decision to quit the Murdoch empire and begin mapping out a new freelance career. I had reached a position where I no longer wanted my work to be determined by one man and his latest whim. I wanted to take control of my own life again.

On my return to New York I took David Corvo out to lunch to explain my plan of action. I told him the show would not launch on 23 October; and that I had doubts that it would ever happen. I told him I intended to tell Rupert that, because of concern about my on-air acceptability to an American audience, I did not wish to play any role as co-anchor or co-host. But I was not prepared to stay only as executive editor. If it was still Fox's intention to proceed with

Full Disclosure I would help launch it, build up the story bank then depart at Christmas.

Corvo was distraught. 'Even if you launch the show just as executive editor,' he said, 'that still leaves the question of who's going to anchor the show. We only have a month to find a replacement – we'll never get a name in that time. And what do we do with all the stories on which you're the reporter?'

'I don't know, David, and I'm not sure I care any more. They are not problems of my making.'

Next day I flew to Tokyo to interview the daughter of a Japanese gangster who we believed was in cahoots with Donald Trump to take control of the Empire State Building. Since the gangster was in jail for failing to meet fire-safety requirements in a Tokyo hotel that went up in flames and killed over thirty people, I felt there would be a certain interest in his family owning one of America's most famous landmarks. I had no idea if the story would ever be broadcast and I had stopped caring: I had never been to Tokyo and that was good enough reason for going (it also meant I could visit my godson in Hong Kong).

I was still going through the motions of preparing items for *Full Disclosure* because it was proving impossible to pin Rupert down even for a meeting, much less a decision. I flew to Austin, Texas to interview people for a story on the Endangered Species Act. It had been passed twenty years ago and had been hailed as a great environmental measure that had saved thousands of animals in danger of extinction. We were going to show that at a cost of billions of dollars it had actually saved none – but was a serious infringement of individual property rights.

I interviewed a number of irate Texans complaining about land that had become worthless because of the Act. One woman took me to a plot that she had been forbidden to develop because the federal government had designated it as the sort of land that certain birds might use as a habitat on their way south. None of the said birds had ever been seen on the land; but the fact they *might* land there one day was enough for the federal government to blight it. It was the sort of contrarian story that no network news magazine had attempted at that time and was certain to outrage America's powerful environment lobby groups.

But back in New York matters were moving to a resolution of sorts. Les Hinton took me to La Caravelle, a fancy midtown restaurant, for lunch on 25 October: he was clearly on an errand from Rupert. He gently explained that John Matoian was dead set against doing any kind of network news magazine, but he was particularly against doing one with 'the existing talent' – American broadcastspeak for Neil and Regan.

'I can understand that,' I replied. 'No traditional American TV executive is going to choose me to do one of their news magazines. It was a typical off-the-wall Rupert decision: it could have been a stroke of genius or a disaster. But it was his decision – and like most of Rupert's gut instincts the moment you subject it to the usual criteria of what works on American TV then it doesn't stand scrutiny. But we've always known that.'

'Rupert's worried that if he asks you just to be executive editor, with no on-air role, then you'll quit,' said Les. I said nothing: I liked Les and I knew he was trying to resolve the issue but I saw no reason why I should show my hand to him by revealing that I had already decided to quit. This was a conversation I should be having direct with Rupert.

'Rupert needs to make up his mind what kind of show he wants and what he wants me to do in it,' I eventually replied. 'Then he can make me an offer and I'll be able to tell him if I accept it or not.'

'Rupert fears the whole momentum will go out of Fox News and the team will split up if you go,' added Les.

'Then he should make me a very good offer,' I replied coyly.

Les then indicated that Rupert was increasingly attracted to a late-night daily news show. I said nothing: our talk was friendly enough but I was determined not to show my hand to Les.

Then it was the turn of David Evans, one of Rupert's reliable Aussies. I was still in the office at 7.45 p.m. when he called me from Los Angeles. He had just spoken to Rupert.

'We didn't come to any conclusions,' he said. There's a surprise, I thought. 'But we could be looking at a five nights a week show. We've been looking at the ratings for news magazines and you'd have to say that sentiment was turning against that sort of format.'

In fact, though there was a glut of news magazines and some would certainly fall by the wayside it was still a remarkably resilient format. But I could see the way the wind was blowing and saw no reason to argue the point. I teased him instead. The previous Sunday (23 October) had been the date pencilled in for the launch of *Full Disclosure* to go up against *60 Minutes*.

'You know, David, I watched *60 Minutes* last Sunday. It was not a great show. They had some pretty dull, dated stuff on the Stealth bomber, fascism in the Ukraine and DNA. We would have had far better stories: our investigative piece about Donald Trump, the Japanese gangster and their attempted takeover of the Empire State Building, Judith's excellent profile of Dominick Dunne on the OJ trial and that controversial piece on the wave of false sexual harassment cases.'

'Nobody has any doubts about the journalism that you can deliver,' said Evans, 'or that you would beat the pants off them. The question is whether you would work on-air in America.'

'That's been the issue ever since Rupert offered me this job back in April,' I snapped back at him. 'It was an issue while I negotiated my contract. And it's been an issue ever since I arrived here. Look, David, just make up your bloody minds what you want me to do, ask me if I'll do it and I'll give you an immediate answer. And if you can't do that then I'll take the decision for you: I have slightly better alternative employment prospects than an unemployed steelworker in Scunthorpe, you know.'

'I understand,' said David, taken aback by my anger. 'What you say is perfectly reasonable.' There was no point in fuming at him: he was just the messenger. It simply confirmed my suspicions: *Full Disclosure* was never going to happen; and I was already laying the groundwork for a new career.

Samir Shah, the head of the BBC's political programmes that originate from its Millbank studios in Westminster, had called me out of the blue in New York to enquire if I would be returning to London after my New York secondment. I told him in confidence that things were not going according to plan in America and that I expected to be spending more time in London in the New Year. He asked if I would be interested in presenting his new, late-night political chat show, *The Midnight Hour*. I said it was certainly a conversation I'd be interested in having. We clinched the deal on my next visit to London, with the understanding that there would be no demands on my time until my contract with Rupert had expired.

Paul Dacre, the editor of the *Daily Mail*, had heard that I might be about to walk away from *The Sunday Times* and Fox and asked if I'd be interested in doing a column for him. Suddenly a new life was unfolding before me: professionally challenging and lucrative. Under my separation agreement with Rupert I was already guaranteed a pay-off plus a two-year column from *The Sunday Times*. To that I could add another highly paid column from the *Daily Mail* and a TV show for the BBC, which would take me back into British television and lead to more work (Channel 4 was also talking about a show, which eventually materialized as *Is This Your Life?*). The editor of *Vanity Fair* had also approached me to be a contributing editor and I had already signed a contract with Macmillan to write this book, a fact of which I had advised Rupert.

Two columns, two television shows, a book and *Vanity Fair*: I was putting together a portfolio of work that would be enormously exciting, pay twice as much as *The Sunday Times* and give me three times as much freedom. Whatever Rupert's latest whim on the TV front I was in a strong position to walk away, which was what I was still determined to do. I had not long to wait to test the strength of my new convictions.

Twenty-four hours after David Evans's call I was in a taxi on my way uptown to a cocktail party with Geordie Greig, the *Sunday Times*' New York correspondent, when Pamela Goddard, my superb English PA in New York, called me on the mobile: 'Rupert just called. He's arrived in New York and wants to have dinner with you.'

'But I'm on my way to a party,' I groaned.

'I can always say I couldn't find you,' said Pam, helpfully. She was my most loyal ally at Fox.

I thought for a moment then realized that if he wanted dinner he must have something to tell me; I certainly had something to tell him. There was no point in spinning the thing out any further. I told Geordie I'd have to forgo the party. We repaired to a nearby hotel for a stiff drink and a final run-through of what I should say. Geordie was a friend as well as a colleague and I had already taken him into my confidence. An hour later I was dining with Rupert in an Italian restaurant near his apartment.

As usual, we spent most of the meal talking about everything but the business at hand. He wanted to know what I thought of Tony Blair (Rupert was clearly impressed). He said he had turned 'dead against' John Major and thought he was 'useless and finished'.

Conversation then turned to the Royal Family. *The Economist* had just gone controversially republican with an anti-monarchy editorial. 'That's really my view,' said Rupert, 'but I wouldn't have the guts to let *The Times* or *The Sunday Times* run an editorial like *The Economist*'s: it would annoy too many of our readers. Do you think the Royal Family is finished now?' He clearly hoped it was. We discussed the monarchy's prospects for another twenty minutes.

Then he revealed that he had just visited Bill Gates in Seattle. 'I've been trying to agree some kind of strategic alliance with him,' Rupert explained. 'Something like News Corporation taking twenty per cent of Microsoft in return for him having access to all our products – provided they have pole position in his new Windows '95.' (The deal never happened.)

Rupert was his usual friendly, fascinating self but they were pouring the coffee before he finally turned to the only subject that really interested me that night.

'I don't think we want to do a news magazine any more,' he said eventually. 'Matoian has scared the pants off me: there are too many of them, their ratings are falling and he's convinced me Fox needs to concentrate on getting its entertainment programming right.' I was about to tell him I had guessed that and was going to resign from Fox and *The Sunday Times* when he raised his latest wheeze.

'I'm anxious,' he said, 'to have a go with news five nights

a week, maybe at 11.30 p.m. I need your energy and your attitude to drive the show as executive editor. I'd love us to be on air by 1 February.'

The man's mad, I thought to myself. It's almost November, there's Christmas coming and he wants us to be ready to go five nights a week by 1 February. And on a network that can't even get its act together to do a show once a week. I also noticed there was no mention of an on-air role for me.

'Rupert, what I do best and what I enjoy most,' I began calmly, 'is being at the centre of controversy. Dealing with and highlighting issues in an original and forthright way. Influencing public opinion and policymakers on issues I care about. And I like being in the public eye while I'm doing it. I enjoy the public debate – I always have, ever since school.

'I understand that I might not be suited to doing that in America, but I didn't ask to come here: you said you wanted me. You have given me the freedom at *The Sunday Times* largely to do what I wished and I am very grateful for that. I know that at times what I've done has caused you distress, but you've let me get on with it. If I can't continue in this vein in America then maybe it's best if we have an amicable parting of the ways. I'll go my own way and do what I like best – without causing you further embarrassment.'

'If we part I hope it will be amicable,' he replied, 'and of course you must do what you want. But I need you to do this daily show.' For some reason I did not feel flattered; in fact, I felt irritated. My heart sank at the prospect of developing another show that would probably never happen.

'Let me say this to you, Rupert, for your benefit, not mine,' I said slowly but firmly. 'I don't think you have any idea of the infrastructure needed to get a show like this on the air five nights a week. It will take the news-gathering facilities of a network news division to do it properly.

'What happens, for example, if at 8 p.m. New York time

there's a news flash that Clinton has been assassinated by Hamas? [The president was in the Middle East that week.] Who or what would we have there to cover this event in three hours' time?'

He thought for a moment. 'We'd have Visnews [the British video wire service],' he said eventually.

'Yes, but that's just wallpaper, everybody gets that, we'd have no reporter on the ground, no correspondents, no specialists there or here.'

'Well, we could get the reaction from Arkansas.'

He was winging it. 'Look, Rupert,' I said, now a little riled. 'Nobody gives a stuff about the reaction in Arkansas if the President has just been assassinated. But suppose we did want it: who or what do we have in Arkansas?' There was no reply.

I reminded him that several months ago I had suggested a late-night daily show. I had proposed that it would begin at 11 p.m. and last an hour, beginning with the hard news of the day and getting progressively softer as the hour went on: the idea was to begin with a senior public figure on the story of the day and finish an hour later with some film star. The plan had been to pre-empt ABC's formidable *Nightline*, which began at 11.30 p.m., and provide a serious alternative to the late-night comedy talk shows hosted by David Letterman and Jay Leno.

We had both agreed that an hour with the right mix of network news between 11 p.m. and midnight would be an original addition to American programming and a sensible alternative to Fox running the same sort of early evening news as the other networks. But we had also agreed that we should get the news magazine up and running first, then use it as a base to go for the late-night show.

Rupert had taken much of this on board but now he was thinking of doing only half-an-hour and starting at 11.30

p.m., which would put the show head-to-head with the well-established *Nightline*. 'I don't think I can get the Fox affiliates to take a news show for an hour at 11 p.m. They make too much money from re-running things like *I Love Lucy*. We'd probably have to launch at 11.30 only on the O & Os [those stations directly owned and operated by Fox] and see where we go from there.'

Great, I thought to myself. We've gone from a prime-time network news magazine to an 11.30 p.m. showing going out on a handful of Fox stations. This is not what I came to America to do.

'Is this a real commitment to go daily,' I enquired, 'or just another off-the-top-of-the-head idea? What happens if Matoian doesn't like a late news show either? I don't want to waste another six months developing another show that never happens.'

He apologized for the frustrations of recent months and said he was very attracted to a daily news programme. Since it would not be in prime time it would not concern Matoian so much. I walked him home and agreed to sleep on it and meet again next day: I could hardly turn it down flat for it would mean under my existing contract a $3 million salary spread over two years. I called David Corvo when I returned home to tell him the weekly news magazine was effectively dead and that the emphasis was now on a daily show. He sighed and repeated his concerns about the huge resources it would take – and Fox's commitment to it.

Just before midnight the phone rang. It was Les Hinton. He was lobbying on Rupert's behalf that I take charge of the daily show. 'He fears the whole operation will fall apart if you don't,' repeated Les.

'Who cares?' I thought to myself and went to bed. Despite the prospect of a huge salary I no longer wanted my life to be determined by Rupert's latest whim, especially since it was so easily changed by the folks out in LA. We had gone from a news magazine to compete with *60 Minutes* on a Sunday, then to follow *Melrose Place* on a weekday, then back to a Sunday, to be launched in August, then September, then October, then December, then January, then not at all. Now it was to be five nights a week from February. I was tired and bored with it all: I've had enough, I thought, as I fell into restless sleep.

The lobbying from Rupert's men continued the next morning. 'He wants you to be the guiding spirit *behind* the camera,' said one. 'He really desperately needs you to kick-start the daily show.' At 2.45 p.m. I was summoned to Rupert's office.

I began the conversation by saying, 'Now that we're not doing a weekly magazine,' when he interrupted to say, 'I've not counted that out. Let me see some more stories before I come to a decision.' I was flabbergasted – and furious. It was the only time in eleven years I lost my temper with him.

'Yes you bloody did count it out!' I shouted. 'Don't you dare deny that was the purpose of last night's dinner!' I was on my feet, ready to walk out.

'Well, I would prefer a late-night show,' he said sheepishly. I sat down again, still simmering, staring angrily at him. It was the kind of confrontation he hates. But there was something else I wanted to get off my chest. Word had reached me that Rupert had started telling his associates that I was being unreasonable: 'He's only prepared to do *The Andrew Neil Hour*, he wants to be the great controversialist in America. It won't work.' I wanted to correct that.

'As you are well aware, Rupert,' I continued, 'I have only ever asked for a limited on-air role. Our original agreement was that I would be chief reporter if there was no host; or co-host if we decided on traditional anchors. I've never asked for more than that – and only in the context of a weekly magazine. I have no ambitions to anchor a late-night show in America. It wouldn't work.

'My main concern is the one I expressed last night: I don't want to waste another six months developing a show only to have it canned by some faceless flake who knows nothing about news in Los Angeles.' But this was a conversation he wanted to avoid, or at least postpone.

'Let's meet in LA in a few days,' he said, still keen to procrastinate. 'We can brainstorm the whole idea with all concerned, including Matoian. Then you can decide what you want to do. If we part company we have to depart friends.'

But I was not in a friendly mood. David Corvo and Emily Rooney were waiting anxiously in my office when I returned. 'I'll swing for that guy if he jerks me about much more,' I said angrily. I had come close to walking out on the spot. 'You know he denied canning the magazine and actually said he wanted to see a few more stories before finally deciding!'

'What did you say?' asked Emily.

'I told him to f—— off – but *not* in so many words.' I smiled: I was beginning to calm down.

'Stories have nothing to do with it,' said Corvo. 'We could have the best stories in the world and this show would never happen. The people in LA just don't want it – and they have Rupert's ear.' He was right.

'We'll have to go through this charade in LA,' I told them, 'but I feel it only fair to tell you that I'm out of here.' They were both disappointed for they feared that Rupert was right about it all falling apart if I left; but I had myself to look after. I decided to put my position on paper so that Rupert was under no misapprehensions when it came to our meeting – and to protect myself should it all turn sour. My priority now was to protect the financial parachute I had secured in London.

'I want to clarify something in advance [of the LA meeting] that concerns me,' I faxed Rupert. 'We always recognized that having me as the main on-air talent in a weekly news magazine, either as chief correspondent or co-host, was something of a risk. It was a risk, however, that we both seemed to think worth taking last May. It may even have worked, especially since we were moving toward a larger studio presence for the correspondents, with me *primus inter pares* among them as their editor rather than as a traditional anchor. This is the format we would have used had we aired last Sunday.

'As I said to you this afternoon, however, it is a very different matter to have a Brit as anchor of a nightly news show in America, even a late-night one. About as sensible as having an American anchor ITV's *News at Ten*, and I think the chances of success so slight that I wouldn't wish even to try. So we need not disagree about that.

'What I am uncertain about is whether you have in mind any on-air presence for me at all. If so I would wish it to be clarified quite precisely so there is no disagreement later on. If not, and my function is to be confined to the offscreen senior driving force of the show, then I have to decide if I want to be a backroom boy for the next couple of years. I suppose it partly depends on what the financial rewards will be, but it also depends on what I think I will enjoy most in the next stage of my career.

'My other concern is that I don't want to spend a further six months developing another show that is also killed off because of the changing views/priorities of Fox executives in LA that I have never even met, much less worked with. My confidence that commitments categorically given will be lived up to has been shaken by recent events. The past six months have been a welcome and well-paid transition from *The Sunday Times* but they have also left me frustrated at being so vulnerable to decisions and forces outside my control. I also do not believe it is understood just how huge a commitment a nightly show is compared with a weekly news magazine.'

I faxed this to his office that night so it would be waiting for him when he arrived in his LA office next morning. I then wrote an article for *The Sunday Times* on the mid-term congressional elections (it was time to get my hand in as a columnist) and instructed my interior designer to begin work on the second phase of the renovation of my house in France (I had a feeling I'd be spending more time there).

The crucial meeting with Rupert and the folks in LA was set for Thursday, 3 November, then postponed until Monday, 7 November (which rather revealed where it was in his priorities). I decided to stick to my original LA schedule so I left New York for a relaxing weekend at one of my favourite hotels, the Four Seasons in Beverly Hills. It would be fair to say I was feeling somewhat 'demob happy'.

I dined with David Corvo at the Four Seasons the night before the meeting with Rupert. I told him that I had learned that he was now saying to his cronies that it was my 'dereliction' that had killed the weekly show. I had 'lost interest in it and slackened off'. Corvo shook his head in disbelief. I smiled: 'My source says we're dealing with a lunatic! Of course, we're not: but it's all a bit irrational and I have had enough of his whimsical unpredictability. He's also saying, by the way, that he's now happy to see me on air, that American viewers will take to me over time.'

'Maybe they will,' said David. 'It's always been the unknown factor.'

'It's going to stay unknown, David. He's saying it to

encourage me to stay for at least six months to launch his daily show. I won't be doing it.'

*

THE MEETING WAS DUE TO START at 9 a.m. in a little boardroom off Rupert's office. He came rushing in at 9.28 a.m. with yellow legal pad and green Pentel in hand, apologizing for being late, and going straight to the top of the table to face a full house of senior Fox executives.

'Everything is open for discussion,' he began. 'We have to establish a Fox news capability and we can do it weekly or daily.' He then handed over to John Matoian, who went through his familiar mantra about the proliferation of news magazines, some of them going head to head with each other at 10 p.m., producing a slump in their ratings. Only NBC's *Dateline* was improving, he said, and that was because it followed *Frasier*, the popular sitcom. Worst of all, he added, the ratings for news magazines were down most in the 18–34 age group, and that's where the Fox audience was concentrated: 'There can only be one conclusion – don't do another news show.'

I said nothing. The weekly show was already dead: this was just its formal funeral. But I ostentatiously took notes of what everybody said: I wanted Rupert to know that whatever commitments he made were being recorded.

'If the *Frasier*/*Dateline* combination works,' asked Rupert, 'why not *Melrose Place* and *Full Disclosure*?' He was putting up only token resistance, to give us the impression the weekly shows were still a matter for debate.

'Because the *Melrose* audience has alternative places to go after it's finished,' said Matoian. 'They won't transfer to *Full Disclosure*.'

'Look,' butted in Corvo, who had become agitated, 'ratings were never the gameplan here. They were not the reason we were asked to do a news show. It was to be a long-term investment in a quality news magazine which would lead to Fox developing its own news capability. News magazines are slow burners, they don't happen overnight, you have to invest in them and establish credibility. But if they work they have a far longer franchise than any entertainment programme.'

'Well, there is an opportunity at 11 p.m.,' said Matoian, ducking the points Corvo had made, 'for something with a news magazine feel.' Since that was outside the prime-time core network schedule for which Matoian was responsible, he cared less what was shown then.

'We could clear eleven o'clock with our O & Os,' said Rupert on cue, 'though I don't think the affiliates would want it before 11.30 p.m. But five nights a week is more forgiving than a weekly magazine; if you have a weak show one night, you can come back strongly the next. But Andrew thinks it needs to be an hour long to be distinctive and he's right.'

'The affiliates won't take an hour,' piped up another Fox executive, 'and we don't have the infrastructure for a show like this. CBS has two hundred uplinks all over the country.'

But Rupert was undaunted: 'It's not as frightening as you make it. We could put together twenty uplinks right now. So let's agree that we'll do a nightly show and discuss how we go about it. I want a dry run in a couple of months and aim to be on air within five – and let's shoot for an hour.'

Fox's chief bean counter and owner of the best handle-bar moustache in Hollywood, Chase Carey, said that five nights a week would be expensive; David Evans said again that the affiliates would not want an hour. But Rupert would not be deflected: he was anxious to show that though he had backed down over the weekly magazine, he was determined to proceed with a major commitment to news. His reputation as a news man was on the line, specifically in front of me.

'Who can we get to front it?' he asked, ignoring their objections. 'How about Bryant Gumbel?' Gumbel was the famous black anchor on NBC's *Today* breakfast show.

Rupert then proceeded to answer his own question: 'I've heard some pretty negative things about him. He's difficult to work with, can't vary the pace in his interviews and is too left. This show should be politically incorrect – not necessarily right-wing or conservative but definitely not PC.' It sounded as if he was reading from my script.

'I think it's a bit academic, Rupert,' I mumbled, speaking for the first time. 'I don't see Gumbel giving up NBC News for a late-night programme on a few Fox stations.'

'You're right,' said Rupert. 'We need to develop our own stars.'

The meeting continued with Rupert the only person in the room showing any enthusiasm for the project under discussion. You could almost hear the other Fox executives sharpening their knives to kill his new baby at birth. The proceedings ended without any real decisions being taken. As he rose from the table Emily Rooney asked one last question: 'So we've killed the magazine?'

'Yes,' said Rupert. 'Let's get focused on this.' Just what 'this' was remained something of an enigma.

'We need to meet alone in your office,' I said firmly and headed for it without waiting on his answer. We sat down on his white sofas, a coffee table between us. He started talking politics, first about how well the Republicans would do in the next day's Congressional elections, then he repeated his belief that John Major was 'finished'.

'You don't think John Witherow's too much of a knee-jerk Tory?' he asked about my successor. I was a little taken aback by the question – Rupert is not normally worried about editors who are too Tory – but I quickly worked out he was worried that John might not be happy to put *The Sunday Times* behind Tony Blair at his proprietor's request.

'I think he's much more of a traditional Tory than me,' I replied. 'But I'm really more anxious to talk about my future.'

'I know,' said Rupert, finally realizing there was no escape from this conversation. 'I need you to drive this new daily show.'

'I'm sorry, Rupert,' I replied, 'I don't want to do it. If it was just the two of us calling all the shots, like *The Sunday Times*, then I would stay. But it's not. I have lost faith in Fox to deliver a news show like this. You may want one but almost everybody else here does not and I don't want to be at the mercy of people in LA who know nothing about news and for whose judgements I have no respect, even if they have your ear. I want to press the parachute.'

My thinking was clear: though it would have been financially attractive to stay on an annual salary of $1.5 million to launch a daily show, even if it was never likely to happen, I was well aware that the longer I was away from London, lost in the obscurity of the back room at Fox, the more job offers from Britain would dry up. The freelance portfolio I had already put together could not rival what Rupert was offering in money terms but it would give me a handsome income by British standards – and it offered freedom and job satisfaction; neither were on offer from Rupert.

Rupert started to remonstrate with me but the phone went. Irritated, he picked it up, then a smile crossed his face. It was his wife, Anna, he had become a grandfather: Elisabeth had just given birth to her first child.

'Congratulations, Grandad,' I smiled.

He began to resume his argument, then stopped. I think he saw I was adamant. 'All right,' he said, 'press the parachute.' We stood up to shake hands and said goodbye: it was a curiously low-key ending to eleven tumultuous years but at least it was amicable. I think we both realized that if we did not part now it was certain to end in tears later.

I had a right to feel angry that he had reneged on his side of the bargain when he asked me to come to America, that he had not delivered on promises so easily given in London. But I had gone to America with my eyes open, knowing it was a long shot and regarding it more as a lucrative transition than the start of a new career.

We had not failed with *Full Disclosure*; it was worse than that: we had not been given the chance to fail. The conventional wisdom is that it would probably have bombed. But who knows? Maybe it would have been distinctive and controversial enough to have carved out a strong niche in American television. My decision to walk away altogether, however, was vindicated by subsequent events at Fox. Two years after that handshake there is still no weekly Fox news magazine, the late-night daily show never happened, neither did Judith Regan's television career and David Corvo has gone to NBC. Several other senior broadcast executives have come and gone in the fruitless quest to give Fox a credible news presence. After a cull of the weaker ones, news magazines continue to do well on the other networks, contrary to Matoian's predictions two years ago.

Roger Ailes, a veteran of the Reagan White House and CNBC (a cable news channel), has been charged with creating a twenty-four-hour Fox News channel in a market already crowded with round-the-clock news. In Rupert's original scheme of things, a twenty-four-hour news channel was to be the final piece in his TV news jigsaw. Now it might be the first: at least the folks at Fox will be happy – it means no news need contaminate their precious entertainment schedules on the Fox network.

'Let's keep in close touch: I'd like to be able to call on you whenever I need you,' said Rupert as I left his office.

In fact, I never heard from him again. Rupert is not the sort of man to keep in touch when he has no further use for you, even if you have done eleven years' sterling service for him. But it did not matter: my years as a Murdoch man were over. They had been mainly the best of times and only periodically the worst of times; but now it was time for life after Rupert. I felt curiously elated, despite my apprehension about what might now lie in store. As I left the Fox lot for the last time in the bright California sunshine I felt a huge black cloud lift from my shoulders.

INDEX